The Making of Colossians

Suomen Eksegeettisen Seuran julkaisuja
Toimittanut Jaakko Hyttinen

ISSN 0356-2786
ISBN 951-9217-41-X
ISBN 3-525-53629-1

Vammalan Kirjapaino Oy 2003

PUBLICATIONS OF THE FINNISH EXEGETICAL SOCIETY 86

OUTI LEPPÄ

The Making of Colossians

A Study on the Formation and Purpose of a Deutero-Pauline Letter

The Finnish Exegetical Society in Helsinki
Vandenhoeck & Ruprecht in Göttingen
2003

Preface

The present study is a slightly revised form of my Th.D. dissertation which was approved by the University of Helsinki in November 2000. The preparation of the dissertation was a ten-year-long voyage of exploration. When I started the task I knew next to nothing about Colossians but its secrets opened for me little by little. At first I started to study the Christology of Colossians. However, when Professor Lars Aejmelaeus advised me to read Professor E.P. Sanders' pioneering article "Literary Dependence in Colossians" (JBL 1966) and Professor Heikki Räisänen counselled me to familiarize myself with the important articles dealing with the relationship between Colossians and the Gospel of Mark written by Professor Wolfgang Schenk in the 1980's, I noticed that the literary dependence between Colossians and other early Christian writings was the subject I wanted to concentrate on. This was the right decision. This study is a good ground for further investigations in Colossians, for instance with regard to the Christology.

My special thanks are due to Professor Heikki Räisänen. I appreciate very much his willingness to devote his time and energies to guiding my dissertation. He always had time to read my work and to give me feedback very rapidly. I have also had the privilege of participating in the research project "Formation of Early Christian Ideology" led by Professor Räisänen (Department of Biblical Studies at the University of Helsinki, Finland). Furthermore, I wish to express my great gratitude to Professor Lars Aejmelaeus. Since he himself has been working on the questions of literary dependence for years, his advice has been priceless for me. I am grateful to Professor Jarmo Kiilunen who, during the preliminary examination of my dissertation, read it through very carefully and noticed many mistakes in the Greek texts. Professor E.P. Sanders kindly read part of my dissertation when he visited Helsinki in October 1998 as the guest of the Finnish Graduate School of Theology. He made many valuable comments on my work which helped me to progress.

I wish to express my warm thanks to my husband Rev. Heikki Leppä who just completed his dissertation on the relationship between Acts and Galatians (Luke's Critical Use of Galatians. Helsinki 2002). As we have interests in similar area, he has been able to give me many good pieces of advice. For English language-editing, I am deeply grateful to Margot Stout Whiting. If any mistakes remain, they are due to my own negligence. I also want to thank all my fellow-students and colleagues at the Department of Biblical Studies who have in various ways contributed to the completion of my dissertation. In addition, I am grateful to many friends at the Department of Church History where I was working as a secretary when I started the dissertation. Their support was very important for me at the beginning of my post-graduate studies.

The dissertation was often hard work. I spent several evenings and nice summer days (very infrequent in Finland) in the library or sitting in front of my computer. However, during the time of my post-graduate studies I also experienced moments of great pleasure. I remember especially the evening Professor Michael

Goulder and Clare Goulder visited our home. Their visit made our party unforgettable. In addition, it has been very pleasant, and useful, to meet scholars from all over the world at the meetings of the Society of Biblical Literature (SBL). Thanks to Dr. Matthew S. Collins who is responsible for the International Meetings of the SBL where I several times had the valuable opportunity to present a paper. In addition, I owe my thanks to Dr. Jennifer Berenson Maclean, Dr. Angela Standhartinger, Dr. Eduard Verhoef, and Dr. Rainer Reuter who sent me copies of their work before they were available in our library or otherwise accessible to me. With all of them I also have had stimulating discussions at the meetings of the SBL and correspondence after the conferences. Furthermore, I am very grateful to Professors Andrew T. Lincoln and Robert M. Royalty, Jr. who sent me copies of their papers read at the Annual Meeting of the SBL in San Francisco in 1997. Though I was present at the session, it was helpful to get copies of the presentations afterwards.

During the course of my studies I received financial aid from several sources. Most important was the opportunity to have several full-time research periods at the Research Unit for Early Jewish and Christian Culture and Literature at the Department of Biblical Studies at the University of Helsinki. The Finnish Graduate School of Theology sponsored me for two months. I have also been supported by grants from the Emil Aaltonen Foundation and the University of Helsinki. I am grateful to all of these institutions. Furthermore, I wish to thank the Finnish Exegetical Society for including my work in its series of publications.

The most important source of support, however, was my family. In addition to my husband Heikki, thanks are owed to our dear children Maria, Johannes, Teresa, Sofia, and Henrik. They continuously reminded me of what is important in life: the skill to find joy in small, everyday incidents. Thus they kept me from being absorbed in the dissertation completely. Finally, I dedicate this book to my father, Professor Rauno Hämäläinen, who taught me the love for learning. His support has been indispensable during all my studies from elementary school through the preparation of this dissertation.

Helsinki, December 2002 Outi Leppä

Contents

1. Introduction

1.1. Colossians as Pseudepigraphy

Colossians (Col) presents Paul as the sender of the letter. However, there are such differences between Col and other Paul's epistles that Ernst Theodor Mayerhoff had already disputed the Pauline authorship of Col in 1838. He based his thesis on significant lexical, grammatical, stylistic, and theological peculiarities and concluded that Paul could not be regarded as the author of Col.[1] It has to be noted that Col has the appearance of being a genuine Pauline epistle. As in 2 Cor 1:1 and Phil 1:1, Paul and Timothy are named the senders of the letter (Col 1:1). In addition, Col 4:18 refers to the imprisonment of Paul in a similar manner to Philem and Phil and gives the impression that it contains Paul's own personal signature in the same way as 1 Cor 16:21, Gal 6:11, and Philem 19. The structure of the letter also corresponds to that of the authentic Pauline letters: there is a dogmatic section (Col 1:15-2:23) followed with an ethical section (Col 3:1-4:1), both of which are framed by the introduction and the conclusion resembling those of Paul.

Nevertheless, Mayerhoff's thesis has been widely accepted and over the past few decades two investigations following Mayerhoff have been frequently cited. Eduard Lohse studied the language of Col statistically and noticed that the vocabulary of Col is exceptional: e.g. there are 34 words which are hapax legomena in the NT and 28 words which reappear in the NT but not in the other Pauline letters. In addition, it is striking that although the author of Col (A/Col) struggles against a legalistic doctrine, the terms which would be expected to occur in such a confrontation are missing: ἁμαρτία (sin), δικαιοσύνη (righteousness), δικαιόω (to justify), νόμος (law), and πιστεύω (to believe). Lohse noted, however, that the appearance of hapax legomena and unusual expressions in other Pauline letters must not be overlooked and refers to the study of Zahn which demonstrates that Gal includes 31 hapax legomena and 39 words which appear in the NT but not in any other letter of the Pauline corpus. Thus he concluded that the question of the authorship cannot be solved on the grounds of the statistics alone.[2]

Lohse also examined the style of Col and Walter Bujard continued the task in a thorough manner. They noticed e.g. the following characteristics of Col: conjunctions are used less and in a different way than in Paul, loosely joined infinitive constructions are often made use of, participle constructions occur frequently, synonyms and expressions belonging to the same stem are piled together, series of dependent genitives are heaped up, and the nouns are repeatedly attached to phrases with the preposition ἐν (in). All these features also occur in the

---

[1] Mayerhoff, Der Brief an die Kolosser, mit vornehmlicher Berücksichtigung der drei Pastoralbriefe kritisch geprüft. Berlin 1838.

[2] Lohse, Colossians and Philemon. A Commentary on the Epistles to the Colossians and to Philemon. Hermeneia. Philadelphia, PA: Fortress Press 1971 (1st ed. in German in 1968), 84-88, which is referred to also by Schweizer 1982, 16, Gnilka 1980, 17 and Kümmel 1987, 341.

other Pauline letters but not as frequently as in Col. Most striking still is the peculiarity of the sentence structure and sequence. Unlike in the major Pauline letters which use quite consistent argumentative style, in Col the sentences are loosely joined together and the argumentation is less logical. While Lohse regards the style as liturgical and caused by the influence of utilized traditions, Bujard calls it associative because he assumes it to be due to the associations of A/Col. Whichever way the style is defined, the writer's way of thinking differs so much from that of Paul that is difficult to believe that Paul was the author of Col. Lohse still contended that on the basis of the observations made about the language and style no decision can be reached on the question of the authorship. However, Bujard drew the conclusion that Col cannot be a genuine Pauline letter.[3]

The difference between Col and the authentic Pauline letters is even more clearly seen when studying the theology of the letters. A/Col has produced new formulations in Christology, eschatology, ecclesiology, the concept of the apostle, and the understanding of baptism. It is also remarkable that the differences are not limited to the sections that argue against "philosophy". Thus they cannot be explained by saying that they are due to the circumstances of this controversy. In addition, the concept of the apostle Paul in Col 1:24, that he is "completing what is lacking in Christ's afflictions", is often taken to refer to the martyrdom of Paul and the letter was thus written after the death of Paul.[4] Based on the theological peculiarities, Lohse also concluded that Paul cannot be considered to be the author of Col.[5]

This interpretation is followed by most scholars: Col is generally regarded as unauthentic on the grounds of the differences in language and style as well as in theological concepts between Col and the letters of Paul.[6] A minority of scholars still do not accept the arguments against the authenticity of Col but regard it as a letter written by Paul.[7] In addition, some explain the differences between Col and

---

[3] Lohse 1971, 88-91. Bujard, Stilanalytische Untersuchungen zum Kolosserbrief als Beitrag zur Methodik von Sprachvergleichen. SUNT 11. Göttingen: Vandenhoeck & Ruprecht 1973.

[4] Schenke 1975, 512; Lindemann 1983, 11; Betz 1995, 513; Gnilka 1980, 5; Standhartinger 1999, 167.

[5] Lohse 1971, 177-181.

[6] See Gnilka 1980, 11-17; Vielhauer 1975, 200; Furnish 1992a, 1094; Conzelmann 1990, 176-177; Lindemann 1979, 38; 1983, 11; Pfammatter 1987, 54-55; Kiley 1986, 73; Schenke & Fischer 1978, 165-167; Pokorný 1987, 1-2; Hübner 1997, 9-10; Standhartinger 1999, 2; Nielsen 1985, 104; Müller 1988, 13-18; Wilson 1977, 17-21. Contra Barclay 1997, 18-35 who has recently criticized the studies of Lohse and Bujard and leaves open the question of the authorship of Col. Though Barclay rightly contends that the problem cannot be solved on the grounds of the bare statistics, it is surprising that he neglects the arguments concerning the theological differences. For the arguments advanced against the authenticity of Col, see Kiley 1986, 37-73.

[7] E.g. Kümmel 1987, 341-342; Cannon 1981, 220-291; O'Brien 1982, xliv-xlix; Hendriksen 1971, 29-31; R. P. Martin 1981, 30-40; Arnold 1995, 7. Arnold presents the alternative as "a fairly strong stream of scholarship" and enumerates the scholars who accept it. However, he mentions only a few names of those who prefer the opposite alternative, and thus does not describe the situation properly.

other Pauline letters by assuming that Paul and his co-worker, usually named Timothy, who is mentioned as a co-sender of the letter in Col 1:1, wrote the letter together.[8] A few scholars accept the unauthenticity of Col but emphasize that Col was not composed by a later writer but by some of Paul's co-workers during his lifetime.[9] The arguments advanced against the authenticity of Col are too strong to be neglected, however. The co-worker hypothesis is not convincing either since, as Kiley states, "Paul, either in collaboration with someone or giving general guidelines to another, is still Paul".[10] It also seems unlikely that during Paul's lifetime some of his disciples would have written a letter which puts forth a theology which diverges so much from Paul. Accordingly, the differences between Col and the other Pauline letters can be explained most naturally by assuming that Col is pseudonymous and was written by a later author, which is also taken as the starting point of this study.

Writing in the name of another person was customary in the ancient world: it appears both in Greek and Jewish literature, especially in the Jewish apocalyptic writings.[11] The motives for producing pseudepigraphic works[12] were various. When the libraries in the Museum of Alexandria and in Pergamum were enlarged, it is said that gold was promised to people who were able to present a book of an ancient author and thus pseudepigraphic writings were also composed out of the desire for financial gain.[13] Sometimes authors sought to defame, like for example Diotimus, who produced fifty letters of low value as if they were written by Epicurus. Much more often than malice, the motive was respect and innocent admiration which influenced the formation of pseudonymous works. For example, the Neo-Pythagoreans so respected Pythagoras, the founder of the philosophical school, that they attributed their treatises to him. One reason for this habit was the modesty of the disciples against presenting under their own name the ideas which they conceived to be their masters'. It is also worth noting that a treatise written by

---

[8] So Dunn 1996, 35-39; Nikolainen 1987, 11; Schweizer 1982, 15-24; Bruce 1988, 30; Ollrog 1979, 232, 241f; Luz 1998, 186-190. According to Luz, the fact that Eph utilizes Col indicates that A/Eph takes Col as a genuine Pauline epistle. It is not still self-evident that the disciples of Paul form their works modelled on the genuine texts only. They may also imitate each other's letters which belong to the same tradition. Cf. Dunn 1996, 36-37: "the fact that (post-Pauline) Ephesians did make such use of Colossians suggests that Colossians itself may have provided something of a model for Ephesians — that is, as an expression of 'late Paulinism' or as written by a Pauline disciple close to Paul".

[9] Hartman 1985, 200-201; Ludwig 1974, 230-231.

[10] Kiley 1986, 46.

[11] Gnilka 1980, 23; Kiley 1986, 17-23; Schweizer 1982, 19; Barclay 1997, 18. See also Speyer 1971.

[12] Like Kiley 1986, (34-35), this study calls Col both pseudonymous and an example of pseudepigraphy.

[13] Metzger 1972, 5-6; Kiley 1986, 20.

an unknown author would be much less likely to have been read. Thus, to ensure readership, it was sometimes necessary to use the name of a famous person.[14]

Since there is no evidence that Paul's letters were sold and nothing in Col seems to be construed as slander towards Paul, it is most likely that a disciple of Paul, who has an important message for others, writes in the name of his (her)[15] respected teacher. He wants to write in a new situation in a way he thinks Paul would have done if still alive.[16] The deutero-Pauline letters, Col, Eph, and the Pastorals, were written in order to keep Paul, though absent in body, present in spirit (cf. Col 2:5).[17]

It is widely assumed that the followers of Paul formed some kind of Pauline "school", the center of which is usually assumed to be situated in Ephesus.[18] There are still different opinions about the character of the school. According to Lohse, Schenke, Müller, and Kiley it was set up after the death of Paul in order to protect his heritage, while Conzelmann, Ollrog, Ludwig, Gnilka, and Hartman assume that the school already started to develop during Paul's lifetime.[19] In addition, while Kiley and Ludwig seem to regard it as a definite group of Paul's followers, Müller, Schenke, and Ollrog emphasize that Paul's heritage was preserved separately in several places.[20]

Col is addressed to the city of Colossae, which was located in the upper valley of the Lycus river in Asia Minor. In ancient times, Colossae was a prominent city. It was wealthy due to its wool industry and its advantageous location on the main road from Ephesus to the east. In Hellenistic times, when Col was written, Colossae was overshadowed by its neighboring cities Laodicea and Hierapolis and had lost its prominence. According to Tacitus, parts of the Lycus valley, especially Laodicea, were destroyed by an earthquake in A.D. 60 – 61. Later Orosius wrote that three cities — Laodicea, Hierapolis, and Colossae — were destroyed. It is not certain whether these reports refer to the same event. Unlike Laodicea, Colossae

---

[14] Further in Metzger 1972, 5-12; Brox 1975, 51-57; Kiley 1986, 17-23; Speyer 1971, 131-149. Contra Verhoef 2001 and Baum 2001 who contest the interpretation that pseudepigraphy was an accepted phenomenon in the ancient world. Verhoef contends that the pseudepigraphic character of the deutero-Pauline letters was not known, otherwise they would have been regarded as forgeries and would not have been accepted in the canon. Baum argues that pseudepigraphic writings were generally considered attempts to deceit and thus taken as literary forgeries.

[15] We do not know whether the author of Col was male or female but for the sake of convenience I use only masculine personal pronouns.

[16] Similarly e.g. Gnilka 1980, 24-26; E. P. Sanders, 1966, 44; Lohse 1971, 181-183; Kiley 1986, 21-23; Lindemann 1983, 13; Vielhauer 1975, 200.

[17] Gnilka 1980, 25, following Brox 1975, 112.

[18] See e.g. Lohse 1971, 182 n. 17; Pokorný 1987, 15; Gnilka 1980, 22; Ludwig 1974, 213; Pfammatter 1987, 54-55; Hübner 1997, 16.

[19] Lohse 1971, 181-183; Schenke 1975; Müller 1988; Kiley 1986, 95-103; Conzelmann 1966; Ludwig 1974, 230-231; Gnilka 1980, 21; Hartman 1985, 200-201; Ollrog 1979, 227-231.

[20] Kiley 1986, 94 ff; Ludwig 1974, 193-228; Müller 1988, 325; Schenke 1975, 508-509; Ollrog 1979, 228-231.

disappears from the literature after the catastrophe.[21] It is thus uncertain whether Colossae was rebuilt at all or whether the congregation still remained there. If there was a Christian community at the time Col was written, it was probably very small.[22]

Besides the uncertainty about the situation of Colossae at the time Col was written, it has to be noted that we have no other evidence except Col about the congregation of Colossae.[23] The fact that many of the same names are mentioned in Col and Philem, Onesimus among them, suggests a connection between these letters. Some scholars argue that Philem is addressed to Colossae and it gives us more information about the congregation. However, nothing in Philem indicates that the recipient of the letter, Philemon, lived in Colossae. The interpretation that Philem is aimed at Colossae is only due to the appearance of the same names in Col and Philem.[24] Therefore, only when Col is taken as a genuine letter of Paul it is reasonable to assume that, like Col, Philem was addressed to Colossae. If Col is regarded as unauthentic, it does not help find the town Philem was aimed at.[25] Accordingly, Philem does not provide any information about the congregation at Colossae.

In addition, while the author of Col is a pseudo-Paul, it is also quite possible that the letter has a pseudo-addressee.[26] It is therefore more probable that Col was aimed at a larger circle of readers in Asia Minor than the ancient city of Colossae.[27] In addition, it is possible that A/Col himself belonged to the community the letter is addressed to.[28] Why then A/Col did address his letter to Colossae which was at his time an insignificant town, if a town at all? The explanation may be that it is easier to aim a fictive letter at a small or fictive community than at a prominent city. Had he addressed his letter to Ephesus, there would have been more people

---

[21] Further in Lohse 1971, 8-9; Schweizer 1982, 13-14; Gnilka 1980, 1-3; R. P. Martin 1981, 2-3; Bruce 1988, 3 ff.

[22] Lohse 1971, 181. Cf. Lindemann 1983, 13; 1999, 203-204; Schweizer 1982, 13-14.

[23] Lohse 1971, 2; Pfammatter 1987, 53; Lindemann 1983, 9, 81.

[24] See e.g. Lohse 1971, 186; O'Brien 1982, 265-266; Winter 1987, 2; R. P. Martin 1981, 144-147.

[25] Cf. Gnilka 1982, 5-6; Schenk 1987b, 3480.

[26] Standhartinger 1999, 10-16; 2000, 124. Cf. Schenk 1987a, 3335; Hartman 1995, 25; Furnish 1992a, 1095. In addition, Bauckham states that a pseudepigraphic letter has usually a supposed addressee. He concludes, however, that Col is an authentic letter because the author does not describe the specific situation as a pseudepigrapher usually does but takes it for granted; Bauckham 1988, 475, 490.

[27] Lohse 1971, 181; Schenke & Fischer 1978, 167-168; Pokorny 1987, 17; Wilson 1997, 16-17; Schenk 1987a, 3335. Cf. Kiley 1986, 104; Nielsen 1985, 103; Standhartinger 1999, 13-16, who assume that the readership aimed at whas even broader.

[28] Cf. Lindemann 1983, 86; 1999, who regards Col to be addressed to Laodicea and assumes that A/Col was living there.

noticing that the letter is not genuine.[29] Even if writing in the name of another person was so customary in A/Col's time that some readers noted the fictive character of the letter, it would still have been more reasonable to set a fictive writing in a possibly non-existent town rather than in a living and well-known city.

In Col 2:6-23 the recipients of the letter are warned about "philosophy" (φιλοσοφία). The teachers confronted are not named: in Col 2:8, 16 they are mentioned only by the indefinite someone (τις). Thus we can only try to estimate what was the content of their "philosophy" on the basis of the description in Col 2:6-23. The warning about the persons who are trying to lead the community astray is still generally taken as the main purpose of Col.[30] Tracing the content of the teaching has been problematic, however. For example, the following alternatives have been put forth: Jewish-Christian gnosticism, a Christianized mystery cult, mystical Jewish ascent, Hellenistic Philosophy, syncretistic folk religion, but no consensus has been reached.[31] Barclay has recently stated that the question is "an unsolved, and insoluble, mystery".[32]

Since Hooker in 1973 contended that perhaps the target of Col was not a specific "error" but A/Col had a general warning in view instead, the alternative has now and then been stated. While Hooker, who regards Col as written by Paul, assumes that the warnings arose from the general pressure to conform to the pagan and Jewish environment[33], Nielsen, who does not accept Col as authentic, interprets the warnings still broader: "... the writer's aim is not to counter some specific form of teaching in a particular location, but to commend Paul's interpretation of Christ as the one corrective for a whole range of errors".[34] Nielsen states also that Col "was not directed to a particular church".[35] Furthermore, Kiley explains that Col "warns against possible future developments which may distract from Christ (some of which distractions may have been real at the time of writing)"[36] and assumes that "the heresy-warning could be part of the program in Col to say that Paul's teaching survives the vicissitudes of time"[37]. Following Kiley and Nielsen, Standhartinger

---

[29] It has to be noted that A/Eph himself is unlikely to have addressed his letter to Ephesus. The words ἐν Ἐφέσῳ in the introductory greeting are omitted in many of the earliest and most important manuscripts and thus are likely to have been added by some later scribe or editor; see Furnish 1992b, 535; Lincoln 1990, 1.

[30] See Lohse 1971, 2-3; Haapa 1978, 10; Kümmel 1987, 338-340; Gnilka 1980, 163; Pfammatter 1987, 53-54; Hendriksen 1971, 22-23.

[31] For the history of scholarship on the Colossian philosophy, see Barclay 1997, 39-48; DeMaris 1994, 18-40.

[32] Barclay 1997, 54. Cf. Nielsen 1985, 106: "It is a vast understatement to say ... that no complete agreement has been reached."

[33] Hooker 1973, 329-331, who is followed by Wright 1990, 463-464, and Schenk 1987a, 3350. Cf. Dunn 1995, 180-181, who maintains that in Colossae there was no "false teaching" or "heresy" but "a synagogue apologetic promoting itself as a credible philosophy".

[34] Nielsen 1985, 107.

[35] Nielsen 1985, 121.

[36] Kiley 1986, 65.

[37] Kiley 1986, 105.

takes Col as a testament of Paul, a letter from heaven ('Himmelsbrief'), which was written after his death in order to protect Paul's heritage in the future.[38] At least Standhartinger no longer believes Col to be an actual letter.

Since Ephesus is generally regarded as the center of the Pauline school tradition and it is located in Asia Minor, not far from Colossae, it is also generally taken as the city where Col most probably was composed.[39] When taken as an example of pseudepigraphy written after Paul's lifetime, Col is often dated to ca. A.D. 70. Gnilka argues for so early a date with the fact that A/Col seems to have the martyrdom of Paul in his mind.[40] Some scholars prefer a little later date, but usually not later than the 80s of the first century.[41]

1.2. The Relationship between Colossians and the Authentic Letters of Paul

1.2.1. Literary Dependence in Colossians: State of the Question

When Col is taken as a deutero-Pauline letter, written by a disciple of Paul after the death of the Apostle, the question arises about the relationship between Col and the genuine Pauline epistles: does A/Col use them as models? In 1966 E. P. Sanders started the discussion with his article Literary Dependence in Colossians.[42] He assumed that A/Col may have used the authentic letters of Paul as literary sources. In order to deny the authenticity of Col, Sanders demonstrated that in many parts of Col there are conflated texts from several genuine letters of Paul (Rom, 1 Cor, 2 Cor, Gal, Phil, 1 Thess). The phenomenon indicates literary dependence which makes it improbable that the texts were written by Paul. In the case of Pauline authorship, we would have to assume that Paul either memorized his previous letters or carried about with him the copies and consulted them when composing a new letter, which seems very unlikely because, like Sanders states,"... there is no

---

[38] Standhartinger 1999, 16, 182-193, 284. Cf. Hübner 1997, 13, who states that Col is addressed to fictive recipients.

[39] Lohse 1969, 219; 1971, 182 n. 17; Pokorný 1987, 15; Gnilka 1980, 22; Pfammatter 1987, 54-55; Schenke & Fischer 1978, 168; Hübner 1997, 16. Also those who accept Col as authentic or at least written in Paul's lifetime usually assume that it was written in Ephesus since it is near Colossae and it is a place where Paul once was in prison. See Schweizer 1982, 24-26; Luz 1998, 184-185; R. P. Martin 1981, 30; Ollrog 1979, 232. Contra Kümmel 1987, 348; and Hartman 1985, 201, who see Caesarea or Rome the most probable solutions and Bruce 1988, 32; O'Brien 1982, xlix-liv; Hendriksen 1971, 22-23; Dunn 1996, 41, who prefer Rome.

[40] Gnilka 1980, 23. Cf. Pfammmatter 1987, 54-55; Schenke & Fischer 1978, 168; Hübner 1997, 10.

[41] Pokorný 1987, 15: about A.D. 70 or later; Lindemann 1983, 11; 1999, 205: A.D. 70 – 80; Wilson 1997, 22: "sometime in the 70s or 80s of the first century"; Lohse 1971, 182 n. 17: "around A.D. 80".

[42] JBL 85, 28-45.

evidence for the literary dependence of any one of Paul's seven undisputed letters upon another".[43]

Sanders methodologically followed C. Leslie Mitton who had investigated in detail the character of Eph and found conflations of several genuine Pauline letters in the text.[44] Sanders further developed the criteria indicating literary dependence. Unlike Mitton, who also takes as parallels passages in which the thought is the same, Sanders emphasizes that only verbal and verbatim resemblances between the texts can show possible literary dependence. He places in parallel only "passages in which three or more words are in agreement within a short space". In addition, "a two-word phrase in verbatim agreement will be considered enough for a parallel, provided that the two words are sufficiently significant and unusual".[45] According to Sanders, the term "literary dependence" includes quotation from memory. Thus, it is not necessary to assume that A/Col had the texts he imitates in front of him when writing or, as Sanders puts it, to "call to mind the picture of a writer unrolling a scroll to a certain point and copying it".[46]

In order to show literary dependence Sanders formulated the following four questions:

> 1. Is there evidence of the conflation of two or more passages from various places in Paul's letters into one passage in Colossians, or of serial quotation of two or more phrases from various places in Paul's letters in one passage of Colossians? ...
> 2. Are non-Pauline characteristics intermixed with verbatim agreement? ...
> 3. Is the phrase quoted such as would be likely to be a stock phrase or a favorite expression, or is it such as to show literary dependence?
> 4. Are the words the same because the argument is the same, or are the same words applied to a different point?[47]

He argued that the evidence for literary dependence which we derive from the questions is cumulative: if we frequently receive "non-Pauline answers", the evidence becomes strong. In addition, the questions help us to notice how the text of an imitator would be likely to differ from that of Paul.[48]

Sanders studies the passages Col 1:15-16, 1:20-22a, 1:26-27, 2:12-13, and 3:5-11 finding verbal agreement with several texts from Rom, 1 Cor, 2 Cor, Gal, Phil, and 1 Thess. He concludes that in these verses the evidence for literary dependence is indisputable but emphasizes that his investigation "by no means exhausts the verbatim agreements between Colossians and the Pauline epistles". Sanders notes that the evidence is mostly limited to the first two chapters. Between the verses Col 2:13 and 3:4 he finds only six words which may suggest a literary dependence

---

[43] E. P. Sanders 1966, 29-31.
[44] Mitton, The Epistle to the Ephesians. Its Authorship, Origin and Purpose. Oxford: Clarendon Press 1951.
[45] E. P. Sanders 1966, 30.
[46] E. P. Sanders 1966, 30 n. 9.
[47] E. P. Sanders 1966, 32-33.
[48] E. P. Sanders 1966, 33.

between Col and the genuine Pauline letters and at Col 3:11 the evidence stops. After that only Col 3:15 shows verbal agreement pointing to a possible literary dependence on Phil 4:7. Thus Sanders does not find any evidence for literary dependence in Col 3:16-4:18 and states that it is compatible with the theory of John Knox, according to which the latter part of Col is authentic.[49]

Wolfgang Schenk published in the 1980's two articles about Col.[50] He agrees with Sanders that at least some parts of Col have a literary dependence upon the authentic letters of Paul[51] and adds some new conclusions e.g. that the phrase τὰ στοιχεῖα τοῦ κόσμου (Col 2:8, 20) depends upon Gal 4:3-9.[52] In addition, he refers to the generally accepted interpretation according to which the frame of Col, the beginning and the conclusion, is modelled on that of Philem which suggests that A/Col knew and utilized Philem. Especially the fact that all five names (Aristarchus, Mark, Epaphras, Luke, and Demas) occurring in Philem 23-24 are enumerated in Col 4:10-14 indicates literary dependence between Col and Philem.[53] Schenk also calls attention to verbal agreements between Col and Mk. He notes e.g. that the phrase ἐπὶ τῆς γῆς is typical of Col (1:16,20; 3:2,5) as well as Mk (4:26-31) and, in addition, both Col 1:6, 10 and Mk 4:8 include the unnatural order "to bear fruit and grow".[54] The resemblances Schenk mentions are mostly limited to the first chapter of Col but the reason for this seems to be only the fact that he concentrates on this part of Col because he regards Col 1:15-20 as the core of the letter.[55] Therefore, the other parts of Col may also include agreements with Mk.

Like Schenk, also e.g. Lars Aejmelaeus, Petr Pokorný, Charles M. Nielsen, V. P. Furnish, Richard E. DeMaris, and Rainer Reuter follow Sanders' conclusion that literary dependence upon the genuine Pauline letters occurs in Col.[56] In addition, Lars Hartman follows Sanders' conclusion stating that A/Col was acquainted with Paul's epistles but rejects the literary dependence of Col and the thesis that Col is deutero-Pauline. Instead he takes Col to have been written by a co-worker of Paul within his lifetime and assumes that the Pauline school had already preserved the copies of Paul's letters at that time.[57] Furnish describes Sanders' method in his

---

[49] E. P. Sanders 1966, 43-45.

[50] Schenk, Christus, das Geheimnis der Welt, als dogmatisches und ethisches Grundprinzip des Kolosserbriefes. EvT 43 (1983), 139-155. Schenk, Der Kolosserbrief in der neueren Forschung (1945-1985). ANRW II 25.4. (1987), 3327-3364.

[51] Schenk 1983, 139; Schenk 1987a, 3341.

[52] Schenk 1987a, 3338-3340.

[53] Schenk 1987a, 3338-3339. Cf. Schenke & Fischer 1978, 167-168; Hübner 1997, 117; Lindemann 1979, 39; Wikenhauser & Schmid 1973, 473; Gnilka 1980, 21-22; Kiley 1986, 83-84; Müller 1988, 296-297; Standhartinger 1999, 81-84; Lohse 1971, 175-177; Vielhauer 1975, 200; Haapa 1978, 11-12; Wilson 1997, 21.

[54] Schenk 1983, 148-151 (see nn. 34 and 36); 1987a, 3343 n. 54.

[55] Schenk 1983, 147.

[56] See L. Aejmelaeus 1987a, 56-57; Pokorný 1987, 1; Nielsen 1985, 120, 108; Furnish 1992a, 1094; DeMaris 1994, 43; Reuter 1997, 23. Cf. VanKooten 1995, 1 n. 1.

[57] Hartman 1985, 197, 200-201; 1986, 139-141; 1995, 35.

article about Colossians in the Anchor Bible Dictionary with the words "carefully formulated criteria for identifying verbal agreements".[58] It is also remarkable that a few scholars follow Sanders methodologically: Lars Aejmelaeus when investigating Paul's speech at Miletus (Apt 20:18-35)[59] and the relationship between 1 Thess 5:1-11 and Lk 21:34-36[60], Anneli Aejmelaeus in her study on the heritage of Paul in 1 Pet[61], Rainer Reuter in his article on the relationship between Luke and 1 Clem[62], and Heikki Leppä when studying Luke's use of Galatians.[63]

Kenneth J. Neumann compared disputed Pauline letters (Eph, Col, 2 Thess) with the authentic ones and also with non-Pauline literature (Hebrews, 1 Clement, Ignatius, Philo, Epictetus, and Josephus)[64] and found Eph and Col to be closer to the genuine Paulines than the Pastorals or other NT writings. It is worth noting that, referring to Mitton (he does not seem to know the article of Sanders), he concludes that "[t]he similarity of the disputed letters to Pauline style could be due to literary dependence".[65]

However, Sanders' point of view has remained a relatively ignored aspect of scholarship: several scholars have criticized Sanders' method and contest his conclusions concerning literary dependence. The similarities between Col and the authentic letters of Paul are generally taken to be due to the Pauline school tradition rather than direct acquaintance with his letters. Helga Ludwig contends in her study Der Verfasser des Kolosserbriefes. Ein Schüler des Paulus that A/Col utilizes Pauline phrases and theology so independently that he cannot be a later writer copying Paul's letters.[66] Similarly, Hartman contends that A/Col is "an independent theologian" who does not use Pauline letters "slavishly or mechanically" and thus cannot be a later author.[67] It is not necessary to assume, however, that a later writer cannot modify the texts he is utilizing. Imitating is more than just copying: in philosophical schools people were taught to imitate the thoughts of famous persons in addition to the style of language.[68] A person living in Paul's lifetime as well as a later author would be able to utilize his phrases and theology independently. It is also interesting that unlike Ludwig, scholars generally assume that the shaping of the Pauline theology indicates a later author rather than one living in Paul's lifetime. In addition, Sanders does not assume that A/Col has no other connection

---

[58] Furnish 1992, 1094.
[59] L. Aejmelaeus 1987a, see pp. 101-190.
[60] L. Aejmelaeus 1985, 95-96, 134. See also Dunderberg 1994, 26-27.
[61] A. Aejmelaeus 1992.
[62] Reuter 1999.
[63] H. Leppä 2002.
[64] Neumann, The Authenticity of the Pauline Epistles in the Light of Stylostatistical Analysis. SBLDS 120. Atlanta 1990.
[65] Neumann 1990, 218-219.
[66] Ludwig 1974, 24, 193 ss.
[67] Hartman 1986, 140.
[68] See e.g. Balz 1969, 411-412.

to Paul but his letters: he regards him as a disciple of Paul who was naturally also otherwise acquainted with other aspects of Paul's heritage besides his letters.

A. J. M. Wedderburn criticizes Sanders in the following words: "... I am inclined to date Colossians at an earlier date when its author was more likely to be recalling from memory the teaching of Paul than to be fabricating a patchwork of citations and allusions on the basis of his collected letters".[69] It is doubtful whether Wedderburn understands the method of Sanders correctly. Since Sanders assumes that A/Col is recalling from memory some texts of the letters, the term literary dependence only means to him that A/Col seems to be acquainted with a definite verse. He does not presuppose that A/Col has a collection of the letters in front of him.

Eduard Lohse, Andreas Lindemann, and Ludwig explain away the verbatim agreement Sanders noticed between Col 1:26-27 and 1 Cor 2:7, Rom 16:25-26, Rom 9:23-24 by emphasizing that A/Col here makes use of a revelation schema developed in the Pauline tradition.[70] However, the interpretation does not explain the other resemblances Sanders found. It is a surprising detail that Lohse and Lindemann (as well as Standhartinger, see p. 21) who otherwise contest literary dependence in Col still contend that the striking similarity between the final greetings of Col and Philem shows that A/Col is a pseudepigrapher who was acquainted with Philem while Sanders contests the literary dependence in the latter part of Col which includes verses Col 4:10-14.

Mark Kiley continued the investigation on the literary dependence in Col in his study Colossians as Pseudepigraphy published in 1986. Kiley criticizes Sanders sharply. In Kiley's view, the "scissors-and-paste method" of Sanders neglects the possibility that the verbal similarities between Col and Paul can be due to a group "keeping alive in their discussions and literary productions a fund of Paul's language which is not dependent on his letters".[71] In addition, he contends that the occurrence of similar words cannot indicate literary dependence because "any number of New Testament texts which are ignorant of each other use the same words", for example both Jas and Mk discuss πίστις.[72] He also states that Sanders "sidesteps the surest criteria for providing literary dependence" because his method does not necessitate that the texts A/Col utilizes occur in the same order in Col and in the texts which are imitated. In addition, he calls attention to the detail that Sanders assumes Col 1:26-27 to depend on Rom 16:25-26, the textual history of

---

[69] Wedderburn 1987, 73; cf. 1993, 62. Similarly Dunn 1996, 37 n. 46, calls Sanders' method a "patchwork quilt" hypothesis which is "no more credible than the older source-critical theories of the Pentateuch or the Synoptic Gospels". Also according to R. P. Martin 1981, 39, the doubts over Sanders' method are considerable.

[70] Lohse 1971, 74 n. 42, 182; Lindemann 1979, 118 n. 28, 120; Ludwig 1974, 87. Cf. Hübner 1988, 229-230. However, Pokorný 1987, 87 assumes referring to Sanders that the phrase τὸ πλοῦτος τῆς δόξης might recall Rom 9:23.

[71] Kiley 1986, 69.

[72] Kiley 1986, 70.

which is a complex one: Rom 16:25-27 may have been added to Rom after Col was written.[73]

Kiley's critique does not do justice to Sanders. It is not true that Sanders neglects the possibility of oral tradition since the third question which according to Sanders' method should be asked (see p. 16) takes into consideration the possibility that some of the verbal agreements do not indicate literary dependence but are due to the use of similar phrases. Nor does Sanders assume that one common word in the texts points to a literary dependence between them, like Kiley claims. Since Sanders does not suggest that Col is modelled on any single letter of Paul and, in addition, according to his definition literary dependence includes quotation from memory, it is not necessary to assume that passages appear in the same order in Col and the letters imitated. Only the last argument of Kiley is well-grounded: it is true that the date of Rom 16:25-26 is uncertain and thus the text may be later than Col. However, this one detail does not invalidate the method of Sanders since in case Rom 16:25-26 is later than Col, the verbal agreement can indicate that it depends on Col.

Kiley puts forth the thesis that Col uses Phil and Philem as its primary models of construction. He inspects six passages in Phil and three in Philem which include language similar to Col, used in the same way and occurring in the same sequence in the letters.[74] Kiley compares these texts with the parallels in other authentic Pauline letters and notices that in all cases the passages in Philem and Phil resemble Col most. His conclusion is that "one is able to say with some confidence that Phil and Philem were known as such to the Col author and were used by him as major models of construction".[75] All other verbal agreements between Col and the authentic Pauline letters he assumes to be influenced by common parlance or Pauline tradition which he defines as "some sort of acquaintance with Paul's language in a group". Nevertheless, Kiley finds it possible that A/Col had all the genuine letters before him but chose to utilize only Philem and Phil.[76]

Sanders and Kiley investigate the literary dependence differently. While Sanders studies verbatim agreements between a few verses, Kiley compares the structures of all the letters. Thus their conclusions are different. For example Kiley assumes that Col 1:15-20 is modelled on Phil 2:6-11 but in Sanders' view it conflates 2 Cor 4:4, Rom 1:20, 1 Cor 8:5-6, Rom 11:36, and 2 Cor 5:18.[77] This indicates that Sanders and Kiley do not define literary dependence in the same way. Kiley seems to assume that the imitator has the text he follows in front of him but

---

[73] Kiley 1986, 71-72. Similarly Schenk 1983, 139, n. 7.

[74] The parallels between Phil and Col: 1) Phil 1:9 // Col 1:9, 2) Phil 2:6-11 // Col 1:15-20, 3) Phil 2:15 // Col 1:22, 4) Phil 3:3-4 // Col 2:11,13,18,23, 5) Phil 3:19-20 // Col 3:1-5, 6) Phil 4:18 // Col 4:12. The parallels between Philem and Col: 1) Philem 4-5 // Col 1:3-4, 2) Philem 13 // Col 4:9, 3) Philem 23-24 // Col 4:10-13.

[75] Kiley 1986, 75-91, quotation from p. 84.

[76] Kiley 1986, 91-103, quotation from p. 94.

[77] E. P. Sanders 1966, 35-38.

Sanders emphasizes quotation from memory which makes possible the conflation of several texts. In addition, it is interesting that besides Philem, e.g. Schweizer and Lohse see the structure of Col as resembling that of Rom, not Phil as Kiley assumes.[78] Thus it is not self-evident that A/Col uses Phil as the primary model of construction.

Angela Standhartinger studies once more the formation of Col in her recent publication Studien zur Entstehungsgeschichte und Intention des Kolosserbriefes (1999). She repeats the criticism stated against Sanders by Lohse and Lindemann, that Col 1:26-27 here makes use of a revelation schema developed in the Pauline tradition.[79] In addition, she criticizes Kiley's assumption that the agreements have to occur in the same order in the texts which have literary dependence on each other and claims that Kiley is not able to show the literary dependence between Col and Phil.[80] Standhartinger concludes that A/Col had Philem in front of him but other verbal agreements with Pauline letters are due to the acquaintance with the oral tradition.[81]

This survey has shown that, on the one hand, Sanders' thesis that A/Col was acquainted with all the genuine letters of Paul has been generally contested. On the other hand, Hartman accepts the thesis and combines it interestingly with his own opinion that Col was written by a co-worker of Paul within his lifetime by assuming that even so early the Pauline school preserved the copies of Paul's letters. Mostly scholars still seem to have problems with the suggestion that the authentic epistles of Paul, apart from Philem, would have been available to A/Col and sometimes it is even argued that it was not possible for him to know the Pauline letters, since the corpus was not yet formed at the time Col was written.[82] However, Philem is a tiny letter addressed to a private person while Col is aimed at a congregation and thus, excluding the beginning and the conclusion of the epistle, the structure of it resembles much more other letters of Paul. So it would be surprising if only Philem was the model for Col.

1.2.2. The Place of Colossians in the Pauline Corpus

This chapter will examine the place of Col in the Pauline corpus in order to work out whether it seems to be possible that A/Col knew the authentic epistles of Paul. The earliest known form of the collection of Paul's letters of which we have definite documentary knowledge contained 10 letters: Rom, 1-2 Cor, Gal, Eph, Phil, Col, 1-2 Thess, Philem. The Pastorals were omitted but the deutero-Pauline

---

[78] See Schweizer 1982, 15-16; Lohse 1969, 219.
[79] Standhartinger 1999, 67.
[80] Standhartinger 1999, 87-89.
[81] Standhartinger 1999, 151-152.
[82] See e.g. Gnilka 1980, 22. Contra Müller 1988, 322, 301, who seems to assume that A/Col knew several letters of Paul.

letters Eph, Col, and 2 Thess were already included. The ten-letter collection is attested in Marcion ca. A.D. 140 but it is very unlikely that Marcion was the first to collect the letters since, for example, 1 Clem shows acquaintance with some of the Pauline epistles.[83] There are two main theories about the formation of the ten-letter collection.

Goodspeed followed by Mitton stated that Paul's letters were almost completely neglected after the recipients of the epistles had read them but about A.D. 90 an intimate disciple of Paul in Ephesus collected all the letters he could find. According to Goodspeed, the collector wrote Eph which shows constant use of the materials of the nine other letters, especially Col and Philem which he seems to have known better than the others. Eph was meant to serve as a summary of Paul's main teaching and as an introduction to the collection and was thus put at the beginning of it as a cover letter. Goodspeed based his theory on the observation that there is no echo of Paul's writings in Acts. He concluded that the collection of Paul's letters was published after Acts and the collector was also inspired by Acts, which tells so much about the life of Paul.[84]

Goodspeed's theory is problematic. The absence of any echo of Paul's writings in Acts is not self-evident: according to several scholars, Acts even depends on the Pauline corpus.[85] In addition, Mowry criticizes Goodspeed's theory by suggesting the possibility that individual letters were circulated and read locally although the author of Acts did not know them.[86] Mitton, who otherwise follows Goodspeed, also acknowledges the problems. He states that the association of the collection of Pauline corpus with the publication of Acts is not an indispensable item for the theory and, in addition, that the theory can be modified so as not to be wholly inconsistent with the assumption of gradual development of the Pauline corpus. Mitton contends that perhaps the purpose of Eph was not to introduce the Pauline corpus as an entirely new work, as Goodspeed stated, but "rather to commend it in its completed form to Christian communities" and assumes that Eph was formed when all the Pauline letters had reached Asia Minor where only Col and Philem were known earlier.[87]

Mitton studied in detail the origin of Eph and compared the parallels between Eph and the letters of Paul which he regarded as authentic (Rom, 1-2 Cor, Gal, Phil, Col, 1-2 Thess, Philem). He concluded that the author of Eph knew Col and

---

[83] Kümmel 1987, 479-480; cf. Mowry 1944, 73; Gamble 1992, 853-854; Knox 1942, 54-55, 172-176; von Harnack 1926, 6-7.

[84] Goodspeed 1974 (first published in 1926), 20-32; 1951; Mitton 1951; 1955. In addition, Knox 1942, 57-60, accepts the thesis that Paul's letters were neglected at first and only later collected but, unlike Goodspeed and Mitton, Knox dates Acts to the middle of the second century and thus denies the suggestion that Acts led to the formation of the Pauline corpus; Knox 1942, 173.

[85] See Enslin 1938; 1970; Thiering 1967, 139-189; Lindemann 1979, 165-173; L. Aejmelaeus 1987a, 41-72; Walker 1985, 3-23; Salo 1991; H. Leppä 2002.

[86] Mowry 1944, 76, 78. Cf. Schenke 1975, 512.

[87] Mitton 1951, 52-53. For the details criticized in Goodspeed's theory, see Furnish 1992b, 541.

Philem very well, he "wrote with a copy of Colossians ready to hand" and "seems to have some special attachment to the epistle to Philemon", but was also familiar with all the letters of Paul, "with the possible exception of 2 Thess".[88] Thus Mitton's results indicate that when Eph was composed, all the genuine Pauline letters were available. In addition, 2 Thess seems to be unauthentic and later than Eph, though Mitton did not acknowledge it himself.

An alternative theory, however, has been put forth that there was an early circulation of the letters. Before Goodspeed the theory was represented e.g. by von Harnack.[89] The letters are assumed to have been read aloud to each community and exchanged with neighboring congregations (cf. 1 Thess 5:27, Col 4:16).[90] Lohse states that Rom above all was "read and studied again and again".[91] It is also generally assumed that the ten-letter corpus of Paul was formed step by step in a long and gradual process: at first smaller collections took shape which later were brought together. However, there is no consensus concerning the stages of the process but several theories have been promulgated.

Mowry, following Mitton's thesis that the ten-letter corpus was not created until after Acts was written but preferring early circulation, contended that the letters were at first collected in three places: the hinterland of Asia Minor, Macedonia, and Achaea. Gal, Col, and Philem were brought together in Asia Minor, 1 Thess and Phil in Macedonia, and 1 Cor and Rom in Achaea. Later the Corinthian church produced a composite 2 Cor and 2 Thess was composed in Macedonia with the help of 1 Thess. Mowry based her theory on the results of literary criticism: Rom 16 was added to Rom 1-15 and the composite 2 Cor was produced, and individual letters were also locally gathered.[92]

Schmithals assumed that the first collection contained the main letters of Paul: 1 Cor, 2 Cor, Gal, Phil, 1 Thess, 2 Thess, and Rom to which Eph, Col, and Philem were added later.[93] Schenke followed Schmithals, modifying his theory. Like Mowry, he takes 2 Thess to be unauthentic and thus does not assume it was included in the first corpus. Moreover, he stated that the corpus did not contain 2 Cor in the form we know it now because it is a composite letter. Accordingly, in Schenke's view the first collection contained 1 Cor, (2 Cor), Gal, Phil, 1 Thess, Rom to which Philem, Col, Eph, 2 Thess as well as 1 Pet and the Pastorals were added later. He assumes that the letters were collected in two centers, in Corinth and in Ephesus. The latter is also the place where the deutero-Pauline Eph and Col

---

88 Mitton 1951, 246-248.

89 von Harnack 1926, 6-27. Further in Mitton 1955, 11 ff.

90 L. Aejmelaeus 1987a, 61; Mowry 1944, 85; Campenhausen 1968, 170; von Harnack 1926, 10-11, 20-21; Hartman 1985, 200-201.

91 Lohse 1969, 218-219; 1971, 181-183, followed by Nielsen 1985, 120.

92 Mowry 1944.

93 Schmithals 1965, 175-201. Contra Gamble 1975, who does not accept Schmithals' idea of a single early edition of the Pauline corpus although he prefers the early circulation of the epistles.

were composed. At first Col was formed using the frame of Philem and then Eph was modelled on Col, upon which Eph also has a literary dependence.[94]

Trobisch has a totally different theory. He contends that Paul himself collected together Rom, 1 Cor, 2 Cor, and Gal. At the beginning of the second century the collection extended to a thirteen-letter corpus when Eph, Phil, Col, 1 Thess, 2 Thess, Philem, and the Pastorals were added. This happened at Ephesus. Later the collection contained 14 letters, adding Heb to the others.[95] Recently Richards has put forth the suggestion that the collection of Paul's letters originated with Paul himself. He notes that in the 1st century letter-writers routinely preserved copies of their letters and assumes that Paul did this as well.[96]

Among the theories about the formation of the Pauline corpus, that of Goodspeed does not allow at all that A/Col knew the genuine Pauline letters since Col was included in the first corpus ever collected and there was no circulation of the letters before that. However, the theory includes so many problems that even his follower Mitton accepted an early circulation. Though Mitton assumed that the letters were published together and thus, apart from Col and Philem, not available to the public before that, it is very unlikely that the letters were hidden so that nobody could read them. Mitton seems to assume that at the same time Col and Philem were known in Ephesus, the other letters were circulating outside Asia Minor, which is natural if Col is taken as authentic. But if Col is taken as unauthentic, is it not possible that when all the letters had reached Asia Minor, Col was written followed by Eph? This alternative would allow for A/Col's acquaintance with all the genuine Pauline letters.

All the theories which accept early circulation make it possible that A/Col knew at least some authentic letters of Paul. According to Mowry's model, it seems to be probable that A/Col knew only Gal and Philem which were circulating in Asia Minor where Col was written. Trobisch's theory suggests it is very likely that A/Col was acquainted with the letters Paul himself collected together (Rom, 1 Cor, 2 Cor, and Gal). In addition, if the letters were read in congregations before they were gathered together, A/Col may have known some of the letters which were added to the corpus at the same time as Col (Eph, Phil, 1 Thess, 2 Thess, Philem, and the Pastorals), probably Phil, 1 Thess, or Philem which are earlier than Col. Schmithals and Schenke's theory facilitates the idea that A/Col was familiar with the first collection of Pauline letters: 1 Cor, (2 Cor), Gal, Phil, (1) Thess, and Rom. In addition, it is possible that he knew some of the letters which were added together to the corpus and thus may have been circulating in the area where Col

[94] Schenke 1975, see especially pp. 513-514, 516. Cf. Lohse 1972, 13, who assumes that there must have been letter collections in the centers of the Pauline mission, in Ephesus and Corinth. He does not try to define the compositions of the collections.

[95] Trobisch 1989. In addition, Lindemann 1979, 30, contends that there have been smaller collections before the formation of the ten-letter corpus.

[96] Richards 1998.

was composed (Philem, Eph, and 2 Thess). Thus an acceptance of Schmithals and Schenke's theory means that A/Col may have been familiar with all the undisputed Pauline letters (Rom, 1-2 Cor, Gal, Phil, 1 Thess, Philem) with the exception of 2 Cor which may have been only available in part. Finally, according to Richards' theory, all the letters may have been available to A/Col.

The survey of the theories concerning the formation of the Pauline corpus has shown that the idea of the early circulation of the letters among the congregations, at least regionally, is generally accepted. Therefore, it is very unlikely that the pseudepigraphic writer of Col was not at all familiar with genuine Pauline letters. Rather, it seems probable that he was acquainted with some, or even all of them. Thus Sanders' thesis concerning the literary dependence in Col cannot be ignored by saying that it was not possible for A/Col to know the authentic Pauline letters.

1.3. Examples of Literary Dependence in Ancient Writings

1.3.1. The Literary Dependence of 2 Peter on Jude

The purpose of this chapter is to examine in detail the literary relationship between 2 Pet and Jude. Because almost all scholars agree that 2 Pet is dependent on Jude[97], this analysis will help to define literary dependence. It was noted above that Sanders, Kiley, and Ludwig have very different opinions about the criteria for literary dependence and, moreover, especially Lohse, Lindemann, and Standhartinger emphasize that apart from those between Col and Philem, all agreements between the texts derive from a common oral tradition. Thus the task of defining literary dependence is important. The analysis of the relationship between 2 Pet and Jude will demonstrate something about the similarities between two texts dependent on each other.

The resemblances between 2 Pet and Jude are most obvious between verses 2 Pet 2:1-18, 3:1-3 and Jude 4-16, 17-18.[98] There 2 Pet seems to imitate Jude nearly verse by verse.[99] However, the only fully identical clauses are 2 Pet 2:17b and Jude 13b.[100] Besides the obvious resemblances, many scholars draw attention to the fact

---

[97] See Bauckham 1992, 1100; Fornberg 1977, 34, 58; Schelkle 1964, 138-139; Grundmann 1974, 106; Kelly 1969, 227. According to Morton & McLeman 1966, 16 the dependence of 2 Pet on Jude would today be called plagiarism. The priority of 2 Pet was supported by Luther. Later it has been accepted e.g. by Bigg 1987 (first published in 1901), 216, 242. According to Reicke 1964, 190 "the best assumption is that both epistles derive from a common tradition which may well have been oral rather than written". In addition, Guthrie 1990, 923-925 denies the literary dependence between 2 Pet and Jude.

[98] Schelkle 1964, 138-139; Vielhauer 1975, 596; Kelly 1969, 225; Bauckham 1992, 1100; Grundmann 1974, 102; Fornberg 1977, 33-34; Watson 1988, 160, 189.

[99] See e.g. Fornberg 1977, 33-34 and Watson 1988, 164-169.

[100] Kelly 1969, 226. 2 Pet 2:17b: ... οἷς ὁ ζόφος τοῦ σκότους τετήρηται. Jude 13b: ... οἷς ὁ ζόφος τοῦ σκότους εἰς αἰῶνα τετήρηται.

that 2 Pet 1:5 is similar to Jude 3 and 2 Pet 1:12 to Jude 5.[101] Furthermore, it is often stated that the beginnings of the letters (2 Pet 1:2 // Jude 2) and the conclusions of them (2 Pet 3:14,18 // Jude 24-25) resemble each other.[102] The connection between the two letters is illustrated in the following table.

2 Pet	Jude
1:2	2
1:5	3
1:12	5
2:1-18	4-16
3:1-3	17-18
3:14, 18	24-25

The table illustrates that most of the resemblances between 2 Pet and Jude occur in the same order in the texts. However, there is one exception: 2 Pet 1:12 imitates Jude 5 but 2 Pet 2 starts again to imitate the text of Jude from v. 4 onwards. In addition, it is noteworthy that, excluding the most obvious resemblances between 2 Pet 2:1-3:3 and Jude 4-18, the similarities occur only in one or two verses. Next it is necessary to examine in detail three examples of the resemblances. First, to look at the agreement between verses 2 Pet 2:12-13, 15 and Jude 10-12 , second, the resemblances between verses 2 Pet 1:5, 12, 2:1-3 and Jude, 3, 5, 4, and third, the similarities between the beginnings and the conclusions of the letters. In the following table — as well as in other tables — the words exactly in the same form are in boldface and other similar words are underlined.

---

[101] Vielhauer 1975, 596; Grundmann 1974, 102; Kelly 1969, 226; Schelkle 1964, 138; Fornberg 1977, 34.

[102] Kelly 1969, 226; Schelkle 1964, 138; Grundmann 1974, 102. Vielhauer 1975, 596, mentions only the similarity between the conclusions of the letters.

2 Pet 2:12-15	Jude 10-12
12 **Οὗτοι δὲ ὡς ἄλογα ζῷα** γεγεννημένα φυσικὰ εἰς ἅλωσιν καὶ φθορὰν ἐν οἷς ἀγνοοῦσιν βλασφημοῦντες, ἐν τῇ φθορᾷ αὐτῶν καὶ φθαρήσονται	10 **Οὗτοι δὲ** ὅσα μὲν οὐκ οἴδασιν βλασφημοῦσιν, ὅσα δὲ φυσικῶς **ὡς** τὰ **ἄλογα ζῷα** ἐπίστανται, ἐν τούτοις φθείρονται.
13 ἀδικούμενοι μισθὸν ἀδικίας, ... σπίλοι καὶ μῶμοι ἐντρυφῶντες **ἐν ταῖς** ἀπάταις αὐτῶν **συνευωχούμενοι** ὑμῖν,	12 Οὗτοί εἰσιν οἱ **ἐν ταῖς** ἀγάπαις ὑμῶν σπιλάδες **συνευωχούμενοι** ἀφόβως ...
14 ὀφθαλμοὺς ἔχοντες μεστοὺς μοιχαλίδος καὶ ἀκαταπαύστους ἁμαρτίας, δελεάζοντες ψυχὰς ἀστηρίκτους, καρδίαν γεγυμνασμένην πλεονεξίας ἔχοντες, κατάρας τέκνα˙	
15 καταλείποντες εὐθεῖαν ὁδὸν ἐπλανήθησαν, ἐξακολουθήσαντες τῇ ὁδῷ **τοῦ Βαλαὰμ** τοῦ Βοσόρ, ὃς μισθὸν ἀδικίας ἠγάπησεν	11 οὐαὶ αὐτοῖς, ὅτι τῇ ὁδῷ τοῦ Κάϊν ἐπορεύθησαν καὶ τῇ πλάνῃ **τοῦ Βαλαὰμ** μισθοῦ ἐξεχύθησαν καὶ τῇ ἀντιλογίᾳ τοῦ Κόρε ἀπώλοντο.

The first example, the relation between Jude 10-12 and 2 Pet 2:12-15, is part of the most obvious resemblance between Jude and 2 Pet. Accordingly, it should be the strongest of the examples of the literary dependence of 2 Pet upon Jude. Jude 10 tells about people (οὗτοι δέ) who slander (βλασφημοῦσιν) whatever they do not understand (ὅσα ... οὐκ οἴδασιν) and who are destroyed (φθείρονται) by those things that they know by instinct (φυσικῶς) like irrational animals (ὡς τὰ ἄλογα ζῷα). Similarly 2 Pet 2:12 describes people (οὗτοι δέ) who are like irrational animals (ὡς ἄλογα ζῷα), mere creatures of instinct (φυσικά), who slander (βλασφημοῦντες) what they do not understand (οἷς ἀγνοοῦσιν) and will be destroyed (φθαρήσονται). Thus the author of 2 Pet imitates clearly the text of Jude. It is remarkable, however, that he does not copy it. Only the words οὗτοι δέ and ὡς (τὰ) ἄλογα ζῷα are repeated verbatim. Other common words are either used in a different form (βλασφημέω, φθείρω) or replaced by a word, which has the same stem (φυσικός, φυσικῶς). The noun φθορά is employed twice in 2 Pet 2:12, which has the same stem as the verb φθείρω used in Jude 10. In addition, the notion that people do not understand is written with different words (ὅσα ... οὐκ οἴδασιν / οἷς ἀγνοοῦσιν). When modifying the word order, the author of 2 Pet breaks up the structure of Jude. Most significant is the changing of the place of the phrase ὡς ἄλογα ζῷα. The meaning of it is difficult to understand in 2 Pet. Consequently, it has been interpreted in many different ways.[103] However, all scholars agree that the meaning of the phrase differs in 2 Pet from that in Jude. Accordingly, neither the words nor the thoughts of Jude are strictly repeated in 2 Pet.

---

[103] Cf. Kelly 1969, 338-339; Watson 1988, 179-180; Grundmann 1974, 104; Fornberg 1977, 48-49.

2 Pet 2:13 continues to describe the evil people. This description resembles the text of Jude 12 although the only common word is the verb συνευωχέομαι, 'to feast together', which occurs in the same form συνευωχούμενοι in both texts. However, the verb συνευωχέομαι is very unusual: 2 Pet 2:13 and Jude 12 are the only texts in early Christian literature where it appears.[104] This fact points to the dependence between 2 Pet 2:13 and Jude 12. In Jude 12 the people are said to be blemishes on the love-feasts (ἐν ταῖς ἀγάπαις ὑμῶν σπιλάδες συνευωχούμενοι) which looks similar to the mention in 2 Pet 2:13, σπίλοι ... ἐν ταῖς ἀπάταις αὐτῶν συνευωχούμενοι ὑμῖν, although the words used are different. It must be noted that some textual variants of 2 Pet read ἀγάπαις and some manuscripts of Jude ἀπάταις. However, the change of pronouns (ὑμῶν – αὐτῶν) makes it unlikely that ἀγάπαις was the original reading of 2 Pet, or that the copy of Jude which was used by the author of 2 Pet already had the reading ἀπάταις. Thus A/Pet must have made an alteration when rewriting the text of Jude 13.[105] This resemblance shows us that a pseudepigrapher sometimes chooses words which look similar instead of using the same words as the text he imitates.

It is also worthy of note that the author of 2 Pet does not follow the text of Jude verse by verse. As was noted above, 2 Pet 2:12 follows Jude 10 and 2 Pet 2:13 follows Jude 12. However, 2 Pet 2:14 has no parallel in Jude; the text has been expanded by the author of 2 Pet.[106] In addition, in 2 Pet 2:15 the writer starts again to imitate Jude. Jude 11 mentions the road of Cain (ὁδὸς τοῦ Κάϊν) and the error of Balaam (πλάνη τοῦ Βαλαάμ) which people follow for the sake of gain (μισθός). The author of 2 Pet has clearly this description in mind when he in 2:15 tells about the people who "have left the straight road" (εὐθεῖαν ὁδόν) and "gone astray" (ἐπλανήθησαν) "following the road of Balaam" (ὁδὸς τοῦ Βαλαάμ), and "who loved the wages (μισθός) of doing wrong". This agreement shows again that the author of 2 Pet does not repeat automatically the text he imitates. Instead of mentioning the error of Balaam (πλάνη), the author of 2 Pet refers to the road of Balaam and uses the verb πλανάω. Moreover, he repeats the nouns ὁδός and μισθός which are used in Jude only once. The emphasis of the text has also been changed. Cain and Korah are not mentioned at all; all interest is focused on Balaam.[107]

---

[104] See Bauer 1988, 1573.
[105] Bauckham 1983, 266; Fornberg 1977, 49-50. Cf. Schelkle 1964, 213-214; Kelly 1969, 340-341.
[106] See Fornberg 1977, 33.
[107] Similarly Fornberg 1977, 40.

2 Pet	Jude
1:5 ... **σπουδὴν πᾶσαν** παρεισενέγκαντες ἐπιχορηγήσατε ἐν τῇ πίστει ὑμῶν τὴν ἀρετήν	3 Ἀγαπητοί, **πᾶσαν σπουδὴν** ποιούμενος γράφειν ὑμῖν περὶ τῆς κοινῆς ἡμῶν σωτηρίας ...
1:12 Διὸ μελλήσω ἀεὶ **ὑμᾶς** ὑπομιμνήσκειν περὶ τούτων καίπερ **εἰδότας** καί	5 Ὑπομνῆσαι δὲ **ὑμᾶς** βούλομαι, **εἰδότας** [ὑμᾶς] πάντα ...
2:1 Ἐγένοντο δὲ καὶ ψευδοπροφῆται ἐν τῷ λαῷ, ὡς καὶ ἐν ὑμῖν ἔσονται ψευδοδιδάσκαλοι, οἵτινες παρεισάξουσιν αἱρέσεις ἀπωλείας καὶ τὸν ἀγοράσαντα αὐτοὺς **δεσπότην ἀρνούμενοι**. ἐπάγοντες ἑαυτοῖς ταχινὴν ἀπώλειαν, 2:2 καὶ πολλοὶ ἐξακολουθήσουσιν αὐτῶν ταῖς ἀσελγείαις δι' οὓς ἡ ὁδὸς τῆς ἀληθείας βλασφημηθήσεται, 2:3 καὶ ἐν πλεονεξίᾳ πλαστοῖς λόγοις ὑμᾶς ἐμπορεύσονται, οἷς **τὸ κρίμα** ἔκπαλαι οὐκ ἀργεῖ καὶ ἡ ἀπώλεια αὐτῶν οὐ νυστάζει.	4 παρεισέδυσαν γάρ τινες ἄνθρωποι, οἱ πάλαι προγεγραμμένοι εἰς τοῦτο **τὸ κρίμα**, ἀσεβεῖς, τὴν τοῦ θεοῦ ἡμῶν χάριτα μετατιθέντες εἰς ἀσέλγειαν καὶ τὸν μόνον **δεσπότην** καὶ κύριον ἡμῶν Ἰησοῦν Χριστὸν **ἀρνούμενοι**.

The second example shows us how the text of Jude 3-5 is used in 2 Pet. Both 2 Pet 1:5 and Jude 3 use the same phrase σπουδὴν πᾶσαν to describe the eagerness to do something but the contexts are different. Jude describes the eagerness of the author of the letter to write about salvation. In 2 Pet the phrase is used to exhort to make every effort to support the faith. Here the evidence for literary dependence does not seem strong at first because the texts only use the same two-word phrase. However, this phrase does not occur anywhere else in the NT exactly in the same form, although e.g. Paul uses many times the noun σπουδή (Rom 12:8, 11, 2 Cor 7:11, 12, 8:7, 8, 16). The connection between 2 Pet 1:5 and Jude thus shows that sometimes a slight verbatim agreement reveals a literary dependence.

The relationship between 2 Pet 1:12 and Jude 5 is also an example of minor resemblance which, however, proves a literary dependence. In both texts the writer uses the same verbs ὑπομιμνήσκω and οἶδα to remind the recipients of the letter of the things he assumes they know. Of the verbs, οἶδα is in the same form εἰδότας in both texts but ὑπομιμνήσκω appears in 2 Pet in the present tense instead of the aorist used in Jude. Thus the agreement is not verbatim. The verb οἶδα and the pronoun ὑμεῖς are common words in early Christian literature but the verb ὑπομιμνήσκω is unusual. It occurs in the NT only seven times (Lk 22:61, Jn 14:26, 2 Tim 2:14, Titus 3:1, 2 Pet 1:12, 3 Jn 10 and Jude 5). Of these, only in 2 Pet 1:12 and in Jude 5 is ὑπομιμνήσκω used with οἶδα. Accordingly, so few similarities between two texts, only three words in common, can reveal the literary dependence.

In Jude 4 the recipients of the letter are warned about some people who have intruded (παρεισέδυσαν) among them. Next it is emphasized that the people were long ago (πάλαι) designated for condemnation (τὸ κρίμα). In what follows, the writer states that the people pervert the grace of our God into licentiousness (ἀσέλγεια) and deny (ἀρνέομαι) our only Master (δεσπότης), Jesus.

2 Pet 2:1-3 seems to follow Jude 4. In 2 Pet 2:1 is a similar warning about the false teachers although the subject and time of the intrusion are different. Instead of the people, who are in Jude 4 the intruders, in 2 Pet 2:1 the opinions brought in (παρεισάξουσιν) are destructive. Jude speaks about present time but 2 Pet describes the future, which is an artificial device; the writer wants his letter to be a testament.[108] In addition, the verbs used in the texts are different (παρεισάγω, παρεισδύομαι). However, they have the same double prefix παρεισ-. Next, 2 Pet 2:1 describes the people who deny the Master which in Jude is the last thing mentioned. Thus these mentions do not appear in the same order in the texts but it is noteworthy that the words used (δεσπότην ἀρνούμενοι) are exactly the same. It shows that in spite of this verbatim agreement, the writer of 2 Pet shapes the text independently, it is typical of him to add his own thoughts to the text and so make it suitable for his own situation.[109]

In 2 Pet 2:2 the meaning of the noun ἀσέλγεια seems to be different from Jude. In Jude it has its usual moral meaning, licentiousness, but in 2 Pet the words "many will follow their licentiousness" (ταῖς ἀσελγείαις) seems to refer to the false teachers.[110] 2 Pet 2:3 mentions, like Jude, that the condemnation of the people was long ago designated. Only the word ἔκπαλαι differs a little from the one used in Jude (πάλαι).

The relationship between Jude 4 and 2 Pet 2:1-3 shows clearly that the author of 2 Pet does not copy the text he imitates. Only part of the agreements are verbatim. It is also noteworthy that the words and thoughts common to the texts do not occur in the same order. Moreover, the writer of 2 Pet has changed some details of the text of Jude. Thus he imitates Jude quite freely. Besides the imitation, the writer of 2 Pet adds to the text so many thoughts of his own that 2 Pet 2:1-3 is much longer than Jude 4. This act is characteristic of a pseudepigrapher.[111] In addition, it is noteworthy that Jude 3-5 is imitated in 2 Pet 1:5, 1:12 and 2:1-3 which are not situated near each other. It proves that a pseudepigrapher sometimes sprinkles reminiscences of an earlier text all over his own text.

---

[108] Vögtle 1994, 183; Kelly 1969, 326; Schelkle 1964, 206; Grundmann 1974, 87-88, 103. Contra Bigg 1987, 220-221.
[109] Grundmann 1974, 106-107.
[110] Watson 1988, 174; Fornberg 1977, 37.
[111] E.g. Schelkle 1964, 139, defends the priority of Jude by this argument. According to Kelly 1969, 226, the tendency in the early Church was towards enlargement of the texts.

2 Pet	Jude	1 Pet
1:2 **χάρις ὑμῖν καὶ εἰρήνη πληθυνθείη** ἐν ἐπιγνώσει τοῦ θεοῦ ...	2 ἔλεος **ὑμῖν καὶ εἰρήνη** καὶ ἀγάπη **πληθυνθείη**.	1:2 ... **χάρις ὑμῖν καὶ εἰρήνη πληθυνθείη**.
3:14 ... ἄσπιλοι **καὶ** ἀμώμητοι αὐτῷ εὑρεθῆναι ἐν εἰρήνῃ	24 ... στῆσαι κατενώπιον τῆς δόξης αὐτοῦ ἀμώμους ἐν ἀγαλλιάσει,	1:19 ... ὡς ἀμνοῦ ἀμώμου **καὶ** ἀσπίλου Χριστοῦ
3:18 ... ἐν ... γνώσει **τοῦ κυρίου ἡμῶν** καὶ σωτῆρος **'Ἰησοῦ Χριστοῦ. αὐτῷ** ἡ δόξα **καὶ νῦν καὶ εἰς** ἡμέραν αἰῶνος. [**ἀμήν.**]	25 μόνῳ θεῷ σωτῆρι ἡμῶν διὰ **'Ἰησοῦ Χριστοῦ τοῦ κυρίου ἡμῶν** ... **καὶ νῦν καὶ εἰς** πάντας τοὺς αἰῶνας, **ἀμήν**.	5:10 'Ὁ δὲ θεὸς πάσης χάριτος, ὁ καλέσας ὑμᾶς εἰς τὴν αἰώνιον αὐτοῦ δόξαν ἐν Χριστῷ ['Ἰησοῦ] ... 5:11 **αὐτῷ** τὸ κράτος **εἰς** τοὺς αἰῶνας, **ἀμήν**.

The greeting χάρις ὑμῖν καὶ εἰρήνη πληθυνθείη in 2 Pet 1:2 resembles the one in Jude 2 (ἔλεος ὑμῖν καὶ εἰρήνη ... πληθυνθείη). However, in 1 Pet 1:2 exactly the same words are used as in 2 Pet 1:2. Because 2 Pet and Jude have so many other resemblances, it is obvious that the beginning of Jude is familiar to the author of 2 Pet. Yet the verbatim agreement between 2 Pet 1:2 and 1 Pet 1:2 strongly points to a literary connection between 1 and 2 Pet and the choice of wording seems to have been influenced by 1 Pet 1:2.[112] It is probable that the author of 2 Pet shaped the greeting to resemble the beginning of 1 Pet either consciously (intending 1 and 2 Pet to be a pair) or unconsciously (it was more familiar to him than the beginning of Jude).

The conclusion of 2 Pet, verse 3:18, resembles both Jude 25 and 1 Pet 5:10-11. Yet it has clearly more in common with the former than with the latter. Therefore, it seems that the author of 2 Pet imitates the conclusion of Jude. Besides using slightly different words from Jude, he also transforms the thought. In Jude the Savior is God (through Christ) but in 2 Pet the Savior is Christ.[113] The connection between 2 Pet 3:14 and Jude 24 is not as clear as the one between 2 Pet 3:18 and Jude 25. In 2 Pet 3:14 the adjective ἀμώμητος occurs which is connected to the adjective ἄσπιλος instead of ἄμωμος used in Jude 24. It is remarkable that the words ἄσπιλοι καὶ ἀμώμητοι in 2 Pet 3:14 resemble the words ἀμώμου καὶ ἀσπίλου in 1 Pet 1:19.[114] Thus it seems that the author of 2 Pet imitates the conclusion of Jude but recalls at the same time the words ἀμνοῦ ἀμώμου καὶ

[112] Fornberg 1977, 13; Kelly 1969, 298; Schelkle 1964, 186; Grundmann 1974, 67.
[113] Grundmann 1974, 123; Kelly 1969, 375. 2 Pet 3:18 and 2 Tim 4:18 are the only doxologies in the NT in which Christ alone is without doubt the object.
[114] Similarly Schelkle 1964, 235; Kelly 1969, 369.

ἀσπίλου used in 1 Pet 1:19. Accordingly, the pseudonymous author of 2 Pet conflates words and phrases from various texts.

We have now looked at three examples of the resemblances between 2 Pet and Jude and noticed that the author of 2 Pet does not copy automatically the text he imitates, as Ludwig assumes a pseudepigrapher would do, but usually shapes his text quite independently. Therefore, the common words between the texts do not always occur in the same order. The author of 2 Pet also sometimes modifies the structure of the text; he does not follow the earlier text verse by verse. In addition, he can also connect the words in a new context or give them a new meaning. Sometimes he even sprinkles the reminiscences of an earlier text to all over his text. Therefore, the relationship between 2 Pet and Jude is inconsistent with Kiley's definition that the parallels between the texts depending on each other had to occur in the same order and with the same meaning.

It is also noteworthy that verbatim agreements seldom occur. Generally the common words are used in a different form. The author of 2 Pet can also use instead of a noun, a verb which belongs to the same stem. Sometimes he chooses words which look similar to the words used in the text imitated. Moreover, it is typical of the author to add his own thoughts to the text and so make it suitable for his own situation. Sometimes he repeats many times the words used in an earlier text. Thus the text written by the author of 2 Pet is longer.

Moreover, it has been noted that the author of 2 Pet sometimes simultaneously has in mind more than one text which influences his choice of wording. In addition, he does not follow Jude strictly, although he clearly tries to imitate it. According to Kelly, there are two explanations for this problem. Either "he is a self-conscious stylist" or "he did not have the earlier trait on his desk before him as he wrote, but preferred to trust his memory".[115] Thus there is no reason to assume that a pseudepigrapher usually follows only one letter verse by verse. It is possible to have in mind at the same time more than one text.

Connections between 2 Pet 1:5 // Jude 3 and 2 Pet 1:12 // Jude 5 prove that, if only one of the words is unusual in early Christian literature, two or three common words can be enough evidence for a literary dependence. Thus analyzing the literary relationship between 2 Pet and Jude has clearly shown that the use of common words refers to a literary dependence between the texts, as Sanders assumes.

1.3.2. The Relationship of Ephesians to Other Pauline Letters

The relationship between Eph and Col is evidently the closest within the Pauline corpus.[116] The most obvious verbatim agreement between Eph and Col is in the

---

[115] Kelly 1969, 227.

[116] Mitton 1951, 55; 1983, 11; Lincoln 1990, xlvii, emphasizes also that "within the NT as a whole (it) is rivaled only by that among the synoptic Gospels and that between 2 Peter and Jude."

postscripts of the letters. Eph 6:21-22 repeats twenty-nine consecutive words (including the prepositions and the articles) from Col 4:7-8 which are exactly the same and in the same order. The only difference between the texts is that the words καὶ σύνδουλος are omitted in Eph.[117] This verbatim agreement points clearly to a literary dependence. Moreover, it is so long that the author of Ephesians (A/Eph) seems to have consulted a copy of Col or he must have had a good reason for remembering the text so exactly.[118] Furthermore, there are extensive resemblances between Eph 1:1-2 and Col 1:1-2, Eph 1:10 and Col 1:20, Eph 4:16 and Col 2:19, and Eph 2:5 and Col 2:12.[119] In addition to having much thematic material in common, the sequence of verses in Eph generally corresponds to the sequence of parallel verses in Col. However, some parallels break the orderly sequence of progression and some counterparts overlap. A/Eph does not follow the text of Col verse by verse. This is the reason why scholars are not entirely agreed on the parallels between Eph and Col.[120]

On the grounds of the similarities between Eph and Col, in 1838 Mayerhoff noticed that one must reckon with the literary dependence of one letter on the other. Accepting the Pauline authorship of Eph, he defended its priority. He assumed Col to have been written by a later writer. However, a few years later (1843) De Wette, accepting the Pauline authorship of Col but not Eph, defended the priority of Col. On the other hand, Holtzmann stated that both Eph and Col derive from an authentic Pauline letter, the proto-Colossians.[121] Since 1951 when Mitton examined in detail the relationship between Eph and other Pauline letters, the literary dependence between Eph and Col has been accepted by most scholars. In addition, most scholars are now agreed on the priority of Col.[122]

The dependence of Eph on Col is supported by the fact that some passages in Eph seem like elaborations of passages in Col (Eph 2:1-10 of Col 2:12-13, Eph 5:21-33 of Col 3:18-19).[123] In addition, Mitton noted that some passages in Eph seem to conflate two from Col. This phenomenon is obvious, for example, between Col 1:14, 1:20 and Eph 1:7, Col 1:9, 1:4 and Eph 1:15-16, and Col 2:13, 3:6 and

---

[117] Lincoln 1990, lii; Mitton 1951, 58-59; 1983, 11. Cf. Lindemann 1985, 11; Gnilka 1971, 8. Eph 6:21-22 / Col 4:7-8: ... πάντα γνωρίσει ὑμῖν Τύχικος ὁ ἀγαπητὸς ἀδελφὸς καὶ πιστὸς διάκονος (καὶ σύνδουλος) ἐν κυρίῳ, ὃν ἔπεμψα πρὸς ὑμᾶς εἰς αὐτὸ τοῦτο, ἵνα γνῶτε τὰ περὶ ἡμῶν καὶ παρακαλέσῃ τὰς καρδίας ὑμῶν.

[118] Mitton 1951, 59, 75; Lincoln 1990, lv. Cf. Best 1997, 92; Vielhauer 1975, 210.

[119] Schnackenburg 1982, 27; Lindemann 1975, 44; Furnish 1992b, 537.

[120] Cf. Furnish 1992b, 536; Lincoln 1990, xlix; Mitton 1951, 64.

[121] For the history of the interpretation, see Merkel 1987, 3212-3220; Mitton 1951, 71-74; Furnish 1992b, 537; Lindemann 1975, 45-46; Maclean 1995, 1-6.

[122] See Furnish 1992b, 537; Pfammatter 1987,9; Lindemann 1975, 44-48; 1979, 122; 1985, 11; Lincoln 1990, l; 1993, 84; Vielhauer 1975, 209-210; Schnackenburg 1982, 29; Müller 1988, 313; VanKooten 1995, 73-74. According to Morton & McLeman 1966, 16 the relationship between Eph and Col would today be called plagiarism.

[123] Furnish 1992b, 537.

Eph 2:1-5.[124] It is also often stated that the theology of Eph represents a development beyond that of Col.[125]

However, the dependence of Eph on Col has not been accepted by all. In 1958 Coutts defended the priority of Eph.[126] In addition, van Roon stated in 1974 that Eph and Col are dependent upon a third text that served as a blueprint for both.[127] Some scholars have denied the literary dependence between Eph and Col. They sought to explain that the letters derive from common traditions which have been adapted differently in each.[128] Best recently rejected the literary dependence between Eph and Col stating that "similarities and dissimilarities of the two letters can be explained most easily on the assumption of distinct authors who were members of the same Pauline school and had discussed together the Pauline theology they had inherited".[129] This hypothesis of the Pauline school resembles the interpretation of Gnilka who, unlike Best, defends the dependence of Eph on Col. However, he considers problematic the way Col seems to be used in Eph, like a mosaic the parts of which are at first detached and then brought together again. Thus he assumes that the authors of the letters were members of the same school and, even though Eph is modelled on Col, both letters also utilize the same Pauline traditions.[130] Yet Gnilka, in his interpretation, connects the hypothesis of the Pauline school and traditions with literary dependence. These two models of interpretation do not seem to contradict each other: they can be used together. In spite of the differing opinions, the literary dependence of Eph on Col is so widely accepted that I take it for the starting point of this study.

Besides Col, Eph also seems to be dependent on authentic Pauline letters. Mitton and Lincoln assume that A/Eph knew all of them.[131] However, Lincoln limits his discussion to "clearer and more substantial parallels" than Mitton.[132] Furnish criticized Mitton by stating that many of the parallels Mitton presents may

---

[124] Mitton 1951, 64-67; Lincoln 1990, li-lii; Furnish 1992b, 537; VanKooten 1995, 15-74. Contra Coutts 1958, 204-205, who does not accept Eph 1:7 to be a conflation of Col 1:14 and 1:20. He criticizes Mitton's argument according to which the word ἀπολύτρωσιν is so similar in meaning to εἰρηνοποίησας that it calls to the writer's mind the following phrase διὰ τοῦ αἵματος τοῦ σταυροῦ αὐτοῦ. However, the phrase διὰ τοῦ αἵματος is so unusual in the Pauline letters (occurs only in Col 1:20 and Eph 1:7) that it also defends the dependence between Col 1:20 and Eph 1:7. Thus, the similarity between the words ἀπολύτρωσιν and εἰρηνοποίησας is not the only argument for this interpretation. Cf. Best 1997, 87, and van Roon 1974, 414.

[125] Schnackenburg 1982, 28-29; Lindemann 1975, 46; Furnish 1992b, 537; Mitton 1951, 69-71, 82-97; Lincoln 1990, liii-lv.

[126] Coutts 1958. Cf. van Roon 1974, 426.

[127] van Roon 1974, 429-30.

[128] Schille 1957; Dahl 1963, 72. According to Bruce 1988, 232 and Guthrie 1990, 527-528 Eph is one of the authentic Pauline letters.

[129] Best 1997, 96.

[130] Gnilka 1971, 11-13. Cf. Bruce 1988, 229-230.

[131] Mitton 1951, 118-158, 266; 1983, 13-15; Lincoln 1990, lvi-lviii. According to Vielhauer 1975, 214 "der Eph zeigt Berührungen mit allen früheren Paulusbriefen".

[132] Lincoln 1990, lvi.

be only "widely used stock phrases". Nevertheless, Furnish emphasizes that Eph seems particularly to be dependent on Rom and 1 Cor[133] but Lindemann only assumes the dependence of Eph on 1 Cor to be probable.[134] Accordingly, the dependence of Eph on all authentic Pauline letters is accepted only by a few scholars, although it is generally agreed that A/Eph knew some of them. The close relationship between Eph and the genuine Pauline letters is also acknowledged by some scholars who do not defend the literary dependence between Eph and other Pauline letters.[135]

Mitton states that besides the most obvious parallel between Eph and Col (Eph 6:21-22 // Col 4:7-8), the letters have three parallels which have seven exactly corresponding consecutive words (Eph 1:1-2 // Col 1:1-2, Eph 3:2 // Col 1:25 and Eph 3:9 // Col 1:26) and two parallels which have an exact correspondence of five consecutive words (Eph 1:7 // Col 1:14, and Eph 4:16 // Col 2:19).[136] In the following table is an example of these parallels, the relationship between Eph 3:2 and Col 1:25.

Eph 3:2	Col 1:25
... **τὴν οἰκονομίαν** τῆς χάριτος **τοῦ θεοῦ** τῆς δοθείσης **μοι εἰς ὑμᾶς**	... **τὴν οἰκονομίαν τοῦ θεοῦ** τὴν δοθεῖσάν **μοι εἰς ὑμᾶς** ...

Besides using seven consecutive words similar to Col 1:25 (like Mitton, I also here count the articles and the prepositions), A/Eph adds between them the word τῆς χάριτος. Moreover, the writer changes the form of the participle from τὴν δοθεῖσάν to τῆς δοθείσης. Probably the Pauline phrases κατὰ τὴν χάριν τοῦ θεοῦ τὴν δοθεῖσάν μοι (1 Cor 3:10) or διὰ τῆς χάριτος τῆς δοθείσης μοι (Rom 12:3) have caused the changes.[137]

Mitton also noted six passages where Eph does not follow Col exactly; words are omitted, added, or changed in order, but still the parallels are close (Eph 1:4 // Col 1:22, Eph 2:5 // Col 2:13, Eph 4:2 // Col 3:12, Eph 4:22-24 // Col 3:8-10, Eph 4:32 // Col 3:12, and Eph 5:19-20 // Col 3:16-17).[138]

---

[133] Furnish 1992b, 537.
[134] Lindemann 1979, 129; 1985, 13.
[135] See Bruce 1988, 231; van Roon 1974, 432-435.
[136] Mitton 1951, 58; 1983, 11; cf. Lincoln 1990, xlviii; Vielhauer 1975, 210. According to Mitton these parallels represent "the largest measure of exact correspondence between the two epistles". However, he emphasizes that the relationship between Eph 1:1-2 and Col 1:1-2 is of little significance because it is an opening greeting similar to other letters, too. Thus Best 1997, 76, unnecessarily criticizes Mitton for presenting these parallels. Cf. van Roon 1974, 416.
[137] Contra Best 1997, 90-91, who does not believe we can define the direction of dependence.
[138] Mitton 1951, 58-63.

Eph 4:22-24

22 ἀποθέσθαι ὑμᾶς κατὰ τὴν προτέραν ἀναστροφὴν **τὸν παλαιὸν ἄνθρωπον** τὸν φθειρόμενον κατὰ τὰς ἐπιθυμίας τῆς ἀγάπης,
23 ἀνανεοῦσθαι δὲ τῷ πνεύματι τοῦ νοὸς ὑμῶν
24 καὶ ἐνδύσασθαι τὸν καινὸν ἄνθρωπον τὸν **κατὰ** θεὸν κτισθέντα ...

Col 3:8-10

8 ... ἀπόθεσθε καὶ ὑμεῖς τὰ πάντα, ὀργήν, θυμόν, κακίαν, βλασφημίαν, αἰσχρολογίαν ἐκ τοῦ στόματος ὑμῶν·
9 μὴ ψεύδεσθε εἰς ἀλλήλους, ἀπεκδυσάμενοι **τὸν παλαιὸν ἄνθρωπον** σὺν ταῖς πράξεσιν αὐτοῦ
10 καὶ ἐνδυσάμενοι τὸν νέον τὸν ἀνακαινούμενον εἰς ἐπίγνωσιν **κατ'** εἰκόνα τοῦ κτίσαντος αὐτόν,

According to Mitton, the relationship between Eph 4:22-24 and Col 3:8-10 is "an instance of a characteristic trait of the relationship between these two epistles". A/Eph takes from Col the contrast between "putting off the old" and "putting on the new" and the idea of being renewed according to the likeness of God. The texts have so much in common that they must be dependent on each other.[139] However, A/Eph does not copy the text of Col but rearranges and develops the borrowed ideas. He emphasizes putting off the old man instead of the vices. Thus the exhortation is not so concrete as the one in Col.[140]

Eph 1:15-16

15 **Διὰ τοῦτο** κἀγὼ ἀκούσας **τὴν** καθ' ὑμᾶς **πίστιν ἐν** τῷ κυρίῳ **'Ιησοῦ καὶ τὴν ἀγάπην** τὴν **εἰς πάντας τοὺς ἁγίους**
16 **οὐ** παύομαι εὐχαριστῶν **ὑπὲρ ὑμῶν** μνείαν ποιούμενος ἐπὶ τῶν προσευχῶν μου

Col 1:9 **Διὰ τοῦτο** καὶ ἡμεῖς, ἀφ' ἧς ἡμέρας ἠκούσαμεν, **οὐ** παυόμεθα **ὑπὲρ ὑμῶν** προσευχόμενοι ...

Col 1:4 ἀκούσαντες **τὴν πίστιν** ὑμῶν **ἐν** Χριστῷ **'Ιησοῦ καὶ τὴν ἀγάπην** ἣν ἔχετε **εἰς πάντας τοὺς ἁγίους**

As was already noted above, the conflation of two passages from Col is a characteristic of A/Eph. The relationship between Eph 1:15-17 and Col 1:9, 4 is an example of this phenomenon. Both in Col 1:9 and 4 are described the things Paul heard from the recipients of the letter. Thus the verb ἀκούω is the link between

139 Mitton 1951, 61; Lindemann 1985, 85-86. Contra Best 1997, 84-85, who assumes that "A/Col and A/Eph have taken up and used the same idea independently". Cf. van Roon 1974, 429.
140 Lindemann 1985, 85-86. Cf. Mitton 1951, 61.

these texts which causes the conflation of them in Eph.[141] Eph 1:15-16 also resembles Philem 4-5, yet the relationship with Col 1:9, 4 is closer.[142]

Eph 5:21-23	Col 3:18	
21 ῾Υποτασσόμενοι	18 **Αἱ γυναῖκες**,	
ἀλλήλοις ...	ὑποτάσσεσθε **τοῖς**	1 Cor 11:3
22 **αἱ γυναῖκες τοῖς**	**ἀνδράσιν ὡς** ἀνῆκεν ἐν	
ἰδίοις **ἀνδράσιν ὡς** τῷ	**κυρίῳ**.	... παντὸς ἀνδρὸς ἡ
κυρίῳ,		κεφαλὴ ὁ Χριστός ἐστιν,
23 ὅτι **ἀνήρ** ἐστιν	Col 1:18	**κεφαλὴ** δὲ **γυναικὸς** ὁ
κεφαλὴ τῆς **γυναικὸς** ὡς		**ἀνήρ** ...
καὶ ὁ Χριστὸς **κεφαλὴ**	**καὶ αὐτός** ἐστιν ἡ	
τῆς ἐκκλησίας, **αὐτὸς**	**κεφαλὴ τοῦ σώματος τῆς**	
σωτὴρ **τοῦ σώματος**˙	**ἐκκλησίας**	

Eph 5:21-23 seems to be the result of a conflation of two passages from Col (3:18, 1:18) with a passage from 1 Cor (11:3).[143] A/Eph exhorts women to be subject to their husbands because "the husband is the head of the wife just as Christ is the head of the church". He clearly connects the exhortation from Col 3:18, in which women are exhorted to be subject to their husbands, to the thought from Col 1:18, according to which Christ is the head of the body. It is noteworthy that exhortations similar to Eph 5:22 and Col 3:18 do not appear anywhere else in the Pauline corpus: thus Eph 5:21-22 has to depend on Col 3:18.[144] In addition, Eph 5:23 includes three nouns common to Col 1:18. Although the nouns κεφαλή, σῶμα, and ἐκκλησία are frequently used in the Pauline letters, they occur together, besides in Col 1:18 and Eph 5:23, only in Eph 1:22-23 which describes Christ as the head of the church similarly to Eph 5:23 and thus probably is also derived from Col 1:18.[145] However, Eph 1:22-23 does not resemble Col 1:18 as much as Eph 5:23 does. It is noteworthy that sometimes ordinary words common to the texts which do not frequently occur together in early Christian literature, may show a literary dependence between the texts. Neither Col 3:18 nor Col 1:18 include the thought that husband is the head of the wife but it is mentioned in 1 Cor 11:3. Besides Eph

---

[141] Mitton 1951, 65. Cf. Furnish 1992b, 537; Lincoln 1990, li; VanKooten 1995, 19-21. Contra van Roon 1974, 418, who states that "Eph 1:15, 16 and Col 1:9 contain traditional turns of phrase which account for the particularly strong resemblance between the two epistles". According to Lindemann 1985, 27, Eph 1:15 is possibly dependent on Col 1:9. Schnackenburg 1982, 71-72, interprets Eph 1:15-16 as following Col 1:4 but the use of the name Lord Jesus instead of Christ Jesus is an echo of Philem 5.

[142] Contra Best 1997, 88, who assumes that both Eph and Col depend on Philem 4-7.

[143] Similarly Mitton 1951, 145-146. Contra van Roon 1974, 435.

[144] Lincoln 1990, lvii; Furnish 1992b, 536-537.

[145] Eph 1:22-23: ... αὐτὸν ἔδωκεν κεφαλὴν ὑπὲρ πάντα τῇ ἐκκλησίᾳ, ἥτις ἐστὶν τὸ σῶμα αὐτοῦ ...

5:23, it is the only verse in the Pauline epistles which includes the thought. The texts also include three nouns in common which are even in the same form. Thus, Eph 5:21-23 seems to depend on 1 Cor 11:3 in addition to Col 3:18 and 1:18.[146]

Eph 4:17-19	Rom 1:21-24
17 Τοῦτο οὖν λέγω καὶ μαρτύρομαι ἐν κυρίῳ, μηκέτι ὑμᾶς περιπατεῖν, καθὼς καὶ τὰ ἔθνη περιπατεῖ **ἐν** ματαιότητι τοῦ νοὸς **αὐτῶν**, 18 ἐσκοτωμένοι τῇ διανοίᾳ ὄντες, ἀπηλλοτριωμένοι τῆς ζωῆς τοῦ θεοῦ διὰ τὴν ἄγνοιαν τὴν οὖσαν ἐν αὐτοῖς, διὰ τὴν πώρωσιν τῆς καρδίας **αὐτῶν**, 19 οἵτινες ἀπηλγηκότες ἑαυτοὺς παρέδωκαν τῇ ἀσελγείᾳ **εἰς** ἐργασίαν ἀκαθαρσίας πάσης ἐν πλεονεξίᾳ.	21 διότι γνόντες τὸν θεὸν οὐχ ὡς θεὸν ἐδόξασαν ἢ ηὐχαρίστησαν, ἀλλ᾽ ἐματαιώθησαν **ἐν** τοῖς διαλογισμοῖς **αὐτῶν** καὶ ἐσκοτίσθη ἡ ἀσύνετος **αὐτῶν** καρδία. ... 24 Διὸ παρέδωκεν αὐτοὺς ὁ θεὸς ἐν ταῖς ἐπιθυμίαις τῶν καρδιῶν αὐτῶν **εἰς** ἀκαθαρσίαν τοῦ ἀτιμάζεσθαι τὰ σώματα αὐτῶν ἐν αὐτοῖς·

As was already noted, besides Col, A/Eph seems sometimes to imitate the authentic Pauline letters. Eph 4:17-19 uses several phrases similar to Rom 1:21-24 (ἐν ματαιότητι ... αὐτῶν, ἐσκοτωμένοι ... τῆς καρδίας αὐτῶν, ἑαυτοὺς παρέδωκαν ... εἰς ... ἀκαθαρσίας). Thus A/Eph clearly has the text of Rom in his mind although he does not copy the text of it but only borrows the phrases. This kind of resemblance Mitton calls a "sustained" parallel.[147]

Eph 3:8	1 Cor 15:9-10	Gal 1:15-16
Ἐμοὶ τῷ ἐλαχιστοτέρῳ πάντων ἁγίων ἐδόθη **ἡ χάρις** αὕτη, **τοῖς ἔθνεσιν** εὐαγγελίσασθαι ...	9 Ἐγὼ γάρ εἰμι ὁ ἐλάχιστος τῶν ἀποστόλων ... 10 ... καὶ **ἡ χάρις** αὐτοῦ ἡ εἰς ἐμὲ οὐ κενὴ ἐγενήθη ...	15 ... καλέσας διὰ τῆς χάριτος αὐτοῦ ... 16 ... ἵνα εὐαγγελίζωμαι αὐτὸν ἐν **τοῖς ἔθνεσιν** ...

Eph 3:8 seems to imitate the description of Paul's call to his mission in 1 Cor 15:9-10. The resemblance between the texts is so obvious that many scholars present it as an example of literary dependence.[148] The texts have in common one noun

[146] Furnish 1992b, 536-537; Lincoln 1990, lvii. According to Lindemann 1985, 13 the literary dependence between Eph 5:23 and 1 Cor 11 is possible but not certain.

[147] Mitton 1951, 120-121. According to Lindemann 1985, 84, A/Eph possibly knew Rom 1:24. Schnackenburg 1982, 199-201, emphasizes that Paul uses in Rom 1:19-21 vocabulary similar to Eph 4:17-19. However, he does not assume a literary dependence between the texts.

[148] Furnish 1992b, 537; Mitton 1951, 128; Lincoln 1990, lvii. According to Lindemann 1985, 13 the literary dependence is possible. Schnackenburg 1982, 137, draws attention to the similarity

(χάρις), one adjective (ἐλάχιστος), and two pronouns (ἐγώ, αὐτός), which, however, are too customary to be counted. Only χάρις is in the same form in both texts. However, although the texts have only two words in common, excluding the pronouns, the resemblance between them is so obvious that the literary dependence seems probable.

Eph 3:8 also uses words similar to Gal 1:15-16. Mitton noticed that Eph 3:8 seems to be the result of a conflation of 1 Cor 15:9-10 and Gal 1:15-16. The mention of the grace (χάρις) is the link between the texts.[149] This interpretation is supported by the fact that the phrase εὐαγγελίζομαι τοῖς ἔθνεσιν does not occur anywhere else in the Pauline letters. Although Eph 3:8 and Gal 1:15-16 have only three common words, excluding the usual pronoun αὐτός, it is obvious that the texts are dependent on each other.

Eph 1:20-23

20 Ἣν ἐνήργησεν ἐν τῷ Χριστῷ ἐγείρας **αὐτὸν ἐκ νεκρῶν** καὶ καθίσας **ἐν δεξιᾷ αὐτοῦ** ἐν τοῖς ἐπουρανίοις
21 ὑπεράνω πάσης ἀρχῆς **καὶ** ἐξουσίας **καὶ** δυνάμεως καὶ κυριότητος καὶ παντὸς ὀνόματος ὀνομαζομένου ...
22 καὶ **πάντα ὑπέταξεν ὑπὸ τοὺς πόδας αὐτοῦ** καὶ αὐτὸν ἔδωκεν κεφαλὴν ὑπὲρ πάντα τῇ ἐκκλησίᾳ,
23 ἥτις ἐστὶν τὸ σῶμα αὐτοῦ, **τὸ πλήρωμα** τοῦ **τὰ πάντα ἐν πᾶσιν** πληρουμένου.

1 Cor 15:24

... ὅταν καταργήσῃ πᾶσαν ἀρχὴν **καὶ** πᾶσαν ἐξουσίαν καὶ δύναμιν.

Phil 2:9-10

9 ... θεὸς ... ἐχαρίσατο αὐτῷ τὸ ὄνομα τὸ ὑπὲρ πᾶν ὄνομα,
10 ... ἐπουρανίων ...

1 Cor 15:27-28

27 **πάντα** γὰρ **ὑπέταξεν ὑπὸ τοὺς πόδας αὐτοῦ.**
28 ... ἵνα ᾖ ὁ θεὸς [**τὰ**] **πάντα ἐν πᾶσιν.**

Col

2:12 ... τῆς ἐνεργείας τοῦ θεοῦ τοῦ ἐγείραντος **αὐτὸν ἐκ νεκρῶν**·
3:1 ... τὰ ἄνω ζητεῖτε, οὗ ὁ Χριστός ἐστιν **ἐν δεξιᾷ** τοῦ θεοῦ καθήμενος·
1:16 ... εἴτε κυριότητες εἴτε ἀρχαὶ εἴτε ἐξουσίαι·

1:18 καὶ αὐτός ἐστιν ἡ κεφαλὴ τοῦ σώματος τῆς ἐκκλησίας ὅς ἐστιν ἀρχή, πρωτότοκος ἐκ τῶν νεκρῶν, ἵνα γένηται **ἐν πᾶσιν** αὐτὸς πρωτεύων,
1:19 ὅτι ἐν αὐτῷ εὐδόκησεν πᾶν **τὸ πλήρωμα** κατοικῆσαι

The relationship between Eph 1:20-23, Col 2:12, 3:1, 1:16-19, and 1 Cor 15:24-28 is an example of A/Eph's habit of conflating words from Col with words from authentic Pauline letters. Eph 1:20-23 follows the text of 1 Cor 15 in order and thus seems to depend on it.[150] The words πάντα ὑπέταξεν ὑπὸ τοὺς πόδας αὐτοῦ in 1

---

between Eph 3:8 and 1 Cor 15:9 although he does not assume them to be literary dependent on each other.

149 Mitton 1951, 152-153.

150 Furnish 1992b, 537; Mitton 1951, 128-129. Contra van Roon 1974, 434. Schnackenburg 1982, 76-77, draws attention to the similarity between Eph 1:21 and 1 Cor 15:24 although he does not

Cor 15:27 and Eph 1:22 are, of course, derived from Ps 110:1 (109:1 LXX) and Ps 8:7. It is noteworthy that the resemblances between Eph 1:22 and the texts of the Psalms are not verbatim as is the agreement between Eph 1:22 and 1 Cor 15:27.[151] Eph 1:22 seems to depend on 1 Cor 15:27.[152]

Besides 1 Cor 15, phrases from Col 2:12, 1:16-19 also seem to have influenced the shaping of the text. The connection between Eph 1:21-23 and Col 1:18 was already noted above. Moreover, the dependence of Eph 1:20 on Col 3:1 seems probable because both texts describe Christ as seated (καθίζω /κάθημαι) at the right hand of God (ἐν δεξιᾷ αὐτοῦ / τοῦ θεοῦ). These two verses are the only cases in the Pauline letters where the phrase ἐν δεξιᾷ αὐτοῦ / τοῦ θεοῦ is used with the verb καθίζω or κάθημαι.[153] Eph 1:21 even seems to be "a deliberate attempt to provide a comprehensive summary of Paul's previous teaching".[154] It is interesting that Eph 1:21 seems to pile up ἀρχή, ἐξουσία, and δύναμις from 1 Cor 15:24 with κυριότης from Col 2:12 and ὄνομα from Phil 2:9-10, although the dependence on the last one is not as clear as on the others. Eph 1:20-21 and Phil 2:9-10 use only three common words πᾶς, ὄνομα, and ἐπουράνιος, of which only the last one is unusual in early Christian literature. It is worth noting that ἐπουράνιος is used several times in 1 Cor 15:40-49. However, these verses do not include the thought that Christ is seated or named above every name. Thus, it is possible that the thought is derived from Phil 2:9-10.[155] It is also interesting that in spite of the use of similar words, the theology of Eph differs from Col. In Col 1:19 πλήρωμα means the divine fullness which has taken up residence in Christ but in Eph 1:23 it refers to the Church.[156]

---

assume a literary dependence between the texts.

[151] Ps 110:1 (109:1 LXX): Κάθου ἐκ δεξιῶν μου, ἕως ἂν θῶ τοὺς ἐχθρούς σου ὑποπόδιον τῶν ποδῶν σου. Ps 8:7: ... πάντα ὑπέταξας ὑποκάτω τῶν ποδῶν αὐτοῦ.

[152] Similarly Lincoln 1982, 41-42. Contra Lindemann 1985, 31.

[153] See Mitton 1951, 285-286. According to Lincoln 1990, lvi Eph 1:21-22 is a conflation of 1 Cor 15:24, 27 and Col 1:16. Lindemann 1985, 30, assumes Eph 1:21-22 to be dependent on Col 2:12 but in his view the direct literary dependence on 3:1 is not as clear. Contra Best 1997, 89, according to whom "there is nothing peculiar about the language of either Eph 1:20 or the Colossian passages (2:12, 3:1) to suggest that either depends on the other". Cf. van Roon 1974, 418. Schnackenburg 1982, 76-77, mentions the similarity between Eph 1:21 and Col 1:16, Phil 2:9 although he does not assume a literary dependence between the texts.

[154] Mitton 1983, 13.

[155] Similarly Mitton 1983, 13.

[156] Lincoln 1990, liv; Lindemann 1985, 33.

Eph 3:11-12	Rom 5:1-2
11 ... ἣν ἐποίησεν ἐν τῷ Χριστῷ Ἰησοῦ τῷ κυρίῳ ἡμῶν, 12 ἐν ᾧ **ἔχομεν τὴν** παρρησίαν καὶ **προσαγωγὴν** ἐν πεποιθήσει διὰ τῆς πίστεως αὐτοῦ.	1 Δικαιωθέντες οὖν ἐκ πίστεως **εἰρήνην ἔχομεν πρὸς τὸν** θεὸν διὰ τοῦ κυρίου ἡμῶν Ἰησοῦ Χριστοῦ 2 **δι'** οὗ καὶ τὴν **προσαγωγὴν** ἐσχήκαμεν [τῇ πίστει] εἰς τὴν χάριν ταύτην ...
Eph 2:17-18	
17 ... εὐηγγελίσατο **εἰρήνην** ... 18 ὅτι **δι'** αὐτοῦ ἔχομεν **τὴν προσαγωγὴν** οἱ ἀμφότεροι ἐν ἑνὶ πνεύματι **πρὸς τὸν** πατέρα.	

The similarities between Rom 5:1-2 and Eph 3:11-12, 2:17-18 show how some passages from the authentic Pauline letters are recurring in Eph. Both Eph 3:11-12 and 2:17-18 seems to depend on Rom 5:1-2 which indicates that A/Eph perhaps was deeply impressed with the text[157] although he does not imitate the same elements from Rom twice. While Eph 3:11-12 imitates the thought "in Christ Jesus our Lord ... we have access to God ... through faith" (ἐν τῷ Χριστῷ Ἰησοῦ τῷ κυρίῳ ἡμῶν, ἐν ᾧ ἔχομεν τὴν ... προσαγωγὴν ἐν πεποιθήσει διὰ τῆς πίστεως αὐτοῦ)[158], Eph 2:17-18 connects the access to God with peace like Rom 5:1-2. Yet both Eph 3:11-12 and 2:17-18 had to be derived from Rom 5:1-2 because these are the only verses in the Pauline corpus in which the word προσαγωγή, "access" occurs.

Eph 2:12	1 Thess 4:5-13
... **ἐλπίδα μὴ ἔχοντες** καὶ ἄθεοι ἐν τῷ κόσμῳ	5 ... καθάπερ καὶ τὰ ἔθνη τὰ μὴ εἰδότα τὸν θεόν, 13 ... ἵνα μὴ λυπῆσθε καθὼς **καὶ οἱ λοιποὶ** οἱ **μὴ ἔχοντες ἐλπίδα.**
Eph 2:3	
... καὶ ἤμεθα τέκνα φύσει ὀργῆς ὡς **καὶ οἱ λοιποί·**	

Likewise, it seems significant that Eph 2:12 and 2:3 are both dependent on 1 Thess 4:5, 13. Eph 2:12 links together the thoughts from 1 Thess 4:5 and 13 to describe

157 Mitton 1951, 122, 136. Cf. Lincoln 1990, lvii.
158 Although Eph 3:11-12 does not mention God, the context reveals that it refers to the access to God.

the condition of the gentiles.[159] This interpretation is supported by the fact that Eph 2:12 and 1 Thess 4:13 are the only verses in the Pauline letters in which the phrase ἐλπίδα μὴ ἔχοντες appears. The use of the same phrase indicates a literary dependence when it is unusual and occurs in the same form in the texts. [160] In addition, Eph 2:3 uses the phrase καὶ οἱ λοιποί from 1 Thess 4:13. The phrase οἱ λοιποί is used also e.g. in Rom 1:13, 11:7 and 1 Cor 9:5, yet they are not such close parallels with Eph 2:3 as 1 Thess 4:13.

Eph 2:8-9

8 **Τῇ** γὰρ **χάριτί** ἐστε σεσῳσμένοι **διὰ**
πίστεως· καὶ τοῦτο οὐκ ἐξ ὑμῶν, θεοῦ τὸ
δῶρον·
9 οὐκ **ἐξ ἔργων**, ἵνα μή τις καυχήσηται.

Rom 3:20-27

20 διότι **ἐξ ἔργων** νόμου οὐ
δικαιωθήσεται πᾶσα σὰρξ ἐνώπιον
αὐτοῦ, διὰ γὰρ νόμου ἐπίγνωσις
ἁμαρτίας.
21 Νυνὶ δὲ χωρὶς νόμου δικαιοσύνη θεοῦ
πεφανέρωται μαρτυρουμένη ὑπὸ τοῦ
νόμου καὶ τῶν προφητῶν,
22 δικαισοσύνη δὲ θεοῦ **διὰ πίστεως**
Ἰησοῦ Χριστοῦ εἰς πάντας τοὺς
πιστεύοντας. οὐ γάρ ἐστιν διαστολή,
23 πάντες γὰρ ἥμαρτον καὶ ὑστεροῦνται
τῆς δόξης τοῦ θεοῦ
24 δικαιούμενοι δωρεὰν **τῇ** αὐτοῦ **χάριτι**
διὰ τῆς ἀπολυτρώσεως τῆς ἐν Χριστῷ
Ἰησοῦ·
25 ὃν προέθετο ὁ θεὸς ἱλαστήριον διὰ
[τῆς] πίστεως ἐν τῷ αὐτοῦ αἵματι εἰς
ἔνδειξιν τῆς δικαιοσύνης αὐτοῦ διὰ τὴν
πάρεσιν τῶν προγεγονότων
ἁμαρτημάτων
26 ἐν τῇ ἀνοχῇ τοῦ θεοῦ, ...
27 Ποῦ οὖν ἡ καύχησις; ἐξεκλείσθη. ...
28 λογιζόμεθα γὰρ δικαιοῦσθαι πίστει
ἄνθρωπον χωρὶς ἔργων νόμου.

[159] Similarly Lincoln 1990, lvii; Mitton 1951,136, 133. However, I do not agree with Mitton's interpretation that "Eph 2:12 links together the two remarkable phrases from 1 Thess 4:5 and 13". In my view ἄθεοι and τὰ μὴ εἰδότα τὸν θεόν mean the same but we cannot call them the same phrases. Moreover, it is not useful to present the parallels between 1 Thess 4:11 // Eph 4:28, as Mitton does, because the phrase ἐργάζομαι ταῖς χερσίν, common to them, occurs also in Col 4:12, as also Mitton himself notes.
[160] The phrase ἐλπίδα ἔχοντες is used in 2 Cor 3:12 and 10:15.

Eph 2:8-9 seems to summarize the teaching of Rom 3:20-27.[161] This summary is more complete than the one written by Paul himself in Rom 3:28. However, Mitton exaggerates when he regards Eph 2:8-9 as "a most complete summary of Paul's theology of salvation by grace through faith".[162] It is only a summary of Rom 3:20-27 which, however, repeats all the important details. Mitton's suggestion that Rom 3:20-4:2 reappears, besides in Eph 2:8-9, in Eph 1:19, 2:5, and 1:7 is not convincing either. Neither Eph 1:19 nor 2:5 have much in common with Rom 3:20-4:2. In addition, Eph 1:7 does not seem to be derived from Rom 3 but to be a conflation of Col 1:14 and Col 1:20, as also Mitton himself mentions.[163]

A few examples of the relationship between Eph and other Pauline letters have now been examined in detail. Sometimes parallels between Eph and Col include many consecutive words which are exactly the same and in the same order. However, this kind of agreement is unusual. Ordinarily the words from an earlier text are omitted, added, or changed in order in Eph. Although the sequence of passages in Eph generally corresponds to the sequence of parallels in Col, the orderly sequence is sometimes broken and some counterparts overlap. Thus the relationship between Eph and Col resembles the dependence of 2 Pet on Jude. However, unlike the author of 2 Pet, A/Eph ordinarily conflates separate passages from Col. Some parts of Eph also seem to be conflations of two passages from the genuine Pauline letters; sometimes words and phrases from Col and the genuine letters are mixed. It is also noteworthy that sometimes the texts which seem to be dependent on each other include only two or three similar words, excluding the pronouns. The words may be common in early Christian literature in general but do not necessarily occur together. In addition, A/Eph often uses the words he borrows in a new context. Sometimes a passage from another letter seems to have impressed the writer so much that he several times repeats parts of it.

Like the author of 2 Pet, A/Eph seems to borrow from the earlier texts quite freely. Excluding the agreement between Eph 6:21-22 and Col 4:7-8, it does not seem that A/Eph has a copy of Col in front of him when writing.[164] On the other hand, the resemblances between the texts are so obvious that A/Eph seems to be familiar with a written copy of Col. Mitton describes this phenomenon:

> The borrowing is exceedingly free. There is nothing rigid or mechanical about it. It is not at all the kind of borrowing that can be associated with a writer who has a document open in front of him as he writes and laboriously incorporates sections from it into his own work. It suggests rather that the author of Ephesians was thoroughly familiar with Colossians, so that his mind could move easily along the lines of developing argument in that epistle, and also could readily associate together similar phrases from different parts of the epistle. ... His

[161] Furnish 1992b, 537; Mitton 1951, 121; Lincoln 1990, lvii. Lindemann 1985, 41, refers to the similarity between Eph 2:8-9 and Rom 3:20-27 although according to him the texts does not seem to be dependent on each other.

[162] Mitton 1951, 155; 1983, 13-14. Also Lindemann 1979, 124, criticizes Mitton's interpretation.

[163] Mitton 1951, 121, cf. 65.

[164] Because of that Schnackenburg 1982, 29, questions how literary the dependence is.

> acquaintance with Colossians is not dependent on what he reads in a document, but it is a familiarity which has become part of his own mental equipment.[165]

In addition, according to Lincoln

> [t]he similarities and yet the development in the use of terms and themes indicate a stage of further reflection since the time of Colossians. During it the writer has been able to employ the earlier material by way of inspiration for his own fresh interpretation of the same Pauline tradition in a new situation.

Lincoln emphasizes that "[w]hether the nature of the dependence should be designated as literary is almost academic". However, he assumes that "it is highly likely ... that the dependence of Ephesians on Colossians should be seen as in some sense a literary one".[166] Moreover, Mitton describes the conflation of the Pauline materials:

> A writer or speaker may purposely combine into a single whole two sentences of quite separate origin, because they are both associated in his mind as dealing with the same theme. More often the process is largely or entirely unconscious. The writer or speaker is aware that he is using phrases which are familiar to him, though he could not clearly assign to them their origin, and they link themselves together in his mind spontaneously and almost automatically. Or again, sometimes a writer may think that he is reproducing from some source familiar to him, and without his realizing it, familiar words from another source are incorporated. He has intended faithfully to reproduce his original source, but extraneous matter of a similar nature creeps in without his knowing it.[167]

Accordingly, the relationship of Eph to other Pauline letters shows that A/Eph does not usually seem to have a copy of Col in front of him when writing but he borrows quite freely, probably due to memorization, from the earlier texts. However, because he seems to know the texts in literary form, the nature of the dependence should be designated to be in some sense a literary one.[168]

It has been shown that A/Eph uses Pauline letters, especially Col, as models for his text. There remains the question of for what purpose did he imitate Paul? Goodspeed assumed that Eph was written as a cover letter for the collection of Pauline letters in order to introduce them and it thus imitates them all. All details of Goodspeed's theory have not been accepted as convincing (see pp. 22-23). Nevertheless, Eph is seen to be written to a new generation of Christians in order

---

[165] Mitton 1951, 57-58, 63. Similarly Lincoln 1990, lv.

[166] Lincoln 1990, lv. Contra VanKooten 1995, 73-74, according to whom Lincoln is underestimating the literary dependence when describing the phenomenon to be "in some sense a literary one".

[167] Mitton 1951, 138-139. Cf. Lincoln's description of the relationship between Eph and the authentic Pauline letters; Lincoln 1990, lviii.

[168] Contra VanKooten 1995, 73-74, who emphasizes that "there is certainly literary dependence of Eph on Col" which cannot be called to be "in some sense a literary one" or to be "due to memorisation". However, VanKooten himself does not define literary dependence at all.

to remind them of the Pauline teachings. Paul's words are used because A/Eph is stating what Paul himself had insisted on.[169] It can be said that A/Eph uses Col and the Pauline tradition in the same way Jewish exegetes often worked on Scripture. The usage resembles one form of midrashic interpretation, the "anthological style", which employed phrases or catchwords from familiar texts, sometimes conflating the texts imitated. For A/Eph the Pauline material seems to be the authoritative tradition which he reformulates for a new situation.[170] It is also possible that he even regards his text as an authoritative interpretation of Paul.[171]

1.3.3. Pseudo-Ignatius as an Imitator

Besides in the NT, there are also other ancient pseudepigraphic letters, e.g. those of Pseudo-Plato and Pseudo-Ignatius. Like the Pauline letters, the corpus of Plato's letters includes thirteen epistles and the authenticity of some of the letters is disputed.[172] Gulley, among others, has suspected that the 7th and 8th letters are spurious. He also maintains that they reveal the writer's acquaintance with Plato's Republic and Laws.[173] They do not, however, (pace Gulley) seem to have verbatim agreements with the authentic writings of Plato. Therefore, this relationship does not accord well with the examples given in the previous chapter.[174]

A collection of Ignatius' letters from the second century A.D. consists of the letters to the Ephesians (Ign, Eph), Magnesians (Ign, Mag), Trallians (Ign, Tral), Philadelphians (Ign, Philad), Romans (Ign, Rom), Smyrnaeans (Ign, Smyr), and to Polycarp of Smyrna (Ign, Pol). This collection, called the "middle recension", is generally accepted as including the authentic letters of Ignatius.[175] A collection which includes only some of Ignatius' genuine epistles is sometimes called the "short recension".[176] In the fourth century A.D. an imitator made interpolations to the genuine letters of the "middle recension" and probably the same person wrote six new letters: to Antioch (Ant), Philippi (Phil), Tarsus (Tar), Hero, Maria of

---

169 Mitton 1983, 28-29. Cf. Schnackenburg 1982, 30-31; Lindemann 1985, 12-14.
170 Lincoln 1990, lviii.
171 So VanKooten 1995, 122.
172 Leisegang 1950, 2522-2524.
173 Gulley 1971, 117-130. Cf. Edelstein 1966, who suspects the 7th letter of Plato is spurious after comparing it with other parts of Plato's corpus.
174 Contra Kiley 1986, 24, who presents the 7th and 8th letters of Plato as examples of texts constructed like Col.
175 See Schoedel 1985, 4-5, 7; 1992, 384; Brox 1976, 182; M. P. Brown 1963, XI, 124; Amelungk 1899, 508; Kiley 1986, 24. Contra Rius-Camps 1980, Joly 1979, and Weijenborg 1969. According to Rius-Camps there were originally only four letters: Rom, Mag, Tral, and Eph. Then Mag was divided and part of it worked up into a letter to Philad. Similarly Eph was divided and part of it worked up into a letter to Smyr. Joly states that the letters of the "middle recension" are a forgery of about A.D. 160 to 170. According to Weijenborg the "middle recension" is a shortened version of the "long recension"; see Schoedel 1980, who reviews Rius-Camps 1980, Joly 1979, and Weijenborg 1969; cf. Schoedel 1985, 5-7.
176 Schoedel 1992, 385; M. P. Brown 1963, XII; Rius-Camps 1980, 13.

Kastabala (Mary) and her reply to Ignatius. This interpolated collection, the "long recension" is thus unauthentic.[177]

In 1899 Amelungk compared side-by-side the spurious letters with Ignatius' genuine epistles. He found so many agreements between the texts that the spurious letters seem to be based on Ignatius' genuine letters. It is noteworthy that sometimes Pseudo-Ignatius seems to follow the texts of the genuine letters in the interpolated form they occur in the "long recension".[178] Accordingly, it seems that the imitator first interpolated the genuine letters of Ignatius and then wrote the spurious letters modelled on them. Moreover, the letters of Pseudo-Ignatius include quotations from and allusions to the LXX and the NT.[179] According to Amelungk's comparison, the letter to Hero, written by a pseudepigrapher, follows mainly in order Ignatius' authentic letter to Polycarp.[180] However, the relationship of the letter to Tarsus to Ignatius' letters is different.[181]

---

[177] Amelungk 1899, 509; Kiley 1986, 24; Brox 1976, 182, 185; M. P. Brown 1963, XI-XII, XIV, 124; Schoedel 1992, 384. Like the writers of the pseudepigraphic letters, Josephus uses the Letter of Aristeas as a source in his Jewish Antiquities in chapter XII (see Shutt 1992, 381; Pelletier 1962). According to Lincoln 1990, lv, this relationship also resembles the one between Eph and Col because "Josephus has omitted, conflated and embellished material from his source". However, unlike A/Eph, Josephus seems to follow his source, the Letter of Aristeas, mainly in order although he makes omissions and additions to the text. In addition, pace Lincoln, there is no conflation of the texts (see Pelletier 1962, 307-327). VanKooten 1995, 3-4, 73, also criticizes Lincoln because of that detail in his interpretation. It is also remarkable that the literary form of Jewish Antiquities differs from Eph: it is an example of historiography, not a letter. Thus, the relationship between Jewish Antiquities and the Letter of Aristeas does not seem to be a good parallel for the relationship between Col and the authentic Pauline letters.

[178] See Amelungk 1899, 539-548, who presents many examples of the agreements between the texts excluding Ignatius' letter to Maria of Kastabala of which he presents only a few examples. Kiley 1986, 24, also mentions the article of Amelungk and emphasizes that Pseudo-Ignatius' letters are pseudepigraphic letters constructed like Col.

[179] M. P. Brown 1963, 114-119. Cf. Brox 1976, who studies the relationship between the Pastoral letters and the letters of Pseudo-Ignatius. According to him both emphasize similarly the possibility to select young men for bishops and presbyters.

[180] Amelungk 1899, 539-540.

[181] See Amelungk 1899, 541-542.

Ps-Ign, Tar

Inscr **᾿Ιγνάτιος, ὁ καὶ Θεοφόρος**, τῇ σεσωσμένῃ ἐν Χριστῷ **ἐκκλησίᾳ** ...

1:1 **᾿Απὸ Συρίας μέχρι ῾Ρώμης θηριομαχῶ**, οὐχ ὑπὸ ἀλόγων **θηρίων** βιβρωσκόμενος (ταῦτα γάρ, ὡς ἴστε, θεοῦ θελήσαντος ἐφείσαντο τοῦ Δανιήλ), ὑπὸ δὲ **ἀνθρωπομόρφων**, οἷς ὁ ἀνήμερος θὴρ ἐμφωλεύων νύττει με ὁσημέραι καὶ τιτρώσκει.

1:2 **ἀλλ᾿ οὐδενὸς** <u>λόγον</u> **ποιοῦμαι** τῶν δεινῶν, οὐδὲ ἔχω **τὴν ψυχὴν τιμίαν ἐμαυτῷ, ὡς** ἀγαπῶν αὐτὴν μᾶλλον ἢ τὸν κύριον. διὸ ἕτοιμός εἰμι **πρὸς πῦρ, πρὸς θηρία**, πρὸς ξίφος, πρὸς <u>σταυρὸν</u>, **μόνον ἵνα <u>Χριστὸν</u>** ἴδω τὸν σωτῆρά μου καὶ θεὸν, **τὸν ὑπὲρ** ἐμοῦ **ἀποθανόντα**.

1:3 **παρακαλῶ οὖν ὑμᾶς ἐγὼ ὁ δέσμιος** Χριστοῦ, ὁ **διὰ γῆς καὶ θαλάσσης** ἐλαυνόμενος· **στήκετε ἐν τῇ πίστει ἑδραῖοι**, ὅτι **ὁ δίκαιος ἐκ πίστεως ζήσεται**· γίνεσθε ἀκλινεῖς, ὅτι κύριος **κατοικίζει μονοτρόπους ἐν οἴκῳ**.

Ign, Smyr Inscr **᾿Ιγνάτιος, ὁ καὶ Θεοφόρος, ἐκκλησίᾳ** θεοῦ πατρός ...

Ign, Rom 5:1 **᾿Απὸ Συρίας μέχρι ῾Ρώμης θηριομαχῶ, διὰ γῆς καὶ θαλάσσης**, ... δεδεμένος δέκα λεοπάρδοις ...

Ign, Smyr 4:1-2 ... ἀπὸ τῶν **θηρίων** τῶν **ἀνθρωπομόρφων** ... δέδωκα τῷ θανάτῳ, **πρὸς πῦρ**, πρὸς μάχαιραν, **πρὸς θηρία**;

Acts 20:24 **ἀλλ᾿ οὐδενὸς** <u>λόγου</u> **ποιοῦμαι τὴν ψυχὴν τιμίαν ἐμαυτῷ ὡς** τελειῶσαι τὸν δρόμον μου

Ign, Rom 5:3 **πῦρ** καὶ <u>σταυρὸς</u> **θηρίων** τε συστάσεις, ... **μόνον ἵνα** ᾿Ιησοῦ <u>Χριστοῦ</u> ἐπιτύχω.

Ign, Rom 6:1 ... εἰς **Χριστὸν** ᾿Ιησοῦν, ... **τὸν ὑπὲρ** ἡμῶν **ἀποθανόντα**·

Eph 4:1 **Παρακαλῶ οὖν ὑμᾶς ἐγὼ ὁ δέσμιος** ἐν κυρίῳ

Ps-Ign, Eph 10:2 ... **στήκετε** ὑμεῖς **ἐν τῇ πίστει ἑδραῖοι** (cf. Ps-Ign, Eph 20:1)

Ign, Eph 10:2 πρὸς τὴν πλάνην αὐτῶν ὑμεῖς **ἑδραῖοι τῇ πίστει**

Rom 1:17 **ὁ** δὲ **δίκαιος ἐκ πίστεως ζήσεται** (cf. Hab 2:4)

Ps 67:7 LXX ὁ θεὸς **κατοικίζει μονοτρόπους ἐν οἴκῳ**

The inscription of Tar mentions Ignatius as the sender of the letter who is also called Theophorus. The name usually appears in the greetings of Ignatius' letters as his epithet for himself. The names of the recipients follow. The inscription of Tar resembles the one of Ign, Smyr and also many other inscriptions of Ignatius' letters (e.g. Tral, Eph, Mag). Thus the author of Tar clearly wants the letter to look like an authentic text of Ignatius.

The first chapter of Tar begins with the words ἀπὸ Συρίας μέχρι ῾Ρώμης θηριομαχῶ similar to the fifth chapter of Rom. Because the descriptions of the struggles for Christ in Ign, Rom 5:3 and Tar 1:2 also much resemble each other, the author clearly imitates the text of Ign, Rom 5:1.[182] Besides Ign, Rom 5, he also seems to recall Ign, Rom 6:1 because both texts use similar words Χριστὸν ... τὸν ὑπὲρ ... ἀποθανόντα[183] and have in mind Ign, Smyr 4:1-2 which uses the words πρὸς πῦρ, πρὸς θηρία and mentions the beasts in the form of men (θηρίων ἀνθρωπομόρφων) like Tar 1:1-2.[184] Tar 1:1-3, therefore, seems to be the result of a conflation of Ign, Rom 5-6 and Ign, Smyr 4:1-2.[185] In addition, the author uses the phrase στήκετε ἐν τῇ πίστει ἑδραῖοι, common to the Ignatian corpus. It appears exactly in the same form in the interpolated Ign, Eph 10:2 and 20:1 (Στήκετε ... ἑδραῖοι ἐν τῇ πίστει) and, without the verb ἵστημι, in the authentic form of Ign, Eph 10:2.[186]

Tar 1:1-3 does not only have verbatim agreement with the letters of Ignatius but the words ἀλλ' οὐδενὸς λόγον ποιοῦμαι ... τὴν ψυχὴν τιμίαν ἐμαυτῷ, ὡς ... in Tar 1:2 are clearly a quotation from Acts 20:24.[187] The imitating of other early Christian literature continues in Tar 1:3. The words παρακαλῶ οὖν ὑμᾶς ἐγὼ ὁ δέσμιος match exactly the words in Paul's letter to the Ephesians (4:1). In addition, Rom 1:17 and Ps 67:7 LXX are quoted at the end of Tar 1:3.[188] Besides Rom 1:17, the words ὁ δίκαιος ἐκ πίστεως ζήσεται also appear in Hab 2:4, which Paul clearly imitates in Rom. However, Tar 1:3 resembles more Rom 1:17 than Hab 2:4 which adds the word μου after the words ἐκ πίστεως. Thus Tar 1:3 seems to depend on Rom 1:17 but unlike Paul, who in Rom 1:17 writes καθὼς γέγραπται before the quotation, Pseudo-Ignatius uses Rom 1:17 without any mention that there is a quotation.

---

[182] M. P. Brown 1963, 99; Funk & Diekamp II, 132; Amelungk 1899, 541. The text of Tar 1 which Amelungk uses differs a little from the version of Funk & Diekamp used in this study. The words ὁ δέσμιος Χριστοῦ, ὁ διὰ γῆς καὶ θαλάσσης ἐλαυνόμενος are in a different place. In addition, I have left out from the comparison the words μὲ δεδεμένον ἀπὸ Συρίας ... ἐν Ῥώμῃ θηριομαχῆσαι from Eph 1 — although Amelungk regards them as a parallel — because they do not resemble Tar 1 very much.

[183] See Funk & Diekamp II, 134.

[184] Also Funk & Diekamp II, 133, and Amelungk 1899, 541, refer to Smyr 4:1-2.

[185] M. P. Brown 1963, 112-113 emphasizes that "[p]articular designations given by Pseudo-I[gnatius] to the heretical teachers are drawn largely from the animal kingdom". However, also in the authentic forms of Rom 5:1-3 and Smyr 4:1-2 heretical teachers are described as wild beasts and beasts in the form of men.

[186] See Funk & Diekamp II, 134. Besides Ps-Ign, Eph 10:2 and 20:1, Amelungk 1899, 541 mentions Ps-Ign, Polyc 3:2 which includes the same phrase in a little different form (στῆθι δὲ ἑδραῖος ὡς ἄκμων τυπτόμενος).

[187] Also Funk & Diekamp II, 132, mentions Acts 20:24 as a parallel to Tar 1:2.

[188] See Funk & Diekamp II, 134.

Ps-Ign, Tar	Ps-Ign, Eph 12:2 **Παύλου** συμμύσται **ἐστε**
2:2 **Παύλου** γάρ **ἐστε** πολῖται καὶ μαθηταί, τοῦ **ἀπὸ** Ἱεροσολύμων **καὶ κύκλῳ μέχρι τοῦ Ἰλλυρικοῦ** πεπληρωκότος **τὸ εὐαγγέλιον** καὶ **τὰ στίγματα τοῦ Χριστοῦ** ἐν τῇ σαρκὶ περιφέροντος.	Ign, Eph 12:2 **Παύλου** συμμύσται Rom 15:19 ὥστε με **ἀπὸ** Ἰερουσαλὴμ **καὶ κύκλῳ μέχρι τοῦ Ἰλλυρικοῦ** πεπληρωκέναι **τὸ εὐαγγέλιον τοῦ Χριστοῦ** Gal 6:17 ἐγὼ γὰρ **τὰ στίγματα τοῦ** Ἰησοῦ ἐν τῷ σώματί μου βαστάζω.

Tar 2:2 and Ign, Eph 12:2 both mention that the recipients of the letter are followers of Paul.[189] The form of the text written by Pseudo-Ignatius is again a little closer to Tar than the authentic one. After the reference to Paul, the author quotes Rom 15:19, again without mentioning that he uses another text as a model. In addition, at the end of Tar 2:2 the writer imitates the style of Paul from Gal 6:17 when describing the carrying of the marks of Christ.[190] Because the noun στίγμα does not occur anywhere else in the Ignatian corpus or the NT, Tar 2:2 seems to depend on Gal 6:17.

Ps-Ign, Tar	Ps-Ign, Smyr 1:1 ... εἰς τὸν κύριον ἡμῶν Ἰησοῦν Χριστόν, τὸν **τοῦ θεοῦ** υἱόν, τὸν πρωτότοκον **πάσης κτίσεως**, τὸν θεὸν λόγον, τὸν μονογενῆ υἱόν, ...
4:1 Καὶ οὗτος ὁ γεννηθεὶς **ἐκ γυναικὸς** υἱός ἐστι **τοῦ θεοῦ**, καὶ ὁ σταυρωθεὶς πρωτότοκος **πάσης κτίσεως** καὶ θεὸς λόγος, καὶ αὐτὸς ἐποίησε τὰ πάντα. 4:2 λέγει γὰρ ὁ ἀπόστολος· **Εἷς θεὸς ὁ πατήρ, ἐξ οὗ τὰ πάντα, καὶ εἷς κύριος Ἰησοῦς Χριστός, δι᾽ οὗ τὰ πάντα.** καὶ πάλιν· **Εἷς γὰρ θεὸς καὶ εἷς μεσίτης θεοῦ καὶ ἀνθρώπων, ἄνθρωπος Ἰησοῦς Χριστός**, καί· **Ἐν αὐτῷ ἐκτίσθη τὰ πάντα**, τὰ **ἐν** οὐρανῷ **καὶ ἐπὶ γῆς, ὁρατὰ καὶ ἀόρατα· καὶ αὐτός ἐστι πρὸ πάντων, καὶ τὰ πάντα ἐν αὐτῷ συνέστηκεν.**	Gal 4:4: ... ἐξαπέστειλεν ὁ θεὸς τὸν υἱὸν αὐτοῦ, γενόμενον **ἐκ γυναικός**, ... 1 Cor 8:6 ... **εἷς θεὸς ὁ πατὴρ ἐξ οὗ τὰ πάντα** καὶ ἡμεῖς εἰς αὐτόν, **καὶ εἷς κύριος Ἰησοῦς Χριστὸς δι᾽ οὗ τὰ πάντα** καὶ ἡμεῖς δι᾽ αὐτοῦ. 1 Tim 2:5 **Εἷς γὰρ θεός, εἷς καὶ μεσίτης θεοῦ καὶ ἀνθρώπων, ἄνθρωπος Χριστὸς Ἰησοῦς** Col 1:16-17 ὅτι **ἐν αὐτῷ ἐκτίσθη τὰ πάντα ἐν** τοῖς οὐρανοῖς **καὶ ἐπὶ** τῆς **γῆς**, τὰ **ὁρατὰ καὶ** τὰ **ἀόρατα, ... καὶ αὐτός ἐστιν πρὸ πάντων καὶ τὰ πάντα ἐν αὐτῷ συνέστηκεν**

---

[189] Amelungk 1899, 541-542.
[190] Funk & Diekamp II, 134, mentions the similarity between Tar 2:2 and Gal 6:17.

Tar 4:1 describes Christ using the same words as in Ps-Ign, Smyr 1:1. In addition, the text of Tar 4:1 resembles Col 1:15-16 and Jn 1:1-3.[191] Still, the similarity with Ps-Ign, Smyr 1:1 is more obvious.[192] This resemblance shows clearly that the author of Tar knows the text of the "long recension". The text of the "middle recension", the authentic text of Ignatius, does not include in Smyr 1 the words πρωτότοκος πάσης κτίσεως or λόγος at all. It describes Christ in a different way. Moreover, θέος is not coupled with λόγος in the authentic letters of Ignatius[193] nor are the words πρωτότοκος πάσης κτίσεως used. In the interpolated texts these words also appear in Ps-Ign, Eph 20:1[194] which, however, does not resemble Tar 4:1 as much as Ps-Ign, Smyr 1:1. Besides imitating Smyr 1:1, Tar 4:1 seems to echo Gal 4:4 as both texts use the words ἐκ γυναικός.

Tar 4:2 quotes three Pauline texts: 1 Cor 8:6, 1 Tim 2:5, and Col 1:16-17.[195] The author uses the words λέγει γὰρ ὁ ἀπόστολος, καὶ πάλιν, and καί to indicate that he quotes the Pauline texts. Although he changes the texts a little, he imitates them more strictly than he follows Smyr 1:1 in Tar 4:1. Pseudo-Ignatius utilizes here the Pauline letters in the same way as Paul usually quotes the LXX. Thus, they seem to be canonical scriptures for Pseudo-Ignatius, while Ignatius' letters are imitated to give an impression that Tar is one of the authentic letters.

Ps-Ign, Tar

6:4 πῶς οὖν ὁ τοιοῦτος ψιλὸς ἄνθρωπος καὶ ἐκ Μαρίας ἔχων τὴν ἀρχὴν τοῦ εἶναι, ἀλλ' οὐχὶ θεὸς λόγος καὶ υἱὸς μονογενής; **ἐν ἀρχῇ** γὰρ **ἦν ὁ λόγος, καὶ ὁ λόγος ἦν πρὸς τὸν θεόν, καὶ θεὸς ἦν ὁ λόγος.** καὶ ἐν ἄλλοις· **Κύριος ἔκτισέ με ἀρχὴν ὁδῶν αὐτοῦ εἰς ἔργα αὐτοῦ· πρὸ τοῦ αἰῶνος ἐθεμελίωσε με, πρὸ δε πάντων βουνῶν γεννᾷ με.**

Jn 1:1 **'Εν ἀρχῇ ἦν ὁ λόγος, καὶ ὁ λόγος ἦν πρὸς τὸν θεόν, καὶ θεὸς ἦν ὁ λόγος.**

Prov 8:22-25 **κύριος ἔκτισέν με ἀρχὴν ὁδῶν αὐτοῦ εἰς ἔργα αὐτοῦ, πρὸ τοῦ αἰῶνος ἐθεμελίωσέν με** ... **πρὸ δε πάντων βουνῶν γεννᾷ με.**

In Tar 6:4 the author first describes Christ in his own words. After that he quotes Jn 1:1 and Prov 8:22-25 one after another.[196] Again there is no clear mention that the text includes quotations. Only when the author begins to imitate Prov do the words καὶ ἐν ἄλλοις indicate that a new argument begins. Nothing reveals that

[191] Col 1:15-16: πρωτότοκος πάσης κτίσεως, ὅτι ἐν αὐτῷ ἐκτίσθη τὰ πάντα. Jn 1:1-3: 'Εν ἀρχῇ ἦν ὁ λόγος, καὶ ὁ λόγος ἦν πρὸς τὸν θεόν, καὶ θεὸς ἦν ὁ λόγος ... πάντα δι' αὐτοῦ ἐγένετο.
[192] Funk & Diekamp II, 136, presents Col 1:15-16, Jn 1:1, and Ps-Ign, Smyr 1:1 as parallels to Tar 4:1.
[193] M. P. Brown 1963, 51-52.
[194] Ps-Ign, Eph 20:1: 'Ιησοῦ Χριστοῦ, τοῦ μονογενοῦς αὐτοῦ υἱοῦ, τοῦ καὶ πρωτοτόκου πάσης κτίσεως.
[195] See Funk & Diekamp II, 136.
[196] See Funk & Diekamp II, 138.

there is a quotation: it would be possible as well that the argument was formulated by the author of Tar himself.

Ps-Ign, Tar	
	Ign, Pol 6:2 **ὀναίμην ὑμῶν** διὰ παντός.
8:1 **᾽Οναίμην ὑμῶν** ἐν κυρίῳ. Νήφετε· πᾶσαν ἕκαστος **κακίαν ἀπόθεσθε** καὶ τὸν θηριώδη **θυμόν**, καταλαλιάν, συκοφαντίαν, ... **ἐνδύσασθε** δὲ **τὸν κύριον** ἡμῶν **᾽Ιησοῦν Χριστόν, καὶ τῆς σαρκὸς πρόνοιαν μὴ ποιεῖσθε εἰς ἐπιθυμίας**.	Ign, Pol 2:3 νῆφε, ὡς θεοῦ ἀθλητής Col 3:8 ... **ἀπόθεσθε** καὶ ὑμεῖς τὰ πάντα, ὀργήν, **θυμόν, κακίαν**, βλασφημίαν ... Rom 13:14 ἀλλὰ **ἐνδύσασθε τὸν κύριον Ιησοῦν Χριστὸν καὶ τῆς σαρκὸς πρόνοιαν μὴ ποιεῖσθε εἰς ἐπιθυμίας.**
8:2 **οἱ πρεσβύτεροι** ὑποτάσσεσθε **τῷ ἐπισκόπῳ, οἱ διάκονοι τοῖς πρεσβυτέροις**, ὁ λαὸς τοῖς διακόνοις. **ἀντίψυχον ἐγὼ** τῶν φυλαττόντων ταύτην τὴν εὐταξίαν·	Ps-Ign, Philad 4:7 **οἱ διάκονοι τοῖς πρεσβυτέροις** ὡς ἱερεῦσιν, **οἱ πρεσβύτεροι** καὶ οἱ διάκονοι καὶ ὁ λοιπὸς κλῆρος ἅμα παντὶ τῷ λαῷ καὶ τοῖς στρατιώταις καὶ τοῖς ἄρχουσι καὶ τῷ καίσαρι **τῷ ἐπισκόπῳ** ... Ign, Philad 4:1 ... ὡς εἷς ἐπίσκοπος ἅμα τῷ πρεσβυτερίῳ καὶ **διακόνοις** τοῖς συνδούλοις μου· Ign, Pol 2:3 κατὰ πάντα σου **ἀντίψυχον ἐγὼ** καὶ τὰ δεσμά μου, ἃ ἠγάπησας

The verb ὀνίνημι in the form ὀναίμην (2nd aorist optative middle) used in Tar 8:1 is a peculiarity of Ignatius (cf. Mag 2:1, 12:1, Rom 5:2, Eph 2:2, Pol 1:1, 6:2). The verb is rare in other texts of the Apostolic Fathers and even outside Christian literature.[197] In addition, the recipients of the letter are called upon to be sober, using the exhortation νήφετε typical of the Ignatian corpus (e.g. Ign, Pol 2:3, Ps-Ign, Eph 10:4). The phrase ἀντίψυχον ἐγὼ occurring in Tar 8:2 is also a characteristic of the genuine epistles of Ignatius (e.g. Pol 2:3, 6:1, Eph 21:1), as well as of Pseudo-Ignatius' texts (e.g. Mary 3:3, Phil 14, Ant 7:2).[198] Besides imitating Ignatius, the author quotes Paul's letters to the Romans (13:14).[199]

[197] M. P. Brown 1963, 18-19, 54-55, who also emphasizes that ὀναίμην is used once in the NT, in Philem 20 which thus makes it "highly probable that Ign had read and become well acquainted with Philemon as, in general, with Pauline phraseology".
[198] Similarly M. P. Brown 1963, 31, 54-55, 63. Unlike in Tar 8:2, in other cases Pseudo-Ignatius connects the verb γενοίμην with the phrase ἀντίψυχον ἐγώ. See also Amelungk 1899, 542 and Funk & Diekamp II, 141.
[199] See Funk & Diekamp II, 142.

Although the resemblance with Col 3:8 is not as clear as with Rom 13:14, Tar 8:1 also seems to echo Col 3:8.

Tar 8:2 mentions the same officers of the church as Ignatius generally does: bishops (ἐπίσκοποι), deacons (διάκονοι), and presbyters (πρεσβύτεροι) (see Mag 2:1, 6:1, Philad 4:7, Tral 2:2-3, 3:1, Smyr 8:1).[200] Once again the text of Ignatius in the interpolated form, Ps-Ign, Philad 4:7, most resembles Tar.[201] There is still not enough evidence to assume a literary dependence between Tar 8:2 and Ps-Ign, Philad 4:7.

This comparison shows that the author of Tar does not use any single one of Ignatius' genuine epistles as his primary model but he recalls phrases and words from several letters. However, sometimes he seems to have a particular text of Ignatius in his mind. Tar 1:1-3 especially seems clearly to depend on Rom 5:1-3 and Smyr 4:1-2, and Tar 4:1 on Smyr 1:1. The author of Tar seems to know the whole collection of Ignatius' letters and to recall texts from all over the letters, putting them down one after another when writing. The same phenomenon is obvious in all examples studied in detail in this chapter and the other parts of Tar seem to be formed in the same way.[202] By borrowing from and copying the genuine letters, Pseudo-Ignatius clearly maintains the illusion of authenticity.[203] It is interesting that the relationship between Tar and the genuine epistles of Ignatius resembles the connection between Eph and the earlier Pauline letters examined in detail in the previous chapter: the author of Tar uses words and phrases typical of Ignatius and conflates texts from his letters. Thus the relationship of Col to the authentic Pauline letters is possibly analogous to these examples.

The author of Tar also sometimes imitates the style of Paul. Moreover, he often inserts into his text long quotations from Paul, other early Christian literature, or the LXX. Although he does not routinely mention when he quotes other texts — Tar 4:2 being an exception — the literary obligations clearly are the most distinguishing feature of his style. In his letters Pseudo-Ignatius uses direct quotations from and identifiable allusions to the LXX and the NT much more than Ignatius does. Thus both the LXX and the NT seem to be canonical scriptures for Pseudo-Ignatius.[204] However, he does not use Ignatius' letters as sources in the same way as these canonical texts which he generally quotes verbatim. Ignatius' letters are for him only models which he imitates. Because A/Col is a writer of a pseudepigraphic letter like Pseudo-Ignatius, we can have reason to assume that the text of Col might be shaped similarly.

---

[200] M. P. Brown 1963, 19-20.
[201] Also Amelungk 1899, 542, and Funk & Diekamp II, 142, presents Ps-Ign, Philad 4:7 as a parallel to Tar 8:2.
[202] See the notes in Funk & Diekamp II, 133-145.
[203] M. P. Brown 1963, 62. Cf. Brox 1976, 185.
[204] M. P. Brown 1963, 114-119.

The comparisons of the texts have shown that the letters of Pseudo-Ignatius are modelled on the authentic letters of Ignatius. Moreover, large parts of the text are composed of quotations from and allusions to the LXX and the NT. Without any doubt, the character of the letters is somehow fictional.[205] Why then were these pseudepigraphic letters written? The texts of Pseudo-Ignatius reveal that he knew the underlying ideas behind many heresies, e.g. Nicolaitans, Ebionites, and that of Marcion but most of all his letters are involved with the Arian controversy.[206] For example Prov 8:22-25, which was "a favourite text in the Arian controversy" is cited in Tar 6:4.[207] In addition, in Tar 4:1 Christ is called θεὸς λόγος which is an unknown phrase in the authentic letters of Ignatius. Pseudo-Ignatius probably uses it to emphasize the real nature of Christ against the Arians for whom it was unthinkable to regard the divine Logos in Christ as equal to God. Accordingly, Pseudo-Ignatius seems to interpolate the authentic letters of Ignatius and write the six new letters in order to oppose the heresies of his time, especially the Arian controversy. This detail is interesting because, as was noted above, the warning about the persons who are trying to lead astray is generally regarded as the main purpose for the writing of Col. Therefore, it seems that two pseudepigraphers, Pseudo-Ignatius and A/Col may have similar motives for writing their letters.

1.4. Thesis and Methodology

This study takes as its starting point the pseudonymity of Col: I assume the letter was written by a disciple of Paul who wrote in Paul's name after his death. The purpose of this dissertation is to show how the deutero-Pauline author formed the text of Col. Though Sanders, Ludwig, Kiley, and Standhartinger have already investigated the formation of Col, they have reached such different conclusions that it is reasonable to undertake the task again. My thesis is that Col has a literary dependence upon several or all the undisputed Pauline letters (Rom, 1 Cor, 2 Cor, Gal, Phil, 1 Thess, Philem) just as Eph depends on earlier Pauline epistles, and the letters of Pseudo-Ignatius on those of Ignatius. In addition, I will consider whether the conclusions concerning the formation of Col illuminate the problematic question of the purpose of Col: whom is the letter aimed at and what is the "philosophy"?

In order to find the texts A/Col imitates, the whole text of Col will be compared with its closest parallels from the authentic Pauline letters. Col may, however, also depend upon some other texts, e.g. upon Mk as Schenk contends. In

---

[205] So Brox 1976, 182, 188, who states that Pseudo-Ignatius also imitates the fictive style of Pseudo-Paul as the writer of the Pastoral letters. Cf. Amelungk 1899, 538, 554, who calls the spurious letters "Fiction" and the author of them "Fictor".

[206] See Brox 1976, 186; Amelungk 1899, 522 ss, 560; M. P. Brown 1963, 115.

[207] M. P. Brown 1963, 115, referring to Lightfoot.

case any parallels do not occur in Paul's letters, I seek them from other early Christian literature (ECL) — excluding Eph which was noted as depending upon Col — from the LXX, or from other ancient Greek texts using the CD Rom Thesaurus linguae graecae (TLG). When searching for parallels, there is always the danger of parallelomania, exaggerations about the meaning of the resemblances, which has been noted by Sandmel followed by Donaldson.[208] To avoid it, the whole text is systematically searched for parallels. Then the evidence is cumulative and the conclusions more reliable than those reached on the grounds of only some parts of the text. Reuter has recently presented the text of Col with its closest parallels in his Synopsis. The purpose of my study is different from that of Reuter's, however. While his Synopsis, as a reference work, places in parallel all verbal agreements between Col and other NT letters, I am attempting to find only those which possibly were the prototypes for Col. In addition, my study is not limited to NT letters but the parallels with Col in other ECL, as well as in other ancient literature, are also taken under consideration.[209]

The study follows Sanders methodologically. I assume that only verbal and verbatim agreements show possible literary dependence, not similar thoughts. Thus only passages which use similar words are placed in parallel.[210] This is also compatible with the fact that the imitation of style is one characteristic of pseudepigraphic works.[211] It is logical that a pseudepigrapher frequently uses the same words as the text he imitates.

Donaldson states that "the identification of a genealogical parallel requires some hard evidence of a relationship between the two elements in question".[212] Since the dates of early Christian writings as well as of other ancient Greek literature are still not fixed, I search for the parallels at first on the grounds of verbal and verbatim agreement also from the texts which have not been reliably established available to A/Col. Only after all the parallels are collected can final conclusions about the probability of the relationships between the texts be considered. If a writing includes only a few parallels to Col, it is not probable that A/Col utilizes it but if there are several resemblances, the cumulative evidence points to a dependence between the texts. In addition, the procedure tests the method: if parallels are mostly found from the texts which probably were available to A/Col, the method is valid; if otherwise, it is inaccurate.

---

[208] Sandmel 1962; Donaldson 1983.

[209] Reuter, Synopse zu den Briefen des Neuen Testaments. Synopsis of the New Testament Letters. Teil I: Kolosser-, Epheser-, II. Thessalonicherbrief. Vol. I: Colossians, Ephesians, II. Thessalonians. Arbeiten zur Religion und Geschichte des Urchristentums; Bd.5. Frankfurt am Main: Peter Lang 1997.

[210] Similarly H. Leppä 2002, 32-33: "The only way to show that someone has known some source they do not mention is to show verbal agreement. We should find the same words together or the same words in the same context. It is even better if the agreement is verbatim."

[211] Schweizer 1982, 19, following Speyer 1971, 82; cf. Brox 1973, 12.

[212] Donaldson 1983, 199.

Like Sanders and Mitton, I include quotation from memory in the term literary dependence and suggest that conflations of several texts indicate literary dependence.[213] Conflations of texts were noted as characteristic of pseudepigraphic works in previous chapters. Since literary dependence can be influenced by quotation from memory, there is no need to assume that the passages imitated occur in the same order in Col and in the text imitated. Neither the authors of Eph and 2 Pet, nor Pseudo-Ignatius follow in order the texts they imitate. Sanders' results also indicate that A/Col does not take over large sections from other writings, like the writers of Eph and 2 Pet, as well as Pseudo-Ignatius, but imitates single verses, phrases, and expressions only, as Reuter also suggests.[214]

Though I include quotation from memory in literary dependence, I do not neglect the possibility that some letters of Paul may have been in front of A/Col when he was writing. It is still probable that the texts are mostly quoted from memory. There are two possible ways by which A/Col may have familiarized himself with the Pauline letters he recalls: he may have heard them read aloud in public or read himself sometime previously, or both. In addition, the texts may be quoted from memory intentionally but it is also possible that sometimes the quotation is unintentional; the writer does not try to imitate another text but the reader can notice that he has in mind a definite passage familiar both to the writer and to the reader.[215] All that is really important is that A/Col seems to be acquainted with a specific passage.

The comparisons between pseudepigraphic works and their models revealed that it is not typical of a later author to copy the genuine texts. Rather are they utilized quite independently: the words from earlier texts are omitted, added, or the order changed. In addition, it was noted that a pseudepigrapher sometimes uses the words from the texts he imitates in a new context or gives them a new meaning in order to make it suitable for his own situation, as also Sanders contends in his second and fourth criteria pointing to literary dependence.[216] Therefore, it would be expected that the Pauline words and phrases will occur in Col rather in different contexts than applied to the same point as in the genuine letters. An imitator can also use instead of a noun, a verb which has the same stem or vice versa. Sometimes he chooses words which look similar to the words used in the text imitated and he may also repeat many times the words used in an earlier text. Thus the longer text is usually written by an imitator. If a pseudepigrapher is deeply

---

[213] Cf. L. Aejmelaeus 1987a, 101, 190; 1985, 104, 134.

[214] Reuter 1999, calls the former habit of utilizing earlier texts as "incorporation" and the latter as "selective use of materials". He contends that also the author of Acts uses other writings, among them 1 Clem, in the same way.

[215] Cf. Maclean 1995, 15-16, who investigates the relationship of Eph to other Pauline letters defines "direct literary dependence" as result of "contact with Paul's letters, whether read in public or in private. It is detected by evidence that the author had knowledge not just of terms, but of specific passages from those letters."

[216] Cf. Donaldson 1983, 194.

impressed with some text, it may recur in his text. He does not, however, usually repeat the same elements but utilizes different words and thoughts from the text. Sometimes an imitator seems to summarize the teaching of his model. The phenomena typical of other pseudepigraphers may also be characteristic of A/Col.

When studying the parallels between pseudepigraphic writings and their models, it was mentioned that in case one of the words is unusual in ECL, the agreement of two or three words can reveal literary dependence. Sometimes also the occurrence of three common words can indicate literary dependence in cases where it is exceptional that the words appear together. Like Sanders, I assume that when parallels include three or more words in agreement or a two-word phrase, provided that the two words are sufficiently significant and unusual, the resemblance points to literary dependence.[217] The criteria exclude the occurrence of the "stock phrases", favorite expressions appearing often in Paul which also in Sanders' opinion do not show literary dependence.[218] Naturally the use of the Pauline "stock phrases" suggests A/Col's acquaintance with Pauline letters but since they cannot show a literary dependence upon a particular text, they are excluded. In addition, pronouns, conjunctions, and prepositions are too common to be counted among the three words but they are taken note of in verbatim expressions.

It is reasonable to classify the resemblances indicating literary dependence into groups because e.g. some of the verbatim agreements Sanders found include much more than three identical words.[219] In this study the resemblances indicating literary dependence are divided into two groups, those pointing to a possible literary dependence which include three (or two unusual) similar words and those indicating a probable literary dependence which have more than three words in agreement. In addition, minor resemblances which do not meet the criteria for literary dependence but still include a remarkable agreement will be investigated because they indicate A/Col's use of Pauline phrases and give us additional information about A/Col's method of forming the text.

Sanders' criteria that the words have to appear "within a short space" is too vague. Thus I suggest instead that the similar words have to occur within five lines in the text imitated in the edition Nestle & Aland, Novum Testamentum Graece. 27. ed. Stuttgart 1993.[220] In order to clarify the comparisons, the text of Col is

---

[217] Cf. Dunderberg 1994, 26. Maclean 1995, 14 n. 58, rejects Sanders' demand for verbatim agreement of three words because it is not compatible with the definition of allusion she adopts. This does not mean that the criteria of Sanders cannot be utilized in this study since Maclean does not investigate Col but Eph and, besides, does not want to prove the literary dependence in Eph but to study a few allusions very closely parallel to Col or the authentic Paulines (see Maclean 1995, 14-16).

[218] Similarly Mitton 1951, 101-102; Maclean 1995, 14; Dunderberg 1994, 26-27.

[219] See E. P. Sanders 1966, 37-39.

[220] Cf. H. Leppä 2002, 34: "One or two similar words do not prove very much. Two authors writing about the same events can employ the same word by coincidence. But if the words are not typical of the later author, the argument becomes stronger. In addition the number of similar words

presented with its closest parallels in tables. The common words of the texts which are exactly in the same form are written in bold and other similar words are underlined. The parallels will be classified into the following groups:

1) Probable literary dependence
The parallels include more than three similar words (nouns, verbs, or adjectives) within five lines in the text imitated. The definition includes words which have the same stem. In order to find the relevant parallels, the habits characteristic of pseudepigraphers are drawn attention to: verbatim imitation, conflations, the repetition of the words of the texts imitated, the use of the words in a new context or in a new sense. In addition, the rare occurrence of a word or the fact that some words do not generally appear together sometimes reveal literary dependence. Though the NT is only one part of ECL, it is sometimes used as an example when estimating how common some word is because the number of occurrences of the words in the NT can be easily found from concordances. In the tables, the numbers of the verses are both in bold and underlined in the heading, e.g. **<u>1 Cor 2:7</u>**.

2) Possible literary dependence
The parallels include at least three similar words (verbs, nouns, or adjectives) within five lines in the text imitated. The use of two common words is enough if they are very unusual in ECL. When a word used in Col occurs only once in the genuine Pauline letters, it especially indicates literary dependence between the texts. In order to find the relevant parallels, the above-mentioned habits characteristic of pseudepigraphers are highlighted. Since a pseudepigrapher is an imitator, verbatim agreements of at least three other words (conjunctions, pronouns, and prepositions) are also taken to indicate a possible literary dependence if they are unusual. In the tables, the numbers of the verses are in bold in the heading, e.g. **Phil 2:30**.

3) The use of similar style
The parallels use two or three similar words which are very customary in ECL. However, the resemblance does not seem to be due to a coincidence but to the use of similar phrases or style.[221] In addition, when the resemblance between the texts does not meet the criteria for a literary dependence yet it seems that A/Col may be acquainted with a particular text, the verb "echo" is used (e.g. "it is possible that

---

compared to the length of the section is also important."

[221] Maclean 1995, 15, calls the phenomenon "indirect literary dependence" which "resulted from the public reading of Paul's letters and participation in a community whose liturgical terminology had been deeply influenced by Paul and his writings. It is evidenced by a general familiarity with Paul's terminology, but not with specific pericopes from his letters".

Col 1:25 echoes 1 Cor 3:10").[222] In the tables the numbers of these verses are neither underlined nor in bold, e.g. 1 Cor 7:28. The cases when A/Col repeats the words and phrases which already occurred in Col are also taken note of.

It is worth noting that the parallel texts cannot be compared with each other like weights or lengths of physical objects. The classification into three groups is only an approximation: every case has to be estimated individually. The mode of the procedure is as follows: At first in chaps. 2-6 the whole text of Col is analyzed in order to find its closest parallels and the texts are presented in the tables. In addition, preliminary remarks about the habit A/Col utilizes Paul's texts are made. In chap. 7 the parallels between Phil 1 and other undisputed Pauline letters are studied in order to make sure that the parallels between Col and the authentic letters differ from those between genuine Pauline texts and chap. 8 contains the conclusions about literary dependence in Col. Finally, the definitive conclusions about the formation and purpose of Col are drawn in chaps. 9-10.

---

[222] Cf. H. Leppä 2002, 33 : "The use of the letter could be just a distant echo of something he had heard much earlier."

2. The Beginning of the Letter (Col 1:1-14)

2.1. Introductory Greeting and Thanksgiving (Col 1:1-8)

Col 1:1-2	**2 Cor 1:1-2**	**1 Cor 1:1-3**
1 **Παῦλος ἀπόστολος Χριστοῦ 'Ιησοῦ διὰ θελήματος θεοῦ καὶ Τιμόθεος ὁ ἀδελφὸς**	1 **Παῦλος ἀπόστολος Χριστοῦ 'Ιησοῦ διὰ θελήματος θεοῦ καὶ Τιμόθεος ὁ ἀδελφὸς** τῇ ἐκκλησίᾳ τοῦ θεοῦ τῇ οὔσῃ ἐν Κορίνθῳ σὺν **τοῖς ἁγίοις** ...	1 **Παῦλος** κλητὸς **ἀπόστολος Χριστοῦ 'Ιησοῦ διὰ θελήματος θεοῦ καὶ** Σωσθένης **ὁ ἀδελφὸς**
2 **τοῖς** ἐν Κολοσσαῖς **ἁγίοις** καὶ πιστοῖς ἀδελφοῖς **ἐν Χριστῷ, χάρις ὑμῖν καὶ εἰρήνη ἀπὸ Θεοῦ πατρὸς ἡμῶν**.	2 **χάρις ὑμῖν καὶ εἰρήνη ἀπὸ θεοῦ πατρὸς ἡμῶν** καὶ κυρίου 'Ιησοῦ Χριστοῦ.	2 τῇ ἐκκλησίᾳ τοῦ θεοῦ τῇ οὔσῃ ἐν Κορίνθῳ, ἡγιασμένοις **ἐν Χριστῷ** 'Ιησοῦ, κλητοῖς **ἁγίοις** ... 3 **χάρις ὑμῖν καὶ εἰρήνη ἀπὸ Θεοῦ πατρὸς ἡμῶν** καὶ κυρίου 'Ιησοῦ Χριστοῦ.
	Phil 1:1	
	... **τοῖς ἁγίοις ἐν Χριστῷ** 'Ιησοῦ ...	

The introductory greeting of Col in verse 1:1 agrees word for word with 2 Cor 1:1a. The texts include eight consecutive nouns which are exactly the same and in the same order. In addition, Col 1:1 very much resembles 1 Cor 1:1. They have only two differences. First, in 1 Cor Paul is mentioned as having been "called to be an apostle" (κλητός) which is missing in Col. Secondly, 1 Cor mentions brother Sosthenes also as a sender of the letter instead of brother Timothy mentioned in Col as well as in many other Pauline letters (Phil, Philem, 2 Cor, 1 and 2 Thess). Accordingly, Col 1:1 has verbatim agreement with both 1 Cor 1:1 and 2 Cor 1:1 long enough to point to a probable literary dependence between the texts. Though most of the words common to the greetings occur often in the Pauline epistles, the definition "an apostle of Christ Jesus" (ἀπόστολος Χριστοῦ 'Ιησοῦ) appears other than in the greetings of Col, 1 Cor, and 2 Cor, only in the later texts of 1 Tim 1:1 and 2 Tim 1:1. In addition, the phrase "by the will of God" (διὰ θελήματος θεοῦ) is not customary in the Pauline letters: besides 1 Cor 1:1 and 2 Cor 1:1, it occurs only in Rom 15:32, 2 Cor 8:5, Eph 1:1, and 2 Tim 1:1.

The definition "the saints and faithful brothers in Christ" (ἁγίοις καὶ πιστοῖς ἀδελφοῖς ἐν Χριστῷ) in Col 1:2 does not have a parallel anywhere in the introductory greetings of the Pauline letters.[223] However, the adjective "saint"

[223] Similarly Dunn 1996, 49; Pfammatter 1987, 37. The words resemble most the phrase τοῖς ἁγίοις τοῖς οὖσιν [ἐν 'Εφέσῳ] καὶ πιστοῖς ἐν Χριστῷ 'Ιησοῦ in Eph 1:1 which clearly depends on Col 1:2.

(ἅγιος) often appears in the beginnings of the letters. In Rom 1:7 the letter is addressed to "God's beloved, called to be saints" (ἀγαπητοῖς θεοῦ, κλητοῖς ἁγίοις), in 1 Cor 1:2 to those who are "called to be saints" (κλητοῖς ἁγίοις), in 2 Cor 1:1 to "the saints" (τοῖς ἁγίοις), and in Phil 1:1 to "the saints in Christ Jesus" (τοῖς ἁγίοις ἐν Χριστῷ 'Ιησοῦ). Of these, the phrase in Phil most resembles the wording of Col although the phrase ἐν Χριστῷ 'Ιησοῦ in Col lacks the word 'Ιησοῦς.[224] Therefore, A/Col possibly had in his mind the words of Phil 1:1 although the resemblance, one noun and one adjective in common, both ordinarily used in the ECL, does not meet the criteria for literary dependence. Neither in the introductory greeting of 2 Cor nor in that of Phil, which otherwise resemble Col 1:1-2, are the recipients of the letter called brothers. However, this is common in other Pauline letters (see e.g. 1 Cor 1:10, Gal 1:11, 1 Thess 1:4, 2 Thess 1:3).

The words "grace to you and peace from God our Father" (χάρις ὑμῖν καὶ εἰρήνη ἀπὸ θεοῦ πατρὸς ἡμῶν) used in the end of Col 1:2 occur generally in the introductory greetings of the Pauline letters (see Rom 1:7, 1 Cor 1:3, 2 Cor 1:2, Gal 1:3, Eph 1:2, Phil 1:2, 2 Thess 1:2, Philem 1:3). Unlike Col, in all other cases, however, the phrases are continued by the words "and the Lord Jesus Christ" (καὶ κυρίου 'Ιησοῦ Χριστοῦ).[225] For this reason many later manuscripts also include the addition in Col 1:2. Since Christology has central significance in Col, it is not likely that the omission of the words καὶ κυρίου 'Ιησοῦ Χριστοῦ was for any theological reasons.[226] The explanation for the omission may simply be that as a pseudonymous writer A/Col failed to remember the greeting typical of Paul exactly.[227]

It has been noted that Col 1:1 has verbatim agreement with both 1 Cor 1:1 and 2 Cor 1:1 and that in Col 1:2 A/Col may have in mind the words "to the saints in Christ Jesus" (τοῖς ἁγίοις ἐν Χριστῷ 'Ιησοῦ) used in Phil 1:1. However, all these texts belong to the introductory greetings of the letters and are thus shaped with similar forms, which makes it natural that the texts resemble each other.[228] Thus it is possible that the genuine Pauline letters also have similar agreements with each other as Col has with 2 Cor and Phil. It was already noted that the introductions of 1 and 2 Cor are similar. In the same way, the beginning of 1 Thess much resembles that of 2 Thess. However, these cases are exceptional: the letters having the same recipients are intentionally composed to look similar. In order to find out if the relationship between the introductory greeting of Col and other Pauline introductions differs from those between the authentic Pauline texts, Phil 1:1-2 is

---

[224] The phrase ἐν Χριστῷ 'Ιησοῦ is used besides in Phil, in the introductory greetings of 1 Cor and 2 Tim.
[225] Also 1 Thess 1:1 differs from the others: it includes only the words χάρις ὑμῖν καὶ εἰρήνη.
[226] Lohse 1971, 10-11. Cf. Dunn 1996, 52; Hübner 1997, 43-44; Nikolainen 1987, 16-17; O'Brien 1982, 6; Hendriksen 1971, 44-45; Bruce 1988, 39.
[227] Similarly Hübner 1997, 43-44, refers to the fact that only the deutero-Pauline writer of Col mysteriously leaves out the words καὶ κυρίου 'Ιησοῦ Χριστοῦ.
[228] VanKooten 1995, 78, has noticed that the prescript of Eph has a higher rate of identical words with the text of Col than other parts of Eph.

here compared with the beginnings of the other genuine Pauline letters, as Col 1:1-2 was compared with them. Phil is a good choice for this study because it is almost precisely the same length as Col and thus it could be expected that the structures of the letters are similar. Moreover, there is only one letter to the Philippians in the Pauline corpus as there is only one to the Colossians.[229]

Phil 1:1-2	Rom 1:1,7	2 Cor 1:1-2
1 **Παῦλος** καὶ **Τιμόθεος** <u>δοῦλοι</u> **Χριστοῦ 'Ιησοῦ** **πᾶσιν τοῖς ἁγίοις** ἐν Χριστῷ 'Ιησοῦ **τοῖς** **οὖσιν ἐν** Φιλίπποις σὺν ἐπισκόποις καὶ διακόνοις, 2 **χάρις ὑμῖν καὶ εἰρήνη** **ἀπὸ θεοῦ πατρὸς ἡμῶν** **καὶ κυρίου 'Ιησοῦ** **Χριστοῦ.**	1 **Παῦλος** <u>δοῦλος</u> **Χριστοῦ 'Ιησοῦ** ... 7 **πᾶσιν τοῖς οὖσιν ἐν** 'Ρώμῃ ... κλητοῖς **ἁγίοις,** **χάρις ὑμῖν καὶ εἰρήνη** **ἀπὸ θεοῦ πατρὸς ἡμῶν** **καὶ κυρίου 'Ιησοῦ** **Χριστοῦ.**	1 **Παῦλος** ἀπόστολος **Χριστοῦ 'Ιησοῦ** διὰ θελήματος θεοῦ καὶ **Τιμόθεος** ὁ ἀδελφὸς ... σὺν **τοῖς ἁγίοις πᾶσιν** **τοῖς οὖσιν ἐν** ὅλῃ τῇ 'Αχαΐᾳ, 2 **χάρις ὑμῖν καὶ εἰρήνη** **ἀπὸ θεοῦ πατρὸς ἡμῶν** **καὶ κυρίου 'Ιησοῦ** **Χριστοῦ.**

Like Col, Phil 1:1 mentions Timothy with Paul as a sender of the letter which is common in the Pauline letters (see p. 59). In addition, they are described as "servants of Christ Jesus" (δοῦλοι Χριστοῦ 'Ιησοῦ). In Rom 1:1 the same words are used of Paul. Moreover, Phil 1:1 and Rom 1:7 define the recipients of the letter quite similarly (Phil: πᾶσιν ... τοῖς οὖσιν ἐν Φιλίπποις, Rom: πᾶσιν τοῖς οὖσιν ἐν 'Ρώμῃ) and both also call them saints (Phil: ἅγιοι, Rom: κλητοὶ ἅγιοι). Yet in 1 Cor the recipients of the letter are also called the saints (κλητοὶ ἅγιοι) like in Rom.[230] Besides Rom 1:7, the introduction of 2 Cor resembles the text of Phil: both mention Timothy and the definitions of the recipients are similar (2 Cor 1:1: σὺν τοῖς ἁγίοις πᾶσιν τοῖς οὖσιν ἐν ὅλῃ τῇ 'Αχαΐᾳ, Phil 1:1: πᾶσιν τοῖς ἁγίοις ... τοῖς οὖσιν ἐν Φιλίπποις σύν ...).

Though Phil 1:1-2 resembles the introductions of Rom and 2 Cor, the similarities between the texts differ from those between Col 1:1 and the genuine Pauline letters. The introduction of Phil does not have so long a verbatim agreement with any other text as Col 1:1 has with 2 Cor 1a and 1 Cor 1:1. Moreover, Phil uses similar phrases to other genuine Pauline letters unlike Col where they have been modified. The choice of wording ἁγίοις καὶ πιστοῖς ἀδελφοῖς ἐν Χριστῷ (Col 1:2) is evidently a new combination of Pauline phrases.

---

229 Similarly E. P. Sanders 1966, 30-35, compares the nature and extent of the parallels between Col and the undisputed Pauline letters with those of the resemblances between Phil and the other genuine texts.

230 Also E. P. Sanders 1966, 34, and Mitton 1951, 322, note the use of the similar phrases in 1 Cor 1:2 and Phil 1:1.

In addition, the expression ἐν Χριστῷ 'Ιησοῦ used in authentic Pauline letters in Col 1:2 lacks the word 'Ιησοῦς.

It is also noteworthy that Phil 1:2 includes the formula χάρις ὑμῖν καὶ εἰρήνη ἀπὸ θεοῦ πατρὸς ἡμῶν καὶ κυρίου 'Ιησοῦ Χριστοῦ like almost all Pauline letters. In Phil the words are exactly in the same form as in the other letters. However, A/Col has left out the end of the formula (καὶ κυρίου 'Ιησοῦ Χριστοῦ) and thus seems to be an imitator who does not remember the phrase so exactly as Paul himself.

The comparison between Phil 1:1-2 and the introductory greetings of the other authentic Pauline letters has shown that the relationship of Col 1:1-2 to the texts of the genuine Pauline epistles is exceptional. A/Col modifies the Pauline phrases in Col 1:2, unlike Phil 1:1-2 which uses the same wordings as other epistles. Moreover, no other introductory greeting has so obvious a verbatim agreement with other texts than Col 1:1 has with 2 Cor 1a and 1 Cor 1:1. Therefore there is a reason to assume that A/Col is imitating either 2 Cor 1:1a or 1 Cor 1:1. Both resemblances include much more than three words in common and thus meet the criteria for a probable literary dependence. Because Col 1:1 matches exactly 2 Cor 1:1a, having eight consecutive nouns which are exactly the same and in the same order, the first alternative is more probable.[231] The obvious resemblance between Col 1:1 and 1 Cor 1:1 cannot, however, be neglected. It is also possible that A/Col knew only 1 Cor 1:1 and modified it or that both 2 Cor 1:1a and 1 Cor 1:1 were familiar to him. Thus also the resemblance between Col 1:1 and 1 Cor 1:1 will be taken under consideration when analyzing the relationships between the letters in chapters 8 and 9. In addition, A/Col may have had in mind the words τοῖς ἁγίοις ἐν Χριστῷ 'Ιησοῦ in Phil 1:1 when he calls the recipients of his letter ἁγίοις καὶ πιστοῖς ἀδελφοῖς ἐν Χριστῷ in Col 1:2 although the resemblance is insufficient to indicate literary dependence.[232]

Many scholars draw attention to the verbatim agreement between Col 1:1 and 2 Cor 1:1a but do not draw any conclusions from it.[233] However, the resemblance is too obvious to be neglected. Ludwig's interpretation is also problematic. On the one hand, she suggests that Col 1:1-2 conflates 2 Cor 1:1-2 and Phil 1:1-2 and thus

---

[231] Similarly Nielsen 1985, 108, takes Col 1:1 as depending upon 2 Cor 1:1a. Cf. Lindemann 1979, 115, who assumes that A/Col probably knew the text of 2 Cor 1:1. Contra Standhartinger 1999, 72-73, according to whom the choice of wording in 2 Cor 1:1 is not closer to Col 1:1 than those in the introductory greetings of other genuine Pauline letters.

[232] Schenk 1987a, 3340, interprets a little differently that the primary model of Col is the introductory greeting of Philem which is modified in verse 1 according to 2 Cor 1:1 and in verse 2 according to Rom 1:7. Lohse 1969, 219, assumes that Col 1:1-2 has been modelled on the introduction of Rom. Besides the verbal resemblances, he defends this interpretation by the fact that among the Pauline letters it was especially Rom which was read and studied in the Pauline churches. Cf. Hübner 1997, 43.

[233] See Dunn 1996, 47; Hartman 1985, 14; Nikolainen, 1987, 15; Lohse 1971, 6; Kiley 1986, 86; Cannon 1981, 173-174; Luz 1998, 192. Pokorný 1987,27 mentions only the resemblance between 1 Cor 1:1 and Col 1:1 but does not note the more obvious similarity to 2 Cor 1:1.

depends on them. On the other hand, she is trying to deny the literary dependence by emphasizing that A/Col shapes his text independently: he does not imitate Paul's texts.[234] This interpretation includes several problems. First, the verbatim agreement between Col 1:1 and 2 Cor 1:1 is so long that it clearly is an imitation. A/Col does not show any independent modifying of the text. Secondly, it is not possible that the text of Col is simultaneously modelled on 2 Cor and written independently. Thirdly, Ludwig's opinion of the literary dependence is problematic. If Col 1:1-2 conflates 2 Cor 1:1-2 and Phil 1:1-2, it must depend on them. The fact that A/Col modifies the texts does not prevent the literary dependence.[235]

Col 1:3-5a	**Philem 4-5**	**1 Thess 1:2-3**
3 **Εὐχαριστοῦμεν τῷ θεῷ** πατρὶ **τοῦ κυρίου ἡμῶν Ἰησοῦ Χριστοῦ πάντοτε περὶ ὑμῶν** προσευχόμενοι, 4 ἀκούσαντες **τὴν πίστιν** ὑμῶν ἐν Χριστῷ Ἰησοῦ **καὶ τὴν ἀγάπην ἣν** ἔχετε **εἰς πάντας τοὺς ἁγίους** 5a διὰ τὴν ἐλπίδα τὴν ἀποκειμένην ὑμῖν ἐν τοῖς οὐρανοῖς	4 Εὐχαριστῶ **τῷ θεῷ** μου **πάντοτε** μνείαν σου ποιούμενος ἐπὶ τῶν προσευχῶν μου, 5 ἀκούων σου **τὴν ἀγάπην καὶ τὴν πίστιν, ἣν** ἔχεις πρὸς τὸν κύριον Ἰησοῦν καὶ **εἰς πάντας τοὺς ἁγίους** **2 Cor 1:3** Εὐλογητὸς ὁ θεὸς καὶ πατὴρ **τοῦ κυρίου ἡμῶν Ἰησοῦ Χριστοῦ** ...	2 **Εὐχαριστοῦμεν τῷ θεῷ πάντοτε περὶ** πάντων **ὑμῶν** μνείαν ποιούμενοι ἐπὶ τῶν προσευχῶν ἡμῶν, ἀδιαλείπτως 3 μνημονεύοντες ὑμῶν τοῦ ἔργου τῆς πίστεως καὶ τοῦ κόπου τῆς ἀγάπης καὶ τῆς ὑπομονῆς τῆς ἐλπίδος **τοῦ κυρίου ἡμῶν Ἰησοῦ Χριστοῦ** ἔμπροσθεν τοῦ θεοῦ καὶ πατρὸς ἡμῶν

The thanksgiving in Col 1:3-5a resembles very much those in Philem 4-5 and in 1 Thess 1:2-3. All texts include similar giving of thanks to God and in all are praised the faith and love of the recipients of the letter. In addition, some phrases of the prayer in Col are verbatim with 1 Thess: the words εὐχαριστοῦμεν τῷ θεῷ ... πάντοτε περί ... ὑμῶν ... τοῦ κυρίου ἡμῶν Ἰησοῦ Χριστοῦ in Col 1:3 match exactly the words in 1 Thess 1:2-3. It is also noteworthy that the noun προσευχή used in 1 Thess 1:3 has the same stem as the verb προσεύχομαι occurring in Col 1:3. Moreover, the noun πατήρ is used in both texts (Col 1:3 // 1 Thess 1:3), although the contexts are different.

Besides the above-mentioned details, the triad of faith (πίστις), love (ἀγάπη), and hope (ἐλπίς) appearing in Col 1:3-5 also occurs in 1 Thess 1:2-3, even in the

[234] Ludwig 1974, 60-65.
[235] Also Kiley 1986, 98, neglects the verbatim agreement between Col 1:1 and 2 Cor 1:1a because he contends that Col 1:1-2 depends only upon Phil 1:1-2.

same order. Instead, in Philem 4-5 hope is not mentioned although love and faith appear. When describing love and faith, the text of Col, however, seems to follow Philem sometimes verbatim. The words τὴν πίστιν καὶ τὴν ἀγάπην are in the same form although the order is reversed. Both texts are continued by a relative clause which uses the words ἣν + ἔχω. In addition, the verb "to hear" (ἀκούω) appears in both texts and, moreover, the words "for all the saints" (εἰς πάντας τοὺς ἁγίους) in Philem 5 match exactly the words in Col 1:4. The expression "in Christ Jesus" (ἐν Χριστῷ 'Ιησοῦ) does not occur in Philem 5 but the words "for the Lord Jesus" (πρὸς τὸν κύριον 'Ιησοῦν) are employed instead.

Accordingly, both 1 Thess 1:2-3 and Philem 4-5 resemble Col 1:3-5a so much that the agreements between the texts meet the criteria for a probable literary dependence. The resemblance between 1 Thess 1:2-3 and Col 1:3-5a seems to be stronger. Still, the verbatim agreement between Philem 4-5 and Col 1:3-5a is remarkable. The words in Col which exactly match 1 Thess are all common to many thanksgivings in the Pauline letters (εὐχαριστοῦμεν τῷ θεῷ ... πάντοτε περί ... ὑμῶν ... τοῦ κυρίου ἡμῶν 'Ιησοῦ Χριστοῦ). It is noteworthy that the verb εὐχαριστέω, "to thank", is in plural only in the thanksgivings of 1 Thess and Col. However, this similarity between Philem and Col is not good evidence for literary dependence. It is self-evident that a writer can make these kinds of shaping himself. It is natural that the verb is used in the plural in Col because Timothy is mentioned as a co-sender of the letter.[236] Unlike the resemblances between 1 Thess and Col, the verbatim agreement between Philem and Col seems to be unique. The expression ἣν + ἔχω ... εἰς πάντας τοὺς ἁγίους is not used elsewhere in the Pauline letters.

Though Col 1:3-5a seems more likely to depend upon Philem 4-5 than upon 1 Thess 1:2-3, there are still two problems left: God is not called Father (πατήρ) in Philem as in Col and 1 Thess and, moreover, all three parts of the triad faith, love, and hope do not occur in Philem, as in 1 Thess and Col. Like in Col, God is, however, called Father in 2 Cor 1:3 which also includes the words τοῦ κυρίου ἡμῶν 'Ιησοῦ Χριστοῦ similar to Col 1:3. Because it was already noted that between Col 1:1-2 and 2 Cor 1-2 there is a resemblance indicating a probable literary dependence, it is very likely that the dependence of Col on 2 Cor continues in Col 1:3. Since the two agreements, the one between Col 1:1-2 and 2 Cor 1:1-2 and that between Col 1:3 and 2 Cor 1:3, occur consecutively, they belong together and thus also the latter one, though alone not meeting the criteria, is classified as a probable literary dependence.

The triad faith–love–hope is well known in the Pauline epistles (e.g. Rom 5:1-5, 1 Cor 13:13, 1 Thess 5:8) as well as in other early Christian literature (e.g. Heb

---

[236] Similarly Hendriksen 1971, 46; Hartman 1985, 19; O'Brien 1982, 9; Haapa 1978, 24; Nikolainen 1987, 17. Dunn 1996, 55-56, however, overdoes it when interpreting that the plural form of the verb implies double authorship unique to Col. In 1 Thess the verb is used in plural like in Col. Cf. Nielsen 1985, 110, according to whom "we" in the intercession is "patently artificial".

10:22-24).[237] It is thus possible that A/Col knew the tradition and was familiar with the triad without having in mind 1 Thess 1:2-3. However, the triad occurs only in 1 Thess (1:2-3 and 5:8) in the same order faith–love–hope as in Col which indicates that A/Col knew both 1 Thess 1:2-3 and Philem 4-5 and thus the triad was familiar to him from 1 Thess 1:2-3. Therefore, the agreement between Col 1:3-5a and 1 Thess 1:2-3 will be taken into consideration in chapters 8 and 9.[238]

Though it is possible that A/Col knew the triad faith–love–hope as a traditional phrase, it does not mean that the verbatim agreement between Col, 1 Thess, and Philem can completely be neglected, like Lindemann and Ludwig assume.[239] Ludwig also stresses, referring to Bujard, that A/Col shapes his text independently because he uses participles instead of causal clauses beginning with the conjunction ὅτι common to the authentic Pauline letters (e.g. Rom 1:8, Phil 1:6). According to Ludwig, this independence evidences that Col cannot have a literary dependence on Philem.[240] Ludwig is right that Bujard has demonstrated A/Col's habit of using participles more often than Paul does. However, Ludwig does not draw attention to the fact that in this case the words ἀκούων σου τὴν ἀγάπην καὶ τὴν πίστιν which includes a participle are also employed in Philem 5 and, moreover, resemble the words ἀκούσαντες τὴν πίστιν used in Col 1:4. Thus in this case it is possible that the text which is imitated has caused the use of a participle.

Bujard has shown that the style of Col 1:3-8 is exceptional: the thought of A/Col is associative, which differs from the authentic Pauline texts. A characteristic of the style is the meandering of the text. The meaning of faith and love are

---

[237] This is emphasized e.g. by O'Brien 1982, 10-11; Hartman 1985, 19-20, R. P. Martin 1981, 47; Bruce 1988, 41; Hendriksen 1971, 47.

[238] Similarly Kiley 1986, 83-84, 93; Schenk 1987a, 3340; Pokorný 1987, 31; Best 1997, 88, assume that Col 1:3-5a probably depends on Philem 4-5. Besides, according to Gnilka 1980, 32, Dunn 1996, 55-56, Luz 1998, 194, and Haapa 1978, 24, Philem 5 is a close parallel to Col 1:4-5. Cf. Hübner 1997, 44. In addition, Pokorný and Dunn draw also attention to the resemblance between Col 1:3-5 and 1 Thess 1:3. According to Lohse 1971, 15, Col 1:3 resembles most Rom 1:8. As was mentioned above (p. 88 n. 10) he assumes the beginning of Col to be wholly modelled on the introduction of Rom. Also Mullins 1984, 288-293, neglects the possibility that the thanksgiving of Col might have been modelled on Philem. He defends his interpretation with two arguments. First, there are nine themes presented in the thanksgiving in Philem (ἀγάπη, πίστις, ὁ κύριος Ἰησοῦς, ἅγιοι, κοινωνία, ἀγαθόν, χαρά, παράκλησις, σπλάγχνα) of which only five are repeated in Col. Moreover, in Col six new themes (ἐλπίς, ἐν τῷ λόγῳ τῆς ἀληθείας τοῦ εὐαγγελίου, χάρις, σύνδουλος, διάκονος, πνεῦμα) are added. According to Mullins the reproduction of so few themes similar to Philem is not enough to assume a literary dependence. Mullins' second argument is based on the use of thanksgiving themes in Col. Because Col develops the themes later in the letter like other Pauline letters, it is an authentic Pauline letter, not an example of pseudepigraphy. The problem of Mullins' interpretation is similar to the one of Ludwig's: he assumes that a later writer cannot modify independently the text he uses

[239] Lindemann 1979, 118-119; Ludwig 1974, 67-68, 37. Also O'Brien 1977, 101, mentions that here is utilized "the primitive Christian triad". However, according to him, the texts of Col, Philem, and Phil are so similar because they all, including Col, are authentic Pauline letters.

[240] Ludwig 1974, 35-37, following Bujard 1973, 60.

discussed in Col at slightly greater length than in 1 Thess or Philem. The style is seen most clearly in the description of hope, which continues from Col 1:5 to 8.[241] The fact that A/Col modifies the text does not, however, prevent literary dependence, as Ludwig assumes. It is possible that a later writer modifies the text he imitates to resemble his own style.

In Col 1:5a, hope is defined as being laid up in the heavens (διὰ τὴν ἐλπίδα τὴν ἀποκειμένην ὑμῖν ἐν τοῖς οὐρανοῖς). The phrase "in the heavens" (ἐν τοῖς οὐρανοῖς) occurs often in the Gospel tradition.[242] Some of the cases resemble Col 1:5a a little: the reward which is great in the heavens is described in Mt 5:12, in Lk 10:20 Jesus exhorts his disciples to rejoice that their names are written in the heavens, and in Lk 12:33, 18:22 he tells about a treasure in the heavens. However, besides the phrase ἐν τοῖς οὐρανοῖς, the texts do not otherwise resemble Col 1:5a.

Besides these examples from the Gospel tradition, some texts in other early Christian literature also resemble Col 1:5a. The verb ἀπόκειμαι is used in 2 Tim 4:8 when the writer tells about the crown of righteousness which is reserved for him. 1 Pet 1:4 tells about an inheritance that is kept in heavens (ἐν οὐρανοῖς), Heb 6:18 about the hope set before us (τῆς προκειμένης ἐλπίδος), and Heb 9:27 about the fact that it is appointed for mortals to die once (καὶ καθ᾽ ὅσον ἀπόκειται τοῖς ἀνθρώποις ἅπαξ ἀποθανεῖν). None of these texts, however, is either very close to Col 1:5a or has verbatim agreement with it. In ECL there is no close parallel to the definition of hope in Col 1:5a.[243]

---

[241] Bujard 1973, 79-80, 86.

[242] Mt 5:12,16, 6:1,9, 7:11,21, 10:33, 16:17,19, Mk 11:25,26, 12:25, 13:25, Lk 10:20, 12:33, 18:22. Besides Col 1:5a, the phrase ἐν τοῖς οὐρανοῖς appears twice in Col, in 1:16 and 1:20. Moreover, Col 1:23 tells about the promise of the Gospel (ἀπὸ τῆς ἐλπίδος τοῦ εὐαγγελίου) which has been proclaimed to every creature under heaven using the phrase ὑπὸ τὸν οὐρανόν.

[243] Neither are the parallels found in Jewish literature very close; see Lohse 1971, 18 nn. 46 and 47; Dunn 1996, 59, and Hartman 1985, 20, who refer e.g. to the following texts:
2 Macc 12:45: εἶτε' ἐμβλέπων τοῖς μετ' εὐσεβείας κοιμωμένοις κάλλιστον ἀποκείμενον χαριστήριον.
4 Macc 8:11: οὐ διαλογιεῖσθε τοῦτο, ὅτι οὐδὲν ὑμῖν ἀπειθήσασιν πλὴν τοῦ μετὰ στρεβλῶν ἀποθανεῖν ἀπόκειται.
Job 38:23: ἀπόκειται δέ σοι εἰς ὥραν ἐχθρῶν, εἰς ἡμέραν πολέμου καὶ μάχης.

Col 1:5b-6	2 Cor 6:7	Gal 2:5, 14
5b ἣν προ-ηκούσατε **ἐν τῷ λόγῳ τῆς ἀληθείας τοῦ εὐαγγελίου** 6 τοῦ παρόντος εἰς **ὑμᾶς**, **καθὼς καὶ ἐν** παντὶ **τῷ κόσμῳ** ἐστὶν καρπο-φορούμενον **καὶ** αὐξανόμενον **καθὼς καὶ ἐν ὑμῖν**, ἀφ' ἧς ἡμέρας ἠκούσατε καὶ ἐπέγνωτε τὴν χάριν τοῦ θεοῦ ἐν ἀληθείᾳ·	**ἐν λόγῳ ἀληθείας** Rom 1:13 ἐλθεῖν πρὸς **ὑμᾶς** ... ἵνα τινὰ καρπὸν σχῶ **καὶ ἐν ὑμῖν καθὼς καὶ ἐν** τοῖς λοιποῖς ἔθνεσιν. Rom 1:8, Mt 26:13 **ἐν** ὅλῳ **τῷ κόσμῳ** **Mk 4:8** καὶ ἄλλα ἔπεσεν εἰς τὴν γῆν τὴν καλὴν καὶ ἐδίδου καρπὸν ἀναβαίνοντα **καὶ** αὐξανόμενα καὶ ἔφερεν ἓν τριάκοντα καὶ ἓν ἑξήκοντα καὶ ἓν ἑκατόν.	ἀλήθεια **τοῦ εὐαγγελίου** 2 Cor 11:9, cf. Gal 4:18,20 καὶ παρὼν πρὸς **ὑμᾶς** Mk 4:20, cf. Mt 13:23, Lk 8:15 καὶ ἐκεῖνοί εἰσιν οἱ ἐπὶ τὴν γῆν τὴν καλὴν σπαρέντες, οἵτινες ἀκούουσιν τὸν λόγον καὶ παραδέχονται καὶ καρποφοροῦσιν ἓν τριάκοντα καὶ ἓν ἑξήκοντα καὶ ἓν ἑκατόν. Phil 1:5 ... εἰς τὸ εὐαγγέλιον ἀπὸ τῆς πρώτης ἡμέρας ἄχρι τοῦ νῦν

Col 1:5b-6 continues the describing of hope which was started in Col 1:5a. The verb "to hear beforehand" (προακούω) does not appear anywhere else in the Pauline letters or in ECL.[244] Because it is typical of A/Col to add prefixes to Pauline words,[245] the verb προακούω is apparently his creation. To the verb "to hear" (ἀκούω) used in Col 1:4 has been added prefix προ-. In addition, the phrase "in the word of the truth of the gospel" (ἐν τῷ λόγῳ τῆς ἀληθείας τοῦ εὐαγγελίου) used in Col 1:5b is unique in ECL before Col.[246] These long series of dependent genitives are characteristic of A/Col.[247] The phrase seems to be the result of a combination of two Pauline phrases, ἐν λόγῳ ἀληθείας (2 Cor 6:7)[248] and ἡ ἀλήθεια τοῦ εὐαγγελίου (Gal 2:5, 14).[249]

---

[244] See Bauer 1988, 1407.

[245] E. P. Sanders 1966, 37.

[246] Eph 1:13 which apparently depends upon Col 1:5 shapes the phrase to the form ἀκούσαντες τὸν λόγον τῆς ἀληθείας, τὸ εὐαγγέλιον τῆς σωτηρίας ὑμῶν.

[247] Lohse 1971, 88; Bujard 1973, 156.

[248] Also Ludwig 1974, 38, emphasizes that the phrase in 2 Cor 6:7 is similar to the one in Col 1:5. The same kind of phrase is also used in 2 Tim 2:15 and Jas 1:18.

[249] Similarly, according to Dunn 1996, 61, the formulation ἐν τῷ λόγῳ τῆς ἀληθείας τοῦ εὐαγγελίου "probably ... contains an echo of the same phrase used in Gal 2:5 and 14". Also Reuter

In the beginning of Col 1:6, the phrase "which has come to you" (πάρειμι πρὸς ὑμᾶς) is used which appears in the genuine Pauline epistles in 2 Cor 11:9, Gal 4:18, and 20. The words καὶ παρὼν πρὸς ὑμᾶς in 2 Cor 11:9 resemble most the words τοῦ παρόντος εἰς ὑμᾶς used in Col 1:6 because both phrases include a participle. However, the similarity does not indicate literary dependence because it is typical of A/Col to use participles but A/Col only uses the Pauline phrase πάρειμι πρὸς ὑμᾶς in Col 1:6.

In Rom 1:13, Paul says that he has often intended to come to the Romans in order to reap some harvest among them. This description includes some interesting verbal resemblances with Col 1:6. The words καρπὸν σχῶ describing the reaping of the harvest in Rom 1:13 resemble the verb καρποφορέω, "to bear fruit", used in Col; they have the same stem. In addition, the words "and among you as also" (καὶ ἐν ὑμῖν καθὼς καὶ ἐν) occur in Col 1:6 although in different order and the adverb καθὼς is repeated (καθὼς καὶ ἐν ... καθὼς καὶ ἐν ὑμῖν).

Moreover, instead of the words "among the rest of the gentiles" (ἐν τοῖς λοιποῖς ἔθνεσιν) in Rom 1:13, in Col 1:6 the phrase "in all the world" (ἐν παντὶ τῷ κόσμῳ) appears, the meanings of which are very much alike. The phrase ἐν παντὶ τῷ κόσμῳ is exceptional but similar phrases including "whole" (ὅλος) instead of "all" (πᾶς) occur once in the genuine Pauline letters (ἐν ὅλῳ τῷ κόσμῳ in Rom 1:8), sometimes in the Gospel tradition (ἐν ὅλῳ τῷ κόσμῳ in Mt 26:13; τὸν κόσμον ὅλον in Mk 8:36, Mt 16:26, Lk 9:25; εἰς ὅλον τὸν κόσμον in Mk 14:9), and once in other letters (περὶ ὅλου τοῦ κόσμου in 1 Jn 2:2). In addition, in Rom 3:19 (γένηται πᾶς ὁ κόσμος) the pronoun πᾶς is connected with the noun κόσμος like in Col 1:6. These words do not, however, form a phrase similar to Col 1:6.[250] Thus the phrase ἐν παντὶ τῷ κόσμῳ seems to be a modification of the phrase ἐν ὅλῳ τῷ κόσμῳ sometimes occurring in ECL. One reason for the modification is probably the habit of A/Col of often using the noun πᾶς (see Col 1:4, 6, 9, 10, 11) which will be taken under consideration when analyzing Col 1:9-11.

Although Col 1:6 and Rom 1:13 resemble each other very much, the verbatim agreement is not remarkable. Besides the similarity between the phrase καρπὸν σχῶ and the verb καρποφορέω, there is only one choice of wording repeated verbatim (καὶ ἐν ὑμῖν καθὼς καὶ ἐν) which is also quite standard in Greek. Thus the similarity between the texts does not meet the criteria for literary dependence.[251]

1997, 56-57, presents 2 Cor 6:7 and Gal 2:5,14 as parallels to Col 1:5b.

[250] The phrase πᾶς ὁ κόσμος also occurs a few times in the texts of Philo.
Philo, De Somniis Liber I, 243: πᾶς ὁ οὐρανὸς καὶ ὁ κόσμος ἀνάθημα Θεοῦ τοῦ πεποιηκότος τὸ ἀνάθημα.
Philo, Quis Rer Div Heres, 99: τοὺς μὲν γὰρ τὰς γνώμας χαλδαΐζοντας οὐρανῷ πεπιστευκέναι, τὸν δ' ἐνθένδε μεταναστάντα τῷ ἐπόχῳ τοῦ οὐρανοῦ καὶ ἡνιόχῳ τοῦ παντὸς κόσμου, Θεῷ, φασὶν οἱ χρησμοί.

[251] Also Pokorný 1987, 36, presents Rom 1:13 as a parallel to Col 1:6. Kiley 1986, 94, and Ludwig 1974, 69, emphasize that Col 1:6 is not dependent upon Rom 1:13 but the verbal resemblance is caused by the use of the same Pauline tradition. In addition, Kiley 1986, 97-99, interprets Phil 1:12 to be a closer parallel to Col 1:6 than Rom 1:13, because "that theme of preaching, which, like Col

In Col 1:6, the gospel is described as bearing fruit and growing (καρποφορούμενον καὶ αὐξανόμενον) which includes an unnatural order. Generally a plant first grows up and then bears fruit. However, a similar unnatural order occurs in Mk 4:8 in the parable of the sower where the words ἐδίδου καρπόν ... καὶ αὐξανόμενα, resembling the ones in Col 1:6, are employed to describe how the seed which fell in the good soil is bringing forth grain and growing up.[252] The words καρποφορούμενον καὶ αὐξανόμενον resemble a little the phrase αὐξάνεσθε καὶ πληθύνεσθε used of human reproduction in the OT (Gen 1:22, 28, 8:17, 9:1) and of Israel's population increase (Jer 3:16, 23:3).[253] However, there is no parallel resembling Col 1:6 as much as Mk 4:8. It is also noteworthy that both synoptic parallels to Mk 4:8 (Mt 13:1-9 and Lk 8:4-8) change the order to the natural one. Because neither the noun καρπός nor the verb καρποφορέω appears together with the verb αὐξάνω anywhere else in the Gospels, except in Mk 4:8, or in the Pauline letters, except in Col 1:6 and in Col 1:10, the verbal agreement between Col 1:6 and Mk 4:8, the occurrence of two similar words, meets the criteria for a possible literary dependence.

In addition, the choice of wording "you heard in the word ... it is bearing fruit" (ἣν προηκούσατε ἐν τῷ λόγῳ ... καρποφορούμενον) in Col 1:5b-6 resemble the words "they hear the word .. and bear fruit" (ἀκούουσιν τὸν λόγον ... καὶ καρποφοροῦσιν) used in Mk 4:20 in the interpretation of the parable of the sower.[254] Like Mk 4:8, Mk 4:20 also describes the seed which fell in the good soil. The verb καρποφορέω appears otherwise in the Gospels only in Mt 13:23 and Lk 8:15, which are parallels to Mk 4:20, and in Mk 4:28, which belongs to the context of Mk 4:20. It also appears only twice in the authentic Pauline letters, in Rom 7:4, 5, where the hearing of the word is not mentioned. This suggests that Col 1:5b-6 conflates the descriptions of the seed which fell in the good soil from the parable of the sower and its interpretation. The use of the verbs καρποφορέω and αὐξάνω together again in Col 1:10 seems to be a repetition typical of an imitator. Since Mk 4:20 and its parallels, Mt 13:23 and Lk 8:15, all employ similar formulations, it cannot be decided which one is the closest parallel to Col[255] and thus the agreement

---

1.5-8, lacks mention of the ἔθνοι, is also present in Phil 1.12". However, Kiley's interpretation does not seem to be valid because the verbal agreement is more obvious between Rom 1:13 and Col 1:6 than that between Phil 1:12 and Col 1:6.

[252] The similarity is emphasized also by Schenk 1983, 148 n. 34; 1987a, 3343 n. 54; Gnilka 1980, 35.

[253] This is maintained by Hartman 1985, 20; R. P. Martin 1981, 48-49; O'Brien 1982, 13; Schweizer 1982, 36. Contra Gnilka 1980, 35, who assumes the phrase to come from apocalyptical texts (4 Esd 3:20, 9:31).

[254] Similarly Pokorný 1987, 36, presents Mk 4:20 as a parallel to Col 1:6. Schenk 1987a, 3343 n. 54; 1983, 148-149, emphasizes the resemblance between Mk 14:9 and Col 1:6 which, however, do not have any other verbal agreement but the similar phrases ἐν παντὶ τῷ κόσμῳ and εἰς ὅλον τὸν κόσμον.

[255] Mt 13:23: ὁ δὲ ἐπὶ τὴν καλὴν γῆν σπαρείς, οὗτός ἐστιν ὁ τὸν λόγον ἀκούων καὶ συνιείς, ὃς δὴ καρποφορεῖ καὶ ποιεῖ ὃ μὲν ἑκατόν, ὃ δὲ ἑξήκοντα, ὃ δὲ τριάκοντα. Lk 8:15: τὸ δὲ ἐν τῇ

between Col 1:5b-6 and Mk 4:20 does not meet the criteria for literary dependence. However, the most probable alternative is that Mk 4:8 and 20 are conflated in Col since the texts describe the seed which fell in the good soil with very similar words.

The obvious resemblance between Col 1:6 and Mk 4:8 has been acknowledged by many scholars.[256] Most of them do not try to interpret the reason for the similarity but some of them suggest that A/Col knew the Gospel tradion, either orally or in some written form.[257] However, the phrase to bear fruit and grow, the unnatural order, occurs in the Gospels only in Mk 4:8. It does not even appear in the synoptic parallels of Mk 4:8. This suggests that it may be due to Markan redaction[258] which gives a reason to assume a close relationship between Mk 4:8 and Col 1:5b-6.[259]

The interpretation includes the problem of the date. As was mentioned in the introduction, Col is generally considered to have been composed soon after the death of Paul, about A.D. 70 – 80. It was thus written about the same time as Mk, which is dated soon after the Jewish War, around A.D. 70.[260] Accordingly, it is not self-evident that A/Col was familiar with the finished Gospel. Here A/Col shows knowledge of the parable of the sower in the form it occurs in Mk and its later interpretation which originates within the church.[261] It is generally assumed that behind Mk 4:1-25 lies at least two pre-Markan stages. At first, the parable of the sower was brought together with other parables in Mk 4 (the seed growing by itself and the mustard-seed) and at the second stage, the parable and its interpretation were brought together.[262] It is thus possible that A/Col knew the second stage, the parable of the sower and its interpretation from oral tradition, but not the text of Mk. The alternative that he knew Mk or part of Mk is still more probable because the unnatural order of bearing fruit and growing occurs only in Mk and thus may be Markan redaction. The question about the relationship between Col and Mk will be discussed further after analyzing all the resemblances.

The noun χάρις used in Col 1:6 often appears in the thanksgivings of the Pauline letters, e.g. in 1 Cor 1:3 which, as noted, resembles Col 1:3. However, the phrase ἡ χάρις τοῦ θεοῦ ἐν ἀληθείᾳ does not appear anywhere else. Because it is typical of A/Col to attach nouns to phrases with the preposition ἐν, the phrase ἡ χάρις τοῦ θεοῦ ἐν ἀληθείᾳ seems to be a creation of A/Col.[263]

καλῇ γῇ, οὗτοί εἰσιν οἵτινες ἐν καρδίᾳ καλῇ καὶ ἀγαθῇ ἀκούσαντες τὸν λόγον κατέχουσιν καὶ καρποφοροῦσιν ἐν ὑπομονῇ.

256 See Schenk 1983, 148 n. 34; 1987a, 3343 n. 54; O'Brien 1977, 102; 1982, 13; Schweizer 1982, 36; Gnilka 1980, 35; R. P. Martin 1981, 48-49; Nikolainen 1987, 18-19; Bruce 1988, 42.

257 Bruce 1988, 42; O'Brien 1977, 102.

258 Similarly Räisänen 1990, 119.

259 Similarly Schenk 1983, 148 n. 34; 1987a, 3343 n. 54.

260 Gnilka 1978, 34; Pesch 1989, 14; Johnson 1960, 20; Achtemeier 1992, 543.

261 Schweizer 1971, 92; Mann 1986, 266; Johnson 1960, 87.

262 Jeremias 1985, 14 n. 11, followed by Räisänen 1990, 85-86. Cf. Schweizer 1971, 94-95.

263 Similarly Lohse 1971, 88; Bujard 1973, 154.

Col 1:7-8	Philem 23	**1 Cor 4:17**, 21
7 καθὼς ἐμάθετε ἀπὸ	Ἐπαφρᾶς ὁ	17 Τιμόθεον, **ὅς ἐστίν**
Ἐπαφρᾶ τοῦ ἀγαπητοῦ	**συναιχμάλωτός** μου ἐν	μου τέκνον ἀγαπητὸν καὶ
συνδούλου ἡμῶν, **ὅς**	Χριστῷ Ἰησοῦ	πιστὸν ἐν κυρίῳ, ὃς ὑμᾶς
ἐστιν πιστὸς ὑπὲρ ὑμῶν		ἀναμνήσει τὰς ὁδούς μου
διάκονος τοῦ **Χριστοῦ**,	**2 Cor 11:23**	τὰς ἐν Χριστῷ ...
8 ὁ καὶ δηλώσας ἡμῖν		21 ... **ἐν** ἀγάπῃ **πνεύματί**
τὴν ὑμῶν ἀγάπην **ἐν**	διάκονοι **Χριστοῦ** εἰσιν;	τε πραΰτητος;
πνεύματι.		

Col 1:7 mentions Epaphras as a fellow servant (σύνδουλος) of Paul. The noun σύνδουλος seems to be typical of A/Col because in the Pauline letters it only appears in Col, in 1:7 and 4:7.[264] Epaphras is mentioned in the Pauline letters, as well as in other ECL, only in Col 4:12 and Philem 23. Like Col 1:7, Philem 23 also uses a συν-compound, συναιχμάλωτος, "a fellow-prisoner", to define the status of Epaphras and mentions that he is serving Christ. Although the verbal agreement between the texts is slight, with only two common nouns, Epaphras and Christ, of which the latter is very usual and συν-compounds resembling each other, the fact that Epaphras is only twice mentioned in ECL makes it very likely that A/Col has taken up the name from Philem.[265] Thus the agreement between Col 1:7 and Philem 23 meets the criteria for a possible literary dependence.

Besides Philem 23, the description of Epaphras resembles the portrait of Timothy in 1 Cor 4:17. Both men are similarly described as faithful (πιστός) and beloved (ἀγαπητός). In addition, the grammatical constructions of the sentences are alike. Both texts include two relative clauses one after another (Col 1:7-8: ὅς ἐστιν ... ὁ καὶ δηλώσας ἡμῖν // 1 Cor 4:17: ὅς ἐστίν ... , ὃς ὑμᾶς ἀναμνήσει). The description of Epaphras in Col 1:7-8 and that of Timothy in 1 Cor 4:17 have an agreement of three similar nouns and relative clauses resembling each other, which meets the criteria for a probable literary dependence.

Col 1:8 also tells how Epaphras has made known to the senders of the letter "your (Colossians') love in the Spirit" (ἡ ὑμῶν ἀγάπη ἐν πνεύματι). The phrase does not appear anywhere else in the Pauline letters. It is a construction in which a noun is attached to a phrase with the preposition ἐν, like in the phrase ἡ χάρις τοῦ θεοῦ ἐν ἀληθείᾳ in Col 1:6, and thus seems to be a creation of A/Col.[266] Still, it is interesting that the phrase resembles the words "with love in a spirit of gentleness" (ἐν ἀγάπῃ πνεύματί τε πραΰτητος) in the context of 1 Cor 4:17, in v. 21, which describes Paul.[267] It indicates that this phrase also is modelled on 1 Cor 4. However, the distance between verses 17 and 21 is so long that they must be studied

[264] In addition, it is used in Mt (18:28, 29, 31, 33; 24:49) and Rev (6:11, 19:10, 22:9).
[265] Similarly Schenk 1987a, 3340.
[266] Similarly Bujard 1973, 154; Lohse 1971, 88.
[267] Cf. Rom 15:30: διὰ τῆς ἀγάπης τοῦ πνεύματος.

separately and thus the resemblance between Col 1:8 and 1 Cor 4:21 does not meet the criteria for literary dependence.

One of the epithets given to Epaphras in Col 1:7-8, a servant of Christ, διάκονος τοῦ Χριστοῦ, does not appear either in Philem 23 or in 1 Cor 4:17. It also seems to be atypical of the Pauline letters. In the genuine epistles, people are described as servants of Christ only once, in 2 Cor 11:23. Later, the expression appears in 1 Tim 4:6. Though the words in common, Χριστός, διάκονος, εἰμι, are very customary in ECL, here it does not seem to be a stock phrase. Therefore, the verbal agreement between Col 1:7-8 and 2 Cor 11:23 just meets the criteria indicating a possible literary dependence.

The associative style can be seen even better in Col 1:5b-8 than it was seen in Col 1:3-5a. In Col 1:3-5a A/Col uses Philem 4-5 as his primary model but in Col 1:5b-8 words and phrases from different texts are woven together without having any prototype. However, the resemblances between the texts reveal that A/Col must have known Pauline texts and perhaps also the parable of sower in Mk 4.

2.2. Intercession (Col 1:9-14)

Col 1:9-11a	Col 1:3-6	**1 Thess 2:12-13**
9 **Διὰ τοῦτο καὶ ἡμεῖς,** **ἀφ' ἧς ἡμέρας** ἠκούσαμεν, οὐ παυόμεθα ὑπὲρ **ὑμῶν** **προσευχόμενοι καὶ** αἰτούμενοι, ἵνα πληρωθῆτε τὴν ἐπίγνωσιν τοῦ θελήματος αὐτοῦ **ἐν** **πάσῃ σοφίᾳ** καὶ συνέσει πνευματικῇ, 10 περιπατῆσαι **ἀξίως** τοῦ κυρίου εἰς πᾶσαν ἀρεσκείαν, ἐν παντὶ ἔργῳ ἀγαθῷ καρποφοροῦντες **καὶ** αὐξανόμενοι τῇ ἐπιγνώσει **τοῦ θεοῦ,**	3 ... πάντοτε περὶ **ὑμῶν** **προσευχόμενοι,** 4 ἀκούσαντες ... 6 τοῦ παρόντος εἰς ὑμᾶς, καθὼς καὶ ἐν παντὶ τῷ κόσμῳ εστὶν καρπο- φορούμενον **καὶ** αὐξανόμενον καθὼς καὶ ἐν ὑμῖν, **ἀφ' ἧς ἡμέρας** ἠκούσατε καὶ ἐπέγνωτε τὴν χάριν **τοῦ θεοῦ** ἐν ἀληθείᾳ· **1 Cor 12:8** ᾧ μὲν γὰρ διὰ τοῦ πνεύματος δίδοται λόγος σοφίας, ἄλλῳ δὲ λόγος γνώσεως ...	12 ... εἰς τὸ περιπατεῖν ὑμᾶς **ἀξίως** τοῦ θεοῦ ... 13 Καὶ **διὰ τοῦτο καὶ** **ἡμεῖς** εὐχαριστοῦμεν τῷ θεῷ ... Rom 15:14 πεπληρωμένοι πάσης [τῆς] γνώσεως Dan 1:4, cf. 17 ... καὶ ἐπιστήμονας **ἐν** **πάσῃ σοφίᾳ** ... 1 Thess 4:1 ... περιπατεῖν καὶ ἀρέσκειν θεῷ
	Mk 11:24	2 Cor 9:8, cf. Rom 2:7
11a ἐν πάσῃ δυνάμει δυναμούμενοι κατὰ τὸ κράτος **τῆς δόξης αὐτοῦ** εἰς πᾶσαν ὑπομονὴν καὶ μακροθυμίαν	**διὰ τοῦτο** λέγω ὑμῖν, πάντα ὅσα προσεύχεσθε **καὶ** αἰτεῖσθε 1 Kings 26:25 (cf. 1 Macc 5:40) ... καὶ ποιῶν ποιήσεις καὶ δυνάμενος δυνήσει.	... εἰς πᾶν ἔργον ἀγαθόν Isa 2:10, 19, 21 ἀπὸ **τῆς δόξης** τῆς ἰσχύος **αὐτοῦ**

The intercession in Col 1:9-14 repeats many details from the thanksgiving (Col 1:3-6). Like Col 1:3, Col 1:9 describes how Paul and his companions are praying for the Colossians (ὑπὲρ ὑμῶν προσευχόμενοι // περὶ ὑμῶν προσευχόμενοι). In addition, the phrase "from the day" (ἀφ' ἧς ἡμέρας) from verse 6 is repeated as well as the verb "to hear" (ἀκούω) from verse 4. Instead of the verb "to observe" (ἐπιγινώσκω) occurring in v. 6, Col 1:9 and 10 use the noun "knowledge" (ἐπίγνωσις), which has the same stem. The exceptional phrase "to bear fruit and grow" (καρποφορούμενον καὶ αὐξανόμενον) from v. 6 reappears in v. 10 (καρποφοροῦντες καὶ αὐξανόμενοι).[268]

Besides Col 1:3-6, the intercession in Phil 1:5-6, 9-11 agrees verbally with Col 1:9-10, which is illustrated in the following table.

Col 1:9-11a	Phil 1:5-6, 9-11
9 Διὰ τοῦτο καὶ ἡμεῖς, ἀφ᾽ ἧς **ἡμέρας** ἠκούσαμεν, οὐ παυόμεθα ὑπὲρ **ὑμῶν** προσευχόμενοι καὶ αἰτούμενοι, **ἵνα** πληρωθῆτε τὴν ἐπίγνωσιν τοῦ θελήματος αὐτοῦ ἐν πάσῃ σοφίᾳ καὶ συνέσει πνευματικῇ, 10 περιπατῆσαι ἀξίως τοῦ κυρίου εἰς πᾶσαν ἀρεσκείαν, ἐν παντὶ ἔργῳ ἀγαθῷ καρποφοροῦντες καὶ αὐξανόμενοι τῇ **ἐπιγνώσει** τοῦ θεοῦ, 11a ἐν πάσῃ δυνάμει δυναμούμενοι κατὰ τὸ κράτος τῆς δόξης αὐτοῦ εἰς πᾶσαν ὑπομονὴν καὶ μακροθυμίαν	5 ... ἀπὸ τῆς πρώτης **ἡμέρας** ... 6 ... ὁ ἐναρξάμενος ἐν ὑμῖν ἔργον ἀγαθόν ... 9 Καὶ τοῦτο προσεύχομαι, **ἵνα** ἡ ἀγάπη **ὑμῶν** ... περισσεύῃ ἐν **ἐπιγνώσει** καὶ πάσῃ αἰσθήσει ... 11 πεπληρωμένοι καρπὸν δικαιοσύνης ... εἰς δόξαν καὶ ἔπαινον θεοῦ.

When Col 1:9-11 is compared with Phil 1:5-6, 9-11 it can be seen that the common words are mostly the same as those which also occur in Col 1:3-6: ἀπὸ τῆς ... ἡμέρας (Phil 1:5) // ἀφ᾽ ἧς ἡμέρας (Col 1:6,9), προσεύχομαι ... ὑμῶν (Phil 1:9) // ὑμῶν προσευχόμενοι (Col 1:3,9), ἐν ἐπιγνώσει (Phil 1:9) // ἐπέγνωτε (Col 1:6), τῇ ἐπιγνώσει (Col 1:10). In addition to these similarities, Phil 1:5-6, 9-11 uses, however, some other words and phrases common to Col 1:9-11: ἐν ὑμῖν ἔργον ἀγαθόν (Phil 1:6) // ἐν παντὶ ἔργῳ ἀγαθῷ (Col 1:10), πεπληρωμένοι (Phil 1:11) // πληρωθῆτε (Col 1:9), εἰς δόξαν (Phil 1:11) // τῆς δόξης (Col 1:11) of which the verb πληρόω, "to make full", and the noun δόξα, "glory" are very customary in ECL. In addition, the mentioning of good works (ἔργον ἀγαθόν) is a typical Christian expression. It appears twice in the genuine Pauline letters (2 Cor 9:8, Rom 2:7)[269] and in later texts these kinds of phrases are usual as well (cf. 2 Thess 2:17, 1 Tim 5:10, 2 Tim 2:21, 3:17, Titus 1:16, 3:1). Accordingly, the use of similar words in Col 1:9-11 and Phil 1:5-6, 9-11 does not point to a literary dependence

[268] Similarly Lohse 1971, 24; Cannon 1981, 180-181; Dunn 1996, 67, 69; O'Brien 1982, 18; Bujard 1973, 88; Haapa, 1978, 27; Nikolainen 1987, 20-21; Pokorný 1987, 37-38; R. P. Martin 1981, 50; Hartman 1985, 29; Luz 1998, 197.

[269] Similarly Standhartinger 1999, 123. C.f. Hübner 1997, 51. Schweizer 1982, 42 presents only 2 Cor 9:8 as a parallel to Col 1:10 and emphasizes that the expression "is not typical of Paul".

between the texts.[270] It is more probable that Col 1:9-11 repeats the same words already employed in Col 1:3-6.

The words περιπατῆσαι ἀξίως τοῦ κυρίου, "that you might walk worthily of the Lord", in Col 1:10 form a loosely joined infinitive construction which is a characteristic of A/Col.[271] The choice of wording resembles the words περιπατεῖν ὑμᾶς ἀξίως τοῦ θεοῦ in 1 Thess 2:12. Moreover, exactly the same words διὰ τοῦτο καὶ ἡμεῖς, "for this reason we also" are used in 1 Thess 2:13, as in Col 1:9.[272] Since the words διὰ τοῦτο καὶ ἡμεῖς do not occur anywhere else in the Pauline letters and, in addition, the verb περιπατέω appears together with the adverb ἀξίως elsewhere only in Eph (4:1) which depends upon Col, the agreement between Col 1:9-10 and 1 Thess 2:12-13 is worth noting. Thus the agreement of the verb περιπατέω, the adverb ἀξίως, and the unusual choice of wording διὰ τοῦτο καὶ ἡμεῖς points to a possible literary dependence between Col 1:9-10 and 1 Thess 2:12-13.[273]

The verbs προσεύχομαι and αἰτέω occurring in Col 1:9 can both be used in the sense "to pray" and are thus synonyms. Although the verbs are very commonplace in ECL, they do not ordinarily appear together. A simple explanation for this exceptional occurrence may be the habit of A/Col of piling synonyms together.[274] However, the description of Jesus' exhortation to pray and ask in Mk 11:24 uses the verbs προσεύχομαι and αἰτέω together.[275] The words διὰ τοῦτο also appear in Mk 11:24 like in Col 1:9. Although the words common to Col 1:9 and Mk 11:24 are too frequently used to suggest a literary dependence between the texts, the use of the verbs προσεύχομαι and αἰτέω together may, however, be an echo of Mk 11:24.[276]

---

[270] Similarly Ludwig 1974, 71-73. Contra Kiley 1986, 76, 81, who takes Col 1:9 to depend on Phil 1:9. Cf. Schenk 1987a, 3341: "Die Fürbitte um Erkenntnis im Proömium 1,9-11 ist von Phil 1,9-11 angeregt".

[271] Bujard 1973, 57; Lohse 1971, 89.

[272] Also Lohse 1971, 24 n. 3, notes the similarity. According to Schweizer 1982, 41 n. 3, the same introductory formula is found besides 1 Thess 2:13, in 1 Thess 3:5, Rom 13:6, Mt 24:44, Lk 11:49, Jn 12:18. It has to be noted, however, that precisely the same words διὰ τοῦτο καὶ ἡμεῖς occur only in Col 1:9 and 1 Thess 2:13.

[273] Similarly E. P. Sanders 1966, 44, takes Col 1:10 to depend on 1 Thess 2:12. According to Ludwig 1974, 36-37, the infinitive construction περιπατῆσαι ἀξίως τοῦ κυρίου in Col 1:10 is modelled on the phrases in 1 Thess 2:12 and Phil 1:27. However, she fails to notice that the construction resembles much more the one in 1 Thess 2:12 (περιπατεῖν ὑμᾶς ἀξίως τοῦ θεοῦ) than the one in Phil 1:27 (ἀξίως τοῦ εὐαγγελίου τοῦ Χριστοῦ πολιτεύεσθε). Cf. Schweizer 1982, 42; Dunn 1996, 71; Haapa 1978, 28; Pokorný 1987, 40; Hartman 1985, 31. Contra Standhartinger 1999, 121, 124-126, who neglects to notice the similarity between 1 Thess 2:12 and Col 1:10 and assumes that the similarity between Col 1:9 and 1 Thess 2:13 is due to the oral Pauline tradition.

[274] So Lohse 1971, 88.

[275] The words ὅσα ἂν αἰτήσητε ἐν τῇ προσευχῇ are used in Mt 21:22 which, however, do not resemble Col 1:9 as much as Mk 11:24. Also Lohse 1971, 25 n. 8, comments on the similarity between Col 1:9 and Mk 11:24.

[276] Cf. O'Brien 1982, 20, who emphasizes that in Mk 11:24 the verbs used in Col 1:9 "have an exact parallel".

The expression πληρωθῆτε τὴν ἐπίγνωσιν, "be filled with the knowl-edge", in Col 1:9 resembles the words πεπληρωμένοι πάσης τῆς γνώσεως, "filled with all knowledge", in Rom 15:14 and thus seems to be Pauline.[277] Instead, the phrase "in all wisdom", ἐν πάσῃ σοφίᾳ, occurs in the Pauline corpus only in a later text, Eph 1:8. However, it is used in Dan 1:4, 17 to describe how wisdom is imparted to young men. Therefore, it may be an echo of Dan.

Like Col 1:9, 1 Cor 12:8 employs the noun σοφία. The noun γνῶσις appears in 1 Cor 12:8 which has the same stem as the noun ἐπίγνωσις occurring in Col 1:9 and the noun πνεῦμα which has the same stem as the adjective πνευματικός in Col 1:9. The resemblance thus meets the criteria for a possible literary dependence. The occurrence of these three terms together in Col 1:9 may be an echo of 1 Cor 12:8. However, the terms σοφία, γνῶσις, and πνεῦμα are so customary in ECL and especially in Jewish wisdom literature that the verbal agreement between Col 1:9 and 1 Cor 12:8 may also be a coincidence.

The noun ἀρεσκεία, "desire to please", used in Col 1:10 is a hapax legomenon in the NT and seems to be also unique otherwise in ECL.[278] In the LXX it appears only in Prov 31:30. However, the verb ἀρέσκω, "to please", is often employed in ECL. Especially the words περιπατεῖν καὶ ἀρέσκειν θεῷ in 1 Thess 4:1 resemble the words περιπατῆσαι ... εἰς πᾶσαν ἀρεσκείαν in Col 1:10. Since the verbs περιπατέω and ἀρέσκω both are frequently used in ECL (περιπατέω occurs 95 times in the NT and ἀρέσκω 17 times) the use of only two words in common does not meet the criteria for literary dependence.[279] It is worth noting that in the genuine Pauline letters the verbs περιπατέω and ἀρέσκω appear together only in 1 Thess 4:1 which indicates that Col 1:10 may echo 1 Thess 4:1.

The phrases κατὰ τὸ κράτος τῆς δόξης αὐτοῦ, "with all the strength of his glorious power", and ἐν πάσῃ δυνάμει δυναμούμενοι, "being empowered with all power", which describe the power of God in Col 1:11, do not have parallels in ECL before Col. Only the words τὸ πλοῦτος τῆς δόξης αὐτοῦ, "the riches of his glory", in Rom 9:23 somewhat resemble Col 1:11. However, the accumulation of power terminology has a lot of parallels in Jewish literature.[280] For example the phrase ἀπὸ τῆς δόξης τῆς ἰσχύος αὐτοῦ, "from the glory of his majesty", in Isa 2:10, 19, 21 resembles the words κατὰ τὸ κράτος τῆς δόξης αὐτοῦ in Col 1:11.[281] It seems thus that A/Col imitates the style used in the LXX. In addition, the phrase ἐν πάσῃ δυνάμει δυναμούμενοι is similar to the expression δυνάμενος δυνήσει in 1 Kings 26:25 and 1 Macc 5:40 which repeats the verb δύναμαι twice. The characteristic

---

[277] Similarly Standhartinger 1998, 122.
[278] See Bauer 1988, 211.
[279] Contra Hübner 1997, 51, who assumes a possible literary dependence between 1 Thess 4:1 and Col 1:10.
[280] Arnold 1995, 303; Dunn 1996, 73; Lohse 1971, 30-31. Arnold and Lohse emphasize that these kinds of expressions appear especially in the Qumran texts.
[281] Similarly Arnold 1995, 303.

of A/Col of combining expressions which have the same stem (cf. 1:29, 2:11, 2:19)[282] also has parallels in the LXX. Like in Col 1:11, the synonyms ὑπομονή and μακροθυμία denoting "patience" sometimes appear together in the catalogues of virtues (e.g. 2 Cor 6:4-6, Jas 5:10-11, 2 Tim 3:10). It is unlikely that the usage in Col is influenced by the catalogs but rather it may be due to A/Col's habit of piling up synonyms (cf. Col 1:9).[283]

As was already mentioned when analyzing the parallels to the phrase ἐν παντὶ τῷ κόσμῳ in Col 1:6, both in Col 1:4-6 and in Col 1:9-10 the pronoun πᾶς is often used: εἰς πάντας τοὺς ἁγίους (1:4), ἐν παντὶ τῷ κόσμῳ (1:6), ἐν πάσῃ σοφίᾳ (1:9), εἰς πᾶσαν ἀρεσκείαν, ἐν παντὶ ἔργῳ ἀγαθῷ (1:10), ἐν πάσῃ δυνάμει δυναμούμενοι ... εἰς πᾶσαν ὑπομονὴν καὶ μακροθυμίαν (1:11).[284] Of these, the phrase εἰς πάντας τοὺς ἁγίους probably depends on Philem 4 and the expression ἐν πάσῃ σοφίᾳ may be an echo of Dan 1:4, 17 but the other cases do not seem to be due to the texts imitated. Accordingly, the repetition of πᾶς must be a habit of A/Col[285] which also confirms the assumption that the phrase ἐν παντὶ τῷ κόσμῳ in Col 1:6 is a modification of the phrases τὸν κόσμον ὅλον / ἐν ὅλῳ τῷ κόσμῳ occurring in ECL.

---

282 Lohse 1971, 88.

283 Similarly Lohse 1971, 88.

284 This is observed also by Cannon 1981, 180-181; Lohse 1971, 24; O'Brien 1982, 18.

285 Similarly Bujard 1973, 159; Pokorný 1987, 40; Hartman 1985, 30.

Col 1:11b-14

11b **Μετὰ χαρᾶς**
12 εὐχαριστοῦν-τες **τῷ πατρὶ** τῷ ἱκανώσαντι ὑμᾶς εἰς τὴν μερίδα τοῦ κλήρου τῶν ἁγίων ἐν τῷ **φωτί**·
13 **ὃς ἐρρύσατο ἡμᾶς ἐκ τῆς ἐξουσίας** τοῦ **σκότους** καὶ μετέστησεν εἰς τὴν βασιλείαν **τοῦ υἱοῦ** τῆς ἀγάπης **αὐτοῦ**,
14 ἐν ᾧ ἔχομεν τὴν ἀπολύτρωσιν, τὴν **ἄφεσιν** τῶν **ἁμαρτιῶν**·

Phil 1:4, 1 Thess 1:6

μετὰ χαρᾶς

Wis 5:5

... ἐν υἱοῖς θεοῦ καὶ ἐν ἁγίοις ὁ κλῆρος αὐτοῦ ἐστιν;

2 Cor 3:6

ὃς καὶ ἱκάνωσεν **ἡμᾶς** ...

2 Cor 6:14-15,18

14 ... ἢ τίς κοινωνία **φωτὶ** πρὸς σκότος; 15 τίς δὲ συμφώνησις Χριστοῦ πρὸς Βελιάρ, ἢ τίς μερὶς πιστῷ μετὰ ἀπίστου; ...
18 καὶ ἔσομαι ὑμῖν εἰς πατέρα καὶ ὑμεῖς ἔσεσθέ μοι εἰς υἱοὺς καὶ θυγατέρας,

Col 1:3

Εὐχαριστοῦμεν **τῷ** θεῷ **πατρί** ...

Acts 26:18

ἀνοῖξαι ὀφθαλμοὺς αὐτῶν, τοῦ ἐπιστρέψαι ἀπὸ **σκότους** εἰς φῶς καὶ **τῆς ἐξουσίας** τοῦ σατανᾶ ἐπὶ τὸν θεόν, τοῦ λαβεῖν αὐτοὺς **ἄφεσιν ἁμαρτιῶν** καὶ κλῆρον ἐν τοῖς ἡγιασμένοις πίστει τῇ εἰς ἐμέ.

Mk 1:11,15

11 ... ὁ υἱός μου ὁ ἀγαπητός ...
15 ἤγγικεν ἡ βασιλεία τοῦ θεοῦ·

The phrase μετὰ χαρᾶς, "with joy", (Col 1:11b) appears twice in the genuine Pauline letters, in Phil 1:4 and in 1 Thess 1:6. It is also occasionally employed in the Gospels and Heb.[286] Thus A/Col uses here a common Christian expression. Thanks is given to the Father (εὐχαριστοῦντες τῷ πατρί) in Col 1:12 similarly to Col 1:3 (εὐχαριστοῦμεν τῷ θεῷ πατρί).[287] Some scholars assume that the verb εὐχαριστοῦντες functions as a participial imperative which is introducing a confession beginning in verse 12 and thus verses 12-14 belong to the same section as verses 15-20 indicating in what sense the following hymn is to be understood.[288] The switching from the second person plural pronoun used in the summons of verse 12 (ὑμᾶς) to the first person plural in verse 13 (ἡμᾶς) is sometimes considered as showing that verse 13 reflects a credal statement.[289]

---

[286] Mt 13:20, Mk 4:16, Lk 8:13, 10:17, 24:52, Heb 10:34, 13:17.

[287] Similarly Bujard 1973, 99, and Hübner 1997, 52, note the repetition.

[288] According to Cannon 1981, 14-16 εὐχαριστέω "is a technical term introducing a confession" which shows that "everything after the participle εὐχαριστοῦντες in verse 12-14 is traditional confessional material". Cf. Lohse 1971, 32, 40; R. P. Martin 1981, 53; Nikolainen 1987, 20. Schweizer 1982, 40; Käsemann 1965, 158-167, even prefers to see Col 1:12-20 as a baptismal liturgy.

[289] Lohse 1971, 36; Nikolainen 1987, 22.

The interpretation includes several problems. First, though the new section begins in verse 12, the change from the second person to the first person does not happen until verse 13. Cannon tries to solve this problem by explaining that in verse 12 the pronoun should be read ἡμᾶς, as some manuscripts have it.[290] Second, εὐχαριστοῦντες should not be detached from the preceding participles in verses 9-11[291] which suggests that Col 1:12 includes a thanksgiving similar to Col 1:3. Third, it is a habit of A/Col to switch from the second person plural to the first person plural and vice versa (cf. Col 1:3,9). It seems thus that in verse 12 he describes the Colossians using the second person but in verse 13 he emphasizes that he himself belongs to the people he describes and thus uses the first person.[292]

In addition, Col 1:11b-14 has been seen as utilizing "traditional phrases"[293] or "traditional confessional materials"[294] because of the participial style occurring in Col 1:12 (τῷ ἱκανώσαντι, "who has been authorizing") and the relative style used in Col 1:13 (ὃς ἐρρύσατο ἡμᾶς, "who has delivered us") as well as in Col 1:14 (ἐν ᾧ ἔχομεν, "in whom we have"). The interpretation is also defended by the fact that the verses include many terms seldom or never used either in Col or otherwise in the Pauline corpus. The noun κλῆρος, "lot", and the phrases ἅγιοι ἐν τῷ φωτί, "the saints in the light", and βασιλεία τοῦ υἱοῦ τῆς ἀγάπης αὐτοῦ, "the kingdom of the son of his love", do not have parallels in the Pauline letters and, in addition, the verb ἱκανόω, "to authorize", is used elsewhere only in 2 Cor 3:6 in the NT. The noun μερίς, "share", appears in the Pauline corpus, only in 2 Cor 6:15.[295]

In spite of the exceptional style and terminology, Col 1:11b-14 still has some parallels. The verb ἱκανόω was also noted as occurring in 2 Cor 3:6. In both cases it appears in a similar context. While in Col 1:12 is described how God enables people to share in the inheritance of the saints in the light, in 2 Cor 3:6 it is mentioned that some people are made competent to be ministers of a new covenant. Moreover, in both texts the verb ἱκανόω occurs in the context of a relative clause (2 Cor 3:6: ὃς καὶ ἱκάνωσεν ἡμᾶς // Col 1:13: ὃς ἐρρύσατο ἡμᾶς).[296] Because the similar words are, apart from one verb, only pronouns, the verbal agreement does not meet the criteria for literary dependence. Nevertheless, it is possible that the beginning of Col 1:13 is not utilizing traditional phrases, as has been contended, but echoing the style of 2 Cor 3:6. It has to be noted also that the participial style

290 Cannon 1981, 16-17.
291 Dunn 1996, 68.
292 Bujard 1973, 83-84, who takes the switch of the personal pronouns to belong to the associative style of A/Col.
293 So Lohse 1971, 32.
294 So Cannon 1981, 14.
295 Lohse 1971, 32-33, 40 n. 63; Cannon 1981, 13-23; Sappington 1991, 196; Arnold 1995, 288.
296 Cf. also 2 Cor 1:10 which uses the verb ῥύομαι in a similar relative clause (ὃς ἐκ τηλικούτου θανάτου ἐρρύσατο ἡμᾶς). In addition, in the LXX, the verb ῥύομαι usually describes God's helping and saving intervention (see e.g. Wis. 2:9, 16:8).

is more typical of A/Col than of Paul (see Col 1:6).[297] Therefore, it is not exceptional that A/Col uses the verb ἱκανόω in a participial form. Similarly the relative style ἐν ᾧ ἔχομεν in Col 1:14 seems to be the characteristic of A/Col. He also uses the same kinds of relative clauses beginning with the words ἐν ᾧ in Col 2:3, 11, 13.

It was noted that because of the exceptional nouns κλῆρος and μερίς, and the phrase ἅγιοι ἐν τῷ φωτί, Col 1:11b-14 is sometimes assumed to utilize traditional phrases. However, these words form the phrase εἰς τὴν μερίδα τοῦ κλήρου τῶν ἁγίων ἐν τῷ φωτί, which heaps up a series of dependent genitives typical of A/Col,[298] and the noun φῶς is attached to the phrase with the preposition ἐν which, as was already seen in Col 1:6 and 8, is another characteristic of A/Col. The exceptional style seems thus rather to be due to the characteristics of A/Col than to the utilizing of traditional phrases. Lohse's interpretation is inconsistent when he, on the one hand, recognizes both the characteristics of A/Col appearing in the phrase εἰς τὴν μερίδα τοῦ κλήρου τῶν ἁγίων ἐν τῷ φωτί but, on the other hand, interprets the phrase ἅγιοι ἐν τῷ φωτί as indicating the utilization of traditional phrases.[299] A phrase cannot both be formed by A/Col and borrowed from the tradition.

In addition, it was noted that the phrase βασιλεία τοῦ υἱοῦ τῆς ἀγάπης αὐτοῦ is assumed to be traditional because it does not have parallels in the Pauline letters. Since the complicated phrase heaps up a series of dependent genitives, it seems, however, to be shaped by A/Col rather than traditional.[300] The choice of wording βασιλεία τοῦ υἱοῦ τῆς ἀγάπης αὐτοῦ resembles the way how in the synoptic Gospels Jesus is described as God's beloved Son, ὁ υἱός μου ὁ ἀγαπητός, in the baptismal story in Mk 1:11/ Mt 3:17/ Lk 3:22 (cf. Mk 9:7, Mt 17:5, Lk 20:13).[301] "Kingdom of God" is mentioned in the context of Mk 1:11, but not until in 1:15.[302] Though Mk 1:11,15 is the closest parallel to Col, the verbal agreement between Col 1:13 and Mk 1:11, 15, three similar words in common (υἱός, ἀγάπη/ἀγαπητός, βασιλεία) but within a distance longer than five lines in the Nestle & Aland version, does not meet the criteria for literary dependence. Anyway the words βασιλεία τοῦ υἱοῦ τῆς ἀγάπης αὐτοῦ echo the way how in the synoptic Gospels

---

[297] Bujard 1973, 59.
[298] Bujard 1973, 154.
[299] See Lohse 1971, 32-33, 88.
[300] Similarly Bujard, 1973, 156. Lohse 1971, 32-33, 88, interprets again inconsistently that the phrase both indicates the traditional style of the passage and is formed by A/Col.
[301] Similarly O'Brien 1977, 98; Lohse 1971, 38; Dunn 1996, 79; Hartman 1985, 29; Pokorný 1987, 45; Gnilka 1980, 49; Hübner 1997, 53; Sappington 1991, 196; Schweizer 1982, 48; Cannon 1981, 20.
[302] Schenk 1987a, 3342-3344; 1983, 148-149, exaggerates the agreement between Col and Mk when he presents as parallels ὅς ἐστιν (Col 1:15) // σὺ εἶ (Mk 1:11), ἐν αὐτῷ εὐδόκησεν (Col 1:19) // ἐν σοὶ εὐδόκησα (Mk 1:11), τὴν ἄφεσιν τῶν ἁμαρτιῶν (Col 1:14) // τὴν ἄφεσιν τῶν ἁμαρτιῶν (Mk 1:4). See p. 90 n. 345.

Jesus is described as God's beloved Son and Mk 1:11,15 is the closest parallel to Col 1:13.

The phrase ἄφεσις ἁμαρτιῶν, "the forgiveness of sins", used in Col 1:14 occurs often in the Gospels (Mt 26:28, Mk 1:4, Lk 1:77, 3:3, 24:47) and in Acts (2:38, 5:31, 10:43, 13:38, 26:18) but nowhere else in the Pauline letters.[303] A/Col uses here a common Christian expression which, however, is not typical of Paul.[304] It was already noted that the nouns κλῆρος and μερίς are atypical of Paul: the former is not used in his letters and the latter is used only in 2 Cor 6:15. However, they are both often used in the LXX when mentioning a part or share received in the apportionment of land (e.g. Deut 10:9, 32:9, Josh 19:9, cf. Act 8:32). Moreover, κλῆρος is used in Dan 12:13 and Wis 5:5 in an eschatological sense, like in Col 1:12.[305] Since the words in Wis 5:5 πῶς κατελογίσθη ἐν υἱοῖς θεοῦ καὶ ἐν ἁγίοις ὁ κλῆρος αὐτοῦ ἐστιν; "why has he been numbered among the children of God and why is his lot among the saints?" closely resembles Col 1:12-13, the choice of wording εἰς τὴν μερίδα τοῦ κλήρου, "to share in the inheritance" may recall the promise first made to Abram (Gen 13:14-17) and renewed to the Jewish people.[306]

Like the inheritance of the saints in Col 1:12-13, the lot of God's chosen ones is called the lot of light in the writings of Qumran. The opposite of it, the lot of Belial, is called the lot of darkness, like in Col. Because of the similarity, scholars often consider the texts of Qumran as a background for these verses of Col.[307] However, we must not neglect the parallels in ECL. The same thought that God and his chosen ones belong to the world of light and his enemies to the world of darkness also appears in the Gospels. In Mt 5:14 Jesus says to his disciples: "You are the light of the world" (Ὑμεῖς ἐστε τὸ φῶς τοῦ κόσμου). The followers of Jesus are called the children of light, υἱοὶ φωτός, e.g in Jn 12:36 and Jesus calls himself the light of the world in Jn 8:12, 9:5. The phrase ἡ ἐξουσία τοῦ σκότους used in Col 1:13 also occurs in Lk 22:53. The difference between the children of light and darkness also appears in 1 Thess 5:5.[308]

However, the closest early Christian parallels to Col 1:11b-14 are Acts 26:18 and 2 Cor 6:14-15. Acts 26:18 describes the difference between the authorities of light and darkness in the same way as Col 1:11b-14. The nouns κλῆρος (lot), φώς (light), σκότος (darkness), ἐξουσία (power), and the verb ἁγιάζω (to sanctify) appear in Acts 26:18 as in Col 1:11b-14 and both texts also use the phrase ἄφεσιν

[303] Cf. Heb 10:18: ... ἄφεσις ... περὶ ἁμαρτίας.
[304] Bruce 1988, 53; Lohse 1971, 39.
[305] Pokorný 1987, 43.
[306] R. P. Martin 1981, 54; Lohse 1971, 35; Gnilka 1980, 46-47; Pokorný 1987, 43; O'Brien 1982, 26; Hübner 1997, 52; Strack & Billerbeck III, 625. Cannon 1981, 20-22 calls the phenomenon "the Exodus motif" which points to the use of traditional materials.
[307] See Lohse 1971, 35; O'Brien 1982, 26; Arnold 1995, 289-290; Hartman 1985, 28; Haapa 1978, 29; Nikolainen 1987, 22; Hübner 1997, 52. However, Dunn 1996, 76, stresses the parallels in other Jewish literature more than the others. Cf. Bruce 1988, 51.
[308] Cf. also Acts 20:32: ... δοῦναι τὴν κληρονομίαν ἐν τοις ἡγιασμένοις πᾶσιν.

ἁμαρτιῶν (the forgiveness of sins).[309] Including five similar words and one phrase, the resemblance between Col 1:11b-14 and Acts 26:18 meets the criteria for a probable literary dependence. Because Acts is generally dated later than Col, somewhere between 80 and 100[310], we cannot assume Col to depend on Acts on the grounds of this single contact point. Since it was noted in the introduction that according to some scholars Acts depends on the Pauline corpus (see p. 22), a more probable explanation for the resemblance is the alternative that the author of Acts knew Colossians.

Col 1:11b-13 and 2 Cor 6:14-15 use three similar nouns φῶς, σκότος, and μερίς.[311] φώς and σκότος frequently occur in ECL. However, μερίς is quite rare: e.g. in the NT it appears elsewhere only in Lk 10:42 and Acts 8:21, 16:12, and later it appears in 1 Clem (29:2, 35:8). Thus the verbal agreement between Col 1:11b-13 and 2 Cor 6:14-15 meets the criteria for a possible literary dependence. In addition, in 2 Cor 6:18, which belongs to the same context as 2 Cor 6:14-15, God is called Father (πατήρ) and believers are called God's sons (υἱοί), while in Col 1:11b-13 God is called Father and Christ is called Son (υἱός). It is true that the above-mentioned parallels prove the contrast between light and darkness to be a theme in ECL. However, we cannot neglect the verbal agreement between 2 Cor 6:14-15 and Col 1:11b-13.[312] It is interesting that in the Qumran texts, which were noted as being a background for Col and are often seen behind 2 Cor 6:14-15 also[313], God is seldom called Father.[314] Moreover, from the standpoint of Col, the use of the noun υἱός is exceptional: it appears in Col only twice, in Col 1:13 and in 3:6.[315]

It has to be noted that 2 Cor 6:14-15 belongs to the passage 2 Cor 6:14-7:1 which does not fit well into its context and reflects a situation different from 2 Cor's other components and is thus assumed to be interpolated. The text also includes so many non-Pauline features that it is also generally doubted whether it was written by Paul.[316] It is not known, however, when the text was added. There

---

[309] Similarly according to O'Brien 1982, 26; Hendriksen 1971, 62; Luz 1998, 198; and Hartman 1985, 28, Acts 26:18 and Col 1:12-14 are closely related passages.
[310] See Conzelmann 1987, xxxiii; Pesch 1986, 28; Bruce 1988, 12.
[311] Similarly Reuter 1997, 68-70, presents Col 1:12-13 and 2 Cor 6:14-15 as parallels but fails to notice that the noun μερίς is a word in common in both texts.
[312] Also Arnold 1995, 291, comments on the resemblance between 2 Cor 6:14-15 and Col 1:11b-14 but he interprets the similarity as being caused by the same writer, Paul.
[313] See L. Aejmelaeus 1987b, 54-57, following e.g. Wikenhauser & Schmid 1973, 440-441, and Vielhauer 1975, 153. Cf. Klauck 1986, 60.
[314] Pokorný 1987, 45 n. 30, emphasizes that the texts from Qumran are not perfect parallels because in the Qumran texts God is called Father in 1 QH 9,35 only. It has to be remembered that after 1987 many new Qumran texts have been found. There may thus be more texts where God is called Father. Nevertheless, it does not seem to be typical of the Qumran texts.
[315] Also Hartman 1985, 29, notes this detail.
[316] See Lindemann 1979, 22; Klauck 1986, 60; L. Aejmelaeus 1987b, 45-66; Furnish 1984, 371-383. Betz (1973) even regards it as an anti-Pauline fragment which originates from Paul's opponents in Gal.

is no textual evidence that 2 Cor existed without 2 Cor 6:14-7:1.[317] Thus the doubtful origin of the passage does not prevent A/Col from being acquainted with 2 Cor 6:14-18. It is possible that he knew 2 Cor 6:14-7:1.

Col 1:11b-14 includes the common Christian expressions μετὰ χαρᾶς and ἄφεσις τῶν ἁμαρτιῶν, the first one also being typical of Paul. In addition, the text echoes the way in which Jesus is described in the synoptic Gospels as God's beloved Son and the promise made to the Jewish people described in the LXX. Besides these echoes from tradition, the text still reflects many characteristics of A/Col. The relative clause ὃς ἐρρύσατο ἡμᾶς ἐκ in Col 1:13 may be an imitation of the Pauline style in 2 Cor 1:10 and 3:6. Like in this section, participles are often used throughout the letter. The verbal similarity between Col 1:11b-13 and 2 Cor 6:14-15 also indicates literary dependence. Thus A/Col's own style of writing is so obvious in Col 1:11b-14 that the text does not seem to utilize traditional phrases or confessional materials. In addition, Col 1:11b-14 is unlikely to belong to the following hymn in Col 1:15-20 but rather it is part of the thanksgiving section of Col 1:3-11.[318]

[317] See e.g. Furnish 1984, 383.

[318] Cf. O'Brien 1982, 19-20, 25: "He is, after all, reporting his *prayer* in this epistolary style"; Cf. Pokorný 1987, 42-43.

3. The Lord of the Church and Paul's Ministry (Col 1:15-2:5)

3.1. Christ the Lord in Creation and Redemption (Col 1:15-20)

3.1.1. The Literary Form and Background of the Text

The style of the verses Col 1:15-20 differs from the context. Unlike the previous verses 13-14 and what follows in 21-23, there is no reference to the community but the text demonstrates the world-wide validity and effect of the Christ-event using hymnic style. The marks of the style are the following: 1) Verse 1:15 begins with a relative pronoun "who" (ὅς) which is typical of hymns (cf. Rom 4:25, Phil 2:6, 1 Tim 3:16, and Heb 1:3). 2) There seem to be two strophes, each introduced by the relative clause ὅς ἐστιν, "who is" (1:15a and 18b). Both strophes include a causal clause beginning with ὅτι (1:16, 19), which is followed by the explanations beginning with the words καὶ αὐτός, "and he" (1:17, 18) and καὶ δι' αὐτοῦ, "and through him" (1:20). The theme of the first strophe is creation; the second one describes redemption.[319] 3) Verses Col 1:15-20 contain a great number of terms which either do not occur at all elsewhere in the Pauline letters or are used otherwise with a different meaning. The phrase εἰκὼν τοῦ θεοῦ, "the image of God" (1:15) is seen again only in 2 Cor 4:4, the adjective ὁρατός, "visible" (1:16) is a hapax legomenon in the NT, and the adjective ἀόρατος, "invisible" (1:15-16) appears in the authentic Pauline letters only once, in Rom 1:20.[320] It is not used anywhere but in Colossians as a contrast to ὁρατός. In addition, the noun θρόνος, "throne" (1:16) and the verb συνίστημι in the perfect form συνεστηκέναι, "to be established" (1:17) do not appear elsewhere in the Pauline corpus and the noun κυριότης "dominion" occurs elsewhere only in Eph 1:21. It is also noteworthy that in a Christological context Paul never speaks of Christ as ἀρχή, "beginning", as in Col 1:18, but once as ἀπαρχή, "first fruits" (1 Cor 15:20). In addition, the verbs πρωτεύω, "to be the first" (1:18) and εἰρηνοποιέω, "to make peace" (1:20) are hapax legomena in the NT and κατοικέω, "to dwell" (1:19) occurs only in Col 1:19, 2:9 and in Eph 3:17. Similarly the verb ἀποκαταλλάσσω, "to reconcile" (1:20), appears only in Eph, in 2:16. In addition, the phrase αἷμα τοῦ σταυροῦ αὐτοῦ, "blood of his cross" (1:20) does not appear elsewhere in the NT.[321]

On these grounds, it is generally agreed that A/Col has included in the text an already formed traditional hymn.[322] Lohse also emphasizes that "these observations

---

[319] See Lohse 1971, 41; Schweizer 1982, 56-57. Cf. Dunn 1996, 83-84; Pfammatter 1987, 61; R. P. Martin 1981, 63; O'Brien 1982, 32-33; Haapa 1978, 31; Nikolainen 1987, 23-24.

[320] Besides Rom 1:20, it appears in the NT only in 1 Tim 1:17 and Heb 11:27.

[321] Lohse 1971, 43, followed by Cannon 1981, 27-28; Schweizer 1982, 56; Nikolainen 1987, 24.

[322] Lindemann 1983, 25; Conzelmann 1990, 182; Pokorný 1987, 48-52; Schweizer 1982, 55; Lohse 1971, 42; Hendriksen 1971, 66-70; Pfammatter 1987, 61; R. P. Martin 1981, 61-66; Gnilka 1980, 53-54; Bujard 1973, 88; Baugh 1985, 227-230; Schenke & Fischer 1978, 164; Wedderburn 1993, 14; Maclean 1995, 37-38, 208; Hübner 1997, 55; Cannon 1981, 23-27; Wilson 1997, 232, 235-236;

exclude the possibility that the author of this letter could have composed these verses himself by using traditional phrases".[323] However, this interpretation includes several problems. First, the words and phrases never or seldom used in the *Pauline* letters do not prove that the text is a quotation from a hymn if the scholars consider Col to be a *deutero-Pauline* letter, as most of those who accept the theory do.[324] The differences in the terminology can then be characteristics of A/Col. Second, the possible backgrounds of the hymn suggested by scholars have been remarkably varied. The following suggestions have been the most influential: pre-Christian Gnosticism, Rabbinic Judaism, Hellenistic Judaism.[325] The variety of assumptions diminishes the plausibility of the theory. Third, it is noteworthy that the text does not form a matching rhythmic pattern: the first strophe is much longer than the second one and the irregularity of the verses can be seen at first glance. Scholars have tried to explain away the problem by suggesting that primitive Christian hymns were probably composed in free rhythm and thus did not consist of regularly constructed verses.[326] Moreover, many parts of the text which interrupt the matching pattern are taken for additions to the authentic hymn. There is, however, no consensus amongst the scholars about the secondary parts of Col 1:15-20. In the following diagram, all parts of the text which have been suggested to be interpolations have been put in parentheses.

Luz 1998, 199-200. For more about the history of the interpretation of Col 1:15-20 as a hymn see Gabathuler 1965, 11-124 and Burger 1975, 3-26.

[323] Lohse 1971, 42. According to Cannon 1981, 28, "Lohse's conclusion ... is an extreme statement" but "the evidence at least suggests a non-Pauline provenance for the hymn".

[324] See e.g. Lohse 1971, 88-91; Schweizer 1982, 18.

[325] See O'Brien 1982, 37-40; Lohse 1971, 45-46; Cannon 1981, 34-38. Drake 1995, 123-144, states that A/Col used "*scriptio continua* as a ploy for ironical intent, and by so doing made possible the Colossian riddle". According to Drake, "Colossians' cryptic visual structures brought surprising ironical tensions to the conventional world of rhetoric".

[326] Lohse 1971, 44; Hübner 1997, 56.

15 a) ὅς ἐστιν εἰκὼν τοῦ θεοῦ τοῦ ἀοράτου,
b) πρωτότοκος πάσης κτίσεως,
16 a) ὅτι ἐν αὐτῷ ἐκτίσθη τὰ πάντα
b) (ἐν τοῖς οὐρανοῖς καὶ ἐπὶ τῆς γῆς,)
c) [(τὰ ὁρατὰ καὶ τὰ ἀόρατα,
d) εἴτε θρόνοι εἴτε κυριότητες εἴτε ἀρχαὶ εἴτε ἐξουσίαι·)
e) τὰ πάντα δι' αὐτοῦ καὶ εἰς αὐτὸν ἔκτισται.]
17 a) [καὶ αὐτός ἐστιν πρὸ πάντων
b) καὶ τὰ πάντα ἐν αὐτῷ συνέστηκεν
18 a) καὶ αὐτός ἐστιν ἡ κεφαλὴ τοῦ σώματος (τῆς ἐκκλησίας·)]
b) ὅς ἐστιν ἀρχή,
c) πρωτότοκος ἐκ τῶν νεκρῶν,
d) (ἵνα γένηται ἐν πᾶσιν αὐτὸς πρωτεύων)
19 ὅτι ἐν αὐτῷ εὐδόκησεν πᾶν τὸ πλήρωμα κατοικῆσαι
20 a) καὶ δι' αὐτοῦ ἀποκαταλλάξαι τὰ πάντα εἰς αὐτόν,
b) [εἰρηνοποιήσας (διὰ τοῦ αἵματος τοῦ σταυροῦ αὐτοῦ,) δι' αὐτοῦ]
c) (εἴτε τὰ ἐπὶ τῆς γῆς εἴτε τὰ ἐν τοῖς οὐρανοῖς.)

Most scholars agree that the words τῆς ἐκκλησίας in verse 18a must be an interpretive addition to the authentic hymn because it is curious that at the first, cosmologically-oriented strophe, Christ is described the "head of the body, the church". This statement would better match with the second strophe which includes soteriological statements.[327] Similarly, the words διὰ τοῦ αἵματος τοῦ σταυροῦ αὐτοῦ in 20b seem to be a Christological interpretation which is usually taken for an addition by A/Col.[328]

In addition, the lines describing the "all things", τὰ πάντα, (τὰ ὁρατὰ καὶ τὰ ἀόρατα, εἴτε θρόνοι εἴτε κυριότητες εἴτε ἀρχαὶ εἴτε ἐξουσίαι) in 16cd are sometimes taken for a secondary enumeration.[329] Moreover, some scholars consider verses 17a - 18a to be a "middle strophe" added by A/Col because the verses do not have a parallel at the end of the second strophe.[330] Sometimes line 16e is also seen to belong to the "middle strophe".[331]

The final clause in verse 18d has been also regarded as an addition because the ἵνα-clause does not match the structure: it has no parallel in the hymn. This

---

[327] Lohse 1971, 45; Schweizer 1982, 57; Gnilka 1980, 59; Lindemann 1983, 25; Käsemann 1960, 36f; Pokorný 1987, 50-52; R. P. Martin 1981, 56; Haapa 1978, 33; Nikolainen 1987, 24; Dunn 1996, 95; Hübner 1997, 56; Robinson 1957, 286; Bammel 1961, 95; Gabathuler 1965, 131; Wedderburn 1993, 16.

[328] Käsemann 1960, 37; Lohse 1971, 45; Ludwig 1974, 80; Schweizer 1982, 59; Gnilka 1980, 57; Wedderburn 1993, 16; Lindemann 1983, 25; Pokorný 1987, 50-52; R. P. Martin 1981, 56-57; Nikolainen 1987, 24; Hübner 1997, 56.

[329] R. P. Martin 1981, 56; Kehl 1967, 37; Gabathuler 1965, 131; Burger 1975, 26; Robinson 1957, 283, 286; Murphy-O'Connor 1995, 233-234. Cf. Schweizer 1982, 57.

[330] Kehl 1967, 37; Burger 1975, 13-15, 26; Murphy-O'Connor 1995, 234; Pfammatter 1987, 61; Bruce 1988, 55-56; Gnilka 1980, 56-57; R. P. Martin 1981, 55.

[331] Gabathuler 1965,129; Burger 1975,13.

interpretation is defended by the fact that the verb πρωτεύω is a hapax legomenon in the NT, as was already mentioned.[332] Many scholars also take the whole of line 20b, including the participle εἰρηνοποιήσας and the words δι' αὐτοῦ, to be secondary.[333] Line 20c has been considered an addition because it seems to be an artificial combination of the contents of 16b and the style of 16cd.[334] Recently, Murphy-O'Connor has stated that line 16 b is also secondary.[335]

When all parts of the text which have been considered to be glosses are marked in the text, we can see that the interpretations vary a great deal. The part which all scholars assume to have been belonged to the authentic hymn is very limited. It is remarkable that many of the extraordinary words which have been seen to prove that the text was an already formed hymn before Col, occur in the parts of the text which are interpreted as additions and thus were not part of the authentic hymn but were written by A/Col. The use of the unusual terminology is thus not so strong an argument for regarding Col 1:15-20 as a traditional hymn, as some scholars contend.

Besides the generally presented arguments for regarding Col 1:15-20 as a hymn, Ludwig states that Col 1:15-20 lacks nearly all characteristics typical of A/Col: participle constructions, dependent relative clauses, loosely joined infinitive constructions, repeating words and phrases, piling synonyms together, interpretive appositions, piling genitives together, and attaching adverbials to nouns with the preposition ἐν. She emphasizes that these characteristics appear often in Col 1:3-14 but seldom in Col 1:15-20. She finds only the participle εἰρηνοποιήσας (1:20) and interpretative apposition αὐτός ἐστιν ἡ κεφαλὴ τοῦ σώματος τῆς ἐκκλησίας (1:18).[336] However, Col 1:15-20 seems to include more examples of the characteristics of A/Col. In 1:18 occurs the participle πρωτεύων. It is not a loosely joined participle which are especially typical of A/Col but, as Ludwig herself states, A/Col often uses all kinds of participles. In addition, in 1:20 genitives are piled together (διὰ τοῦ αἵματος τοῦ σταυροῦ αὐτοῦ). It is also noteworthy that phrases are repeated often in the text. The words ἐν τοῖς οὐρανοῖς and ἐπὶ τῆς γῆς appear twice (1:16, 20), the phrase ἐν αὐτῷ three times (1:16, 17, 19), and τὰ πάντα four times (1:16, 17, 20). The customary adjective πρωτότοκος also occurs twice (1:15, 18). Furthermore, the relative clauses in Col 1:15-20 do not differ from the ones in Col 1:3-14 which, according to Ludwig, are typical of A/Col. The relative clause ὃς ἐρρύσατο ἡμᾶς in Col 1:13 resembles the clauses beginning with the words ὅς ἐστιν in verses 1:15 and 18. Accordingly, Ludwig's interpretation is not conclusive. So many characteristics typical of A/Col appear in Col 1:15-20 that on the grounds of the stylistic peculiarities, there is no reason to assume that the text is not written by him.

The number of solutions amongst the scholars concerning Col 1:15-20 as pre-existing hymn makes the interpretation suspect. Some of the scholars admit this

---

332 Kehl 1967, 37; Bammel 1961, 95; Gabathuler 1965, 131; Burger 1975, 26; Schweizer 1982, 57.
333 Burger 1975, 26; Kehl 1967, 37; Murphy-O'Connor 1995, 234; Robinson 1957, 286; Gabathuler 1965, 131.
334 Robinson 1957, 286; Gabathuler 1965, 131; Kehl 1967, 37; R. P. Martin 1981, 56; Murphy-O'Connor 1995, 233-234.
335 Murphy-O'Connor 1995, 233-235. His interpretation is based on an assumption that the redactors of Col 1:15-20 and Phil 2:6-11 act similarly.
336 Ludwig 1974, 32-35, 48-49.

themselves.[337] The interpretation has been criticized most keenly by those who take Col for an authentic Pauline letter[338] but also some of the scholars who accept Col as a deutero-Pauline letter do not regard Col 1:15-20 as a hymn which existed before Col.[339] Those who assume Col to be an authentic letter emphasize that he himself has formed the hymn utilizing traditional materials.[340] However, we can assume as well that the deutero-Pauline author of Col composed the text putting together distinct statements which already existed.[341] When analyzing Col 1:1-14, it was pointed out that A/Col seems to compose the text imitating the genuine Pauline letters and some texts from the LXX. My hypothesis is that Col 1:15-20 was formed similarly.

---

[337] E.g. Cannon 1981, 23-27; R. P. Martin 1981, 62; Hartman 1985, 42; Gnilka 1980, 51.

[338] Kümmel 1987, 342-343; Moule 1958, 61; Caird 1976, 174-175, 1-6; Baugh 1985, 227-230; Gibbs 1971, 98-99; O'Brien 1982, 35-36; Dunn 1996, 84; Goulder 1995, 612 n. 45. Cf. Gyllenberg 1969, 110-111, who does not mention at all that Col 1:15-20 has been suggested to be based on a traditional hymn. Hooker 1973, 316-317, emphasizes that "there is, however, no real evidence, in spite of the ingenuity of exegetes, that such a hymn ever existed."

[339] O'Neill 1979, 87-89; Schenk 1983, 146, who doubts whether the other similar texts (e.g. Phil 2:6-11) are also based on early Christian hymns.

[340] Kümmel 1987, 343; O'Brien 1982, 35-36. Cf. Dunn 1996, 84-85.

[341] So O'Neill 1979, 87-100.

3.1.2. Col 1:15-20 as a Praise to Christ Written by the Author of Colossians

Col 1:15-20

15 **ὅς ἐστιν εἰκὼν τοῦ θεοῦ** τοῦ ἀοράτου, πρωτότοκος πάσης **κτίσεως**,

16 ὅτι ἐν αὐτῷ ἐκτίσθη τὰ πάντα **ἐν** τοῖς οὐρανοῖς καὶ **ἐπὶ** τῆς γῆς, τὰ ὁρατὰ καὶ **τὰ ἀόρατα**, εἴτε θρόνοι εἴτε κυριότητες εἴτε ἀρχαὶ εἴτε ἐξουσίαι. **τὰ πάντα δι' αὐτοῦ καὶ εἰς αὐτὸν** ἔκτισται.

17 καὶ αὐτός ἐστιν **πρὸ πάντων** καὶ τὰ πάντα ἐν αὐτῷ συνέστηκεν,

18 καὶ αὐτός **ἐστιν ἡ κεφαλὴ** τοῦ σώματος τῆς ἐκκλησίας· ὅς ἐστιν ἀρχή, πρωτότοκος **ἐκ** τῶν **νεκρῶν**, ἵνα γένηται ἐν πᾶσιν αὐτος πρωτεύων,

19 ὅτι **ἐν αὐτῷ εὐδόκησεν** πᾶν τὸ πλήρωμα κατοικῆσαι

20 και **δι' αὐτοῦ** ἀποκαταλλάξαι **τὰ πάντα εἰς αὐτόν**, εἰρηνοποιήσας διὰ **τοῦ αἵματος τοῦ** σταυροῦ αὐτοῦ, [δι' αὐτοῦ] εἴτε **τὰ ἐπὶ τῆς γῆς** εἴτε **τὰ ἐν τοῖς οὐρανοῖς**.

2 Cor 4:4

... **ὅς ἐστιν εἰκὼν τοῦ θεοῦ**.

1 Cor 8:5-6

5 ... εἴτε **ἐν** οὐρανῷ εἴτε **ἐπὶ γῆς**, ὥσπερ εἰσὶν θεοὶ πολλοὶ καὶ κύριοι πολλοί,
6 ἀλλ' ἡμῖν εἷς θεὸς ὁ πατὴρ ἐξ οὗ **τὰ πάντα καὶ** ἡμεῖς **εἰς αὐτόν**, καὶ εἷς κύριος Ἰησοῦς Χριστὸς δι' οὗ **τὰ πάντα καὶ** ἡμεῖς **δι' αὐτοῦ**.

Rom 11:36

ὅτι ἐξ αὐτοῦ καὶ **δι' αὐτοῦ καὶ εἰς αὐτὸν τὰ πάντα**·

1 Cor 11:3

... παντὸς ἀνδρὸς **ἡ κεφαλὴ** ὁ Χριστός **ἐστιν**

1 Cor 12:27-28

27 Ὑμεῖς δέ ἐστε σῶμα Χριστοῦ καὶ μέλη ἐκ μέρους.
28 Καὶ οὓς μὲν ἔθετο ὁ θεὸς ἐν τῇ ἐκκλησίᾳ

Col 1:16

ὅτι ἐν αὐτῷ ἐκτίσθη **τὰ πάντα ἐν τοῖς οὐρανοῖς καὶ ἐπὶ τῆς γῆς** ... **τὰ πάντα δι' αὐτοῦ** καὶ **εἰς αὐτὸν** ἔκτισται·

1 Cor 10:16

τοῦ αἵματος τοῦ Χριστοῦ

Rom 8:29

... τῆς εἰκόνος **τοῦ** υἱοῦ αὐτοῦ, εἰς τὸ εἶναι αὐτὸν πρωτότοκον ἐν πολλοῖς ἀδελφοῖς·

Rom 1:20

τὰ γὰρ **ἀόρατα** αὐτοῦ ἀπὸ **κτίσεως** κόσμου ...

1 Cor 15:24

... ὅταν καταργήσῃ πᾶσαν ἀρχὴν καὶ πᾶσαν ἐξουσίαν καὶ δύναμιν.

Prov 8:22-27

22 κύριος ἔκτισέν με ἀρχὴν ὁδῶν αὐτοῦ...
24 πρὸ τοῦ τὴν γῆν ποιῆσαι ...
25 ... **πρὸ** δὲ **πάντων** βουνῶν γεννᾷ με. ...
27 ἡνίκα ἡτοίμαζεν τὸν οὐρανόν

1 Cor 15:20

... Χριστὸς ἐγήγερται **ἐκ νεκρῶν** ἀπαρχὴ τῶν κεκοιμημένων.

Ps 67:17 LXX

... τὸ ὄρος, ὃ **εὐδόκησεν** ὁ θεὸς κατοικεῖν **ἐν αὐτῷ**;

2 Cor 5:18

τὰ δὲ **πάντα** ἐκ τοῦ θεοῦ τοῦ καταλλάξαντος ἡμᾶς ἑαυτῷ **διὰ** Χριστοῦ ...

1 Cor 1:17

ὁ σταυρὸς **τοῦ** Χριστοῦ

Many of the rare words in Col 1:15-20 appear in verses 15-16. As was mentioned above, the adjective ὁρατός, visible, is a hapax legomenon in the NT and ἀόρατος, invisible, which is used both in Col 1:15 and 1:16 occurs in the undisputed letters of Paul only in Rom 1:20, and it appears later e.g. in Tim 1:17 and Heb 11:27. Besides the use of the exceptional adjective ἀόρατος, Col 1:15-16 and Rom 1:20 also resemble each other otherwise. While Rom 1:20 describes the invisible nature of God since the creation using the words τὰ γὰρ ἀόρατα αὐτοῦ ἀπὸ κτίσεως, according to Col 1:15 Christ is the image of the invisible God (εἰκὼν τοῦ θεοῦ τοῦ ἀοράτου) and the firstborn of all creation (πρωτότοκος πάσης κτίσεως). In Col 1:16 the adjective ἀόρατος is repeated in the juxtaposition visible – invisible (τὰ ὁρατά – τὰ ἀόρατα). The noun κτίσις appears in Col 1:15 even in the same form as in Rom 1:20 (κτίσεως) as well as the adjective ἀόρατος when it is used the second time in the text in Col 1:16 (τὰ ἀόρατα). Thus it seems possible that Col 1:15-16 echoes Rom 1:20. Though the texts include only two similar words, because of the rare occurrence of the adjective ἀόρατος and the repetition of it in Col, the resemblance meets the criteria for a possible literary dependence. Accordingly, the exceptional occurrence of ἀόρατος does not necessitate that Col 1:15-20 belongs to a pre-existing hymn, but indicates that Col 1:15 depends on Rom 1:20.[342]

Likewise, the curiosity of the words ὅς ἐστιν εἰκὼν τοῦ θεοῦ in the Pauline letters does not presuppose that Col 1:15 is based on an earlier hymn. The fact that only Col 1:15 and 2 Cor 4:4 use the words exactly in the same form points rather to a literary dependence. In addition, the similarity of the contexts, both dealing with light and darkness (2 Cor 4:6 // Col 1:11-13), indicates a connection between the texts.[343] The words ὅς ἐστιν εἰκὼν τοῦ θεοῦ also resemble Gen 1:27: καὶ ἐποίησεν ὁ θεὸς τὸν ἄνθρωπον, κατ' εἰκόνα θεοῦ ἐποίησεν αὐτόν. Thus it is often assumed that Gen 1:27 and the Jewish literature which developed the same theme (e.g. Wis 7:26, Philo, Leg All 1:43) is the background of Col 1:15.[344] Because of the verbatim agreement between 2 Cor 4:4 and Col 1:15, the dependence between them is more probable than the possibility that they both derive from Gen 1:27. On the grounds of the verbatim agreement of the words ὅς ἐστιν εἰκὼν τοῦ θεοῦ, the resemblance between Col 1:15 and 2 Cor 4:4 meets the criteria for a possible literary dependence.[345]

---

[342] Similarly E. P. Sanders 1966, 35.
[343] Contra Hübner 1997, 59, who emphasizes that Col 1:11 is not in the direct context of Col 1:15.
[344] See e.g. Hendriksen 1971, 71; Bruce 1988, 58; O'Brien 1982, 43; Haapa 1978, 31; Pokorný 1987, 62; Gnilka 1980, 59-60; Schnabel 1985, 256; Nikolainen 1987, 25; Hooker 1973, 323.
[345] Similarly E. P. Sanders 1966, 36-37, who emphasizes the precise agreement between Col 1:15 and 2 Cor 4:4. Cf. Hübner 1997, 59: "Sollte er, wie zu vermuten ist, 2Kor gekannt haben, so hatte er 2Kor 4,4 vor Augen gehabt...". Contra Lindemann 1979, 117, according to whom Paul and A/Col knew the same tradition and thus use similar phrases. The possible dependence between Col 1:15 and 2 Cor 4:4 also rules out Schenk's interpretation, according to which the words ὅς ἐστιν are derived from the baptismal story of Jesus (see p. 80 n. 302). Although scholars often mention the similarity between Col 1:15 and 2 Cor 4:4, they do not usually assume a literary dependence

The phrase πρωτότοκος πάσης κτίσεως is unique in ECL. Except for Col 1:16, it does not appear before Origen (Contra Celsum VI, 38) and Pseudo-Ignatius (Tar 4:1), the latter clearly depending on Col 1:16-17 (see pp. 49-50). Accordingly, it is clearly a creation of A/Col. Like in Col 1:15, the noun εἰκών and the adjective πρωτότοκος appear together in Rom 8:29. The verbal agreement is interesting because the adjective πρωτότοκος does not occur anywhere else in the Pauline corpus and is also otherwise atypical of ECL (it occurs in Lk 2:7, Heb 1:6, 11:28, 12:23, Rev 1:5). Many scholars emphasize the similarity between Col 1:15 and Rom 8:29 but do not usually assume any connection between the texts.[346] Because of the two words in common, of which the adjective πρωτότοκος appears so seldom in the ECL, the verbal agreement between Col 1:15 and Rom 8:29 meets the criteria for a possible dependence and thus Col 1:15 seems to conflate 2 Cor 4:4, Rom 1:20, and Rom 8:29. As a pseudepigrapher, A/Col uses the words he takes up from Rom 1:20 and Rom 8:29 in a new context. While in Rom 1:20 the words ἀόρατα ... ἀπὸ κτίσεως describe God's eternal power which has been seen ever since the creation and πρωτότοκος is used about Christ as the firstborn in the future glory in Rom 8:29, in Col 1:15 the phrase πρωτότοκος πάσης κτίσεως describes Christ as the firstborn of all creation.

Col 1:16 has an even closer parallel in the genuine Pauline letters than those of v. 15. Col 1:16 and 1 Cor 8:5-6 similarly describe the rulers in heaven and on earth and both also use phrases resembling Stoic formulations. However, instead of the phrase εἴτε ἐν οὐρανῷ εἴτε ἐπὶ γῆς used in 1 Cor 8:5, A/Col uses the words ἐν τοῖς οὐρανοῖς καὶ ἐπὶ τῆς γῆς which are more typical of him. The phrase ἐπὶ τῆς γῆς also occurs in Col 1:20, 3:25 and the phrase ἐν τοῖς οὐρανοῖς in Col 1:5, 20 but they are only seldom used in the genuine Pauline letters: ἐν τοῖς οὐρανοῖς occurs only in 2 Cor 5:1 and ἐπὶ τῆς γῆς only in Rom 9:28, neither of which otherwise resembles Col 1:16.[347] Instead, in the Gospels the phrases ἐν τοῖς οὐρανοῖς and ἐπὶ τῆς γῆς are often used, and in Mt 16:19 both are found together.[348] Although the phrases are so normal in the Gospels that there is no reason to assume a connection between Col 1:16 and Mt 16:19, the use of the phrases ἐν τοῖς οὐρανοῖς and ἐπὶ τῆς γῆς in Col may be an echo of the Gospels.[349]

---

between the texts; see Conzelmann 1990, 183; Pfammatter 1987, 61-62; Dunn 1996, 87; Hartman 1985, 35; Bruce 1988, 57; Hendriksen 1971, 72; Pokorný 1987, 63; Gnilka 1980, 61; Wedderburn 1993, 24; O'Brien 1982, 42-45; R. P. Martin 1981, 57.

[346] See O'Brien 1982, 42-45; Pokorný 1987, 70; Pfammatter 1987, 63-64; Hartman 1985, 35; Strack & Billerbeck III, 626.

[347] Cf. Phil 2:10: ἵνα ἐν τῷ ὀνόματι Ἰησοῦ πᾶν γόνυ κάμψῃ ἐπουρανίων καὶ ἐπιγείων καὶ καταχθονίων.

[348] The phrase ἐπὶ τῆς γῆς appears in Mk 2:10, 4:1, 26, 31, 31, 6:47, 8:6, 9:3, 20, 14:35, Mt 6:19, 9:6, 16:19, 18:18, 19, 23:9, 35, 28:18, Lk 5:24, 18:8, 21:23, 25, Jn 6:21, 17:4. The occurrence of the phrase ἐν τοῖς οὐρανοῖς in the Gospels is listed in p. 93 n. 20.

[349] Cf. Schenk 1983, 148 n. 36; 1987a, 3331, 3343 n. 54, who takes the occurrence of the phrase ἐπὶ τῆς γῆς in Col to be due to Mk because it appears in Mk ten times and in Col four times and is thus typical of both. Moreover, Schenk emphasizes that in Mk the phrase is used in Mk 4:26, 31 when describing the kingdom of God (βασιλεία) which is also characteristic of Col.

On the other hand, it is also possible that the phrases are familiar to A/Col from Paul, who uses both once.[350]

Besides using phrases diverging a little from 1 Cor 8:5-6, A/Col also describes differently the rulers in heaven and on earth. Instead of gods and lords mentioned in 1 Cor 8:5-6 (θεοὶ πολλοὶ καὶ κύριοι πολλοί), Col 1:16 lists thrones, dominions, rulers, and powers (θρόνοι, κυριότητες, ἀρχαί, ἐξουσίαι). Thus only the nouns κύριοι and κυριότητες resemble each other. Although the throne of God is often mentioned in ECL, the reference to many thrones in heaven in Col 1:16 is exceptional. It has parallels only in Mt 19:28 / par. Lk 22:30 and Rev 4:4, 11:16. However, rulers and powers (ἀρχαί, ἐξουσίαι) are often mentioned together.[351] In the authentic Pauline letters they occur together only in 1 Cor 15:24. Since the contexts of Col 1:16 and 1 Cor 15:24 are similar, both describing the kingdom of God the Father and Christ as his Son, it seems to be possible that the mention of ἀρχαί and ἐξουσίαι in Col 1:16 is an echo of 1 Cor 15:24.[352]

The clearest resemblance between Col 1:16 and 1 Cor 8:5-6 is the use of similar Stoic formulation. The choice of wording "all things ... through him and for him" (τὰ πάντα δι' αὐτοῦ καὶ εἰς αὐτόν) in Col 1:16 resemble very much the words τὰ πάντα ... εἰς αὐτόν ... τὰ πάντα ... δι' αὐτοῦ appearing in 1 Cor 8:6. A similar formulation also appears in Rom 11:36 in the form δι' αὐτοῦ καὶ εἰς αὐτὸν τὰ πάντα which better matches Col 1:16. Therefore it seems that Col 1:16 is modelled on 1 Cor 8:5-6 but the author remembers the words of the Stoic formula in the form used in Rom 11:36 because they appear there in a more convenient order.[353] These kinds of formulae are not unique. The formulation "in him we live and move and have our being" (ἐν αὐτῷ γὰρ ζῶμεν καὶ κινούμεθα καὶ ἐσμέν) appears in Acts 17:28 and Marcus Aurelius (Ad se ipsum 4: 23) uses the words "O Nature ... all things come from you, subsist in you, go back to you" (ὦ φύσις, ἐκ σοῦ πάντα, ἐν σοὶ πάντα, εἰς σὲ πάντα, quite similar to Col 1:16, as many scholars emphasize.[354] However, the formulations occurring in 1 Cor 8:6 and Rom 11:36 are clearly closer to Col 1:16 than the others, which indicates literary dependence. In addition, there are the other verbal agreements between Col 1:16 and 1 Cor 8:5-6. It is thus more probable that Col 1:16 conflates 1 Cor 8:6 and Rom 11:36 than that the verbatim agreement results only from the use of similar phrases or the same oral tradition.[355] Although A/Col seems to imitate the Stoic formula from Paul's

---

[350] Cf. E. P. Sanders 1966, 35-36.
[351] See Col 1:18, 2:10, 15, Lk 12:11, 20:20, 1 Cor 15:24, Eph 1:21, 3:10, 6:12, Titus 3:1.
[352] Also Pokorný 1987, 65, states 1 Cor 15:24 as a parallel to Col 1:16.
[353] Similarly E. P. Sanders 1966, 36. Cf. Luke's use of 1 Clem 18:1 in Acts 13:17-23. According to Reuter 1999, Luke imitates 1 Clem but the choice of wording is also influenced by LXX texts.
[354] See Lohse 1971, 49; E. P. Sanders 1966, 36; Hartman 1985, 35, 54; Dunn 1996, 91; Haapa 1978, 32; Gnilka 1980, 64; Hübner 1997, 60; Luz 1998, 202. Pöhlmann 1973, 57, lists also other similar formulae.
[355] Cf. E. P. Sanders 1966, 36, who leaves open the question. Contra Standhartinger 1999, 147; Pokorný 1987, 49 n. 6. Many scholars present 1 Cor 8:5-6 as a parallel to Col 1:16 although they do not assume a literary dependence between the texts; see O'Brien 1982, 45; Lindemann 1983,

letters, as a pseudepigrapher he uses it differently. While in 1 Cor 8:6 and Rom 11:36 the words describe God, in Col 1:16 they are applied to Christ.[356] The resemblance between Col 1:16 and 1 Cor 8:5-6, including three similar nouns and the same kind of Stoic formulations, clearly meets the criteria for a possible literary dependence. Though Col 1:16 and Rom 11:36 do not use any similar nouns, the verbatim agreement between the formulations has to be regarded as indicating a possible literary dependence.

The use of the verb κτίζω, "to create", in Col 1:16 may be due to the noun κτίσεως, "creation", in Rom 1:20.[357] The verb κτίζω does not appear either in Rom 1:20 or in other Pauline texts which A/Col seems to imitate[358] but it is often used in the LXX when describing how God created Wisdom before the creation of the world (e.g. Prov 8:22, Sir 1:4, 24:9).[359] Besides the verb κτίζω, the words πρὸ δὲ πάντων βουνῶν γεννᾷ με, "before the hills, I was brought forth", (v. 25) are also used in Prov 8, which resemble the words αὐτός ἐστιν πρὸ πάντων, "he is before all things", in Col 1:17.[360] In addition, both Prov 8 and Col 1:16-18 mention the beginning (ἀρχή), heaven (οὐρανός), and earth (γή). Though the use of the verb κτίζω in Col differs from the LXX, there God creates Wisdom but in Col all things are created in Christ, it is possible that Col 1:16 not only resembles[361] but also echoes Prov 8:22-27[362].

The words "in him all things hold together" (τὰ πάντα ἐν αὐτῷ συνέστηκεν) in Col 1:17 do not have any parallel in the Pauline corpus. In other ECL only in 2 Pet 3:5 is the verb συνίστημι used, resembling Col 1:17 when describing how the earth was formed out of water and by means of water by the word of God (γῆ ἐξ ὕδατος καὶ δι' ὕδατος συνεστῶσα τῷ τοῦ θεοῦ λόγῳ). However, Col 1:17 has closer parallels in Hellenistic Judaism. Philo speaks of the four principles "from which the world has been established", ἐξ ὧν συνέστηκεν ὁ κόσμος (Rer Div Her

---

27; Gnilka 1980, 64; Pfammatter 1987, 63-64; Arnold 1995, 257; Hartman 1985, 35; Haapa 1978, 32; Conzelmann 1990, 184; Wedderburn 1993, 26. Excluding O'Brien, Arnold, and Haapa, they also mention the similarity between Col 1:16 and Rom 11:36.

[356] E. P. Sanders 1966, 36. Cf. Barclay 1997, 80, 82.

[357] So E. P. Sanders 1966, 35.

[358] The verb κτίζω is used in the authentic Pauline letters only twice, in Rom 1:25 and 1 Cor 11:9.

[359] Prov 8:22: κύριος ἔκτισέν με ἀρχήν. Sir 1:4: προτέρα πάντων ἔκτισται σοφία. Sir 24:9: πρὸ τοῦ αἰῶνος ἀπ' ἀρχῆς ἔκτισέν με.

[360] The words αὐτός ἐστιν πρὸ πάντων in Col 1:17 describe, similarly to the phrase πρωτότοκος πάσης κτίσεως in Col 1:16, not only the temporal priority of the universe but also suggests Christ's superiority over it; Lohse 1971, 52; Bruce 1988, 65; Wedderburn 1993, 28.

[361] The resemblance between Col 1:16-18 and Prov 8:22-27 is noticed by most scholars; see Arnold 1995, 256 n. 30, 260-261; Murphy-O'Connor 1995, 236; Sappington 1991, 173; Hooker 1973, 330; Strack & Billerbeck III, 626; R. P. Martin 1981, 58; Gnilka 1980, 60-63; Hartman 1985, 53; Lindemann 1983, 25; Bruce 1988, 60; Conzelmann 1990, 183; Haapa 1978, 31; Nikolainen 1987, 25-26; O'Brien 1982, 43; Pfammatter 1987, 62; Dunn 1996, 89-93, 97; Wedderburn 1993, 18; Goulder 1994, 102; Hübner 1997, 59.

[362] Cf. Dunn 1996, 89; Hübner 1997, 59; Murphy-O'Connor 1995, 235-236; O'Brien 1982, 43; Bruce 1988, 60. According to Lincoln 1997, 2, in Col 1:15-20 "... all the attributes of Wisdom from the Hellenistic Jewish tradition are seen as embodied in Christ".

281). His text is derived from the Platonic and Stoic philosophy in which the verb συνεστηκέναι was used to denote the unity of the world. The closest parallel to Col 1:17 is Pseudo-Aristotle, De Mundo 6 397b which describes "that all things are from God and are constituted ... by God" (ὡς ἐκ θεοῦ πάντα καὶ διὰ θεὸν συνέστηκεν). Although Col 1:17 is unlikely to depend directly on Pseudo-Aristotle, De Mundo 6 397b, the phrase τὰ πάντα ἐν αὐτῷ συνέστηκεν seems to echo the phraseology of Platonic and Stoic philosophy.[363] Some scholars try to deny this connection, emphasizing that the parallels from the Jewish Wisdom tradition are closer to Col 1:17. However, none of the texts they present e.g. Ps 103:24 LXX, Prov 3:19, Wis 8:5,[364] Wis 1:7,[365] Eccl 43:26,[366] and Ps 33:6 (32:6 LXX)[367] agree verbatim with Col 1:17.

In Col 1:18 Christ is described as "the head of the body of the church" (ἡ κεφαλὴ τοῦ σώματος τῆς ἐκκλησίας). In the genuine Pauline letters, body often symbolizes the congregation (cf. 1 Cor 6:15, 12:12-13, 27-28, 10:17, Rom 12:5). The closest parallel to Col 1:18 is 1 Cor 12:27-28 which, unlike the others, uses the term ἐκκλησία. Although the words in common between the texts, σῶμα, ἐκκλησία, and εἰμι are very ordinary in ECL, the fact that the nouns σῶμα and ἐκκλησία do not usually appear together indicates a possible literary dependence between the texts.

Paul never describes Christ as the head of the church, as in Col 1:18, but the church as the body of Christ.[368] Nevertheless, the hierarchy described in 1 Cor 11:3 resembles Col 1:18. It suggests that Christ is the head of every man, the husband the head of his wife, and God the head of Christ. The verbal agreement between Col 1:18 and 1 Cor 11:3, one noun and one verb in common, does not meet the criteria for literary dependence. However, the words ἐστιν (ἡ) κεφαλή match verbatim and both texts describe Christ, although Col 1:18 refers to him using the pronoun αὐτός. It is also remarkable that Eph 5:23 seems to conflate Col 1:18 and 1 Cor 11:3 : it can be seen from the following table that Eph 5:23 combines the idea that the husband is the head of the wife from 1 Cor 11:3 and the thought that Christ is the head of the church from Col 1:18. Thus A/Eph seems to notice, consciously or unconsciously, that Col 1:18 echoes 1 Cor 11:3. This suggests a connection between Col 1:18 and 1 Cor 11:3 which should be classified as an agreement

---

[363] Cf. Lohse 1971, 52; Hübner 1997, 61; Hartman 1985, 54; Wedderburn 1993, 17; Pokorný 1987, 73.

[364] See Dunn 1996, 91-93. Ps 103:24 LXX: πάντα ἐν σοφίᾳ ἐποίησας. Prov 3:19: ὁ θεὸς τῇ σοφίᾳ ἐθεμελίωσεν τὴν γῆν. Wis 8:5: τί σοφίας πλουσιώτερον τῆς τὰ πάντα ἐργαζομένης.

[365] See Sappington 1991, 174; O'Brien 1982, 47-48. Wis 1:7: ὅτι πνεῦμα κυρίου πεπλήρωκεν τὴν οἰκουμένην, καὶ τὸ συνέχον τὰ πάντα γνῶσιν ἔχει φωνῆς.

[366] See O'Brien 1982, 48. Eccl 43:26: ἐν λόγῳ αὐτοῦ σύγκειται τὰ πάντα.

[367] See Bruce 1988, 62. Ps 33:6 (32:6 LXX): τῷ λόγῳ τοῦ κυρίου οἱ οὐρανοὶ ἐστερεώσαν.

[368] Hendriksen 1971, 76; Dunn 1996, 96; Schweizer 1982, 72; Lohse 1971, 55; Hartman 1985, 45-46; Haapa 1978, 33; Bruce 1988, 68; Wedderburn 1993, 59.

pointing to a possible literary dependence. Therefore, Col 1:18 seems to be the result of a conflation of 1 Cor 11:3 and 12:27-28.[369]

Eph 5:23	Col 1:18	1 Cor 11:3
ὅτι ἀνήρ ἐστιν κεφαλὴ τῆς γυναικὸς ὡς καὶ ὁ Χριστὸς κεφαλὴ τῆς ἐκκλησίας	καὶ αὐτός ἐστιν ἡ κεφαλὴ τοῦ σώματος τῆς ἐκκλησίας˙	... παντὸς ἀνδρὸς ἡ κεφαλὴ ὁ Χριστός ἐστιν, κεφαλὴ δὲ γυναικὸς ὁ ἀνήρ ...

However, it should not be forgotten that Col 1:18 also resembles the Stoic conception of the cosmic body. The Stoic view was also adopted in Hellenistic Judaism. E.g. Philo speaks of the world as a body over which the Logos is set as the head (Som I,128, II, 207, Op Mund 119, Fug 110, 182).[370] The closest parallel to Col 1:18 is Som I,128: "occupying the place which the head does in the whole body and sets it up close to his understanding" (ὡσανεὶ σώματος ἡνωμένου κεφαλὴν πλησίον ἱδρύεται διανοίας τῆς ἑαυτοῦ). Therefore, it is probable that the Stoic conception of the cosmic body was familiar to A/Col, although he clearly adopted the allegory of the church as the body of Christ from Paul.[371]

The words ὅς ἐστιν ἀρχή in Col 1:18b correspond to the relative clause ὅς ἐστιν εἰκών in Col 1:15a. In addition, the relative clause is followed by the words πρωτότοκος ἐκ τῶν νεκρῶν which resemble the words πρωτότοκος πάσης κτίσεως in v. 15a. Accordingly, verses 15a and 18b are constructed similarly. As was already mentioned, Paul never speaks about Christ as ἀρχή but once, in 1 Cor 15:20, as ἀπαρχή. Besides this verbal similarity, both Col 1:18 and 1 Cor 15:20 mention that Christ has been raised from the dead using the same words ἐκ νεκρῶν. Thus 1 Cor 15:20 is often presented as a parallel to Col 1:18.[372] Though the resemblance does not meet the criteria for literary dependence, Col 1:18 possibly echoes 1 Cor 15:20.

It is not clear what is the subject of the sentence ἐν αὐτῷ εὐδόκησεν πᾶν τὸ πλήρωμα κατοικῆσαι in Col 1:19. The phrase ἐν αὐτῷ seems to exclude Christ as the subject.[373] However, it cannot be decided with certainty whether God, or the fullness is the more probable subject of "was pleased". Some scholars consider that

---

[369] Similarly Hübner 1997, 61. Cf. Martin 1981, 34, and Kümmel 1987, 343-34. Contra Lohse 1971, 55, who emphasizes that "the understanding of the church in Col cannot be explained as a simple evolution from earlier beginnings within Pauline theology". According to Murphy-O'Connor 1995, 240-241, who regards Col as a genuine Pauline letter, 1 Cor 12:12-27 is later than Col 1:18.
[370] Lohse 1971, 54-55; 1965, 205; Wedderburn 1993, 18.
[371] Similarly Wedderburn 1993, 12-13, 18. Contra O'Brien 1982, 50, according to whom "there is no need to look for Stoic antecedents as the source of the writer's ideas". Cf. Bruce 1988, 68.
[372] Pokorný 1987, 70; Haapa 1978, 33; Nikolainen 1987, 28; Lindemann 1983, 27; Gnilka 1980, 70; Hartman 1985, 36.
[373] O'Brien 1982, 51.

God should be supplied as the subject of the sentence.[374] The most influential suggestion, however, is that the subject of the sentence is "the fullness of deity". The parallel in Col 2:9 also supports this interpretation. There the whole fullness of deity is clearly the subject of the same verb κατοικέω.[375]

The choice of wording ἐν αὐτῷ εὐδόκησεν ... κατοικῆσαι resembles Ps 67:17 LXX, ὃ εὐδόκησεν ὁ θεὸς κατοικεῖν ἐν αὐτῷ, which tells about the mountain that God desired for his abode. In addition, the verb εὐδοκέω is used similarly to Col 1:19 in the Gospels (Mk 1:11, Mt 3:17, 17:5, Lk 3:22) when describing how God is pleased with his Son (ἐν σοὶ εὐδόκησα). The Gospel texts do not resemble Col 1:19 as much as Ps 67:17 LXX which matches it partly verbatim.[376] Though the agreement between the texts, only two verbs in common, does not meet the criteria for literary dependence, Col 1:19 may echo Ps 67:17 LXX.[377]

The fullness in Christ is mentioned in the same way as in Col 1:19, in Jn 1:16, Eph 1:23, 3:19, and 4:13 which all are later than Col. However, the expression may be derived from the fullness of God which is frequently emphasized in the OT. Jer 23:24 describes how God fills heaven and earth (μὴ οὐχὶ τὸν οὐρανὸν καὶ τὴν γῆν ἐγὼ πληρῶ) and according to Isa 6:1, the hem of God's robe fills the temple when he is sitting on a throne (εἶδον τὸν κύριον καθήμενον ἐπὶ θρόνου ὑψηλοῦ καὶ ἐπηρμένου, καὶ πλήρης ὁ οἶκος τῆς δόξης αὐτοῦ). It thus seems possible that the mention of the fullness in Christ is likewise the words ἐν αὐτῷ εὐδόκησεν ... κατοικῆσαι derived from the LXX.[378]

The Stoic formula δι' αὐτοῦ ... τὰ πάντα εἰς αὐτόν is repeated in the beginning of Col 1:20 from Col 1:16. The phrases τὰ ἐπὶ τῆς γῆς and τὰ ἐν τοῖς οὐρανοῖς also occurred in Col 1:16.[379] However, the verb ἀποκαταλλάσσω, "to reconcile", (Col 1:20, 22[380]) appears here for the first time in all of ancient Greek literature known to us. Since it was noted that it is typical of A/Col to add prefixes

---

[374] E.g. Hendriksen 1971, 78-79; Delling 1973, 303. See also O'Brien 1982, 51, who himself, however, does not defend the decision.

[375] O'Brien 1982, 51; Bruce 1988, 72-73; Arnold 1995, 262; Lindemann 1983, 28; Pokorný 1987, 72; Haapa 1978, 33-34; Wedderburn 1993, 32, 34.

[376] Contra Schenk 1987a, 3342-3343; 1983, 148-149, who assumes that Col 1:19 depends on Mk 1:11 (see p. 80 n. 302). Also Pokorný 1987, 72, emphasizes the similarity between Col 1:19 and Mk 1:11.

[377] Cf. Arnold who emphasizes that "the roots of the ... phrase go deep into the OT and LXX". In addition, the similarity between Col 1:19 and Ps 67:17 LXX is noticed by many scholars. See Arnold 1995, 262; Delling 1973, 303; Murphy-O'Connor 1995, 236; Wedderburn 1993, 32; Lohse 1971, 58; Schweizer 1982, 77-78; Gnilka 1980, 71; O'Brien 1982, 52; Haapa 1978, 34; Pokorný 1987, 72; Dunn 1996, 101.

[378] Similarly Arnold 1995, 262-264; Dunn 1996, 99-100; Wedderburn 1993, 31; Schnabel 1985, 257-258; Schweizer 1982, 78; O'Brien 1982, 51-52.

[379] Also Dunn 1996, 104, calls attention to the repetition. Contra E. P. Sanders 1966, 37-38, who neglecting to notice the similarity between Col 1:16 and 20, emphasizes the agreement between 1 Cor 8:5 and Col 1:20.

[380] Instead of ἀποκαταλλάξαι some textual critics follow in verse 20 the more difficult reading, the passive ἀποκατηλλάγητε; O'Brien 1982, 64; Hendriksen 1971, 96.

to the Pauline verbs in Col 1:5b where he employed the unusual verb προακούω instead of the more usual ἀκούω, it seems that A/Col uses the verb ἀποκαταλλάσσω instead of the Pauline verb καταλλάσσω.[381]

Paul uses the verb καταλλάσσω in Rom 5:10, 1 Cor 7:11, and 2 Cor 5:18, 19, 20, of which 2 Cor 5:18 resembles Col 1:20 most.[382] The choice of wording τὰ δὲ πάντα ἐκ τοῦ θεοῦ τοῦ καταλλάξαντος ... διὰ Χριστοῦ in 2 Cor 5:18 is similar to that in Col 1:20, δι' αὐτοῦ ἀποκαταλλάξαι τὰ πάντα ... διὰ ... αὐτοῦ. However, the resemblance does not meet the criteria for literary dependence because, besides the verb (ἀπο)καταλλάσσω, the texts include only one pronoun (πᾶς) and one preposition (διά) in common, which also seem to be due to the repetition of Col 1:16. Nevertheless, the use of the verb ἀποκαταλλάσσω in Col 1:20 may be influenced by 2 Cor 5:18. It is possible that A/Col recalls the choice of wording in 2 Cor 5:18 which resembles the one he himself uses in Col 1:16 and so picks up the verb καταλλάσσω adding the prefix ἀπο-.[383]

The clause εἰρηνοποιήσας διὰ τοῦ αἵματος τοῦ σταυροῦ αὐτοῦ, "making peace through the blood of his cross" (Col 1:20) includes a loosely joined participle construction which is a characteristic of A/Col.[384] In addition, the phrase διὰ τοῦ αἵματος τοῦ σταυροῦ αὐτοῦ (Col 1:20) is unique in ECL.[385] It includes the same kind of series of dependent genitives as verses 1:5, 12, 13 and therefore is apparently a formation of A/Col which connects together two Pauline phrases, τό αἷμα τοῦ Χριστοῦ (1 Cor 10:16, cf. 11:27) and ὁ σταυρὸς τοῦ Χριστοῦ (1 Cor 1:17).[386]

The verb εἰρηνοποιέω, "to make peace", is very exceptional in biblical Greek; it is a hapax legomenon in the NT, and in the LXX it occurs only once (Prov 10:10). In addition, the noun εἰρηνοποιός appears only once in the NT (Mt 5:9) and so does the phrase ποιῶν εἰρήνην (Eph 2:15). In other Greek literature of the first century A.D., εἰρηνοποιέω and εἰρηνοποιός are also seldom used. Philo and Cornutus use εἰρηνοποιός once each and Plutarch twice.[387] Philo, Spec Leg II, 192 resembles Col 1:20 most. There God is described as a peacemaker

---

[381] E. P. Sanders 1966, 37; Arnold 1995, 266; Dunn 1996, 102; Büchsel 1974, 258; Hübner 1997, 62-63. Studying the TLG confirms the argument. The verb ἀποκαταλλάσσω can be found during the years 800 B.C. – A.D. 100 only in Col 1:20,22 and Eph 2:16.

[382] Also Hübner 1997, 62-63, E. P. Sanders 1966, 37, and Pokorný 1987, 74, emphasize the similarity between Col 1:20, 2 Cor 5:18 and Rom 5:10-11.

[383] Similarly E. P. Sanders 1966, 37-38, who neglecting the verbatim agreement between Col 1:16 and 20, emphasizes even more the possibility that Col 1:20 depends on 2 Cor 5:18. Contra Lindemann 1979, 117, according to whom the resemblances between Col 1:20 and 2 Cor 5:18 are caused by the knowledge of the same tradition.

[384] Bujard 1973, 60.

[385] The closest parallel is the phrase διὰ τοῦ αἵματος αὐτοῦ in Eph 1:7.

[386] E. P. Sanders 1966, 38, and Lohse 1971, 88, both assume that A/Col has made the construction διὰ τοῦ αἵματος τοῦ σταυροῦ αὐτοῦ modelled on Pauline phrases. Contra Coutts 1958, 205, who suggests that A/Col connects together the phrases ἐν τῷ αἵματι τοῦ Χριστοῦ (Eph 2:13) and ἐν ἑνὶ σώματι τῷ θεῷ διὰ τοῦ σταυροῦ (Eph 2:16).

[387] See Bauer 1988, 459; Foerster 1973, 419-420; TLG.

between the parts of the universe which are fighting against each other.[388] It is possible that the idea of making peace in Col is derived from the longing for the stability of the universe which was commonplace in the Hellenistic literature of the time.[389] However, it can also be due to the Jewish idea of peacemaking between God and people, Creator and creature.[390] The phrase ποιήσωμεν εἰρήνην αὐτῷ in Isa 27:5 especially resembles the text of Col.[391]

The analysis of Col 1:15-20 supports my hypothesis. The comparison between Col and other texts has shown that A/Col probably composed Col 1:15-20 by imitating words and phrases familiar to him from the authentic Pauline letters and from the LXX.[392] The occurrence of many characteristics peculiar to A/Col: adding prefixes to Pauline verbs, loosely joined participle constructions and other participle constructions, repeating words and phrases, interpretive appositions, and piling genitives together, defends the interpretation. It does not seem probable that A/Col used Phil 2:6-11 as his primary model[393] because the words and phrases appearing in Col 1:15-20 resemble much more the aforementioned distinct Pauline texts. Accordingly, there is no reason to assume that A/Col included in the text a pre-existing hymn.[394]

---

[388] Philo, Spec Leg II, 192: διὰ τοῦτο καθάπερ ἐπώνυμον ἑορτὴν ὀργάνου πολεμικοῦ σάλπιγγος ἀπέφηνεν ὁ νόμος, ἐπ' εὐχαριστίᾳ τοῦ εἰρηνοποιοῦ θεοῦ καὶ εἰρηνοφύλακος.

[389] So Schweizer 1982, 80-81; DeMaris 1994, 130-131; Gnilka 1980. 75. Cf. Hartman 1985, 49.

[390] So Dunn 1996, 103-104. Cf. Strack & Billerbeck III, 627. See Isa 11:6-9, 65:17,25, Jub 1:29, 23:26-29.

[391] Bauer 1988, 459, and Foerster 1973, 419, note also that in Isa 27:5 Aq. Sym. Theod. εἰρηνοποιήσει appears instead of the LXX ποιήσωμεν εἰρήνην. According to Pokorný 1987, 74, the choice of wording might have been influenced by Isa 57:19: εἰρήνην ἐπ' εἰρήνην τοῖς μακρὰν καὶ τοῖς ἐγγὺς οὖσιν· which in my view does not resemble Col 1:20 as much as Isa 27:5.

[392] Cf. O'Neill 1979, 87-95, who contends that A/Col puts together distinct statements from the public language of the Jewish community to which he belongs. Furthermore, according to O'Neill, the grammar of Col 1:9-23 is odd because of Hebraisms. Similarly A. Aejmelaeus 1992, 216, assumes that 1 Pet 2:21-25 are not based on an already existing early Christian hymn but composed by the author of 1 Pet who uses words and phrases similar to Isa 53 and the Pauline letters.

[393] So Kiley 1986, 76-78, who defends his decision with the following arguments: both texts are of about the same length, they are both used as a basis of the teaching later in the letters, both celebrate the cosmic victory of their central figure, both are edited by the authors of the letters with a reference to the cross. See Standhartinger's criticism on Kiley's interpretation (1999, 88).

[394] Contra E. P. Sanders 1966, 38-39, who explains that Col 1:15-16 seems to depend on 2 Cor 4:4, Rom 1:20, 1 Cor 8:5-6, and Rom 11:36 but leaves open the question whether there existed a hymn or not. Cf. Pokorný 1987, 49 n. 6: "Die Analyse von Sanders ... wonach Kol. 1,15-16 Sätze und Wortverkoppelungen aus 2. Kor. 4,4; Röm. 1,20; 1. Kor. 8,5 f. und Röm. 11,36 enthält, muß nicht zu dem Schluß führen, daß jene zwei Verse durch den Absender unter Anlehnung an Paulus formuliert sind. Wir sehen, daß die Übereinstimmungen die in der hellenistischen Sprache allgemein verbreiteten Phrasen betreffen ...". Goulder 1995, 612 n. 45, also emphasizes that Col 1:15-18 uses the same words and phrases as 2 Cor 4:4, Rom 8:22, 29, 1 Cor 8:5, and 1 Cor 15:20, 24 but assumes the similarity to be the result of the authenticity of Col. Ludwig 1974, 140-141, and Luz 1998, 200, state that Paul and A/Col use similar words because they both knew the same early Christian hymn.

3.2. Reconciliation Accomplished and Applied (Col 1:21-23)

Col 1:21-23

21 Καὶ ὑμᾶς ποτε ὄντας ἀπηλλοτριω-μένους καὶ ἐχθροὺς τῇ διανοίᾳ **ἐν τοῖς** ἔργοις τοῖς πονηροῖς,
22 νυνὶ δὲ ἀποκατήλλαξεν **ἐν** τῷ **σώματι** τῆς **σαρκὸς αὐτοῦ διὰ τοῦ θανάτου παραστῆσαι** ὑμᾶς ἁγίους καὶ ἀμώμους καὶ ἀνεγκλήτους κατενώπιον αὐτοῦ
23 εἴ γε ἐπιμένετε τῇ πίστει τεθεμελιωμένοι καὶ **ἑδραῖοι** καὶ μὴ μετακινούμενοι ἀπὸ τῆς ἐλπίδος τοῦ εὐαγγελίου οὗ ἠκούσατε, τοῦ κηρυχθέντος ἐν **πάσῃ κτίσει** τῇ ὑπὸ τὸν οὐρανόν, οὗ ἐγενόμην ἐγὼ Παῦλος διάκονος.

Rom 5:10-11

10 εἰ γὰρ ἐχθροὶ ὄντες κατηλλάγημεν τῷ θεῷ **διὰ τοῦ θανάτου** τοῦ υἱοῦ αὐτοῦ
...
11 ... Ἰησοῦ Χριστοῦ δι᾽ οὗ νῦν τὴν καταλλαγὴν ἐλάβομεν.

Sir 23:17

ἄνθρωπος πόρνος **ἐν σώματι σαρκὸς αὐτοῦ**

Rom 11:22-23

22 ... ἐὰν ἐπιμένῃς τῇ χρηστότητι ...
23 ... μὴ ἐπιμένωσιν τῇ ἀπιστίᾳ

Ezek 14:4-5

4 ... ἐγὼ κύριος ἀποκριθήσομαι αὐτῷ ἐν οἷς ἐνέχεται ἡ διάνοια αὐτοῦ,
5 ... κατὰ τὰς καρδίας αὐτῶν τὰς ἀπηλλοτριωμένας ἀπ᾽ ἐμοῦ **ἐν τοῖς** ἐνθυμήμασιν αὐτῶν.

2 Cor 11:2

... παρθένον ἁγνὴν **παραστῆσαι** τῷ Χριστῷ·

1 Cor 15:58

... **ἑδραῖοι** γίνεσθε, ἀμετακίνητοι ...

Mk 16:15

... κηρύξατε τὸ εὐαγγέλιον **πάσῃ** τῇ **κτίσει**.

When analyzing verse Col 1:20, it was noted that the verb ἀποκαταλλάσσω seems to depend on the Pauline verb καταλλάσσω. In Col 1:22 it occurs again. Col 1:21-22 very much resembles Rom 5:10-11. Besides the verb (ἀπο)καταλλάσσω, both use the adverb νυν(ί), "now", and the phrases ἐχθροὶ ὄντες, "you were enemies", and διὰ τοῦ θανάτου, "through death", the latter even appearing in the same form. Both texts also emphasize the contrast between once and now: once we were enemies — now we have been reconciled. Since the texts use two similar nouns (ἐχθρός, θάνατος) and two similar verbs (εἰμί, (ἀπο)καταλλάσσω) within two lines in Rom, the resemblance between Col 1:21-22 and Rom 5:10 meets the criteria for a probable literary dependence.[395] The probable dependence of Col

[395] Similarly E. P. Sanders 1966, 39, who emphasizes that "almost every word or phrase" in Col 1:21-22a "which does not come from Rom 5:10 is not to be found in Paul at all". Therefore he assumes that this passage "seems clearly to depend literarily upon Rom 5:10".Cf. Ludwig 1974, 76, who regards Rom 5:10 as a model for Col 1:21-22 which A/Col develops and shapes to fit into his own thought. This explanation, which clearly assumes a literary dependence between Col 1:21-22 and Rom 5:10, clashes with Ludwig's overall interpretation according to which A/Col knows Pauline words and phrases only through oral tradition. Contra Standhartinger 1999, 128-129, who

1:21-22 on Rom 5:10 assures the assumption stated in the previous chapter that the verb ἀποκαταλλάσσω is based on the Pauline verb καταλλάσσω. However, A/Col uses the verb differently from Paul: in Pauline letters, God alone is the subject of καταλλάσσω but, in Col the subject of ἀποκαταλλάσσω is also Christ.[396]

Col 1:22 uses the phrase ἐν τῷ σώματι τῆς σαρκὸς αὐτοῦ, "in the body of his flesh", which is unique in ECL.[397] The same kind of formulation ἐν σώματι σαρκὸς αὐτοῦ occurs once in the LXX, in Sir 23:17.[398] Though the agreement of two usual nouns does not meet the criteria for literary dependence between these texts, it indicates that A/Col may have been acquainted with Sir 23:17 and recalls the exceptional phrase from it.

It is emphasized in Col 1:21 that the Colossians were once doing evil deeds, using the words ἐν τοῖς ἔργοις τοῖς πονηροῖς. A similar phrase ἀπὸ παντὸς ἔργου πονηροῦ occurs in 2 Tim 4:18, which does not, however, suggest any connection between the texts. In addition, these kinds of expressions appear several times in the Johannine literature (Jn 3:19, 7:7, 1 Jn 3:12, 2 Jn 11:2, 3 Jn 10:2). Besides the phrase πονηρὰ τὰ ἔργα, Jn 3:19 also includes other words common to Col: it uses the nouns φῶς and σκότος (cf. Col 1:12-13), and κόσμος (cf. Col 1:6, 2:8,20).[399] However, the use of similar words occurring all over the text of Col does not point to literary dependence between Jn 3:19 and Col. More likely the resemblance is due to the fact that the texts were written approximately at the same time and in the same milieu, Asia Minor: the terms were in the air.

The verb ἀπαλλοτριόω, "to estrange", occurs elsewhere in the Pauline corpus only in Eph 2:12 and 4:18. The noun διάνοια, "mind", is not used in the authentic Pauline letters. However, ἀπαλλοτριόω appears in the LXX occasionally when describing people who are estranged from God (e.g. Ps 58:3, 69:8, Jer 19:4, Ezek 14:4-5,7). Among these, the wording of Ezek 14:4-5 resembles Col 1:21. Besides the verb ἀπαλλοτριόω, both texts use the noun διάνοια. In addition, the structures of the phrases ἐν τοῖς ἐνθυμήμασιν αὐτῶν and ἐν τοῖς ἔργοις τοῖς πονηροῖς resemble each other.[400] It is thus possible that the wording of Col 1:21 is influenced by the use of the verb ἀπαλλοτριόω in the LXX. The use of the verb ἀπαλλοτριόω in Eph 2:12, which probably depends on Col 1:21, also points to the

---

takes the similarity between Col 1:21 and Rom 5:10 to be due to the oral Pauline tradition. Schweizer 1982, 90, and Hübner 1997, 62-63, note the resemblances between Rom 5:10 and Col 1:21-22a and, in addition, Gnilka 1980, 76, emphasizes that Col 1:20, 2 Cor 5:20 and Rom 5:10 include similar thought. None of them assume, however, a literary dependence among the texts.

[396] Büchsel 1974, 258; Lindemann 1983, 31; Luz 1998, 207.

[397] In Col 2:11 this phrase occurs in the form τό σῶμα τῆς σαρκός.

[398] This is noticed also by Schweizer 1982, 91; Gnilka 1980, 90; Dunn 1996, 109; Pokorný 1987, 77; Bruce 1988, 78.

[399] Jn 3:19: τὸ φῶς ἐλήλυθεν εἰς τὸν κόσμον καὶ ἠγάπησαν οἱ ἄνθρωποι μᾶλλον τὸ σκότος ἢ τὸ φῶς· ἦν γὰρ αὐτῶν πονηρὰ τὰ ἔργα.

[400] Also Dunn 1996, 105; Gnilka 1980, 89; and Hartman 1985, 49, refer to Ezek 14:5 as a parallel to Col 1:21.

interpretation. Namely Eph 2:12 describes that when people were estranged they were strangers to the covenants of promise, without God.

The clause παραστῆσαι ὑμᾶς ἁγίους καὶ ἀμώμους καὶ ἀνεγκλήτους κατενώπιον αὐτοῦ, "to present you holy and blameless and irreproachable before him", in Col 1:22b seems to be a complicated construction which A/Col has formed. The words παραστῆσαι ὑμᾶς forms a loosely joined infinitive construction characteristic of A/Col, the same kind of construction he already used in Col 1:10.[401] The adjectives ἅγιος, ἄμωμος, and ἀνέγκλητος all have approximately the same meaning. Typically, then, A/Col is here piling up the synonyms (cf. 1:9, 11).[402] The adverb κατενώπιον appears in the LXX (see Josh 1:5, 3:7, 21:44, 23:9, Dan 5:22) but it does not occur in ECL before Col.[403] Instead, the word ἐνώπιον is utilized when standing before God is described.[404] Since adding prefixes to verbs has been noted to be a characteristic of A/Col, it seems that likewise here he adds a prefix to an adverb.

Besides ἐνώπιον, the verb παρίστημι,"to present", is frequently used in ECL in the context of bringing someone to God or Christ.[405] Nevertheless, there is no close parallel to Col 1:22. It resembles mostly 2 Cor 11:2 which emphasizes the hope that the recipients of the letter are going to be presented pure before Christ.[406] Apart from the use of the verb παρίστημι, verbal agreement indicating literary dependence between the texts is missing.

The adjective ἅγιος is very common in ECL. However, both ἄμωμος and ἀνέγκλητος occur only once in the undisputed letters of Paul, ἄμωμος in Phil 2:15[407] and ἀνέγκλητος in 1 Cor 1:8[408]. The thought of Col 1:22 recalls both Phil 2:15 and 1 Cor 1:8. In Phil 2:15 Paul hopes that the Philippians are going to be "children of God without blemish (ἄμωμα) in the midst of a crooked and perverse generation". In 1 Cor 1:8 Paul promises that God will strengthen the Corinthians so that they may be blameless (ἀνεγκλήτους) on the day of our Lord Jesus Christ. It is thus possible that A/Col recalls the words ἄμωμος and ἀνέγκλητος from these texts. However, Col 1:22 has only one adjective in common with 1 Cor 1:8, as well as with Phil 2:15, which is not enough to indicate a literary dependence between the texts.[409]

---

[401] Similarly Bujard 1973, 57; Lohse 1971, 89.

[402] Lohse 1971, 88.

[403] Later Eph (1:4) follows Col. Cf. Jude 24. For the use of the adverb κατενώπιον in the LXX, see Sollamo 1979, 21, 116, 119, 131.

[404] The adverb ἐνώπιον occurs often in the Gospel of Luke, in Acts and in the Book of Revelation which according to Sollamo 1983 indicates that "the development towards greater use of ἐνώπιον inevitably denotes a gradual increase of the influence of the LXX on the language of the NT."

[405] Lk 2:22, Rom 6:13, 12:1, 14:10, 2 Cor 4:14, 11:2. Similarly in Deut it is described how the levitical priests stand before the Lord, cf. Deut 18:5,7; Gnilka 1980, 91.

[406] Similarly Standhartinger 1999, 129-130, presents 2 Cor 11:2 as a parallel to Col 1:22.

[407] Besides Phil 2:15, it appears in Eph 1:4, 5:27, Heb 9:14, 1 Pet 1:19, Jude 24, Rev 14:5.

[408] It is also used in 1 Tim 3:10 and Titus 1:6.

[409] Similarly Standhartinger 1999, 88, 129. Contra Kiley 1986, 78-79, 82, who assumes that Col 1:22 is dependent on Phil 2:15 because ἄμωμος occurs only in Phil 2:15 in the genuine Pauline

The choice of wording εἴ γε ἐπιμένετε τῇ πίστει, "provided that you continue in the faith", in Col 1:23 resembles the one in Rom 11:22-23, ἐὰν ἐπιμένῃς τῇ χρηστότητι ... ἐὰν μὴ ἐπιμένωσιν τῇ ἀπιστίᾳ, "provided that you continue in kindness ... if they do not continue in unbelief". Similar uses of the verb ἐπιμένω, "to continue", occur a few times in the authentic Pauline letters, e.g. in Rom 6:1, Phil 1:24, and once in deutero-Pauline letters, in 1 Tim 4:16. Thus Col 1:23 seems to begin with Pauline style.[410] The verb θεμελιόω, "to lay the foundation", does not appear in Paul but is ordinary in the OT when describing God's founding activity in creation (e.g. in Ps 8:4 LXX, 23:2, 101:26, Isa 48:13, 51:13) and the establishing of his city on Mt. Zion (e.g. in Ps 47:9 LXX, Isa 14:32). However, Paul speaks a few times about building on a foundation which someone else has laid, using the noun θεμέλιον (see 1 Cor 3:10-12, Rom 15:16-20). Accordingly, the thought that the foundation ought to be well established is familiar to Paul also. Piling up the synonyms τεθεμελιωμένοι, "established", and ἑδραῖοι, "steadfast", in Col 1:23 is, however, a speciality of A/Col.[411]

The closest Pauline parallel to Col 1:23 is 1 Cor 15:58. It includes the exhortation ἑδραῖοι γίνεσθε, ἀμετακίνητοι, "be steadfast, immovable", very similar to the choice of wording ἑδραῖοι καὶ μὴ μετακινούμενοι, "steadfast and not shifting", in Col 1:23. The words common to both texts are very exceptional. The adjective ἑδραῖος appears elsewhere in the Pauline letters only in 1 Cor 7:37. Otherwise, it is used only later in texts of the apostolic fathers (Ign, Pol 3:1 and Ign, Eph 10:2) in ECL. In addition, both the verb μετακινέω and the adjective ἀμετακίνητος are unique in ECL. Although 1 Cor 15:58 includes only one noun (ἑδραῖος) in common with Col 1:23 and the adjective ἀμετακίνητος having the same stem as the verb μετακινέω in Col 1:23, all the words are so rare that the agreement of two words meets the criteria for a possible literary dependence.[412]

The choice of wording εὐαγγελίου ... τοῦ κηρυχθέντος ἐν πάσῃ κτίσει, "the gospel ... which has been proclaimed in all creation", in Col 1:23b resembles very much the exhortation of Jesus in Mk 16:15: κηρύξατε τὸ εὐαγγέλιον πάσῃ τῇ

---

letters and, moreover, both verses follow a hymn.

[410] Gnilka 1980, 91; O'Brien 1982, 69; Dunn 1996, 119.

[411] Similarly Lohse 1971, 88.

[412] Contra Coutts 1958, 201-202, who assumes that Col 1:23a is modelled on Eph 3:17 because in his opinion the dependence of Eph 3:17 on Col is more difficult to explain. He suggests that if Eph depends on Col, the words in Eph 3:17 are derived from Col 1:1:23a (θεμελιόω, πίστις), 2:2 (ἐν ἀγάπῃ), and 2:7 (ῥιζόω, πίστις). In addition, if Col depends on Eph all the words in Col 1:23a, which are common to Eph and Col, (πίστις, θεμελιόω /θεμέλιος), are derived from Eph 3:17. It has to be noted that Coutts' interpretation explains only the source of two words in Col 1:23, of which πίστις is very ordinary in the NT. However, it does not explain at all where the other words in Col 1:23, which are not common to Eph and Col, come from, e.g. ἑδραῖος. Thus the dependence of Eph on Col does not explain the similarities any better than the dependence of Col on Eph. In the commentaries, 1 Cor 15:58 is usually presented as a parallel to Col 1:23 although no literary dependence is assumed; see Dunn 1996, 111; O'Brien 1982, 70; Lohse 1971, 66; R. P. Martin 1981, 68; Pokorný 1987, 78.

κτίσει, "proclaim the gospel to the whole creation".[413] Both use the verb κηρύσσω, the noun εὐαγγέλιον, and the phrase πᾶς κτίσις. Since similar exhortations to preach the good news are ordinary in the Gospels, the resemblance may be due to common parlance. However, none of the Gospel parallels use the phrase πάσῃ τῇ κτίσει (see Mk 13:10, 14:9, Mt 28:18-19, Lk 24:47). In addition, apart from Col 1:23 and Mk 16:15, the verb κηρύσσω does not appear together with the noun κτίσις in ECL before Origen, Contra Celsum II 13, 63, which clearly depends on Col 1:23.[414] Therefore the agreement between Col 1:23b and Mk 16:15, one verb and two nouns, which do not generally appear together, meets the criteria for a possible literary dependence.

It has to be noted, however, that Mk 16:15 belongs to the longer ending of Mk (16:9-20) which was not connected to the Gospel until the second century A.D.[415] Therefore, it is very unlikely that A/Col was acquainted with the text but rather it seems possible that Mk 16:15 depends upon Col 1:23.[416] However, the longer ending of Mk "... even at first glance ... appears to be a collage of a series of resurrection traditions."[417] It is also noteworthy that Mk 16:20 uses three verbs which are not otherwise found in the Gospels but only in the epistles, one of them in Col (συνεργέω in Rom 8:28, 1 Cor 16:16, 2 Cor 6:1, Jas 2:22, βεβαιόω in Rom 15:8, 1 Cor 1:6,8, 2 Cor 1:21, Col 2:7, Heb 2:3, 13:9, ἐπακολουθέω in 1 Tim 5:10,24, 1 Pet 2:21).[418] Therefore, I take it as likely that Mk 16:15 could depend on Col 1:23.

The words "I, Paul, became a servant" (ἐγενόμην ἐγὼ Παῦλος διάκονος) in the end of Col 1:23 do not have a definite model in the authentic Pauline letters. Paul uses often the words ἐγὼ Παῦλος (Gal 5:2, 1 Thess 2:18, Philem 19). In addition, he sometimes calls himself one of the servants, διάκονοι (1 Cor 3:5, 2 Cor 6:4, 11:23) but he never uses the word in the singular like in Col 1:23.[419] Thus the choice of wording ἐγενόμην ἐγὼ Παῦλος διάκονος seems to be a formulation of A/Col which he, as a later writer, uses in order to emphasize the authority of Paul.[420]

---

[413] Similarly O'Brien 1982, 70. Cf. Hartman 1985, 58; Gnilka 1980, 91; Hendriksen 1971, 85; Haapa 1978, 36; Nikolainen 1987, 30.

[414] Similarly Borrett 1967, 323. Origen, Contra Celsum II 13, 63: κεκηρυγμένον τὸ Ἰησοῦ Χριστοῦ εὐαγγέλιον "ἐν πάσῃ κτίσει τῇ ὑπὸ τὸν οὐρανόν".

[415] See e.g. Pesch 1977, 544; Johnson 1960, 266; Gnilka 1979, 352-354.

[416] Cf. Kelhoffer 2000, 192: "although the possibility ... of some borrowing of terms cannot be excluded, there is no indication that Col 1:21-23 directly influenced Mark 16:15.

[417] Mann 1986, 673. Cf. Johnson 1960, 266.

[418] Mann 1986, 676.

[419] Also Schweizer 1982, 96, and Lohse 1971, 67, emphasize this difference.

[420] Cf. Nielsen 1985, 110. Contra Dunn 1996, 112; O'Brien 1982, 71; R. P. Martin 1981, 68-69, according to whom the words show that Col is an authentic Pauline letter.

3.3. The Apostle as a Proclaimer of God's Mystery (Col 1:24-2:5)

Col 1:24

Νῦν χαίρω ἐν τοῖς παθήμασιν ὑπὲρ **ὑμῶν** καὶ ἀνταναπληρῶ τὰ ὑστερήματα τῶν θλίψεων **τοῦ Χριστοῦ ἐν τῇ σαρκί μου** ὑπὲρ **τοῦ σώματος** αὐτοῦ, ὅ **ἐστιν** ἡ ἐκκλησία

Phil 2:30

ὅτι διὰ τὸ ἔργον **Χριστοῦ** μέχρι θανάτου ἤγγισεν ... ἵνα ἀναπληρώσῃ τὸ **ὑμῶν** ὑστέρημα τῆς πρός με λειτουργίας.

1 Cor 7:28

θλῖψιν δὲ **τῇ σαρκὶ** ἕξουσιν

Col 1:18

καὶ αὐτός **ἐστιν** ἡ κεφαλὴ **τοῦ σώματος** τῆς ἐκκλησίας·

2 Cor 7:9

νῦν χαίρω, ... ὅτι ἐλυπήθητε εἰς μετάνοιαν·

2 Cor 1:5

... περισσεύει τὰ παθήματα **τοῦ Χριστοῦ** εἰς ἡμᾶς

Rom 7:18, Gal 4:14

ἐν τῇ σαρκί μου

In Col 1:24-2:5, Christ is described as a mystery of God. The pericope includes two parts, Col 1:24-28 and Col 1:29-2:1, which both also tell about the struggle of the Apostle Paul for the work of Christ. Col 1:24 begins with a characteristic Pauline theme, rejoicing in sufferings (e.g. Rom 5:3, 12:12, 2 Cor 6:10, 7:4, 8:2, 13:9, Phil 2:18, 1 Thess 1:6). In addition, Col 1:24 uses the verb χαίρω to describe Paul's rejoicing for the sake of the recipients of the letter as Paul does in 2 Cor 7:9 and in 7:16 the former of which resembles Col 1:24 more than the latter.

The verb ἀνταναπληρόω employed in Col 1:24 is unique in ECL. Instead, the verb ἀναπληρόω often appears. In 1 Cor 16:17 and Phil 2:30 it is used with the noun ὑστέρημα as its object like the verb ἀνταναπληρόω in Col 1:24.[421] The same phrase "completing what is lacking" also occurs in 2 Cor 9:12, 11:9, only the verb is in a little different form, προσαναπληρόω.[422] Besides using the same phrase, Phil 2:30 resembles Col 1:24 in another way: it describes how Epaphroditus came close to death for the work of Christ while in Col 1:24 Paul is told to suffer for the work of Christ. Therefore it seems possible that A/Col had Phil 2:30 in mind when writing Col 1:24. Since it is typical of him to add prefixes to the Pauline verbs, it is not surprising that he adds the prefix ἀντ- to the verb ἀναπληρόω which does not essentially change the meaning of the verb: ἀναπληρόω means "to fill up" in Phil 2:30 as does ἀνταναπληρόω in Col 1:24.[423] The detail that Col 1:24 does not

---

[421] Similarly Dunn 1996, 116, Ludwig 1974, 86 n. 89, O'Brien 1982, 79-80, and Standhartinger 1999, 131, emphasize the use of the similar phrases in Col 1:24, 1 Cor 16:17, and Phil 2:30.
[422] Lohse 1971, 71 n. 24; Bruce 1988, 81; Gnilka 1980, 97. Cf. Standhartinger 1999, 131
[423] Similarly Gnilka 1980, 97. See Delling 1973, 305, 307; Liddell & Scott 1953, 116, 149; Bauer 1988, 118, 144.

portray the same person as Phil 2:30 does not prevent the literary dependence between the texts, because it is typical of a later writer to use phrases and words in a new sense from the text imitated.[424] The agreement between Col 1:24 and Phil 2:30, the use of two similar nouns and one verb, meets the criteria for a possible literary dependence.[425]

The complicated formulation ἀνταναπληρῶ τὰ ὑστερήματα τῶν θλίψεων τοῦ Χριστοῦ, brings to mind that in his sufferings Paul completes the still incomplete afflictions of Christ, which is surprising. Moreover, it is interesting that the phrase θλίψεων τοῦ Χριστοῦ is unique: the noun θλῖψις does not refer anywhere else in the Pauline letters to Christ's afflictions but instead to those of Paul (e.g. Rom 8:18, 2 Cor 1:8, 2:4, 6:4, 7:4, Phil 4:14). When referring to Christ's afflictions, the phrase τὰ παθήματα τοῦ Χριστοῦ is used (2 Cor 1:5, Phil 3:10). Scholars have tried to solve the problem of the complicated formulation by many different interpretations.[426] The best explanation may be, however, that A/Col as a later writer uses the noun θλῖψις in a different way from the genuine letters and, in addition, after the martyrdom of Paul, wants to protect his uniqueness: the death of Paul completes the afflictions of Christ.[427] Eph 3:13, which seems to depend on Col 1:14, defends this interpretation. There A/Eph interprets the afflictions (θλῖψις) as Paul's.[428]

The fact that A/Col typically imitates Paul's letters adding new formulations supports this interpretation of Col 1:24. Like in Col 1:18, at the end of Col 1:24 the Pauline metaphor of the church as the body of Christ is employed but the relative clause begins with the formulaic phrase ὅ ἐστιν which is typical of A/Col (cf. Col 3:14).[429] It is worthy of note that, besides the aforementioned 2 Cor 7:9 and Phil 2:30, Col 1:24 echoes many texts from the authentic Pauline letters. Both the words ἦμεν ἐν τῇ σαρκί, τὰ παθήματα ... ἐνηργεῖτο in Rom 7:5 and περισσεύει τὰ παθήματα τοῦ Χριστοῦ εἰς ἡμᾶς in 2 Cor 1:5 resemble Col 1:24.[430] Moreover, the words θλῖψιν ... τῇ σαρκὶ ἕξουσιν in 1 Cor 7:28 describing the distress of those who marry are similar to Col 1:24. In addition, the phrase ἐν τῇ σαρκί μου in Col 1:24 is typical of Paul (Rom 7:18, Gal 4:14). Though the resemblances are too slight to indicate a literary dependence, the complicated formulation of Col 1:24

---

[424] Contra Kiley 1986, 87-88.

[425] Similarly Ludwig 1974, 86, mentions the use of the similar phrases ἀνταναπληρῶ τὰ ὑστερήματα + gen in Col 1:24 and Phil 2:30. Moreover, she describes how A/Col revises the text of Phil 2:30 which thus seems to be familiar to him. However, this interpretation clashes again (cf. p. 142 n. 77) with Ludwig's overall interpretation according to which A/Col does not know the genuine letters of Paul but only oral tradition. Contra Standhartinger 1999, 131-132, and Luz 1998, 187-188, who deny the literary dependence.

[426] See Gnilka 1980, 94-98; Schweizer 1982, 101-106; O'Brien 1982, 77-80; Lohse 1971, 69-72; 1965, 210-211; Müller 1988, 228.

[427] Cf. Nielsen 1985, 113; Pfammatter 1987, 67; Standhartinger 1999, 168. See p. 10.

[428] Eph 3:13: διὸ αἰτοῦμαι μὴ ἐγκακεῖν ἐν ταῖς θλίψεσίν μου ὑπὲρ ὑμῶν, ἥτις ἐστὶν δόξα ὑμῶν.

[429] Lohse 1971, 89.

[430] Also O'Brien 1982, 75-76, Dunn 1996, 114; Haapa 1978, 37, and Gnilka 1980, 95 present 2 Cor 1:5 as a parallel to Col 1:24.

seems to be a result of the conflation of many different phrases characteristic of the Pauline letters. Since the choice of wording τὰ ὑστερήματα τῶν θλίψεων τοῦ Χριστοῦ includes a series of dependent genitives noted to be characteristic of A/Col,[431] it clearly is his formulation.

Col 1:25-28

25 ἧς **ἐγενόμην ἐγὼ διάκονος κατὰ τὴν** οἰκονομίαν **τοῦ θεοῦ τὴν δοθεῖσάν μοι** εἰς ὑμᾶς πληρῶσαι τὸν λόγον **τοῦ θεοῦ,**
26 **τὸ μυστήριον** τὸ ἀποκεκρυμμένον ἀπὸ **τῶν αἰώνων** καὶ ἀπὸ τῶν γενεῶν — νῦν δὲ ἐφανερώθη τοῖς ἁγίοις αὐτοῦ,
27 οἷς ἠθέλησεν **ὁ θεὸς** γνωρίσαι τί τὸ πλοῦτος **τῆς δόξης** τοῦ μυστηρίου τούτου ἐν τοῖς ἔθνεσιν, ὅ ἐστιν **Χριστὸς ἐν ὑμῖν, ἡ ἐλπὶς τῆς δόξης·**
28 ὃν ἡμεῖς καταγγέλλομεν νουθετοῦντες πάντα ἄνθρωπον καὶ διδάσκοντες πάντα ἄνθρωπον **ἐν πάσῃ σοφίᾳ**, ἵνα παραστήσωμεν πάντα ἄνθρωπον τέλειον ἐν Χριστῷ·

Col 1:23b

οὗ **ἐγενόμην ἐγὼ** Παῦλος **διάκονος**

1 Cor 4:1

1 οἰκονόμους μυστηρίων **θεοῦ** ...

1 Cor 2:7, 1, 6

7 ἀλλὰ λαλοῦμεν **θεοῦ** σοφίαν ἐν μυστηρίῳ τὴν ἀποκεκρυμμένην, ἣν προώρισεν ὁ θεὸς πρὸ **τῶν αἰώνων** εἰς δόξαν ἡμῶν ...
1 ἦλθον οὐ καθ' ὑπεροχὴν λόγου ἢ σοφίας καταγγέλλων ὑμῖν **τὸ μυστήριον τοῦ θεοῦ** ...

6 Σοφίαν δὲ λαλοῦμεν ἐν τοῖς τελείοις

1 Cor 3:10

Κατὰ τὴν χάριν **τοῦ θεοῦ τὴν δοθεῖσάν μοι**

Rom 9:22-24

22 εἰ δὲ θέλων **ὁ θεὸς** ...
23 ἵνα γνωρίσῃ τὸν πλοῦτον **τῆς δόξης** αὐτοῦ ...

24 ... καὶ ἐξ ἐθνῶν

Rom 8:10, Gal 4:19, 2 Cor 13:5

Χριστὸς ἐν ὑμῖν

Rom 5:2

ἡ ἐλπὶς τῆς δόξης

Col 1:9

ἐν πάσῃ σοφίᾳ

Col 1:22

παραστῆσαι ὑμᾶς ἁγίους καὶ ἀμώμους καὶ ἀνεγκλήτους κατενώπιον αὐτοῦ

In 1:25 A/Col continues to describe the ministry of the Apostle, repeating the words ἐγενόμην ἐγὼ διάκονος, "I became the servant", from Col 1:23.[432] By that

[431] Similarly Lohse 1971, 88. See Col 1:5, 12, 13, 20.
[432] Dunn 1996, 113, emphasizes that the writer picks up the clause "of which I Paul became a minister" from Col 1:23 and fills it out. Cf. Hübner 1997, 67; Nielsen 1985, 110.

means the later writer wants again to emphasize the authority of Paul.[433] The choice of wording "according to God's commission that was given to me" (κατὰ τὴν οἰκονομίαν τοῦ θεοῦ τὴν δοθεῖσάν μοι) does not have a parallel in the Pauline letters. However, in 1 Cor 3:10 occur the words κατὰ τὴν χάριν τοῦ θεοῦ τὴν δοθεῖσάν μοι which are nearly the same.[434] The only difference between the phrases is that in Col 1:25 the commission (οἰκονομία) is mentioned instead of the grace (χάρις) in 1 Cor 3:10.[435] It is noteworthy that the words τὴν χάριν τὴν δοθεῖσαν appear elsewhere a few times in the genuine Pauline letters (Rom 12:6, 15:15, Gal 2:9) and thus seem to form a stock phrase. The other occurrences do not resemble Col 1:25 as much as 1 Cor 3:10, however. Therefore, the use of the identical choice of wording κατὰ τὴν ... τοῦ θεοῦ τὴν δοθεῖσάν μοι suggests a possible literary dependence between Col 1:25 and 1 Cor 3:10.[436]

In addition, the expression "the commission of God" (οἰκονομία τοῦ θεοῦ) which belongs together with the revelation of the mystery mentioned in Col 1:26 echoes 1 Cor 4:1 where Paul describes himself and other teachers as the stewards of God's mysteries (οἰκονόμοι μυστηρίων θεοῦ).[437] Having three nouns in common, the resemblance between Col 1:26 and 1 Cor 4:1 also meets the criteria for a possible literary dependence.

The phrase ὁ λόγος τοῦ θεοῦ, "the word of God", employed in Col 1:25 appears sometimes in the genuine Pauline letters (Rom 9:6, 1 Cor 14:36, 2 Cor 2:17, 4:2)[438]. None of these texts, however, otherwise resemble Col but the best parallel to the choice of wording πληρῶσαι τὸν λόγον τοῦ θεοῦ, "to make the word of God fully known", in Col 1:25 is in Rom 15:19 which similarly emphasizes that the Gospel should be fully proclaimed using the words πεπληρωκέναι τὸ εὐαγγέλιον τοῦ Χριστοῦ.[439] However, the verbal resemblance between the texts does not meet the criteria for literary dependence. It is remarkable that the choice of wording πληρῶσαι τὸν λόγον τοῦ θεοῦ is a loosely joined infinitive construction which is characteristic of Col (cf. 1:10, 22)[440] and thus seems to be a formulation of A/Col.

---

[433] Pokorný 1987, 82; Nielsen 1985, 110. Contra Luz 1998, 209, who assumes that the writer is Paul who wants to maintain his apostolic status to the congregation he does not know personally.
[434] Similarly Dunn 1996, 113, draws attention to the similarity between Col 1:25 and 1 Cor 3:10.
[435] In Eph 3:2 the phrase τὴν οἰκονομίαν τῆς χάριτος τοῦ θεοῦ τῆς δοθείσης μοι εἰς ὑμᾶς is used which seems to be a conflation of Col 1:25 and the Pauline phrases.
[436] Cf. Standhartinger 1999, 132, who does not take the resemblance between Col 1:25 and 1 Cor 3:10 to indicate literary dependence. Hübner 1997, 69, emphasizes the connection between Gal 2:9 and Col 1:25.
[437] Similarly Gnilka 1980, 99. Also Lohse 1971,72, Hartman 1985, 66, O'Brien 1982, 81, R. P. Martin 1981, 71, and Haapa 1978, 38 presents 1 Cor 4:1 as a parallel to Col 1:25.
[438] Cf. Jn 15:25, 18:9: πληρωθῇ ὁ λόγος.
[439] Similarly Lohse 1971, 73; Hübner 1997, 69; Ludwig 1974, 86; Bruce 1988, 84 n. 212; O'Brien 1982, 82; Schweizer 1982, 106; Lindemann 1983; 34; Hartman 1985, 66. Contra Kiley 1986, 90, who emphasizes the similarity between Col 1:25 and Phil 1:14 which is not at all as remarkable as that between Col 1:25 and Rom 15:19.
[440] Similarly Bujard 1973, 57; Lohse 1971, 89.

The description of the mystery in Col 1:26-27 emphasizes the difference "once hidden ... now revealed" like many other letters in the Pauline corpus (1 Cor 2:7-10, Rom 16:25-27, Eph 3:3-10, 1 Tim 3:16, 2 Tim 1:9-10, Titus 1:2), and also e.g. 1 Pet 1:20. In addition to the early Christian letters, in Dan (2:18-19, 27-30) God is seen as a revealer of mysteries (ἔστι θεὸς ἐν οὐρανῷ ἀνακαλύπτων μυστήρια). Thus the description clearly depends on Jewish apocalyptic usage.[441] Because the emphasis between "once hidden ... now revealed" appears commonly in the Pauline corpus, it is often assumed that the texts use the same revelation schema. The beginning of the process is found in 1 Cor 2:7-10 which was then developed in later texts.[442] In addition, 1 Cor 2:7 and Rom 16:25-27 are generally regarded as the closest parallels to Col 1:25-27.[443]

When comparing Col 1:25-27 and 1 Cor 2:7, we notice that their descriptions of the mystery once hidden – now revealed are very much alike. The wording of Col, θεοῦ, τὸ μυστήριον τὸ ἀποκεκρυμμένον ἀπὸ τῶν αἰώνων ... ὁ θεός ... τῆς δόξης, seems to follow the words of 1 Cor, θεοῦ ... ἐν μυστηρίῳ τὴν ἀποκεκρυμμένην ... ὁ θεὸς πρὸ τῶν αἰώνων εἰς δόξαν, even nearly in the same order. Because the phrases ἀπὸ τῶν αἰώνων and ἀπὸ τῶν γενεῶν do not occur anywhere else in the Pauline letters but in Col 1:26, it seems that A/Col prefers the wording ἀπὸ τῶν αἰώνων instead of πρὸ τῶν αἰώνων occurring in 1 Cor 2:7. Besides, he typically adds the synonymous term ἀπὸ τῶν γενεῶν.[444] Since the texts have three nouns (θεός, μυστήριον, δόξα) in common, similar forms from the verb ἀποκρύπτω (passive present perfect participle), and the phrases ἀπὸ τῶν αἰώνων and πρὸ τῶν αἰώνων resembling each other, which even appear within two lines in 1 Cor, the agreement between Col 1:26-27 and 1 Cor 2:7 meets the criteria for a probable literary dependence and thus indicates that the texts not only develop the same revelation schema but also depend on each other.

Although Rom 9:22-24 does not describe the revelation of the mystery like Col 1:27, it is noteworthy that it employs similar words. The choice of wording "God, desiring ... in order to make known the riches of his glory ... also from the Gentiles" (θέλων ὁ θεὸς ... ἵνα γνωρίσῃ τὸν πλοῦτον τῆς δόξης αὐτοῦ ... καὶ ἐξ ἐθνῶν) is in striking agreement with the words "God desired to make known how great among the Gentiles are the riches of the glory" (ἠθέλησεν ὁ θεὸς γνωρίσαι τί τὸ πλοῦτος τῆς δόξης ... ἐν τοῖς ἔθνεσιν) in Col 1:27. Thus Col 1:27 seems to follow Rom 9:22-24. In addition, the rare occurrence of the phrase τὸ πλοῦτος τῆς

---

441 Dunn 1996, 119-120. Cf. Bruce 1988, 85; O'Brien 1982, 84; Hartman 1985, 66; Nikolainen 1987, 32; Haapa 1978, 39; Hübner 1997, 70; Lohse 1971, 74.

442 Lührmann 1965, 117-140; Lindemann 1975, 74; 1979, 118; Schweizer 1982, 107-108; Nikolainen 1987, 32; Lohse 1971, 74 n. 42; Ludwig 1974, 87; Gnilka 1980, 104; Haapa 1978, 39; Hartman 1985, 66; R. P. Martin 1981, 71; Luz 1998, 209. Contra Murphy-O'Connor 1995, 241, who regards Col as an authentic Pauline letter and dates 1 Cor 2:6-9 later than Col 1:27.

443 See O'Brien 1982, 84; Pfammatter 1987, 68; R. E. Brown 1959, 70-72; Dunn 1996, 121; Lindemann 1979, 118.

444 Similarly Lohse 1971, 88; Bujard 1973, 148. Contra Dunn 1996, 119, who emphasizes that the words αἰών and γενεά are often linked in the OT (e.g. Isa 51:9, Sir 24:33, Tobit 1:4).

δόξης supports the literary dependence. It appears elsewhere in the Pauline corpus only in Eph (1:18, 3:16), which is a later text.[445] By connecting the words τοῦ μυστηρίου τούτου to the phrase, A/Col shapes the phrase τὸ πλοῦτος τῆς δόξης τοῦ μυστηρίου τούτου which is a series of dependent genitives characteristic of his style.[446] It is also noteworthy that he uses the phrase "the riches of the glory" in a new context. Since Rom 9:22-24 and Col 1:27 include three nouns (θεός, δόξα, ἔθνος) and two similar verbs (θέλω, γνωρίζω) in common, and both also employ the unique phrase τὸ πλοῦτος τῆς δόξης which, apart from the noun ἔθνος, appear within five lines in Rom even in the same order, the literary dependence between the texts should be classified as probable.

On the grounds of the above-mentioned verbal agreements, Sanders assumes that Col 1:26-27 depends on 1 Cor 2:7 and Rom 9:23-24 but he neglects the resemblance between Col 1:27 and Rom 9:22 (θέλων ὁ θεός // ἠθέλησεν ὁ θεός). Instead, he contends that the choice of wording νῦν δὲ ἐφανερώθη is an imitation of the words φανερωθέντος δὲ νῦν from Rom 16:26 and thus takes Col 1:26 to be the result of the conflation of 1 Cor 2:7, Rom 9:23-24 and 16:25-26.[447] As was already noted in the introduction, the problems in the interpretation of this pericope have primarily caused Sanders' whole thesis on the literary dependence in Colossians to remain a relatively neglected aspect of scholarship. The verbatim agreement has been explained by emphasizing that Col utilizes the revelation schema which had been developed in the tradition or contending that the authors of many texts which are ignorant of each other use the same words. In addition, attention has been drawn to the fact that the date of Rom 16:25-26 is uncertain and thus the text may be later than Col (see p. 20).

It is true that Sanders' interpretation includes some problems. It cannot be ignored that Rom 16:25-27 is regarded as a later addition to the authentic Pauline Rom and thus of unclear date.[448] Sanders himself also refers to the possibility that Rom 16:25-27 is a later addition to Rom[449] but assumes that it more probably is earlier than Col. In addition, he contends that "the other evidence of conflation in Col 1:26-27 makes it unlikely that Rom 16:25 is dependent upon Colossians".[450]

---

[445] Cf. Pokorný 1987, 87. Contra van Roon 1974, 434-435 and Standhartinger 1999, 67. The latter denies the literary dependence between Col 1:27 and Rom 9:23 because Phil 4:19 also uses the phrase τὸ πλοῦτος αὐτοῦ ἐν δόξῃ ἐν Χριστῷ Ἰησοῦ which resembles the phrase τὸ πλοῦτος τῆς δόξης. However, Phil 4:19 does not use exactly the same phrase. In addition, Standhartinger fails to notice that, besides the phrase τὸ πλοῦτος τῆς δόξης, Col 1:27 and Rom 9:23 also use other common words. It is noteworthy that Hübner 1997, 71, O'Brien 1982, 86, and Gnilka 1980, 102 refer to the use of the similar phrase in Col 1:27 and Rom 9:23 although they do not assume the texts depend on each other.

[446] Similarly Lohse 1971, 88; Bujard 1973, 156; O'Brien 1982, 86. Cf. Col 1:5, 12, 13, 20, 24.

[447] E. P. Sanders 1966, 39-40.

[448] About the textual history of Rom 16:25-27, see Wilckens 1978, 22-24; Lindemann 1979, 26-28; Lührmann 1965, 123 n. 4.

[449] He also presents the possibility that A/Col wrote Rom 16:25, if Rom 16:25-27 is a later addition; E. P. Sanders 1966, 40 n. 23.

[450] E. P. Sanders 1966, 40 n. 25.

There is, however, no reason why a text cannot depend on another text which includes conflation. In addition, Sanders contends the word δέ to be so rare in Colossians (appearing five times) that "[i]ts use here may be due only to its having been in the source (Rom 16:25) used by the author of Colossians"[451] but does not mention that the words νυνὶ δέ appear already in Col 1:22 and thus seem to be typical of A/Col.

In spite of the problems in Sanders' interpretation, the verbatim agreement between Col 1:25-27, 1 Cor 2:7, and Rom 9:22-24 is so striking that its significance cannot be denied by saying that many texts use the same words. It is true, however, that the schema of revelation similar to Col 1:26-27, 1 Cor 2:7, and Rom 16:25-27 also appears in many other early Christian texts (Eph 3:3-10, 1 Tim 3:16, 2 Tim 1:9-10, Titus 1:2, and 1 Pet 1:20). It is thus possible that the occurrence of the same words is due to the use of the same tradition. Before continuing to search for the possible models of Col, it is necessary to compare the texts utilizing the same schema to be sure that they all do not resemble each other as much as Col 1:25-27, 1 Cor 2:7, and Rom 9:22-24 do. In addition, the place of Rom 16:25-27 in the development of the revelation schema needs to be defined in order to find out if it is later or earlier than Col.

[451] E. P. Sanders 1966, 40.

1 Cor 2:7, 10

ἀλλὰ λαλοῦμεν θεοῦ σοφίαν ἐν μυστηρίῳ τὴν ἀποκεκρυμμένην, ἣν προώρισεν ὁ θεὸς πρὸ τῶν αἰώνων εἰς δόξαν ἡμῶν ... ἡμῖν δὲ ἀπεκάλυψεν ὁ θεὸς ...

Col 1:25-27

... κατὰ τὴν οἰκονομίαν τοῦ θεοῦ τὴν δοθεῖσάν μοι εἰς ὑμᾶς πληρῶσαι τὸν λόγον τοῦ θεοῦ, τὸ μυστήριον τὸ ἀποκεκρυμμένον ἀπὸ τῶν αἰώνων καὶ ἀπὸ τῶν γενεῶν — νῦν δὲ ἐφανερώθη τοῖς ἁγίοις αὐτοῦ, οἷς ἠθέλησεν ὁ θεὸς γνωρίσαι τί τὸ πλοῦτος τῆς δόξης τοῦ μυστηρίου τούτου ἐν τοῖς ἔθνεσιν, ὅ ἐστιν Χριστὸς ἐν ὑμῖν, ἡ ἐλπὶς τῆς δόξης·

Rom 16:25-27
... κατὰ ἀποκάλυψιν μυστηρίου χρόνοις αἰωνίοις σεσιγημένου, φανερωθέντος δὲ νῦν διά τε γραφῶν προφητικῶν κατ' ἐπιταγὴν τοῦ αἰωνίου θεοῦ εἰς ὑπακοὴν πίστεως εἰς πάντα τὰ ἔθνη γνωρισθέντος, ... ἡ δόξα εἰς τοὺς αἰῶνας, ἀμήν.

1 Tim 3:16
... μυστήριον· ὃς ἐφανερώθη ἐν σαρκί, ἐδικαιώθη ἐν πνεύματι, ὤφθη ἀγγέλοις, ἐκηρύχθη ἐν ἔθνεσιν, ἐπιστεύθη ἐν κόσμῳ, ἀνελήμφθη ἐν δόξῃ.

2 Tim 1:9-10
... καλέσαντος κλήσει ἁγίᾳ, ... κατὰ ... χάριν, τὴν δοθεῖσαν ἡμῖν ἐν Χριστῷ Ἰησοῦ πρὸ χρόνων αἰωνίων, φανερωθεῖσαν δὲ νῦν ...

Titus 1:2-3
ἐπ' ἐλπίδι ζωῆς αἰωνίου, ἣν ἐπηγγείλατο ὁ ἀψευδὴς θεὸς πρὸ χρόνων αἰωνίων, ἐφανέρωσεν δὲ καιροῖς ἰδίοις τὸν λόγον αὐτοῦ ἐν κηρύγματι

1 Pet 1:19-21
... Χριστοῦ, προεγνωσμένου μὲν πρὸ καταβολῆς κόσμου φανερωθέντος δὲ ἐπ' ἐσχάτου τῶν χρόνων δι' ὑμᾶς ... καὶ δόξαν αὐτῷ δόντα

Eph 3:2-10, 16
... τὴν οἰκονομίαν τῆς χάριτος τοῦ θεοῦ τῆς δοθείσης μοι εἰς ὑμᾶς ... ὃ ἑτέραις γενεαῖς οὐκ ἐγνωρίσθη ... νῦν ἀπεκαλύφθη τοῖς ἁγίοις ἀποστόλοις αὐτοῦ ... οὗ ἐγενήθην διάκονος κατὰ τὴν δωρεὰν τῆς χάριτος τοῦ θεοῦ τῆς δοθείσης μοι ...
... ἐδόθη ἡ χάρις αὕτη, τοῖς ἔθνεσιν εὐαγγελίσασθαι τὸ ἀνεξιχνίαστον πλοῦτος τοῦ Χριστοῦ καὶ φωτίσαι [πάντας] τίς ἡ οἰκονομία τοῦ μυστηρίου τοῦ ἀποκεκρυμμένου ἀπὸ τῶν αἰώνων ἐν τῷ θεῷ ...
ἵνα γνωρισθῇ νῦν ...
ἵνα δῷ ὑμῖν κατὰ τὸ πλοῦτος τῆς δόξης ...

As was already commented upon, Col 1:26 seems to follow 1 Cor 2:7. It is worth noting that instead of the verb ἀποκαλύπτω employed in 1 Cor 2:10, the verb φανερόω occurs in Col. Because the verb ἀποκαλύπτω, as well as the noun ἀποκάλυψις, do not appear at all in Col but the verb φανερόω occurs four times, it seems that A/Col prefers to use his typical verb.

Eph 3:9 uses the words τὸ μυστήριον τὸ ἀποκεκρυμμένον ἀπὸ τῶν αἰώνων which resemble both 1 Cor 2:7 and Col 1:26. Since the words are exactly the same as in Col 1:26, there is no reason to assume that Eph imitates 1 Cor 2:7 like Col but since it depends on Col, it more probably copies the words from Col 1:26. The choice of wording ἵνα γνωρισθῇ νῦν ... τὸ πλοῦτος τῆς δόξης in Eph 3:2-10, 16 seems to follow Col 1:25-27. A/Eph also employs many phrases and words which A/Col uses but which are not in the text of 1 Cor. The words κατὰ τὴν οἰκονομίαν τοῦ θεοῦ τὴν δοθεῖσάν μοι εἰς ὑμᾶς from Col 1:25 are used twice: in Eph 3:2 (τὴν οἰκονομίαν τῆς χάριτος τοῦ θεοῦ τῆς δοθείσης μοι εἰς ὑμᾶς) and in 3:7 (κατὰ τὴν δωρεὰν τῆς χάριτος τοῦ θεοῦ τῆς δοθείσης μοι). In addition, like in Col 1:26, it is told that the mystery is revealed to the saints (τοῖς ἁγίοις) in Eph 3:5 and both texts also mention the Gentiles, ἔθνη (Col 1:27 // Eph 3:8). Both Col and Eph also emphasize that the revelation happens now, νῦν (Col 1:26 // Eph 3:5) and connects the revelation to the work of Christ (Col 1:27 // Eph 3:8). Furthermore, Eph 3:16 picks up the phrase τὸ πλοῦτος τῆς δόξης from Col 1:27 as well as the verb γνωρίζω in Eph 3:10. Besides the similarities, there is also one interesting difference between Col and Eph. The verb φανερόω, typical of A/Col, does not appear in Eph at all. Instead, A/Eph uses the verb ἀποκαλύπτω like 1 Cor.

Rom 16:25-27 employs the noun ἀποκάλυψις which has the same stem as the verb ἀποκαλύπτω used in 1 Cor 2:7. In addition, the nouns δόξα and θεός which, however, are very customary in ECL, appear in both texts. Though the choice of wording μυστηρίου χρόνοις αἰωνίοις σεσιγημένου in Rom 16:25 resembles the words ἐν μυστηρίῳ τὴν ἀποκεκρυμμένην ... πρὸ τῶν αἰώνων in 1 Cor 2:7, the words τὸ μυστήριον τὸ ἀποκεκρυμμένον ἀπὸ τῶν αἰώνων in Col 1:27 are clearly a closer parallel to 1 Cor 2:7. Accordingly, it does not seem probable that Rom 16:25-27 depends directly on 1 Cor.

It is also noteworthy that Rom 16:25-27 does not seem to follow Eph 3:2-10, 16 because it does not use any phrases similar to Eph but instead similar to Col. As Sanders already noticed, above all, the words φανερωθέντος δὲ νῦν in Rom 16:26 and νῦν δὲ ἐφανερώθη in Col 1:26 resemble each other (see pp. 108-109). Thus it seems possible that Col 1:25-27 and Rom 16:25-27 depend on each other but it is not easy to say at first glance which one is earlier. It is remarkable that Rom 16:25 uses the phrase χρόνοις αἰωνίοις instead of ἀπὸ τῶν αἰώνων which appears in Col 1:26 and Eph 3:9. A similar phrase (πρὸ χρόνων αἰωνίων) also appears in 2 Tim 1:9 and Titus 1:2. Accordingly, the use of the phrase χρόνοις αἰωνίοις indicates that Rom 16:25-27 belongs to the same group as the Pastoral letters and is thus later than Col. Like Eph 3, Rom 16:25-27 includes much more verbal agreement with Col 1:25-27 than the Pastorals. Thus it seems probable that Rom

16:25-27, as a closer parallel to Col, is earlier than the Pastorals but it is not self-evident: a later parallel can copy the text verbatim as well. It is also noteworthy that, like Col 1:25 and Rom 16:26, 1 Tim 3:16, 2 Tim 1:9-10, Titus 1:2-3, and 1 Pet 1:19-21 all use the verb φανερόω which does not appear at all in Eph. Accordingly, all texts representing the revelation schema do not utilize similar words which indicates that those which use them depend on the others. The development seem to be the following: first, A/Col imitated 1 Cor 2:7, then both A/Eph and the author of Rom 16:25-27 followed Col 1:25-27 and later the Pastoral letters and 1 Pet continues the same tradition as Col and Rom 16:25-27.

It has been noted that the other texts which use the same revelation schema as Col do not similarly repeat the words of 1 Cor 2:7 nor do they imitate Rom 9:22-24. Though in Eph 3:8-16 the words τοῖς ἔθνεσιν ... ἵνα γνωρισθῇ νῦν ... τὸ πλοῦτος τῆς δόξης occur, resembling Rom 9:22-24, A/Eph rather seems to imitate Col. The words εἰς πάντα τὰ ἔθνη γνωρισθέντος in Rom 16:26 do not resemble Rom 9:23-24 at all so strikingly as the choice of wording in Col 1:27. Only the use of the final clause ἵνα γνωρισθῇ points to the possibility that A/Eph also follows Rom 9:22-24 in addition to Col 1:25-28. Accordingly, the use of the same words in Col, 1 Cor, and Rom is hardly due to the use of the same tradition only but rather indicates that Col 1:25-27 depends on 1 Cor 2:7 and Rom 9:23-24. In addition, Rom 16:25-27 seems to be later than Col 1:25-26 and thus not a model for it but vice versa.

The dependence between Col 1 and 1 Cor 2 can be seen even clearer when comparing Col 1:28 and 1 Cor 2:1,6 (see p. 106). Both Col 1:28 and 1 Cor 2:1 describe the mystery of God, similarly mentioning the proclaiming in wisdom using the verb καταγγέλλω to which A/Col typically connects the synonyms διδάσκω and νουθετέω.[452] It is also possible that the phrase λόγου ἢ σοφίας occurring in 1 Cor 2:1 influences A/Col to use the phrase ὁ λόγος τοῦ θεοῦ in Col 1:25 and the phrase ἐν πάσῃ σοφίᾳ in Col 1:28. In addition, the adjective τέλειος is used in 1 Cor 2:6, like in Col 1:28.[453] However, it is remarkable that the deutero-Pauline A/Col uses neither τέλειος nor σοφία ironically as Paul does in 1 Cor.[454] The phrase ἐν πάσῃ σοφίᾳ, which was already used in Col 1:9, describes positively the teaching in all wisdom as do the words παρίστημι + τέλειος. The verb παρίστημι was already used in Col 1:22 about the presenting of the people before Christ. Since the distance between 1 Cor 2:1 and 1 Cor 2:7 is more than five lines in the Nestle & Aland version, their agreements with Col must be handled separately. However, like the agreement between Col 1:25-27 and 1 Cor 2:7, also that between Col 1:25-28 and 1 Cor 2:1, the use of one verb (καταγγέλλω) and

[452] Cf. Col 1:9, 11, 22, 23, 26.
[453] Kiley 1986, 89, emphasizes the similarity of Col 1:28 to Phil 3:15 which also employs the adjective τέλειος but, however, does not resemble Col 1:28 as much as 1 Cor 2:1,6-7.
[454] Cf. Gnilka 1980, 104.

four nouns (λόγος, σοφία, μυστήριον, θεός) in common, meets the criteria for a probable literary dependence.

The mystery is described by the words ὅ ἐστιν Χριστὸς ἐν ὑμῖν, ἡ ἐλπὶς τῆς δόξης, "which is Christ in/among you, the hope of glory" in Col 1:27. Since the phrase Χριστὸς ἐν ὑμῖν occurs in Rom 8:10, Gal 4:19, and 2 Cor 13:5 and, in addition, the phrase ἡ ἐλπὶς τῆς δόξης appears in Rom 5:2, A/Col seems to connect two Pauline phrases together here, like in Col 1:20, (see p. 97).

Col 1:29-2:1	1 Cor 4:12	1 Cor 9:25
29 εἰς **ὃ καὶ** κοπιῶ **ἀγωνιζόμενος κατὰ τὴν ἐνέργειαν αὐτοῦ** τὴν ἐνεργουμένην **ἐν ἐμοὶ** ἐν δυνάμει.	**καὶ** κοπιῶμεν ἐργαζόμενοι ...	πᾶς δὲ **ὁ ἀγωνιζόμενος** ...
	Phil 3:21	Phil 2:13
	... τῆς δόξης **αὐτοῦ κατὰ τὴν ἐνέργειαν** ...	ὁ ἐνεργῶν **ἐν** ὑμῖν
		Phil 4:13
	1 Cor 11:3	
		ἐν τῷ ἐνδυναμοῦντί με
1 **Θέλω** γὰρ **ὑμᾶς εἰδέναι** ἡλίκον **ἀγῶνα** ἔχω ὑπὲρ ὑμῶν καὶ τῶν ἐν Λαοδικείᾳ καὶ ὅσοι οὐχ ἑόρακαν τὸ πρόσωπόν μου **ἐν σαρκί**,	**Θέλω** δὲ **ὑμᾶς εἰδέναι** ...	Phil 1:30
	Gal 1:22	τὸν αὐτὸν **ἀγῶνα** ἔχοντες
	ἤμην δὲ ἀγνούμενος τῷ προσώπῳ ταῖς ἐκκλησίαις τῆς Ἰουδαίας ...	Rom 8:9 etc
		ἐν σαρκί

The struggle of the Apostle is described again in Col 1:29, like in Col 1:24. A/Col employs the verb κοπιάω, "to work hard", which is also regularly used in the authentic Pauline letters for the hard work of the ministry.[455] In addition, it utilizes the metaphor of the athletic contest typical of Paul. The choice of wording in Col 1:29 (εἰς ὃ καὶ κοπιῶ ἀγωνιζόμενος) resembles both that in 1 Cor 4:12 (καὶ κοπιῶμεν ἐργαζόμενοι) and the one in 1 Cor 9:25 (πᾶς δὲ ὁ ἀγωνιζόμενος) and thus may be a result of the conflation of them. Similarly, the choice of wording κατὰ τὴν ἐνέργειαν αὐτοῦ τὴν ἐνεργουμένην ἐν ἐμοὶ ἐν δυνάμει could be a combination of the Pauline phraseology used in Phil 3:21 (τῆς δόξης αὐτοῦ κατὰ τὴν ἐνέργειαν), in Phil 2:13 (ὁ ἐνεργῶν ἐν ὑμῖν), and in Phil 4:13 (ἐν τῷ ἐνδυναμοῦντί με). It is noteworthy that A/Col typically connects the noun

---

[455] Dunn 1996, 126; O'Brien 1982, 90; Gnilka 1980, 104-105.

ἐνέργεια and the verb ἐνεργέω which have the same stem.[456] In addition, in the phrase ἐν ἐμοὶ ἐν δυνάμει a noun is attached to a phrase with the preposition ἐν which is characteristic of A/Col.[457] Though the verbal agreements between Col 1:29 and the Pauline texts are too slight to indicate a literary dependence on any specific verse, A/Col clearly seems to imitate the Pauline style by conflating phrases characteristic of Paul.[458] However, he adapts the phrases to fit to his own style by connecting them together in complicated combinations.

Col 2:1, like Col 1:24 and 29, tells about the struggle of the Apostle. In addition, in Col 2:1-5 the purpose of his ministry is again, as in Col 1:25-27, described as the knowledge of the mystery of God. Thus verses 1:24-2:5 are taken as a unit even by those scholars who divide the passage into two sections, Col 1:24-29 and Col 2:1-5.[459] Col 2:1 begins with the words Θέλω γὰρ ὑμᾶς εἰδέναι, "for I want you to know", utilizing a Pauline formula, a "disclosure form" which generally appears in the transition from the opening epistolary thanksgiving to the body in the letters.[460] A "disclosure form" generally includes the verb παρακαλέω but sometimes θέλω is used, as in Col 2:1 (cf. Rom 1:13, 11:25, 1 Cor 10:1, 11:3, 2 Cor 1:8, 1 Thess 4:13, 5:12).[461]

However, it is noteworthy that the words θέλω γὰρ ὑμᾶς εἰδέναι in Col 2:1 are almost identical with the words θέλω δὲ ὑμᾶς εἰδέναι in 1 Cor 11:3, a unique phrase: the other disclosures do not bear the same resemblance.[462] In addition, Col 2:1 and 1 Cor 11:3 are the only occurrences which lack the vocative address, generally ἀδελφοί.[463] Because the "disclosure form" belongs to the literary style of the letters, it is problematic to assume that the occurrence of the same phrase is due to the tradition used in the conversations of the Pauline school.[464] Though Col 2:1 and 1 Cor 11:3 have only two verbs in common (θέλω, οἶδα), the similarity

---

456 Similarly Lohse 1971, 88.Cf. Col 1:11. Dunn 1996, 127 assumes that A/Col uses the semitic doubling of noun and verb.

457 See Col 1:6, 8, 12. Similarly Bujard 1973, 29; Lohse 1971, 88.

458 Many scholars present especially 1 Cor 4:12, 9:25, Phil 2:13, 3:21, 4:13 as parallels to Col 1:29 although they do not assume a literary dependence; see Gnilka 1980, 104-105; Pokorný 1987, 88; O'Brien 1982, 90-91; R. P. Martin 1981, 73; Hartman 1985, 68; Ludwig 1974, 87-88; Kiley 1986, 90; Wilson 1997, 73; Hübner 1997, 72-73.

459 See Lindemann 1983, 33-38; Hendriksen 1971, 101; Schweizer 1982, 115; Pokorný 1987, 89; Dunn 1996, 128.

460 Standhartinger 1999, 118-119; O'Brien 1982, 74, following Mullins 1964 who termed this a "disclosure form". The formulas were also studied by J. T. Sanders 1962.

461 See J. T. Sanders 1962, 349 ff.

462 Besides the disclosures, the words θέλω ὑμᾶς followed by an infinitive also occur in 1 Cor 7:32, 10:20, 14:5, 16:7 which, however, do not resemble Col 2:1 as much as 1 Cor 11:3.

463 Mullins 1964, 48.

464 So Ludwig 1974, 42, who assumes that A/Col knew the formula either from the tradition used in the conversations of the Pauline school or from popular philosophy. However, she also suggests that the phrase θέλω γὰρ ὑμᾶς εἰδέναι utilizes 1 Cor 11:3 verbatim ("die Redewendung θέλω γὰρ ὑμᾶς εἰδέναι benützt Paulus wortwörtlich in 1.Kor 11,3") and thus accepts the literary dependence between Col 2:1 and 1 Cor 11:3.

between the disclosure forms compared to other texts indicates a possible literary dependence between the texts.[465]

Col 2:1 utilizes the same metaphor of the athletic contest as the preceding verse, now employing the phrase ἀγῶνα ἔχω which also occurs in Phil 1:30. Though the verbal agreement between the verses does not meet the criteria for literary dependence, A/Col evidently imitates the style of Paul as he did in Col 1:29 and he may also recall Phil 1:30.[466]

The phrase "seeing someone's face" used in Col 2:1 is typical of Paul (cf. 1 Cor 13:12, 2 Cor 10:7, Gal 1:22, 2:11, 1 Thess 2:17, 3:10). From the Pauline parallels, Gal 1:22 which describes how Paul was unknown by sight to some congregations resembles Col 2:1 most. Though the phrase ἐν σαρκί also occurs routinely in the Pauline letters,[467] the choice of wording πρόσωπόν μου ἐν σαρκί used in Col 2:1 is unique. Since it resembles the words ἐν τῇ σαρκί μου used earlier in Col (1:24), it seems to be a formation of A/Col. It refers to the situation after Paul's death when one can no longer see his face[468] and points to the interpretation that Col "is written for all who have not seen Paul's face".[469]

[465] Though many scholars present 1 Cor 11:3 as the closest parallel to Col 2:1 and some of them emphasize the verbatim agreement between the texts, none of them, however, assume the texts to depend on each other; see Hübner 1997, 73: "fast wörtlich in 1Kor 11,3"; Lindemann 1983, 36: "wörtliche Übereinstimmung". Cf. Schweizer 1982, 115; Gnilka 1980, 108; R. P. Martin 1981, 74; Haapa 1978, 40; Hartman 1985, 68.

[466] Cf. Kiley 1986, 89: "The ἀγών of the Apostle in Phil 1.30 is reflected in his ἀγών at Col 1.29-2.1."

[467] See Rom 7:5, 8:3 (ἐν τῇ σαρκί), Rom 8:8-9, 2 Cor 10:3, Gal 2:20, 6:12, Phil 1:22, 3:3-4, Philem 16 (ἐν σαρκί)

[468] Cf. Standhartinger 1998, 281; Nielsen 1985, 107.

[469] Nielsen 1985, 114.

Col 2:2-3

2 ἵνα παρακληθῶσιν αἱ καρδίαι αὐτῶν συμβιβασθέντες ἐν ἀγάπῃ καὶ **εἰς** πᾶν πλοῦτος τῆς πληροφορίας τῆς συνέσεως, εἰς **ἐπίγνωσιν** τοῦ μυστηρίου **τοῦ θεοῦ**, Χριστοῦ,
3 ἐν ᾧ εἰσιν πάντες οἱ θησαυροὶ τῆς **σοφίας καὶ γνώσεως** ἀπόκρυφοι.

2 Thess 2:17

παρακαλέσαι ὑμῶν τὰς καρδίας ...

Col 1:27

τὸ πλοῦτος τῆς δόξης τοῦ μυστηρίου

1 Cor 2:1

... λόγου ἢ **σοφίας** καταγγέλλων ὑμῖν τὸ μυστήριον **τοῦ θεοῦ**.

Rom 11:33

Ὦ βάθος πλούτου καὶ **σοφίας καὶ γνώσεως θεοῦ**·

Prov 2:2-6

2 ...παραβαλεῖς καρδίαν σου εἰς σύνεσιν,...
4 ... καὶ ὡς θησαυροὺς ἐξερευνήσῃς αὐτήν,
5 τότε συνήσεις φόβον κυρίου καὶ **ἐπίγνωσιν θεοῦ** εὑρήσεις.
6 ὅτι κύριος δίδωσιν σοφίαν, καὶ ἀπὸ προσώπου αὐτοῦ γνῶσις καὶ σύνεσις·

Sir 1:25

Ἐν θησαυροῖς **σοφίας** παραβολαὶ ἐπιστήμης

The teaching of the mystery started in Col 1:25-28 continues in Col 2:2. Instead of the perfect passive participle τὸ ἀποκεκρυμμένον, "kept concealed", used in Col 1:26, the adjective ἀπόκρυφος, "stored up" is employed in Col 2:3.[470] The definition of the mystery also differs a little: in Col 1:27 the mystery is Christ in you (Χριστὸς ἐν ὑμῖν) but in Col 2:2 it is Christ himself.[471] In the beginning of Col 2:2 is an exhortation to encourage the hearts (ἵνα παρακληθῶσιν αἱ καρδίαι αὐτῶν) which does not have a parallel in the authentic Pauline letters but appears in Col 4:8 (παρακαλέσῃ τὰς καρδίας ὑμῶν), in Eph 6:22 (παρακαλέσῃ τὰς καρδίας ὑμῶν), and in 2 Thess 2:17 (παρακαλέσαι ὑμῶν τὰς καρδίας). Thus it seems to be a characteristic of deutero-Pauline letters.[472] As was noted in the introduction, Eph seems to depend on Col but it is not as clear whether 2 Thess is earlier or later than Col. Therefore, it is possible that Col 2:2 echoes 2 Thess 2:17.

In addition, the phrase συμβιβάζω ἐν ἀγάπῃ in Col 2:2 has the closest parallel in a letter later than Col, in Eph 4:16.[473] Although in Eph 4:16 twenty words are added between the verb συμβιβάζω and the words ἐν ἀγάπῃ, it seems to be possible that Eph 4:16 depends on Col 2:2. Thus most scholars take the verb

---

[470] O'Brien 1982, 95.
[471] Pokorný 1987, 89-90.
[472] Similarly Dunn 1996, 130, mentions that the use of the phrase "is confined to the disputed Paulines".
[473] Eph 4:16: ... συμβιβαζόμενον διὰ πάσης ἁφῆς τῆς ἐπιχορηγίας κατ' ἐνέργειαν ἐν μέτρῳ ἑνὸς ἑκάστου μέρους τὴν αὔξησιν τοῦ σώματος ποιεῖται εἰς οἰκοδομὴν ἑαυτοῦ ἐν ἀγάπῃ.

συμβιβάζω in the sense of "unite" similarly to Eph 4:16 and interpret the unique phrase συμβιβάζω ἐν ἀγάπῃ to mean "being knit together".[474]

The complicated choice of wording πᾶς πλοῦτος τῆς πληροφορίας τῆς συνέσεως, "all riches of full assurance of understanding", in Col 2:2 is unique in ECL. It resembles the words τὸ πλοῦτος τῆς δόξης τοῦ μυστηρίου which appeared in Col 1:27, both including a series of dependent genitives typical of A/Col[475], and thus seems to be a formation of A/Col. Similarly, the choice of wording εἰς ἐπίγνωσιν τοῦ μυστηρίου τοῦ θεοῦ in Col 2:2, consisting of a series of dependent genitives, seems to be the style of A/Col.[476]

Although the expression τὸ μυστήριον τοῦ θεοῦ, "the mystery of God", used in Col 2:2 did not occur in Col 1:25-28, it is remarkable that it appears in 1 Cor 2:1 and 4:1, which A/Col seems to imitate in Col 1:25-28, but nowhere else in the Pauline corpus. It seems that now, when describing the mystery again, A/Col remembers the phrase τὸ μυστήριον τοῦ θεοῦ which is familiar to him from 1 Cor 2:1 and 4:1.

The words "the treasures of wisdom and knowledge" (οἱ θησαυροὶ τῆς σοφίας καὶ γνώσεως) in Col 2:3 do not have a parallel in ECL. It is also worth noting that the term θησαυρός occurs elsewhere in the Pauline corpus only in 2 Cor 4:7 which does not otherwise resemble Col 2:3.[477] However, the term θησαυρός, as well as the terms μυστήριον, σοφία, ἐπίγνωσις, γνῶσις, and σύνεσις used in Col 2:2-3, evokes Jewish wisdom tradition. Like Col 2:2-3, Isa 45:3 tells about treasures which are hidden.[478] Moreover, Sir 41:14 mentions hidden wisdom and unseen treasure.[479] The closest parallel to Col 2:3 is Sir 1:25 which employs the same phrase "treasures of wisdom" (οἱ θησαυροὶ τῆς σοφίας). Though the use of two similar nouns which also occur often in the LXX is not sufficient evidence to point to literary dependence between the texts, it is possible that A/Col is familiar with Sir 1:25 and he adds the words "and knowledge" (καὶ γνώσεως) to the phrase "the treasures of wisdom".[480]

Like in Col 2:3, wisdom and knowledge are connected in Rom 11:33: "O the depth of the riches and wisdom and knowledge of God" (Ὦ βάθος πλούτου καὶ

---

474 O'Brien 1982, 93. Cf. R. P. Martin 1981, 75; Hendriksen 1971, 103.

475 Similarly Bujard 1973, 156; Lohse 1971, 88. See Col 1:5, 12, 13, 18, 20, 24, 27.

476 Similarly Lohse 1971, 88.

477 2 Cor 4:7: Ἔχομεν δὲ τὸν θησαυρὸν τοῦτον ἐν ὀστρακίνοις σκεύεσιν.

478 Isa 45:3: καὶ δώσω σοι θησαυροὺς σκοτεινούς, ἀποκρύφους ἀοράτους ἀνοίξω σοι, ἵνα γνῷς ... E.g. Schnabel 1985, 259; Dunn 1996, 132; R. P. Martin 1981, 76; Gnilka 1980, 111; Hartman 1985, 69; Lindemann 1983, 37; Pfammatter 1987, 69; Müller 1988, 233; Wilson 1997, 127, and Schweizer 1982, 118 n. 6, present Isa 45:3 as a parallel to Col 2:2-3.

479 Sir 41:14: σοφία δὲ κεκρυμμένη καὶ θησαυρὸς ἀφανής. Cf. Philo, Cong 127.6: ὥσπερ θησαυρόν τινα σοφίας μόνος ἀνευρηκώς. Plato, Phileb 15e: ἡσθεὶς ὥς τινα σοφίας ηὑρηκὼς θησαυρόν.

480 Cf. Bruce 1988, 91 n. 12; Hendriksen 1971, 105. Also Strack & Billerbeck III, 627; Dunn 1996, 132; R. P. Martin 1981, 76 n. 6; Müller 1988, 233; Schweizer 1982, 118, present Sir 1:25 as a parallel to Col 2:3.

σοφίας καὶ γνώσεως θεοῦ).[481] It is also noteworthy that in both texts the words occur exactly in the same form σοφίας καὶ γνώσεως. Since Col 2:2-3 and Rom 11:33 both also use the noun θεός and thus have three nouns in common, the verbal agreement between Col 2:2-3 and Rom 11:33 meets the criteria for a possible literary dependence. Accordingly, Col 2:3 may conflate Sir 1:25 and Rom 11:33.[482]

The resemblance between Col 2:2-3 and Prov 2:2-6 is also noteworthy. Both texts begin similarly with an exhortation to hear the advice. While according to Prov 2:2, the heart should be inclined to understanding (παραβαλεῖς καρδίαν σου εἰς σύνεσιν), the hearts should be encouraged so that they may have understanding (ἵνα παρακληθῶσιν αἱ καρδίαι αὐτῶν ... εἰς πᾶν πλοῦτος τῆς πληροφορίας τῆς συνέσεως) in Col 2:2. Thus it seems possible that A/Col follows Prov 2:2 but adds his typical series of dependent genitives (πᾶν πλοῦτος τῆς πληροφορίας) in order to define the understanding. Similarly, both texts use the words ἐπίγνωσιν θεοῦ but A/Col adds the preposition εἰς before it because the phrase εἰς ἐπίγνωσιν is one of his characteristic expressions: it is used later in Col 3:10. In addition, he inserts τοῦ μυστηρίου τοῦ between ἐπίγνωσιν and θεοῦ. It is also remarkable that both Col 2:2-3 and Prov 2:2-6 describe wisdom and understanding using the same terms σύνεσις, ἐπίγνωσις, θησαυρός, σοφία, and γνῶσις. Though only those agreements in Prov 2:4-6 occur within as short a space as five lines in the Nestle & Aland version, the five nouns in common meets the criteria for a probable literary dependence. All the terms used are standard in wisdom literature, however, and, in addition, occur in other texts which may be imitated here, except σύνεσις and ἐπίγνωσις which are typical of A/Col (see Col 1:9-10). Accordingly, the verbal agreement between Col 2:2-3 and Prov 2:2-6 should be classified as a possible literary dependence only.[483]

---

[481] Also e.g. O'Brien 1982, 95; R. P. Martin 1981, 75; and Dunn 1996, 132, present Rom 11:33 as a parallel to Col 2:3.

[482] Contra Kiley 1986, 94, who sees the resemblance between Col 2:3 and Rom 11:33 as a result of some sort of acquaintance with Paul's language from the Pauline tradition. In addition, he emphasizes that the words πλοῦτος, σοφία, and γνῶσις occur both in Col 2:2-3 and in Rom 11:33 in the same order. It is odd that Kiley does not assume a literary dependence between Col 2:2-3 and Rom 11:33 because, as noted in the introduction, he himself presents the occurrence of the words in the same order as a criterion for literary dependence. Similar to Kiley, Ludwig 1974, 43, 89, suggests that A/Col was acquainted with the same triad πλοῦτος–σοφία–γνῶσις as Paul. However, there remains the question of why the triad does not appear anywhere else in the Pauline letters.

[483] Cf. R. P. Martin 1981, 76, followed by O'Brien 1982, 96: "the whole train of ideas and words suggests a conscious indebtedness to the figure of wisdom in Proverbs 2:3 ff." In addition, many scholars consider the similarity between Col 2:2-3 and Prov 2:2-6. See Schweizer 1982, 118 n. 6; Lindemann 1983, 37; Gnilka 1980, 111; Hendriksen 1971, 105; Dunn 1996, 132; Pfammatter 1987, 69; Haapa 1978, 41; Arnold 1995, 274; Bujard 1973, 151; Schnabel 1985, 259; Müller 1988, 233; Wilson 1997, 127. However, Nielsen 1985, 118, following Lohse 1971, 82 n. 117, contends that in Col 2:2-3 there is no intentional allusion to an OT passage.

Col 2:4-5	Gal 3:17 etc.	Bel 7
4 **Τοῦτο λέγω**, ἵνα **μηδεὶς** ὑμᾶς παραλογίζηται ἐν πιθανολογίᾳ.	**τοῦτο** δὲ **λέγω**˙	**μηδείς** σε παραλογιζέσθω˙
5 εἰ **γὰρ** καὶ τῇ σαρκὶ ἄπειμι, ἀλλα **τῷ πνεύματι** σὺν ὑμῖν ἐιμι,	**1 Cor 5:3** ἐγὼ μὲν **γάρ**, ἀπὼν τῷ σώματι παρὼν δὲ **τῷ πνεῦματι**	
χαίρων καὶ βλέπων ὑμῶν τὴν **τάξιν** καὶ τὸ στερέωμα τῆς εἰς Χριστὸν πίστεως **ὑμῶν**.	Col 1:3-4 3 Εὐχαριστοῦμεν ... 4 ἀκούσαντες τὴν πίστιν **ὑμῶν** ἐν Χριστῷ 'Ιησοῦ	1 Cor 14:40 πάντα δὲ εὐσχημόνως καὶ κατὰ **τάξιν** γινέσθω.

Col 2:4 begins with a "disclosure form" like Col 2:1. Instead of the more normal verbs παρακαλέω and θέλω, λέγω is used here. The closest parallel to Col 2:4 is Gal 3:17 which similarly employs the words τοῦτο λέγω, "I say this", but it should be noted that these kinds of disclosures appear often in the Pauline letters (cf. 1 Cor 1:12, 7:35, 1 Thess 4:15).[484] Since Col 2:4 is the only example of an imperatival ἵνα following a τοῦτο λέγω construction,[485] A/Col, as a pseudepigrapher, utilizes the Pauline phrase differently from Paul.

With the words ἵνα μηδεὶς ὑμᾶς παραλογίζηται ἐν πιθανολογίᾳ, "so that no one may deceive you with plausible arguments", A/Col for the first time expressly points to the danger facing the recipients of the letter.[486] The terms employed are rare. The verb παραλογίζομαι occurs elsewhere in ECL only in Jas 1:22 and only a few times in the LXX. It is noteworthy that Bel and the Dragon (Bel) 7 is a close parallel to Col 2:4. There Daniel warns the king not to be deceived, using the words μηδείς σε παραλογιζέσθω which are very similar to the choice of wording in Col 2:4.[487] Nevertheless, the resemblance is too slight to indicate any connection between the texts. The noun πιθανολογία, which means the use of plausible arguments, the art of persuading, appears nowhere else in ECL nor is it used in the LXX but it is a well-known word in other texts: for example, Plato uses the noun in the same way as A/Col.[488] As usual, the persuading is also

---

[484] See J. T. Sanders 1962, 353-354; Standhartinger 1999, 120.

[485] O'Brien 1982, 97.

[486] O'Brien 1982, 97; Schweizer 1982, 118; R. P. Martin 1981, 76; Gnilka 1980, 107; Dunn 1996, 133; Luz 1998, 211. According to Sumney 1993, 369, here is already an evaluation of the opponents: "they deceive with good sounding arguments".

[487] Lohse 1971, 83 n. 121, refers to this parallel. In Col 2:18 is again used a similar warning μηδεὶς ὑμᾶς καταβραβευέτω θέλων ἐν ταπεινοφροσύνῃ.

[488] This is noted by Lohse 1971, 83; Dunn 1996, 133; Hartman 1995, 27 n. 5; Standhartinger 1999, 182. See Plato, Theaet 162E: σκοπεῖτε οὖν ... εἰ ἀποδέξεσθε πιθανολογίᾳ τε καὶ εἰκόσι περὶ τηλικούντων λεγομένους λόγους. Cf. Aristotle, Eth Nic 1094B: παραπλήσιον γὰρ φαίνεται

given a negative meaning in Col 2:4. There is a warning against the possibility of being deceived.[489] Since the choice of wording includes very exceptional terms and attaches a noun to the phrase with the preposition ἐν, characteristic of A/Col[490], the writer seems to have formed the caution himself and not modelled it on the authentic Pauline letters.

The metaphor to be absent in body but still present in spirit employed in Col 2:5 also occurs in the genuine Pauline letters in 1 Cor 5:3, in Phil 1:27, and in 1 Thess 2:17.

Col 2:5: εἰ γὰρ καὶ τῇ σαρκὶ ἄπειμι, ἀλλα τῷ πνεύματι σὺν ὑμῖν ἐιμι
1 Cor 5:3: ἐγὼ μὲν γάρ, ἀπὼν τῷ σώματι παρὼν δὲ τῷ πνεῦματι
Phil 1:27: ἵνα εἴτε ἐλθὼν καὶ ἰδὼν ὑμᾶς εἴτε ἀπὼν ἀκούω τὰ περὶ ὑμῶν
1 Thess 2:17: ... ἀπορφανισθέντες ἀφ' ὑμῶν πρὸς καιρὸν ὥρας, προσώπῳ οὐ καρδίᾳ, περισσοτέρως ἐσπουδάσαμεν τὸ πρόσωπον ὑμῶν ἰδεῖν ἐν πολλῇ ἐπιθυμία

When comparing the texts, it can be seen that the words τῇ σαρκὶ ἄπειμι – τῷ πνεύματι σὺν ὑμῖν εἰμι in Col 2:5 resemble very much the words ἀπὼν τῷ σώματι – παρὼν δὲ τῷ πνεύματι in 1 Cor 5:3 and thus it is clearly the closest parallel to Col 2:5 in the authentic Paulines.

It is worth noting that the metaphor is also frequently utilized in other ancient epistolary literature[491] but the contrast between absence and presence is described in many different ways. At least the juxtapositions τὰ γράμματα – θεάσασθαι, τὰ γράμματα – οἱ ὀφθαλμοί, τὰ γράμματα – αὐταὶ ὄψεις, ἡ διάθεσις – ἡ ἀκοή, and τὸ πνεῦμα – τὸ σῶμα occur.[492] Of the parallels outside the Pauline letters, the following texts resemble Col 2:5.

P.Lond.Bell 1926 [IV], 17 f.: εἰ κὲ ἐν σώματι οὐκ ἶκα (= ἧκα) παρὰ τοὺς πόδας σ[ο]υ, ἐν πνεύματι εἶκα πρὸς τοὺς πόδας σου.
B.G.U. IV 1080 [III], 6 ff.: καὶ ἡμεῖς δὲ ἀκοῇ ἀπόντες ὡς παρόντες διαθέσι ηὐφράνθημεν κατευχόμενοι σοι
Synesios, Ep. 138: δύνασθαι τὴν ἐπιστολὴν ... εἶναι παραμυθίαν, παρεχομένην ἐν ἀπουσίᾳ σωμάτων φαντασίαν τῆς παρουσίας.[493]

All the examples are later than Col (from ca. A.D. 200 – 400).[494] It is noteworthy, however, that there is not any single fixed form to express the thought. Thus the

---

μαθηματικοῦ τε πιθανολογοῦτος ἀποδέχεσθαι καὶ ῥητορικὸν ἀποδείξεις ἀπαιτεῖν.
[489] Dunn 1996, 133; Hooker 1973, 317, 325; Lohse 1971, 83; Hübner 1997, 74; T. W. Martin 1996a, 26.
[490] See Bujard 1973, 154; Lohse 1971, 89.
[491] Gnilka 1980, 114; Lohse 1971, 83 n. 124; Nikolainen 1987, 35.
[492] See Koskenniemi 1956, 177.
[493] See the texts mentioned by Koskenniemi 1956, 172-180 and Karlsson 1956, 140.
[494] According to Karlsson 1956, 140, the text of P.Lond.Bell 1926 [IV], 17 f. may be modelled on Col 2:5.

similarity between Col 2:5 and 1 Cor 5:3 points to a literary dependence between the texts although the verbal agreement is not very obvious. It is remarkable that both refer to the absence employing the verb ἄπειμι and the presence is also mentioned quite similarly: both use the noun πνεῦμα, "spirit", and instead of πάρειμι used in 1 Cor 5:3, σύν + ἐιμι occurs in Col 2:5 which do not make any difference to the meaning. In addition, Col uses σάρξ and 1 Cor σῶμα which both denote the bodily absence.[495] Since it was noted when analyzing Col 2:1 to be characteristic of A/Col to use the noun σάρξ, he seems to prefer this noun here.[496] It is also worth noting that the same conjunction γάρ occurs in both texts. Though Col 2:1 and 1 Cor 5:3 include only one verb (ἄπειμι) and one noun (πνεῦμα) in common, the agreement is so remarkable compared to other texts utilizing the same metaphor that it should be classified as a resemblance pointing to a possible literary dependence.[497] By utilizing this Pauline metaphor, A/Col, as a deutero-Pauline author, may also intend to emphasize that the Apostle Paul will always, even after his death, be present in spirit.[498]

Col 2:5 tells how Paul rejoices in the order (τάξις) and the firmness (στερέωμα) of the faith of Colossians. The note of rejoicing in Col 2:5 resembles the theme of thanksgiving in Col 1:3-8[499]: both describe how Paul rejoices at the Colossians' faith in Christ. The terms τάξις and στερέωμα are atypical of Pauline letters. In addition, the noun στερέωμα is unique in all ECL but in the LXX it is used to describe the solid vault of heaven in Gen (1:6, 7, 8, 14 LXX) and in the

---

[495] O'Brien 1982, 98. Contra Schweizer 1982, 119, who assumes that the use of the phrase "in the flesh and not in the body as in 1 Cor 5:3 leads one to believe that here the emphasis lies elsewhere".

[496] Paul also uses sometimes the pair σάρξ – πνεῦμα; see Rom 8:4-6, 9, 13, 1 Cor 5:5, 2 Cor 7:1, Gal 4:29. However, it has to be noted that 2 Cor 7:1 belongs to the passage 2 Cor 6:14-7:1 which is assumed to be interpolated and thus unlikely to be a genuine Pauline text (see pp. 82-83).

[497] Similarly Schenk 1987a, 3341. It is also worth noting that scholars usually present 1 Cor 5:3 as the closest parallel to Col 2:5 although they do not explicitly assume a literary dependence between the texts; see Schweizer 1982, 119; Pokorný 1987, 91; O'Brien 1982, 98; Dunn 1996, 134; Bruce 1988, 92; Hartman 1985, 69; Hübner 1997, 74; Haapa 1978, 42; Nikolainen 1987, 35. Lindemann usually denies the literary dependence of Col but in 1979, 115, states that A/Col knew 1 Cor 5:3f and 2 Cor 10:10f and thus consciously uses a similar Pauline phrase. "Da zu einer solchen Bemerkung im Rahmen des Kol eigentlich kein Anlaβ besteht, mag man vermuten, daβ der Vf sich tatsächlich der aus den beiden Kor bekannten Wendung bewuβt bediente; möglicherweise erschien sie ihm als typisch paulinischer Briefstil." Similarly Ludwig 1974, 89, who also normally emphasizes that A/Col knew Pauline phrases from the tradition, now takes Col 2:5 to be modelled on 1 Cor 5:3. "Die Wendung τῇ σαρκὶ ἄπειμι – τῷ πνεύματι σὺν ὑμῖν in Kol 2,5 stellt eine Umformulierung des bei Paulus vorkommenden Ausdrucks ἀπὼν τῷ σώματι – παρὼν τῷ πνεῦματι von 1.Kor 5,3 dar." Cf. Müller 1988, 233. Kiley 1986, 89, 94, contends that in Col 2:5 A/Col imitates Phil 1:27 but the similarity between Col 2:5 and 1 Cor 5:3 should be ascribed to the common parlance in the Pauline tradition. Kiley's interpretation is problematic because both the thought and the words of Col 2:5 resemble 1 Cor 5:3 much more than Phil 1:27. Like Kiley, also Standhartinger 1999, 120, denies the literary dependence between 1 Cor 5:3 and Col 2:5.

[498] Cf. Lindemann 1983, 37; Nielsen 1985, 114; Müller 1988, 233, 288; Standhartinger 1999, 173-174. Contra Luz 1998, 211, according to whom there is no need to assume that the text is deutero-Pauline.

[499] Similarly Dunn 1996, 143.

Psalms the firmness of Lord which is called upon (e.g. Ps 17:3 LXX, 70:3 LXX). Thus it is possible that the use of the term στερέωμα relates to the LXX.

The term τάξις appears occasionally in ECL, once in Lk (1:8) and several times in Heb (5:6, 10, 6:20, 7:11, 17), but only once in the Pauline letters, in 1 Cor 14:40. It is noteworthy that τάξις denotes the well-ordered Christian behavior in the church in 1 Cor 14:40, like in Col 2:5. Though the agreement of one noun only does not meet the criteria for literary dependence, there is a good reason to assume the use of the term τάξις in Col 2:5 echoes 1 Cor 14:40.[500]

---

[500] Also e.g. O'Brien 1982, 99, and Pokorny 1987, 91, present 1 Cor 14:40 as a parallel to Col 2:5.

4. Immunization Against Dangers (Col 2:6-23)

4.1. Christ in All His Fullness (Col 2:6-15)

Col 2:6-7	**1 Thess 4:1**	Pss Sol 14:4, cf. Sir 24:12
6 ῾Ως οὖν **παρελάβετε** τὸν Χριστὸν ᾽Ιησοῦν τὸν κύριον, ἐν αὐτῷ **περιπατεῖτε**, 7 ἐρριζωμένοι καὶ ἐποικοδομούμενοι **ἐν αὐτῷ** καὶ βεβαιούμενοι τῇ πίστει καθὼς ἐδιδάχθητε, περισσεύοντες ἐν εὐχαριστίᾳ.	... παρακαλοῦμεν ἐν κυρίῳ ᾽Ιησοῦ, ἵνα καθὼς **παρελάβετε** παρ᾽ ἡμῶν ... καθὼς καὶ **περιπατεῖτε**, ἵνα περισσεύητε μᾶλλον. 1 Cor 1:5-6 5 ἐν παντὶ ἐπλουτίσθητε **ἐν αὐτῷ**, ... 6 καθὼς τὸ μαρτύριον τοῦ Χριστοῦ ἐβεβαιώθη ἐν ὑμῖν	ἡ φυτεία αὐτῶν ἐρριζωμένη εἰς τὸν αἰῶνα 1 Cor 3:9-10 9 ... θεοῦ οἰκοδομή ἐστε. 10 ... ἕκαστος δὲ βλεπέτω πῶς ἐποικοδομεῖ. 2 Cor 4:15, cf. 9:12 ... διὰ τῶν πλειόνων τὴν εὐχαριστίαν περισσεύσῃ ...

The warning about "philosophy" (φιλοσοφία), which is usually assumed to be the main theme of the letter, is included in Col 2:6-23. The dangers were first touched upon in Col 2:4 but Col 2:6 begins the section which mainly handles the teachings confronted. As was mentioned in the introduction, there is not, however, any consensus about the identity of the opponents but a wide range of alternatives has been put forth. The passage can be divided in two parts. First, in Col 2:6-15 the Colossians are admonished to persevere in the teaching they received. Second, in Col 2:16-23, Christian liberty from strict regulations is defended.

The parenesis in Col 2:6-7 resembles the exhortation of Col 1:10 (περιπατῆσαι ἀξίως τοῦ κυρίου).[501] When analyzing Col 1:10, it was noted that it possibly depends on 1 Thess 2:12 but is also similar to 1 Thess 4:1. Thus, it is interesting that Col 2:6-7 resembles 1 Thess 4:1 even more than Col 1:10. Both Col 2:6 and 1 Thess 4:1 include the same "indicative-imperative" form which is also a characteristic of Paul (cf. Col 2:20, 3:1-4, Rom 15:7, Gal 5:25, Phil 2:5).[502] In addition, both texts use very similar words (παρελάβετε, ᾽Ιησοῦν τὸν κύριον / ἐν κυρίῳ ᾽Ιησοῦ, περιπατεῖτε, περισσεύοντες / περισσεύητε). Accordingly, Col 2:6-7 may follow 1 Thess 4:1. Although all the words in common are often used in ECL, the most unusual is the verb περισσεύω appearing 39 times in the NT. The

---

[501] Similarly Lohse 1971, 93; O'Brien 1982, 105-106; Nikolainen 1987, 36; Dunn 1996, 140-141; Hübner 1997, 75.

[502] O'Brien 1982, 105-106; Schweizer 1982, 122. Cf. Lindemann 1983, 39; Pokorný 1987, 93.

fact that the verbs παραλαμβάνω and περιπατέω appear in the same form indicates literary dependence. It is also remarkable that the occurrence of five similar words occasionally together would be unlikely. On the grounds of the use of two same nouns and three same verbs occurring within four lines in 1 Thess, the agreement between Col 2:6-7 and 1 Thess 4:1 should be classified as a resemblance indicating a probable literary dependence.[503]

Col 2:7 describes the life in Christ using the metaphor "rooted and built up in him" (ἐρριζωμένοι καὶ ἐποικοδομούμενοι ἐν αὐτῷ). A/Col usually piles synonyms together. Though ῥιζόω and ἐποικοδομέω are not exactly synonyms, the same phenomenon appears here: similar words are piled up together.[504] Another characteristic of A/Col is the use of many participles (ἐρριζωμένοι, ἐποικοδομούμενοι, βεβαιούμενοι, περισσεύοντες).[505]

Besides Col 2:7, the verb ῥιζόω appears in ECL only in Eph 3:17[506] but the noun ῥίζα is sometimes used in the Gospels (Mt 13:6, 21, Mk 4:6, 17, Lk 8:13) and also once in the Pauline letters (Rom 11:17) when describing the importance of the good roots. In Jewish tradition, close parallels to Col 2:6 occur. Pss Sol 14:1, 4 tells how "the Lord is faithful to those who truly love him ... Their planting is firmly rooted forever" (ἡ φυτεία αὐτῶν ἐρριζωμένη εἰς τὸν αἰῶνα). In addition, according to Sir 24:12 Wisdom "took root in an honored people" (ἐρρίζωσα ἐν λαῷ δεδοξασμένῳ). Thus the metaphor to be rooted in Christ in Col 2:7 may echo the use of the verb ῥιζόω in Jewish tradition.[507] The verb ἐποικοδομέω is employed quite similarly to Col 2:7 in the metaphor in 1 Cor 3:6-11 to describe the solid foundation upon which the believers' lives are to be based. Though the verb οἰκοδομέω is commonplace in the Pauline letters (see. e.g. Rom 15:20, 1 Cor 8:1, 14:4, Gal 2:18), 1 Cor 3:10-14 is the only passage in the authentic ones where the verb ἐποικοδομέω is used.[508] Therefore, it is possible that the use of the verb ἐποικοδομέω in Col 2:7 is due to 1 Cor 3:6-11 although the texts have no other words in common.[509]

The choice of wording βεβαιούμενοι τῇ πίστει, "established in the faith", in Col 2:7 resembles the exhortation ἐπιμένετε τῇ πίστει, "continue in the faith", used in Col 1:23. Paul employs the verb βεβαιόω to mean the establishment of the

---

[503] Contra Standhartinger 1999, 125-126, according to whom the similarity is due to the Pauline tradition. Kiley 1986, 89, calls attention to the similarity of the parenesis in Col 2:6 and Phil 4:9 but fails to notice that there is a more remarkable resemblance between Col 2:6 and 1 Thess 4:1. Lohse 1971, 93, presents both 1 Thess 4:1 and Phil 4:9 as the closest parallels to Col 2:6.
[504] Similarly Lohse 1971, 88.
[505] Bujard 1973, 60.
[506] Eph 3:17: ... ἐν ἀγάπῃ ἐρριζωμένοι καὶ τεθεμελιωμένοι.
[507] Similarly Dunn 1996, 141-142. Contra Schenk 1987a, 3343 n. 54, who emphasizes the similarity between Mk 4:17 and Col 2:7.
[508] Later the verb ἐποικοδομέω appears in Eph 2:20 and Jude 20.
[509] 1 Cor 3:6-11 is usually presented as a parallel to Col 2:7; see O'Brien 1982, 107; Lohse 1971, 93-94; Ludwig 1974, 25, 43; Gnilka 1980, 117; Hartman 1985, 82; R. P. Martin 1981, 78; Lindemann 1983, 39; Dunn 1996, 142; Haapa 1978, 44. Cf. 1 Cor 14:12: ... πρὸς τὴν οἰκοδομὴν τῆς ἐκκλησίας ζητεῖτε ἵνα περισσεύητε.

testimony of Christ among people in 1 Cor 1:6, 8 and 2 Cor 1:21. Both Col 2:7 and 1 Cor 1:5 also use the words ἐν αὐτῷ to refer to the connection to Christ.[510] The words περισσεύοντες ἐν εὐχαριστίᾳ also seem to be Pauline: in 2 Cor 4:15 appears a similar phrase τὴν εὐχαριστίαν περισσεύσῃ and in 2 Cor 9:12 the words περισσεύουσα διὰ πολλῶν εὐχαριστιῶν.[511]

Apart from the verb ῥιζόω, A/Col seems to use Pauline terms and phrases in Col 2:6-7 although he does not imitate any particular text. He has collected together in two verses several different words and phrases from the Pauline exhortations. It seems that, as a deutero-Pauline author, A/Col utilizes Paul's own words to strengthen his admonition to persevere in the teaching received.[512] Since just before the exhortations, A/Col referred to the presence of Paul (Col 2:5), here may also be the notion that Paul's interpretation of Christ is authoritative.[513] It cannot, however, be concluded that it was primarily the imprisonment and death of Paul which makes the author anxious about the future of the congregation.[514] More probably, he has an actual danger in mind.

---

[510] Similarly Lohse 1971, 94, presents 1 Cor 1:8 as a parallel to Col 2:7. However, we have no reason to assume that Col 2:7 was influenced by Psalter 41:12 and 119:28 like O'Brien 1982, 107, does who regards Col as a genuine Pauline letter. When Col is taken as a pseudonymous letter, we have no need to search for the source of the verb βεβαιόω outside the Pauline letters. Psalter 41:12 (Ps 40:13 LXX): ... καὶ ἐβεβαίωσάς με ἐνώπιόν σου εἰς τὸν αἰῶνα. Psalter 119:28 (Ps 118:28 LXX): βεβαίωσόν με ἐν τοῖς λόγοις σου.

[511] Similarly Standhartinger 1999, 123.

[512] Cf. Wedderburn 1993, 53-54.

[513] Nielsen 1985, 107. Cf. Royalty 1997, 4.

[514] So Standhartinger 1999, 179.

Col 2:8-11	Gal 5:15, cf. 1 Cor 8:9	Mk 13:5 / Mt 24:4
8 Βλέπετε μή τις ὑμᾶς ἔσται ὁ συλαγωγῶν διὰ τῆς φιλοσοφίας καὶ κενῆς ἀπάτης κατὰ **τὴν παράδοσιν τῶν ἀνθρώπων**, κατὰ **τὰ στοιχεῖα τοῦ κόσμου** καὶ οὐ κατὰ Χριστόν·	**βλέπετε μή** ... Mk 7:8 ... κρατεῖτε **τὴν παράδοσιν τῶν ἀνθρώπων**.	**βλέπετε μή τις ὑμᾶς** πλανήσῃ· **Gal 4:3-4** 3 ... ὑπὸ **τὰ στοιχεῖα τοῦ κόσμου** ἤμεθα δεδουλωμένοι· 4 ὅτε δὲ ἦλθεν **τὸ πλήρωμα** τοῦ χρόνου, ἐξαπέστειλεν ὁ θεὸς τὸν υἱὸν αὐτοῦ ...
9 **ὅτι ἐν αὐτῷ** κατοικεῖ **πᾶν τὸ πλήρωμα** τῆς θεότητος σωματικῶς,	Col 1:19 **ὅτι ἐν αὐτῷ** ... **πᾶν τὸ πλήρωμα** κατοικῆσαι	
10 καὶ **ἐστὲ** ἐν αὐτῷ **πεπληρωμένοι**, ὅς **ἐστιν ἡ κεφαλὴ πάσης** ἀρχῆς καὶ ἐξουσίας.	Col 1:18 καὶ αὐτός **ἐστιν ἡ κεφαλὴ** τοῦ σώματος τῆς ἐκκλησίας· Col 1:16 εἴτε ἀρχαὶ εἴτε ἐξουσίαι	Rom 15:14 ... **ἐστε** ... **πεπληρωμένοι πάσης** [τῆς] γνώσεως ... 1 Cor 15:24 ... πᾶσαν ἀρχὴν **καὶ** πᾶσαν ἐξουσίαν ...
11 Ἐν ᾧ καὶ περιετμήθητε **περιτομῇ** ἀχειροποιήτῳ **ἐν** τῇ ἀπεκδύσει τοῦ σώματος **τῆς σαρκός**, **ἐν** τῇ **περιτομῇ** τοῦ Χριστοῦ,	**Phil 3:2-3** 2 **Βλέπετε** τοὺς κύνας ... 3 ἡμεῖς γάρ ἐσμεν ἡ **περιτομή**, οἱ πνεύματι θεοῦ λατρεύοντες καὶ καυχώμενοι **ἐν** Χριστῷ Ἰησοῦ καὶ οὐκ ἐν σαρκὶ πεποιθότες	**2 Cor 5:1-3** 1 ... οἰκίαν ἀχειροποίητον αἰώνιον ἐν τοῖς οὐρανοῖς. 3 ... καὶ ἐκδυσάμενοι ... Col 1:22 **ἐν** τῷ σώματι **τῆς σαρκὸς** αὐτοῦ

By a strong warning "beware" (βλέπετε μή), the Colossians are in Col 2:8 alerted to the dangers which were first touched upon in Col 2:4. The verb συλαγωγέω does not otherwise appear in ECL. On the grounds of its use in other Greek literature, scholars usually assume that it denotes "carry off as booty or captive".[515] The

[515] Lohse 1971, 94 n. 18, followed by Dunn 1996, 146-147. Cf. O'Brien 1982, 109; R. P. Martin 1981, 79; Bruce 1988, 97-98; Luz 1998, 220.

warning βλέπετε μή is typical of Paul (e.g. 1 Cor 8:9, Gal 5:15)[516] but in Mk 13:5 (par. Mt 24:4) occur exactly the same words βλέπετε μή τις ὑμᾶς as in Col 2:8.[517] In Mk 13:5 people are also similarly warned not to let any one lead them astray. Thus it is possible that A/Col conflates the formulation in Mk 13:5/ Mt 24:4 with the Pauline phrase βλέπετε μή which he, as a pseudo-Paul, has in mind. The words common to Col 2:8 and the Gospel texts are still so customary in ECL that the agreement does not meet the criteria for literary dependence.

The persons who are trying to lead astray are referred to by the indefinite someone (τις). A/Col does not thus reveal the opponents he has in mind. In addition, the future tense (ἔσται) suggests that the author does not yet refer to an actual danger but Col 2:8 is part of the preceding parenesis (Col 2:6-7)[518] and rather advises to look ahead.[519] However, probably most readers of author's time would be able to realize what A/Col has in mind and recognize the persons referred to.[520]

The teaching which leads astray is called philosophy (φιλοσοφία) and empty deceit (κενὴ ἀπάτη). The term φιλοσοφία is unique in ECL but the noun φιλόσοφος appears in Acts 17:18 where the Epicureans and Stoics are called philosophers. Similarly, the noun φιλοσοφία was used to describe all sorts of groups, tendencies and viewpoints within the Greek and Jewish worlds. For example, Josephus defined the different sects of Judaism (Essenes, Sadducees, and Pharisees) to be philosophical schools. In addition, members of various religious groups, even those who practiced magic, called themselves philosophers. Therefore, the use of the term φιλοσοφία leaves it open what sort of teaching was in question.[521] The other definition of the teaching, κενὴ ἀπάτη, is also exceptional. It is doubly condemnatory because both the adjective κενός, "empty", and the noun ἀπάτη, "deceit", show that A/Col rejects the philosophy.[522] Since the term φιλοσοφία was widely used in the ancient Greek and Jewish worlds, there is no need to assume that it is picked up from the opponents who used it to refer to their own teachings.[523]

---

[516] Similarly Lindemann 1983, 39; Pokorný 1987, 94; Haapa 1978, 44; O'Brien 1982, 109; Kiley 1986, 86; Lohse 1971, 94; Ludwig 1974, 42; Standhartinger 1999, 121.

[517] Also O'Brien 1982, 109, presents Mk 13:5 as a parallel to Col 2:8.

[518] Similarly Hübner 1997, 75, calls attention to the context.

[519] Similarly Dunn 1996, 146; T. W. Martin 1996a, 27-28; Bruce 1988, 97. Cf. Hooker 1973, 326; Standhartinger 1999, 182-184; Kiley 1986, 63; Nielsen 1985, 105, who assume that A/Col does not have an actual danger in mind at all.

[520] Cf. R. P. Martin 1981, 79; O'Brien 1982, 109; Wilson 1997, 171; Hartman 1985, 117; Luz 1998, 220.

[521] E.g. Sumney 1993, 373, emphasizes that. See also O'Brien 1982, 109; Lohse 1971, 94-95; Dunn 1996, 147-148; Lindemann 1983, 39; Hartman 1985, 83; Haapa 1978, 44; Nikolainen 1987, 37; R. P. Martin 1981, 79; Bruce 1988, 98. Cf. T. W. Martin 1996a, 30, 33, who assumes that "the opponent employs 'the philosophy' as a means of persuasion and argumentation".

[522] Cf. Dunn 1996, 148; Lohse 1971, 95; O'Brien 1982, 109-110; Royalty 1997, 4.

[523] Similarly Royalty 1997, 4. Contra O'Brien 1982, 109-110; Wilckens 1971, 523; Nikolainen 1987, 37; R. P. Martin 1981, 79; Ludwig 1974, 94.

Next, the philosophy is defined to be "according to human tradition" (κατὰ τὴν παράδοσιν τῶν ἀνθρώπων). The phrase παράδοσις τῶν ἀνθρώπων occurs otherwise in ECL only in Mk 7:8 and it is not used at all in the LXX. The noun παράδοσις and the phrase παράδοσις τῶν πρεσβυτέρων are used a few times in the Gospels but these occurrences are also in the context of Mk 7:8, in Mk 7:3, 5, 9, 13 and in its parallel in Mt (15:2, 3, 6). In addition, the noun παράδοσις appears a few times in the epistles (1 Cor 11:12, Gal 1:14, 2 Thess 2:15, 3:6). Therefore, the noun παράδοσις is, on the one hand, so usual that the agreement between Col 2:8 and Mk 7:8, the use of the same two words which also forms a phrase, does not meet the criteria for literary dependence but, on the other hand, so unusual that it is possible that Col 2:8 echoes Mk 7:8.[524] The contexts are also similar. While in Col 2:8 "human tradition" is against Christ, in Mk 7:8 it is against the commandment of God. Thus both in Mk 7:8 and in Col 2:8 the phrase κατὰ τὴν παράδοσιν τῶν ἀνθρώπων emphasizes that the teaching is not based on divine revelation but is a human fabrication.[525] Such a slanderous characterization of the opponents is hardly due to their own teaching.[526]

Mk 7:8 occurs between the quotation from Isa 29:13 in Mk 7:6-7 and an example of rejecting the commandment of God in Mk 7:9-13 which the author of Mark certainly appropriated from the tradition. Since it also is an interpretation of the citation, it must be Markan redaction.[527] Therefore, the agreement between Col 2:8 and Mk 7:8 suggests that A/Col was acquainted with Mk or at least this part of the Gospel.

The term τὰ στοιχεῖα τοῦ κόσμου occurs in Gal 4:3 in a context similar to Col 2:8: both texts maintain the difference between once and now. According to Gal 4:3-9, people were formerly enslaved to the elements of the universe (τὰ στοιχεῖα τοῦ κόσμου), beings that by nature are not gods, but now, after God sent his Son and they have come to know Christ, they have turned back. Col 2:6-8 emphasizes that the recipients of the letter have received Christ and so they have to see that no one leads them astray with philosophy which is according to the elements of the universe (τὰ στοιχεῖα τοῦ κόσμου) and not according to Christ. Thus in both texts the elements of the universe are described to be the opposite of Christ.

---

[524] Cf. Dunn 1995, 157, according to whom the echo of Mk 7:8 "may be more than coincidental". In addition, the similarity between Col 2:8 and Mk 7:8 is noticed by many scholars; see Lohse 1971, 96; Schenk 1987a, 3343 n. 54; Haapa 1978, 44-45; Nikolainen 1987, 37; Schweizer 1982, 136; Gnilka 1980, 123; Dunn 1996, 148; Hübner 1997, 76; Luz 1998, 220; Arnold 1995, 189 n. 91, 209 n. 43; Hartman 1985, 83, 94; Bruce 1988, 93.

[525] Lohse 1971, 96; O'Brien 1982, 110; Royalty 1997, 4. However, Dunn 1996, 148, exaggerates when interpreting that the use of the phrase παράδοσις τῶν ἀνθρώπων in Col 2:8 "adds strength to the likelihood that the sort of 'philosophy' in mind here was essentially a form of Jewish thought being presented as a 'philosophy' by Jewish apologists."

[526] Similarly Royalty 1997, 4. Contra Ludwig 1974, 94.

[527] Similarly Gnilka 1978, 277. Cf. Scweizer 1971, 143, 145; Grundmann 1977, 188-189.

In addition, both in the context of Col 2:8 and in that of Gal 4:3, the noun πλήρωμα is used in the description of Christ's work. While Gal 4:4 tells that "when the fullness (πλήρωμα) of time had come, God sent his Son", according to Col 2:9, in Christ "the whole fullness (πλήρωμα) of deity dwells bodily". The sense of the noun is not similar in the texts, which is not surprising; it has been noted that A/Col as a pseudepigrapher often uses the words differently from his sources. The words ὅτι ἐν αὐτῷ κατοικεῖ πᾶν τὸ πλήρωμα in Col 2:9 repeat clearly the words ὅτι ἐν αὐτῷ ... πᾶν τὸ πλήρωμα κατοικῆσαι from Col 1:19 and A/Col thus seems to employ the noun πλήρωμα in a way typical of him. Since the term τὰ στοιχεῖα τοῦ κόσμου appears elsewhere in ECL only in Gal 4:3, it is usually assumed that Col 2:8 depends on Gal 4:3.[528] On the grounds of the use of three common nouns, στοιχεῖον, κόσμος, and πλήρωμα, appearing within two lines in Gal, the agreement between Col 2:8-9 and Gal 4:3-4 meets the criteria for a possible literary dependence.

The term "element" was familiar to philosophers when they spoke of the matter out of which everything was formed (e.g. Plato, Theaet 201e; Philo, De Vita Contemplativa 3)[529]. In Hellenistic syncretism, the teaching about the elements was mythologized: the elements were personified as spirits or given the names of deities. They were thought to be under the control of spirit powers. Because "according to the elements of the universe" is the opposite of "according to Christ" who is a person,[530] this seems to be the the sense of the term in Col also.[531] The contrast between "according to the elements of the universe" and "according to Christ" also indicates that A/Col quotes the term τὰ στοιχεῖα τοῦ κόσμου from Paul in order to get help for his argumentation from his teacher.[532] Thus the term τὰ στοιχεῖα τοῦ κόσμου is unlikely to have played a special role in the teaching

---

[528] See Schenk 1987a, 3341; Schenke & Fischer 1978, 160; Pokorný 1987, 96; Hartman 1995, 34-35; Schweizer 1982, 127; 1988, 455-456; Wilson 1997, 28. Contra Delling 1971, 685; Kiley 1986, 93; Lindemann 1979, 117; DeMaris 1994, 54. According to Kiley the expression τὰ στοιχεῖα τοῦ κόσμου can be seen as common parlance because it appears also in Sibylline Oracles 2.206 (καὶ τότε χηρεύσει στοιχεῖα πρόπαντα τὰ κόσμου ἀὴρ γαῖα θάλασσα φάος πόλος ἤματα νύκτες˙). The Sibylline Oracles do not, however, use the term exactly in the same form as Gal and Col: they add the word πρόπαντα between στοιχεῖα and κόσμου. Nor does one occurrence besides Gal and Col prove that the term belongs to common parlance. Lindemann, who assumes that the use of the same term in Col 2:20 and Gal 4:3 is due to the A/Col's adopting of Pauline thinking, neglects the fact that the expression is used only in Gal and Col. Dunn 1995, 169-170, states that "the relative proximity of Colossae and Galatia in the Anatolian hinterland may even suggest that τὰ στοιχεῖα τοῦ κόσμου was a characteristic feature of the apologia of Jewish synagogues in the region". This interpretation exaggerates the significance of the term which, however, occurs only a few times in two letters.

[529] Plato, Theaet 201e: στοιχεῖα, ἐξ ὧν ἡμεῖς τε συγκείμεθα καὶ τἆλλα. Philo, De Vita Contemplativa 3: ἆρά γε τοὺς τὰ στοιχεῖα τιμῶντας, γῆν, ὕδωρ, ἀέρα, πῦρ.

[530] E.g. Hübner 1997, 79, emphasizes this.

[531] Cf. Lohse 1971, 99; O'Brien 1982, 129-132; Hübner 1997, 76-79; Dunn 1996, 149-150; Pfammatter 1987, 72; Gnilka 1980, 125; R. P. Martin 1981, 10-12; Hartman 1985, 118-119; Schweizer 1988, 466; Wedderburn 1993, 8-9.

[532] Cf. Hartman 1985, 119; Schenke & Fischer 1978, 160 ff.

which is confronted.[533] Similarly, all of Col 2:8 has been noted to be a polemical description of the opponents. The terms "philosophy", "empty deceit", and "human tradition" are slanderous characterizations of them, not quotations of their slogans.

The words "in him" (ἐν αὐτῷ) were already used in Col 2:7 but there begins in Col 2:9 a sequence of "in him" clauses which explain the force of "according to Christ": ἐν αὐτῷ (2:9, 10, 15), ἐν ᾧ (2:11, 12). After the alert to the dangers in Col 2:8, in Col 2:9 the author starts to describe the significance of Christ. Col 2:9-10 takes up the language from Col 1:15-20. The fullness (πλήρωμα, Col 1:19), Christ as a head (κεφαλή, Col 1:18), and the rulers and authorities (ἀρχαί and ἐξουσίαι, Col 1:16) are mentioned again.[534] Unlike in Col 1:19, in Col 2:9 the fullness (πλήρωμα) is clearly the subject of the verb κατοικέω (see pp. 95-96). Thus according to Col 2:9, the fullness is pleased to dwell in Christ. Col 2:9 seems to be an explanatory repetition of Col 1:19: the fullness is defined by the words τῆς θεότητος σωματικῶς, "of deity in bodily form".[535] It is remarkable that both the noun θεότης and the adverb σωματικῶς are hapax legomena in the NT. The noun θεότης does not occur in other ECL either[536] but the adverb σωματικῶς is once used in the Papias-fragment.[537]

The term "deity" (θεότης) used in Col 2:9 has to be distinguished from "divine nature" (θειότης). The term θειότης (derived from the adjective θεῖος) describes divinity, the character of God. It is used once in the Pauline letters, in Rom 1:20 and once in the LXX, in Wis 18:9. However, the term θεότης (derived from the noun θεός) describes divine quality, godlikeness.[538] The definition πᾶν τὸ πλήρωμα τῆς θεότητος thus emphasizes that in Christ dwells all fullness of deity, divine quality. This supports the interpretation that the term πλήρωμα may be derived from the OT descriptions in which God fills all the places (see p. 96). The Hellenistic term θεότης is thus used to distinguish the character of God, θειότης, from the bearer of the divine office.[539] The present tense of the verb

---

[533] Similarly Pokorný 1987, 96; Schenke & Fischer 1978, 160 ff; Delling 1971, 685-686; Hartman 1985, 119; Royalty 1997, 4; Luz 1998, 219; Sumney 1993, 374; DeMaris 1994, 55-56, 73, 96. Contra Lohse 1971, 100; Ludwig 1974, 94; Arnold 1995, 189-190; Schweizer 1988, 455-456; T. W. Martin 1996a, 31-34; Wilson 1997, 28.

[534] Similarly Bujard 1973, 99; Pfammatter 1987, 71; Standhartinger 1999, 136; Lindemann 1983, 40; Dunn 1996, 151; Ludwig 1974, 43; O'Brien 1982, 103, 114; Lohse 1971, 92; Gnilka 1980, 118-119; Sappington 1991, 175; Haapa 1978, 45; Luz 1998, 213; Wedderburn 1993, 35 ff; Wilson 1997, 243; Cannon 1981, 48. Cannon emphasizes unnecessarily the traditional character of Col 2:9-10 because he interprets that A/Col himself formed the text on the grounds of Col 1:15-20.

[535] Cf. the descriptions of the fullness in Eph 1:23: ἥτις ἐστὶν τὸ σῶμα αὐτοῦ, τὸ πλήρωμα τοῦ τὰ πάντα ἐν πᾶσιν πληρουμένου, Eph 3:19: ἵνα πληρωθῆτε εἰς πᾶν τὸ πλήρωμα τοῦ θεοῦ, and Jn 1:16: ὅτι ἐκ τοῦ πληρώματος αὐτοῦ ἡμεῖς πάντες ἐλάβομεν.

[536] See Bauer 1988, 728.

[537] Bauer 1988, 1595.

[538] See Gnilka 1980, 128; Lohse 1971, 100; O'Brien 1982, 111-112; Kleinknecht 1974, 123.

[539] Gnilka 1980, 128. Cf. Stauffer 1974, 119.

κατοικέω seems to mean that Col 2:9 describes the resurrected Christ who is now present as the exalted one.[540]

It has been assumed that A/Col chose the term πλήρωμα because the teachers confronted used it when they promised fullness of life. By using the same term, he wants to emphasize that the fullness of life is found in Christ.[541] However, there is no need to assume that either the term πλήρωμα or the verb πληρόω used in Col 2:10 are derived from the teaching confronted. As was noted, the term πλήρωμα may be familiar to A/Col from Gal 4:3-4 and its usage in Col can be derived from the OT. Col 2:10 may also echo Paul's use of the verb πληρόω. Especially the words ἐστὲ ... πεπληρωμένοι πάσης τῆς γνώσεως, "are ... filled with all knowledge", in Rom 15:14 (cf. Phil 1:11) resemble the words ἐστὲ ἐν αὐτῷ πεπληρωμένοι in Col 2:10 which emphasizes that the recipients of the letter have been filled in Christ and are able to find in him everything that is important.[542]

The unique adverb σωματικῶς may have a connection with the noun σῶμα in Col 1:18 because many other words and phrases from Col 1:16-19 are also used.[543] Nevertheless, it does not seem probable that σῶμα refers here to the Church as the body of Christ like in Col 1:18. This interpretation puts too much weight on a single adverb.[544] The more probable interpretation is that σωματικῶς refers to Jesus' life on earth, his real sharing of our humanity.[545]

While in Col 1:18 Christ was said to be the head of the church, in Col 2:10 he is described as the head of all principalities and powers. There is a flashback to Col 1:16 where the rulers and powers (ἀρχαί and ἐξουσίαι) were already mentioned.[546] Because the description of Christ as the head of the church in Col 1:18 may have been influenced by the Stoic conception of the cosmic body, it is possible that the rulers and powers (ἀρχαί and ἐξουσίαι) in Col 2:10 means nearly the same as the elements of the universe (τὰ στοιχεῖα τοῦ κόσμου) in Col 2:8, the personified spirits.[547] However, more than Col 1:16, the wording of Col 2:10

---

[540] Schweizer 1982, 138. Cf. Hendriksen 1971, 111-112; Wedderburn 1993, 37; Lindemann 1983, 41; O'Brien 1982, 112; Hartman 1985, 95. However, the later Christology of "divine nature" is not yet present; Dunn 1996, 151. Cf. Gnilka 1980, 128, and Barclay 1997, 81-82. The latter states that A/Col does not attempt "to define in ontological terms the relationship between Christ and God it portrays. Indeed, with hindsight it seems almost miscievously to invite the Christological battles of later centuries!"

[541] See R. P. Martin 1981, 81; Lindemann 1983, 41; O'Brien 1982, 109; Lohse 1971, 100; Hübner 1997, 80; Wilson 1997, 33. Cf. Conzelmann 1990, 190.

[542] O'Brien 1982, 114; Haapa 1978, 45; Conzelmann 1990, 190; Hübner 1997, 81.

[543] Similarly Gnilka 1980, 119.

[544] O'Brien 1982, 112. Cf. Dunn 1996, 152; Hübner 1997, 81. Contra Lohse 1971, 100-101; Gnilka 1980, 130.

[545] Similarly Dunn 1996, 152; R. P. Martin 1981, 80. Cf. Lindemann 1983, 41; O'Brien 1982, 112; Schweizer 1982, 108. On the grounds of Col 1:15, Pokorný 1987, 103, followed by Hübner 1997, 80, interpret σωματικῶς as describing Jesus as the real image of God.

[546] Cf. Lohse 1971, 101; Hübner 1997, 81; Dunn 1996, 153; Gnilka 1980, 131; R. P. Martin 1981, 81; Pokorný 1987, 103-104; Bruce 1988, 102; Hendriksen 1971, 113.

[547] Cf. Hübner 1997, 80.

resembles 1 Cor 15:24 which it may echo although the common words of the texts are so customary that the resemblance does not meet the criteria for a literary dependence.[548]

When in Col 2:11 the author uses the words περιετμήθητε περιτομῇ "circumcised with circumcision" he typically combines together the expressions which have the same stem.[549] There is described the circumcision of Christ (περιτομῇ τοῦ Χριστοῦ) which is not performed by human hand (περιτομῇ ἀχειροποίητος). In Jewish tradition circumcision is sometimes interpreted allegorically as "the circumcision of the heart" (e.g. Deut 10:16, Jer 4:4, Ezek 44:7). Similarly, Paul in Rom 2:28-29 emphasizes the difference between the external physical circumcision (ἐν τῷ φανερῷ ἐν σαρκὶ περιτομή) and the real circumcision of the heart (περιτομὴ καρδίας). In addition, in Phil 3:3 the Christians who worship in the spirit of God are described to be the circumcision (περιτομή) although they do not have any confidence in the flesh (σάρξ). The context of Phil 3:3 is also similar to Col 2:11. As in Col 2:8, the Colossians are alerted to the persons who are trying to lead astray by the words βλέπετε μή, "beware". Phil 3:2 also warns about those who practice circumcision using the warning βλέπετε. Having four words in common, the nouns circumcision (περιτομή), flesh (σάρξ), Christ (Χριστός) and the verb to beware (βλέπω), which all occur within five lines in Phil, the resemblance between Col 2:11 and Phil 3:2-3 meets the criteria for a probable literary dependence.[550]

The term περιτομὴ ἀχειροποίητος, "circumcision not made by hands", is also unique in the Pauline letters. Though the adjective χειροποίητος, "made by hands", is frequently used in ECL to emphasize the contrast between the constructions of man and the work of God (cf. Mk 14:58, Acts 7:48, 17:24, Eph 2:11, Heb 9:11, 24)[551], the adjective ἀχειροποίητος, "not made by hands", is employed elsewhere only in Mk 14:58 and 2 Cor 5:1. Thus 2 Cor 5:1 is the only case when either χειροποίητος or ἀχειροποίητος appears in the genuine Pauline letters, which indicates that Col 2:11 may depend on 2 Cor 5:1. In addition, it seems possible that the noun ἀπέκδυσις, "putting off", used in Col 2:11 may be derived from the verb ἐκδύω, "to put off", utilized in 2 Cor in the same context as the adjective ἀχειροποίητος, in verses 5:3-4. It is noteworthy that although the use

---

[548] Similarly E. P. Sanders 1966, 44, followed by DeMaris 1994, 43, emphasizes that Col 2:10 resembles 1 Cor 15:24 which points to a dependence between the texts.

[549] Lohse 1971, 88.

[550] Similarly according to Kiley 1986, 79-80, 82, Col 2:11 possibly depends on Phil 3:3. Contra Hübner 1997, 81, who takes Col 2:11 to be due to Rom 2:28-29. According to Lindemann 1979, 118, A/Col and Paul knew similar Jewish traditions (Jub 1:23, Odes Sol 11:1-3) and thus both use the word περιτομή allegorically. Cf. Arnold 1995, 297; Standhartinger 1999, 89. It seems more probable, however, that A/Col, as a pseudo-Paul, knew the thought from Paul rather than that both A/Col and Paul by accident use the Jewish tradition similarly. Dunn 1996, 137, refers to Gal 5:6, 6:15 which also interpret circumcision allegorically but still do not resemble Col 2:11 as much as Phil 3:3-4.

[551] O'Brien 1982, 115-116; Lohse 1971, 102; Dunn 1996, 156.

of the verb ἐνδύω, "to put on", is typical of Paul (see Rom 13:12-14, 1 Cor 15:53-54, Gal 3:27), the verb ἐκδύω, "to put off" occurs only in 2 Cor 5:3-4.[552] In addition, the verb ἀπεκδύομαι appears in the Pauline corpus only in Col (2:15 and 3:9) as well as the noun ἀπέκδυσις used in Col 2:11. The verb ἀπεκδύομαι or the noun ἀπέκδυσις does not occur anywhere else in ECL except in Col.[553]

It is also worth noting that the contexts of Col 2:11 and 2 Cor 5:1-4 resemble each other. A/Col uses the noun ἀπέκδυσις in a unique phrase ἐν τῇ ἀπεκδύσει τοῦ σώματος τῆς σαρκός, "putting off the body of the flesh", which includes a typical series of dependent genitives.[554] The phrase σῶμα τῆς σαρκός already appeared in Col 1:22 denoting the fleshly body of Christ. Thus some scholars suggest that ἀπέκδυσις τοῦ σώματος τῆς σαρκός refers to the death of Christ.[555] It is also possible, however, that it is addressed to the recipients of the letter and thus means the unclothing, the putting off of the old nature, the sins.[556] This resembles the wish "not to be unclothed but to be further clothed, so that what is mortal may be swallowed up by life" in 2 Cor 5:4. Though the verbal agreement between Col 2:11 and 2 Cor 5:1-4 is not very striking, the adjective ἀχειροποίητος and the verb ἀπεκδύω/ἐκδύω are so exceptional that the use of these two words within five lines in 2 Cor meets the criteria for a possible literary dependence.

The circumcision of Christ in Col 2:11 seems to be the baptism which is described in the following verses 12 and 13.[557] The term περιτομή ἀχειροποίητος clearly shows that A/Col sets the circumcision of Christ in antithesis to Jewish circumcision which was done by the hand of man. The circumcision is not described polemically.[558] Rather the circumcision of Christ, the baptism, seems to have taken its place: baptism means for the Christians the same as the circumcision of flesh for the Jews.[559] Since there is not any polemic against circumcision and the verbal agreements indicate that Col 2:11 depends on Phil 3:3 and 2 Cor 5:1-3, it is more probable that, as a pseudepigrapher, A/Col chose to describe circumcision allegorically because Paul did so rather than adopting the term "circumcision" from the teaching confronted.[560]

---

552 Besides, the verb ἐκδύω occurs occasionally in the Gospels (Mk 15:20, Mt 27:28, 31, Lk 10:30).
553 See Bauer 1988, 166.
554 Similarly Lohse 1971, 88; Bujard 1973, 156. Cf. Col 1:5, 12, 13, 18, 20, 24, 27 ja 2:2.
555 See O'Brien 1982, 116-117.
556 Cf. Hübner 1997, 84; Gnilka 1980, 132. It hardly suggests the practices of mystery cults as Lohse 1971, 102, assumes.
557 Lohse 1971, 103; Hendriksen 1971, 116; Haapa 1978, 45; Nikolainen 1987, 39; Hartman 1995, 28; Luz 1998, 221. Cf. Gnilka 1980, 131, who emphasizes that the circumcision of Christ and baptism are not complete parallels. Contra Dunn 1996, 159.
558 Similarly Dunn 1996, 156; O'Brien 1982, 114-15.
559 Cf. Schweizer 1982, 142; Hendriksen 1971.
560 Cf. Schweizer 1982, 142; Hartman 1995, 35. Contra Lohse 1971, 101-102; Gnilka 1980, 133; Dunn 1995, 160-161; 1996, 155-156.

Col 2:12-15
12 συνταφέντες **αὐτῷ** ἐν τῷ βαπτισμῷ, ἐν ᾧ **καὶ** συνηγέρθητε **διὰ** τῆς πίστεως τῆς ἐνεργείας τοῦ **θεοῦ** τοῦ ἐγείραντος **αὐτὸν ἐκ νεκρῶν**·
13 **καὶ** ὑμᾶς **νεκροὺς ὄντας** [ἐν] τοῖς παραπτώμασιν καὶ τῇ ἀκροβυστίᾳ τῆς σαρκὸς ὑμῶν, συνεζωοποίησεν ὑμᾶς **σὺν αὐτῷ**, χαρισάμενος **ἡμῖν πάντα τὰ παραπτώματα**.

14 ἐξαλείψας τὸ καθ᾽ ἡμῶν χειρόγραφον τοῖς δόγμασιν ὃ ἦν ὑπεναντίον ἡμῖν, καὶ αὐτὸ ἦρκεν ἐκ τοῦ μέσου προσηλώσας αὐτὸ τῷ σταυρῷ·
15 ἀπεκδυσάμενος τὰς ἀρχὰς **καὶ** τὰς **ἐξουσίας** ἐδειγμάτισεν ἐν παρρησίᾳ, θριαμβεύσας αὐτοὺς **ἐν** αὐτῷ.

Rom 6:4
συνετάφημεν οὖν **αὐτῷ** διὰ τοῦ βαπτίσματος εἰς τὸν θάνατον, ἵνα ὥσπερ ἠγέρθη Χριστὸς **ἐκ νεκρῶν** ...

Col 1:21
καὶ ὑμᾶς ... **ὄντας**

Rom 6:11
... **καὶ** ὑμεῖς λογίζεσθε ἑαυτοὺς [εἶναι] **νεκροὺς** μὲν τῇ ἁμαρτίᾳ ζῶντας δὲ τῷ θεῷ ...

Rom 8:32
... **σὺν αὐτῷ** τὰ **πάντα ἡμῖν** χαρίσεται;

Col 2:10-11
10 καὶ ἐστὲ ἐν αὐτῷ πεπληρωμένοι, ὅς ἐστιν ἡ κεφαλὴ πάσης ἀρχῆς **καὶ ἐξουσίας**.
11 Ἐν ᾧ καὶ περιετμήθητε περιτομῇ ἀχειροποιήτῳ ἐν τῇ ἀπεκδύσει τοῦ σώματος τῆς σαρκός, ἐν τῇ περιτομῇ τοῦ Χριστοῦ

Heb 6:1-2
1 Διὸ ἀφέντες τὸν τῆς ἀρχῆς τοῦ Χριστοῦ ... μὴ πάλιν θεμέλιον καταβαλλόμενοι ... **πίστεως** ἐπὶ θεόν,
2 βαπτισμῶν διδαχῆς ... ἀναστάσεώς τε **νεκρῶν** ...

Gal 1:1
... **διὰ** ... θεοῦ πατρὸς **τοῦ ἐγείραντος αὐτὸν ἐκ νεκρῶν**

Rom 4:24-25
24 ... τοῖς πιστεύουσιν ἐπὶ τὸν ἐγείραντα Ἰησοῦν τὸν κύριον ἡμῶν **ἐκ νεκρῶν**,
25 ὃς παρεδόθη διὰ **τὰ παραπτώματα** ἡμῶν ...

Rom 8:11
... τὸ πνεῦμα **τοῦ ἐγείραντος** τὸν Ἰησοῦν **ἐκ νεκρῶν** ... ζῳοποιήσει ...

2 Cor 2:14
Τῷ δὲ θεῷ χάρις τῷ πάντοτε θριαμβεύοντι ἡμᾶς **ἐν** τῷ Χριστῷ καὶ τὴν ὀσμὴν τῆς γνώσεως αὐτοῦ φανεροῦντι δι᾽ ἡμῶν ἐν παντὶ τόπῳ·

Both Col 2:12-13 and Rom 6:4 describe how people were buried with Christ in baptism (Col: συνταφέντες αὐτῷ ἐν τῷ βαπτισμῷ / Rom: συνετάφημεν οὖν αὐτῷ διὰ τοῦ βαπτίσματος) and how God raised Christ from the dead (Col: θεοῦ τοῦ ἐγείραντος αὐτὸν ἐκ νεκρῶν / Rom: ἠγέρθη Χριστὸς ἐκ νεκρῶν). In addition, the phrase "you were dead in trespasses ... God made you alive" (καὶ ὑμᾶς νεκροὺς ὄντας ἐν τοῖς παραπτώμασιν ... συνεζωοποίησεν ὑμᾶς) in Col 2:13 much resembles the words "you must consider yourselves dead to sin and alive to God" (καὶ ὑμεῖς λογίζεσθε ἑαυτοὺς [εἶναι] νεκροὺς μὲν τῇ ἁμαρτίᾳ ζῶντας δὲ τῷ θεῷ) in Rom 6:11. Instead of the words καὶ ὑμεῖς ... εἶναι in Rom, A/Col uses the words καὶ ὑμᾶς ... ὄντας which fit his own style: he also uses a similar expression in Col 1:21.[561] It is worth noting that the common words appearing in Rom 6:4, 11 and Col 2:12-13 occur mostly in the same order in the texts and that the verb συνθάπτω does not appear anywhere else in the NT.[562]

Because of the similarities between Col 2:12-13 and Rom 6, there has been nearly a consensus among scholars that A/Col uses here an earlier Christian baptismal tradition which is the same that Paul modifies in Rom 6.[563] However, the resemblance between the texts is so remarkable that nowadays many scholars assume that Col 2:12-13 depends on Rom 6.[564] Since Rom 6:4 and 11 do not occur within five lines in the text, their agreements with Col have to be handled separately. Having two similar verbs (συνθάπτω, συνεγείρω / ἐγείρω) and two similar nouns (βαπτισμός / βάπτισμα, νεκρός) within five lines in Rom, the resemblance between Col 2:12 and Rom 6:4 meets the criteria for a probable literary dependence. Col 2:12-13 and Rom 6:11 also include two similar verbs (ειμί, συζωοποιέω / ζάω) and two similar nouns (νεκρός, θεός). It is uncertain, however, whether the verb εἰμί originally belonged to Rom 6:11.[565] Thus the agreement between Col 2:12-13 and Rom 6:11 should be classified as indicating a possible literary dependence only. Though the resemblance between Col 2:12-13 and Rom 6 is so obvious, some scholars neglect the literary dependence and suggest that the agreement between the texts is due to the acquaintance with Paul's language which is familiar to A/Col from the Pauline tradition.[566] However, these interpretations do not explain at all why only Rom 6:4, 11 resemble Col 2:12-13 much more than any other text of Paul.

Although Col 2:12-13 follows the language of Rom 6, the texts reflect different opinions about eschatology. While Rom 6:4-11 speaks only about the resurrection of Christ and assumes the resurrection of the believers to be in the

---

[561] Similarly Gnilka 1980, 120, Conzelmann 1990, 191, Dunn 1996, 163, and O'Brien 1982, 121, draw attention to the similarity between Col 1:21 and Col 2:13.

[562] Also Schweizer 1982, 143-144; Wedderburn 1987, 74, and O'Brien 1982, 118 call attention to this detail.

[563] The interpretation is supported e.g. by Lohse 1971, 103-104; Burger 1975, 96-97; Luz 1998, 213; Cannon 1981, 48-54. According to Schweizer 1982, 143, Col 2:12 "is dependent on Rom 6:4 or on baptismal tradition already present in Paul". For more about Paul's use of traditional material in Rom 6 see Wedderburn 1987, 37-69.

[564] E. P. Sanders 1966, 40-42, followed by DeMaris 1994, 43; Pokorný 1987, 106; Müller 1988, 122; Hübner 1997, 83. Cf. Gnilka 1980, 135; Haapa 1978, 46; Nikolainen 1987, 39. It is noteworthy that Lindemann 1979, 115-117 neglects the literary dependence but Lindemann 1983, 42-43, suggests that in Col 2:12 A/Col shows knowledge of the letters of Paul and among them Rom. Cf. Conzelmann 1990, 190.

[565] E.g. the manuscripts A D F and G omit it and, in addition, in p46 and 33 the reading cannot be determined with absolute certainty.

[566] See Kiley 1986, 94; Wedderburn 1987, 73; 1993, 49; Standhartinger 1999, 67; 115; 138-140. Cf. Wilson 1997, 120; Luz 1998, 187-188. Ludwig 1974, 45-46, leaves open the question whether A/Col knew Rom 6:4 directly or only through the tradition of the Pauline school.

future, Col assumes that the believers were raised with Christ in baptism.[567] It is remarkable that the verb συνεγείρω appears ECL elsewhere only in Col 3:1 and later in Eph 2:6, and Ign, Pol 6:1[568]. Thus it seems that A/Col has, characteristically, formed it by adding the prefix συν- to the verb ἐγείρω.[569]

In contrast to Rom 6:4, in Col 2:12 the noun βαπτισμός is employed in the sense of baptism instead of the more usual noun βάπτισμα. This is surprising because generally the noun βαπτισμός is used of Jewish ceremonial washing.[570] The noun βαπτισμός occurs otherwise in ECL only in Heb 6:2, 9:10, and Mk 7:4. It is not used at all in the LXX. Thus it is regarded as a new Jewish and Christian term.[571] The closest parallel to Col 2:12 is Heb 6:2. Since it describes the basic teaching about Christ, there βαπτισμός also seems to have something to do with baptism. The noun is used in the plural form which is interpreted as referring to a distinction between Christian baptism and other purification rites.[572] Besides the noun βαπτισμός, Col 2:12 and Heb 6:1-2 also have the nouns πίστις and νεκρός in common. Thus the agreement of three nouns meets the criteria for literary dependence. The difficulties concerning the date of Heb, e.g. according to Attridge it was composed somewhere between A.D. 60 to 100[573], allows the possibility that Col 2:12 depends on Heb 6:2, or vice versa. It has to be noted, however, that besides the noun βαπτισμός, the words in common are very usual. Therefere, on the grounds of this single agreement nothing certain can be concluded.

Rom 6 is not the only Pauline text which resembles Col 2:12-13. Exactly the same words διὰ ... θεοῦ ... τοῦ ἐγείραντος αὐτὸν ἐκ νεκρῶν, "through ... God ... who raised him from the dead" occur in Gal 1:1, as in Col 2:12. Having two nouns (θεός, νεκρός) and one verb (ἐγείρω) in common within two lines in Gal, the verbal agreement between Col 2:12 and Gal 1:1 also meets the criteria for a possible literary dependence. A/Col thus may imitate the words from Gal 1:1 adding, typical of him, the series of dependent genitives διὰ τῆς πίστεως τῆς ἐνεργείας τοῦ θεοῦ, "through faith of the power of God".[574] Similar words "God who raised Christ from the death" (τὸν ἐγείραντα Ἰησοῦν τὸν κύριον ἡμῶν ἐκ νεκρῶν) are also used in Rom 4:24. In addition, both Rom 4:24-25 and Col 2:12-13 mentions the faith (τοῖς πιστεύουσιν / διὰ τῆς πίστεως) and trespasses (τὰ

---

567 Lohse 1971, 103-104; Schweizer 1982, 144-145; Gnilka 1980, 135; Conzelmann 1990, 191; Müller 1988, 68; Hartman 1985, 99; Hübner 1997, 83; Luz 1998, 213; Wilson 1977, 19.

568 Ign, Pol 6:1: συνεγείρεσθε ὡς θεοῦ οἰκονόμοι.

569 Similarly E. P. Sanders 1966, 41.

570 Gnilka 1980, 134; Bruce 1988, 102; O'Neill 1979, 97. Some manuscripts read in Col 2:12 βαπτίσματι. However, it is more probable that βαπτισμός has been changed to the more usual βάπτισμα than vice versa; Bruce 1988, 102 n. 56.

571 Oepke 1974, 545.

572 Attridge 1989, 164; Gyllenberg 1971, 64; Oepke 1974, 545. Cf. Montefiore 1964, 105; Bruce 1990, 140.

573 Attridge 1989, 9. Cf. Lane 1991, lxii-lxiii. Lohse 1972, 127, defines the date more definitely between A.D. 80 and 90.

574 Similarly Lohse 1971, 88, regards the words as a series of dependent genitives characteristic of A/Col.

παραπτώματα), the latter even occurring twice in Col. Therefore, Rom 4:24-25 and Col 2:12-13 include four similar words (πιστεύω / πίστις, ἐγείρω, νεκρός, παράπτωμα) which meets the criteria for a probable literary dependence. Col 2:12, Gal 1:1, and Rom 4:24 all use the words "God who raised Christ from the dead" which seems to be Paul's stock phrase. However, here it seems to serve as "a Stichwort", the phrase which connects the texts together in the mind of A/Col. It seems thus that in Col 2:12, Rom 6:4, Gal 1:1, and Rom 4:24-25 are conflated.[575]

The verb ζωοποιέω, "to make alive", is typical of the genuine Pauline letters (see Rom 4:17, 8:11, 1 Cor 15:22, 36, 45, 2 Cor 3:6, Gal 3:21) but the verb συζωοποιέω, "to make alive together", used in Col 2:13, never appears there. It appears only here and in Eph 2:5 in ECL and, in addition, it is not previously attested.[576] The verb συζωοποιέω seems to be formed by A/Col adding the prefix συ(ν)- to the Pauline verb ζωοποιέω. A/Col may have had in mind Rom 8:11 which uses besides the verb ζωοποιέω, the words τοῦ ἐγείραντος ... ἐκ νεκρῶν and thus employs the same Stichwort "God who raised Christ from the dead" as Gal 1:1 and Rom 4:24.[577] Having two similar verbs and one similar noun, the resemblance between Col 2:12-13 and Rom 8:11 meets the criteria for a possible literary dependence.

The resemblances between Col 2:12-13 and Gal 1:1, Rom 4:24-25, Rom 8:11 support the interpretation that A/Col imitates Rom 6:4, 11 because they clarify why he has reshaped the text. As was already noticed, after the warning about the false teaching in Col 2:8, the teaching "according to Christ" is presented in Col 2:9-14. In Col 2:12-13, A/Col seems to have in mind the details of the resurrection of Christ which he recalls from the Pauline letters with the help of the Stichwort "God who raised Christ from the dead".

Because of the transition from "you" to "us" in verse 13, the words σὺν αὐτῷ χαρισάμενος ἡμῖν πάντα in Col 2:13c are sometimes regarded as a traditional style of preaching which begins a new section — Col 2:13c-15. It is sometimes assumed that A/Col here adopts traditional formulations because there appear many hapax legomena in the NT (χειρόγραφος, προσηλόω, ἀπεκδύομαι) and several participles (χαρισάμενος, ἐξαλείψας, προσηλώσας, ἀπεκδυσάμενος, θριαμβεύσας). In addition, the interpretation has been defended by the use of the words which do not appear anywhere else in the Pauline corpus although they are sometimes used in the NT (ἐξαλείφω, cf. Acts 3:19, Rev 3:5, 7:17, 21:4;

[575] Similarly E. P. Sanders 1966, 40-42, followed by Pokorný 1987, 106. Cf. DeMaris 1994, 43. Contra Wedderburn 1987, 73, according to whom "these relationships might, however, be better explained as independent echoes of a credal formula".

[576] Bultmann 1973a, 875 n. 5. Cf. Bauer 1988, 1548.

[577] Similarly Hübner 1997, 84. Contra E. P. Sanders 1966, 40-41, according to whom the verb συζωοποιέω is derived from the participle ζῶντας in Rom 6:11.

ὑπεναντίος, cf. Heb 10:27; δειγματίζω, cf. Mt 1:19). It has also been noted that the verb θριαμβεύω appears otherwise only once in the NT (2 Cor 2:14).[578]

The style of Col 2:13c-15 is not so exceptional as it has been presented, however. The words σὺν αὐτῷ χαρισάμενος ἡμῖν πάντα in Col 2:13 are nearly the same as the words σὺν αὐτῷ τὰ πάντα ἡμῖν χαρίσεται in Rom 8:32. Though the number of the similar verbs and nouns does not meet the criteria for literary dependence, the verbatim agreement between the formulations, four words in the same form, still indicates a possible literary dependence between Col 2:13 and Rom 8:32.[579] It is remarkable that as a pseudepigrapher A/Col uses the words differently from his teacher. Paul never says that God forgives trespasses. Moreover, the verb χαρίζομαι means in Rom 8:32 "to bestow" but A/Col uses it in the sense "remit, forgive" which occurs in Paul only in 2 Cor 2:7-10.[580] The dependence on Rom 8:32 may also have caused the change from "you" to "us" in verse 13.[581] On the other hand, the transition may be due to the associative style of A/Col. He first describes the trespasses of the Colossians but when he starts to tell about the forgiveness, he remembers that God forgives the trespasses of all people, not only those of the Colossians.[582] It is noteworthy that, as in Col 2:13c-15, in 2:12-13b also occurs the participles (συνταφέντες, ἐγείραντος) and that ἐξαλείψας, προσηλώσας, θριαμβεύσας are participles used instead of relative clauses, which is typical of A/Col.[583] Moreover, the phrase καὶ ὑμᾶς ... ὄντας, which is a repetition of Col 1:21[584], includes a participle construction. The abundant use of participles does not thus point to the use of traditional formulations but is characteristic of A/Col.[585] Accordingly, the style of Col 2:13c-15 does not indicate that A/Col did not compose the text.[586]

That the vocabulary of Col 2:14 is exceptional in the Pauline corpus and also unusual in other ECL cannot be ignored.[587] As was noted, the verb ἐξαλείφω, "erase", "wipe away", appears in the NT only in texts later than Col, in Acts and

---

578 So Lohse 1971, 106. Cf. Wedderburn 1987, 73; Haapa 1978; Deichgräber 1967, 168-169; Cannon 1981, 54-58; Kiley 1986, 92; Wilson 1997, 121; Maclean 1995, 97-99. Cf. also O'Neill 1979, 95-99, who contends that A/Col puts together distinct statements from the public language of the Jewish community to which he belongs.

579 Cf. E. P. Sanders 1966, 41.

580 Similarly E. P. Sanders 1966, 41. Cf. Dunn 1996, 164.

581 Similarly E. P. Sanders 1966, 41 followed by Pokorný 1987, 106. Contra Ludwig 1974, 96 and Wedderburn 1987, 73 who assume that both Rom 8:32 and Col 2:13 use the same early Christian formula.

582 Bujard 1973, 83-84, followed by Pokorný 1987, 113. Cf. Hartman 1985, 100-101; Gnilka 1980, 137; Hendriksen 1971, 118; Dunn 1996, 164; O'Brien 1982, 124; Bruce 1988, 108 n. 88.

583 Bujard 1973, 60.

584 Similarly Hartman 1985, 100.

585 Cf. Hübner 1997, 84-85; Gnilka 1980, 121.

586 Similarly Ludwig 1974, 97; Arnold 1995, 276; Pokorný 1987, 114; Dunn 1977, 139.

587 Many scholars try to solve the problem by assuming that A/Col uses here fragments of traditions and shapes them to fit to his own style; see Gnilka 1980, 121; Pokorný 1987, 115; Schweizer 1982, 135-136; Sappington 1991, 206-207. Cf. O'Neill 1979, 95-99; Hübner 1997, 84-85; Standhartinger 1999, 213. In any case, it is left open as to where the exceptionally words come from.

in Rev. In addition, it is used in 1 Clem 53:3-5. Like in Acts 3:19, the verb ἐξαλείφω is often used of the blotting out of sins in the LXX (e.g. Isa 43:25, Jer 18:23). In addition, in Rev 3:5 and in 1 Clem 53:3-5, it is used of the blotting out of a name from the Book of Life which resembles the descriptions of the book of the living mentioned in Ps 68:29 LXX and Ex 32:33. Therefore, Col 2:14 seems to presuppose the common thought in Judaism that God keeps accounts of man's debts.[588]

In addition, the noun χειρόγραφον, "written decree", which is unique in ECL, appears in the LXX in Tob 5:3, 9:2,5 meaning literally a document written in one's own hand as a proof of obligation.[589] In Jewish apocalyptic literature it denotes, however, a certificate of indebtedness or the heavenly book of living, which seems to be the more probable sense here.[590] Furthermore, the verb προσηλόω, "to nail", used in Col 2:14 in the words "nailing it to the cross", generally assumed to refer to the crucifixion of Jesus[591], occurs otherwise in ECL only later in Mart Pol 13:3. In the LXX it also appears once, in 3 Macc 4:9.[592] Therefore, the exceptional vocabulary of Col 2:14 seems to be due to the Jewish literature, although we cannot define any particular text as being familiar to A/Col. Though the precise sense of the exceptional words is not clear, the main intention of the author seems to be the same as in Col 2:8. Regulations, δόγματα which in Hellenistic Judaism mean the commandments of God, the Old Testament law, refer here to all the regulations (cf. δογματίζω in Col 2:20-22) which are not "according to Christ". Thus they may refer to the teaching confronted.[593]

The use of the words in Col 2:15 is not as exceptional as in verse 14. The rulers and powers (ἀρχαί and ἐξουσίαι) were already mentioned in Col 1:16 and 2:10 and in Col 2:10 also occurred the noun ἀπέκδυσις which has the same stem as the verb ἀπεκδύομαι, "to put off", in Col 2:15. Since ἀπέκδυσις does not occur anywhere else in ECL and ἀπεκδύομαι appears otherwise only in Col 3:9, here seems to be a flashback of Col 2:10.[594] The verb θριαμβεύω, which is later used in Acta Pauli 4:12, occurs in the Pauline corpus elsewhere only in 2 Cor 2:14. It is interesting that both texts describe the triumph of Christ. Although the similarity between the texts does not meet the criteria for literary dependence, the words

---

588 Similarly O'Brien 1982, 124; Lohse 1971, 108; Dunn 1996, 164. Cf. Müller 1988, 124. Moreover, Hübner 1997, 85, assumes that Col 2:15 is derived from Isa 43:25 (ἐγώ εἰμι ἐγώ εἰμι ὁ ἐξαλείφων τὰς ἀνομίας σου καὶ οὐ μὴ μνησθήσομαι) although he maintains that it cannot be proven.

589 Lohse 1974, 435; Dunn 1996, 164.

590 Dunn 1996, 164. Cf. R. P. Martin 1981, 84; O'Brien 1982, 124; Lohse 1974 435.

591 R. P. Martin 1981, 86; Pokorný 1987, 117; Bruce 1988, 110; Gnilka 1980, 140; Hartman 1985, 87; Luz 1998, 223.

592 3 Macc 4:9: ... οἱ μὲν τοῖς ζυγοῖς τῶν πλοίων προσηλωμένοι τοὺς τραχήλους.

593 Lohse 1971, 110; Nikolainen 1987, 42; Hendriksen 1971, 120-121; Dunn 1996, 165; Schweizer 1982, 150-151; Gnilka 1980, 139, Sappington 1991, 218-220.

594 According to Yates 1991, 583-584, ἀπεκδυσάμενος "is a word not found in Greek writers before the Christian era".

θριαμβεύσας αὐτοὺς ἐν αὐτῷ in Col 2:15 resemble so much the words θριαμβεύοντι ἡμᾶς ἐν τῷ Χριστῷ in 2 Cor 2:14 that A/Col may have 2 Cor 2:14 in mind.[595] The verb δειγματίζω means "to exhibit", "to make public".[596] As was already noted, it does not appear in Pauline corpus besides Col 2:15 but is employed in Mt 1:19 in which it is used in describing Joseph's wish not to cite Mary publicly.[597] There is no reason, however, to assume any connection between Mt 1:19 and Col 2:15.

Accordingly, the vocabulary of Col 2:13c-15 is not so exceptional compared with the genuine Pauline letters, as has been contended. While Col 2:13c matches verbatim Rom 8:32, Col 2:15 mentions the rulers and powers (ἀρχαί and ἐξουσίαι) typical of Paul and employs the verb θριαμβεύω, also appearing in 2 Cor. In Col 2:14, the author, however, does not utilize Pauline phraseology at all. Instead, he uses several terms which seem to be due to the Jewish literature and appear now for the first time in ECL. Later the terms are adopted by other Christian writers.

---

595 Similarly Arnold 1995, 276. Contra Kiley 1986, 92 following Ludwig 1974, 97. Cf. Yates 1991, 576-577, who emphasizes the similarity between 2 Cor 2:14 and Col 2:15 but assumes both texts to be genuine Pauline.

596 See Schlier 1973, 31. Cf. O'Brien 1982, 128.

597 O'Brien 1982, 128; Schlier 1973, 31.

4.2. A Defense of Christian Liberty (Col 2:16-23)

Col 2:16-23
16 **Μὴ** οὖν **τις ὑμᾶς**
κρινέτω ἐν βρώσει **καὶ**
ἐν πόσει ἢ **ἐν** μέρει
ἑορτῆς ἢ νεομηνίας ἢ
σαββάτων·
17 ἅ ἐστιν σκιὰ **τῶν**
μελλόντων, τὸ δὲ σῶμα
τοῦ Χριστοῦ.
18 μηδεὶς ὑμᾶς
καταβραβευέτω θέλων ἐν
ταπεινοφροσύνῃ καὶ
θρησκείᾳ τῶν ἀγγέλων,
ἃ ἑόρακεν ἐμβατεύων,
εἰκῇ φυσιούμενος ὑπὸ
τοῦ νοὸς **τῆς σαρκὸς**
αὐτοῦ,
19 καὶ οὐ κρατῶν τὴν
κεφαλήν, ἐξ οὗ πᾶν τὸ
σῶμα διὰ τῶν ἁφῶν καὶ
συνδέσμων
ἐπιχορηγούμενον καὶ
συμβιβαζόμενον αὔξει
τὴν αὔξησιν **τοῦ θεοῦ**.
20 **Εἰ** ἀπεθάνετε **σὺν**
Χριστῷ ἀπὸ τῶν
στοιχείων τοῦ κόσμου, τί
ὡς ζῶντες ἐν κόσμῳ
δογματίζεσθε;
21 **μὴ** ἅψῃ μηδὲ γεύσῃ
μηδὲ θίγῃς,
22 ἅ ἐστιν πάντα εἰς
φθορὰν τῇ ἀποχρήσει,
κατὰ τὰ **ἐντάλματα** καὶ
διδασκαλίας τῶν
ἀνθρώπων,
23 ἅτινά ἐστιν λόγον μὲν
ἔχοντα **σοφίας** ἐν
ἐθελοθρησκίᾳ καὶ
ταπεινοφροσύνῃ [καὶ]
ἀφειδίᾳ σώματος, οὐκ ἐν
τιμῇ τινι πρὸς
πλησμονὴν τῆς σαρκός.

Rom 14:3, 5, **17**
3 ὁ δὲ μὴ ἐσθίων τὸν
ἐσθίοντα **μὴ** κρινέτω
5 Ὃς μὲν γὰρ κρίνει
ἡμέραν παρ᾽ ἡμέραν, ὃς δὲ
κρίνει πᾶσαν ἡμέραν· 17 οὐ
γάρ ἐστιν ἡ βασιλεία τοῦ
θεοῦ βρῶσις **καὶ** πόσις ...

Philo, Conf 190
νομίσαντας τὰ μὲν ῥητὰ
τῶν χρησμῶν σκιάς τινας
ὡσανεὶ σωμάτων εἶναι

1 Cor 9:24, Phil 3:14
... τὸ βραβεῖον ...

Col 1:18
καὶ αὐτός ἐστιν ἡ κεφαλὴ
τοῦ σώματος τῆς ἐκκλησίας·

Gal 4:9-10
9 ... πῶς ἐπιστρέφετε πάλιν
ἐπὶ τὰ ἀσθενῆ καὶ πτωχὰ
στοιχεῖα ...
10 ἡμέρας παρατηρεῖσθε
καὶ μῆνας καὶ καιροὺς καὶ
ἐνιαυτούς

Rom 6:8
εἰ δὲ ἀπεθάνομεν **σὺν**
Χριστῷ, πιστεύομεν ὅτι καὶ
συζήσομεν αὐτῷ

2 Cor 6:17
... καὶ ἀκαθάρτου **μὴ**
ἅπτεσθε

Hos 13:6
...καὶ ἐνεπλήσθησαν εἰς
πλησμονήν, καὶ ὑψώθησαν
αἱ καρδίαι αὐτῶν·

Col 2:8
Βλέπετε **μή τις ὑμᾶς**
ἔσται ὁ συλαγωγῶν ...

Ezek 45:17, cf. Hos 2:13
... **ἐν** ταῖς ἑορταῖς καὶ ἐν
ταῖς νουμηνίαις καὶ ἐν
τοῖς σαββάτοις ...

Heb 10:1
Σκιὰν γὰρ ἔχων ὁ νόμος
τῶν μελλόντων ἀγαθῶν

1 Cor 5:2
καὶ ὑμεῖς πεφυσιωμένοι
ἐστέ ...

Col 1:22
ἐν τῷ σώματι **τῆς σαρκὸς**
αὐτοῦ

Col 1:10
... αὐξανόμενοι τῇ
ἐπιγνώσει **τοῦ θεοῦ**

Col 2:8b
... **κατὰ** τὴν παράδοσιν
τῶν ἀνθρώπων, κατὰ τὰ
στοιχεῖα τοῦ κόσμου καὶ
οὐ κατὰ Χριστόν·

Mk 7:7
διδασκαλίας ἐντάλματα
ἀνθρώπων

1 Cor 2:1
... ἦλθον οὐ καθ᾽
ὑπεροχὴν λόγου ἢ
σοφίας ...

Lucian, Anacharsis 24
τῶν σωμάτων ἀφειδεῖν

In Col 2:16-23, the warning concerning the persons who are trying to lead the community astray is continued. As in Col 2:8, in Col 2:16 they are referred to by the indefinite someone (τις). The warnings μὴ οὖν τις ὑμᾶς κρινέτω in Col 2:16 and μηδεὶς ὑμᾶς καταβραβευέτω in Col 2:18 also resemble the introductory formula βλέπετε μή τις ὑμᾶς ἔσται ὁ συλαγωγῶν used in Col 2:8a. However, the future tense is not used in Col 2:16 or 18 which indicates that now A/Col may be referring to actual dangers.[598]

The prohibitions with regard to food and drink (βρῶσις and πόσις), and the observance of festivals (ἑορτή), the time of the new moon (νεομηνία) or sabbaths (σάββατον) are mentioned in Col 2:16. In the genuine Pauline letters the theme is under consideration in Rom 14 which, like Col 2:16, handles the abstinence from food and drink (v. 17), and also the observance of sacred times (v. 5). Rom 14 also has remarkable verbal agreements with Col 2:16. First of all, it is noteworthy that the nouns βρῶσις, "food", and πόσις, "drink", are used together in ECL only in Col 2:16 and Rom 14:17. E.g. in Rom 14:21 and in 1 Cor 9:4, Paul employs the verbs φαγεῖν, "to eat", and πιεῖν, "to drink". In the LXX, the nouns βρῶσις and πόσις also appear together only once, in Dan 1:10. The noun πόσις is otherwise very exceptional. It occurs elsewhere in ECL, only in Jn 6:55 and only in Dan 1:10 in the LXX.[599]

The second agreement between Rom 14 and Col 2:16 is the similarity of the warnings. The choice of wording μὴ οὖν τις ὑμᾶς κρινέτω ἐν βρώσει καὶ ἐν πόσει in Col resembles the exhortations ὁ δὲ μὴ ἐσθίων τὸν ἐσθίοντα μὴ κρινέτω in Rom 14:3 and μηκέτι οὖν ... κρίνωμεν in Rom 14:13. However, both Rom 14:3 and 14:13 occur so far from Rom 14:17 that the texts must be compared separately to Col 2:16. Because the noun πόσις is so exceptional and it occurs together with βρῶσις so seldom, the agreement between Col 2:16 and Rom 14:17 meets the criteria for a possible literary dependence. However, the words in common between Col 2:16 and Rom 14:3 or 13 are so ordinary that the resemblances do not meet the criteria for literary dependence. It is possible, though, that Col 2:16 echoes Rom 14:3 which resembles Col 2:16 a little more than Rom 14:13 and also includes a prohibition with regard to food.[600] It is also worth noting that Col 2:16 seems like

---

598 Cf. Dunn 1996, 171; Sumney 1993, 367; Lohse 1971, 114; Haapa 1978, 49-50; O'Brien 1982, 138.

599 Luz 1998, 216, mentions two interesting parallels to Col 2:16 in the Letter to Aristeas (142, 162) which both use the adjective βρωτός and the noun πότον together. Especially the first one resembles Col 2:16. Letter to Aristeas 142: ὅπως οὖν μηθενὶ συναλισγούμενοι μηδ᾽ ὁμιλοῦντες φαύλοις διαστροφὰς λαμβάνωμεν, πάντοθεν ἡμᾶς περιέφραξεν ἁγνείαις καὶ διὰ βρωτῶν καὶ ποτῶν καὶ ἁφῶν καὶ ἀκοῆς καὶ ὁράσεως νομικῶς.

600 Cf. Hübner 1997, 87, according to whom A/Col had probably Rom 14:3 in his mind and Lindemann 1979, 117 n. 21: "Oder geht μὴ κρινέτω direkt auf Röm 14,3 zurück?". In addition, Schenk 1987a, 3342 assumes that Col 2:16 depends on Rom 14. Lindemann 1983, 47, and DeMaris 1994, 57, suggest instead that Col 2:16 and Rom 14 discuss similar conflict. It is worth noting that many scholars call attention to the similarity between Col 2 and Rom 14; see Dunn 1995, 163; 1996, 173; Goulder 1994, 28; Behm 1973, 927; Bruce 1988, 114; O'Brien 1982, 139.

a conflation of the exhortation μὴ κρινέτω from Rom 14:3 and the warning βλέπετε μή τις ὑμᾶς ἔσται ὁ συλαγωγῶν used in Col 2:8a.

The use of Pauline style in the beginning of Col 2:16 seems to be intentional because it gives Paul's authority to the warning which starts the section Col 2:16-23. Though A/Col utilizes the formulations from Rom 14, he holds a stronger opinion than Paul concerning the abstinence from food and drink. While Paul states in Rom 14:3 that "those who eat must not despise those who abstain", in Col 2:16-17 all abstinence is condemned. It is "only a shadow of what is to come".

The terms festival (ἑορτή), the time of the new moon (νεομηνία), and sabbath (σάββατον) used in Col 2:16 are all unusual in the Pauline corpus: the noun ἑορτή, which is ordinary in the Gospels, does not occur anywhere else in the Pauline letters. The noun σάββατον appears only once, in 1 Cor 16:2, and the noun νεομηνία, the time of the new moon, occurs only here in the Pauline corpus. However, in Gal 4:10, which like Col 2:16 discusses the observance of holy days, μήν, "month", is mentioned. The fact that the noun μήν can also be used to refer to a new moon or the New Moon festival[601] indicates a connection between Col 2:16 and Gal 4:10. The similarity of the contexts is also remarkable. When A/Col in Col 2:8 for the first time employed the term "elements of the universe", the text was noted as possibly depending upon Gal 4:3 which is the first time the term is used in Gal (see pp. 129-130). Both Col 2:20 and Gal 4:9 again mention the "elements" and both authors emphasize similarly that people must not submit to them though different words are used. In addition, both in Col 2:16 and Gal 4:10 the observance of holy days is criticized though different words are used. Though the agreement between Col 2:16, 20 and Gal 4:9-10 does not meet the criteria for literary dependence, it still seems that as in Col 2:8, A/Col has Gal 4 in mind.[602] It is not likely, however, that the opponents of Col are the same as those in Gal.[603] A/Col, as a later writer, imitates the style of Paul in Gal. It has to be also noted that Gal is not his only model: Col 2:16a was noted as being modelled on Rom 14.

Instead of the list "days, months, seasons, and years" used in Gal 4:10, A/Col enumerates the festival (ἑορτή), the new moon (νεομηνία), and the sabbath (σάββατον), utilizing the normal Jewish way of speaking of the main festivals, special days dedicated to God. E.g. in Hos 2:13 and Ezek 45:17 the words are enumerated in the same order as in Col, however in plural form; in 1 Chr 23:31 and

---

[601] Thornton 1989, 99, followed by T. W. Martin 1996b, 109.

[602] Also Schweizer 1982, 155 n. 3, Goulder 1994, 28, and Lindemann 1983, 47, comment on the similarity between Col 2:16 and Gal 4:10.

[603] Similarly Lohse 1972, 37, who states that the opponents in Col cannot be regarded as the same referred to in Gal. Contra Dunn 1996, 136-137; 1995, 169-170, who emphasizes the similarity between the dangers confronted in Gal and Col. Donelson 1997, 760, is right when criticizing him: "Dunn is perhaps overestimating the parallels he detects between the structure of Colossians and those of ... Galatians. It may be that Colossians is not ordered by a single thesis."

2 Chr 2:3, 31:3 the order diverges a little.[604] Unlike the list in Gal which can be taken either pagan or Jewish, the catalog in Col 2:16 is exclusively Jewish.[605]

The prohibitions in Col 2:16 are presented very briefly but the regular Jewish way of speaking of the main festivals indicates the Jewish character of the opponents, who may also emphasize the observance of sacred times. However, I believe it to be more probable that A/Col adopted the habit of enumerating the main Jewish festivals from the OT rather than that he quotes the catchwords of the opponents.[606] It seems also likely that abstinence from food and drink is important in the teaching confronted and therefore, as in Col 2:8, A/Col in Col 2:16 imitates Pauline style in order to get support for his argumentation from his teacher.[607]

In Col 2:17, it is emphasized that the prohibitions described in Col 2:16 are "only a shadow of what is to come (σκιὰ τῶν μελλόντων), but the substance, the reality (σῶμα) belongs to Christ". A/Col is here employing the contrast "copy – original" which derives from Plato and was also adopted by Philo and Josephus (see Pilo, De Conf Ling, 190; De Migr Abr, 12; Josephus, Jewish War II, 28). In Platonic thought, the copy is called shadow (σκιά) and the original usually image (εἰκών), but sometimes body (σῶμα).[608] Unlike in Platonic thought, in Col 2:17 the shadow is not the copy of the heavenly and eternal "idea" but it is foreshadowing what is to come.[609] Nevertheless, the contrast "copy – original" seems to be familiar to A/Col from Hellenistic philosophers. A similar phrase "the shadow of what is to come" also occurs in Heb 10:1 which, utilizing the same Platonic thought, presents the law as having "only a shadow of the good things to come" (σκιὰν γὰρ ἔχων ὁ νόμος τῶν μελλόντων ἀγαθῶν).[610] The context is also similar to Col. While Col 2:16-17 criticizes the significance of the observance of sacred times or prohibitions with regard to food and drink, Heb 10:1 criticizes the sacrifices. Though the resemblance is notable, it does not meet the criteria for literary dependence.

Since the noun σῶμα denotes the body of Christ, the church in Col 1:18 and Col 2:19, it is often assumed that here also the author has this sense in mind and the

---

[604] Similarly T. W. Martin 1996b, 106-107; DeMaris 1994, 56; Luz 1998, 216; Schweizer 1982, 155; Schenk 1987a, 3351; Gnilka 1980, 145; Dunn 1996, 175; O'Brien 1982, 139; Nikolainen 1987, 43; Haapa 1978, 50; Wilson 1997, 127, call attention to the similarity between Col 2:16 and the LXX texts.

[605] T. W. Martin 1996b, 129.

[606] So Lohse 1971, 115-116: "The "philosophy" made use of terms which stemmed from Jewish tradition, but which had been transformed in the crucible of syncretism to be subject to the service of the elements of the universe". Cf. Arnold 1995, 215; Sappington 1991, 163; DeMaris 1994, 112.

[607] Contra Nielsen 1985, 105, who regards Col 2:16 as too general to assume that A/Col has a definite teaching in view; cf. Hooker 1973, 317.

[608] See Lohse 1971, 116; Pokorný 1987, 121-122; DeMaris 1994, 63; Gnilka 1980, 146-147; R. P. Martin 1981, 92; Dunn 1996, 176; O'Brien 1982, 139-140; Nikolainen 1987, 44; Haapa 1978, 51.

[609] O'Brien 1982, 140; Dunn 1996, 176; Pokorný 1987, 121.

[610] Also Attridge 1989, 269-279, calls attention to the detail that Col 2:17 and Heb 10:1 utilize the same Platonic thought. Cf. Heb 8:5: οἵτινες ὑποδείγματι καὶ σκιᾷ λατρεύουσιν τῶν ἐπουρανίων and Rom 5:14: ᾿Αδὰμ ὅς ἐστιν τύπος τοῦ μέλλοντος.

use of the noun σῶμα instead of εἰκών indicates that the church is the place where the reality of Christ is embodied.[611] However, the double reference is not necessary: the author may use here the noun σῶμα in a sense different from Col 1:18 and Col 2:19.[612]

Col 2:18 begins with the warning μηδεὶς ὑμᾶς καταβραβευέτω. The verb καταβραβεύω as well as the verb βραβεύω employed in Col 3:15 appear nowhere else in ECL and are thus typical of A/Col. However, Paul uses the noun βραβεῖον, "prize", which has the same stem (1 Cor 9:24, Phil 3:14). Since it has been noted as a characteristic of A/Col to reshape the Pauline words, it is possible that the noun βραβεῖον is behind this formulation.[613] Thus the verb καταβραβεύω may mean that no one is allowed to deprive one of one's right to the "prize", Christ,[614] rather than "to pass judgment" or "condemn" as it is usually understood.[615] Neither the resemblance between Col 2:18 and 1 Cor 9:24 nor the one between Col 2:18 and Phil 3:14 meet the criteria for literary dependence.

After the warning, the dangers are described but unfortunately so briefly that we can only try to guess the characteristics of the teaching confronted. The first words θέλων ἐν can be translated "delight in" and so refer to "those practices in which the advocates of the philosophy took pleasure".[616] Another possibility is to interpret the words as meaning "insisting on" and thus to indicate "the desire on the part of the errorists to impose their views on the Colossian church".[617] In either case the words θέλων ἐν describe the eagerness of the opponents.

The next term ταπεινοφροσύνη is normally used in ECL in the positive sense of the Christian grace of "humility" (cf. Col 3:12, Phil 2:3, Eph 4:2, Apt 20:19, 1 Pet 5:5). Thus it is surprising that it here seems to refer to a negative practice. On the grounds of the rare use of the term, it does not seem probable that it depends on Phil 2:3 although it is the only case when the term occurs in the genuine Pauline letters.[618] In the LXX, the term ταπεινοφροσύνη does not appear but the verb ταπεινόω is used in the sense "to fast" (see e.g. Lev 16:29, 31; 23:27; Ps 34:13, Isa 58:3). So the term ταπεινοφροσύνη may in Col also carry the sense

---

[611] See Lohse 1971, 117; R. P. Martin 1981, 91-92; Hartman 1985, 112; Gnilka 1980, 147-148; Pokorný 1987, 122; Conzelmann 1990, 192-193; Nikolainen 1987, 44; Dunn 1996, 176; Schweizer 1982, 156.

[612] Similarly O'Brien 1982, 140.

[613] Similarly R. P. Martin 1981, 92; Gnilka 1980, 148; Dunn 1996, 177-178; Ludwig 1974, 14. According to Kiley 1986, 89, the verb καταβραβεύω may depend literarily on Phil 3:14. However, he fails to notice that the noun is also used in 1 Cor 9:24 which also may be the model of Col 2:18.

[614] Cf. Haapa 1978, 51; R. P. Martin 1981, 92; Nikolainen 1987, 44; Hartman 1985, 106; Dunn 1996, 177-178; Schweizer 1982, 158.

[615] See O'Brien 1982, 141; Sumney 1993, 375; Bruce 1988, 117; Hendriksen 1971, 125; Gnilka 1980, 148; Lohse 1971, 117.

[616] O'Brien 1982, 142. Cf. Haapa 1978, 51; Schweizer 1982, 158; Lohse 1971, 118.

[617] R. P. Martin 1981, 93. In addition Dunn 1996, 178, assumes that the words include "an essentially sectarian attitude" that "my way is superior to yours".

[618] Similarly Kiley 1986, 90. Phil 2:3: μηδὲν κατ' ἐριθείαν μηδὲ κατὰ κενοδοξίαν ἀλλὰ τῇ ταπεινοφροσύνῃ ἀλλήλους ἡγούμενοι.

of mortification or fasting.[619] On the other hand, it may refer to counterfeit "humility": the sort of humility which calls attention to oneself.[620] It has been also assumed that ταπεινοφροσύνη "refers to ascetic practices as a prelude to the reception of heavenly visions".[621] Some scholars also connect it to the next phrase θρησκεία τῶν ἀγγέλων when it means "readiness to serve".[622] In my opinion, the term ταπεινοφροσύνη in Col 2:18 most probably means counterfeit humility because it is used there in a slanderous description of the opponents. The opponents themselves may have used it to describe their humility in a positive sense.[623]

Though the term "worship" (θρησκεία) is used in Acts 26:5 and in Jas 1:26, 27, the term "worship of angels" (θρησκεία τῶν ἀγγέλων) does not appear anywhere else in ECL. Later it appears in Origen, Contra Celsum (V 8, 25) which quotes Col 2:18. Because A/Col does not describe at all the worship he is referring to, several different interpretations have been stated. The term θρησκεία τῶν ἀγγέλων has been interpreted to denote "the worship directed to the angels" (taking the genitive as objective).[624] Since worshiping angels was not usually practiced in Judaism, this interpretation often includes the assumption that the Colossian situation was syncretistic. However, venerating angels was not completely unfamiliar to Judaism. Though they were not worshipped in the cultic sense, they were sometimes called upon for help.[625]

An alternative hypothesis was put forward by F. O. Francis who takes the phrase as denoting "the worship offered by angels to God" (with the genitive being regarded as subjective). Such angelic liturgy is described e.g. in the Qumran texts (cf. Isa 6, Rev 22:8-9). In this interpretation, believers are often understood to participate in heavenly worship with angels.[626]

The next words "which he has seen upon entering" (ἃ ἑόρακεν ἐμβατεύων) are also difficult to understand. The verb ἐμβατεύω is hapax legomenon in ECL.

---

[619] Dunn 1996, 178-179; R. P. Martin 1981, 93; Pokorný 1987, 123. Contra DeMaris 1994, 75.

[620] See Schweizer 1982, 159; Nikolainen 1987, 45; Bruce 1988, 118; Hendriksen 1971, 125; Hartman 1985, 106.

[621] O'Brien 1982, 142.

[622] See Lohse 1971, 117-118; Haapa 1978, 51. Cf. Gnilka 1980, 149 and Lindemann 1983, 149, who assume that ταπεινοφροσύνη refers to the submission to the demands of angels and other cosmic powers. According to Hübner 1997, 88, this interpretation is possible.

[623] Cf. Luz 1998, 216; O'Brien 1982, xxxii; Sumney 1993, 371-372; DeMaris 194, 71.

[624] The interpretation is followed by Lohse 1971, 117-119; R. P. Martin 1981, 93-94; DeMaris 1994, 59-62; Arnold 1995, 101-102; Hendriksen 1971, 126; Lindemann 1983, 48; Pokorný 1987, 96-97; House 1992, 58; Gnilka 1980, 149-150; Hübner 1997, 88; Luz 1998, 217; Hartman 1985, 106-107.

[625] See Arnold 1995, 32-89. Cf. Hartman 1985, 121; Wedderburn 1993, 8-9.

[626] The interpretation is followed by Dunn 1996, 181; Sappington 1991, 159; Bruce 1988, 119; Schweizer 1982, 159-160. Recently, Stuckenbruck 1995, 117-119 criticized these traditional interpretations. He contends that "[t]here is good reason ... to think that the customary alternative posed between a subjective and objective interpretation of τῶν ἀγγέλων is misleading"... "it is no longer necessary to decide whether the writer intended the genitive phrase to denote either the activity of angels or human behavior in which angels are venetrated. Indeed, both motifs are found side by side in a number of early Jewish texts"

Martin Dibelius put forward the interpretation that the verb ἐμβατεύω is a technical term for initiation into a mystery cult and it refers to the visions seen when preparing for initiation. In addition, he assumed that in the circle of the "philosophy" such cultic rites were performed.[627] This interpretation is followed by many scholars.[628] However, there have also been doubts whether the verb ἐμβατεύω should be taken as a technical term of mystery cults because it is also used in the Jewish apocalyptic literature to refer to the visionary entering into the heavenly realm. It is also worth noting that 2 Cor 12:2-4 describes a visionary or mystical journey. Therefore, the words ἃ ἑόρακεν ἐμβατεύων rather refer to the visionary entering into the heavenly realm in order to get special knowledge.[629] The fact that the terms θρησκεία τῶν ἀγγέλων and ἃ ἑόρακεν ἐμβατεύων do not appear in the genuine Pauline letters indicates that angels and visions are characteristics of the teaching opposed. Of course it is also possible, though unlikely, that Col depends here on some lost letter of Paul or another text we do not know.

The words εἰκῇ φυσιούμενος ὑπὸ τοῦ νοὸς τῆς σαρκὸς αὐτοῦ at the end of Col 2:18 describe the character of the people who are trying to lead the others astray. The verb φυσιόω, which means "puffed up", "conceited", occurs in the Pauline corpus elsewhere only in 1 Cor (4:6, 18, 19, 5:2, 8:1, 13:4) which indicates that the verb φυσιόω may be familiar to A/Col from 1 Cor.[630] However, there are no other verbal agreements to prove the connection. The words νοῦς τῆς σαρκὸς αὐτοῦ resemble the words ἐν τῷ σώματι τῆς σαρκὸς αὐτοῦ which were used in Col 1:22 and thus seem to be a formation of A/Col.[631] Though the strict ense of the words "the mind of his flesh" (νοῦς τῆς σαρκὸς αὐτοῦ) is difficult to understand, they must somehow refer to "the worldly mind" of the opponents.[632]

In Col 2:19, one more variation of the body – head image appears. While in Col 1:18 was described how Christ is the head of the body, now the dependence of the body on the head is emphasized.[633] The detailed description of how the body operates corresponds to ancient ideas of physiology.[634] E.g. Aristotle describes the body quite similarly (De partibus animalium 670a, 8-10)[635] Both ἁφαί (joints,

---

[627] Dibelius 1956, 55-65.

[628] See Lohse 1971, 119-121; Haapa 1978, 51-52; Arnold 1995, 155-157; Gnilka 1980, 150-151; Lindemann 1983, 48; Argall 1987; Hübner 1997, 88-89.

[629] O'Brien 1982, 143-145; R. P. Martin 1981, 95; Schweizer 1982, 161; Dunn 1996, 183-184; Sappington 1991, 155-58. Cf. Preisker 1973, 535-536.

[630] Cf. DeMaris 1994, 67, 69. In addition, Wedderburn 1993, 35-36, call attention to the similar use of the verb φυσιόω in Col 2:18 and 1 Cor.

[631] Similarly DeMaris 1994, 68.

[632] See Bruce 1988, 122; Schweizer 1982 162; Dunn 1996, 184-185; Lindemann 1983, 49; Pokorný 1987, 124; Gnilka 1980, 151.

[633] Dunn 1996, 186. Cf. Lohse 1971, 121.

[634] Lindemann 1983, 49; Gnilka 1980, 153; O'Brien 1982, 147; Hartman 1985, 114; Haapa 1978, 52; Dunn 1996, 186; Lohse 1971, 121.

[635] De partibus animalium 670a, 10: Ἔστι δὲ σπλάγχνα τὰ κάτω τοῦ ὑποζώματος κοινῇ μὲν πάντα τῶν φλεβῶν χάριν, ὅπως οὖσαι μετέωροι μένωσι τῷ τούτων συνδέσμῳ πρὸς τὸ σῶμα.

sinews) and σύνδεσμοι (ligaments) are rare terms in ECL.[636] Though the noun σύνδεσμος appears sometimes, e.g. in Acts 8:23, in Eph 4:3, and in Col 3:14, it denotes ligaments only here. The noun ἁφή is also used in Eph 4:15-16 where the whole image is taken further.[637] In the genuine Pauline letters, the body is never described in such detail.

The verb συμβιβάζω, "to bring together", which appeared in Col 2:2 is used at the end of Col 2:19. In both cases the verb is used to describe the unity of the people. Col 2:19 continues with the words αὔξει τὴν αὔξησιν τοῦ θεοῦ, "grows with the growth of God". The thought was already mentioned in Col 1:6 and 10, the latter of which resembles Col 2:19 more. It is remarkable that both in Col 1:6 and 10 the verb αὐξάνω was used. Instead, Col 2:19 uses the shorter form αὔξω and, typically, A/Col adds the noun αὔξησις which has the same stem.[638] It is noteworthy that the noun αὔξησις occurs in the Pauline corpus only here and in Eph 4:16. Therefore, the formulation αὔξει τὴν αὔξησιν τοῦ θεοῦ in Col 2:19 clearly a formation of A/Col.

While in Col 1:17-18 it was emphasized that Christ is the head of the whole world, not only the church, the elements of the universe or rulers and powers are not mentioned in Col 2:19. The church is described as the body of Christ.[639] Thus, it seems that Christ is regarded as the head of the whole cosmos but only the church is described as his body.[640] The words οὐ κρατῶν τὴν κεφαλήν in the beginning of Col 2:19 maintain that anyone who takes pleasure in the religious experiences mentioned in Col 2:18, the humility, angelic worship, visions etc., "is not holding fast to the head" and thus fails to be closely united in Christ. Therefore, A/Col warns about those religious experiences.[641]

It has been noted that Col 2:18 is very fragmentary and thus difficult to understand and almost untranslatable. It is usually explained that A/Col quotes the catchwords of the philosophy and therefore the text is so fragmentary[642] but scholars admit that it is not clear what words are taken from the opponents and used in the polemic against them or when the phrases are A/Col's own formulation.[643] The most probable explanation is that the terms "do not represent

---

[636] O'Brien 1982, 147; Lohse 1971, 121. Dunn 1996, 186, emphasizes that the terms are almost synonymous.

[637] Eph 4:14-16: ... τῆς διδασκαλίας ἐν τῇ κυβείᾳ τῶν ἀνθρώπων ... ἡ κεφαλή, Χριστός, ἐξ οὗ πᾶν τὸ σῶμα συναρμολογούμενον καὶ συμβιβαζόμενον διὰ πάσης ἁφῆς τῆς ἐπιχορηγίας κατ' ἐνέργειαν ἐν μέτρῳ ἑνὸς ἑκάστου μέρους τὴν αὔξησιν τοῦ σώματος.

[638] Cf. 1:11, 29, 2:11. Similarly Lohse 1971, 88.

[639] Dunn 1996, 187. Cf. Hendriksen 1971, 128; Pfammatter 1987, 75; R. P. Martin 1981, 92; Haapa 1978, 52; Bruce 1988, 123.

[640] Gnilka 1980, 152; Lohse 1971, 122; Schweizer 1982, 163; Hartman 1985, 114.

[641] Cf. Lindemann 1983, 49; Dunn 1996, 185; Haapa 1978, 52; O'Brien 1982, 146-148; Hendriksen 1971, 128; Pokorný 1987, 127.

[642] See O'Brien 1982, 141-142; R. P. Martin 1981, 93; Lindemann 1983, 48; Schweizer 1982, 154; Lohse 1971, 117; Sumney 1993, 376-377. Cf. Luz 1998, 214, 217.

[643] See O'Brien 1982, 138; Nikolainen 1987, 43; Lohse 1971, 114.

the opponents' own custom of self-expression, but instead the author's denigrating characterization of their beliefs".[644]

The exhortation "if with Christ you died ... why do you live as if you still belonged to the world?" in Col 2:20 can also be translated "why live as if ...?" and interpreted as a warning against danger which is not yet actual but may occur.[645] The exhortation resembles the orders given in Rom 6:2-8, which has been noted by many scholars. The thought of Rom 6:2 "how can we who died to sin go on living in it?" is near to Col 2:20, although instead of sin, Col criticizes the living according to the elements of the universe, which were already mentioned in Col 2:8. However, the choice of wording in Rom 6:8 resembles Col 2:20 even more than that in Rom 6:2. Both Col 2:20 and Rom 6:8 describe the dying with Christ using similar words εἰ ἀπεθάνετε / ἀπεθάνομεν σὺν Χριστῷ. Besides, in Rom 6:8 is the exhortation to live with Christ while in Col 2:20 it is said indirectly: "why do you live as if you still belonged to the world?". A/Col seems to have Rom 6 in mind and recall the wording of Rom 6:8 but he uses it in his own way, referring to the elements of the universe instead of sin. The agreement between Col 2:20 and Rom 6:8, the use of two similar verbs (ἀποθνῄσκω, ζάω / συζάω) and one identical noun (Χριστός), meets the criteria for a possible literary dependence between the texts.[646]

The verb δογματίζω, "establish or publish a decree" in Col 2:20 is exceptional in ECL: it does not appear otherwise in the Pauline corpus and later it is employed only in 1 Clem (20:4, 27:5). The passive form in Col 2:20 should be understood as "let yourself be regulated". There seems to be a reference back to the regulations mentioned in Col 2:14 using the noun δόγμα which has the same stem as the verb δογματίζω.[647] Similarly, in Col 1:6, 10 the verb αὐξάνω occurs and later in Col 2:19 the verb αὔξω and the noun αὔξησις. It thus seems to be typical of A/Col to repeat verbs and nouns having the same stem.

Col 2:21 includes the briefly presented prohibitions "Do not handle, Do not taste, Do not touch". It is interesting that the first and the third are nearly synonymous. The verbs γεύομαι "to taste" and θιγγάνω "to touch" do not appear anywhere else in the Pauline corpus but sometimes in other ECL. The verb γεύομαι is used in the Gospels, Acts, Heb, and 1 Pet but not in a prohibition as in Col 2:21. The verb θιγγάνω appears in Heb 11:28 and 12:20, the latter of which

---

644 Wilson 1997, 28. Cf. T. W. Martin 1996a, 108-109, who regards Col as a response to the cynic critique but assumes that the scenario presented in the text may exist in the mind of the author.

645 Dunn 1996, 188, and Kiley 1986, 63, following Hooker 1973, 317-318. Contra Goulder 1995, 601 n. 1.

646 Cf. Dunn 1996, 189, who sees in Col 2:20 "a direct echo of Rom 6:8" and also calls attention to the similarities between Col 2:20 and Rom 6:2,10. In addition, Schweizer 1982, 165-166; Pokorný 1987, 127; O'Brien 1982, 149; Lindemann 1983, 50; Hübner 1998, 129, notes the similarity between Col 2:20 and Rom 6:2-10. According to Gnilka 1980, 156, the resemblance between the texts is due to the dependence on baptismal tradition.

647 O'Brien 1982, 149; Hooker 1973, 328; R. P. Martin 1981, 97; Hartman 1985, 107; Gnilka 1980, 157; Dunn 1996, 190.

slightly resembles Col 2:21. There is a prohibition against touching the mountain (κἂν θηρίον θίγῃ τοῦ ὄρους, λιθοβοληθήσεται).

Instead, the verb ἅπτομαι, "to touch", occurs twice in the authentic Pauline letters, in 1 Cor 7:1 and 2 Cor 6:17. Because ἅπτομαι is used in 1 Cor 7:1 when exhorting a man not to touch a woman, the first prohibition of Col 2:21 has also been thought to point to sexual relations.[648] This is, however, unlikely because the following words in Col 2:22 suggest material objects and thus rather than to sexual relations, the prohibitions refer to food and drink, which were also mentioned in Col 2:16.[649] The closest parallel to Col 2:21 is 2 Cor 6:17 where the verb "to touch" is used in a similar context. It appears in a quotation from Isa 52:11 where it is forbidden to touch anything unclean. The prohibition in 2 Cor 6:17 shows the non-Pauline character of 2 Cor 6:14-7:1 (see pp. 82-83) and is the type of legalistic command which is condemned in Col 2:21 rather than the model for it. Accordingly, the prohibitions "Do not handle, Do not taste, Do not touch" are not an imitation of Paul but characteristic of A/Col. Therefore, they seem to be a caricature of the legalistic commands of the opponents.[650]

Col 2:22 describes the character of the prohibitions mentioned in Col 2:21. The expression "according to human commands and teachings" (κατὰ τὰ ἐντάλματα καὶ διδασκαλίας τῶν ἀνθρώπων) resembles the words "according to human tradition" (κατὰ τὴν παράδοσιν τῶν ἀνθρώπων) which appeared in Col 2:8; here are used only the words τὰ ἐντάλματα καὶ διδασκαλίας instead of τὴν παράδοσιν. Thus Col 2:16-22 repeats many details from Col 2:8: the introductory formula μή τις ὑμᾶς in Col 2:16, the elements of the universe (τὰ στοιχεῖα τοῦ κόσμου) in Col 2:20, and now the reference to human commands.

In addition, the prohibitions are taken as "things that perish with use" and are "according to human commands and teachings" (κατὰ τὰ ἐντάλματα καὶ διδασκαλίας τῶν ἀνθρώπων). The definition "things that perish with use" resembles Mk 7:18b-19 which states that "whatever goes into a person from outside cannot defile, since it enters, not the heart but the stomach, and goes out into the sewer", although there is no verbal agreement between the texts.[651] The phrase "human commands and teachings" occurs in Isa 29:13 in the form ἐντάλματα ἀνθρώπων καὶ διδασκαλίας and it is quoted in Mk 7:7 / par Mt 15:9 in the form διδασκαλίας ἐντάλματα ἀνθρώπων. Because ἔνταλμα occurs only in

---

[648] So e.g. Schweizer 1982, 166.
[649] O'Brien 1982, 150; Lindemann 1983, 51; R. P. Martin 1981, 96; Hartman 1985, 115; Bruce 1988, 127; Hendriksen 1971, 131; Haapa 1978, 53; Nikolainen 1987, 46; Lohse 1971, 123-124; Dunn 1996, 190-191; Pokorný 1987, 128-129.
[650] Similarly Lohse 1971, 123; Lindemann 1983, 51; Gnilka 1980, 156-158; Sumney 1993, 369-370. Contra Nielsen 1985, 106, who assumes that A/Col has no particular danger in mind but the recipients of the letter are supposed to fill in their own objects, ones relevant to their own situation.
[651] The similarity between Col 2:22 and Mk 7:19 is also noted by Pokorný 1987, 129; Dunn 1996, 194; Bruce 1988, 114; Haapa 1978, 53; Hartman 1985, 116; Goulder 1994, 28-30. In addition, Goulder states that in Mk 7:19 Jesus was "a Pauline", a disciple of Paul, while the author of Mt, who leaves out the comment "Thus he declared all food clean", was "a Petrine" (Mt 15:20).

these three passages in the NT and besides Isa 29:13, only in Job 23:11-12 in the LXX, it is unlikely that the similarity is accidental.[652]

Although scholars usually draw attention to the similarity among these texts, they, however, assume rather that both Col 2:22 and Mk 7:7 / par Mt 15:9 depend on the wording of Isa 29:13, direct or through the tradition, rather than that there was some connection between Col 2:22 and the Gospels.[653] Still, the similarity between Col 2:22 and Mk 7:19, mentioning the "things that perish with use" points to a connection between Mk and Col because Mk 7:19 does not have a parallel in other Gospels. Although on the grounds of verbal agreement, we are not able to decide whether Col 2:22 depends on Isa 29:13, Mt 15:9, or Mk 7:7, the connection between Col 2:22 and Mk 7:7 is most probable.[654]

In Mk 7:18b-19, the author of Mk may utilize some earlier material since it may be an exposition of the saying in Mk 7:15 which originates with the church. However, the literary dependence between Col and Mk 7 cannot be contested in the manner of Schweizer, who assumes that both Col 2:22 and Mk 7:19 are similar expositions of the saying in Mk 7:15.[655] It is remarkable that Johnson takes the detail that the teaching is given in private as "a sign that it is not part of the well-known tradition".[656] Though Mk 7:18b-19 may utilize tradition that originates with the church, the fact that it has no synoptic parallel still makes it characteristic of Mk.

Col 2:23 begins with the words ἅτινά ἐστιν, "which are". It points back to the regulations, commands and teachings mentioned in vv. 21 and 22 which A/Col wants to characterize once more in conclusion.[657] The regulations are defined to "have a reputation of wisdom" (λόγον μὲν ἔχοντα σοφίας) and thus to be considered as wisdom although they really are not. Since Paul has a similar negative attitude to the wisdom of this world in 1 Cor 1:17, 2:1, and 2:13, A/Col seems to write here in the manner of Paul.

It is generally agreed that the clauses of Col 2:23 are very difficult to understand.[658] In addition, some exegetes have assumed that the text has been

---

[652] Similarly Dunn 1996, 193.

[653] See O'Brien 1982, 151; Lindemann 1983, 51; Bruce 1988, 127; R. P. Martin 1981, 97; Schweizer 1982, 167; Ludwig 1974, 99; Gnilka 1980, 158-159; Arnold 1995, 223; Lohse 1971, 124; Sumney 1993, 370; Wilson 1997, 127.

[654] Similarly Müller 1988, 130, takes Mk 7:19, 6 as the background of Col 2:22. Cf. Luz 1998, 225, who refers only to the similarity between Col 2:22 and Mk 7. In contrast Dunn 1996, 194, Nielsen 1985, 119, and Hübner 1997, 91-92, assume that A/Col knew the same Jesus tradition which arises in Mk 7:1-23 // Mt 15:1-20. In addition, Pokorný 1987, 128-129, suggests that the similarity between Col 2:20 and Mk 7:19 shows that the synoptic tradition is familiar to A/Col. However, nothing indicates that the similarity is due to the synoptic tradition since Mk 7:19 has no parallel in other Gospels.

[655] So Schweizer 1971, 146.

[656] Johnson 1960, 134.

[657] O'Brien 1982, 152; Dunn 1996, 194; Haapa 1978, 54.

[658] See e.g. Lohse 1971, 124-126; Hübner 1997, 92; Dunn 1996, 194; Hartman 1985, 116; Sumney 1993, 370; Nikolainen 1987, 46.

corrupted early and have tried to reconstruct it.[659] Although the strict sense of the verse is impossible to know, it is still clear that here are again enumerated the features of wrong practices. The term ταπεινοφροσύνη occurred already in Col 2:18 where it was interpreted as most probably referring to counterfeit humility. The term ἐθελοθρησκεία does not occur in ancient texts before Col. It has thus been assumed that A/Col quotes a catchword of the philosophy confronted.[660] It is remarkable that the words ἐν ἐθελοθρησκίᾳ seem to repeat the words θέλων ἐν ... θρησκείᾳ from v. 18 only in a little different form.[661] Therefore, it is also possible that the term ἐθελοθρησκεία is formed by A/Col.[662] The term has been interpreted to denote "freely chosen worship".[663] However, many exegetes assume that it also includes the sense "worship performed by men", "self made religion".[664] In any case, ἐθελοθρησκεία is a slanderous term describing the religious practices of the opponents.

The noun ἀφειδία is unique in ECL and it does not occur in the LXX either. However, in the second century A.D. Lucian uses the words "unmindful of their bodies" (τῶν σωμάτων ἀφειδεῖν) when speaking about people practising athletics (Anacharsis 24) which is quite a close parallel to Col 2:23. Although the strict sense of the term ἀφειδία σώματος, "severe treatment of the body", is undefined, it clearly points to ascetic activities, probably fasting, because abstinence from food and drink was already mentioned in v. 16.[665]

Like at the beginning of Col 2:23, at the end of the verse also it is emphasized that strict regulations are without any value (οὐκ ἐν τιμῇ τινι).[666] They are only "for the satisfaction of the flesh" (πρὸς πλησμονὴν τῆς σαρκός). The term πλησμονή is unique in ECL but it is sometimes used in the LXX in a good sense denoting satisfaction, especially with food and drink (see Ex 16:3, Prov 3:10).[667] However, like Col 2:23, Hos 13:6 uses the term in a negative sense. It states how the heart of the satisfied people was proud and they forgot the Lord.[668] Similarly, Col 2:23 maintains that the legalistic way of life satisfies only the flesh, making man proud, but does not have any other significance.[669]

---

[659] Further in Lohse 1971, 124-126, which mentions e.g. Eberhard Nestle, Ernst von Dobschütz, B. G. Hall, and P.L. Hedley.
[660] See O'Brien 1982, 153; Lindemann 1983, 51; Nikolainen 1987, 46; R. P. Martin 1981, 98.
[661] E.g. Bujard 1973, 99; Dunn 1996, 195, and Wilson 1997, 175-176, note the repetition.
[662] Pokorný 1987, 131; Schmidt 1974, 159. Cf. Dunn 1996, 195. Contra Hübner 1997, 93
[663] Arnold 1995, 219; Lohse 1971, 126; Sumney 1993, 371; Schweizer 1982, 168; Haapa 1978, 54; Hartman 1985, 108.
[664] See Luz 1998, 216-217; R. P. Martin 1981, 94, 98; Lindemann 1983, 51; Bruce 1988, 128; Nikolainen 1987, 46; Hendriksen 1971, 133. Cf. DeMaris 1994, 59.
[665] O'Brien 1982, 153; Lindemann 1983, 51-52; Bruce 1988, 129; R. P. Martin 1981, 99; Schweizer 1982, 169; Haapa 1978, 54; Pokorný 1987, 131; Pfammatter 1987, 76; Lohse 1971, 126-27.
[666] Dunn 1996, 196; O'Brien 1982, 154.
[667] O'Brien 154-155; Dunn 1996, 196.
[668] Dunn 1996, 196; Hartman 1985, 108.
[669] Cf. Lindemann 1983, 52; Bruce 1988, 129; R. P. Martin 1981, 99; Haapa 1978, 55; O'Brien 1982, 153; Lohse 1971, 127.

It has been noted that A/Col always refers to the opponents by the indefinite someone (τις) and also their characteristics are very briefly described. Moreover, many of the warnings can be explained as being directed towards possible dangers. It has thus been assumed that A/Col has not any particular teaching in mind but the warnings arose from the general pressure to conform to the pagan and Jewish environment[670] or that the author has in mind all possible dangers which may occur after Paul's death.[671] However, it has to be noted that in Gal 1:7 Paul also uses the indefinite τις when he refers to the opponents.[672] Thus A/Col may only imitate the Pauline style. It is also difficult to believe that A/Col would take the trouble to compose a letter without having any actual danger in mind.

Abstinence from food and drink as well as the observance of holy days probably had a role in the teaching confronted. A/Col's usage of a regular Jewish way of speaking of the main festivals also indicates the Jewish character of the opponents. In addition, the prohibitions "Do not handle, Do not taste, Do not touch" seem to be a caricature of the legalistic commands of the opponents. The fact that the terms θρησκεία τῶν ἀγγέλων, "angelic worship", and ἃ ἑόρακεν ἐμβατεύων, "which he has seen upon entering", are not due to any Pauline or other text we know indicates that they are characteristics of some actual dangers of A/Col's own time. Therefore, the main identifying marks of the opponents are "angelic worship" and visions. These both are typical of the apocalyptic strands of Christianity among which Revelation (Rev) was written. Rev describes the visions of John of Patmos, John the seer, who was the leader of the group. He probably came with his followers from Palestine to Asia Minor after the Jewish War ca. A.D. 70.[673] Though Col is unlikely to have been addressed to the city of Colossae, it still seems to have been written in Asia Minor (see pp. 12-13) which is also the place where Rev was formed.[674] Since Rev is dated ca. A.D. 95,[675] it is unlikely that the text in the form we have it today was familiar to A/Col. Yet quite probably John the seer and his followers had influence in Asia Minor during the few decades before Rev was written, which makes it reasonable to think that Col was written in response to those strands of Christianity which Rev represents.[676]

Angels have an important role in Rev. They are praising Christ and worshiping God in the heavenly throne room (Rev 5:11, 7:11-12). John is also

---

[670] Hooker 1973, 329-331, followed by Schenk 1987a, 3350; and Wright 1990, 463-464. See also the interpretation of Dunn presented in p. 21 n. 33.

[671] Nielsen 1985, 107: "the writer's aim is not to counter some specific form of teaching in a particular location, but to commend Paul's interpretation of Christ as the one corrective for a whole range of errors". Cf. Standhartinger 1999, 181-193, and Kiley 1986, 65, 105, see also pp. 20-21.

[672] Cf. Arnold 1988, 71, who criticizes Kiley for overlooking the fact that Paul generally used the indefinite τις when speaking of opponents.

[673] Roloff 1984, 17. Cf. Royalty 1997, 1.

[674] Collins 1992, 701-702; Roloff 1984, 17.

[675] Caird 1966, 6; Collins 1992, 701; Roloff 1984, 19.

[676] Cf. Royalty 1997, 2, who takes John of Patmos and his followers as possible opponents of Col since Rev is generally assumed to has been composed in stages.

intending to fall at their feet, but he is denied this (Rev 22:8-10). Angels are also delivering messages to churches (Rev 2-3). What is meant by "the angels of the communities" is disputed. Latin church fathers interpreted them as bishops, which is unlikely. Since otherwise in Rev, the term "angel" is used only of superterrestrial beings, the more probable explanation is that the author has in mind the guardian angels of the cities familiar to the Hellenistic tradition.[677] Therefore, when A/Col refers to "worship of angels" and "dwelling on visions" he may well have in mind such visions described in Rev.[678]

Other characteristics of the opponents are also compatible with Rev. It contains clear condemnation of Christians on matters of food. Churches in Pergamum and Thyatira are condemned for tolerating the eating of meat sacrificed to idols (Rev 2:14, 20) and the Ephesians are praised for rejecting the teaching of the Nicolaitans which also included the eating of idol meat (Rev 2:6).[679] The Jewish character of the Christianity represented in Rev is also clear. People are condemned for tolerating the eating of idol meat. The text constantly quotes the OT and also resembles Jewish apocalypses.[680] It is thus quite possible that A/Col defends Paul's heritage of Christian liberty against the apocalyptic Christianity represented in Rev.

In Rev 1:2, John is said to testify "to the word of God". Similarly, A/Col describes Paul as making "the word of God fully known" (Col 1:25). The choice of wording is not typical of Paul himself but clearly a formation of A/Col. This suggests that here may be two competing interpretations of "the word of God" which would also explain A/Col's notion that Paul's interpretation of Christ is authoritative (see p. 126). As is usual in apocalypticism, the visions described in Rev represent the expectation that this world will come to an end soon (Rev 1:1,3, 4:1, 22:6,10). Though Col does not explicitly reject the apocalyptic expectation, Col and Rev hold different opinions about eschatology. In Col 1:26-27 "the word of God" is defined as "Christ among you (ἐν ὑμῖν), the hope of glory". Thus "Christ among you" is the content of mystery, "the word of God". Since "hope" already lies prepared in heaven (Col 1:5), in Col there is no longer any expectation that the world will come to an end soon, unlike in Rev. Col represents realized eschatology.[681]

The Christology of Col matches well with the explanation that the opponents are those circles in which Rev was composed. In the beginning of Rev, in 1:5, Christ is described as "the firstborn of the dead" (πρωτότοκος τῶν νεκρῶν) like in Col 1:18 and as "the ruler of the kings of the earth". Nevertheless, Rev is very theocentric: God is praised as the Almighty (παντοκράτωρ) again and again (1:8,

---

[677] Ford 1975, 386-387. Cf. Roloff 1984, 45-46.

[678] Cf. Royalty 1997, 3-4.

[679] Similarly Royalty 1997, 3. For the Nicolaitans see Räisänen 1995; Watson 1992.

[680] See Ford 1975, 22-26.

[681] Cf. Lohse 1971, 76: "it is no longer a matter of various mysteries concerning God's eschatological plan as in Jewish apocalyptic", see also 180. Cf. Royalty 1997, 2-3; Schweizer 1982, 109-110.

4:8, 11:17, 15:3, 16:7,14, 19:6,15, 21:22).[682] In contrast, in Col God is seldom mentioned but Christ has a central position: in Christ "the whole fullness of deity dwells bodily" (2:9). In addition, A/Col often describes Christ using characteristics which also Paul applies to God e.g. he is "before all things, and in him all things hold together" (1:17). The high Christology of Col could oppose the theocentric character occurring in the visions described in Rev.[683]

It seems quite possible that A/Col opposes such an apocalyptic movement represented in Rev. It suggests that Paul's heritage and the apocalyptic strand in Rev represent two different types of Christianity. The apocalyptic movement in Rev takes a position which seems to be consistent with the Apostolic Decree (Acts 15:29). Those tolerating the eating of idol meat are condemned in Rev 2:14-15.[684] On the contrary, Col 2:16, 21 clearly oppose all such regulations concerning food. Similar debate between two early Christian groups was called attention to some generations ago by the scholars of the Tübingen school who regarded the Nicolaitans rejected in Rev as followers of Paul.[685] The view remained a relatively neglected aspect of scholarship but is still sometimes stated.[686] The detail that Col 2 and Rom 14:17, which Col 2:16 is following, have been suggested as among the "possible roots of the Nicolaitan position"[687] also supports the interpretation that Col represents the debate between two strands of early Christianity: Paul's heritage of Christian liberty and an apocalyptic visionary group that observed stricter regulations.[688]

---

[682] The term παντοκράτωρ is normal in the LXX but appears in the NT only in Rev and in the passage 2 Cor 6:14-7:1 which is noteworthy for including many non-Pauline, according to Betz even anti-Pauline features (see p. 82 n. 316). The character of 2 Cor 6:14-7:1 resembles also in some aspects the Christianity represented in Rev. God is praised as the Almighty (2 Cor 6:18) and there is a prohibition against touching anything unclean (2 Cor 6:17). Since A/Col in Col 1:11b-13 reveals acquaintance with this passage and in Col 2:21 condemns similar prohibitions presented in 2 Cor 6:17, there rises the question whether 2 Cor 6:14-7:1 is formed among the same strand of Christianity as Rev.

[683] Cf. Royalty 1997, 5, who takes the Christology of Col as one of the highest in the NT and assumes that it opposes the theocentric nature Rev represents. Similarly Barclay 1997, 82, states that Col "contains some of the 'highest' Christology in the New Testament."

[684] Cf. Collins 1986, 316-318, followed by Räisänen 1995, 1605 ss.

[685] Further in Räisänen 1995, 1603 ss.

[686] See Caird 1966, 39-40; Rowland 1987, 262; Räisänen 1995; H. Leppä 2002, 171-172.

[687] Räisänen 1995, 1631.

[688] Goulder 1994, 50, 160, 172, also takes Col as representing the debate between two strands of early Christianity: Paul and his disciples, "the Paulines", and Peter and his followers, "the Petrines". He regards Col as a genuine Pauline letter which is debating with the Petrines who are trying to force the Paulines into observing Jewish ways. Col is attaching the Petrine law doctrine, the insistence on sabbath, food and purity rules as well as the visions. Rev is, in Goulder's opinion, "a semi-Pauline writing", "a bridge writing", between the Paulines and the Petrines; Goulder 1994, 183, 186. Cf. Lindemann 1999, 196, 208-210 who regards the opponents as Christians living in Laodicea and Barclay 1997, 53 who states that "the 'heresy' is being sponsored by Christians".

5. The Rule of Christ in the Life of the Believers (Col 3:1-4:1)

5.1. Catalogs of Vices and Virtues (Col 3:1-17)

Col 3:1 begins the hortatory section of the letter which continues through 4:1. The passage includes first the catalogs of vices (Col 3:1-11) and virtues (Col 3:12-17) which are then followed by the household rules (Col 3:18-4:1).

Col 3:1-4

1 **Εἰ** οὖν **συνηγέρθητε** τῷ **Χριστῷ**, τὰ **ἄνω** ζητεῖτε, οὗ ὁ **Χριστός** **ἐστιν ἐν δεξιᾷ** τοῦ **θεοῦ** **καθήμενος**·
2 τὰ **ἄνω** φρονεῖτε, μὴ **τὰ** ἐπὶ τῆς γῆς.
3 **ἀπεθάνετε** γὰρ καὶ ἡ ζωὴ ὑμῶν κέκρυπται σὺν τῷ Χριστῷ ἐν τῷ θεῷ·
4 ὅταν ὁ **Χριστὸς** φανερωθῇ, ἡ ζωὴ ὑμῶν, τότε καὶ ὑμεῖς σὺν αὐτῷ φανερωθήσεσθε ἐν δόξῃ.

Col 2:20, 12

20 **Εἰ ἀπεθάνετε** σὺν **Χριστῷ** ...
12 ... ἐν ᾧ καὶ **συνηγέρθητε** ...

Rom 8:34

... **Χριστὸς** ... ὅς καί **ἐστιν ἐν δεξιᾷ τοῦ θεοῦ**

Lk 22:67-69

67 ... εἰ σὺ εἶ ὁ **χριστός**,
...
69 ... ἔσται ὁ υἱὸς τοῦ ἀνθρώπου **καθήμενος** ἐκ δεξιῶν τῆς δυνάμεως **τοῦ θεοῦ**.

Phil 3:14, **19-21**

14 ... τὸ βραβεῖον τῆς **ἄνω** κλήσεως ...
19 ... οἱ **τὰ** ἐπίγεια φρονοῦντες.
20 ... Ἰησοῦν Χριστόν,
21 ὃς μετασχηματίσει τὸ σῶμα τῆς ταπεινώσεως ἡμῶν σύμμορφον τῷ σώματι τῆς δόξης αὐτοῦ ...

Phil 1:21

Ἐμοὶ γὰρ τὸ ζῆν **Χριστὸς** ...

The parenesis before the catalog of vices refers back to the preceding verses. The words Εἰ οὖν συνηγέρθητε τῷ Χριστῷ, "so if you have been raised with Christ", (Col 3:1) repeat the words ἐν ᾧ καὶ συνηγέρθητε, "you were also raised with him", in Col 2:12 and ἀπεθάνετε γάρ, "for you have died", in Col 3:3 refers back to εἰ ἀπεθάνετε σὺν Χριστῷ, "if with Christ you died", in Col 2:20. In addition, the structure of the clause εἰ οὖν συνηγέρθητε τῷ Χριστῷ in 3:1 resembles the one in Col 2:20, εἰ ἀπεθάνετε σὺν Χριστῷ.[689]

The exhortation "to seek that which is above" (τὰ ἄνω ζητεῖτε) in Col 3:1 is unique in ECL. In addition, the term τὰ ἄνω occurs elsewhere only in Jn 8:23. The words clearly refer to the heavenly world which is also familiar to Paul when he mentions "the Jerusalem which is above" (ἡ ἄνω Ἰερουσαλήμ) in Gal 4:26 and

[689] Similarly Lohse 1971, 132; Schweizer 1982, 172; Ludwig 1974, 105; Luz 1998, 225; Hübner 1997, 97; R. P. Martin 1981, 100-101; Lindemann 1983, 53; Haapa 1978, 55-56; O'Brien 1982, 158; Schweizer 1982, 175.

the "upward call" (τὸ βραβεῖον τῆς ἄνω κλήσεως) in Phil 3:14.[690] In Col 3:2, the exhortation is repeated and clarified by presenting the opposite of it, the things that are on earth (τὰ ἐπὶ τῆς γῆς).[691] The choice of wording τὰ ἄνω φρονεῖτε resembles the words τὰ ἐπίγεια φρονοῦντες in Phil 3:19 which, however, provide a clear antithesis to it.[692] In addition, Col 3:4 and Phil 3:20-21 describe the future appearance of Christ in glory very similarly. The resemblance between Col 3:1-4 and Phil 3:19-21, the use of two of the same nouns (Χριστός, δόξα) and one verb (φρονέω) within five lines in Phil, meets the criteria for a possible literary dependence. Unfortunately, the use of the adverb ἄνω in Phil 3:14 appears too far away and so cannot be included with the common words.[693] Col 3:4 also resembles Phil 1:21. The words "Christ, our life" (ὁ Χριστὸς ..., ἡ ζωὴ ὑμῶν) are similar to the words "for to me, living is Christ" (Ἐμοὶ γὰρ τὸ ζῆν Χριστός). Although the verbal agreement is too slight to indicate literary dependence, Col 3:4 may also echo Phil 1:21.[694]

Col 3:1 mentions that Christ is seated at the right hand of God. The thought, which appears only once in the authentic Pauline letters (Rom 8:34) but is a stock phrase in other ECL (see e.g. Mk 14:62, Mk 16:19, Mt 26:64, Lk 22:69, Acts 2:3,35, Heb 1:13; Eph 1:20), is due to Ps 109:1 LXX (κάθου ἐκ δεξιῶν μου). It is worth noting, however, that some parallels in ECL are clearly closer to Col 3:1 than the Psalm text. The words ἐστιν ἐν δεξιᾷ τοῦ θεοῦ exactly match Rom 8:34. Though the verb κάθημαι, "to be seated", does not appear in Rom 8:34, it is used in the Gospel texts, of which Lk 22:69 (ἔσται ... καθήμενος ἐκ δεξιῶν τῆς δυνάμεως τοῦ θεοῦ) resembles Col 3:1 most.[695] Thus it seems that the choice of wording in Col 3:1, ἐστιν ἐν δεξιᾷ τοῦ θεοῦ καθήμενος, follows Rom 8:34, adding the verb κάθημαι in the participle form καθήμενος which is used in the Gospels. Since Col 3:1 uses the noun Χριστός like Rom 8:34 and repeats verbatim three consecutive words from it (ἐστιν ἐν δεξιᾷ τοῦ θεοῦ), the resemblance meets the criteria for a possible literary dependence.[696] In addition, A/Col seems to be acquainted with some or several of the Gospel texts which are based on Ps 109:1 LXX.[697] Since Col 3:1 seems to depend on Rom 8:34, there is no reason to

---

[690] Cf. 2 Clem 19:4: ἐκεῖνος ἄνω μετὰ τῶν πατέρων ἀναβιώσας.

[691] A similar juxtaposition ἐν τῷ οὐρανῷ ἄνω – ἐπὶ τῆς γῆς κάτω also occurs in Acts 2:19 and frequently in the LXX (see Ex 20:4, Deut 4:39, 5:8, Josh 2:11, 3 Kings 8:23). Cf. Jn 8:23.

[692] This is also noted by Kiley 1986, 82; E. P. Sanders 1966, 44; Haapa 1978, 56; O'Brien 1982, 160-161, 164; Arnold 1995, 306. Cf. Pokorný 1987, 135; Dunn 1996, 205.

[693] E.g. Pokorný 1987, 135; Bruce 1988, 137; O'Brien 1982, 167-168; Luz 1998, 226; Arnold 1995, 305-306, present Phil 3:20-21 as a close parallel to Col 3:4.

[694] Also e.g. Ludwig 1974, 107; Gnilka 1980, 176; and O'Brien 1982, 167, note the similarity between Col 3:4 and Phil 1:21.

[695] A/Eph also uses the verb κάθημαι in Eph 1:20: ... Χριστῷ ... καθίσας ἐν δεξιᾷ αὐτοῦ ἐν τοῖς ἐπουρανίοις.

[696] Also Gnilka 1980, 172 and Bruce 1988, 132 n. 2, comment on the similarity between Col 3:1 and Rom 8:34.

[697] Cf. Nielsen 1985, 118: "it seems reasonable to suggest that the author of Colossians found the fragment in some Christian writing."

emphasize the connection between Col and Ps by saying that Col 3:1 quotes or draws obviously from Ps 109:1 LXX, as most scholars do.[698]

Col 3:5-11
5 Νεκρώσατε **οὖν τὰ μέλη τὰ ἐπὶ τῆς γῆς**, πορνείαν ἀκαθαρσίαν πάθος ἐπιθυμίαν κακήν, καὶ τὴν πλεονεξίαν, ἥτις **ἐστὶν εἰδωλολατρία**,

6 δι' ἃ ἔρχεται ἡ **ὀργὴ** τοῦ **θεοῦ** [ἐπὶ τοὺς υἱοὺς τῆς ἀπειθείας].

7 **ἐν** οἷς **καὶ** ὑμεῖς περιεπατήσατέ **ποτε**, ὅτε ἐζῆτε ἐν τούτοις·

8 **νυνὶ δὲ** ἀπόθεσθε **καὶ** ὑμεῖς τὰ πάντα, ὀργήν, θυμόν, κακίαν, βλασφημίαν, αἰσχρολογίαν ἐκ τοῦ στόματος ὑμῶν·

9 μὴ ψεύδεσθε εἰς ἀλλήλους, ἀπεκδυσάμενοι τὸν παλαιὸν ἄνθρωπον σὺν ταῖς πράξεσιν αὐτοῦ

10 **καὶ** ἐνδυσάμενοι τὸν νέον τὸν ἀνακαινούμενον **εἰς ἐπίγνωσιν κατ' εἰκόνα** τοῦ κτίσαντος **αὐτόν**,

Col 3:2
τὰ ἄνω φρονεῖτε, μὴ **τὰ ἐπὶ τῆς γῆς**.

Rom 13:12b-14
12b ἀποθώμεθα **οὖν** τὰ ἔργα τοῦ σκότους ...
13 ὡς ἐν ἡμέρᾳ εὐσχημόνως περιπατήσωμεν, μὴ κώμοις καὶ μέθαις, ...
14 ἀλλὰ ἐνδύσασθε τὸν κύριον Ἰησοῦν Χριστὸν καὶ τῆς σαρκὸς πρόνοιαν μὴ ποιεῖσθε εἰς ἐπιθυμίας.

Col 1:21-22
Καὶ ὑμᾶς **ποτε** ὄντας ...
ἐν τοῖς ἔργοις τοῖς πονηροῖς,
νυνὶ δὲ ἀποκατήλλαξεν

Rom 6:6
ὁ παλαιὸς ἡμῶν ἄνθρωπος συνεσταυρώθη

Col 2:2
εἰς ἐπίγνωσιν τοῦ μυστηρίου τοῦ θεοῦ

Gen 1:27
κατ' εἰκόνα θεοῦ ἐποίησεν **αὐτόν**

Gal 3:27-28
... Χριστὸν ἐνεδύσασθε.

Rom 6:13
μηδὲ παριστάνετε **τὰ μέλη** ὑμῶν ὅπλα ἀδικίας τῇ ἁμαρτίᾳ, ἀλλὰ ... τῷ θεῷ ὡσεὶ ἐκ νεκρῶν ζῶντας ...

Gal 5:19-20
19 ἅτινά **ἐστιν** πορνεία, ἀκαθαρσία, ἀσέλγεια,
20 **εἰδωλολατρία**, ... θυμοί

1 Thess 4:3, 5
3 ἀπὸ τῆς πορνείας, ...
5 μὴ ἐν πάθει ἐπιθυμίας ...

1 Cor 5:11
ἢ πλεονέκτης ἢ εἰδωλολάτρης

Rom 1:18
Ἀποκαλύπτεται γὰρ **ὀργὴ θεοῦ** ...

1 Thess 1:10
ἐκ τῆς ὀργῆς τῆς ἐρχομένης.

Col 2:11
ἐν τῇ ἀπεκδύσει τοῦ σώματος τῆς σαρκός

[698] See Dunn 1996, 203-204; R. P. Martin 1981, 101. Cf. Lohse 1971, 133; Arnold 1995, 306; Nikolainen 1987, 48-49; O'Brien 1982, 162; Conzelmann 1990, 196; Hartman 1985, 131; Luz 1998, 225; Hübner 1997, 98; Wilson 1997, 127.

11 ὅπου **οὐκ ἔνι** **Ἕλλην** καὶ **Ἰουδαῖος**, **περιτομὴ** καὶ **ἀκροβυστία**, βάρβαρος, Σκύθης, **δοῦλος**, **ἐλεύθερος**, **ἀλλὰ** [**τὰ**] **πάντα** καὶ **ἐν πᾶσιν** Χριστός.	**οὐκ ἔνι Ἰουδαῖος** οὐδὲ **Ἕλλην**, οὐκ ἔνι **δοῦλος** οὐδὲ **ἐλεύθερος**, ... πάντες γὰρ ὑμεῖς εἷς ἐστε **ἐν** Χριστῷ Ἰησοῦ.	**Gal 6:15** οὔτε γὰρ **περιτομή** τί ἐστιν οὔτε **ἀκροβυστία** **ἀλλὰ** καινὴ κτίσις. Rom 1:14 Ἕλλησίν τε καὶ βαρβάροις, σοφοῖς τε καὶ ἀνοήτοις ὀφειλέτης εἰμί **1 Cor 15:28** ἵνα ᾖ ὁ θεὸς [**τὰ**] **πάντα** **ἐν πᾶσιν**.

The catalog of vices begins in Col 3:5 with the demand to put to death the parts of you which are on the earth (νεκρώσατε ... τὰ μέλη τὰ ἐπὶ τῆς γῆς). The text refers back to 3:2 which contained the exhortation to seek that which is above and not that on the earth (τὰ ἐπὶ τῆς γῆς).[699] The verb νεκρόω occurs otherwise in the Pauline corpus only in Rom 4:19 but it is also used in Heb 11:12. However, neither of the texts resemble Col 3:2: both employ the verb νεκρόω literally when describing the old body of Abraham while Col 3:2 uses it in a figurative sense.[700] On the one hand, it is noteworthy that in ECL the word νεκρός is sometimes used figuratively both as an adjective and as a noun (see Lk 15:24, 32, Rom 7:8, 6:13, Col 2:13, Heb 6:1, 9:14, Jas 2:17, 26, Rev 3:1, Ign, Philad 6:1, Herm 9:21). Rom 6:13: "no longer present your members (τὰ μέλη) to sin as instruments of wickedness, but ... to God as those who have been brought from death (ἐκ νεκρῶν) to life" especially is quite similar to Col 3:5. On the other hand, the later Stoics also use the verb νεκρόω figuratively; e.g. Epict, Diss I, 5,4[701] resembles Col 3:2. Although the agreement between Col 3:2 and Rom 6:13 does not meet the criteria for literary dependence, it is possible that Col 3:2 echoes the choice of wording in Rom 6:13.[702] It may also be influenced by the Stoic figurative use of the verb νεκρόω.

The composition, the words used, and the thought of the exhortation in Col 3:5-10 resemble Rom 13:12b-14. The first clauses νεκρώσατε οὖν τὰ μέλη τὰ ἐπὶ τῆς γῆς, "put to death, therefore, whatever on you is earthly" (Col 3:5) and ἀποθώμεθα οὖν τὰ ἔργα τοῦ σκότους, "let us then lay aside the works of darkness" (Rom 13:12b) are formed similarly. In addition, Col 3:5-10 and Rom 13:12b-14 include both the juxtaposition "to lay aside – to put on" (ἀποτίθημι – ἐνδύομαι) and use the verb περιπατέω, "to walk", and the noun ἐπιθυμία, "desire". It is also

---

699 Similarly R. P. Martin 1981, 103; Dunn 1996, 212; Haapa 1978, 60; Hendriksen 1971, 144; O'Brien 1982, 174, 176.

700 Bultmann 1973b, 894.

701 Epict, Diss I, 5,4: οἱ δὲ πολλοὶ τὴν μὲν σωματικὴν ἀπονέκρωσιν φοβούμεθα ..., τῆς ψυχῆς δ' ἀπονεκρουμένης οὐδὲν ἡμῖν μέλει.

702 Similarly Lindemann 1983, 55. Cf. Bultmann 1973b, 894.

noteworthy that the verbs ἀποτίθημι and ἐνδύομαι are not frequently used together. For example, in the NT they appear together elsewhere only in Eph 4:22-24. Since three of the words in common, the verbs ἀποτίθημι, περιπατέω, and ἐνδύομαι, appear within five lines in Rom, the verbal agreement between Col 3:5-10 and Rom 13:12b-14 indicates a possible literary dependence.[703] The structure of the text also resembles Col 1:21-22. Both Col 3:7-8 and Col 1:21-22 employ the juxtaposition "once – but now" (ποτε – νυνὶ δέ) in order to describe the contrast between the earlier and current life.[704]

Lists of vices and virtues were common in ancient world. In ECL occur e.g. the following catalogs of vices: Rom 1:29-32, 1 Cor 5:9-11, 6:9-10, 2 Cor 12:21, Gal 5:19-23, 1 Thess 4:3-6, 1 Pet 4:3, Mk 7:21-23, Did 5, and Barn 20. The catalog of vices in Col is divided into two distinct lists. Both Col 3:5 and 8 enumerate five vices which are probably based on a fivefold enumeration from the Persian tradition.[705] Like Col 3:5, Gal 5:19 starts the list by mentioning πορνεία (fornication) and ἀκαθαρσία (impurity), which also in both lists are later followed by the vices εἰδωλολατρία (idolatry) and θυμός (wrath, anger) even in the same order (Col 3:5, 8 / Gal 5:20). The texts also use a very similar choice of wording, ἥτις ἐστίν, "which is", (Col 3:5) and ἅτινά ἐστιν, "which are", (Gal 5:19).

The agreement between the beginnings of the catalogs, the same two vices in succession, is remarkable because, in spite of the great number of different lists, the vices πορνεία and ἀκαθαρσία are not enumerated one after another anywhere else in the first century A.D. Later, in the second and third centuries they sometimes appear together: Clement of Alexandria lists them one after another three times and Origen eight times. In addition, they occur in the Epistulae de virginitate (I 8, 2) which belongs to the unauthentic writings attached to the name of Clement of Rome, the Pseudo-Clementines. Of the texts, e.g. Clement of Alexandria, Paedagogus III 71,1, clearly follows Col 3:5-6 while e.g. Epistulae de

---

[703] Similarly E. P. Sanders 1966, 42-43, followed by Pokorný 1987, 139, assumes that "Col 3:5-10 has been built around Rom 13:12ff." Cf. Schweizer 1982, 195: "this passage is closely connected with Rom 13:12-14" and Müller 1988, 172. Contra many scholars who comment on the resemblance between the texts but instead of literary dependence, take the agreements to be due to the use of the same tradition, sometimes defined as the baptismal tradition because the juxtaposition "to lay aside" – "to put on" is interpreted as referring to baptism; see T. W. Martin 1996a, 194, n. 2; Lohse 1971, 149; Luz 1998, 227; Lohse 1971, 136; Gnilka 1980, 186; Lindemann 1979, 118 n. 31. However, this interpretation does not explain at all why Col 3:5-11 and Rom 13:12b-14 use so many of the same words and e.g. Rom 6:13 does not although it includes very similar thought.

[704] Similarly Schweizer 1982, 192; Lohse 1971, 140; Hartman 1985, 146; O'Brien 1982, 174, 185; Dunn 1996, 218; Luz 1998, 227.

[705] Lohse 1971, 137; Hartman 1985, 135; Schweizer 1982, 185-186. Contra O'Brien 1982, 177, who does not see any need to look for Persian analogies.

virginitate I 8, 2 seems to imitate Gal 5:19f.[706] The agreement between Col 3:5, 8 and Gal 5:19-20 is obvious: four of the same nouns and the similar choice of wording ἥτις ἐστίν / ἅτινά ἐστιν which occur within two lines in Gal and, in addition, the enumerating of the vices πορνεία and ἀκαθαρσία in succession which is unique in the texts of the first century A.D. Therefore, the resemblance clearly meets the criteria for a probable literary dependence.[707]

Besides Gal 5:19-20, the catalog of vices in 1 Thess 4:3, 5 and the one in 1 Cor 5:11 have some interesting agreements with Col 3:5. In 1 Thess 4:3, 5 are enumerated πορνεία (fornication), πάθος (passion), and ἐπιθυμία (evil desire) exactly in the same order as in Col 3:5. In addition, the rare occurrence of the noun πάθος in the Pauline corpus points to a dependence between the texts: it appears, except in Col 3:5 and in 1 Thess 4:5, only in Rom 1:26 near a list of vices (see v. 29). The resemblance between Col 3:5 and 1 Thess 4:3, 5, three nouns in common within two lines in the text imitated, meet the criteria for a possible literary dependence. 1 Cor 5:11 lists ἢ πλεονέκτης ἢ εἰδωλολάτρης, "greedy or an idolater", resembling the choice of wording in Col 3:5, τὴν πλεονεξίαν, ἥτις ἐστὶν εἰδωλολατρία, "greed which is idolatry". The agreement is noteworthy because the vices greed and idolatry are not otherwise enumerated in succession in the catalogs of vices in ECL, except in Eph 5:5 which is later and probably follows Col 3:5[708]. In addition, the nouns εἰδωλολάτρης and εἰδωλολατρία are unusual in the genuine Pauline letters: while the former occurs only in 1 Cor 5:10-11, 6:9, and 10:7, the latter is used in 1 Cor 10:14 and Gal 5:20. Accordingly, the resemblance between Col 3:5 and 1 Cor 5:11, the use of two similar nouns, meet the criteria for a possible literary dependence.[709]

Though many scholars call attention to the resemblances between Col 3:5 and the authentic Pauline texts, they still do not, apart from Sanders, assume any dependence between the texts. Instead, the similarities are taken to be due to the use of the same tradition.[710] For example, Schweizer states that Col 3:5 and Gal

---

706 Clement of Alexandria, Paedagogus III 71,1: Νεκρώσατε οὖν τὰ μέλη τὰ ἐπὶ τῆς γῆς, πορνείαν, ἀκαθαρσίαν, πάθος, ἐπιθυμίαν κακὴν καὶ τὴν πλεονεξίαν, ἥτις ἐστὶν εἰδωλολατρεία, δι' ἃ ἔρχεται ἡ ὀργὴ τοῦ θεοῦ. Epistulae de virginitate I 8, 2: ἅτινά εἰσιν πορνεία, ἀκαθαρσία, ἀσέλγεια, εἰδωλολατρεία, φαρμακεία, ἔχθραι, ἔρεις, ζῆλοι, θυμοί, ...

707 Similarly E. P. Sanders 1966, 42-43, contends that Col 3:5 is built around Gal 5:19-20. Following Sanders, Pokorný 1987, 139, maintains that the list in Col 3:5 has the closest parallel in Gal 5:19 ff. Besides, many scholars note the similarity between the texts; see R. P. Martin 1981, 103; Lindemann 1983, 56-57; Haapa 1978, 60; Hübner 1997, 102; Lohse 1971, 139; Dunn 1996, 214; Luz 1998, 227-228.

708 Eph 5:5: ... πᾶς πόρνος ἢ ἀκάθαρτος ἢ πλεονέκτης, ὅ ἐστιν εἰδωλολάτρης.

709 Also Cannon 1981, 83-84, 87; R. P. Martin 1981, 103; Haapa 1978, 60; Lohse 1971, 139; Hübner 1997, 102, Hendriksen 1971, 146, call attention to the similarity between Col 3:5 and 1 Thess 4:3, 5.

710 See e.g. Luz 1998, 227 ff.; Lohse 1971, 136; R. P. Martin 1981, 107; Cannon 1981, 103 ff; Lindemann 1979, 118. Kiley 1986, 93, does not even want to admit that the agreement between Col 3:5 and Gal 5:19-20 is due to the Pauline tradition but emphasizes, referring to the occurrence of the term πορνεία in the Shepherd of Hermas, that the similarity is due to the common parlance. However, the occurrence of one similar vice does not invalidate the close similarity between the

5:19b, 20a go back to the basic community parenesis which was first presented in 1 Thess 4:3-6.[711] Schweizer's interpretation does not, however, explain the close resemblance between Col and Gal: the use of the similar phrases ἥτις ἐστίν / ἅτινά ἐστιν and the enumerating of the vices εἰδωλολατρία and θυμός are not derived from 1 Thess 4:3-6.[712] Accordingly, the resemblances between Col 3:5, Gal 5:19-20, 1 Thess 3, 5, and 1 Cor 5:11 do not seem to be due to the use of the same tradition but rather point to literary dependence between the texts. Since all of the vices mentioned in Col 3:5 are enumerated in Gal 5:19-20, 1 Thess 4:3, 5, or 1 Cor 5:11, it seems that A/Col has in mind these authentic Pauline catalogs and conflates them.[713]

Col 3:6 contains the warning that "the wrath of God is coming on those who are disobedient". The catalogs of vices are frequently set within the framework of God's judgment (cf. 1 Thess 4:3-6, 1 Cor 5:10-13, Rom 1:18-32, Gal 5:19-21). The expression "the wrath of God" (ὀργὴ θεοῦ) used in Col 3:6 appears also in Rom 1:18.[714] Besides, 1 Thess 1:10 mentions the rescue from "the wrath that is coming" (ἐκ τῆς ὀργῆς τῆς ἐρχομένης). Although the resemblances do not meet the criteria for literary dependence, the words ἔρχεται ἡ ὀργὴ τοῦ θεοῦ in Col 3:6 may echo Rom 1:18 and 1 Thess 1:10.[715] The words "on those who are disobedient" (ἐπὶ τοὺς υἱοὺς τῆς ἀπειθείας) do not have a parallel in the genuine Pauline letters. It is also uncertain whether they belonged to the authentic text of Col 3:6 because the words are missing in the old manuscripts p46 and B. However, most old manuscripts include them[716] and, in addition, the words are used exactly in the same form in Eph 5:6 which also otherwise matches Col 3:6.[717] Thus it seems probable that the words ἐπὶ τοὺς υἱοὺς τῆς ἀπειθείας belonged to the authentic text of Col which was then imitated by A/Eph.[718]

In Col 3:8 is another catalog of five vices: in this verse ὀργή (anger), θυμός (wrath), κακία (malice), βλασφημία (slander), and αἰσχρολογία (abusive language) are enumerated. Unlike the first list, the one in Col 3:8 includes vices atypical of the genuine Pauline catalogs: ὀργή does not otherwise appear, apart

---

lists in Col and Gal. Note also Schweizer 1982, 185: "the catalogues clearly bear the stamp of a tradition that can be identified only in Paul's writings".

711 Schweizer 1982, 189-190.

712 Nor is convincing the supposition of Hartman 1987, 240, according to which Col 3:5,8 are dependent on the Decalogue. Hartman is referring to Gnilka 1980, 185, but as a matter of fact, Gnilka only suggests that Col 3:5, 8 seems almost to depend on the Decalogue.

713 Similarly E. P. Sanders 1966, 42-43.

714 Besides, it occurs in Jn 3:36.

715 According to Dunn 1996, 216, 1 Thess 1:10 is the closest parallel to Col 3:6. Cf. Lohse 1971, 139; Gnilka 1980, 183; Haapa 1978, 62. In addition, R. P. Martin 1981, 104; Schweizer 1982, 18; Bruce 1988, 144; Lohse 1971, 139, mentions Rom 1:18 as a parallel to Col 3:6.

716 ℵ A C D F G H I Ψ 075. 0278. 33. 1739. 1881 *m*.

717 Eph 5:6: ... διὰ ταῦτα γὰρ ἔρχεται ἡ ὀργὴ τοῦ θεοῦ ἐπὶ τοὺς υἱοὺς τῆς ἀπειθείας. Cf. Eph 2:2: ἐν αἷς ποτε περιεπατήσατε ... ἐν τοῖς υἱοῖς τῆς ἀπειθείας.

718 Similarly Lindemann 1983, 55. Contra Pokorný 1987, 141, who assumes that the words are interpolated later.

from Eph 4:31 which is later than Col. θυμός is the only one which occurred in the texts that A/Col seems to imitate in v. 5, κακία appears only in Rom 1:29, αἰσχρολογία is not included in the catalogs of vices until in Did 5:1, and, in addition, βλασφημία is not at all used in the authentic Pauline letters although it occurs in all Gospels, e.g. in the catalog of vices in Mk 7:22 /par. Mt 15:19.

The context of Mk 7:22 also resembles Col 3:8: while it is stated in Mk 7:21-23 that the evil things which defile a person come from within, Col 3:8 lists as a vice the abusive language from your mouth.[719] The resemblance does not meet, however, the criteria for literary dependence: except βλασφημία, no other common words occur. Therefore, the catalog of vices in Col 3:8 does not seem to have any prototypes in the genuine Pauline letters, nor does the exhortation presented after the list in Col 3:9 "do not lie to one another" (μὴ ψεύδεσθε εἰς ἀλλήλους).[720] Nothing indicates that the vices are those which were most current at the time Col was written. Rather, Col 3:8 seems to include a general parenesis valid to all churches because the vices listed are the kinds usually occurring in human communities.[721]

Col 3:9 restates that the recipients of the letter "have stripped off the old self with its practices" (ἀπεκδυσάμενοι τὸν παλαιὸν ἄνθρωπον σὺν ταῖς πράξεσιν αὐτοῦ). As was already noted, the verb ἀπεκδύομαι is typical of A/Col: it appears only in Col 2:15 and 3:9 in ECL. Furthermore, the noun ἀπέκδυσις occurs only in Col 2:11. The phrase ἀπέκδυσις τοῦ σώματος τῆς σαρκός, "putting off the body of the flesh", in Col 2:11 is a close parallel to Col 3:9 which clearly uses the verb ἀπεκδύομαι as the opposite of the Pauline verb ἐνδύομαι used in the following verse.[722] In addition, the expression ὁ παλαιὸς ἄνθρωπος occurs elsewhere only in Rom 6:6 and in Eph 4:22 in ECL. Because the phrase ὁ παλαιὸς ἄνθρωπος is so exceptional, the occurrence of two words in common meets the criteria for a possible literary dependence and the resemblance between Col 3:9 and Rom 6:6 indicates literary dependence.[723]

---

719 On the grounds of the resemblances between Col 3:8 // Mk 7:21-23 and the similarity which was noted between Col 2:22 and Mk 7, Pokorný 1987, 142, assumes that A/Col knows the synoptic tradition utilized in Mk 7:1-23.

720 The last one resembles a little the words οὐ ψεύδομαι, "I am not lying" which Paul sometimes uses (see Rom 9:1, Gal 1:20, 2 Cor 11:31).

721 Cf. Lohse 1971, 136-137: "The exhortations follow traditional forms and sequences of enumeration and do not at all refer to specific problems in the community." O'Brien 1982, 180, and Hartman 1985, 143-144, are not so rigid but still emphasize that we must not jump to conclusions when trying to define the situation among the recipients of the letter. Contra Schweizer 1982, 190: "... Paul mentions only those sins which he fears he may encounter in the community ..." In addition, he contends that similar lists occur in 2 Cor 12:20, Gal 5:20, and Rom 13:13 which all are introduced by the triad of "strife, jealousy, and anger". Col 3:8 does not use at all the words ἔρις, ζῆλος, θυμοί occurring in 1 Cor 12:20 and Gal 5:20. In addition, Rom 13:13 differs from 1 Cor 12:20 and Gal 5:20: it uses only the words ἔριδι καὶ ζήλῳ. Thus (pace Schweizer) Col 3:8 does not seem to include a catalog similar to 2 Cor 12:20, Gal 5:20, and Rom 13:13.

722 Gnilka 1980, 178, notes also the similarity between Col 3:9 and 2:11.

723 Similarly E. P. Sanders 1966, 42-43. Many scholars comment on the similarity between Col 3:9 and Rom 6:6 although they do not assume that the texts depend on each other; see R. P. Martin

The use of the verb ἐνδύομαι in Col 3:10 was noted as probably being due to Rom 13:14. However, instead of the putting on the Lord Jesus Christ in Rom, Col describes the putting on of the new self, which is being renewed (ἐνδυσάμενοι τὸν νέον τὸν ἀνακαινούμενον). The description does not have any close parallel in the genuine Pauline letters although sometimes Paul mentions the renewing quite similarly (see Rom 12:2, 2 Cor 4:16).[724] The renewal is further defined by the words εἰς ἐπίγνωσιν κατ' εἰκόνα τοῦ κτίσαντος αὐτόν. The phrase "in knowledge" (εἰς ἐπίγνωσιν) occurred already in Col 2:2 and was noted to be typical of A/Col.[725] In addition, the words "according to the image of its creator" (κατ' εἰκόνα τοῦ κτίσαντος αὐτόν) resemble Col 1:15 which describes Christ both as the image of God (εἰκὼν τοῦ θεοῦ) and the firstborn of all creation (πρωτότοκος πάσης κτίσεως). The choice of wording τῆς εἰκόνος τοῦ υἱοῦ αὐτοῦ in Rom 8:29 is also somewhat similar to Col 3:10. Though A/Col probably has Col 1:15 in mind because he repeats the same theme, Gen 1:27 (κατ' εἰκόνα θεοῦ ἐποίησεν αὐτόν) is a closer parallel to Col 3:10. Thus Gen 1:27 seems to lie in the background of the text although A/Col does not cite it directly.[726]

Col 3:11 states that "there is no longer Greek and Jew, circumcised and uncircumcised, barbarians, Scythian, slave and free" and thus emphasizes that Christ makes irrelevant any ethnic, cultural, and social distinctions. The thought is familiar to Paul also. 1 Cor 12:13 maintains that all were baptized in the one Spirit — Jews or Greek, slaves or free.[727] In alike manner, Gal 3:27-28 refers to baptism and continues "there is no longer Jew or Greek, there is no longer slave or free, there is no longer male and female". All these three texts enumerate two juxtapositions: Jew – Greek and slaves – free. The only difference is that unlike the others, Col mentions Greek first. However, the choice of wording in Gal resembles Col more than that in 1 Cor: both Col 3:11 and Gal 3:28 begin the catalog with the words οὐκ ἔνι and the choice of wording τὰ πάντα καὶ ἐν πᾶσιν Χριστός in Col resembles the one in Gal, πάντες ... εἷς ἐστε ἐν Χριστῷ 'Ιησοῦ. In addition, before

1981, 107; Bruce 1988, 142; Lindemann 1983, 57; Lohse 1971, 142; Dunn 1996, 220; Ludwig 1974, 109; O'Brien 1982, 190; Hendriksen 1971, 149; Hartman 1985, 148; Gnilka 1980, 187 note 48. However, Kiley 1986, 82, fails to notice the similarity because he compares Col 3:2, 5 with Rom 6:6, not Col 3:9. The mention of the old self "with its practices" (σὺν ταῖς πράξεσιν αὐτοῦ) also resembles a little the exhortation "put to death the deeds of the body" (τὰς πράξεις τοῦ σώματος θανατοῦτε) in Rom 8:13.

[724] Rom 12:2: ... μεταμορφοῦσθε τῇ ἀνακαινώσει τοῦ νοὸς εἰς τὸ δοκιμάζειν ὑμᾶς τί τὸ θέλημα τοῦ θεοῦ. 2 Cor 4:16: ... εἰ καὶ ὁ ἔξω ἡμῶν ἄνθρωπος διαφθείρεται, ἀλλ' ὁ ἔσω ἡμῶν ἀνακαινοῦται. E.g. O'Brien 1982, 190, and Hendriksen 1971, 150, mentions 2 Cor 4:16 as a parallel to Col 3:10.

[725] Differently Pokorný 1987, 143, assumes that the phrase is based on Phil 1:9.

[726] Especially Lohse 1971, 142; O'Brien 1982, 191; and Nielsen 1985, 119, emphasize that this is not an explicit Scripture citation. Cf. R. P. Martin 1981, 107; Hendriksen 1971, 151; Haapa 1978, 64; Hübner 1988, 173; Bruce 1988, 147; Conzelmann 1990, 198; Dunn 1996, 222. Contra Hübner 1997, 104 (cf. Gnilka 1980, 189) who emphasizes that Col 3:10 resembles Col 1:15 and Rom 8:29.

[727] 1 Cor 12:13: ... εἰς ἓν σῶμα ἐβαπτίσθημεν, εἴτε 'Ιουδαῖοι εἴτε Ἕλληνες εἴτε δοῦλοι εἴτε ἐλεύθεροι.

maintaining the irrelevance of any distinctions between people, both texts describe the putting on using the verb ἐνδύομαι which thus seems to be a Stichwort which reminds A/Col of the choice of wording in Gal 3:28.[728] The agreement between Col 3:10-11 and Gal 3:27-28, four nouns, one verb, and one adjective in common occurring within three lines in Gal, clearly meets the criteria for a probable literary dependence between the texts.[729]

The remarkable similarity between Col 3:11 and Gal 3:28 is often commented on and taken to be due to the Pauline tradition.[730] Though the scholars, apart from Sanders, do not explicitly accept a literary dependence between the texts, still some of them emphasize that the relationship is very close. For example, according to Hübner the influence of the Pauline choice of wording is nowhere else in Col as evident as it is between Gal 3:27-28 and Col 3:11[731] and Martin states that in Col 3:11 "the teaching of Gal 3:28 is repeated and amplified".[732] Schweizer suggests that Col 3:11 "takes over from Gal 3:28 the picture of what baptism really means".[733] In addition, Dunn states that the clause "but Christ is all in all" is "a further variation of Gal 3:28".[734] Therefore, it seems that many scholars implicitly accept the literary dependence between Col 3:11 and Gal 3:28.

The choice of wording ὁ θεὸς [τὰ] πάντα ἐν πᾶσιν, "God is all in all", in 1 Cor 15:28 is so close to the words [τὰ] πάντα καὶ ἐν πᾶσιν Χριστός, "Christ is all in all", in Col 3:11 that it is often commented upon.[735] Since in Col 1:16 A/Col seems to imitate a formula from 1 Cor and Rom but transfers a characteristic of God to Christ (see pp.92-93), it is likely that he acts similarly here.[736] It has to be noted that in 1 Cor 12:6 quite similar words θεὸς ὁ ἐνεργῶν τὰ πάντα ἐν πᾶσιν are used, but 1 Cor 15:28 is still a closer parallel to Col 3:11. In addition, the expression τὰ πάντα ἐν πᾶσιν is used only twice in the genuine Pauline letters and both occurrences are in the same letter which indicates that it is not a stock phrase of Paul. Although the pronoun πᾶς is very customary in Greek, the use of the identical words τὰ πάντα ἐν πᾶσιν meets the criteria for a possible literary dependence between Col 3:11 and 1 Cor 15:28. Col 3:11 conflates the expression τὰ πάντα ἐν πᾶσιν with the words πάντες ... εἷς ἐστε ἐν Χριστῷ Ἰησοῦ from Gal

---

[728] Cf. E. P. Sanders 1966, 43.
[729] Similarly E. P. Sanders 1966, 42-43, and Gnilka 1980, 12, assume that Col 3:11 depends on Gal 3:27-28. Cf. Müller 1988, 172.
[730] See Kiley 1986, 94; Ludwig 1974, 109; Lohse 1971, 142-143; Haapa 1978, 64. Cf. Lindemann 1983, 57-58; Dunn 1996, 223; Michel 1971, 449; Wedderburn 1993, 49; T. W. Martin 1996a, 196.
[731] Hübner 1997, 104.
[732] R. P. Martin 1981, 108. Similarly O'Brien 1982, 192.
[733] Schweizer 1982, 196.
[734] Dunn 1996, 227. Cf. Ludwig 1974, 110. See also Gnilka 1980, 188; Hartman 1985, 137; Nielsen 1985, 119; Bruce 1988, 149; Pfammatter 1987, 78; Wilson 1997, 124.
[735] See Lohse 1971, 145; Nikolainen 1987, 52; Schweizer 1982, 200; Dunn 1996, 227; Hartman 1985, 137; O'Brien 1982, 191.
[736] Cf. E. P. Sanders 1966, 43.

3:28[737] and thus A/Col, as a pseudepigrapher, again uses the words differently from Paul.[738]

It is remarkable that Col 3:11 enumerates groups of people who are missing in Gal 3:28: περιτομή, ἀκροβυστία, βάρβαρος, and Σκύθης are added. In addition, the lists in Gal and in 1 Cor are not so long as in Col, which probably is caused by the prolix style of A/Col. The juxtaposition περιτομή – ἀκροβυστία (circumcision – uncircumcision) is typical of Paul: it appears e.g. in 1 Cor 7:19, Gal 5:6, 6:15. Besides employing the juxtaposition, Gal 6:15 emphasizes the significance of the new creation and thus uses the words καινὴ κτίσις which have the same stem as the verbs ἀνακαινόω, "to renew", and κτίζω, "to create", occurring in Col 3:10. Accordingly, Col 3:10-11 and Gal 6:15 employ four similar nouns, verbs, or adjectives, the same or having the same stem, which points to a probable literary dependence.[739]

The "barbarian" (βάρβαρος) and "Scythian" (Σκύθης) are no longer juxtaposed to one another antithetically.[740] The barbarian was a non-Greek who did not speak the language and thus also frequently was not well educated. The Scythians were considered to be a strange kind of barbarian, very rude persons.[741] They were occasionally mentioned in Jewish literature. Josephus, Contra Apionem II 26 describes the Scythians as being "little better than wild beasts".[742] Besides Col 3:11, the Scythians are not mentioned anywhere else in ECL but barbarians appear in Acts 28:2, 4 and Rom 1:14. In Cor 14:11, the term βάρβαρος is employed in its primary usage to refer to a person who speaks a strange, unintelligible language.[743] Because Rom 1:14 enumerates the groups of people like Col 3:11 and Gal 3:28, it is possible that A/Col has Rom 1:14 in mind. Therefore, it seems that the long list in Col 3:11 enumerates different kinds of groups mentioned, except Scythians, in the authentic Pauline texts which A/Col, using his prolix style, combines into a catalog longer than its models.

---

[737] Similarly E. P. Sanders 1966, 42-43. Contra Schweizer 1982, 201, who underestimates the connection when suggesting that "similar phrases were mediated to the NT authors via Hellenistic Judaism". He refers to Philo, Spec Leg I,208 which does not resemble either Col 3:11 or 1 Cor 15:28 very much. Philo, Spec Leg I,208: ἡ δὲ εἰς μέλη τοῦ ζῴου διανομὴ δηλοῖ, ἤτοι ὡς ἓν τὰ πάντα ἢ ὅτι ἐξ ἑνός τε καὶ εἰς ἕν ...

[738] The difference is noted also by E. P. Sanders 1966, 43; Dunn 1996, 227; Schweizer 1982, 200.

[739] The similarity between Col 3:11 and Gal 6:15 is also commented on by R. P. Martin 1981, 108; Gnilka 1980, 188; Pokorný 1987, 143 n. 61; Lohse 1971, 142; Bruce 1988, 147; Haapa 1978, 63.

[740] Similarly Lohse 1971, 144; Pokorný 1987, 143-144; O'Brien 1982, 193; Gnilka 1980, 190. Contra Michel 1971, 449, according to whom "it is hard to say whether Σκύθης is simply an outstanding example of a barbarian people or whether βάρβαρος and Σκύθης are meant to differ from one another culturally, geographically and racially".

[741] O'Brien 1982, 193; Hartman 1985, 137, 150; Lohse 1971, 144; Dunn 1996, 225 f.

[742] Josephus, Contra Apionem II 26: Σκύθαι δὲ φόνοις χαίροντες ἀνθρώπων καὶ βραχὺ τῶν θηρίων διαφέροντες. Cf. 2 Macc 4:47, 3 Macc 7:5.

[743] Dunn 1996, 225.

Col 3:12-15

12 ᾿Ενδύσασθε οὖν, ὡς
ἐκλεκτοὶ τοῦ **θεοῦ** ἅγιοι
καὶ ἠγαπημένοι, σπλάγχνα
οἰκτιρμοῦ χρηστότητα
ταπεινοφροσύνην
πραΰτητα μακροθυμίαν,
13 ἀνεχόμενοι ἀλλήλων
καὶ χαριζόμενοι ἑαυτοῖς
ἐάν τις πρός τινα ἔχῃ
μομφήν· **καθὼς καὶ ὁ**
κύριος ἐχαρίσατο ὑμῖν,
οὕτως καὶ ὑμεῖς·
14 ἐπὶ πᾶσιν δὲ τούτοις τὴν
ἀγάπην, ὅ ἐστιν σύνδεσμος
τῆς τελειότητος.
15 **καὶ ἡ εἰρήνη τοῦ**
Χριστοῦ βραβευέτω ἐν ταῖς
καρδίαις **ὑμῶν**, **εἰς** ἣν καὶ
ἐκλήθητε ἐν ἑνὶ σώματι·
καὶ εὐχάριστοι γίνεσθε.

Rom 8:32-33

32 ... πῶς οὐχὶ καὶ σὺν
αὐτῷ τὰ πάντα ἡμῖν
χαρίσεται;
33 τίς ἐγκαλέσει κατὰ
ἐκλεκτῶν **θεοῦ**;

Gal 5:22-23

22 ... ἐστιν ἀγάπη χαρὰ
εἰρήνη, μακροθυμία
χρηστότης ἀγαθωσύνη,
πίστις
23 πραΰτης ἐγκράτεια·

Rom 15:7

Διὸ προσλαμβάνεσθε
ἀλλήλους, **καθὼς καὶ ὁ**
Χριστὸς προσελάβετο ὑμᾶς
...

Phil 4:7

καὶ ἡ εἰρήνη τοῦ θεοῦ ...
φρουρήσει τὰς καρδίας
ὑμῶν ...

Phil 2:1-3

1 ... εἴ τι παραμύθιον
ἀγάπης ..., εἴ τις σπλάγχνα
καὶ οἰκτιρμοί,
3 ... τῇ ταπεινοφροσύνῃ
ἀλλήλους ἡγούμενοι
ὑπερέχοντας ἑαυτῶν

Col 2:18

μηδεὶς ὑμᾶς
καταβραβευέτω ...

1 Cor 12:13

... **εἰς** ἓν σῶμα
ἐβαπτίσθημεν, εἴτε
᾿Ιουδαῖοι εἴτε Ἕλληνες
εἴτε δοῦλοι εἴτε ἐλεύθεροι
...

In the beginning of the catalog of virtues, in Col 3:12, the recipients of the letter are called God's chosen ones (ἐκλεκτοὶ τοῦ θεοῦ), holy (ἅγιοι) and beloved (ἠγαπημένοι). The idea of a people "chosen by God" was exclusively Jewish (cf. Deut 7:6-7).[744] For example, in Sir 46:1, 47:22 people are called God's elect using the words ἐκλεκτῶν αὐτοῦ and in Isa 42:1, 45:4, and 65:9 God calls Israel his chosen one (ὁ ἐκλεκτός μου). However, in the LXX people are not called ἐκλεκτοὶ τοῦ θεοῦ but a similar expression occurs in Rom 8:33 where the recipients of the letter are, like in Col 3:12, called God's chosen ones. It is noteworthy that this is the only case in the Pauline letters the term is used.[745] In addition, the words ἡμῖν χαρίσεται are employed in Rom 8:32 which resemble the words ἐχαρίσατο ὑμῖν in Col 3:13. It seems thus possible that the choice of wording ἐκλεκτοὶ τοῦ θεοῦ

[744] See e.g. Dunn 1995, 159; 1996, 227-228; O'Brien 1982, 197; Lohse 1971, 146; Bruce 1988, 153; R. P. Martin 1981, 109.

[745] In the Gospels persons are also called chosen ones (ἐκλεκτοί) (e.g. Mk 13:20, 22, 27, Mt 22:14, 24:22, 24, 31, Lk 18:7) but the term ἐκλεκτοὶ τοῦ θεοῦ never occurs.

has been influenced by knowledge of Rom 8:33 and, in addition, the verbal agreement between Col 3:12-13, three words in common (ἐκλεκτός, θεός, χαρίζομαι), just meets the criteria for a possible literary dependence.

Like in Col 3:12, the Colossians are also called holy (ἅγιοι) in Col 1:2, 4, 12, 22, 26. The third definition ἠγαπημένοι, "beloved", has a parallel in 1 Thess 1:4 where the recipients of the letter are also described as beloved by God (ἀδελφοὶ ἠγαπημένοι ὑπὸ τοῦ θεοῦ) and reminded, like in Col 3:12, that they are chosen by God (εἰδότες ... ἐκλογὴν ὑμῶν). The Colossians' love for all the saints is mentioned twice (1:4, 8) but 3:12 is the only case where A/Col calls them beloved. The style of addressing the recipients of the letter in Col 3:12 thus resembles, on the whole, the custom of the undisputed Pauline letters. Instead, the habit of piling up three definitions: God's chosen ones (ἐκλεκτοὶ τοῦ θεοῦ), holy (ἅγιοι), and beloved (ἠγαπημένοι) is not typical of Paul. It has an echo of the OT: for instance, in the classic covenant text Deut 7:6-8 Israel is said to be holy (λαὸς ἅγιος), chosen by God (προείλατο κύριος ὁ θεός), and beloved by God (τὸ ἀγαπᾶν κύριον ὑμᾶς).[746]

In Col 3:12, the metaphor of putting on is used, which already occurred in Col 3:10. While in Col 3:10 it was counselled to put on the new self, now the readers are exhorted to clothe themselves with the virtues. The catalog of virtues is based on a fivefold enumeration like the two catalogs of vices (3:5,8). It is remarkable that, like the list of vices in Col 3:5, the catalog of virtues also has a parallel in Gal 5. Both Col 3:12-15 and Gal 5:22-23 enumerate patience (μακροθυμία), kindness (χρηστότης), and meekness (πραΰτης) which appear together nowhere else in the Pauline corpus; two of them, χρηστότης and μακροθυμία, are also used together in Rom 2:4 and 2 Cor 6:6. In addition, both texts employ the nouns love (ἀγάπη) and peace (εἰρήνη). Accordingly, Col 3:12-15 and Gal 5:22-23 include five of the same nouns which meets the criteria for a probable literary dependence.[747]

In addition to the aforementioned virtues, the catalog in Col includes compassion (σπλάγχνα), sympathy (οἰκτιρμός), and humility (ταπεινοφροσύνη). All these virtues also appear in Phil 2:1-3, even in the same order.[748] It is thus possible that A/Col recalls Phil 2:1-3 and connects together the nouns σπλάγχνα and οἰκτιρμός, which appear one after another in Phil, into the unique phrase σπλάγχνα οἰκτιρμοῦ. In addition, the pronoun ἀλλήλων and noun ἀγάπη are both found in Phil 2:1-3 and Col 3:13. Because of the remarkable similarity, four common nouns within five lines in Phil, the resemblance between Phil 2:1-3 and Col 3:12-13 meets the criteria for a probable literary dependence. Therefore, the

---

746 Dunn 1996, 228. Cf. R. P. Martin 1981, 109-110; Hartman 1985, 150; O'Brien 1982, 197.

747 Cf. Hübner 1997, 106, who takes Gal 5:22 as a Pauline prototype of Col 3:12-15. Also Schweizer 1982, 205, and Haapa 1978, 65, comment on the similarity between the catalogs of virtues in Col 3:12f and Gal 5:22f although they do not contend that the texts depend on each other.

748 Bruce 1988, 153, and Dunn 1996, 228, present also Phil 2:1-3 as a parallel to Col 3:12.

list in Col 3:12-13 could be the result of the conflation of the virtues mentioned in Gal 2:22-23 and Phil 2:1-3.[749]

In the beginning of Col 3:13, the Colossians are told to bear with one another and forgive each other. The habit of using the participle forms of the verbs (ἀνεχόμενοι, χαριζόμενοι) is a characteristic of A/Col[750] but the theme of forgiveness also occurs in the authentic Pauline letters (e.g. in 2 Cor 2:5-11) and in the Gospels (e.g. Mk 11:25 /Mt 6:14). Col 3:13 does not have verbal agreements with these texts, however. In addition, the noun μομφή, "complaint", used in Col 3:13 is unique in ECL.

The choice of wording at the end of Col 3:13 has parallels. Similarly to Col 3:13, in Rom 15:7 people are exhorted to do to one another just as Christ has done to them (καθὼς καὶ ... ὑμᾶς). In addition, the Lord's Prayer in Mt 6:12 includes a similar thought. Neither of the parallels show enough verbal similarity to indicate literary dependence, however. Since the choice of wording in Rom 15:7 resembles Col 3:13 more than that in Mt 6:12, Col 3:13 may echo Rom 15:7.[751] It is also worth noting that A/Col ascribes to Christ a characteristic which belongs to God in the authentic Pauline letters: usually it is God who is said to forgive but in Col 3:13 it is Christ (κύριος).[752]

Col 3:14 emphasizes the worth of love which is an ordinary theme in the genuine Pauline letters (e.g. Rom 8:39, 13:8-10, 1 Cor 13:2, 16:14). However, Col 3:14 is the only case in ECL where love is said to be the bandage of perfection (σύνδεσμος τῆς τελειότητος). The choice of wording resembles the words συμβιβασθέντες ἐν ἀγάπῃ in Col 2:2. In addition, the word σύνδεσμος is used in Col 2:19 to denote a ligament. The phrase σύνδεσμος τῆς τελειότητος seems thus to be a creation of A/Col. Σύνδεσμος has a symbolic meaning for example in Plato, Polit 310a which says of the true idea of the right: "this bond which unites unlike and divergent parts of virtue is more divine".[753]

---

[749] Similarly Köster 1971, 556, emphasizes that the phrase (σπλάγχνα οἰκτιρμοῦ) "can hardly have been coined without literary dependence on ... Phil 2:1". Contra Kiley 1986, 89, 93, who underestimates the verbatim agreements between Phil 2:1-3 and Col 3:12-13 because the similarities occur in different positions in the letters. According to O'Brien 1982, 199, "it is not necessary to posit a literary dependence on ... Phil 2:1" because "the almost identical phrase" heart of mercy is used at Lk 1:78. However, the words διὰ σπλάγχνα ἐλέους θεοῦ in Lk 1:78 do not resemble Col 3:12 as much as those in Phil 2:1.

[750] Bujard 1973, 60.

[751] Similarly O'Brien 1982, 202, notes the resemblance between Col 3:13 and Rom 15:7. Contra Hendriksen 1971, 158, according to whom Col 3:13 has a conscious echo of the Lord's Prayer (Mt 6:12).

[752] O'Brien 1982, 202-203; Hübner 1997, 105-106; Dunn 1996, 231. Hendriksen 1971, 158, harmonizes the thought of Col 3:13 with the authentic Paulines by interpreting that forgiving is one of the virtues of Christ which believers had to imitate.

[753] Plato, Polit 310a: τοῦτον θειότερον εἶναι τὸν σύνδεσμον ἀρετῆς μερῶν φύσεως ἀνομοίων καὶ ἐπὶ τὰ ἐναντία φερομένων. E.g. O'Brien 1982, 203; Lohse 1971, 148-149; and Fitzer 1971, 859, refer to this parallel.

The choice of wording "let the peace of Christ rule in your hearts" (καὶ ἡ εἰρήνη τοῦ Χριστοῦ βραβευέτω ἐν ταῖς καρδίαις ὑμῶν) in Col 3:15 resembles the words "the peace of God ... will guard your hearts" (καὶ ἡ εἰρήνη τοῦ θεοῦ ... φρουρήσει τὰς καρδίας ὑμῶν) in Phil 4:7.[754] Since both texts use two of the same nouns (εἰρήνη, καρδία) and include exactly the same choice of wording καὶ ἡ εἰρήνη τοῦ ... ὑμῶν, the resemblance points to a possible literary dependence between Col 3:15 and Phil 4:7.[755] The verb βραβεύω, which A/Col uses instead of φρουρέω found in Phil 4:7, does not appear in the authentic Pauline letters. However, the verb καταβραβεύω which has the same stem is employed in Col 2:18 and is unique in ECL. Accordingly, A/Col seems here to prefer the verb βραβεύω which he uses elsewhere.

In spite of the similarity, Col 3:15 and Phil 4:7 have one distinctive difference: Col 3:15 mentions the peace of Christ instead of the peace of God. It is also remarkable that in the genuine Pauline letters peace is always a characteristic of God (see Rom 15:33, 16:20, 2 Cor 13:11, Phil 4:9, 1 Thess 5:23). A/Col seems again to imitate the choice of wording of Paul but changes the idea. Thus it is not necessary to harmonize the thought of Col 3:15 with the authentic Pauline letters.[756]

In Col 3:15, the Colossians are reminded that they are called in the one body (ἐκλήθητε ἐν ἑνὶ σώματι) which clearly refers to the image of Christ as the head of the body, the church (1:18, 24, 2:19).[757] Christians are similarly described to be one body in Christ in Rom 12:5 (ἓν σῶμά ἐσμεν ἐν Χριστῷ) and in 1 Cor 12:13 (εἰς ἓν σῶμα ἐβαπτίσθημεν). The choice of wording in 1 Cor 12:13 resembles Col 3:15 more than that in Rom 12:5 but the verbal similarity does not meet the criteria for literary dependence. However, 1 Cor 12:13 was noted as emphasizing the equality of people in alike manner to Col 3:11 (see pp.165-166). Therefore, it is possible that A/Col recalls 1 Cor 12:13.[758]

---

[754] Cf. Rom 5:5 ... ὅτι ἡ ἀγάπη τοῦ θεοῦ ἐκκέχυται ἐν ταῖς καρδίαις ὑμῶν which resembles Col 3:15 but not at all as much as Phil 4:7.

[755] Similarly E. P. Sanders 1966, 44. Cf. Dunn 1996, 233, according to whom Phil 4:7 is "the only close Pauline parallel". Stauffer 1974, 638, takes Phil 4:7 as "an analogous expression" to Col 3:15". In addition, e.g. Lohse 1971, 149; O'Brien 1982, 204; Haapa 1978, 66; Nikolainen 1987, 53; Wilson 1997, 180, comment on the similarity between the phrases in Col 3:15 and Phil 4:7. Contra Kiley 1986, 89, who underestimates the agreement between Col 3:15 and Phil 4:7 because the sentences have different meanings in Col and Phil. It has to be noted, however, that it is typical of a pseudepigrapher to use the words in a different way than the imitated text. Ludwig 1974, 115-116, also notes the similarity and explains that Col 3:15 is modelled on Phil 4:7. On the other hand, she emphasizes that A/Col does not copy the text of Phil. This interpretation necessitates literary dependence which is not in harmony with her hypothesis that A/Col knows only the Pauline tradition, not the letters.

[756] So Dunn 1996, 233, who interprets that "the Christ of Col 1:15-20 and 2:9 is so much the embodiment of God's wisdom and fullness that it comes to the same thing". In addition, Hendriksen 1971, 159, states that "it is the peace of Christ because it was merited for believers by Christ".

[757] Similarly Schweizer 1982, 208.

[758] Cf. E. P. Sanders 1966, 44, according to whom Col 3:15 "perhaps depends upon 1 Cor 12:13".

At the end of verse 15, the Colossians are exhorted to be thankful. The adjective εὐχάριστος is exceptional: it does not occur anywhere else in the Pauline corpus and it appears only once (Prov 11:16) in the LXX [759]. In addition, in the writings of the Apostolic Fathers it is used only in Justin, Apol I 13,2.[760] So the adjective εὐχάριστος may be due to the verb εὐχαριστέω which both Paul and A/Col often employ when giving thanks to God (e.g. Rom 1:8, 14:6, 16:4, 1 Cor 1:4, 1 Thess 2:13, Col 1:3, 12, 3:17).

Col 3:16-17	Col 1:25, 28	Rom 8:11
16 'Ο λόγος τοῦ Χριστοῦ ἐνοικείτω **ἐν ὑμῖν** πλουσίως, **ἐν πάσῃ σοφίᾳ διδάσκοντες καὶ νουθετοῦντες** ἑαυτούς, ψαλμοῖς ὕμνοις ᾠδαῖς πνευματικαῖς ἐν [τῇ] χάριτι ᾄδοντες **ἐν ταῖς καρδίαις ὑμῶν** τῷ θεῷ· 17 καὶ πᾶν ὅ **τι** ἐὰν ποιῆτε ἐν λόγῳ ἢ ἐν ἔργῳ, **πάντα ἐν ὀνόματι κυρίου 'Ιησοῦ, εὐχαριστοῦντες τῷ θεῷ πατρὶ δι' αὐτοῦ.**	25 ... πληρῶσαι τὸν λόγον τοῦ θεοῦ, 28 ... καταγγέλλομεν **νουθετοῦντες** πάντα ἄνθρωπον **καὶ διδάσκοντες** πάντα ἄνθρωπον **ἐν πάσῃ σοφίᾳ**	... διὰ τοῦ ἐνοικοῦντος αὐτοῦ πνεύματος **ἐν ὑμῖν**.
		Col 3:15
		ἐν ταῖς καρδίαις ὑμῶν
		Rom 15:18
	1 Cor 14:26	
	... ὅταν συνέρχησθε, ἕκαστος ψαλμὸν ἔχει, διδαχὴν ἔχει ...	... ὧν οὐ κατειργάσατο Χριστὸς δι' ἐμοῦ ... λόγῳ καὶ ἔργῳ
		Col 1:12
	1 Cor 10:31	**εὐχαριστοῦντες** τῷ **πατρί** ...
	... εἴτε **τι** ποιεῖτε, **πάντα** εἰς δόξαν θεοῦ ποιεῖτε.	Col 1:3
		Εὐχαριστοῦμεν **τῷ θεῷ πατρί** ...
	1 Cor 6:11	
	... ἐδικαιώθητε **ἐν** τῷ **ὀνόματι** τοῦ **κυρίου 'Ιησοῦ** Χριστοῦ ...	Col 1:16
		τὰ πάντα **δι' αὐτοῦ**

Col 3:16 begins with an exhortation "Let the word of Christ dwell in you richly" ('Ο λόγος τοῦ Χριστοῦ ἐνοικείτω ἐν ὑμῖν πλουσίως). This is the only case where A/Col uses the term the word of Christ (λόγος τοῦ Χριστοῦ) and it is never found in the genuine Pauline letters. Instead, the word of God (ὁ λόγος τοῦ θεοῦ) and the word of the Lord (ὁ λόγος τοῦ κυρίου) are common (see e.g. 2 Cor 2:17, 4:2 , 1 Thess 1:8, 4:15). The expression "the word of God" is also employed in Col 1:25 when describing Paul's ministry. So like "the word of God" in Col 1:25, "the word

[759] Prov 11:16: γυνὴ εὐχάριστος ἐγείρει ἀνδρὶ δόξαν.
[760] Justin, Apol I 13,2: ἐκείνῳ δὲ εὐχαρίστους ὄντας διὰ λόγου πομπὰς.

of Christ" in Col 3:16 seems to speak about Paul's message, the Gospel of Christ.[761] In addition, Col 3:16 resembles 1 Cor 3:16 which speaks about the dwelling of God's Spirit (τὸ πνεῦμα τοῦ θεοῦ οἰκεῖ ἐν ὑμιν) and Rom 8:11 uses the same verb as Col 3:16, ἐνοικέω, when describing God's Spirit (διὰ τοῦ ἐνοικοῦντος αὐτοῦ πνεύματος ἐν ὑμῖν). Accordingly, as earlier, in Col 3:16 A/Col ascribes a characteristic of God to Christ and utilizes the Pauline phraseology in his own way.[762]

The choice of wording "teach and admonish one another in all wisdom" (ἐν πάσῃ σοφίᾳ διδάσκοντες καὶ νουθετοῦντες ἑαυτούς) in Col 3:16 refers back to Col 1:28. All the words are exactly in the same form as in Col 1:28 and seem as though copied from it.[763] In addition, the phrase ἐν ταῖς καρδίαις ὑμῶν, used at the end of Col 3:16, already occurred in the previous verse.[764] Col 3:16 mentions the singing (the verb ᾄδω) of psalms (ψαλμοῖς), hymns (ὕμνοις), and spiritual songs (ᾠδαῖς πνευματικαῖς). It is not possible to make fine distinctions among the three terms: they are nearly synonyms.[765] So it seems that A/Col is typically piling synonyms together.[766] The description has a close parallel in a later text, Eph 5:19-20[767], but otherwise the terms are exceptional in the Pauline letters. Elsewhere the noun ὕμνος occurs only in Eph 5:19. In addition, the noun ᾠδή and the verb ᾄδω are used only in Eph 5:19 and later in other ECL in Rev 5:9, 14:3, 15:3. The term ψαλμός is the only one which appears in the authentic Pauline letters, in 1 Cor 14:26. It also occurs sometimes in ECL, e.g. in Lk 20:42, 24:44, in Acts 1:20, 13:33, and in Eph 5:19. Although the resemblance does not meet the criteria for literary dependence, it is possible that Col 3:16 echoes 1 Cor 14:26.[768]

---

[761] Cf. Lohse 1971, 150; Hendriksen 1971, 139, 155; Dunn 1996, 236; R. P. Martin 1981, 115; Lindemann 1983, 62; Pokorný 1987, 147; Haapa 1978, 67.

[762] According to Hartman 1985, 155, we are at the beginning of the time when the written Gospels have the worth of the Scriptures.

[763] Cf. Dunn 1996, 237: "The strong echo of 1:28 ... can hardly be accidental". Also Bujard 1973, 98-99, comments on the similarity and assumes it to be caused by the associative style of the author. Cf. Gnilka 1980, 200; Hübner 1997, 108; R. P. Martin 1981, 115; Hartman 1985, 156; O'Brien 1982, 208; Lohse 1971, 150-151.

[764] This is noted also by O'Brien 1982, 210: Schweizer 1982, 210; Lohse 1971, 151; R. P. Martin 1981, 116; Lindemann 1983, 63.

[765] Cf. O'Brien 1982, 209: Schweizer 1982, 210; R. P. Martin 1981, 115-116; Haapa 1978, 68; Lindemann 1983, 63; Pokorný 1987, 147; Lohse 1971, 151; Luz 1998, 231-232. Contra Hendriksen 1971, 162, according to whom "the term *psalms* has reference, at least mainly, to the Old Testament Psalter; *hymns* mainly to the New Testament songs of praise to God or to Christ; and *spiritual songs* mainly to any other sacred songs dwelling on themes other than direct praise to God or to Christ." See also Dunn 1996, 237-239.

[766] Similarly Lohse 1971, 88.

[767] Eph 5:19-20: λαλοῦντες ἑαυτοῖς [ἐν] ψαλμοῖς καὶ ὕμνοις καὶ ᾠδαῖς πνευματικαῖς, ᾄδοντες καὶ ψάλλοντες τῇ καρδίᾳ ὑμῶν τῷ κυρίῳ, εὐχαριστοῦντες πάντοτε ὑπὲρ πάντων ἐν ὀνόματι τοῦ κυρίου ἡμῶν 'Ιησοῦ Χριστοῦ τῷ θεῷ καὶ πατρί.

[768] Scholars usually present 1 Cor 14:26 as a parallel to Col 3:16; see O'Brien 1982, 209: R. P. Martin 1981, 115; Haapa 1978, 68; Lindemann 1983, 63; Pokorný 1987, 147; Hendriksen 1971, 162; Bruce 1988, 158; Luz 1998, 232.

Col 3:17 begins with the words "and whatever you do, in word or deed, do everything in the name of the Lord Jesus" (καὶ πᾶν ὅ τι ἐὰν ποιῆτε ἐν λόγῳ ἢ ἐν ἔργῳ, πάντα ἐν ὀνόματι κυρίου 'Ιησοῦ) which utilizes Pauline phrases. The words resemble, for example, the following texts: 1 Cor 10:31 "whatever you do, do everything for the glory of God" (εἴτε τι ποιεῖτε, πάντα εἰς δόξαν θεοῦ ποιεῖτε)[769], Rom 15:18 "what Christ has accomplished through me ... by word and deed" (ὧν οὐ κατειργάσατο Χριστὸς δι' ἐμοῦ ... ἐν λόγῳ ἢ ἐν ἔργῳ)[770], and 1 Cor 6:11 "you were justified in the name of the Lord Jesus Christ" (ἐδικαιώθητε ἐν τῷ ὀνόματι τοῦ κυρίου 'Ιησοῦ Χριστοῦ)[771]. The giving thanks to God, Father at the end of Col 3:17 refers back to the beginning of the letter. It conflates the words εὐχαριστοῦντες τῷ πατρί from the intercession (Col 1:12) and the words εὐχαριστοῦμεν τῷ θεῷ πατρί from the introductory greeting (Col 1:3).[772] Moreover, the last addition δι' αὐτοῦ which refers to Christ may echo the Stoic formula used in Col 1:16.

5.2. Household Rules (Col 3:18-4:1)

5.2.1. The Origin of the Christian Haustafel

The rules for the household are presented in Col 3:18-4:1: the admonitions addressed to wives and husbands, children and fathers, and slaves and masters which are commonly designated by the German term "Haustafel". In ECL, the corresponding household rules appear only in Eph 5:21-6:9 which is generally assumed to depend on Col.[773] Quite close parallels also occur in the Pastoral letters, in 1 Tim 2:8-15, 6:1-2, in Titus 2:1-10, and in 1 Pet 2:18-3:7, of which the latter resembles the Colossian household code most; the others are rather rules for the church.[774] In addition, some admonitions in the writings of the Apostolic Fathers have something in common with Col (see Did 4:9-11; Barn 19:5-7; 1 Clem 1:3, 21:6-9, 38:2; Pol, Phil 4:2-6:3). Since all early Christian parallels are included in

[769] Also Ludwig 1974, 116-117; Bruce 1988, 160; O'Brien 1982, 210; Dunn 1996, 240; and Pokorný 1987, 48, present 1 Cor 10:31 as a parallel to Col 3:17.

[770] The juxtaposition λόγος – ἔργον also occurs in 2 Cor 10:11, Lk 24:19, Acts 7:22, and 2 Thess 2:17.

[771] The similarity between Col 3:17 and 1 Cor 6:11 is also mentioned by Lindemann 1983, 63; R. P. Martin 1981, 117; O'Brien 1982, 211. The phrase ἐν ὀνόματι κυρίου 'Ιησοῦ also appears in Rom 1:5, 1 Cor 1:10, 5:4, 6:11 in the genuine Pauline letters and later in 2 Thess 1:12.

[772] Bujard 1973, 99, assumes that the repetition is caused by the associative thought of the author. The similarity is also noted by Hendriksen 1971, 161; O'Brien 1982, 212; Pokorný 1987, 148.

[773] See e.g. Crouch 1972, 35; Schnackenburg 1982, 246; Schweizer 1982, 213; Hübner 1997, 110.

[774] Gnilka 1980, 207; Pfammatter 1987, 79.

the letters generally dated later than Col, Col 3:18-4:1 is usually taken as the oldest Christian Haustafel.[775]

The section Col 3:18-4:1 is a free-standing unit which is not closely related to the context. Furthermore, the exhortations are briefer and more abrupt than the preceding ones. It has thus been assumed that the household code may have been derived from earlier traditional material.[776] In Hellenistic, and specifically Stoic, moral philosophy there was a habit of listing the duties which were fitting (καθῆκον) for a conscientious man to fulfil (see e.g. Epictetus, Diss II 17, 31).[777] Therefore, Dibelius (1913), followed by his pupil Weidinger, claimed that the origin of the Christian household rules was to be found in that Stoic schema.[778] Lohmeyer accepted the thesis that the Colossian Haustafel has a pre-Christian background but regarded it as Jewish rather than Hellenistic. He noted the concept of fearing the Lord (see Col 3:22) as a motive for ethical behavior. He also emphasized that women, slaves, and children were often mentioned together in Jewish texts from the time of Deuteronomy to Rabbinic times.[779] Later, in the 1950's, Rengstorf[780] and Schroeder[781] sought to explain the rules for the household as being uniquely Christian.

In the early 1970's, Crouch went through a large number of ancient texts and concluded that, although there is no exact parallel to the Colossian Haustafel, the closest equivalents to Col 3:18-4:1 are in the texts of Hellenistic Judaism which had adopted the Stoic custom of listing duties. He also repeated Lohmeyer's thesis that women, slaves, and children are often mentioned in the texts of Judaism in the same order as in the Colossian household rules.[782] Since Crouch's work, it has been widely assumed that the Christian household code depends on the Stoic schema and this came into Christian exhortation through Hellenistic Judaism.[783] As the closest example of the parallels to the household rules in Col, Crouch presents Philo, Hyp VII 14 which describes how "the husband seems competent to transmit knowledge

---

775 See Dibelius 1953, 49; Pokorný 1987, 169; Hartman 1985, 163; 1997, 179; Crouch 1972, 32; Hübner 1997, 110; Ludwig 1974, 118; Standhartinger 1999, 248; Nikolainen 1987, 55.

776 See e.g. Dunn 1996, 242; Lohse 1971, 154; Ludwig 1974, 117; Cannon 1981, 120-137; Pfammatter 1987, 79; Crouch 1972, 9-18. Cf. Cope 1985, 49, who states that a later editor added the passage to the letter.

777 Epictetus, Diss II 17, 31: ἐγὼ θέλω μὲν καὶ ἀπαθὴς εἶναι καὶ ἀτάραχος, θέλω δ᾽ ὡς εὐσεβὴς καὶ φιλόσοφος καὶ ἐπιμελὴς εἰδέναι τί μοι πρὸς θεούς ἐστι καθῆκον, τί πρὸς γονεῖς, τί πρὸς ἀδελφούς, τί πρὸς τὴν πατρίδα, τί πρὸς ξένους.

778 Dibelius 1953, 45-50 (1st ed. 1913); Weidinger 1928.

779 Lohmeyer 1954 (10th ed.), 152-160.

780 Rengstorf 1953.

781 Schroeder 1976. His unpublished dissertation from 1959 (Die Haustafeln des Neuen Testaments. Ihre Herkunft und ihr theologisher Sinn) was not available to me.

782 Crouch 1972, 104-105.

783 See Lohse 1971, 155-157; Schweizer 1982, 213-215; Conzelmann 1990, 199; Gnilka 1980, 212; R. P. Martin 1981, 118; Nikolainen 1987, 55; Ludwig 1974, 117-118; Haapa 1978, 69. Cf. Lindemann 1983, 63, who mentions only the influence of the Stoic schema.

of the laws to his wife, the father to his children, the master to his slaves".[784] However, like Philo, Hyp VII 14, other Hellenistic household rules were usually also addressed only to a male, adult, and free person who is told how he should behave in relationship to women, children, and slaves (see e.g. Philo, Spec Leg II 224-41; Hyp VII 1-9; De Decal 165-167; Ps-Phocylides 175-227, Josephus, Ap II 190-219). No parallel has been found which gives orders to wives, children, and slaves besides free men.

Around 1980 Lührmann, Balch, and Berger introduced a new stage in research on the codes: they assumed that the early Christian Haustafel has clearer parallels in the philosophical treatises from Plato and Aristotle onwards, which handle household management (οἰκονομία, οἰκονόμος)[785] (see e.g. Aristotle, Politica I 1253b1-14).[786]

Despite all efforts, the problem concerning the origin of the Colossian household rules has not been solved. As Barclay recently pointed out, it is hardly surprising if we find the same members of the household mentioned elsewhere as in Colossians but yet the truth is that "there is no *precise* analogy to the form and theme of the Colossian code".[787] Furthermore, Hartman, followed by Barclay and Wedderburn, has emphasized that it is not correct to speak about a "schema" which was borrowed and formed into a "household code" because there is no evidence of such a literary form ready to be used by early Christians. Instead, Col 3:18-4:1 is indebted to the attitudes and social conventions of the Greco-Roman world.[788] There have also been doubts about the existence of "a house-table schema" in the

---

[784] Philo, Hyp VII 14: καὶ ἀνὴρ γυναικὶ καὶ παισὶ πατὴρ καὶ δούλοις δεσπότης ἱκανὸς εἶναι δοκεῖ τοὺς νόμους παραδιδόναι. Crouch 1972, 106-107. In addition, he assumes that "this idealistic statement of the duty of husbands, fathers, and masters to provide wives, children and slaves with a knowledge of the Law was a part of the traditional material which Philo incorporated into his *De Hypothetica*".

[785] Lührmann 1980; Balch 1981; Berger 1984. Cf. Lincoln 1997, 3: "Colossians' wisdom teaching takes up an early Christian version of accumulated reflection on household management from the Aristotelian and Hellenistic Jewish tradition ...."

[786] Aristotle, Politica I 1253b3-8: οἰκονομίας δὲ μέρη ἐξ ὧν πάλιν οἰκία συνέστηκεν˙ οἰκία δὲ τέλειος ἐκ δούλων καὶ ἐλευθέρων. ἐπεὶ δ᾽ ἐν τοῖς ἐλαχίστοις πρῶτον ἕκαστον ζητητέον, πρῶτα δὲ καὶ ἐλάχιστα μέρη οἰκίας δεσπότης καὶ δοῦλος, καὶ πόσις καὶ ἄλοχος, καὶ πατὴρ καὶ τέκνα. For the history of interpretation further in Hartman 1987, 237-239; 1997, 179-182; Crouch 1972, 18-31; O'Brien 1982, 215-218; Cannon 1981, 137-150.

[787] Barclay 1997, 70. Cf. Lincoln 1990, l; Ludwig 1974, 118; Rengstorf 1953, 134. Thus Best 1997, 81, is unable to prove his assumption that there was a traditional Haustafel which both A/Col and A/Eph used independently.

[788] Hartman 1997 (the article was first published in 1988); Wedderburn 1993, 20-21; Barclay 1997, 69-70. Cf. Cannon 1981, 161: "it seems clear that both pre-Christian Jewish and Hellenistic ideas influenced its mode of expression, but there is no evidence of literary dependence on a pre-Christian code". Angela Standhartinger recently presented the law-codes of Ps.-Zaleukos (228.13) and Ps. Charondas (61.1-62.34) and an inscription from Philadelphia as parallels to the Colossian household code and concluded that "Col 3:18-4:1 can be seen as deriving from the law-code model employed by popular street philosophers"; Standhartinger 2000. However, these parallels are not so close to Col that there were any evidence of literary dependence and the tree texts are quite few to show the existence of law-code model either.

early Christian tradition because household rules occur very seldom and, in addition, apart from Eph 5:21-6:9, the other ones only bear some resemblance to the Colossian Haustafel.[789] Accordingly, the background of Col 3:18-4:1 is left open.

[789] Hartman 1997, 191. Cf. O'Brien 1982, 218.

5.2.2. The Admonitions to Wives and Husbands, Children and Fathers, Slaves and Masters

Col 3:18-4:1
18 **Αἱ γυναῖκες**,
ὑποτάσσεσθε τοῖς ἀνδράσιν
ὡς ἀνῆκεν **ἐν** κυρίῳ.
19 Οἱ ἄνδρες, ἀγαπᾶτε τὰς
γυναῖκας καὶ μὴ
πικραίνεσθε πρὸς αὐτάς,
20 Τὰ τέκνα, ὑπακούετε
τοῖς γονεῦσιν κατὰ **πάντα**,
τοῦτο γὰρ εὐάρεστόν ἐστιν
ἐν κυρίῳ.
21 Οἱ πατέρες, μὴ
ἐρεθίζετε τὰ τέκνα ὑμῶν,
ἵνα μὴ ἀθυμῶσιν.
22 Οἱ **δοῦλοι**, **ὑπακούετε**
κατὰ πάντα τοῖς κατὰ
σάρκα κυρίοις, μὴ ἐν
ὀφθαλμοδουλίᾳ ὡς
ἀνθρωπάρεσκοι, ἀλλ᾽ **ἐν**
ἁπλότητι καρδίας
φοβούμενοι τὸν κύριον.
23 **ὃ ἐὰν ποιῆτε**, ἐκ ψυχῆς
ἐργάζεσθε **ὡς** τῷ κυρίῳ καὶ
οὐκ ἀνθρώποις,
24 **εἰδότες** ὅτι ἀπὸ κυρίου
ἀπολήμψεσθε τὴν
ἀνταπόδοσιν τῆς
κληρονομίας. **τῷ κυρίῳ**
Χριστῷ δουλεύετε˙
25 ὁ γὰρ ἀδικῶν κομίσεται
ὃ ἠδίκησεν, καὶ οὐκ **ἔστιν**
προσωποληµψία.
1 Οἱ κύριοι, τὸ δίκαιον καὶ
τὴν ἰσότητα τοῖς δούλοις
παρέχεσθε, **εἰδότες** ὅτι καὶ
ὑμεῖς ἔχετε κύριον **ἐν**
οὐρανῷ.

1 Cor 14:34-35
34 **αἱ γυναῖκες** ...
ὑποτασσέσθωσαν, ...
35 ... ἐν οἴκῳ τοὺς ἰδίους
ἄνδρας ἐπερωτάτωσαν˙

Eccl 9:9
ἰδὲ ζωὴν μετὰ γυναικός, ἧς
ἠγάπησας

Philem 16
οὐκέτι ὡς δοῦλον ἀλλ᾽ ὑπὲρ
δοῦλον ... ἐν σαρκὶ καὶ ἐν
κυρίῳ.

Gal 1:10
... εἰ ἔτι ἀνθρώποις ἤρεσκον,
Χριστοῦ δοῦλος οὐκ ἂν ἤμην.

Wis 1:1
... περὶ τοῦ κυρίου ... **ἐν**
ἁπλότητι καρδίας ζητήσατε
αὐτόν.

Col 3:17
καὶ πᾶν **ὅ** τι **ἐὰν ποιῆτε** ...
πάντα ἐν ὀνόματι κυρίου
᾽Ιησοῦ

Rom 16:18
... **τῷ κυρίῳ** ἡμῶν **Χριστῷ** οὐ
δουλεύουσιν ...

Rom 2:9-11
9 θλῖψις ... ἐπὶ πᾶσαν ψυχὴν
ἀνθρώπου τοῦ
κατεργαζομένου τὸ κακόν, ...
11 οὐ γάρ **ἐστιν προσωπο-**
λημψία παρὰ τῷ θεῷ.

Philo, De Spec Leg IV 231
ἔστι γὰρ ἰσότης ... μήτηρ
δικαιοσύνης.

Philem 8
... **ἐν** Χριστῷ παρρησίαν
ἔχων ἐπιτάσσειν σοι τὸ
ἀνῆκον

2 Cor 2:9
... εἰς **πάντα** ὑπήκοοί ἐστε.

Rom 12:1-2, 14:18, Phil 4:18
εὐάρεστος τῷ θεῷ

Rom 6:16
... **δοῦλοί** ἐστε ᾧ **ὑπακούετε**

Pss Sol 4:7, cf. Ps 52:6
ἀνακαλύψαι ὁ θεὸς τὰ ἔργα
ἀνθρώπων ἀνθρωπαρέσκων

Deut 6:5 / Mk 12:30
καὶ ἀγαπήσεις κύριον τὸν
θεόν σου ... ἐξ ὅλης τῆς
ψυχῆς σου ...

1 Thess 2:4
οὐκ ὡς ἀνθρώποις
ἀρέσκοντες

Heb 11:8
... ἤμελλεν λαμβάνειν εἰς
κληρονομίαν ...

2 Cor 5:10-11
10 ... ἵνα κομίσηται ἕκαστος
τὰ διὰ τοῦ σώματος πρὸς ἃ
ἔπραξεν ...
11 **Εἰδότες** οὖν τὸν φόβον
τοῦ κυρίου ...

1 Cor 8:5-6
5 ... **ἐν οὐρανῷ** ... εἰσὶν ...
κύριοι πολλοί,
6 ἀλλ᾽ ἡμῖν ... εἷς κύριος

The first admonition is addressed to wives. In the genuine Pauline letters, the relationship between wives and husbands is discussed in 1 Cor 7:1-16, 11:2-16, 14:34-35. The exhortation "wives be subject to your husbands" (αἱ γυναῖκες, ὑποτάσσεσθε τοῖς ἀνδράσιν) employs the same words as 1 Cor 14:34-35: "women ... should be subordinate" and "ask their husbands at home" (αἱ γυναῖκες ... ὑποτασσέσθωσαν, ... ἐν οἴκῳ τοὺς ἰδίους ἄνδρας ἐπερωτάτωσαν). The resemblance between Col 3:18 and 1 Cor 14:34-35, the use of two of the same nouns (γυνή, ἀνήρ) and one verb (ὑποτάσσω), meets the criteria for a possible literary dependence. The verbal agreement is interesting because in ECL in the texts dealing with the relationship between wives and husbands, the verb ὑποτάσσω, "to subject", is otherwise used only in Eph 5:21-22, in Titus 2:5, and in 1 Pet 3:1, 5.[790]

Eph 5:21-22: Ὑποτασσόμενοι ... αἱ γυναῖκες τοῖς ἰδίοις ἀνδράσιν ὡς τῷ κυρίῳ
Titus 2:5: ... τὰς νέας φιλάνδρους ... ὑποτασσομένας τοῖς ἰδίοις ἀνδράσιν
1 Pet 3:1, (cf. v. 5): ... [αἱ] γυναῖκες, ὑποτασσόμεναι τοῖς ἰδίοις ἀνδράσιν

The comparison of the texts shows that, like in Col 3:18, in Eph 5:21-22, in Titus 2:5, and in 1 Pet 3:1, 5 wives are also exhorted to be subject to their husbands, which does not explicitly appear in 1 Cor 14. In addition, the texts use the word ἴδιος, "one's own", which occurs in 1 Cor 14:35 but not in Col 3:18. Since Eph 5:21-22, Titus 2:5, and 1 Pet 3:1, 5 seem thus to conflate Col 3:18 and 1 Cor 14:34-35, Col 3:18 must be earlier than Eph, Titus, 1 Pet. It is remarkable that in other ancient Greek literature the verb ὑποτάσσω seldom appears in a similar context: only two texts have been found, Plutarch, Moralia 142E and Historia Alexandri Magni (Ps-Callisthenes) I 22, 4.[791] The texts of Hellenistic Judaism generally use other terms. For example, Josephus, Ap II 201 and Philo, De Hyp VII 3, which Crouch regards as the closest parallels to Col 3:18, employ the verbs ὑπακούω, "to obey", and δουλεύω, "to serve", when describing the wife as inferior to her husband.[792] Since 1 Cor 14:34-35 is clearly a closer parallel to Col 3:18 than the above-mentioned texts of Josephus and Philo, a literary dependence between Col 3:18 and 1 Cor 14:34-35 is very likely.[793]

---

[790] Rengstorf 1953, 135, notes the fact that the verb ὑποτάσσω does not occur in this context in the writings of the Apostolic Fathers.

[791] Plutarch, Moralia 142E: ὑποτάττουσαι [αἱ γυναῖκες] μὲν γὰρ ἑαυτὰς τοῖς ἀνδράσιν ἐπαινοῦνται. Historia Alexandri Magni (Ps-Callisthenes) I 22, 4: πρέπον γάρ ἐστι τὴν γυναῖκα τῷ ἀνδρὶ ὑποτάσσεσθαι. Rengstorf 1953, 131-133, followed by O'Brien 1982, 221, emphasizes this detail. According to Rengstorf, this proves that the use of the verb in connection with women is specifically Christian. Still, the non-Christian parallels make this problematic, as Crouch 1972, 111, remarks.

[792] Crouch 1972, 84-85. Josephus, Ap II 201: γυνὴ χείρων, φησίν, ἀνδρὸς εἰς ἅπαντα. τοιγαροῦν ὑπακουέτω, μὴ πρὸς ὕβριν, ἀλλ' ἵν' ἄρχηται. Philo, De Hyp VII 3: γυναῖκας ἀνδράσι δουλεύειν, πρὸς ὕβρεως μὲν οὐδεμιᾶς, πρὸς εὐπείθειαν δ' ἐν ἅπασι·

[793] Cf. Crouch 1972, 110, 122-123, 131-145, who points out that both 1 Cor 14:33b-36 and Col 3:18 are a defense against local expressions of enthusiastic tendencies among the Hellenistic churches.

It must be noted, however, that the verses 1 Cor 14:34-35 belong to the section 1 Cor 14:33b-36 which may be a later interpolation to the text: it upsets the context and is in opposition to 1 Cor 11:2-16 where the active participation of women in the church is presupposed and, in addition, it includes peculiarities of linguistic usage and thought.[794] Since, in case there is an interpolation, we still do not know when the interpolation was added to the text, it is possible that 1 Cor 14:34-35 already was part of the text with which A/Col was acquainted.

The admonition to wives is accompanied by the motivating statement "as is fitting in the Lord" (ὡς ἀνῆκεν ἐν κυρίῳ). The word ἀνῆκεν resembles the expression τὸ καθῆκον used by Stoic philosophers when listing the duties which were "fitting" for a conscientious man to fulfil.[795] So the statement is generally taken as a characteristically Stoic feature which was passed to Christianity through the Hellenistic synagogue and christianized by adding the words ἐν κυρίῳ.[796] It is remarkable, however, that the word ἀνῆκεν is not identical with the Stoic expression καθῆκον and, besides, it is seldom used in a similar sense.[797] The direct connection between the expressions is not self-evident. Yet it is worth noting that the verb ἀνήκω occurs in the Pauline letters in Philem 8 and Eph 5:4, the former resembling Col 3:18. There Paul commands Philemon in Christ to do his duty (ἐν Χριστῷ ... ἐπιτάσσειν σοι τὸ ἀνῆκον). Though the resemblance does not meet the criteria for literary dependence, it is still possible that the motivating statement ὡς ἀνῆκεν ἐν κυρίῳ in Col 3:18 is modelled on the use of the expression τὸ ἀνῆκον in Philem 8 rather than on the Stoic expression καθῆκον directly.

The second admonition in Col 3:19 advises husbands to love (ἀγαπᾶτε) their wives. It is generally assumed that the use of the verb ἀγαπάω refers to the term "agape" and so we are dealing here with specifically Christian material.[798] However, the addition "do not threat them harshly" (μὴ πικραίνεσθε πρὸς αὐτας) points rather to the interpretation that love here means "the loving care of a husband for his wife" which does not include anything specifically Christian.[799] Apart from Eph 5:25, no similar exhortation appears in early Christian rules for the

---

Though he does not assume literary dependence between the texts, he emphasizes that there are "two direct points of contact between I Cor. 14:34ff. and the Colossian *Haustafel*" (144). In addition, Cannon 1981, 156; Pokorný 1987, 152; O'Brien 1982, 221; Dunn 1996, 246; R. P. Martin 1981, 118; Gnilka 1980, 217; Hartman 1985, 159, 164, note the similarity between Col 3:18 and 1 Cor 14:34-35. Contra Schenk 1987a, 3343 n. 54, who maintains the analogy between Col 3:18ff and Mk 10:2-16 which, in my view, do not much resemble each other.

[794] See Conzelmann 1975, 246; Lang 1986, 199; Lindemann 1979, 25-26. Contra Rengstorf 1953, 131, who assumes that 1 Cor 14:34 is certainly Pauline and Crouch 1972, 133-137, who contends that 1 Cor 14:33b-36 is not in opposition to 1 Cor 11:2-16.

[795] See Schlier 1974b, 438-439.

[796] Dunn 1996, 244; O'Brien 1982, 222; Pokorný 1987, 152; Gnilka 1980, 211-212, 217; Bruce 1988, 164; Haapa 1978, 69; Schweizer 1982, 221; Lohse 1971, 157 n. 23. Cf. Ludwig 1974, 118.

[797] See Schlier 1974a, 360, Schweizer 1982, 221 n. 40.

[798] See Dunn 1996, 248; Schweizer 1982, 222; O'Brien 1982, 223; Lindemann 1983, 65; cf. Haapa 1978, 70; Gnilka 1980, 218; Lohse 1971, 158.

[799] Crouch 1972, 111-112. Cf. Bruce 1988, 164; Lohmeyer 1954, 156.

household, nor is it found in any other Hellenistic household rules.[800] The closest parallels to the second admonition seem to be in the LXX where the verb ἀγαπάω is used to refer to the love of a man for a woman (see Gen 24:67, 29:18, Judg 16:4, Eccl 9:9, 1 Esd 4:25, Tobit 10:13). Especially Eccl 9:9: ἰδὲ ζωὴν μετὰ γυναικός, ἧς ἠγάπησας, "enjoy life with the wife whom you love", resembles Col 3:19.[801] In any case, no prototype for Col 3:19 has been found.

The verb πικραίνω employed in Col 3:19 occurs in an ethical context in the sense "to embitter, anger" only here in the NT[802], and it is not used in another Haustafel in this context.[803] The verb appears in Rev 8:11, 10:9, 10, but there it occurs in the concrete sense "to make bitter". However, the verb πικραίνω was frequently used by classical writers from Plato onwards.[804] The closest parallel to Col 3:19 seems to be in the text of Hellenistic philosophy, in Plutarch, Moralia 457A where those who "behave harshly to women" (πρὸς γύναια διαπικραίνονται) are condemned.[805] In addition, in the Apostolic Fathers, in Barn 19:7 and in Did 4:10, the noun πικρία is used in the household rules in connection with treatment of slaves.[806]

Children are exhorted to obey (ὑπακούω) their parents in Col 3:20. The admonition is remarkable because it was exceptional in ancient times that children were treated as human beings in their own right.[807] The exhortation to children, like the one to slaves, is put more strongly than that to wives. The verb ὑπακούω is used in the active imperative while in Col 3:18 the verb ὑποτάσσω occurs in the middle voice. The phrase "in all things" (κατὰ πάντα) further strengthens the injunction.[808] The verb ὑπακούω is frequently used in the genuine Pauline letters but not in a similar sense as here. Instead, it refers to one's submission to Christ, the Gospel, and the apostolic teaching (see Rom 6:17, 10:16, Phil 2:12, cf. 2 Thess 1:8, Mk 1:17, 4:41).[809] The admonition "to obey ... in all things" (ὑπακούετε ... κατὰ πάντα) in Col 3:20 may echo the words "you are obedient in everything" (εἰς πάντα ὑπήκοοί ἐστε) in 2 Cor 2:9.

Rom 1:30 mentions people who are rebellious towards parents but the juxtaposition "parents – children" (οἱ γονεῖς – τὰ τέκνα) appears in the authentic Pauline letters only in 2 Cor 12:14. Because neither of the texts otherwise resemble

---

800 See Lohse 1971, 158 note 28; Crouch 1972, 111-114.

801 Crouch 1972, 112-113, regards the Jewish texts as the closest parallels to Col 3:19 taking B. Yebamoth 62b as the most striking one.

802 This is emphasized by Lohmeyer 1954, 156, and Lohse 1971, 158, n. 29.

803 Crouch 1972, 113.

804 O'Brien 1982, 223, and Lohse 1971, 158 n. 29. See Bauer 1988, 1323.

805 The similarity between these texts is usually noted by the commentaries, see e.g. Lohmeyer 1954, 156; Bruce 1988, 164; Lohse 1971, 158 n. 30; Dunn 1996, 249.

806 Barn 19:7: οὐ μὴ ἐπιτάξῃς δούλῳ σου ἢ παιδίσκῃ ἐν πικρίᾳ. Did 4:10: οὐκ ἐπιτάξεις δούλῳ σου ἢ παιδίσκῃ ... ἐν πικρίᾳ σου. Also Crouch 1972, 113 n. 82, comments on this detail.

807 Schweizer 1982, 223; Pokorný 1987, 153; Gnilka 1980, 220; Dunn 1996, 250.

808 O'Brien 1982, 224. Cf. Gnilka 1980, 219; Pokorný 1987, 153; Bruce 1988, 165; Schweizer 1982, 223.

809 Schweizer 1982, 223; O'Brien 1982, 224.

Col 3:20, it does not seem to be modelled on either of them. Therefore, no close parallel to Col 3:20 appears in ECL before Col; the only identical admonition in Eph 6:1-2 is later.

However, the unequivocal nature of the admonition to children is reminiscent of the OT.[810] The basic injunction is the fourth commandment "honor your father and your mother" (τίμα τὸν πατέρα σου καὶ τὴν μητέρα, see Exod 20:12, Deut 5:16) but other similar admonitions also appear (see Exod 21:15, Lev 20:9, Prov 1:8, 6:20, 30:17). It is worth noting that Eph 6:1-3, which clearly follows Col 3:20, also cites Exod 20:12.[811] In addition, some Jewish Hellenistic texts discuss the relationship between parents and children (e.g. Philo, Hyp VII 3; Spec Leg II, 232-233; De Dec 165-167; Josephus, Ap II, 206, 217). Depending on the fourth commandment, the admonitions generally employ the verb τιμάω instead of ὑπακούω (see Josephus, Ap II 206; Philo De Dec 165, Spec Leg 234). However, sometimes also in the Jewish texts (e.g. in Philo, Spec Leg II 232) as well as in other Hellenistic texts (see Epictetus, Diss II 10, 7) the verb ὑπακούω is used.[812] Neither these Jewish parallels nor the other Hellenistic texts concerning the relationship between parents and children (e.g. Epictetus, Ench XXX; Diss II 14,8, Plato, Republic IV 425b) seem to be prototypes for Col 3:20.[813] However, the instruction in Col 3:20 is a close parallel to Col 3:22.[814] It is possible that the use of the verb ὑπακούω in Col 3:22 has influenced the choice of wording in Col 3:20.[815]

Like the exhortation to wives, the admonition to children is also followed by a motivating statement. The words "this is pleasing in the Lord" (εὐάρεστόν ἐστιν ἐν κυρίῳ) resemble the expression "pleasing in God" (εὐάρεστον τῷ θεῷ) which appears once in the LXX, in Sap 4:10 (cf. 9:10), but is more often used by Paul, e.g. in Rom 12:1-2, 14:18, and Phil 4:18. The verb εὐαρεστέω is also sometimes employed in Hellenistic moral teaching in a context similar to Col 3:20: for example, Epictetus, Diss. I 12, 8 uses the words πῶς ἂν εὐαρεστοίην τῇ θείᾳ.[816]

---

[810] Pokorný 1987, 153; Hendriksen 1971, 170; Hartman 1985, 160; O'Brien 1982, 224.

[811] Eph 6:1-3: Τὰ τέκνα, ὑπακούετε τοῖς γονεῦσιν ὑμῶν [ἐν κυρίῳ]· τοῦτο γάρ ἐστιν δίκαιον. τίμα τὸν πατέρα σου καὶ τὴν μητέρα, ἥτις ἐστὶν ἐντολὴ πρώτη ἐν ἐπαγγελίᾳ, ἵνα εὖ σοι γένηται καὶ ἔσῃ μακροχρόνιος ἐπὶ τῆς γῆς.

[812] Philo, Spec Leg II 232: διὰ τοῦτ' ἔξεστι τοῖς πατράσι καὶ κακηγορεῖν πρὸς τοὺς παῖδας καὶ ἐμβριθέστερον νουθετεῖν καί, εἰ μὴ ταῖς δι' ἀκοῶν ἀπειλαῖς ὑπείκουσι, τύπτειν ... Epictetus, Diss II 10, 7: Μετὰ τοῦτο μέμνησο, ὅτι υἱὸς εἶ. τίς τούτου τοῦ προσώπου ἐπαγγελία; πάντα τὰ αὑτοῦ ἡγεῖσθαι τοῦ πατρός, πάντα ὑπακούειν ... Crouch 1972, 114, emphasizes that "the words κατὰ πάντα have their parallel in the Hellenistic Jewish statements about the submission of women. De Hyp 7.3: ἐν ἅπασι. Contra Apionem ii. 201: εἰς ἅπαντα".

[813] Cf. Crouch 1972, 114, who contends that the exhortation to children has "no direct parallel to similar non-Christian statements".

[814] Similarly Dunn 1996, 249.

[815] Crouch 1972, 114.

[816] Epictetus, Diss. I 12, 8: ὁ δὲ παιδευόμενος ταύτην ὀφείλει τὴν ἐπιβολὴν ἔχων ἐλθεῖν ἐπὶ τὸ παιδεύεσθαι 'πῶς ἂν ἑποίμην ἐγὼ ἐν παντὶ τοῖς θεοῖς καὶ πῶς ἂν εὐαρεστοίην τῇ θείᾳ διοικήσει.

The expression εὐάρεστον τῷ θεῷ used in Sap 4:10 is the closest parallel to the words εὐάρεστόν ἐστιν ἐν κυρίῳ in Col 3:20.[817] It is worth noting that A/Col again ascribes the characteristic of God to Christ.

In Col 3:21, fathers are exhorted not to provoke, to irritate (ἐρεθίζω) their children, that they may not lose heart (ἀθυμέω). The admonition is addressed only to fathers although in the previous verse both parents were mentioned. Probably the reason is simply that in contemporary society the father had the authority and power as the head of the house (patria potestas).[818] The verb ἐρεθίζω appears otherwise in the Pauline letters only in 2 Cor 9:2 in a different sense meaning "to provoke", "to stir up" in a positive sense. Though the verb ἐρεθίζω is atypical of ECL, it is used in a negative sense, as in Col 3:21, often in Jewish and Hellenistic literature (e.g. 1 Macc 15:40; Philo, Ebr 16; Josephus, Bell II 414; Ant IV 169; Epictetus, Ench XX).[819] The verb ἀθυμέω, "to be disheartened", does not appear anywhere else in the Pauline letters but it is frequently employed in the LXX (Deut 28:65, 1 Kings 1:6-7, 15:11, 2 Kings 6:8) and in other Jewish literature (Josephus, Bell VI 94; Ant IX 87). The admonition to fathers is not unique. Ps-Phocylides 207 is cautioning against extreme severity towards children and in Plutarch, Moralia 13D, fathers are exhorted not to behave harshly and austerely.[820] Neither of the texts, however, are close enough to be a prototype for Col 3:21.[821]

As was already mentioned, the admonition to slaves in Col 3:22 parallels the injunction to children. Both use the verb ὑπακούω, "to obey", and the phrase κατὰ πάντα, "in all things", which strengthen the injunction.[822] Paul discusses the status of the slaves in 1 Cor 7:17-23 and in Rom 6 he uses the term δοῦλος metaphorically when describing people as servants of sin. Though neither of these texts seem to be a prototype for Col 3:22-25, they include some similar choices of wording. First, δοῦλός ἐστιν Χριστοῦ, "is a slave of Christ", in 1 Cor 7:22 resembles the phrase τῷ κυρίῳ Χριστῷ δουλεύετε, "you serve the Lord Christ", in Col 3:24. Second, δοῦλοί ἐστε ᾧ ὑπακούετε, "you are slaves of the one whom you obey", in Rom 6:16 uses the same words as the injunction οἱ δοῦλοι, ὑπακούετε, "slaves, obey", in Col 3:22. The first verbal agreement does not point to literary dependence because it is typical of Paul to describe the Christians as slaves of Christ or the Lord using the verb δουλεύω or the noun δοῦλος (cf. Rom

---

[817] Similarly Hübner 1997, 110; R. P. Martin 1981, 120; O'Brien 1982, 225; Gnilka 1980, 219. Contra Lohse 1971, 156, followed by Ludwig 1974, 118, who emphasizes that the reference to what is "pleasing" (εὐάρεστον) corresponds to Hellenistic moral teaching.

[818] Gnilka 1980, 220; Pokorný 1987, 154; O'Brien 1982, 225; Hendriksen 1971, 172 n. 150; Bruce 1988, 165; Haapa 1978, 70; Nikolainen 1987, 56. Contra Schweizer 1982, 223, who explains referring to Heb 11:23 that "fathers" in the plural sometimes include both parents.

[819] Epictetus, Ench XX: ὅταν οὖν ἐρεθίσῃ σέ τις, ἴσθι, ὅτι ἡ σή σε ὑπόληψις ἠρέθικε.

[820] Ps-Phocylides 207: παισὶν μὴ χαλέπαινε τεοῖσ', ἀλλ' ἤπιος εἴπης. Plutarch, Moralia 13D: οὐδὲ γὰρ αὖ πάλιν τοὺς πατέρας ἔγωγ' ἀξιῶ τελέως τραχεῖς καὶ σκληροὺς εἶναι τὴν φύσιν.

[821] Nor does Crouch 1972, 115-116, find any close parallel to Col 3:21.

[822] The similarity is commented on by Pokorný 1987, 154; Schweizer 1982, 224; O'Brien 1982, 226; Hartman 1985, 170; Lindemann 1983, 66.

12:11, 14:18, 16:18). A/Col seems rather to use here a phrase characteristic of Paul. Yet Paul never connects κύριος and Χριστός one after another like A/Col here does.[823] The closest resemblance among the Pauline texts is the choice of wording in Rom 16:18: τῷ κυρίῳ ἡμῶν Χριστῷ οὐ δουλεύουσιν.[824] The second similarity is more remarkable than the first one. Since in the genuine Pauline letters, the verb ὑπακούω is connected to slaves only in Rom 6, it seems possible that the choice of wording in Col 3:22 is influenced by Rom 6. Still, the words δοῦλος and ὑπακούω are so ordinary that the resemblance does not meet the criteria for literary dependence.

In Col 3:22, masters are defined as "lords in terms of the flesh" (κατὰ σάρκα κυρίοις) while Christ is called the Lord (κυρίος). The words κατὰ σάρκα κυρίοις appear otherwise in the Pauline epistles only in Eph 6:5-6 which seems to follow the admonition to slaves in Col.[825] However, the juxtaposition ἐν σαρκὶ – ἐν κυρίῳ, "in the flesh – in the Lord" is used in Philem 16 to describe how Onesimus, on the one hand, is a slave (δοῦλος) of Philemon but, on the other hand, is more than a slave (ὑπὲρ δοῦλον), a beloved brother in the Lord. A/Col thus may have in mind here the juxtaposition of Philem 16 which he modifies. The agreement between Col 3:22 and Philem 16, the use of three of the same nouns (δοῦλος, κυρίος, σάρξ) also meets the criteria for a possible literary dependence.

Like the expression κατὰ σάρκα κυρίοις, the terms ὀφθαλμοδουλία, "eye-service", and ἀνθρωπάρεσκος, "manpleaser", as well as the phrase ἐν ἁπλότητι καρδίας, "with sincerity of heart", also appear only in Eph 6:5-6 in the Pauline epistles. In addition, the term ὀφθαλμοδουλία does not occur anywhere else in ancient Greek literature and thus seems to be coined by A/Col.[826] The phrase ἐν ἁπλότητι καρδίας is used in Jewish literature (see TestLevi 13:1, TestReub 4:1: ἐν ἁπλότητι καρδίας ἐν φόβῳ κυρίου, TestSim 4:5) and it already occurred in the LXX, in Wis 1:1 and in 1 Chr 29:17, the former of which is a closer resemblance to Col 3:22 than the latter because the context is similar. While Col 3:22 mentions fearing the Lord, Wis 1:1 discusses searching for the Lord. Accordingly, the use of the phrase ἐν ἁπλότητι καρδίας may be recalled from the LXX.[827]

Similarly, the term ἀνθρωπάρεσκος appears sometimes in the LXX (see Pss Sol 4:7, 8, 19, Ps 52:6) but not at all in the authentic Pauline letters. However, in Gal 1:10 and 1 Thess 2:4 a similar phrase ἀνθρώποις ἀρέσκω is used. It is

---

[823] This is also emphasized by Lohse 1971, 161 n. 65; Haapa 1978, 72; Nikolainen 1987, 60.

[824] O'Brien 1982, 229; Hendriksen 1971, 175; and Hartman 1985, 161, call attention to the similarity between Col 3:24 and Rom 16:18. Contra Pokorný 1987, 155, who emphasizes the similarity between Col 3:24 and Rom 12:11.

[825] Eph 6:5-6: Οἱ δοῦλοι, ὑπακούετε τοῖς κατὰ σάρκα κυρίοις μετὰ φόβου καὶ τρόμου ἐν ἁπλότητι τῆς καρδίας ... μὴ κατ' ὀφθαλμοδουλίαν ὡς ἀνθρωπάρεσκοι ἀλλ' ὡς δοῦλοι Χριστοῦ.

[826] See Bauer 1988, 1212. The uniqueness of the term is also noted e.g. by Lohse 1971, 160; and Dunn 1996, 254.

[827] Also Standhartinger 1999, 251, notes that the phrase ἐν ἁπλότητι καρδίας is known in the Jewish tradition,

remarkable that the theme of Gal 1:10 also resembles Col 3:22-24. Both mention the serving of Christ and, moreover, the verbal agreement between the texts, two of the same nouns (Χριστός, δοῦλος) and the expressions ἀνθρωπάρεσκος / ἀνθρώποις ἀρέσκω resembling each other, meets the criteria for a possible literary dependence. So it seems that A/Col may have in mind the words "if I were still pleasing people, I would not be a servant of Christ" (εἰ ἔτι ἀνθρώποις ἤρεσκον, Χριστοῦ δοῦλος οὐκ ἂν ἤμεν) from Gal 1:10[828] but instead of the phrase ἀνθρώποις ἀρέσκω, he uses the noun ἀνθρωπάρεσκος, familiar from the LXX.[829]

The admonition "to fear the Lord" is ordinary in the OT (see Deut 6:13, Ps 111:10, 110:10 LXX) but it also occurs in ECL, e.g. in Acts 9:31, in 2 Cor 5:11, and in Rev 15:4, and thus it is not self-evident that it indicates the Jewish background of the Haustafel as Lohmeyer stated (see p. 175). Like in the OT, in Rev 15:4 and in Acts 9:31 the expression refers to God.[830] Since 2 Cor 5:10 mentions the judgment seat of Christ, the fear of the Lord in the following verse seems to refer to Christ rather than to God.[831] It is also possible that the fear of God is meant because 2 Cor 5:11 emphasizes that we are well known to God.[832] In any case, the exhortation to fear the Lord in Col 3:22 clearly refers to Christ.[833] Typically, A/Col ascribes a characteristic of God to Christ. Besides mentioning the fear of the Lord, Col 3:22-25 and 2 Cor 5:10-11 also have other similarities: both use the verb form εἰδότες and the verb κομίζω when describing the judgment according to deeds. The resemblance is remarkable because the fear of the Lord is mentioned nowhere else in the Pauline letters and the verb κομίζω is otherwise used only in Eph 6:8. Furthermore, the agreement between Col 3:22-25 and 2 Cor 5:10-11, the use of four similar words (κομίζω, εἰδότες, φοβέω/φόβος, κύριος) occurring within two lines in 2 Cor, meets the criteria for a probable literary dependence.[834]

Col 3:23 begins with the words ὃ ἐὰν ποιῆτε, "whatever your task", which are a repetition from Col 3:17. The admonition which in v. 17 was addressed to all members of the congregation is picked up again and directed to the slaves only.[835] It is also possible that in Col 3:23-25 the author has in mind other people besides

---

[828] Similarly Hübner 1997, 113, and Standhartinger 1999, 250, comment on the similarity between the choice of wording in Gal 1:10 and Col 3:22.

[829] Lohmeyer 1954, 158, and Standhartinger 1999, 250-251, call attention to the fact that the noun ἀνθρωπάρεσκος occurs in the LXX.

[830] Though in Acts 9:27 Christ is called the Lord, it seems probable that the fear of the Lord in Acts 9:31 has to be understood in the light of the OT; see Schneider 1982, 40 n. 68. In addition, the expression "to fear God" is used in Acts 10:2, 22, in 1 Pet 2:17, and in Rev 14:7.

[831] Barnett 1997, 279 n. 3.

[832] So Furnish 1984, 322; R. P. Martin 1986, 120.

[833] Cf. O'Brien 1982, 227; Lohse 1971, 160.

[834] Also Bruce 1988, 169-170, and O'Brien 1982, 231, note the similarity between Col 3:25 and 2 Cor 5:10.

[835] Similarly O'Brien 1982, 228; Hübner 1997, 113; Schweizer 1982, 225. Cf. Ludwig 1974, 121; and Crouch 1972, 10. Bujard 1973, 98, emphasizes that the repetition is caused by the associative style of A/Col.

slaves because the exhortations are suitable to all Christians.[836] While in v. 17 everything was to be done in the name of the Lord Jesus, now all tasks should be done as for the Lord (ὡς τῷ κυρίῳ) not as for the people (οὐκ ἀνθρώποις). Similarly in 1 Cor 14:2 the juxtaposition not to speak to people (οὐκ ἀνθρώποις) but to God is employed and in 1 Thess 2:4 not to please people (οὐκ ὡς ἀνθρώποις ἀρέσκοντες) but God.[837] So the juxtaposition "as for the Lord – not for the people" seems to be an imitation of a Pauline phrase. Since it was already mentioned that 1 Thess 2:4 employs the phrase ἀνθρώποις ἀρέσκω which resembles the noun ἀνθρωπάρεσκος used in Col 3:22, it is possible that Col 3:23 also echoes it.

The admonition to work "with all your soul" (ἐκ ψυχῆς) in Col 3:23 may echo the injunction "you shall love the Lord your God with all your heart, and with all your soul" (καὶ ἀγαπήσεις κύριον τὸν θεόν σου ... ἐξ ὅλης τῆς ψυχῆς σου) familiar from Deut 6:5 and cited in Mk 12:30/ Mt 22:37.[838] The formulations in Mk 12:30 and Deut 6:5 are the closest to Col because they use the same preposition, ἐκ, while the preposition ἐν is employed in Mt 22:37.[839] Therefore, Col 3:23 seems to echo either Deut 6:5 or Mk 12:13.

The words "from the Lord you will receive the reward of the inheritance" (ἀπὸ κυρίου ἀπολήμψεσθε τὴν ἀνταπόδοσιν τῆς κληρονομίας) in Col 3:24 do not have a parallel in the Pauline letters. The noun ἀνταπόδοσις, "reward", does not occur anywhere else and the noun κληρονομία, "inheritance", is used only in Gal 3:18 when describing the promises God gave to Abraham. Though Gal 3:18 does not otherwise verbally agree with Col 3:24, the use of the noun "inheritance" still points in the direction that Col 3:24 also refers to the promises given to Abraham.[840]

The closest parallel to Col 3:24 is Heb 11:8 which tells about the inheritance Abraham received with the words ἤμελλεν λαμβάνειν εἰς κληρονομίαν. In the LXX, the noun ἀνταπόδοσις often means "punishment" (see Ps 90:8, 93:2, Hos 9:7, Isa 34:8, 59:18, 63:4, 66:6) but sometimes it is also used in the sense "reward" like in Col (see Judg 9:16, Ps 102:2, Isa 61:2). An interesting parallel is Isa 59:18-19 which employs the noun ἀνταπόδοσις when describing how the Lord will repay his adversaries according to their deeds so that His name will be feared.[841] Thus it seems that the LXX usage of the noun ἀνταπόδοσις has influenced its use in Col 3:24. In addition, the giving of the inheritance is such a common idea in the OT that there can hardly be any connection between Col 3:24 and Heb 11:8. The agreement is more probably due to both writers' acquaintance with the LXX.

---

[836] Similarly A. Aejmelaeus 1992, 210-212, assumes that in 1 Pet 2:18ff the writer has in mind not only the slaves but other Christians also.

[837] Cf. Eph 6:7: μετ' εὐνοίας δουλεύοντες ὡς τῷ κυρίῳ καὶ οὐκ ἀνθρώποις.

[838] The similarity is also noted by Dunn 1996, 255-256; Nikolainen 1987, 60; R. P. Martin 1981, 122; Pokorný 1987, 154; Hartman 1985, 161.

[839] Mt 22:37: ... ἀγαπήσεις κύριον τὸν θεόν σου ... ἐν ὅλῃ τῇ ψυχῇ σου.

[840] Cf. Dunn 1996, 257.

[841] Isa 59:18-19: ὡς ἀνταποδώσων ἀνταπόδοσιν ὄνειδος τοῖς ὑπεναντίοις. καὶ φοβηθήσονται οἱ ἀπὸ δυσμῶν τὸ ὄνομα κυρίου.

The phrase οὐκ ἔστιν προσωπολημψία, "there is no partiality", used in Col 3:25, also appears in Rom 2:11, Eph 6:9, and TestJob 43:13. The noun προσωπολημψία is formed from the expression λαμβάνειν πρόσωπον, "to raise the face", to denote respect for persons — this appears both in the LXX (e.g. in Sir 35:13) and in ECL (see Gal 2:6, Lk 20:21, Barn 19:4, Did 4:3).[842] The noun προσωπολημψία does not, however, occur in the LXX, and it appears in ECL, besides in Col 3:25, Rom 2:11, Eph 6:9, and TestJob 43:13, only in Jas 2:1, and Pol, Phil 6:1.[843] In addition, in other ancient Greek texts it appears only in the TestJob, the exact date of which is indefinite. The noun may thus be formed by Paul.[844] The fact that the noun προσωπολημψία otherwise occurs only in a few writings which seem to be later than Col indicates that Col 3:25 not only uses a phrase similar to Rom 2:11 but also depends on it.

The contexts of Col 3:25 and Rom 2:11 are also very much alike: while the former emphasizes that "for the wrongdoer will be paid back for whatever wrong has been done" (ὁ γὰρ ἀδικῶν κομίσεται ὃ ἠδίκησεν), according to the latter "there will be anguish ... for everyone who does evil" (ἐπὶ πᾶσαν ψυχὴν ἀνθρώπου τοῦ κατεργαζομένου τὸ κακόν). Though described with different words, the texts include the same thought. In addition, the choices of wording in Col 3:23 and Rom 2:9 resemble each other: both use the noun ψυχή, and the verb κατεργάζομαι, which has the same stem as ἐργάζομαι in Col 3:23, occurs in Rom 2:9. Thus it seems possible that when A/Col wrote the text, Rom 2:9-11 inspired the words ἐκ ψυχῆς ἐργάζεσθε.

Besides the verbal and verbatim agreement, there is also other evidence pointing to the dependence between Col 3:23-25 and Rom 2:9-11, namely the agreement between Col 3:25-4:1 and Eph 6:8-9.[845]

---

[842] Lohmeyer 1954, 159; Lohse 1973, 779-780; Dunn 1996, 258; Gnilka 1980, 223; O'Brien 1982, 231. Cf. Hays 1989, 44.

[843] The following words having the same stem also appear: the verb προσωπολημπτέω in Jas 2:9, the noun προσωπολήπτης in Acts 10:34, and the adverb ἀπροσωπολήπτως in 1 Pet 1:17, 1 Clem 1:3, Barn 4:12, TestJob 4:8.

[844] So Gnilka 1980, 223. Also Dunn 1996, 258, and Bruce 1988, 170 n. 215, emphasize that the noun προσωπολημψία is not attested before the NT documents. Contra Lohse 1971, 162 n. 70; 1973, 780 n. 3, (followed by O'Brien 1982, 231) who claims that the noun προσωπολημψία "is found for the first time in the NT but was probably in use already in Hellenistic Judaism". However, he does not present any text to prove his assumption, for which he is also criticized by Gnilka 1980, 224 n. 99.

[845] Cf. TestJob 43:13: δίκαιός ἐστιν Κύριος, ἀληθινὰ αὐτοῦ τὰ κρίματα· παρ' ᾧ οὐκ ἔστιν προσωπολημψία·

Eph 6:8-9	Col 3:25-4:1	Rom 2:9-11
8 **εἰδότες ὅτι** ἕκαστος ἐάν τι ποιήσῃ **ἀγαθόν**, τοῦτο **κομίσεται** παρὰ κυρίου εἴτε δοῦλος εἴτε ἐλεύθερος.	25 ὁ γὰρ ἀδικῶν **κομίσεται** ὃ ἠδίκησεν, **καὶ οὐκ ἔστιν προσωπολημψία**.	9 θλῖψις ... ἐπὶ πᾶσαν ... τοῦ κατεργαζομένου τὸ κακόν, Ἰουδαίου τε πρῶτον καὶ Ἕλληνος·
9 Καὶ **οἱ κύριοι**, τὰ αὐτὰ ποιεῖτε πρὸς αὐτούς, ἀνιέντες τὴν ἀπειλήν, **εἰδότες ὅτι** καὶ αὐτῶν **καὶ** ὑμῶν ὁ κύριός ἐστιν **ἐν** οὐρανοῖς **καὶ προσωπολημψία οὐκ ἔστιν** παρ᾽ αὐτῷ.	1 **Οἱ κύριοι**, τὸ δίκαιον καὶ τὴν ἰσότητα τοῖς δούλοις παρέχεσθε, **εἰδότες ὅτι καὶ** ὑμεῖς ἔχετε κύριον **ἐν** οὐρανῷ.	10 δόξα ... παντὶ τῷ ἐργαζομένῳ τὸ **ἀγαθόν**, Ἰουδαίῳ τε πρῶτον καὶ Ἕλληνι·
		11 **οὐ** γάρ **ἐστιν προσωπολημψία** παρὰ τῷ θεῷ.

When Col 3:25-4:1 is compared with Eph 6:8-9, it can be seen that the latter follows the former. The exceptional verb κομίζω occurs in both texts in the same form κομίσεται and the unique phrase καὶ οὐκ ἔστιν προσωπολημψία is reused verbatim in Eph, only the words are in a different order καὶ προσωπολημψία οὐκ ἔστιν. In addition, the words εἰδότες ὅτι are repeated twice in Eph and the exhortation to the masters (οἱ κύριοι) resembles its parallel in Col. Both also remind the masters that they have a Master in heaven using the same words, even though they are not repeated verbatim or even in the same order.

Nevertheless, there are three interesting differences between the texts. First, Eph describes the reward of those who do good instead of the wrongdoers mentioned in Col.[846] Second, unlike Col, A/Eph adds the words παρ᾽ αὐτῷ after the phrase καὶ προσωπολημψία οὐκ ἔστιν which resembles the words παρὰ τῷ θεῷ appearing in Rom 2:11. Third, like in Rom but unlike in Col, it is emphasized in Eph that the reward concerns all kinds of people. The examples mentioned are the Jew and the Greek in Rom while in Eph they are the slave and the free. The change is natural because in Eph the text belongs to the injunctions directed to slaves. Accordingly, the comparison shows that Eph 6:8-9 follows Col 3:25-4:1 but makes some changes which seems to be due to Rom 2:9-11. The fact that the reading of Col 3:25-4:1 seems to have brought Rom 2:9-11 to the mind of A/Eph indicates that the text of Col is modelled on that of Rom. Though the verbal agreement between Col 3:23-25 and Rom 2:9-11 is otherwise not very obvious, the use of the exceptional phrase οὐκ ἔστιν προσωπολημψία connected with the evidence from Eph 6:8-9 should be regarded as pointing to a probable literary dependence between the texts.[847]

---

[846] Also Hendriksen 1971, 175, notes the difference.

[847] It is surprising that Dunn 1996, 258; and Bruce 1988, 170 n. 215, emphasize that the noun προσωπολημψία is unusual but still do not assume any connection between Col 3:25 and Rom 2:11. Also Lindemann 1983, 67, neglects the similarity between the phrases in Col 3:25 and in Rom 2:11 by presenting only that Col includes Pauline thought. In addition, Hübner 1997, 113-114,

It is an interesting detail that when speaking about wrongdoers, A/Col uses the verb ἀδικέω which does not occur either in 2 Cor 5:10 or in Rom 2:9 which he otherwise seems to imitate. However, the verb occurs in Philem 18, the context of which also resembles Col 3:25: it refers to the slave Onesimus who might have done wrong to Philemon. Even though the verbal similarity between the texts does not meet the criteria for literary dependence, it is possible that the use of the verb ἀδικέω in Col 3:25 echoes Philem 18.[848] Accordingly, the admonition to slaves in Col 3:22-25 does not seem to have any prototype in the authentic Pauline letters or in other ancient literature. Its phraseology still resembles Philem 16, Gal 1:10, 2 Cor 5:10-11, Rom 2:9-11 and is thus very Pauline.[849]

Masters are exhorted to treat their slaves "justly and fairly" (τὸ δίκαιον καὶ τὴν ἰσότητα) in Col 4:1. The injunction has no parallel in the Pauline letters. The term δίκαιος occurs often but never in this context. The closest parallel in ECL is the use of the term in Mt 20:4. There the landowner promises to pay to the laborers whatever is right (ὃ ἐὰν ᾖ δίκαιον δώσω ὑμῖν).[850] In addition, the term ἰσότης appears in the Pauline letters, besides in Col 4:1, only in 2 Cor 8:13-14 which emphasizes the fair balance between the churches. Normally, like in 2 Cor, ἰσότης means "equality" but in Col 4:1 it is used rather in the sense of "equity, fairness".[851]

The relationship between "justness" and "fairness" was an ordinary theme in the moral teaching of Stoic philosophy. For example, Plutarch discusses the relationship between δικαιοσύνη and ἰσότης and Philo describes ἰσότης as the mother of δικαιοσύνη.[852] These examples show that, like in Col 4:1, in other texts also the terms were used almost as synonyms. In addition, humane treatment for slaves is often urged in Jewish texts (eg. in Sir 4:30, 33:31, 7:20, in Philo, De Dec 167, De Spec Leg II 89-91, III 137-143) but sometimes in other ancient literature too (see Aristotle, Politica 1260b), it was not specifically a Jewish view.[853] It is worth noting that Philo (De Spec Leg II, 90) uses the term "so-called masters" (οἱ λεγόμενοι δεσπόται) which resembles the juxtapositions made between different

---

calls attention to the detail that in Gal 2:6 Paul uses the expression λαμβάνειν πρόσωπον similar to the phrase οὐκ ἔστιν προσωπολημψία but fails to notice that in Rom 2:11 exactly the same phrase occurs.

848 Philem 18: εἰ δέ τι ἠδίκησέν σε. The similarity of language in Col 3:25 and Philem 18 is noted e.g. by R. P. Martin 1981, 124; O'Brien 1982, 230; Haapa 1978, 72.

849 Contra Crouch 1972, 117, who regards Hellenistic Jewish propaganda as the background of the admonition to slaves.

850 Also according to Schrenk 1973, 188, the use of the term δίκαιος in Mt 20:4 is not far from Col 4:1.

851 Stählin 1974, 355; Dunn 1996, 259-260; Gnilka 1980, 224. Contra Schweizer 1982, 227, who prefers the sense "equality".

852 Plutarch, Moralia 719B: ... προσαγορευομένην καὶ διδάσκουσαν ἡμᾶς τὸ δίκαιον ἴσον, ἀλλὰ μὴ τὸ ἴσον δεῖν ποιεῖσθαι δίκαιον. Further in Lohse 1971, 162 n. 74; Dunn 1996, 259-260; Stählin 1974, 354-355.

853 Cf. Crouch 1972, 117-119. Contra Dunn 1996, 259, who emphasizes that "... there may be a conscious dependence on Jewish tradition, which in general treated slaves more favorably than most other traditions ..."

kinds of masters in Col 3:22 and 4:1. In addition, in Philo, De Dec 167, masters are exhorted to show servants the gentleness and kindness by which inequality is equalized which includes a thought similar to Col 4:1 although different words are used.[854]

As was already mentioned, at the end of Col 4:1, the masters (οἱ κύριοι) are reminded that they also have a Master in heaven (κύριος ἐν οὐρανῷ), a phrase which is imitated in Eph 6:9. The juxtaposition κύριοι – κύριος ἐν οὐρανῷ is similar to that in Col 3:22, κατὰ σάρκα κυρίοις – κυρίος. It may also echo 1 Cor 8:5-6 which emphasizes that there are many lords in heaven (ἐν οὐρανῷ ... κύριοι πολλοί) but for us there is one Lord (εἷς κύριος). Therefore, apart from the last words, the admonition to masters does not seem to imitate Pauline letters. Although the use of the terms τὸ δίκαιον and ἰσότης suggests that A/Col is acquainted with the teaching of Stoic philosophy directly or through Hellenistic Judaism, Col 4:1 does not have such a close parallel that its origin could be strictly defined.

To conclude: I contend that the Colossian household code in Col 3:18-4:1 does not directly derive so much from Stoic philosophy or Hellenistic Judaism as has been assumed. The motivating statements ὡς ἀνῆκεν ἐν κυρίῳ and εὐάρεστόν ἐστιν ἐν κυρίῳ hardly seem to be modifications of the Stoic expression καθῆκον. Rather they show the use of the Pauline phraseology which is also obvious throughout the whole text. Only the use of the terms "justness" (τὸ δίκαιον) and "fairness" (ἰσότης) together points to an acquaintance with the teaching of Stoic philosophy directly or through Hellenistic Judaism. It is also interesting that in v. 22 A/Col uses the noun ἀνθρωπάρεσκος, "manpleaser", and the phrase ἐν ἁπλότητι καρδίας, "with sincerity of heart", which both occur in the LXX but not in Paul. Nevertheless, the use of these two expressions does not point to a Jewish character of the text. It is not surprising that A/Col was acquainted with the LXX, the Bible of his time.[855]

It is remarkable that Col 3:18-4:1 includes resemblances to the genuine Pauline letters much more than to other ancient texts. The first admonition to wives depends possibly on the Pauline exhortation to women in 1 Cor 14:34-35. Though other admonitions do not have prototypes in the authentic Pauline letters, they still, apart from the exhortations to husbands and fathers, utilize phrases typical of Paul. It can be seen most clearly in the admonition to slaves: Col 3:22-25 possibly depends on Philem 16 and Gal 1:10 as well as probably upon 2 Cor 5:10-11 and Rom 2:9-11. Accordingly, Col 3:18-4:1 seems to be formed like the other parts of the letter: A/Col wrote it modelled on the genuine Pauline letters.[856]

Col 3:18-4:1 is a free standing unit which is not closely related to the context and the exhortations are briefer and more abrupt than the preceding ones. Still, this

---

[854] Philo, De Dec 167: ... δεσπόταις δ' εἰς ἠπιότητα καὶ πρᾳότητα, δι' ὧν ἐξισοῦται τὸ ἄνισον.
[855] Nor is there much support for Hartman's view (1987, 241-243) that Col 3:18-4:1 has the Decalogue as a point of departure.
[856] Similarly A. Aejmelaeus 1992, 208-210, puts forth that the writer of the Haustafel in 1 Pet 2:13-25 connects several texts from the Pauline letters.

does not necessarily mean that the text has been derived from earlier traditional material. The style of a text is also influenced by its genre.[857] It is also worth noting that Col 3:18-4:1 includes some features characteristic of A/Col: the synonyms τὸ δίκαιον and ἰσότης are used together in v. 4:1; there appear two participles (φοβούμενοι in 3:22, εἰδότες in 1:24, 4:1). In addition, there appear repetitions typical of A/Col: the phrase κατὰ πάντα and the verb ὑπακούω are repeated twice (3:20, 22) and the noun κύριος several times.[858]

In spite of the verbal and verbatim agreements with the authentic Pauline letters, it is true that the form of the Haustafel does not have an equivalent in them. I have not found any proof that the household rules were based either on Stoic philosophy's habit of listing the duties adopted into Hellenistic Judaism or on the philosophical treatises which handle household management. The idea of forming this unity, a Christian Haustafel, may, however, be due to corresponding customs in the Greco-Roman world.[859] Nevertheless, A/Col seems to have formed the first Christian Haustafel without any prototypes but utilizing Pauline phraseology.

[857] See Bujard 1973, 229.
[858] Contra Ludwig 1974, 49, who finds only one phenomenon typical of A/Col: the use of the synonyms τὸ δίκαιον and ἰσότης together.
[859] Cf. Crouch 1972, 120-145, who states that enthusiastic expressions of freedom of women and slaves discussed in 1 Cor 7 and 1 Cor 14:34-36 brought about the need for Christian household rules which were then modelled on the Hellenistic Jewish prototypes and instructions to children, husbands, fathers, and masters were added.

6. Conclusion of the Letter (Col 4:2-18)

6.1. Final Admonitions (Col 4:2-6)

Col 4:2-6	Rom 12:12	Mk 14:38 / par Mt 26:41
2 **Τῇ προσευχῇ** προσκαρτερεῖτε, γρηγοροῦντες ἐν αὐτῇ ἐν εὐχαριστίᾳ,	... **τῇ προσευχῇ** προσκαρτεροῦντες 1 Thess 5:25	γρηγορεῖτε καὶ προσεύχεσθε Col 1:25-28
3 προσευχόμενοι ἅμα **καὶ περὶ ἡμῶν**, ἵνα ὁ θεὸς ἀνοίξῃ ἡμῖν θύραν τοῦ λόγου λαλῆσαι **τὸ μυστήριον τοῦ Χριστοῦ**, δι᾽ ὃ καὶ δέδεμαι,	προσεύχεσθε [**καὶ**] **περὶ ἡμῶν**. **2 Cor 2:12** ... εἰς τὸ εὐαγγέλιον **τοῦ Χριστοῦ** καὶ θύρας μοι ἀνεῳγμένης ἐν κυρίῳ	25 ...εἰς ὑμᾶς πληρῶσαι τὸν λόγον τοῦ θεοῦ, 26 **τὸ μυστήριον**, ... νῦν δὲ ἐφανερώθη ... 28 ... διδάσκοντες πάντα ἄνθρωπον **ἐν** πάσῃ **σοφίᾳ**
4 ἵνα φανερώσω αὐτὸ ὡς δεῖ με λαλῆσαι.		Mk 4:11
5 **Ἐν σοφίᾳ** περιπατεῖτε **πρὸς** τοὺς **ἔξω** τὸν **καιρὸν** ἐξαγοραζόμενοι.	**1 Thess 4:12** ἵνα περιπατῆτε εὐσχημόνως **πρὸς τοὺς ἔξω** ...	... ὑμῖν **τὸ μυστήριον** δέδοται ... τοῖς ἔξω ἐν παραβολαῖς τὰ πάντα γίνεται
6 ὁ λόγος ὑμῶν πάντοτε ἐν χάριτι, ἅλατι ἠρτυμένος, εἰδέναι πῶς δεῖ ὑμᾶς ἑνὶ ἑκάστῳ ἀποκρίνεσθαι.	Dan 2:8 ... **καιρὸν** ὑμεῖς ἐξαγοράζετε	Mk 9:50, cf. Lk 14:34 ... ἐὰν δὲ τὸ ἅλας ἄναλον γένηται, ἐν τίνι αὐτὸ ἀρτύσετε; ἔχετε ἐν ἑαυτοῖς ἅλα καὶ εἰρηνεύετε ἐν ἀλλήλοις.

The conclusion of the letter begins with the exhortations addressed to the whole congregation. Similar admonitions near the end of the letter sometimes also occur in the authentic Pauline letters (cf. 1 Thess 5:12-22, Gal 5:25-6:6, and Phil 4:8-9). The exhortation to devote yourselves to prayer (τῇ προσευχῇ προσκαρτερεῖτε) in Col 4:2 is nearly identical with the admonition in Rom 12:12 (τῇ προσευχῇ προσκαρτεροῦντες). The same kinds of phrases "to be devoted to prayer" also occur in Acts (1:14, 2:42, 6:4)[860] but they do not resemble the exhortation in Col 4:2 as much as that in Rom 12:12. Since the verb προσκαρτερέω is unusual in the Pauline epistles, appearing elsewhere only in Rom 12:12 and 13:6, Col 4:2 may

---

[860] Acts 1:14: οὗτοι πάντες ἦσαν προσκαρτεροῦντες ὁμοθυμαδὸν τῇ προσευχῇ. Acts 2:42: Ἦσαν δὲ προσκαρτεροῦντες τῇ διδαχῇ ... καὶ ταῖς προσευχαῖς. Acts 6:4: ἡμεῖς δὲ τῇ προσευχῇ καὶ τῇ διακονίᾳ τοῦ λόγου προσκαρτερήσομεν.

echo Rom 12:12.[861] The verbal agreement between the texts does not, however, meet the criteria for literary dependence.

The verb γρηγορέω, "to be watchful", occurs in the genuine Pauline letters three times (1 Cor 16:13, 1 Thess 5:6,10) but is never connected with prayer. However, a similar link with prayer appears in the Gospel narration of the events in the Garden of Gethsemane (Mk 14:38, par Mt 26:41), where Jesus advises the disciples to watch and pray (γρηγορεῖτε καὶ προσεύχεσθε).[862] On the one hand, exhortations to be watchful are typical of ECL (see e.g. 1 Thess 5:6, 1 Cor 16:3, Mk 13:34, Mt 25:13) which indicates that the resemblance may be accidental but, on the other hand, the fact that the exhortation "to be watchful" is not frequently connected with prayer points to a connection between Col 4:2 and Mk 14:38 or Mt 26:41. Mk 14:38 is not generally taken to be due to the words of historical Jesus but the later tradition.[863] The resemblance thus indicates A/Col's knowledge of the same tradition as the author of Mk. However, the verbal agreement between Col 4:2 and Mk 14:38 does not meet the criteria for literary dependence and nothing certain about the relationship between the texts can be concluded.[864]

The reference to the thanksgiving at the end of the v. 2 is not surprising because it is typical of A/Col (see 1:3, 12, 2:7, 3:17).[865] In addition, the words γρηγοροῦντες ... ἐν εὐχαριστίᾳ, "being watchful ... in thanksgiving", resemble the words περισσεύοντες ἐν εὐχαριστίᾳ, "overflowing in thanksgiving", used earlier in Col, in 2:7.[866]

Col 4:3-4 includes a typical Pauline request for prayer for himself and his ministry which usually indicates that the letter is drawing to a close (cf. Rom 15:30-32, 1 Thess 5:25, Philem 22). The expression προσεύχομαι + περὶ ἡμῶν used in Col 4:3 occurs once in the authentic Pauline letters, in 1 Thess 5:25, and also in 2 Thess 3:1 and Heb 13:18. Like Col 4:3, 1 Thess 5:25 also adds the conjunction καί before the words περὶ ἡμῶν. It is uncertain, however, whether the conjunction καί originally belonged to 1 Thess 5:25.[867] Still, it is worth noting that the verb γρηγορέω, which occurs otherwise in the genuine Pauline letters only in 1 Cor 16:13, is employed in 1 Thess 5:6, 10. Even though the verbal agreement is

---

861 Similarly Schenk 1987a, 3342, and Haapa 1978, 73, who assume that Col 4:2 follows Rom 12:12. It is noteworthy that Lindemann 1983, 69, regards Rom 12:12 as the closest parallel to Col 4:2. In addition, e.g. Ludwig 1974, 124; Schweizer 1982, 231; Hartman 1985, 181; Pfammatter 1987, 80-81; Müller 1988, 184; Hübner 1997, 115, call attention to the similarity between Col 4:2 and Rom 12:12. Nevertheless Hübner, Ludwig, and Schweizer take the resemblance as due to the use of the Pauline phraseology.

862 Similarly Dunn 1996, 262. Also Hübner 1997, 115; Bruce 1988, 172; and Hendriksen 1971, 179, note that the wording of Col 4:2 resembles Mk 14:38, par Mt 26:41.

863 Bultmann 1958, 288; Schweizer 1971, 310; cf. L. Aejmelaeus 1985, 73-74.

864 Cf. Hübner 1997, 115: "Es ist aber nicht ausgemacht, daβ der AuctCol diese Überlieferung, die Markus erst um 70 in seiner Evangelienschrift rezipierte, bereits gekannt hat."

865 Cf. Dunn 1996, 262.

866 Thus there is no need to assume, like Kiley 1986, 89, that the words τῇ προσευχῇ ... μετὰ εὐχαριστίας from Phil 4:6 are repeated here.

867 E.g. the following manuscripts omit it: ℵ A D' F G.

too slight to meet the criteria for literary dependence, the words used in common are so exceptional that Col 4:3 may echo 1 Thess 5:25.[868]

The 1. person plural used in the beginning of Col 4:3 (ἡμῶν, ἡμῖν) changes to the 1. person singular (δέδεμαι) at the end of the verse. By doing this, a deutero-Pauline writer may emphasize that the letter has the authority of Paul.[869] The expression "have been bound" (δέδεμαι) as signifying imprisonment occurs in ECL also e.g. in Mk 15:7, Jn 18:24, Acts 9:21, 24:27 but is unique in the Pauline letters which usually mention the bonds, δεσμοί, (Phil 1:7, 13, 14, 17, Philem 10, 13) or use the noun prisoner, δέσμιος, (Philem 1, 9). Thus here A/Col, as a pseudepigrapher, employs an expression atypical of Paul.

Like in Col 4:3, the image of an open door is used in missionary contexts twice in the genuine Pauline letters, in 1 Cor 16:9 and 2 Cor 2:12, of which the latter resembles Col 4:3 more than the former.[870] Col 4:3 and 2 Cor 2:12 both mention the proclamation of Christ and, besides, employ the verb ἀνοίγω and the noun θύρα. The texts include three words in common which just meets the criteria for a possible literary dependence. It indicates that A/Col here not only utilizes Pauline phraseology[871] but follows 2 Cor 2:12.

However, A/Col does not speak about the gospel of Christ (τὸ εὐαγγέλιον τοῦ Χριστοῦ) like Paul in 2 Cor 2:12, but the mystery of Christ (τὸ μυστήριον τοῦ Χριστοῦ).[872] So Col 4:3 seems to develop the idea concerning the mystery which has been revealed which was presented in Col 1:25-28. Like in Col 1:25, the gospel is called the word (λόγος) in Col 4:3 and like in Col 1:26, in the following verse, the verb φανερόω, "to reveal", is used. In addition, Col 4:5 employs the phrase ἐν σοφίᾳ which is nearly the same as ἐν πάσῃ σοφίᾳ appearing in Col 1:28. It is also noteworthy that otherwise in the Pauline corpus, the verb φανερόω is not used for Paul's preaching of the gospel.[873] Therefore Col 1:26 seems to have influenced the choice of wording in Col 4:3-4.[874] The words "as I ought to speak" (ὡς δεῖ με λαλῆσαι) in Col 4:4 make use of a loosely joined infinitive construction typical of A/Col (cf. Col 1:10, 22, 25).[875]

Like Col 4:5, 1 Thess 4:12 and 1 Cor 5:12-13 discuss the behavior toward outsiders (τοῖς ἔξω). However, only 1 Thess 4:12 employs the expression

---

[868] Also Ludwig 1974, 124-125; Lohse 1971, 165; R. P. Martin 1981, 126; Lindemann 1983, 69; Hendriksen 1971, 180; O'Brien 1982, 236, note the similarity between Col 4:3 and 1 Thess 5:25.
[869] Cf. Pfammatter 1987, 81; Gnilka 1980, 227-228.
[870] Cf. Acts 5:19 and 14:27 which are not as close parallels to Col 4:3 as those in 1 and 2 Cor.
[871] So R. P. Martin 1981, 126; Dunn 1996, 263; Standhartinger 1999, 133; Luz 1998, 240; Hartman 1985, 182; Müller 1988, 185.
[872] The phrase τὸ μυστήριον τοῦ Χριστοῦ appears otherwise in the Pauline letters only in Eph 3:4.
[873] This is noted by R. P. Martin 1981, 127; Pfammatter 1987, 81; Lohse 1971, 165; Gnilka 1980, 230; Lindemann 1983, 70; Luz 1998, 240. However, 2 Cor 11:6-7 might be an exception.
[874] Also e.g. Dunn 1996, 264; Pfammatter 1987, 81; Pokorný 1987, 157; Lohse 1971, 164; Gnilka 1980, 229; Hübner 1997, 115; Hartman 1985, 183; Lindemann 1983, 70; Müller 1988, 185; Luz 1998, 239, call attention to the similarities between Col 4:3ff. and Col 1:25ff.
[875] Lohse 1971, 89; Bujard 1973, 57. Exactly the same words are elsewhere used in the Pauline letters only in Eph 6:20.

περιπατέω + πρὸς τοὺς ἔξω similarly to Col 4:5.[876] Since the phrase does not occur anywhere else in the Pauline letters and the words πρὸς τοὺς ἔξω match exactly, the resemblance should be classified as indicating a possible literary dependence. Thus I would assume that A/Col here imitates 1 Thess 4:12 rather than only utilizes a Pauline expression.[877]

The description of the mystery in Col 4:3-5 includes interesting similarities with Mk 4:11. While in Mk 4:11 Jesus says to his disciples that the secret (μυστήριον) of the kingdom of God has been given to them, the revelation of the mystery (μυστήριον) of Christ is described in Col 4:3. It is remarkable that the parallels of Mk 4:11 — Mt 13:11 and Lk 8:10 — use the noun μυστήριον in the plural but both Col 4:3 and Mk 4:11 prefer the singular form.[878] In addition, both Col 4:5 and Mk 4:11 mention the outsiders: while it is emphasized in Mk 4:11 that for those outside (τοῖς ἔξω) everything comes in parables, in Col 4:5 is an exhortation to conduct yourselves wisely toward outsiders (πρὸς τοὺς ἔξω).[879] Again, Mk 4:11 differs from its synoptic parallels which do not use the term οἱ ἔξω. Mk 4:11-12 is generally taken as pre-Markan text which the author of Mk inserted here.[880] However, the above-mentioned characteristics in v. 11, which are typical of Mk only, may be due to Markan redaction.[881] Though the verbal agreement between Col 4:3-5 and Mk 4:11 does not meet the criteria for literary dependence, Col 4:5 may echo Mk 4:11. On the other hand, the declaring of the mystery is one of A/Col's favorite themes (cf. Col 1:26-27, 2:2). It is thus also possible that A/Col connects it to the early Christian idea of a dichotomy between insiders and outsiders occurring in 1 Thess 4:12 without dependence on Mk.[882]

The verb ἐξαγοράζω employed in Col 4:5 occurs otherwise in the Pauline letters only twice in Gal (3:13, 4:5) and once in Eph (5:16). The verb means normally "to buy" but in Gal it is used in the sense "to redeem". Col 4:5 and Eph 5:16 employ a similar phrase τὸν καιρὸν ἐξαγοραζόμενοι. The NRSV translates it "making the most of the time". Because it is difficult to understand what this means exactly, scholars often give their own translations or interpretations: "snapping up every opportunity that comes"[883], "buying up the present opportu-

---

[876] 1 Cor 5:12-13: τί γάρ μοι τοὺς ἔξω κρίνειν; οὐχὶ τοὺς ἔσω ὑμεῖς κρίνετε; τοὺς δὲ ἔξω ὁ θεὸς κρινεῖ. Cf. 1 Tim 3:7: δεῖ δὲ καὶ μαρτυρίαν καλὴν ἔχειν ἀπὸ τῶν ἔξωθεν.

[877] So Schweizer 1982, 233; Standhartinger 1999, 125-126. Cf. Lohse 1971, 167; Dunn 1996, 265; Hartman 1985, 184; Lindemann 1983, 70; Müller 1988, 186.

[878] E.g. R. E. Brown 1958, 428; and Räisänen 1990, 109-110, call attention to this difference between the synoptic Gospels.

[879] Also Schenk 1987a, 3343 n. 54; Schweizer 1982, 233; Räisänen 1990, 123 n. 169; Lohse 1971, 164, note that Col and Mk similarly mention the outsiders.

[880] See Mann 1986, 263; Räisänen 1990, 86; Jeremias 1985, 13-15.

[881] Cf. Räisänen 1990, 130-137.

[882] The agreement between Col 4:3-5 and Mk 4:11 is generally taken to be due to the use of the same Christian traditions; see Lohse 1971, 164; Schweizer 1982, 233; Räisänen 1990, 123, 131. Hübner 1988, 186, emphasizes that the contents of Col 4:5 resembles Mk 4:11f. although the use of the phrase πρὸς τοὺς ἔξω may be due to the Pauline phraseology.

[883] O'Brien 1982, 235.

nity"[884], "buying up the time"[885], "do not idle away the time that has been given you"[886]. The verb ἐξαγοράζω is exceptional: in ECL it appears outside the Pauline letters only in MartPol 2:3[887] and in the LXX only once, in Dan 2:8. So it is remarkable that, like in Col 4:5, the verb ἐξαγοράζω is used also together with the noun καίρος in Dan 2:8 although the words do not mean the same as in Col and Eph but rather "to try to gain time".[888] The verb ἐξαγοράζω is so infrequent that the choice of wording in Col 4:5 may echo Dan 2:8. Since the other word in common, καίρος, is very usual both in ECL and in the LXX, the agreement of only two words does not meet the criteria for literary dependence.

The recipients of the letter are exhorted to "let your speech be always with grace, seasoned with salt" (ὁ λόγος ὑμῶν πάντοτε ἐν χάριτι, ἅλατι ἠρτυμένος) in Col 4:6. The noun λόγος refers back to verse 3 which also describes the speaking of the word.[889] In addition, the expression ἐν χάριτι is typical of A/Col: it was already used in Col 3:16. However, the metaphor "seasoned with salt" is exceptional: it does not otherwise occur in the Pauline letters but it is used once in the Gospels. In Mk 9:50 and its parallels in Mt 5:13/ Lk 14:34, the disciples are reminded that salt which has lost its taste is difficult to restore and are commanded to have salt in themselves.[890] Since in Mk 9:50 and Lk 14:34 both the verb ἀρτύω and the noun ἅλας are employed like in Col 4:6, they resemble Col more than the parallel in Mt, but still neither of them is closer to Col than the other. Though the prototype of Col 4:6 is not thus clear, the verbal agreements still indicate some connection between Col and the metaphor presented in Mk 9:50/ Mt 5:13/ Lk 14:34,[891] namely the verb ἀρτύω does not appear otherwise in ECL and the noun "salt", in a little different form ἅλς, is used only in 1 Clem 11:2. In addition, the use of the verb ἀποκρίνομαι may indicate a connection between Col 4:6 and the Gospels: it occurs in the Pauline letters only in Col 4:6 but is normal in the Gospels.[892]

The metaphor "salt that seasons" is familiar to Jewish literature (see e.g. Job 6:6) and Hellenistic texts. Like Col 4:6, Plutarch, Moralia 514F, 685A, connects the metaphor "to speak seasoned with salt" and the noun χάρις, which is noted by

---

884 Bruce 1988, 173.
885 Dunn 1996, 261.
886 Lohse 1971, 169.
887 MartPol 2:3: καὶ προσέχοντες τῇ τοῦ Χριστοῦ χάριτι τῶν κοσμικῶν κατεφρόνουν βασάνων, διὰ μιᾶς ὥρας τὴν αἰώνιον ζωὴν ἐξαγοραζόμενοι.
888 See Lohse 1971, 167-168; Hartman 1985, 178; Schweizer 1982, 234 n. 7; Bruce 1988, 174 n. 17; Nikolainen 1987, 63; Haapa 1978, 75. Cf. Dunn 1996, 265-266, who does not emphasize the difference between the use of the phrase in Col 4:5 and Dan 2:8 but interprets Col 4:3 as an exhortation to gain time "which would otherwise be lost or slip away".
889 Similarly R. P. Martin 1981, 128
890 Also in Ign, Mag 10:2 is exhorted to be salted in Jesus Christ (ἁλίσθητε ἐν αὐτῷ).
891 Schenk 1987a, 3343 n. 54, calls attention to the similarity between Col 4:6 and Mk 9:50.
892 Also Gnilka 1980, 232, comment on the use of the verb atypical of NT letters. In his view, it refers to the struggle the congregation is facing.

some commentators.[893] However, the use of the phrase ἐν χάριτι seems to be typical of A/Col and thus there is no need to see a connection with Plutarch. It is more probable that there is some relationship between the use of similar metaphors in Col 4:6 and the Gospels than that the formulation of Col 4:6 is only based upon an expression current at that time as is generally assumed.[894] In Mk 9:41-50, the author of Mk may have employed a collection of proverbs used for purposes of instruction.[895] The exhortation "have salt in yourselves" may even belong to the original words of Jesus.[896] Therefore, the use of the metaphor "salt that seasons" in Col 4:6 seems to be due to early Christian tradition.

The final admonitions in Col 4:2-6 form an interesting combination of the Pauline phrases and A/Col's own style. The text utilizes phrases from Rom 12:12 and 1 Thess 5:25, 4:12 nearly verbatim and it uses the image of an open door typical of Paul. On the other hand, the text includes many characteristics of A/Col. As was already mentioned, the words ὡς δεῖ με λαλῆσαι make use of a loosely joined infinitive construction typical of A/Col. Another example of the same phenomenon is the use of the verb form εἰδέναι in Col 4:6.[897] The text also includes several repetitions which belong to the associative style of A/Col. The infinitive λαλῆσαι occurs the first time in v. 3 and is repeated in v. 4 (ὡς δεῖ με λαλῆσαι). In addition, the words πῶς δεῖ ὑμᾶς ... ἀποκρίνεσθαι are used in v. 6, resembling the wording of v. 4.[898] It is also interesting that A/Col connects the exhortation "to be watchful" with prayer and uses the idiom "to speak seasoned with salt" neither of which are typical of Paul but occur in the Gospels instead.

---

[893] E.g. Lohse 1971, 169; Dunn 1996, 266; Hübner 1997, 116; Schweizer 1982, 234 n. 8.
[894] So Lohse 1971, 168. Cf. Dunn 1996, 266-267; Schweizer 1982, 234; R. P. Martin 1981, 128; Luz 1998, 240.
[895] Schweizer 1971, 196.
[896] Gnilka 1979, 67; Grundmann 1977, 267.
[897] Similarly Bujard 1973, 57; Lohse 1971, 89.
[898] Bujard 1973, 99, followed by O'Brien 1982, 236.

6.2. Personal Greetings and Instructions (Col 4:7-18)

<table>
<tr><td>Col 4:7-9</td><td>Phil 1:12</td><td>Col 1:7</td></tr>
<tr><td>7 Τὰ κατ᾽ ἐμὲ πάντα
γνωρίσει ὑμῖν Τύχικος ὁ
ἀγαπητὸς ἀδελφὸς καὶ
πιστὸς διάκονος καὶ
σύνδουλος ἐν κυρίῳ,
8 ὃν ἔπεμψα πρὸς ὑμᾶς
εἰς αὐτὸ τοῦτο, ἵνα γνῶτε
τὰ περὶ ἡμῶν καὶ
παρακαλέσῃ τὰς καρδίας
ὑμῶν·
9 σὺν ᾽Ονησίμῳ τῷ πιστῷ
καὶ ἀγαπητῷ ἀδελφῷ, ὅς
ἐστιν ἐξ ὑμῶν. πάντα ὑμῖν
γνωρίσουσιν τὰ ὧδε.</td><td>12 Γινώσκειν δὲ ὑμᾶς
βούλομαι, ἀδελφοί, ὅτι τὰ
κατ᾽ ἐμέ ...

Philem 10-12

10 ... ᾽Ονήσιμον, ...
12 ὃν ἀνέπεμψά σοι,</td><td>... ἀπὸ ᾽Επαφρᾶ τοῦ
ἀγαπητοῦ συνδούλου
ἡμῶν, ὅς ἐστιν πιστὸς
ὑπὲρ ὑμῶν διάκονος τοῦ
Χριστοῦ

Col 2:2

ἵνα παρακληθῶσιν αἱ
καρδίαι αὐτῶν</td></tr>
</table>

The end of Col is taken up with personal greetings (Col 4:7-15), instructions (Col 4:16-17), and the final greeting written in Paul's own hand (Col 4:18) which are also typical of the genuine Pauline letters (cf. 1 Cor 16:19-24, Rom 16:1-23, Philem 23-25). In Col 4:7 it is mentioned that Tychicus will report all the news about Paul using the words τὰ κατ᾽ ἐμέ which also occur in Phil 1:12. In addition, like Col 4:7-8, Phil 1:12 employs the verb γινώσκω, the pronoun ὑμεῖς, and the noun ἀδελφός. The expression τὰ κατ᾽ ἐμέ appears elsewhere in the Pauline letters only in Rom 1:15 in a little different form τὸ κατ᾽ ἐμέ and then later in Eph 6:21, which depends on Col 4:7 (see pp. 32-33). Thus the resemblance between Col 4:7 and Phil 1:12, the use of the unusual expression τὰ κατ᾽ ἐμέ, the verb γινώσκω, and the noun ἀδελφός, meets the criteria for a possible literary dependence. Moreover, the similarity between the contexts of Col 4:7-8 and Phil 1:12 indicates a connection between the texts. While Phil 1:12-13 refers to Paul's imprisonment for Christ and spreading of the gospel (ὥστε τοὺς δεσμούς μου φανεροὺς ἐν Χριστῷ γενέσθαι), Col 4:3 mentions quite similarly the declaring of the mystery of Christ, for which Paul is in prison (λαλῆσαι τὸ μυστήριον τοῦ Χριστοῦ, δι᾽ ὃ καὶ δέδεμαι).[899]

Tychicus is described as a beloved brother (ἀγαπητὸς ἀδελφός), a faithful minister (πιστὸς διάκονος), and a fellow servant (σύνδουλος). Apart from brother

---

[899] Also Lohse 1971, 170; Schweizer 1982, 237; Dunn 1996, 271; O'Brien 1982, 246; Ludwig 1974, 127, call attention to the similar expressions in Col 4:7 and Phil 1:12. Kiley 1986, 90, does not take the resemblance between Col 4:7 and Phil 1:12 to indicate literary dependence because the phrase is bearing different meaning: "τὰ κατ᾽ ἐμὲ are made known by Paul himself in Phil 1.12, but by Tychicus in Col 4.7." Yet both texts refer to the situation of Paul which, in my view, makes the usage quite similar.

(ἀδελφός), all the same epithets were ascribed to Epaphras in Col 1:7.[900] In addition, Onesimus is described as a faithful and beloved brother (πιστὸς καὶ ἀγαπητὸς ἀδελφός) in v. 10. Thus repetitions occur, typical of the author's associative style.[901] Therefore, the use of the same epithets for Tychicus and Epaphras seems rather to belong to the style of the author than to show that the reasons for recommending Tychicus are so similar to those in the case of Epaphras that there is "essential identity" between the men.[902] Similarly, the phrase "to encourage the hearts" (καὶ παρακαλέσῃ τὰς καρδίας ὑμῶν) in Col 4:8 is a repetition from Col 2:2 and the words "tell you about everything" πάντα γνωρίσει/ γνωρίσουσιν ὑμῖν are used both in Col 4:7 and in Col 4:9.

As was noted in the introduction, many scholars state that the enumeration of the same names in Col 4:10-14 and Philem 23-24 (Aristarchus, Mark, Epaphras, Luke, and Demas) points to a dependence between the texts (see p. 17). In addition, both texts define the persons with similar epithets, a fellow prisoner (συναιχμάλωτός) and a co-worker (συνεργός). The name Onesimus does not belong to the list of Philem 23-24 but it occurs in Philem 10. Since these are the only cases where the name appears in the NT, it is generally assumed that there is a connection between Col 4:9 and Philem 10.[903] It is interesting that A/Col does not say anything concrete about Onesimus. He is only mentioned briefly, having some of the same epithets as Tychicus. Therefore, like the other ones, the name Onesimus also seems to be incorporated from Philem into the frame of Col.[904]

In addition, there is a verbal similarity between Col 4:8 and Philem 12. In Col 4:8, the sending of Tychicus is mentioned by using the epistolary aorist ἔπεμψα[905] which appears in Philem 12 when the sending of Onesimus is mentioned. Though the epistolary aorist is typical of Paul (see 1 Cor 4:17, 16:3, 2 Cor 9:3, Phil 2:19, 23, 25, 1 Thess 3:2, 5), it is noteworthy that the relative clause ὃν ἀνέπεμψά σοι in Philem 12 resembles the one in Col 4:8 (ὃν ἔπεμψα πρὸς ὑμᾶς). Even though the verbal similarity between the texts is not remarkable, the fact that the name Onesimus does not occur anywhere else in the Pauline letters indicates a possible literary dependence between Col 4:8-10 and Philem 10-12.[906]

Tychicus is never mentioned in the genuine Pauline letters but the name appears in Acts 20:4 and in the deutero-Pauline letters (Eph 6:21, 2 Tim 4:12, Titus

---

[900] The resemblance between Col 4:7 and 1:7 is also noted by Ludwig 1974, 127; Pokorný 1987, 160-161; Lindemann 1983, 72; Hübner 1997, 118; Hartman 1985, 191; Haapa 1978, 77; Schweizer 1982, 236 n. 1; Hendriksen 1971, 185.

[901] Similarly Bujard 1973, 99. Cf. Hübner 1997, 118

[902] So Hendriksen 1971, 185.

[903] Lohse 1971, 171; Dunn 1996, 273; Luz 1998, 241; R. P. Martin 1981, 130; Gnilka 1980, 235; O'Brien 1982, 248; Schweizer 1982, 238; Hartman 1985, 191; Nikolainen 1987, 65.

[904] Similarly Haapa 1978, 77.

[905] O'Brien 1982, 247-248; Gnilka 1980, 235; Lohse 1971, 171 n. 7; R. P. Martin 1981, 130; Bruce 1988, 176 n. 26.

[906] Cf. Kiley 1986, 83, who regards the mentioning of Onesimus as pointing to a literary dependence between Col 4:9 and Philem 10.

3:12). The name also occurs in inscriptions found in Asia Minor.[907] Those who regard Col as a genuine Pauline letter assume that Tychicus and Onesimus were the bearers of the letter.[908] However, the fact that, according to the authentic letters, Paul never sends two people to report news about him points to a deutero-Pauline character of the text.[909] When Col is taken as a pseudonymous letter, it is generally stated that Tychicus and Onesimus were known as friends of Paul and A/Col, as a later writer, mentions them as the representatives of the Pauline tradition in Asia Minor.[910] In addition, it has been contended that Tychicus may have had a leading role in the Pauline churches at the time the deutero-Pauline letters were written because, unlike the genuine letters, they mention him.[911]

The deutero-Pauline letters do not give many facts about Tychicus. As was already noted, he is given exactly the same characteristics in Col 4:7 as Epaphras in Col 1:7. So it seems that A/Col does not want to say anything personal about him[912] but defines him with the epithets he usually gives to a respected Christian. Eph 6:21 follows and depends on Col 4:7 and so does not give any new information.[913] Like in Col and in Eph, also both in 2 Tim and in Titus, the name Tychicus is only mentioned among the personal greetings at the conclusion of the letter. While in Titus 3:12 Tychicus is said to be sent to Titus, the recipient of the letter, he is sent to Ephesus in 2 Tim 4:12. In addition, it is noteworthy that like Col 4:14, 2 Tim 4:10-11 mentions Demas and Luke, who appear otherwise together only in Philem 24, the probable prototype of Col 4:14. This may indicate the literary dependence of 2 Tim 4:10-12 on Col 4:14 or Philem 24. The evidence is too slight, however, since the texts do not otherwise resemble each other. Consequently, there are not many facts about Tychicus in ECL but it is remarkable that his name is mentioned so many times. Therefore, it is possible that he was an influential person at the time the deutero-Pauline letters were written.

---

907 O'Brien 1982, 247; R. P. Martin 1981, 129.

908 Bruce 1988, 176; O'Brien 1982, 246; R. P. Martin 1981, 129-130.

909 Hartman 1985, 191, also mentions that it is not typical of Paul to send two people to report the news about him.

910 Pfammatter 1987, 82; Pokorný 1987, 161-162; Gnilka 1980, 234-235, 242. Cf. Lohse 1970, 193-194.

911 Gnilka 1980, 234; Nikolainen 1987, 64; Hartman 1985, 191; cf. Dunn 1996, 272; Haapa 1978, 76-77.

912 Cf. Hübner 1997, 118.

913 Hübner 1997, 118. Cf. Lindemann 1983, 72; Hartman 1985, 187; Gnilka 1980, 233.

Col 4:10-14	**Philem 23-24**	
10 **Ἀσπάζεται** ὑμᾶς	23 **Ἀσπάζεταί** σε	2 Cor 7:15
Ἀρίσταρχος ὁ	**Ἐπαφρᾶς ὁ**	
συναιχμάλωτός μου καὶ	**συναιχμάλωτός μου** ἐν	... **ἐδέξασθε αὐτόν**.
Μᾶρκος ὁ ἀνεψιὸς	Χριστῷ Ἰησοῦ,	
Βαρναβᾶ (περὶ οὗ	24 **Μᾶρκος**, **Ἀρίσταρχος**,	
ἐλάβετε ἐντολάς, ἐὰν	**Δημᾶς**, **Λουκᾶς**, οἱ	
ἔλθῃ πρὸς ὑμᾶς, **δέξασθε**	**συνεργοί** μου.	Gal 2:12-13
αὐτόν)		
11 καὶ Ἰησοῦς ὁ		12 ... φοβούμενος τοὺς **ἐκ**
λεγόμενος Ἰοῦστος, οἱ		**περιτομῆς**.
ὄντες **ἐκ περιτομῆς**, οὗτοι	Col 1:7,9	13 ... ὥστε καὶ Βαρναβᾶς
μόνοι **συνεργοὶ** εἰς τὴν		...
βασιλείαν τοῦ θεοῦ,	7 ... ἀπὸ Ἐπαφρᾶ τοῦ ...	
οἵτινες ἐγενήθησάν μοι	συνδούλου ἡμῶν, ...	
παρηγορία.	πιστὸς ὑπὲρ ὑμῶν	
12 **ἀσπάζεται** ὑμᾶς	διάκονος τοῦ **Χριστοῦ** ...	
Ἐπαφρᾶς ὁ ἐξ ὑμῶν,	9 ... οὐ παυόμεθα **ὑπὲρ**	
δοῦλος Χριστοῦ [Ἰησοῦ],	**ὑμῶν** προσευχόμενοι ...	Col 1:28-29
πάντοτε **ἀγωνιζόμενος**	**ἵνα** πληρωθῆτε τὴν	
ὑπὲρ ὑμῶν ἐν ταῖς	ἐπίγνωσιν τοῦ θελήματος	28 ... **ἵνα** παραστήσωμεν
προσευχαῖς, **ἵνα** σταθῆτε	αὐτοῦ ...	πάντα ἄνθρωπον τέλειον
τέλειοι καὶ		ἐν Χριστῷ·
πεπληροφορημένοι ἐν	Rom 10:2	29 εἰς ὃ καὶ κοπιῶ
παντὶ θελήματι τοῦ θεοῦ.		**ἀγωνιζόμενος** ...
13 **μαρτυρῶ γὰρ** αὐτῷ **ὅτι**	**μαρτυρῶ γὰρ** αὐτοῖς **ὅτι**	
ἔχει πολὺν πόνον ὑπὲρ	ζῆλον θεοῦ ἔχουσιν ...	Rom 1:1, cf. Phil 1:1
ὑμῶν καὶ τῶν ἐν		
Λαοδικείᾳ καὶ τῶν ἐν		**δοῦλος Χριστοῦ Ἰησοῦ**
Ἱεραπόλει.		
14 **ἀσπάζεται** ὑμᾶς		
Λουκᾶς ὁ ἰατρὸς ὁ		
ἀγαπητὸς καὶ **Δημᾶς**.		

As was already noted, the final greetings in Col 4:10-14 and in Philem 23-24 both enumerate the names Aristarchus, Mark, Epaphras, Luke, and Demas and also give them similar epithets, a fellow prisoner (συναιχμάλωτός) and a co-worker (συνεργός). In addition, both greetings begin with exactly the same words ἀσπάζεται ... ὁ συναιχμάλωτός μου, "my fellow prisoner greets you". Though the verb ἀσπάζομαι was the conventional word of the time for expressing greetings[914] and is also standard in the final greetings of the genuine Pauline epistles (see Rom 16:21-23, 1 Cor 16:19-20, Phil 4:21), the use of precisely the same words in the

[914] O'Brien 1982, 249; Dunn 1996, 275.

same form is striking. Therefore, the verbal agreement between Col 4:10-14 and Philem 23-24, the list of five of the same names, the similar epithets for the persons, and the same choice of wording at the beginning of the text, clearly meets the criteria for a probable literary dependence.[915]

Nevertheless, the texts also include interesting differences. While in Philem 23 Epaphras is named first and described as a fellow prisoner, in Col 4:10 the epithet is given to Aristarchus who is also mentioned first.[916] This suggests that the imagery given to Aristarchus is figurative.[917] Epaphras is described later in v. 12 with an epithet resembling those given to him in Col 1:7. While he there was presented as a beloved fellow servant (συνδούλος) and as a faithful minister of Christ (διάκονος τοῦ Χριστοῦ), now his epithet is a servant of Christ Jesus (δοῦλος Χριστοῦ 'Ιησοῦ). In the genuine Pauline letters this title is given to Paul in Rom 1:1 and to Paul and Timothy in Phil 1:1. Therefore, as a pseudepigrapher, A/Col uses the epithet differently from the authentic letters when giving it to a person other than Paul.[918]

Col 4:12 describes how Epaphras "is always wrestling in his prayers" so that the recipients of the letter "may stand mature and fully assured in everything that God wills". This description seems to summarize ideas from two earlier parts of Col. Col 1:9 tells how Paul and Epaphras have not ceased "praying for you" (ὑπὲρ ὑμῶν προσευχόμενοι) and Col 1:29 relates how Paul is struggling for the Gospel (ἀγωνιζόμενος). The words "is always wrestling in his prayers" (ἀγωνιζόμενος ὑπὲρ ὑμῶν ἐν ταῖς προσευχαῖς) connect them both together. In addition, the choice of wording "may stand mature and fully assured in everything that God wills" (ἵνα σταθῆτε τέλειοι καὶ πεπληροφορημένοι ἐν παντὶ θελήματι τοῦ θεοῦ) seem to be the result of the conflation of the words ἵνα πληρωθῆτε ... τοῦ θελήματος αὐτοῦ from Col 1:9 and ἵνα παραστήσωμεν ... τέλειον from Col 1:28.[919] Thus the

---

[915] It is surprising that Sanders 1966, 43-45 (followed by Cope 1985, 48-49), does not at all call attention to the remarkable verbal similarity between Col 4:10-14 and Philem 23-24 but emphasizes that the lack of the evidence for literary dependence after 3:15 is compatible with "... the argument for the authenticity of Colossians developed by John Knox ..." which "... only requires Paul to have written the last portion of the letter". Martin 1981, 129, states that instead of Philem 23-24, the nearest equivalent of Col 4:10-14 is Rom 16. Certainly Col 4:10-14 should be compared with Rom 16 in its scope, like Lohse 1971, 172, states (cf. O'Brien 1982, 248-249), but the listing of the same names and the use of similar words show that A/Col has been utilizing Philem 23-24 (cf. Lohse 1970, 194; 1971, 77). Dunn 1996, 276, contends that the conclusions of Col, Rom, and Philem are so similar because all three letters were written during the same imprisonment. This interpretation does not explain at all the verbal closeness between Col 4:10-14 and Philem 23-24 compared to Rom 16. It is also remarkable, like Lohse 1971, 176, states, that the greetings at the end of Rom are different from those in Col: while in Rom 16 greetings are given to a long list of persons, Col 4:10-14 introduces several of Paul's fellow workers.

[916] Similarly Pokorný 1987, 162; Schweizer 1982, 239; and Dunn 1996, 275, note that the description of Aristarchus in Col 4:10 is the same as that of Epaphras in Philem 23.

[917] Similarly Dunn 1996, 275.

[918] Schweizer 1982, 240; Haapa 1978, 79. Cf. O'Brien 1982, 252-253.

[919] The verb πληροφορέω is used here instead of the more standard verb πληρόω; Lohse 1971, 173; O'Brien 1982, 254.

description of Epaphras in Col 1:12 largely corresponds to that which was before said about Paul.[920]

In Col 4:13 Epaphras is praised using the words "for I testify for him that he has" (μαρτυρῶ γὰρ αὐτῷ ὅτι ἔχει) which resembles Rom 10:2: "for I testify for them that ... they have" (μαρτυρῶ γὰρ αὐτοῖς ὅτι ... ἔχουσιν). However, the texts employ only two of the same verbs, which does not meet the criteria for literary dependence. It should also be noted that the words μαρτυρῶ γὰρ ... ὅτι seem to form a stock phrase of Paul because they are used also in Gal 4:15.

Mark is passed over in Philem 24 with a bare mention but in Col 4:10 he is called the cousin of Barnabas who occurs often in ECL and is an important, well-known figure. In authentic Pauline letters, Barnabas appears in 1 Cor 9:6 and Gal 2:1, 9, 13. In addition, Col 4:10 refers to the instructions which the recipients of the letter have been given concerning Mark and counsels welcoming him if he comes to Colossae. The exhortation to welcome Mark (δέξασθε αὐτόν) uses the same verb δέχομαι as Gal 4:14 and 2 Cor 11:16 when describing how Paul was welcomed. In addition, the verb is employed in 2 Cor 7:15 when mentioning how Paul's co-worker Timothy was welcomed in Corinth. Thus, Pauline style appears here but the reference to the instructions given concerning Mark (περὶ οὗ ἐλάβετε ἐντολάς) does not have any parallel in the genuine Pauline letters: there the word ἐντολή generally means the divine commands.[921]

Col 4:11 mentions Jesus, who is also called Justus. The name is the only one which does not occur in Philem 23-24. Therefore, it has been conjectured that instead of "of Jesus" ('Ιησοῦ) the name Jesus ('Ιησοῦς) should be read in Philem 23, although no manuscript supports this interpretation.[922] The name does not otherwise appear in ECL and we thus do not know any more of Jesus Justus than what is told us here.[923] Since the name is not picked up from Philem, he might have been a person living at the time Col was written.

There follows further information about Aristarchus, Mark, and Jesus Justus who are defined to be "those of the circumcision" (οἱ ὄντες ἐκ περιτομῆς) which is an expression typical of the authentic Pauline letters (see Rom 4:12 and Gal 2:12) and normally taken to refer to Jewish Christians.[924] It is noteworthy that Barnabas is mentioned in the context of Gal 2:12, in the following verse 13. The

---

[920] Cf. Dunn 1996, 280; O'Brien 1982, 253; Sappington 1991, 143-144; Hartman 1985, 192-193; Schweizer 1982, 240; Hübner 1997, 120; Lindemann 1999, 202. Contra Kiley 1986, 80, who contends that in Col 4:12 Epaphras is presented as the link between Paul and the community like Epaphroditus in Phil 4:18 and regards the resemblance as a point of contact which refers to a literary dependence between Col and Phil. However, there is no verbal agreement between Col 4:12 and Phil 4:18. Kiley's interpretation is also criticized by Standhartinger 1999, 88.

[921] Cf. Dunn 1996, 277.

[922] See O'Brien 1982, 251; Martin 1981, 132; Lindemann 1983, 74; Lohse 1970, 192.

[923] Hübner 1997, 119; O'Brien 1982, 251; Lohse 1971, 172.

[924] Schweizer 1982, 240; Lindemann 1983, 74; Martin 1981, 132; O'Brien 1982, 251; Bruce 1988, 180 n. 51. Contra Dunn 1996, 278, who assumes that it denotes Jews.

verbal agreement is, however, too slight to indicate literary dependence.[925] In addition, the three men are described using the expression "co-workers for the kingdom of God" (συνεργοὶ εἰς τὴν βασιλείαν τοῦ θεοῦ) which is not typical of Paul[926] nor is the noun "comfort", παρηγορία, used at the end of the verse. Demas is passed over with a bare mention in Col 4:14 but Luke is called "the beloved physician". Like the definition "cousin of Barnabas" given to Mark, the epithet is exceptional: the term physician (ἰατρός) occurs otherwise in ECL only in the Gospels (see e.g. Mt 9:12, Mk 5:26, Lk 4:23). Therefore, the epithet "the beloved physician" seems to be a formation of A/Col.

This comparison has shown that Philem 23-24 is the prototype of Col 4:10-14. A/Col enumerates all the names mentioned in Philem but gives them different epithets and adds one new person, Jesus Justus, who is otherwise unknown. The interpretation that Col and Philem were written at the same time does not explain why A/Col mentions the same names as Philem but describes the persons so differently. Rather the text seems to imitate Philem 23-24 which, on the grounds of the remarkable number of similarities, might actually be in front of the author. In addition, Col 10-14 includes so many unique terms and phrases which do not occur in the genuine Pauline letters that it cannot be an authentic Pauline text.[927] Nor is it probable that Timothy would have written in Paul's lifetime, in his company, a text which mentions the same persons as Philem but describes them so differently.[928] Accordingly, the most probable alternative is that the text has been shaped by a later writer after Paul's death.

One reason to form the conclusion of the letter on the Philem model must have been to link the pseudo-Pauline letter to the apostle's life so that it seems to have been written at the same time as Philem.[929] In addition, the mentioning of two neighboring cities of Colossae, Laodicea and Hierapolis (Col 4:13), indicates the purpose of connecting the letter to a real location. The names familiar from a genuine Pauline letter are used to give an apostolic authorization to the letter[930] and to show that the co-workers of Paul are his followers who continue his work.[931]

---

[925] Contra Schenk 1987a, 3339.

[926] Pfammatter 1987, 83. Cf. Dunn 1996, 279, who states that "the language here, then could be a sign of another hand" than Paul's.

[927] Contra e.g. Bruce 1988, 178; Guthrie 1990, 576-577; O'Brien 1982, 246 ff.; Martin 1981, 129 ff.; Luz 1998, 241-242, who take the text as genuine.

[928] E.g. Dunn 1996, 37-38, states that Col 4:10-14 resembles Philem 23-24 so much because Col was written at about the same time as Philem but actually composed by Timothy.

[929] Lindemann 1983, 75; Pokorný 1987, 160. Pokorný also states that A/Col may have chosen Philem as a model because it was written to the area where Colossae is situated. However, as a matter of fact, we do not know where Philem is addressed. It has been assumed that Philemon was living in Colossae only because the same persons are mentioned in Col and in Philem (see p. 13).

[930] Pokorný 1987, 159; Lohse 1970, 193; 1971, 176-177. Contra Martin 1981, 129.

[931] Gnilka 1980, 236, 242; Pokorný 1987, 163-164; Lohse 1970, 193; 1971, 176; Nikolainen 1987, 66-67.

This would explain why so many fellow workers are presented and they are introduced much more elaborately than Paul's companions are normally.[932]

From among the names mentioned, Epaphras is clearly emphasized most: his character in Col 4:12 even corresponds to what earlier has been said of Paul and he is already presented in Col 1:7 as the person through whom the Gospel was made known in Colossae. Therefore, it has been assumed that Epaphras was the follower of Paul to whom A/Col especially wants to give an apostolic authorization.[933] The leading position given to Epaphras may also be caused simply by the fact that the name occurs first in the list of Philem.

Col 4:15-18	**Philem 2**	
15 ᾿Ασπάσασθε τοὺς ἐν Λαοδικείᾳ ἀδελφοὺς καὶ Νύμφαν **καὶ** τὴν **κατ᾽ οἶκον** αὐτῆς ἐκκλησίαν.	... καὶ **᾿Αρχίππῳ** τῷ συστρατιώτῃ ἡμῶν **καὶ** τῇ **κατ᾽οἶκόν** σου ἐκκλησίᾳ	
16 καὶ ὅταν ἀναγνωσθῇ παρ᾽ ὑμῖν ἡ ἐπιστολή, ποιήσατε ἵνα καὶ ἐν τῇ Λαοδικέων ἐκκλησίᾳ ἀναγνωσθῇ, καὶ τὴν ἐκ Λαοδικείας ἵνα καὶ ὑμεῖς ἀναγνῶτε.	1 Thess 5:27 ... ἀναγνωσθῆναι τὴν ἐπιστολὴν πᾶσιν τοῖς ἀδελφοῖς.	**1 Cor 16:21-23**
17 καὶ εἴπατε **᾿Αρχίππῳ·** βλέπε τὴν διακονίαν ἣν παρέλαβες ἐν κυρίῳ, ἵνα αὐτὴν πληροῖς.	Col 1:25 ἐγενόμην ἐγὼ διάκονος ... τὴν δοθεῖσάν μοι εἰς ... πληρῶσαι	**21 ῾Ο ἀσπασμὸς τῇ ἐμῇ χειρὶ Παύλου. ... 23 ἡ χάρις** τοῦ κυρίου ᾿Ιησοῦ **μεθ᾽ὑμῶν.**
18 ῾Ο ἀσπασμὸς τῇ ἐμῇ χειρὶ Παύλου. μνημονεύετέ μου τῶν δεσμῶν. **ἡ χάρις μεθ᾽ ὑμῶν.**	1 Thess 2:9 **Μνημονεύετε** ... τὸν κόπον ἡμῶν καὶ τὸν μόχθον·	Philem 13, cf. Philem 10, Phil 1:7, 13, 14, 17 ἐν τοῖς δεσμοῖς τοῦ εὐαγγελίου

In Col 4:15 greetings are given to Nympha and the church in her house (καὶ τὴν κατ᾽ οἶκον αὐτῆς ἐκκλησίαν).[934] Similarly, Paul greets the church in the house of

[932] Lohse 1971, 176.

[933] Marxsen 1963, 154-155. Cf. Gnilka 1980, 240; Lindemann 1983, 75. Contra Martin 1981, 135; O'Brien 1982, 255, who emphasize that Epaphras is called a fellow servant like the others.

[934] In addition, it is not self-evident whether the greeting to Nympha (Νυμφαν) refers to a man who is called Νυμφᾶς or to a woman with the name Νύμφα because some manuscripts read αὐτῆς, "her" (house), and some αὐτοῦ, "his". Because the mention of a woman has to be considered unusual, αὐτῆς is probably the authentic form. Similarly Pokorný 1985, 164-165; Lohse 1971, 174; Gnilka 1980, 244; Hartman 1985, 189; Haapa 1978, 79; Hübner 1997, 120; Luz 1998, 242-243.

Prisca and Aquila (Rom 16:5, 1 Cor 16:19) and the community that has been assembled in the house of Philemon (Philem 2). Thus A/Col imitates here the style of Paul. While the companions of Paul who were sending the greetings were mentioned in Col 4:10-14, in Col 4:15 the attention turns to those to whom the greetings are addressed. It is interesting that only two persons, Nympha and Archippus, are named, in contrast to the long list of those sending greetings. It points to the fictive character of the greetings: since Colossae is a pseudo-addressee, A/Col is not able to enumerate people living there.[935]

Nympha does not otherwise appear in ECL. Since the name is not mentioned in Philem, she may be a person working at the time Col was written.[936] Because Archippus appears in the authentic Pauline letters only in Philem 2 where also, as in Col 4:15, a house-church is mentioned, it seems likely that Philem 2 is imitated here. Though the sending of greetings to the community assembled in someone's house (καὶ τῇ κατ᾽ οἶκον ... ἐκκλησίᾳ) is a stock phrase of Paul, the fact that Archippus does not otherwise occur in ECL indicates strongly that Col 4:15-17 depends on Philem 2. Thus the agreement of three nouns (᾽Αρχίππος, οἶκος, ἐκκλησία) should be classified as pointing to a possible literary dependence.[937] It is worth noting that Archippus is described differently in the two texts. While he is called a fellow soldier in Philem 2, in Col 4:17 he is ordered to complete (πληρόω) the task (διακονία) he has received. The description much resembles that of Col 1:25 which tells about the mission of Paul to make the word of God fully known. Therefore, it seems that A/Col has picked up the name Archippus from Philem and then describes his mission in the same way as Paul's mission is described in Col 1:25. Similarly, A/Col defined Epaphras in Col 4:12 with the epithets normally ascribed to Paul.[938]

Besides Nympha and the church at her home, the community at Laodicea is greeted. It is stated that this letter is to be read at first among Colossians and then given to the Laodiceans so that they also could read it. Correspondingly, the Colossians should read the letter sent to Laodicea. The verb ἀναγινώσκω means here, as normally in ECL, to "read aloud". Paul similarly commands to read aloud a letter to the whole community in 1 Thess 5:27. It is possible that A/Col has in mind this counsel of Paul. However, he does not only mechanically imitate it but adds the advice about the exchange of the letters. This instruction shows that at the time Col was written the letters were, in addition to being read aloud to each community, disseminated and perhaps also copied and collected.[939] A/Col may

---

[935] Contra Dunn 1996, 283, according to whom this "is consistent with the information that Paul had never previously visited Colossae".
[936] Similarly Pokorný 1987, 165.
[937] Similarly Kiley 1986, 89, regards Col 4:17 as dependent upon Philem 2. Cf. Lindemann 1999, 202 who regards it likely that the name Archippus is just picked up from Philem 2.
[938] According to Gnilka 1980, 246, the admonition to complete the task is addressed to the whole community. Nothing in the text indicates the interpretation, however.
[939] Cf. Lohse 1971, 175; O'Brien 1982, 259; Nikolainen 1987, 67; Haapa 1978, 79; Schweizer 1982, 242; Dunn 1996, 286; Conzelmann 1990, 202; Pfammatter 1987, 83; Müller 1988, 300;

order the letters to be exchanged with the community in Laodicea in order to get Col quickly into circulation.[940] That the letters were read aloud publicly, like the holy scriptures in synagogues, shows that they already had a special significance[941], even a normative position.[942]

There is no letter to the Laodiceans in the Pauline corpus. There have been several efforts to identify the Laodicean letter mentioned in Col 4:16. It has been assumed to be e.g. Philem, Eph, a letter written from Laodicea, or a letter which has been lost (cf. 1 Cor 5:9).[943] Nowadays scholars usually admit, however, that we must remain in doubt about this letter.[944] If the deutero-Pauline character of Col is accepted, the most probable solution to the problem is that the Laodicean letter never existed.[945]

It was a common epistolary technique in the first century to write in one's own hand the last words of the letter which had been dictated.[946] Paul did this in 1 Cor 16:21 and Gal 6:11 (cf. also Philem 19). The words ὁ ἀσπασμὸς τῇ ἐμῇ χειρὶ Παύλου, "the greeting, in my own hand, of Paul", in Col 4:18 are exactly the same as those used in 1 Cor 16:21.[947] Although the greeting "the grace of the Lord Jesus with you" (ἡ χάρις τοῦ κυρίοῦ 'Ιησοῦ μεθ' ὑμῶν) in 1 Cor 16:23 is not so short as that in Col 4:18 "the grace with you" (ἡ χάρις μεθ' ὑμῶν), all other genuine letters use still longer forms (see Rom 16:20, 2 Cor 13:13, Gal 6:18, Phil 4:23, 1 Thess 5:28).[948] A/Col seems thus to imitate the conclusion of 1 Cor.[949] Since the

---

Standhartinger 1999, 287. Contra Martin 1981, 137, who denies that the addition points to the deutero-Pauline character of Col but emphasizes that the reading aloud is similarly mentioned already in 1 Thess 5:27.

[940] So Lohse 1971, 177.

[941] Gnilka 1980, 245.

[942] So Pokorný 1987, 164.

[943] Further in O'Brien 1982, 257-258; Hendriksen 1971, 194-197.

[944] See Dunn 1996, 287; Bruce 1988, 184-185; O'Brien 1982, 257-258.

[945] Similarly Lindemann 1983, 77, who assumes that Col may have been addressed to Laodicea and the letter was mentioned in order to comfort the Laodiceans: though they never received a letter from Paul, he once sent them one which had been lost. Contra Luz 1998, 243.

[946] Lohse 1971, 177; Bruce 1988, 186; Schweizer 1982, 242-243; O'Brien 1982, 259; Hartman 1985, 194.

[947] Luz 1998, 244; Gnilka 1980, 247; Haapa 1978, 81, also call attention to the similarity between Col 4:18 and 1 Cor 16:21. The words are also repeated in 2 Thess 3:17 which, in addition, emphasizes them to be the mark of every letter of Paul.

[948] Besides Col, the short form ἡ χάρις μεθ' ὑμῶν is also used in deutero-Pauline letters 1 and 2 Tim (1 Tim 6:21, 2 Tim 4:22). It is surprising that Standhartinger 1999, 79, presents the genuine Pauline parallels to the greeting of grace in Col 4:18 without calling any attention to the fact that the greeting in Col clearly differs from the other ones in its length.

[949] Similarly Ludwig 1974, 132. Cf. Schweizer 1982, 19, according to whom Col 4:18 "could be an unconscious repetition of the same sentence in 1 Cor 16:21". However, Schweizer states that here "the imitation of style could derive from the author being on intimate terms with Paul" but not a pseudepigrapher. Since he presents the imitation of style as a habit practiced in the rhetorical schools, the interpretation seems only to be an attempt to defend the co-authorship of Paul with Timothy, which he prefers. Müller 1988, 301-302, contests the literary dependence between Col 4:18 and 1 Cor 16:21 because, in his opinion, it is not possible that A/Col was acquainted with 1 Cor which was not written in the same area as Col.

words ὁ ἀσπασμὸς τῇ ἐμῇ χειρὶ Παύλου are repeated verbatim and, in addition, the texts use more than three nouns in common, the resemblance between Col 4:18 and 1 Cor 16:21-23 meets the criteria for a probable literary dependence. A/Col utilizes here the style of Paul in order to give an apostolic authorization to the letter.[950]

In Col 4:18 the imprisonment of Paul is referred to by mentioning his chains (δεσμοί). The same term is used in Philem (10, 13) and in Phil (1:7, 13, 14, 17).[951] Unlike in these genuine letters, in Col is the exhortation to remember (μνημονεύω) Paul's chains, which resembles the admonition in 1 Thess 2:9 to remember the labor and toil of Paul and his companions.[952] By doing this, A/Col is once more trying to give an apostolic authorization to the letter[953], which seems to be typical of the whole conclusion of Col.

---

[950] Similarly Gnilka 1980, 247. Contra Luz 1998, 244.

[951] Also Schenk 1987a, 3339; and Kiley 1986, 89, call attention to the similarity.

[952] Similarly Lohse 1971, 177. Cf. R. P. Martin 1981, 141.

[953] Cf. Haapa 1978, 81. Contra Luz 1998, 240, who states that compared to the description of Paul's imprisonment in 2 Tim (1:16f., 2:9 f., 3:11, 4:6-8, 16-18) that in Col seems to be authentic. According to R. P. Martin 1981, 141, Paul himself (not a later writer) is here "summoning them to respect his authority as a prisoner for the gospel's sake".

7. Resemblances Among the Undisputed Pauline Letters

The purpose of this chapter is to compare the nature and extent of the parallels among undisputed Pauline letters with those between Col and the genuine Pauline letters. Since all Pauline letters include similar sections: introduction, thanksgiving, intercession, exhortations, theological sections, conclusion, and greetings, which more or less resemble each other, it is possible that, among the undisputed Pauline letters, similar agreements occur as they do between Col and the genuine letters. When analyzing the introductory greeting of Col, it was already noted that the resemblances between Col 1:1-2 and the authentic Pauline texts differ from those between Phil 1:1-2 and other authentic Pauline texts. Now the rest of Phil 1 will be compared with other genuine texts. As was mentioned in chapter 2.1., Phil is a good choice for the study because it is almost exactly the same length as Col. Moreover, there is only one letter to the Philippians as there is only one to the Colossians. If there are similar verbal agreements between Phil and the other authentic texts as there are between Col and the authentic texts, then the agreements that have been found do not indicate literary dependence in Col. In case there are no similar verbal agreements between Phil and the other authentic Pauline texts, as there are between Col and the authentic texts, the agreements that have been found suggest literary dependence in Col. It has to be noted, however, that if there are only a few similar resemblances among the authentic Pauline texts, this does not prove that the method employed in this study is not valid. It is the great number of verbal and verbatim agreements between Col and the undisputed Pauline letters which have been discussed.

Phil 1:3-6

3 **Εὐχαριστῶ τῷ θεῷ μου** ἐπὶ πάσῃ τῇ μνείᾳ **ὑμῶν**
4 **πάντοτε** ἐν πάσῃ δεήσει μου ὑπὲρ **πάντων ὑμῶν**, μετὰ χαρᾶς τὴν δέησιν **ποιούμενος**,

Philem 4 **Εὐχαριστῶ τῷ θεῷ μου πάντοτε** μνείαν σου **ποιούμενος** ἐπὶ τῶν προσευχῶν μου

1 Thess 1:2 Εὐχαριστοῦμεν **τῷ θεῷ πάντοτε** περὶ **πάντων ὑμῶν** μνείαν ποιούμενοι ἐπὶ τῶν προσευχῶν ἡμῶν

Rom 1:8-10 ... **εὐχαριστῶ τῷ θεῷ μου** διὰ Ἰησοῦ Χριστοῦ περὶ **πάντων ὑμῶν** ... μνείαν **ὑμῶν** ποιοῦμαι **πάντοτε** ἐπὶ τῶν προσευχῶν μου ...

5 **ἐπὶ** τῇ κοινωνίᾳ **ὑμῶν εἰς τὸ εὐαγγέλιον** ἀπὸ τῆς πρώτης ἡμέρας ἄχρι τοῦ νῦν,	2 Cor 9:13 ... **ἐπὶ** τῇ ὑποταγῇ τῆς ὁμολογίας **ὑμῶν εἰς τὸ εὐαγγέλιον** τοῦ Χριστοῦ καὶ ἁπλότητι τῆς κοινωνίας εἰς αὐτοὺς καὶ εἰς πάντας
6 πεποιθὼς αὐτὸ τοῦτο, ὅτι ὁ ἐναρξάμενος ἐν ὑμῖν ἔργον ἀγαθὸν ἐπιτελέσει ἄχρι ἡμέρας **Χριστοῦ Ἰησοῦ·**	Gal 3:3 ... ἐναρξάμενοι πνεύματι νῦν σαρκὶ ἐπιτελεῖσθε; Rom 2:7, cf. 2 Cor 9:8 καθ' ὑπομονὴν ἔργου ἀγαθοῦ 1 Cor 1:8, cf. Rom 14:6, 1 Cor 5:5, 2 Cor 1:14 ὃς καὶ βεβαιώσει ὑμᾶς ἕως τέλους ἀνεγκλήτους ἐν τῇ ἡμέρᾳ τοῦ κυρίου ἡμῶν **Ἰησοῦ** [**Χριστοῦ**].

The thanksgiving in Phil 1:3-4 resembles those in Philem 4, in 1 Thess 1:2, and in Rom 1:8-10. All of them mention how Paul (in 1 Thess with his companions) thanks God in his prayers every time he remembers the recipients of the letter, and they employ nearly the same words. The only remarkable difference between the texts is that Phil uses the noun δέησις when mentioning the prayers instead of προσευχή occurring in the other texts. The noun δέησις seems to be typical of Phil because it also appears in Phil 1:19 and 4:6, but it is also known in other genuine letters of Paul (see Rom 10:1, 2 Cor 1:11, 9:14). It is worth noting, however, that, unlike the thanksgiving in Col 1:3-4, that in Phil 1:3-4 does not have a single close parallel among the other texts. All three thanksgivings: Philem 4, 1 Thess 1:2, and Rom 1:8-9, resemble Phil 1:3-4 equally. It seems clear that all texts utilize independently the same phraseology typical of the thanksgivings in the Pauline letters.

The nouns εὐαγγέλιον, "gospel", and κοινωνία, "sharing" occur together in 2 Cor 9:13, like in Phil 1:5. In addition, both texts use the words ἐπὶ ... ὑμῶν εἰς τὸ εὐαγγέλιον. Since the nouns εὐαγγέλιον and κοινωνία are commonplace in the Pauline letters, the verbal agreement is not remarkable, however.

Phil 1:6 refers to the good works (ἔργον ἀγαθόν) which is typical of Paul (cf. Rom 2:7 and 2 Cor 9:8). Moreover, like Phil 1:6, Paul tells about the day of Christ in Rom 14:6, 1 Cor 1:8, 5:5, 2 Cor 1:14, among which the choice of wording in 1 Cor 1:8 most resembles that of Phil 1:6. In addition to the typical phraseology of Paul, Phil 1:6 employs the unusual verbs ἐνάρχομαι, "to begin with", and ἐπιτελέω, "to complete". They are otherwise used together in the Pauline letters only in Gal 3:3.[954] These are also the only verses in ECL where ἐνάρχομαι appears. Though the verb ἐπιτελέω is not as exceptional as ἐνάρχομαι, it still occurs only seven times in the authentic Pauline letters. The use of the verbs ἐνάρχομαι and

[954] In 2 Cor 8:6, slightly different verbs προενάρχομαι and ἐπιτελέω are used.

ἐπιτελέω in Phil 1:6 and Gal 3:3 is thus similar to the agreements which have above been accepted as indicating a possible literary dependence between the texts: the two verbs do not otherwise appear together and one of them is very unusual.

Phil 1:7-8

7 Καθώς ἐστιν δίκαιον ἐμοὶ τοῦτο φρονεῖν ὑπὲρ πάντων ὑμῶν διὰ τὸ ἔχειν με ἐν τῇ καρδίᾳ ὑμᾶς, **ἐν** τε **τοῖς δεσμοῖς** μου καὶ ἐν τῇ ἀπολογίᾳ καὶ βεβαιώσει **τοῦ εὐαγγελίου** συγκοινωνούς μου τῆς χάριτος πάντας ὑμᾶς ὄντας.

8 **μάρτυς γάρ μου ὁ θεὸς** ὡς ἐπιποθῶ πάντας ὑμᾶς ἐν σπλάγχνοις Χριστοῦ Ἰησοῦ.

Philem 13, cf. Philem 10

ἐν τοῖς δεσμοῖς τοῦ εὐαγγελίου

1 Cor 9:23

πάντα δὲ ποιῶ διὰ τὸ εὐαγγέλιον, ἵνα συγκοινωνὸς αὐτοῦ γένωμαι.

Rom 1:9

μάρτυς γάρ μού ἐστιν **ὁ θεός**

Philem 20

ἀνάπαυσόν μου τὰ σπλάγχνα ἐν Χριστῷ.

Phil 1:7 includes several formulations typical of Phil. The words τοῦτο φρονεῖν ὑπὲρ πάντων ὑμῶν resemble those in Phil 2:5, τοῦτο φρονεῖτε ἐν ὑμῖν. This kind of phrase does not occur in other Pauline epistles. Moreover, the nouns ἀπολογία, "defense", and εὐαγγελίον, "gospel", are used together another time in Phil (1:16: εἰς ἀπολογίαν τοῦ εὐαγγελίου κεῖμαι) but nowhere else in the Pauline letters. It is worth noting that besides Phil (1:7, 13, 14, 17), Paul mentions his chains (δεσμοί) only in Philem 10, 13. Similarly to Phil 1:7, both the imprisonment and the gospel (εὐαγγέλιον) are mentioned in Philem 13. However, the noun εὐαγγέλιον is quite normal in ECL and δεσμός also occurs six times in the genuine Pauline epistles. Therefore, the similarity between Phil 1:7 and Philem 13, the occurrence of two customary nouns in common, does not meet the criteria used to indicate literary dependence.

Like in Phil 1:7, the noun εὐαγγέλιον and the adjective συγκοινωνός, "partaking", the latter of which is exceptional, are used together in 1 Cor 9:23. In addition to these cases, the adjective συγκοινωνός appears only in Rom 11:17 in the genuine Pauline letters and later in Rev 1:9. Since the adjective συγκοινωνός only occurs three times in the Pauline corpus, the verbal agreement of two words between Phil 1:7 and 1 Cor 9:23 is similar to the resemblances which have accepted as notable enough to point to literary dependence.

The expression "God is my witness" in Phil 1:8 can be taken as a stock phrase of Paul because it is also used in Rom 1:9, 2 Cor 1:23, and 1 Thess 2:5,

10.[955] Nevertheless, it is remarkable that only between Phil 1:8 and Rom 1:9 is there verbatim agreement: both use exactly the same words, μάρτυς γάρ μου ὁ θεός. The resemblance between Phil 1:8 and Rom 1:9 thus might have been classified as indicating a possible literary dependence if it appeared between Col and a genuine Pauline text. There is an agreement of two nouns, σπλάγχνον, "heart, the seat of the feelings", and Χριστός, "Christ" between Phil 1:8 and Philem 20. Both nouns are so customary, however, that the resemblance does not meet the criteria used to indicate literary dependence.

Phil 1:9-11	Philem 4-6
9 Καὶ τοῦτο προσεύχομαι, ἵνα ἡ ἀγάπη ὑμῶν ἔτι μᾶλλον καὶ μᾶλλον περισσεύῃ **ἐν ἐπιγνώσει** καὶ πάσῃ αἰσθήσει	4 ... ἐπὶ τῶν προσευχῶν μου, 5 ἀκούων σου τὴν ἀγάπην καὶ τὴν πίστιν ...
10 **εἰς τὸ δοκιμάζειν ὑμᾶς τὰ διαφέροντα**, ἵνα ἦτε εἰλικρινεῖς καὶ ἀπρόσκοποι **εἰς** ἡμέραν Χριστοῦ,	6 ὅπως ἡ κοινωνία τῆς πίστεώς σου ἐνεργὴς γένηται **ἐν ἐπιγνώσει** παντὸς ἀγαθοῦ τοῦ ἐν ἡμῖν **εἰς** Χριστόν.
11 πεπληρωμένοι καρπὸν δικαιοσύνης τὸν διὰ Ἰησοῦ Χριστοῦ εἰς δόξαν καὶ ἔπαινον θεοῦ.	Rom 12:2 ... **εἰς τὸ δοκιμάζειν ὑμᾶς** ...
	Rom 2:18 ... δοκιμάζεις **τὰ διαφέροντα** ...

The beginning of the intercession in Phil 1:9-10 includes one verb and three nouns in common with Philem 4-6. Thus there is a resemblance of four words which meets, at least in numbers, the criteria used to indicate a probable literary dependence. However, the verb προσεύχομαι (to pray), and the nouns ἀγάπη (love), ἐπίγνωσις (full knowledge), and Χριστός (Christ) are all routine in ECL. Thus, the resemblance between Phil 1:9-10 and Philem 4-6 is similar to that between Col 2:2-3 and Prov 2:4-6 which, in spite of the agreement of five nouns, was classified as indicating a possible literary dependence only. In addition, it is remarkable that, excluding the phrase ἐν ἐπιγνώσει, the words do not appear in the same form and so the intercession in Philem 4-6 does not resemble that in Phil 1:9-11 at all as much as the one in Col 1:3-4 which follows verbatim several phrases from Philem 4-5 (see p. 63).

The choice of wording, εἰς τὸ δοκιμάζειν ὑμᾶς τὰ διαφέροντα, "to determine what is best", used in Phil 1:10 looks like a combination of the words εἰς τὸ δοκιμάζειν ὑμᾶς (Rom 12:2) and δοκιμάζεις τὰ διαφέροντα (Rom 2:18). The conflation is still limited in extent[956]: neither the verbal agreement between Phil 1:10 and Rom 12:2 nor that between Phil 1:10 and Rom 2:18 meets the criteria used to indicate literary dependence. Moreover, these kinds of similarities between Col 1:29 and Phil 2:13, 3:21 were not accepted as suggesting a literary dependence

[955] So E. P. Sanders 1966, 34. See also Mitton 1951, 323.
[956] E. P. Sanders 1966, 33-34. See also Mitton 1951, 323.

(see pp. 114-115). Unlike Phil 1:9-10, verse 11 does not have any parallel in the authentic Pauline letters. Similar phrases are used only later in Eph (1:6, 12, 14, 5:9).[957]

Phil 1:12-17

12 Γινώσκειν δὲ ὑμᾶς βούλομαι, ἀδελφοί, ὅτι τὰ **κατ᾽ ἐμὲ** μᾶλλον εἰς προκοπὴν τοῦ εὐαγγελίου ἐλήλυθεν,	Rom 1:15 οὕτως τὸ **κατ᾽ ἐμὲ** πρόθυμον ...
13 ὥστε τοὺς δεσμούς μου φανεροὺς ἐν Χριστῷ γενέσθαι ἐν ὅλῳ τῷ πραιτωρίῳ καὶ τοῖς λοιποῖς πᾶσιν,	
14 καὶ τοὺς πλείονας τῶν ἀδελφῶν ἐν κυρίῳ πεποιθότας τοῖς δεσμοῖς μου περισσοτέρως τολμᾶν ἀφόβως τὸν λόγον λαλεῖν.	1 Cor 14:19, cf. 1 Cor 14:9 ... θέλω πέντε λόγους τῷ νοΐ μου λαλῆσαι ...
15 τινὲς μὲν καὶ διὰ φθόνον καὶ ἔριν, τινὲς δὲ καὶ δι᾽ εὐδοκίαν τὸν **Χριστὸν** κηρύσσουσιν·	Rom 1:29 ... μεστοὺς φθόνου φόνου ἔριδος ... 1 Cor 1:23, cf. 1 Cor 15:12, 2 Cor 1:19, 4:5 ἡμεῖς δὲ κηρύσσομεν **Χριστόν**
16 οἱ μὲν ἐξ ἀγάπης, εἰδότες ὅτι εἰς ἀπολογίαν τοῦ εὐαγγελίου κεῖμαι,	
17 οἱ **δὲ ἐξ ἐριθείας** τὸν Χριστὸν καταγγέλλουσιν, οὐχ ἁγνῶς, οἰόμενοι θλῖψιν ἐγείρειν τοῖς δεσμοῖς μου.	Rom 2:8 τοῖς **δὲ ἐξ ἐριθείας** καὶ ἀπειθοῦσι τῇ ἀληθείᾳ πειθομένοις ...

Phil 1:12-26 includes a report on the apostle's situation and prospects. As was noted when examining the parallels to Col 4:7, the expression τὰ/τὸ κατ᾽ ἐμέ is used only twice in the authentic Pauline letters, in Phil 1:12 and in Rom 1:15. Still, the use of a single identical expression alone does not meet the criteria used to indicate literary dependence. It is also striking that Col 4:7 and Phil 1:12, which were assumed to depend on each other, include other verbal agreements besides the expression τὰ κατ᾽ ἐμέ, (see p. 198).

The mention of Paul's chains (δεσμοί), which occurred already in Phil 1:7, is repeated in Phil 1:13, 14 and 17. It is worth noting that the expression τὸν λόγον λαλέω, "to speak the word", is commonplace in ECL (see Mk 2:2, 8:32, Lk 24:44) but seldom appears in the authentic Pauline letters. Besides in Phil 1:14, it occurs only in 1 Cor 14:9, 19. The agreement between the texts is still not notable since both the noun λόγος and the verb λαλέω are very customary in ECL. The nouns φθόνος, "envy", and ἔρις, "rivalry", appear together only twice in the authentic Pauline letters, in Phil 1:15 and in Rom 1:29.[958] Neither of the words is unique in

[957] Eph 5:9: ὁ γὰρ καρπὸς τοῦ φωτὸς ἐν πάσῃ ἀγαθωσύνῃ καὶ δικαιοσύνῃ καὶ ἀληθείᾳ. Eph 1:12 (cf. 1:6, 14): εἰς ἔπαινον δόξης αὐτοῦ.
[958] Cf. 1 Tim 6:4.

the Pauline corpus: the noun φθόνος is also used in Gal 5:21 and ἔρις in Rom 13:13, 1 Cor 1:11, 3:3, 2 Cor 12:20, and Gal 5:20. Therefore, the agreement between Phil 1:15 and Rom 1:29 is not such resemblance of two words as those which were classified as indicating a literary dependence between Col and the authentic Pauline letters.

The expression τὸν Χριστὸν κηρύσσω, "to proclaim Christ", in Phil 1:15 is typical of Paul. It is also used in 1 Cor 1:23, 15:12, in 2 Cor 1:19, and 4:5. However, the phrase οἱ δὲ ἐξ ἐριθείας, "those out of selfish ambition", is unusual. It occurs elsewhere only in Rom 2:8. Since there is a verbatim agreement of three words, including conjunctions and prepositions (δὲ ἐξ ἐριθείας), the resemblance is similar e.g. to that between Col 3:11 and 1 Cor 15:28 which was classified as meeting the criteria for a possible literary dependence (see pp. 166-167). It is remarkable, however, that in Col 3:11 the author, besides using similar formulation as 1 Cor 15:28, utilizes it differently when transferring a characteristic of God to Christ but in Phil 1:17 and Rom 2:8 the expression οἱ δὲ ἐξ ἐριθείας is employed similarly to describe bad people.

Phil 1:18-26

18 Τί γάρ; πλὴν ὅτι παντὶ τρόπῳ, εἴτε προφάσει εἴτε ἀληθείᾳ, Χριστὸς καταγγέλλεται, καὶ ἐν τούτῳ χαίρω.	Rom 3:2 πολὺ κατὰ πάντα τρόπον.
Ἀλλὰ καὶ χαρήσομαι, 19 οἶδα γὰρ ὅτι τοῦτό μοι ἀποβήσεται **εἰς σωτηρίαν** διὰ τῆς **ὑμῶν** δεήσεως καὶ ἐπιχορηγίας τοῦ πνεύματος Ἰησοῦ Χριστοῦ	Rom 10:1 ... ἡ δέησις πρὸς τὸν θεὸν ὑπὲρ αὐτῶν **εἰς σωτηρίαν**. 2 Cor 3:12 Ἔχοντες οὖν τοιαύτην **ἐλπίδα** πολλῇ **παρρησίᾳ** χρώμεθα
20 κατὰ τὴν ἀποκαραδοκίαν καὶ **ἐλπίδα** μου, ὅτι ἐν οὐδενὶ αἰσχυνθήσομαι ἀλλ᾽ ἐν πάσῃ **παρρησίᾳ** ὡς πάντοτε καὶ νῦν μεγαλυνθήσεται Χριστὸς **ἐν τῷ σώματί** μου, εἴτε διὰ ζωῆς εἴτε διὰ θανάτου.	2 Cor 10:15 ... **ἐλπίδα** δὲ ἔχοντες αὐξανομένης τῆς πίστεως ὑμῶν ἐν ὑμῖν μεγαλυνθῆναι ...
21 **Ἐμοὶ** γὰρ τὸ ζῆν **Χριστὸς** καὶ τὸ ἀποθανεῖν κέρδος.	1 Cor 6:20, cf. 2 Cor 4:10, Gal 6:17 ... δοξάσατε δὴ τὸν θεὸν **ἐν τῷ σώματι** ὑμῶν.
22 εἰ δὲ τὸ ζῆν **ἐν σαρκί**, τοῦτό μοι καρπὸς ἔργου, καὶ τί αἱρήσομαι οὐ γνωρίζω. 23 συνέχομαι δὲ ἐκ τῶν δύο, τὴν ἐπιθυμίαν ἔχων εἰς τὸ ἀναλῦσαι καὶ σὺν Χριστῷ εἶναι, πολλῷ [γὰρ] μᾶλλον κρεῖσσον· 24 τὸ δὲ ἐπιμένειν [ἐν] τῇ σαρκὶ ἀναγκαιότερον δι᾽ ὑμᾶς. 25 καὶ τοῦτο πεποιθὼς οἶδα ὅτι μενῶ καὶ παραμενῶ πᾶσιν ὑμῖν εἰς τὴν ὑμῶν προκοπὴν καὶ χαρὰν τῆς πίστεως,	Gal 2:20 ... ζῇ δὲ ἐν **ἐμοὶ Χριστός**· ὃ δὲ νῦν ζῶ **ἐν σαρκί**, ἐν πίστει ζῶ τῇ τοῦ υἱοῦ τοῦ θεοῦ ...

26 ἵνα τὸ καύχημα ὑμῶν περισσεύῃ ἐν Χριστῷ Ἰησοῦ ἐν ἐμοὶ διὰ τῆς ἐμῆς παρουσίας **πάλιν πρὸς ὑμᾶς**.	2 Cor 1:16, cf. 2:1 ... **πάλιν** ἀπὸ Μακεδονίας ἐλθεῖν **πρὸς ὑμᾶς** ...

The noun τρόπος occurs only in Phil 1:18 and in Rom 3:2 in the authentic Pauline letters. Since, besides the noun τρόπος, the texts have only the pronoun πᾶς in common, the resemblance is not such as used to indicate literary dependence. It is noteworthy, however, that in the genuine Pauline letters there are sometimes used nouns which do not occur more than twice. The noun ἀποκαραδοκία appears, besides in Phil 1:20, only in Rom 8:19 and the verb αἰσχύνομαι only in 2 Cor 10:8. The phenomenon indicates that an agreement of one noun, though unusual, is not enough to show literary dependence between two texts, as has been assumed in this study.

Phil 1:18-20 includes several agreements of two words with other Pauline texts. Most of the words in common are so normal that the resemblances are not similar to those used to indicate literary dependence. In Phil 1:19 and in Rom 10:1, the prayer to God for salvation is mentioned using the nouns δέησις and σωτηρία which both are commonplace in ECL. In addition, the words παρρησία and ἐλπίς, which are also frequently employed, appear together in both 2 Cor 3:12 and Phil 1:20. In contrast, the verb μεγαλύνω which is used together with the noun ἐλπίς in Phil 1:20 and in 2 Cor 10:15 is rare: it does not occur anywhere else in the authentic Pauline letters. The resemblance of two words thus meets the criteria used to indicate a possible literary dependence. However, the phrase ἐν τῷ σώματι employed in Phil 1:20 is typical of Paul. It appears for example in 1 Cor 6:20, 2 Cor 4:10, and Gal 6:17.

Gal 2:20 closely resembles Phil 1:21-22. Both use the verb ζάω several times and also include the phrases ἐμοὶ Χριστός and ἐν σαρκί. Because of the three words in common (ζάω, Χριστός, σάρξ) and the verbatim agreement of the phrases, the resemblance between Phil 1:21-22 and Gal 2:20 is similar to those which have been used to point to a possible literary dependence between Col and other writings. It is worth noting, however, that in Phil 1:21-22 and Gal 2:20 the same words are used quite similarly referring to Christ, while A/Col usually employs Paul's words differently, ascribing a characteristic of God to Christ. In Phil 1:23-26 the only notable verbal agreement with other Pauline texts is the use of the phrase πάλιν πρὸς ὑμᾶς in v. 26 (cf. 2 Cor 1:16, 2:1). The fact indicates that it is not a characteristic of Paul to imitate his other letters.

Phil 1:27-30

27 Μόνον ἀξίως τοῦ εὐαγγελίου τοῦ Χριστοῦ πολιτεύεσθε, ἵνα εἴτε ἐλθὼν καὶ <u>ἰδὼν</u> <u>ὑμᾶς</u> εἴτε **ἀπὼν** ἀκούω τὰ περὶ **ὑμῶν**, ὅτι στήκετε **ἐν ἑνὶ πνεύματι**, μιᾷ ψυχῇ συναθλοῦντες τῇ πίστει τοῦ εὐαγγελίου
28 καὶ μὴ πτυρόμενοι ἐν μηδενὶ ὑπὸ τῶν ἀντικειμένων, ἥτις ἐστὶν αὐτοῖς ἔνδειξις ἀπωλείας, ὑμῶν δὲ σωτηρίας, καὶ τοῦτο ἀπὸ θεοῦ·
29 ὅτι ὑμῖν ἐχαρίσθη τὸ ὑπὲρ Χριστοῦ, οὐ μόνον τὸ εἰς αὐτὸν πιστεύειν ἀλλὰ καὶ τὸ ὑπὲρ αὐτοῦ πάσχειν,
30 τὸν αὐτὸν ἀγῶνα ἔχοντες, οἷον εἴδετε ἐν ἐμοὶ καὶ νῦν ἀκούετε ἐν ἐμοι.

1 Cor 5:3 ἐγὼ μὲν γάρ, **ἀπὼν** τῷ σώματι παρὼν δὲ τῷ πνεῦματι

1 Thess 2:17: ... ἀπορφανισθέντες ἀφ' **ὑμῶν** πρὸς καιρὸν ὥρας, προσώπῳ οὐ καρδίᾳ, περισσοτέρως ἐσπουδάσαμεν τὸ πρόσωπον **ὑμῶν** <u>ἰδεῖν</u> ...

1 Cor 12:13, cf. 12:9 ... **ἐν ἑνὶ πνεύματι** ... ἐβαπτίσθημεν

The exhortations to the community in Phil 1:27-30 have very little verbal agreement with the instructions in Paul's other letters. The only remarkable detail is that the words ἐν ἑνὶ πνεύματι used in Phil 1:27 also occur in the same form in 1 Cor 12:13 and in the form ἐν τῷ ἑνὶ πνεύματι in 1 Cor 12:9. Phil 1:27 employs the metaphor to be absent in body but still present in spirit which also appears in the genuine letters in 1 Cor 5:3 and in 1 Thess 2:17 and was noted as being used later in Col 2:5 (see pp. 121-122). However, unlike Col which utilizes the words employed in 1 Cor 5:3, the words in Phil 1:27 are different from other parallels. While the only agreement between Phil 1:27 and 1 Cor 5:3 is the use of the verb ἄπειμι, Phil 1:27 and 1 Thess 2:17 have only two words in common, the pronoun ὑμεῖς and the verb ὁράω. Therefore, again it seems that Paul does not generally repeat the same words.

The comparison between Phil 1:3-30 and other genuine Pauline letters has shown that the texts which are written by the same author may sometimes include verbal agreements similar to those used in this study to indicate a possible literary dependence. The following six resemblances have been found: Phil 1:9-10 and Philem 4-6 have more than three standard nouns in common, Phil 1:21-22 and Gal 2:20 have one verb and two nouns in common, Phil 1:6 and Gal 3:3 as well as Phil 1:20 and 2 Cor 10:15 includes verbal agreements of two words, one of which is unusual, and there are also two examples of verbatim agreement of three or more words including conjunctions, pronouns, and prepositions (Phil 1:8 // Rom 1:9, Phil 1:17 // Rom 2:8) .

It is remarkable, however, that the nature and extent of the parallels that have been found differ from the agreements between Col and the genuine Pauline letters. First of all it has to be noted that there is no parallel between Phil and other letters of Paul which meets the criteria used to indicate a probable literary dependence. Nor are there any cases when the same words or phrases are used in a new context and in a different sense which happens when Col and the genuine texts are compared. In addition, Phil 1 does not include any good example of *conflation* of the texts which is characteristic of a comparison of Col and the genuine Pauline letters. The only example of conflation, the one between Phil 1:10 and Rom 12:2, 2:18, is limited in extent. Moreover, the frequency of the verbal agreements with other Pauline letters is much less in Phil than in Col. While Phil 1:3-30 includes six verbal agreements, in Col 1:3-14, 1:21-2:2, which is also in the beginning of the letter and about as long,[959] there are nineteen cases.

The results of the comparison suggest that the occurrence of a few verbal agreements meeting the criteria for a possible literary dependence only is not enough to prove literary dependence between the texts because it can be due to the texts having the same author. However, the regular appearance of such agreements, especially when connected to the use of the words in a different context or sense, points to a dependence. Since no agreement meeting the criteria for a probable literary dependence was found in authentic Pauline texts, there is a reason to assume that such resemblances strongly indicate literary dependence.

It has also been noted that some words occur only twice in the genuine Pauline letters. This supports the criteria used that the occurrence of one similar word, though exceptional, is not enough to show literary dependence between two texts but two or three words in common are needed. Accordingly, the comparison between Phil 1 and other genuine Pauline texts supports the validity of the method used in this study: the continual occurrence of the verbal agreements of at least two words is not typical of the authentic Pauline letters but indicates literary dependence.

---

[959] Both texts are about 57 lines long in Nestle & Aland version. Col 1:15-20 is not used because it is normally regarded as a hymn and the text is not printed using full lines and is thus difficult to measure.

8. Conclusions on Literary Dependence in Colossians

In chapters 2-6, the whole text of Col has been compared with its closest parallels in order to find verbal and verbatim agreements pointing to literary dependence. The results of the comparison are collected in the Appendix: Parallels to Colossians (see pp. 282-287). As expected, the parallels to Col mostly appear in the authentic Pauline letters. The table shows, however, that the literary dependence in Col is not limited to the verses Sanders studied nor did it stop after 3:11, as he claims, but is typical of the whole letter. The resemblance between Col 1:3-5a and Philem 4-5, as well as that between Col 4:10-14 and Philem 23-24, points to a probable literary dependence which supports the general interpretation that the beginning and the conclusion of Col are modelled on Philem. Nevertheless, this is not the whole truth: the introductory greeting in Col 1:1-2 does not seem to follow Philem but to be modelled on 2 Cor 1:1-2 and the thanksgiving in Col 1:3-5a conflates 2 Cor 1:3 and Philem 4-5. Because Col has at least one resemblance which includes verbal or verbatim agreement meeting the criteria for a probable literary dependence with all the genuine Pauline letters (Rom, 1 Cor, 2 Cor, Gal, Phil, Philem, 1 Thess) and a few indicating a possible literary dependence, it does not seem that A/Col knew only Philem, as Standhartinger states, or Phil and Philem, like Kiley claims, but rather was acquainted with several letters, like Sanders assumes.

It is remarkable that, apart from Eph, there are only a few cases when the text of Col resembles other deutero-Pauline letters similarly to the genuine letters: Col 2:2-3 uses a phrase resembling that in 2 Thess 2:17 and Titus 2:5 seems to conflate Col 3:18 and 1 Cor 14:34-35 (see p. 179). In addition, some small likenesses between the introductions and conclusions of Col and the deutero-Pauline letters have been noted (see p. 60 n. 224, p. 207 n. 948). If the resemblances between Col and the genuine Pauline letters were due to the use of the same tradition, as is usually stated, it might be expected that there would be more verbal agreements between Col and other deutero-Pauline letters which belong to the same tradition. Thus, the resemblances between Col and the authentic Pauline letters rather point to literary dependence than to the use of the same tradition as e.g. Ludwig and Lindemann assume.

Besides the Pauline letters, Col has some interesting resemblances with the synoptic Gospels, Heb, and Acts. Acts 26:18 describes the difference between the authorities of light and darkness in the same way as Col 1:11b-14. It is significant that the agreement between the texts even meets the criteria for a probable literary dependence (see pp. 81-82). Since Acts is generally dated later than Col and this is the only remarkable verbal agreement between Col and Acts, it is probable that, if there is any connection between the writings, Acts depends upon Col.

Col and Heb have three notable verbal agreements. Col 3:24 and Heb 11:8 both refer to the inheritance received with the words ἀπολαμβάνω/ λαμβάνω and κληρονομία. This similarity is more probably due to both writers' knowledge of the LXX than dependence between Col and Heb (see p. 186). The use of similar phrase σκιὰ τῶν μελλόντων, "the shadow of what is to come" in Col 2:17 and Heb

10:1 is more remarkable since the contexts are also very similar (see p. 145). Furthermore, the agreement between Col 2:12 and Heb 6:1-2, which meets the criteria for a possible literary dependence, is noteworthy. It is interesting that both Col and Heb use the exceptional noun βαπτισμός with regard to baptism (see p. 137). Though the two last-mentioned agreements are such that they cannot be passed over by saying that they are accidental, the evidence is still too slight to draw any conclusions on the dependence between Col and Heb.

The only notable verbal agreement between Col and Mt, which has no closer parallels in Mk, is the use of the phrase ἐν ὅλῳ τῷ κόσμῳ (Mt 26:13) which resembles the formulation ἐν παντὶ τῷ κόσμῳ in Col 1:6. Since the same phrase also occurs in Rom 1:8, the agreement is not remarkable (see p. 68). The only agreement noted between Lk and Col is not obvious. A/Col seems to be acquainted with some of the Gospel texts which quote Ps 109:1 (LXX) and present Christ as seated on the right hand of God. Lk 22:69 is the closest parallel to Col 3:1. However, Ps 109:1 is so often quoted in the Gospels that the agreement cannot be taken as remarkable. Therefore, it is unlikely that there is any dependence between Col and Mt or Lk.

The similarities between Col and Mk are worth taking a closer look at, as Schenk also claims, because there are many more verbal agreements between the texts than there are between Col and other Gospels or between Col and any other writing outside the Pauline corpus. Two of the agreements meet the criteria for a possible literary dependence, Col 1:5b-6 // Mk 4:8 and Col 1:23 // Mk 16:15. It has to be remembered that Mk 16:15 belongs to the longer ending of Mk (16:9-20) which was not connected to the Gospel until the second century A.D. and therefore it was concluded as being unlikely that A/Col was acquainted with the text but more probable that Mk 16:15 could depend on Col 1:23 (see pp. 102-103). Since this is the only verbal agreement found between Col and the longer ending of Mk, it now seems clearer that Col does not depend on it. The agreement can be due to the dependence of Mk 16:15 on Col 1:23 but on the grounds of this single resemblance, nothing certain can be concluded.

There remains only one verbal agreement between Mk and Col which meets the criteria for a possible literary dependence (Col 1:5b-6 // Mk 4:8). It was noted in the previous chapter that the occurrence of a few verbal agreements meeting the criteria for a possible literary dependence alone does not indicate literary dependence because writings not depending on each other but having the same author sometimes include such resemblances. However, the case between Col and Mk is different: there is no reason to assume that the writings have the same author and Col and Mk do not even represent the same tradition in the same way as deutero-Pauline letters and Paul's authentic epistles do. Therefore, several slight resemblances between Col and Mk, among them one agreement indicating a possible literary dependence, are remarkable.

In addition to ECL, Col bears some resemblance to several texts of the LXX and some of Philo and Lucian (Col 2:16-23 // Philo: Conf 190, Lucian: Anacharsis

24; Col 3:18-4:1 // Philo: Spec Leg IV). The contact points between Col and Philo or Lucian are so slight, however, that they do not indicate any connection between the texts. In contrast, the verbal agreements between Col and the LXX are worth noting because the LXX was the Holy Scripture of the first Christians, which Paul also frequently cites. A/Col probably knew texts from the LXX. Therefore, it is surprising that only one of the agreements between Col and the LXX meets the criteria for a possible literary dependence (Col 2:2-3 // Prov 2:2-6), the others are minor. The fact indicates that A/Col does not cite the LXX in the same way as Paul does.

Though it has been observed that literary dependence is typical of all of Col, there are still some parts which do not have parallels. No resemblance to Col 2:14, which describes "erasing the record that stood against us", has been found although it is clear that its vocabulary is due to Jewish literature (see p. 140-141). In addition, the caution against severity with children is familiar to ancient literature but the admonition to fathers not to provoke their children in Col 3:21 does not have any parallel using similar words (see pp. 181-183). Most significant is the fact that the terms θρησκεία τῶν ἀγγέλων, "angelic worship", and ἃ ἑόρακεν ἐμβατεύων, "which he has seen upon entering", which in Col 2:18 describe the teachings confronted, are unique. Therefore, the conclusion was that the main identifying marks of the opponents are "angelic worship" and visions. Since both of these are typical of Rev, I concluded that Col opposes the apocalyptic strands of Christianity among which Rev was written (see pp. 154-156).

Although nearly all parts of Col depend on other texts, it does not seem to be modelled on any particular Pauline letter but the prototypes of the text change all the time and sometimes many texts are also conflated. Thus, A/Col imitates several texts at the same time, which makes it unlikely that he had all the texts in front of him when writing: mostly the texts must have been in his mind. A/Col also often repeats his own words and modifies and conflates them in the same manner as he uses other texts. This phenomenon is compatible with the associative style of A/Col, which was noted by Bujard. Though the author probably did not consciously cite definite texts, we can call the phenomenon literary dependence because readers who are acquainted with the epistles of Paul are able to recognize the texts he imitates. However, it is also possible that sometimes the borrowing was conscious and some of the texts may occasionally be physically in front of A/Col. Accordingly, Col seems to be formed similarly to Eph (see pp. 43-45), like Sanders also assumed.

Next, I shall compare the amounts of the parallels between Col and the genuine Pauline letters (Rom, 1 Cor, 2 Cor, Gal, Phil, Philem, 1 Thess) and also Mk. Other Gospels, Acts and Heb, are not presented because of the small number of parallels. In addition, the parallels from the LXX are not counted since the occurrences are slight compared to the amount of the text. Table 1 includes the numbers of the agreements which point to a probable literary dependence, Table 2 those indicating a possible literary dependence. Table 3 includes the numbers of other resemblances, those which do not indicate literary dependence. Table 4 presents the numbers of the words each writing includes. The number of the words in Mk does not include its longer ending (Mk 16:9-20) since it has been noted very unlikely that A/Col was acquainted with it. For the same reason, the number of the words in Rom 16:25-27 has not been added to that of Rom (see pp. 112-113). Because the length of the letters varies a great deal, and Mk is much longer than the others, it is necessary to compare the numbers of the parallels to the amount of the text.

Since the agreements between Col 1:1-2 // 2 Cor 1:1-2 and Col 1:3-5a // 2 Cor 1:3 occur one after another, they are counted as a single resemblance. In addition, when a phrase used in Col occurs many times in the same genuine letter, e.g. the reference to the bonds of Paul in Phil 1:7, 13, 14, 17 and in Philem 10, 13, only one resemblance in each letter is counted. Similarly, when the phrase used in Col 1:5b-6 appears both in Gal 2:5 and 14, it is taken as one agreement.

Table 1: Probable Literary Dependence

Rom	1 Cor	2 Cor	Gal	Phil	1 Thess	Philem	Mk
5	5	2	4	2	2	2	-

Table 2: Possible Literary Dependence

Rom	1 Cor	2 Cor	Gal	Phil	1 Thess	Philem	Mk
13	13	5	3	4	3	4	1

Table 3: Other Resemblances

Rom	1 Cor	2 Cor	Gal	Phil	1 Thess	Philem	Mk
23	20	15	9	12	7	2	10

Table 4: Number of Words[960]

Rom	1 Cor	2 Cor	Gal	Phil	1 Thess	Philem	Mk
7057	6820	4477	2232	1629	1481	335	11095

First of all, it is remarkable that all the undisputed Pauline letters include at least two resemblances with Col, pointing to a probable literary dependence and, a few parallels indicating a possible one. Since it was noted in the previous chapter that there are no verbal agreements meeting the criteria used to show a probable literary dependence in the authentic Pauline letters, the result suggests that A/Col was acquainted with all the genuine Pauline letters.

Rom and 1 Cor has the most of agreements indicating a probable (both 5) or a possible literary dependence (both 13). Furthermore, Rom and 1 Cor include more of all kinds of resemblances than other letters (Rom: 23 // 1 Cor 20), which is not very surprising, however, because they are also the longest letters. It is remarkable that though Gal is shorter than Rom or 1 Cor, it includes four resemblances indicating a probable literary dependence which is only one less than that of Rom and 1 Cor. It should be emphasized that the number of parallels in

---

[960] The numbers of the words are from Morgenthaler 1982.

Philem is significant compared to its length. Though it is much shorter than the others, it includes two resemblances indicating a probable literary dependence, like 2 Cor, Phil, and 1 Thess. The number of the parallels pointing to a possible literary dependence in Philem (4) is also noteworthy compared to those of Gal (3) and 1 Thess (3).

The numbers of other resemblances in Table 3 are not as important as those indicating literary dependence. Still, the occurrence of 10 agreements in Mk is remarkable. The amount is small compared to the length of the Gospel but is still exceptional because, outside Pauline letters, no other text has so many agreements with Col. The numbers of the resemblances will be put into proportion with the length of each writing in order to have a better opportunity to compare the frequency of the occurrences. The following tables present the numbers of the occurrences per 1000 words.

Table 1: Probable Literary Dependence
occurrences / 1000 words

Rom	1 Cor	2 Cor	Gal	Phil	1 Thess	Philem	Mk
0.7	0.7	0.4	1.8	1.2	1.4	6.0	-

Table 2: Possible Literary Dependence
occurrences / 1000 words

Rom	1 Cor	2 Cor	Gal	Phil	1 Thess	Philem	Mk
1.8	1.9	1.1	1.3	2.5	2.0	11.9	0.1

Table 3: Other Resemblances
occurrences / 1000 words

Rom	1 Cor	2 Cor	Gal	Phil	1 Thess	Philem	Mk
3.3	2.9	3.4	4.0	7.4	4.7	6.0	0.9

When the numbers of the occurrences are put into proportion with the length of each writing, it can be seen that the frequency of resemblances indicating a probable literary dependence is great in Philem (6.0) and also remarkable in Gal (1.8). In addition, the frequency is clearly higher in 1 Thess (1.4) and in Phil (1.2) than in Rom (0.7) and in 1 Cor (0.7) where the numbers of the occurrences were higher. The frequency of the appearances is the least (0.4) in 2 Cor. Accordingly, when the numbers of the appearances are put into proportion with the length of each text, it can be seen that the great numbers of resemblances in the longest letters, 1 Cor and Rom, are not remarkable, as was assumed earlier. Apart from 2 Cor, the frequencies of the parallels in shorter letters are greater. Since it has been noted that the appearance of the resemblances meeting probable literary dependence is the most reliable indicator of a connection between the texts, the result suggests that Gal and Philem have been the most basic models for Col.

When the resemblances suggesting a possible literary dependence are taken into account, it is remarkable that the numbers of occurrences in Philem (11.9) is again much greater than in the others. In contrast, the frequency of the appearances in Gal (1.3) is surprising: it is smaller than those in Phil (2.5), in 1 Thess (2.0), in

1 Cor (1.9), and in Rom (1.8) while the frequency of the occurrences indicating a probable literary dependence in Gal was much higher than in those letters. The explanation for the difference will be considered in the next chapter. In addition, it is worth noting that the frequency of the occurrences of agreements indicating either a possible literary dependence or a probable one is the smallest in 2 Cor, which suggests that it is not one of the most basic models for Col.

To conclude: the numbers of the resemblances between Col and the genuine Pauline letters suggest that A/Col was acquainted with all the letters of Paul (Rom, 1 Cor, 2 Cor, Gal, Phil, Philem, 1 Thess). In addition, the agreements between Col and Mk may indicate some connection between them. The result that Philem and Gal include more verbal agreements indicating a probable literary dependence than the others, compared to the length, suggests that Gal and Philem have been the most central models for Col. In contrast, the small frequency of the occurrences of agreements indicating literary dependence in 2 Cor suggests that it is not one of the central models for Col. On the grounds of the comparisons in this chapter is not, however, possible to say anything reliable about the significance of each writing in the formation of Col. This matter will be under consideration in the next chapter.

9. Writings Familiar to the Author of Colossians

9.1. Philemon

The following tables illustrate the resemblances between Philem and Col. The first one (Table Philem A, p. 324) includes the texts in the order they occur in Philem and the second one (Table Philem B, p. 325) from the standpoint of Col. Since so few agreements not meeting the criteria for literary dependence have been found between Col and Philem, all the parallels are presented.

As was noted in the previous chapter, the fact that the thanksgiving in Col 1:3-4 seems probably to depend on that in Philem 4-5, as well as the final greetings in Col 4:10-14 on those in Philem 23-24, supports the general interpretation that the frame, the beginning and the conclusion of Col, is modelled on Philem. Thus, Philem is some kind of "primary model" for Col, as Kiley, followed by Standhartinger, assume. Since the agreement between Philem 23-24 and Col 4:10-14 is very strong, the same five persons are mentioned and the same epithets, although ascribed to different persons, it is probable that A/Col even had Philem in front of him when writing.

It is interesting, however, that Col does not follow Philem in order. Archippus, who in Philem is mentioned as one of the recipients in the beginning of the letter (Philem 2), is greeted at the end of the letter in Col (Col 4:17). Similarly, Epaphras is not mentioned in Philem until the conclusion (Philem 23) but already in the introduction in Col (Col 1:7). Since Philem is so short, A/Col may have glanced it through several times during the composing of Col. A/Col seems to pick up most of the names he mentions from Philem: besides Archippus and Epaphras, he adds Onesimus from Philem 10 and Timothy from Philem 1. Paul is also described as being in prison like in Philem 10 and 13. Accordingly, Philem has given the frame to Col and is intentionally imitated in order to link the pseudo-Pauline letter to the apostle's life. A/Col tries to give the impression that Paul wrote Col about the same time as Philem, during the same imprisonment. In addition, a few phrases similar to Philem are used in the household rules: the words "be subject ... as is fitting" (ὑποτάσσεσθε ... ὡς ἀνῆκεν) in Col 3:18 resembles Philem 8 and the expression "lords in terms of the flesh" (κατὰ σάρκα κυρίοις) may be due to the juxtaposition δοῦλος ἐν σαρκί – δοῦλος ἐν κυρίῳ in Philem 16.

Table Philem A

Philem	Col
2 ... καὶ **Ἀρχίππῳ** τῷ συστρατιώτῃ ἡμῶν **καὶ** τῇ **κατ' οἶκόν** σου ἐκκλησίᾳ	4:15-17 Ἀσπάσασθε ... Νύμφαν **καὶ** τὴν **κατ' οἶκον** αὐτῆς ἐκκλησίαν. ... καὶ εἴπατε **Ἀρχίππῳ·**
4-5 Εὐχαριστῶ **τῷ θεῷ** μου **πάντοτε** μνείαν σου ποιούμενος ἐπὶ τῶν προσευχῶν μου, ἀκούων σου **τὴν ἀγάπην καὶ τὴν πίστιν, ἣν** ἔχεις πρὸς τὸν κύριον Ἰησοῦν καὶ **εἰς πάντας τοὺς ἁγίους**	1:3-4 Εὐχαριστοῦμεν **τῷ θεῷ** πατρὶ τοῦ κυρίου ἡμῶν Ἰησοῦ Χριστοῦ **πάντοτε** περὶ ὑμῶν προσευχόμενοι, ἀκούσαντες **τὴν πίστιν** ὑμῶν ἐν Χριστῷ Ἰησοῦ **καὶ τὴν ἀγάπην ἣν** ἔχετε **εἰς πάντας τοὺς ἁγίους**
8 ... **ἐν** Χριστῷ παρρησίαν ἔχων ἐπιτάσσειν σοι τὸ ἀνῆκον	3:18 Αἱ γυναῖκες, ὑποτάσσεσθε τοῖς ἀνδράσιν ὡς ἀνῆκεν **ἐν** κυρίῳ.
	4:18 ... μνημονεύετέ μου τῶν δεσμῶν.
10-13 ... ὃν ἐγέννησα ἐν τοῖς δεσμοῖς, Ὀνήσιμον, ... **ὃν ἀνέπεμψά** σοι, ... ἐν τοῖς δεσμοῖς τοῦ εὐαγγελίου	4:8-9 **ὃν ἔπεμψα** πρὸς ὑμᾶς ... σὺν Ὀνησίμῳ ...
16 οὐκέτι ὡς δοῦλον ἀλλ' ὑπὲρ δοῦλον ... ἐν σαρκὶ καὶ ἐν κυρίῳ.	3:22 Οἱ δοῦλοι, ὑπακούετε κατὰ πάντα τοῖς κατὰ σάρκα κυρίοις, ... φοβούμενοι τὸν κύριον.
23-24 **Ἀσπάζεταί** σε **Ἐπαφρᾶς ὁ συναιχμάλωτός μου** ἐν Χριστῷ Ἰησοῦ, **Μᾶρκος, Ἀρίσταρχος, Δημᾶς, Λουκᾶς**, οἱ **συνεργοί** μου.	1:7 καθὼς ἐμάθετε ἀπὸ Ἐπαφρᾶ τοῦ ἀγαπητοῦ **συνδούλου** ἡμῶν, ὅς ἐστιν πιστὸς ὑπὲρ ὑμῶν διάκονος τοῦ Χριστοῦ
	4:10-14 **Ἀσπάζεται** ὑμᾶς **Ἀρίσταρχος ὁ συναιχμάλωτός μου** καὶ **Μᾶρκος** ὁ ἀνεψιὸς Βαρναβᾶ ... καὶ Ἰησοῦς ὁ λεγόμενος Ἰοῦστος,... οὗτοι μόνοι **συνεργοὶ** εἰς τὴν βασιλείαν τοῦ θεοῦ, οἵτινες ἐγενήθησάν μοι παρηγορία. **ἀσπάζεται** ὑμᾶς **Ἐπαφρᾶς** ὁ ἐξ ὑμῶν, δοῦλος Χριστοῦ [Ἰησοῦ], ... **ἀσπάζεται** ὑμᾶς **Λουκᾶς** ὁ ἰατρὸς ὁ ἀγαπητὸς καὶ **Δημᾶς**.

Table Philem B

Col	Philem
1:3-4 Εὐχαριστοῦμεν **τῷ θεῷ** πατρὶ τοῦ κυρίου ἡμῶν Ἰησοῦ Χριστοῦ **πάντοτε** περὶ ὑμῶν προσευχόμενοι, ἀκούσαντες **τὴν πίστιν** ὑμῶν ἐν Χριστῷ Ἰησοῦ **καὶ τὴν ἀγάπην ἣν** ἔχετε **εἰς πάντας τοὺς ἁγίους**	**4-5** Εὐχαριστῶ **τῷ θεῷ** μου **πάντοτε** μνείαν σου ποιούμενος ἐπὶ τῶν προσευχῶν μου, ἀκούων σου **τὴν ἀγάπην καὶ τὴν πίστιν, ἣν** ἔχεις πρὸς τὸν κύριον Ἰησοῦν καὶ **εἰς πάντας τοὺς ἁγίους**
1:7 καθὼς ἐμάθετε ἀπὸ Ἐπαφρᾶ τοῦ ἀγαπητοῦ **συν**δούλου ἡμῶν, ὅς ἐστιν πιστὸς ὑπὲρ ὑμῶν διάκονος τοῦ Χριστοῦ	**23** ... Ἐπαφρᾶς ὁ **συν**αιχμάλωτός μου ἐν Χριστῷ Ἰησοῦ,
3:18 Αἱ γυναῖκες, ὑποτάσσεσθε τοῖς ἀνδράσιν ὡς ἀνῆκεν **ἐν** κυρίῳ.	8 ... **ἐν** Χριστῷ παρρησίαν ἔχων ἐπιτάσσειν σοι τὸ ἀνῆκον
3:22 Οἱ δοῦλοι, ὑπακούετε κατὰ πάντα τοῖς κατὰ σάρκα κυρίοις, ... φοβούμενοι τὸν κύριον.	**16** οὐκέτι ὡς δοῦλον ἀλλ' ὑπὲρ δοῦλον, ... ἐν σαρκὶ καὶ ἐν κυρίῳ
4:8-9 **ὃν ἔπεμψα** πρὸς ὑμᾶς ... σὺν Ὀνησίμῳ ...	**10-12** ... Ὀνήσιμον, ... **ὃν** ἀν**έπεμψά** σοι
4:10-14 **Ἀσπάζεται** ὑμᾶς **Ἀρίσταρχος ὁ συναιχμάλωτός μου** καὶ **Μᾶρκος** ὁ ἀνεψιὸς Βαρναβᾶ ... καὶ Ἰησοῦς ὁ λεγόμενος Ἰοῦστος, ... οὗτοι μόνοι **συνεργοὶ** εἰς τὴν βασιλείαν τοῦ θεοῦ, οἵτινες ἐγενήθησάν μοι παρηγορία. **ἀσπάζεται** ὑμᾶς **Ἐπαφρᾶς** ὁ ἐξ ὑμῶν, δοῦλος Χριστοῦ [Ἰησοῦ], ... **ἀσπάζεται** ὑμᾶς **Λουκᾶς** ὁ ἰατρὸς ὁ ἀγαπητὸς καὶ **Δημᾶς**.	**23-24** **Ἀσπάζεταί** σε **Ἐπαφρᾶς ὁ συναιχμάλωτός μου** ἐν Χριστῷ Ἰησοῦ, **Μᾶρκος, Ἀρίσταρχος, Δημᾶς, Λουκᾶς,** οἱ **συνεργοί** μου.
4:15-17 Ἀσπάσασθε ... Νύμφαν **καὶ** τὴν **κατ' οἶκον** αὐτῆς ἐκκλησίαν. ... καὶ εἴπατε **Ἀρχίππῳ**·	2 ... καὶ **Ἀρχίππῳ** τῷ συστρατιώτῃ ἡμῶν **καὶ** τῇ **κατ' οἶκόν** σου ἐκκλησίᾳ
4:18 ... μνημονεύετέ μου τῶν δεσμῶν.	13, cf. 10 ἐν τοῖς δεσμοῖς τοῦ εὐαγγελίου

It has to be noted that the beginning and the conclusion of Col are not, however, modelled on Philem only. Though both Col and Philem present brother Timothy also as a sender of the letter besides Paul, the text seems rather to imitate 1 Cor 1:1 or 2 Cor 1:1 than Philem 1 (see pp. 59-63). In addition, the influence of 2 Cor may also continue in Col 1:3-4, which seems to conflate Philem 4-5 and 2 Cor 1:3 or imitate 1 Thess 1:2-3 (see pp. 63-66). It is also remarkable that Col 4:18 mentions Paul's writing in his own hand, like Philem 19, but the choice of wording follows 1 Cor 16:21-23 instead. The reason for recalling the formulations from other letters may be the fact that like Col, they are addressed to congregations and thus their introductory greetings and conclusions are more suitable prototypes of Col than those of Philem, which is written to a private person.

9.2. Galatians

The following tables illustrate the resemblances between Col and Gal. The first one enumerates them from the standpoint of Gal (Table Gal A). Because the agreements can be seen in the order they appear in Col in the Appendix (pp. 394-399), they are not enumerated again here. In the second and third table, the resemblances pointing to literary dependence are examined more closely, first from the standpoint of Gal (Table Gal B) and then from that of Col (Table Gal C).

Table Gal A

Gal		Col	Gal		Col
1:	**1**	2:12	4:	**3-4**	2:8-9
	10	3:22, 24		9-10	2:16, 20
	22	2:1		14	1:24
				18, 20	1:6
2:	5	1:5b		19	1:27
	12-13	4:10-11			
	14	1:5b	5:	15	2:8
				19-20	3:5, 8
3:	**27-28**	3:10-11		**22-26**	3:12-15
			6:	**15**	3:10-11

Table Gal B

Gal	Col
1:1 ... **διὰ** ... θεοῦ πατρὸς **τοῦ ἐγείραντος αὐτὸν ἐκ νεκρῶν**	2:12 ... **διὰ** τῆς πίστεως τῆς ἐνεργείας τοῦ **θεοῦ τοῦ ἐγείραντος αὐτὸν ἐκ νεκρῶν**·
1:10 ... εἰ ἔτι ἀνθρώποις ἤρεσκον, Χριστοῦ δοῦλος οὐκ ἂν ἤμην.	3:22, 24 ... μὴ ἐν ὀφθαλμοδουλίᾳ ὡς ἀνθρωπάρεσκοι, ... τῷ κυρίῳ Χριστῷ δουλεύετε·
3:27-28 ... Χριστὸν ἐνεδύσασθε. **οὐκ ἔνι Ἰουδαῖος** οὐδὲ **Ἕλλην**, οὐκ ἔνι **δοῦλος** οὐδὲ **ἐλεύθερος**, ... πάντες γὰρ ὑμεῖς εἷς ἐστε **ἐν** Χριστῷ Ἰησοῦ.	3:10-11 καὶ ἐνδυσάμενοι τὸν νέον ... ὅπου **οὐκ ἔνι Ἕλλην** καὶ Ἰουδαῖος, περιτομὴ καὶ ἀκροβυστία, βάρβαρος, Σκύθης, **δοῦλος, ἐλεύθερος**, ἀλλὰ [τὰ] πάντα καὶ **ἐν** πᾶσιν Χριστός.
4:3-4 ... ὑπὸ **τὰ στοιχεῖα τοῦ κόσμου** ἤμεθα δεδουλωμένοι· ὅτε δὲ ἦλθεν **τὸ πλήρωμα** τοῦ χρόνου, ἐξαπέστειλεν ὁ θεὸς τὸν υἱὸν αὐτοῦ	2:8-9 Βλέπετε μή τις ὑμᾶς ἔσται ὁ συλαγωγῶν ... κατὰ **τὰ στοιχεῖα τοῦ κόσμου** καὶ οὐ κατὰ Χριστόν· ὅτι ἐν αὐτῷ κατοικεῖ πᾶν **τὸ πλήρωμα** τῆς θεότητος σωματικῶς
5:19-20 ... ἅτινά **ἐστιν** πορνεία, ἀκαθαρσία, ἀσέλγεια, **εἰδωλολατρία**, ... θυμοί, ...	3:5, 8 ... πορνείαν ἀκαθαρσίαν πάθος ἐπιθυμίαν κακήν, καὶ τὴν πλεονεξίαν, ἥτις **ἐστὶν εἰδωλολατρία**, ... θυμόν, ...
5:22-23 ... ἐστιν ἀγάπη χαρὰ εἰρήνη, μακροθυμία χρηστότης ἀγαθωσύνη, πίστις πραΰτης ἐγκράτεια·	3:12-15 ... χρηστότητα ταπεινοφροσύνην πραΰτητα μακροθυμίαν, ... ἐπὶ πᾶσιν δὲ τούτοις τὴν ἀγάπην, ὅ ἐστιν σύνδεσμος τῆς τελειότητος. καὶ ἡ εἰρήνη τοῦ Χριστοῦ βραβευέτω ...
6:15 οὔτε γὰρ **περιτομή** τί ἐστιν οὔτε **ἀκροβυστία ἀλλὰ** καινὴ κτίσις.	3:10-11 ... τὸν ἀνακαινούμενον εἰς ἐπίγνωσιν κατ᾽ εἰκόνα τοῦ κτίσαντος αὐτόν, ὅπου οὐκ ἔνι Ἕλλην καὶ Ἰουδαῖος, **περιτομὴ** καὶ **ἀκροβυστία** ... **ἀλλὰ** [τὰ] πάντα καὶ ἐν πᾶσιν Χριστός.

Table Gal C

Col	Gal
2:8-9 Βλέπετε μή τις ὑμᾶς ἔσται ὁ συλαγωγῶν ... κατὰ **τὰ στοιχεῖα τοῦ κόσμου** καὶ οὐ κατὰ Χριστόν· ὅτι ἐν αὐτῷ κατοικεῖ πᾶν **τὸ πλήρωμα** τῆς θεότητος σωματικῶς	**4:3-4** ... ὑπὸ **τὰ στοιχεῖα τοῦ κόσμου** ἤμεθα δεδουλωμένοι· ὅτε δὲ ἦλθεν **τὸ πλήρωμα** τοῦ χρόνου, ἐξαπέστειλεν ὁ θεὸς τὸν υἱὸν αὐτοῦ
2:12 ... **διὰ** τῆς πίστεως τῆς ἐνεργείας τοῦ **θεοῦ τοῦ ἐγείραντος αὐτὸν ἐκ νεκρῶν**·	**1:1** ... **διὰ** ... **θεοῦ** πατρὸς **τοῦ ἐγείραντος αὐτὸν ἐκ νεκρῶν**
3:5, 8 ... πορνείαν ἀκαθαρσίαν πάθος ἐπιθυμίαν κακήν, καὶ τὴν πλεονεξίαν, ἥτις **ἐστὶν εἰδωλολατρία**, ... θυμόν, ...	**5:19-20** ... ἅτινά **ἐστιν** πορνεία, ἀκαθαρσία, ἀσέλγεια, **εἰδωλολατρία**, ... θυμοί, ...
3:10-11 καὶ ἐνδυσάμενοι τὸν νέον τὸν ἀνακαινούμενον εἰς ἐπίγνωσιν κατ' εἰκόνα τοῦ κτίσαντος αὐτόν, ὅπου **οὐκ ἔνι Ἕλλην** καὶ 'Ιουδαῖος, **περιτομὴ** καὶ **ἀκροβυστία**, βάρβαρος, Σκύθης, **δοῦλος**, **ἐλεύθερος**, **ἀλλὰ** [τὰ] πάντα καὶ **ἐν** πᾶσιν Χριστός.	**3:27-28** ... Χριστὸν ἐνεδύσασθε. **οὐκ ἔνι 'Ιουδαῖος** οὐδὲ **Ἕλλην**, οὐκ ἔνι **δοῦλος** οὐδὲ **ἐλεύθερος**, ... πάντες γὰρ ὑμεῖς εἷς ἐστε **ἐν** Χριστῷ 'Ιησοῦ. **6:15** οὔτε γὰρ **περιτομή** τί ἐστιν οὔτε **ἀκροβυστία ἀλλὰ** καινὴ κτίσις.
3:12-15 ... χρηστότητα ταπεινοφροσύνην πραΰτητα μακροθυμίαν, ἀνεχόμενοι ἀλλήλων ... ἐπὶ πᾶσιν δὲ τούτοις τὴν ἀγάπην, ὅ ἐστιν σύνδεσμος τῆς τελειότητος. καὶ ἡ εἰρήνη τοῦ Χριστοῦ βραβευέτω ...	**5:22-23** ... ἐστιν ἀγάπη χαρὰ εἰρήνη, μακροθυμία χρηστότης ἀγαθωσύνη, πίστις πραΰτης ἐγκράτεια·
3:22, 24 ... μὴ ἐν ὀφθαλμοδουλίᾳ ὡς ἀνθρωπάρεσκοι ... τῷ κυρίῳ Χριστῷ δουλεύετε·	**1:10** ... εἰ ἔτι ἀνθρώποις ἤρεσκον, Χριστοῦ δοῦλος οὐκ ἂν ἤμεν.

The agreements between Col and Gal are not centered in any particular part of Gal but occur here and there (see Table Gal A). Though Col does not imitate the greetings, the conclusion, or other texts typical of a letter from Gal, it is worth noting that A/Col shows acquaintance with Gal 1:1, the first verse of the letter, as well as 6:15 which belongs to the last verses of the epistle. This indicates that he had familiarized himself with the whole letter.

The situation is different from the standpoint of Col. The agreements indicating literary dependence between Col and Gal are centered in Col 2:8-3:24 (see Table

Gal C). All resemblances thus occur either in the part which includes the warning about the persons who are trying to lead the community astray (Col 2:6-23) or in the exhortations to believers (Col 3:1-4:1). Most of all, the catalogs of vices and virtues (Col 3:1-17) seem to be modelled on Gal. The lists have a probable literary dependence upon Gal 5:19-20, 22-23, 6:15, and 3:27-28. In addition, the exceptional term "the elements of the universe" (τὰ στοιχεῖα τοῦ κόσμου), which describes the philosophy, possibly depends on Gal (4:3).

Since A/Col does not follow Gal in order and also conflates two texts from it, Gal 3:27-28 and 6:15, it is unlikely that A/Col had Gal in front of him when writing. Rather seems it possible that he had read it through before composing this part of his letter or that he otherwise was well acquainted with it and thus recalls the texts so well. This would also explain the surprising result reached in chap. 8 (see pp. 222-223). The frequency of the occurrence of the agreements indicating probable literary dependence between Gal and Col may be higher than the one suggesting possible literary dependence because A/Col knows the text of Gal very well.

Another explanation for exact imitation may be that A/Col does not often follow the argumentation of Paul but only picks up the conclusions which, as summaries, are easy to recall. Gal 3:27-28 summarizes the discussion about law in Gal 3 and Gal 6:15 does the same for that on circumcision in Gal 6. Moreover, at the end of Gal 5, the catalogs of vices and virtues are conclusions of the previous discussion. A/Col's habit of using Gal is understandable. It is natural that he is more interested in Paul's conclusions than the arguments Paul uses in a specific situation. He may also think that Paul has settled the questions concerning law and circumcision and thus only imitates the conclusions. A/Col himself handles the questions very little. Col 2:11, which explains circumcision metaphorically as the circumcision of Christ, is the only case when the question about circumcision is referred to and the term νόμος, "law", does not occur in Col at all.

A/Col's acquaintance with Gal may also explain the problem of Col 2:14 which uses several unique terms, has no parallel including verbal agreement and is also difficult to understand (see pp. 139-140, 220). Gal 3:1-2 reveals that the opponents who have bewitched the Galatians maintain the works of the law. Paul criticizes the Galatians and reminds them that "It was before your eyes that Jesus Christ was publicly exhibited as crucified". In addition, it is emphasized in Gal 3:17 that the law does not nullify the promise previously ratified by God and that it was Christ who redeemed people from the curse of the law. At the end of the verse, the crucifixion of Christ is also referred to with the quotation "Cursed is everyone who hangs on a tree". Similarly, Col 2:14 mentions the nailing to the cross which probably refers to the crucifixion of Christ. Therefore, it seems possible that when writing the words "erasing the record which stood against us with its legal demands", A/Col may have in mind the description about the law which does not nullify the promise in Gal 3. Like the record with its legal demands in Col 2:14, the law in Gal 3 was set aside when Christ was crucified.

The juxtapositions Greek – Jew and slave – free from Gal 3:27-28 are imitated in Col 3:11 but the pair male – female, mentioned in Gal 3:28, is not present. However, the question concerning men and women is dealt with in the household rules. The fact that no prototype for the household code in Col 3:18-4:1 was found raises the question: is it not possible that Gal 3:27-28 has inspired A/Col to form the rules? The admonitions to masters to treat their slaves well, as well as their wives and children in the Haustafel could be based on the idea "there is no longer slave or free, there is no longer male and female; for all of you are one in Christ Jesus" in Gal 3:27-28. That all are one in Christ still does not mean to A/Col that all are equal: wives must be subject to their husbands and children have to obey their parents as well as slaves their masters.

The observation that A/Col imitates Gal only when warning about the dangers and in the exhortations following them is compatible with the finding that A/Col seems to quote the term "the elements of the universe" (τὰ στοιχεῖα τοῦ κόσμου) from Paul in order to get help for his argumentation from his teacher (see p. 130). Like Paul, A/Col uses the term to describe the teaching confronted as being the opposite of Christ. The term is used twice both in Col and Gal (Gal 4:3, 9, Col 2:8, 20) and people are similarly warned against being enslaved to "the elements of the universe". Neither Col nor Gal mention the names of the oppo-nents but refer them only by the indefinite someone, τις (Gal 1:7, Col 2:8). Both authors also emphasize that the elements of the universe belong to the past and the same juxtaposition τότε – νῦν, "formerly – now", is employed (Gal 4:8-9, Col 1:21-22).

Furthermore, while Paul in Gal 1:11 emphasizes that the Gospel proclaimed by him "is not of human origin" (οὐκ ἔστιν κατὰ ἄνθρωπον) and in Gal 1:14 says: "I was ... zealous for the traditions of my ancestors" (τῶν πατρικῶν μου παραδόσεων), Col 2:8 takes the philosophy confronted as being of human origin using the term "according to human tradition" (κατὰ τὴν παράδοσιν τῶν ἀνθρώπων). A/Col thus emphasizes the same idea as Paul in Gal though utilizing different terms. The change is understandable. The expression "the traditions of my ancestors" refers to teachings and practices developed in the Pharisaic schools.[961] A/Col, as a later writer, and a representative of the second Christian generation, probably did not have a Pharisaic background like Paul and thus prefers the term "human tradition" which may depend on Mk 7:8 (see pp. 129). Accordingly, Paul's style when warning about false teachers and describing their character in Gal is used as the prototype for the argumentation in Col.

Both in Gal and Col are also exhortations not to observe special days and festivals (Gal 4:10, Col 2:18). However, A/Col employs the regular Jewish way of speaking of the main festivals (the sabbaths, new moons, and festivals) instead of enumerating special days, months, seasons, and years like Gal 4:10. This change is also understandable. The list in Gal can be regarded as either pagan or Jewish.

---

[961] Longenecker 1990, 30; Fung 1988, 57; Lührmann 1978, 31; Dunn 1993,60.

Therefore, A/Col prefers the regular Jewish way of speaking in order to better oppose the Jewish character of the teaching represented in Rev (see pp.144-145).

Gal 1:7-8 is also compatible with the characteristics of the opponents in Col. There Paul refers to those who are confusing the Galatians and says "even if we or an angel from heaven should proclaim to you a gospel contrary to what we proclaimed to you, let that one be accursed!" Furthermore, in Gal 3:19 he says that the law "was ordained through angels by a mediator". Thus it seems that A/Col intentionally chose Gal as the prototype for the descriptions of the dangers because the opponents in Gal are so similar to his: both practice Jewish habits, the observance of holy days among them. In addition, A/Col may remember Paul's reference to angels. Nevertheless, the opponents in Gal cannot be regarded as the same as those in Col (see p. 144). Nor is Gal the only model for opposing the persons who are trying to lead the community astray. For example, the warning not to judge anyone in matters of food and drink in Col 2:16 seems to be modelled on Rom 14 rather than on Gal (see pp. 143-144).

9.3. 1. Corinthians

Unlike those between Col and Gal, the agreements indicating literary dependence between Col and 1 Cor are not centered in any particular part of Col but occur all over the text (see the Appendix). The following three tables illustrate the resemblances between 1 Cor and Col like those of Gal in the previous chapter. In Table 1 Cor B (pp. 334-335), Col 2:23 and 4:1 are put in the parenthesis because their agreements with 1 Cor do not meet the criteria for literary dependence. They are still presented because the agreement indicating a probable literary dependence between 1 Cor 2:1-7 and Col 1:25-28 as well as that pointing to a possible one between 1 Cor 2:1-7 and Col 2:2-3 suggest that A/Col has also 1 Cor 2 in mind in Col 2:23. Similarly, the possible dependence between 1 Cor 8:5-6 and Col 1:16 indicates that Col 4:1 may also have been modelled on 1 Cor 8:5-6.

Table 1 Cor A

1 Cor		Col	1 Cor		Col
1:	**1-3**	1:1-2	9:	24	2:18
	5-6	2:7		25	1:29
	17	1:20			
			10:	16	1:20
2:	1	2:23		31	3:17
	1	2:2-3			
	1, 6-7	1:25-28	11:	3	1:18
				3	2:1
3:	9-10	2:7			
	10	1:25	12:	6	3:11
				13	3:15
4:	**1**	1:25-26		**8**	1:9-10
	12	1:29		**27-28**	1:18
	17, 21	1:7-8			
			14:	26	3:16
5:	2	2:18		**34-35**	3:18
	3	2:5		40	2:5
	11	3:5			
			15:	20	1:18
6:	11	3:17		24	1:16
				24	2:10
7:	28	1:24		**28**	3:11
				58	1:23
8:	**5-6**	1:16			
	5-6	4:1	16:	**21-23**	4:18
	9	2:8			

Table 1 Cor B

1 Cor	Col
1:1-3 **Παῦλος** κλητὸς **ἀπόστολος Χριστοῦ Ἰησοῦ διὰ θελήματος θεοῦ καὶ** Σωσθένης **ὁ ἀδελφὸς** τῇ ἐκκλησίᾳ τοῦ θεοῦ τῇ οὔσῃ ἐν Κορίνθῳ, ἡγιασμένοις **ἐν Χριστῷ** Ἰησοῦ, κλητοῖς **ἁγίοις** ... **χάρις ὑμῖν καὶ εἰρήνη ἀπὸ θεοῦ πατρὸς ἡμῶν** καὶ κυρίου Ἰησοῦ Χριστοῦ.	1:1-2 **Παῦλος ἀπόστολος Χριστοῦ Ἰησοῦ διὰ θελήματος θεοῦ καὶ** Τιμόθεος **ὁ ἀδελφὸς τοῖς** ἐν Κολοσσαῖς **ἁγίοις** καὶ πιστοῖς ἀδελφοῖς **ἐν Χριστῷ, χάρις ὑμῖν καὶ εἰρήνη ἀπὸ θεοῦ πατρὸς ἡμῶν**.
2:1, 6-7 ... ἦλθον οὐ καθ' ὑπεροχὴν λόγου ἢ **σοφίας** καταγγέλλων ὑμῖν **τὸ μυστήριον τοῦ θεοῦ**. ... Σοφίαν δὲ λαλοῦμεν ἐν τοῖς τελείοις ... ἀλλὰ λαλοῦμεν **θεοῦ** σοφίαν ἐν μυστηρίῳ τὴν ἀποκεκρυμμένην, ἣν προώρισεν ὁ θεὸς πρὸ **τῶν αἰώνων** εἰς δόξαν ἡμῶν **3:10 Κατὰ τὴν** χάριν **τοῦ θεοῦ τὴν δοθεῖσάν μοι** **4:1** ... οἰκονόμους μυστηρίων **θεοῦ**.	1:25-28 ἧς ἐγενόμην ἐγὼ διάκονος **κατὰ τὴν** οἰκονομίαν **τοῦ θεοῦ τὴν δοθεῖσάν μοι** εἰς ὑμᾶς πληρῶσαι τὸν λόγον **τοῦ θεοῦ, τὸ μυστήριον** τὸ ἀποκεκρυμμένον ἀπὸ **τῶν αἰώνων** καὶ ἀπὸ τῶν γενεῶν - νῦν δὲ ἐφανερώθη τοῖς ἁγίοις αὐτοῦ, οἷς ἠθέλησεν ὁ θεὸς γνωρίσαι τί τὸ πλοῦτος τῆς δόξης τοῦ μυστηρίου τούτου ἐν τοῖς ἔθνεσιν, ὅ ἐστιν Χριστὸς ἐν ὑμῖν, ἡ ἐλπὶς τῆς δόξης· ὃν ἡμεῖς καταγγέλλομεν νουθετοῦντες πάντα ἄνθρωπον καὶ διδάσκοντες πάντα ἄνθρωπον ἐν πάσῃ σοφίᾳ, ἵνα παραστήσωμεν πάντα ἄνθρωπον τέλειον ἐν Χριστῷ·
	2:2-3 ... εἰς ἐπίγνωσιν τοῦ μυστηρίου **τοῦ θεοῦ**, Χριστοῦ, ἐν ᾧ εἰσιν πάντες οἱ θησαυροὶ τῆς σοφίας καὶ γνώσεως ἀπόκρυφοι.
	(2:23 ἅτινά ἐστιν λόγον μὲν ἔχοντα **σοφίας** ...)
4:17, 21 ... Τιμόθεον, **ὅς ἐστίν** μου τέκνον ἀγαπητὸν καὶ πιστὸν ἐν κυρίῳ, ὃς ὑμᾶς ἀναμνήσει τὰς ὁδούς μου τὰς ἐν Χριστῷ ... **ἐν** ἀγάπῃ **πνεύματί** τε πραΰτητος;	1:7-8 καθὼς ἐμάθετε ἀπὸ Ἐπαφρᾶ τοῦ ἀγαπητοῦ συνδούλου ἡμῶν, **ὅς ἐστιν** πιστὸς ὑπὲρ ὑμῶν διάκονος τοῦ Χριστοῦ, ὁ καὶ δηλώσας ἡμῖν τὴν ὑμῶν ἀγάπην **ἐν πνεύματι**.
5:3 ἐγὼ μὲν **γάρ**, ἀπὼν τῷ σώματι παρὼν δὲ **τῷ πνεύματι**	2:5 εἰ **γὰρ** καὶ τῇ σαρκὶ ἄπειμι, ἀλλα **τῷ πνεύματι** σὺν ὑμῖν εἰμι
5:11 ... ἢ πλεονέκτης ἢ εἰδωλολάτρης ...	3:5 ... καὶ τὴν πλεονεξίαν, ἥτις ἐστὶν εἰδωλολατρία

8:5-6 καὶ γὰρ εἴπερ εἰσὶν λεγόμενοι θεοὶ εἴτε **ἐν οὐρανῷ** εἴτε **ἐπὶ γῆς**, ὥσπερ εἰσὶν θεοὶ πολλοὶ καὶ κύριοι πολλοί, ἀλλ' ἡμῖν εἷς θεὸς ὁ πατὴρ ἐξ οὗ τὰ πάντα καὶ ἡμεῖς **εἰς αὐτόν**, καὶ εἷς κύριος 'Ιησοῦς Χριστὸς δι' οὗ **τὰ πάντα καὶ** ἡμεῖς **δι' αὐτοῦ**.	1:16 ὅτι ἐν αὐτῷ ἐκτίσθη τὰ πάντα **ἐν** τοῖς οὐρανοῖς καὶ **ἐπὶ** τῆς **γῆς**, τὰ ὁρατὰ καὶ τὰ ἀόρατα, εἴτε θρόνοι εἴτε κυριότητες εἴτε ἀρχαὶ εἴτε ἐξουσίαι· **τὰ πάντα δι' αὐτοῦ καὶ εἰς αὐτὸν** ἔκτισται· (4:1 ... εἰδότες ὅτι καὶ ὑμεῖς ἔχετε κύριον **ἐν οὐρανῷ**.)
11:3 Θέλω δὲ **ὑμᾶς εἰδέναι** ...	2:1 **Θέλω** γὰρ **ὑμᾶς εἰδέναι** ...
12:8 ᾧ μὲν γὰρ διὰ τοῦ πνεύματος δίδοται λόγος σοφίας, ἄλλῳ δὲ λόγος γνώσεως ...	1:9 ... ἵνα πληρωθῆτε τὴν ἐπίγνωσιν τοῦ θελήματος αὐτοῦ ἐν πάσῃ σοφίᾳ καὶ συνέσει πνευματικῇ
12:27-28 'Υμεῖς δέ ἐστε σῶμα Χριστοῦ καὶ μέλη ἐκ μέρους. Καὶ οὓς μὲν ἔθετο ὁ θεὸς ἐν τῇ ἐκκλησίᾳ ...	1:18 καὶ αὐτός ἐστιν ἡ κεφαλὴ τοῦ σώματος τῆς ἐκκλησίας·
14:34-35 αἱ γυναῖκες ... ὑποτασσέσθωσαν, ... ἐν οἴκῳ τοὺς ἰδίους ἄνδρας ἐπερωτάτωσαν·	3:18 **Αἱ γυναῖκες**, ὑποτάσσεσθε τοῖς ἀνδράσιν ...
15:28 ... ἵνα ᾖ ὁ θεὸς **[τὰ] πάντα ἐν πᾶσιν**.	3:11 ... ἀλλὰ **[τὰ] πάντα** καὶ **ἐν πᾶσιν** Χριστός.
15:58 ... **ἑδραῖοι** γίνεσθε, ἀμετακίνητοι ...	1:23 ... **ἑδραῖοι** καὶ μὴ μετακινούμενοι ...
16:21-23 'Ο ἀσπασμὸς τῇ ἐμῇ χειρὶ Παύλου. ... **ἡ χάρις** τοῦ κυρίου 'Ιησοῦ **μεθ' ὑμῶν.**	4:18 **'Ο ἀσπασμὸς τῇ ἐμῇ χειρὶ Παύλου.** ... **ἡ χάρις μεθ' ὑμῶν.**

Table 1 Cor C

Col	1 Cor
1:1-2 **Παῦλος ἀπόστολος Χριστοῦ ᾽Ιησοῦ διὰ θελήματος θεοῦ καὶ** Τιμόθεος **ὁ ἀδελφὸς τοῖς** ἐν Κολοσσαῖς **ἁγίοις** καὶ πιστοῖς ἀδελφοῖς **ἐν Χριστῷ, χάρις ὑμῖν καὶ εἰρήνη ἀπὸ θεοῦ πατρὸς ἡμῶν.**	1:1-3 **Παῦλος** κλητὸς **ἀπόστολος Χριστοῦ ᾽Ιησοῦ διὰ θελήματος θεοῦ καὶ** Σωσθένης **ὁ ἀδελφὸς** τῇ ἐκκλησίᾳ τοῦ θεοῦ τῇ οὔσῃ ἐν Κορίνθῳ, ἡγιασμένοις **ἐν Χριστῷ** ᾽Ιησοῦ, κλητοῖς **ἁγίοις** ... **χάρις ὑμῖν καὶ εἰρήνη ἀπὸ θεοῦ πατρὸς ἡμῶν** καὶ κυρίου ᾽Ιησοῦ Χριστοῦ.
1:7-8 καθὼς ἐμάθετε ἀπὸ ᾽Επαφρᾶ τοῦ ἀγαπητοῦ συνδούλου ἡμῶν, **ὅς ἐστιν** πιστὸς ὑπὲρ ὑμῶν διάκονος τοῦ Χριστοῦ, ὁ καὶ δηλώσας ἡμῖν τὴν ὑμῶν ἀγάπην **ἐν πνεύματι.**	4:17, 21 ... Τιμόθεον, **ὅς ἐστίν** μου τέκνον ἀγαπητὸν καὶ πιστὸν ἐν κυρίῳ, ὃς ὑμᾶς ἀναμνήσει τὰς ὁδούς μου τὰς ἐν Χριστῷ ... **ἐν** ἀγάπῃ **πνεύματί** τε πραΰτητος;
1:9 ... ἵνα πληρωθῆτε τὴν ἐπίγνωσιν τοῦ θελήματος αὐτοῦ ἐν πάσῃ σοφίᾳ καὶ συνέσει πνευματικῇ	**12:8** ᾧ μὲν γὰρ διὰ τοῦ πνεύματος δίδοται λόγος σοφίας, ἄλλῳ δὲ λόγος γνώσεως ...
1:16 ὅτι ἐν αὐτῷ ἐκτίσθη τὰ πάντα **ἐν** τοῖς οὐρανοῖς καὶ **ἐπὶ** τῆς **γῆς**, τὰ ὁρατὰ καὶ τὰ ἀόρατα, εἴτε θρόνοι εἴτε κυριότητες εἴτε ἀρχαὶ εἴτε ἐξουσίαι˙ **τὰ πάντα δι᾽ αὐτοῦ καὶ εἰς αὐτὸν** ἔκτισται˙	**8:5-6** καὶ γὰρ εἴπερ εἰσὶν λεγόμενοι θεοὶ εἴτε **ἐν** οὐρανῷ εἴτε **ἐπὶ γῆς**, ὥσπερ εἰσὶν θεοὶ πολλοὶ καὶ κύριοι πολλοί, ἀλλ᾽ ἡμῖν εἷς θεὸς ὁ πατὴρ ἐξ οὗ τὰ πάντα καὶ ἡμεῖς **εἰς αὐτόν**, καὶ εἷς κύριος ᾽Ιησοῦς Χριστὸς δι᾽ οὗ **τὰ πάντα καὶ** ἡμεῖς **δι᾽ αὐτοῦ**.
1:18 καὶ αὐτός ἐστιν ἡ κεφαλὴ τοῦ σώματος τῆς ἐκκλησίας˙	**12:27-28** ῾Υμεῖς δέ ἐστε σῶμα Χριστοῦ καὶ μέλη ἐκ μέρους. Καὶ οὓς μὲν ἔθετο ὁ θεὸς ἐν τῇ ἐκκλησίᾳ ...
1:23 ... **ἑδραῖοι** καὶ μὴ μετακινούμενοι ...	**15:58** ... **ἑδραῖοι** γίνεσθε, ἀμετακίνητοι ...

1:25-28 ἧς ἐγενόμην ἐγὼ διάκονος **κατὰ τὴν** οἰκονομίαν **τοῦ θεοῦ τὴν δοθεῖσάν μοι** εἰς ὑμᾶς πληρῶσαι τὸν λόγον **τοῦ θεοῦ, τὸ μυστήριον** τὸ ἀποκεκρυμμένον ἀπὸ **τῶν αἰώνων** καὶ ἀπὸ τῶν γενεῶν — νῦν δὲ ἐφανερώθη τοῖς ἁγίοις αὐτοῦ, οἷς ἠθέλησεν ὁ Θεὸς γνωρίσαι τί τὸ πλοῦτος τῆς δόξης τοῦ μυστηρίου τούτου ἐν τοῖς ἔθνεσιν, ὅ ἐστιν Χριστὸς ἐν ὑμῖν, ἡ ἐλπὶς τῆς δόξης· ὃν ἡμεῖς καταγγέλλομεν νουθετοῦντες πάντα ἄνθρωπον καὶ διδάσκοντες πάντα ἄνθρωπον ἐν πάσῃ σοφίᾳ, ἵνα παραστήσωμεν πάντα ἄνθρωπον τέλειον ἐν Χριστῷ·	**3:10 Κατὰ τὴν** χάριν **τοῦ θεοῦ τὴν δοθεῖσάν μοι** **4:1** ... οἰκονόμους μυστηρίων **θεοῦ** ... **2:1, 6-7** ... ἦλθον οὐ καθ' ὑπεροχὴν λόγου ἢ σοφίας καταγγέλλων ὑμῖν **τὸ μυστήριον τοῦ θεοῦ**. ... Σοφίαν δὲ λαλοῦμεν ἐν τοῖς τελείοις ... ἀλλὰ λαλοῦμεν **θεοῦ** σοφίαν ἐν μυστηρίῳ τὴν ἀποκεκρυμμένην, ἣν προώρισεν ὁ θεὸς πρὸ **τῶν αἰώνων** εἰς δόξαν ἡμῶν
2:1 **Θέλω** γὰρ **ὑμᾶς εἰδέναι** ...	**11:3 Θέλω** δὲ **ὑμᾶς εἰδέναι** ...
2:2-3 ... εἰς ἐπίγνωσιν τοῦ μυστηρίου **τοῦ θεοῦ**, Χριστοῦ, ἐν ᾧ εἰσιν πάντες οἱ θησαυροὶ τῆς **σοφίας** καὶ γνώσεως ἀπόκρυφοι.	**2:1** ... λόγου ἢ **σοφίας** καταγγέλλων ὑμῖν τὸ μυστήριον **τοῦ θεοῦ**.
2:5 εἰ **γὰρ** καὶ τῇ σαρκὶ ἄπειμι, ἀλλα **τῷ πνεύματι** σὺν ὑμῖν εἰμι	**5:3** ἐγὼ μὲν **γάρ**, ἀπὼν τῷ σώματι παρὼν δὲ **τῷ πνεῦματι**
3:5 ... καὶ τὴν πλεονεξίαν, ἥτις ἐστὶν εἰδωλολατρία	**5:11** ... ἢ πλεονέκτης ἢ εἰδωλολάτρης ...
3:11 ... ἀλλὰ [**τὰ**] **πάντα** καὶ **ἐν πᾶσιν** Χριστός.	**15:28** ... ἵνα ᾖ ὁ θεὸς [**τὰ**] **πάντα ἐν πᾶσιν**.
3:18 **Αἱ γυναῖκες**, ὑποτάσσεσθε τοῖς ἀνδράσιν ...	**14:34-35 αἱ γυναῖκες** ... ὑποτασσέσθωσαν, ... ἐν οἴκῳ τοὺς ἰδίους ἄνδρας ἐπερωτάτωσαν·
4:18 **Ὁ ἀσπασμὸς τῇ ἐμῇ χειρὶ Παύλου**. . ... **ἡ χάρις μεθ' ὑμῶν.**	**16:21-23 Ὁ ἀσπασμὸς τῇ ἐμῇ χειρὶ Παύλου**. ... **ἡ χάρις** τοῦ κυρίου Ἰησοῦ **μεθ' ὑμῶν.**

The agreements pointing to literary dependence between 1 Cor and Col are located all over 1 Cor which indicates that A/Col was acquainted with the whole letter (see Table 1 Cor A). Four of the resemblances meet the criteria for a probable literary dependence. First, the introductory greeting in Col 1:1-2 employs the same words as the greeting in 1 Cor 1:1-3. Second, in the conclusion of the letter in Col 4:18, Paul's writing in his own hand is mentioned with exactly the same words as at the end of 1 Cor, in 1 Cor 16:21-23, and the greetings that follow also resemble each other. Third, the epithets given to Epaphras in Col 1:7-8 seem to be modelled on those of Timothy in 1 Cor 4:17, 21. Fourth, the description of the mystery which was once hidden but now revealed in Col 1:25-28 probably depends on 1 Cor 2:1, 6-7.

Three of the agreements meeting the criteria for a probable literary dependence belong somehow to the frame of Col: one is in the introduction of the letter, one in its conclusion, and one occurs when a person is introduced. In addition, there are two agreements indicating a possible literary dependence which appear in the texts typical of a letter: Col 2:1 uses a Pauline "disclosure form" "I want you to know" (Θέλω ... ὑμᾶς εἰδέναι) similar to 1 Cor 11:3. The metaphor in Col 2:5 "to be absent in body but still present in spirit" resembles 1 Cor 5:3. This strongly indicates that A/Col has not only heard teachings from 1 Cor but also read the epistle. It has to be remembered, however, that 1 Cor 1:1-3 is not the closest parallel to Col 1:1-2. That is 2 Cor 1:1-2. Nevertheless, the occurrence of several other resemblances between Col and 1 Cor in the parts typical of a letter indicates that the introductory greeting of 1 Cor was familiar to A/Col. It is also possible that A/Col intentionally uses 1 Cor, in addition to Philem, as a prototype for the frame of the letter. Nothing, however, indicates that he had 1 Cor in front of him when writing. All the resemblances are such that they can be recalled from memory.

It is interesting that some texts from 1 Cor seem to be recurring in Col. 1 Cor 2:1, 6-7 is imitated in Col 1:25-28, 2:2-3, and 2:23 and both Col 1:16 and Col 4:1 seem to follow 1 Cor 8:5-6. When we compare 1 Cor 2:1-7 and Col 1:25-28, 2:2-3, 2:23, we can see that A/Col does not three times imitate the same elements from 1 Cor 2 (see Table 1 Cor B): Col 1:25-28 mainly follows 1 Cor 2:1-7 but only some words are repeated in Col 2:2-3 and 2:23. Similarly, 1 Cor 8:5-6 recurs in Col but each time different elements are utilized. 1 Cor 8:5-6 states that there are many so-called gods and lords in heaven and on earth, but for us there is only one Lord. In contrast, Col 1:16 mentions only many rulers in heaven and earth while Col 4:1 emphasizes only one Lord in heaven. The phenomenon is the same as that which occurs between Eph and other Pauline letters. It was noted that A/Eph imitates several times texts with which he is deeply impressed but does not pick up the same words and phrases every time (see p. 41).

Besides the description of the mystery which was once hidden but is now revealed, there are also some other teachings in Col which have prototypes in 1 Cor. The description of Christ as the head of the church in Col 1:18 may depend on 1 Cor 12:27-28 and there is also a possible dependence between the catalogs of vices in Col and 1 Cor (Col 3:5 // 1 Cor 5:11) as well as between the admonitions to wives to be subject to their husbands (Col 3:18 // 1 Cor 14:34-35). Accordingly, A/Col imitates parts of the frame of 1 Cor and utilizes its teachings several times and thus seems to be very well acquainted with 1 Cor. It is noteworthy that there are several parts of 1 Cor of which A/Col reveals no knowledge, e.g. 1 Cor 13. This does not, however, indicate that these parts of 1 Cor were not familiar to him because all Paul's texts cannot be imitated in one letter.

9.4. Romans

The agreements pointing to literary dependence between Col and Rom appear quite regularly all over Col (see the Appendix). Table Rom A shows that the situation is similar from the standpoint of Rom. It is remarkable that there are five resemblances indicating a probable literary dependence between Col and Rom. The findings suggest that A/Col was well acquainted with Rom.

Table Rom A

Rom	Col	Rom	Col
1: 1	4:12	8: **11**	2:12-13
8	1:6	**29**	1:15
13	1:6	**32**	2:13
14	3:11	**32-33**	3:12-13
18	3:6	**34**	3:1
20	1:15		
22-23	1:23	9: **22-24**	1:27
2: 7	1:10	10: 2	4:13
9-11	3:23-25		
		11: **33**	2:2-3
4: **24-25**	2:12-13	**36**	1:16
5: 2	1:27	12: 1-2	3:20
10-11	1:21-22	12	4:2
6: **4**	2:12	13: **12b-14**	3:5-10
6	3:9		
8	2:20	14: 3, 5	2:16
11	2:13	**17**	2:16
13	3:5	18	3:20
16	3:22		
7: 5	1:24	15: 7	3:13
18	1:24	14	1:9
		14	2:10
8: 9	2:1	18	3:17
10	1:27		
11	3:16	16: 18	3:24

Like between Col and 1 Cor, the phenomenon of recurring also appears between Col and Rom: Rom 8:32-33 is first imitated in Col 2:13 and again in Col 3:12-13 (see Table Rom B). It is worth noting again that A/Col does not employ the same elements from the prototype both times. At first, he picks up the words σὺν αὐτῷ ... πάντα ἡμῖν + χαρίζομαι in Col 2:13 and then in Col 3:12-13 ἐκλεκτοὶ τοῦ θεοῦ + χαρίζομαι.

Rom is usually imitated in Col when the text is dealing with Christ (see Table Rom C). Six such agreements indicating either a probable or a possible literary dependence are clustered in Col 1:15-2:3. Col 1:15-16 utilizes Rom 8:29, 1:20, and 11:36 when presenting Christ as the image of God and as the firstborn of all creation and Col 1:21-22, which describes reconciliation through the death of Christ, follows Rom 5:10-11. In addition, the description of Christ as the mystery of God in Col 1:27, 2:2-3 resembles both Rom 9:22-24 and 11:33. In Col 2:6-23, in the part with the warnings about the dangers, Rom is utilized twice. However, Rom is again used as a model for the description of Christ in Col 2:20. Only in Col 2:16, when warning not to let anyone judge in matters of food and drink, is Rom used in another context. In addition, Rom is utilized in the exhortations in Col 3:1-25.

Rom is clearly one of the models for the Christology of Col but not the only one. In a previous chapter, it was noted that 1 Cor is often also utilized when Christ is described. Sometimes the texts from Rom and 1 Cor are conflated in Col. For example Col 1:15-16 utilizes, besides Rom (8:29, 1:20, 11:36), also 1 Cor (8:5-6) and Col 1:27, 2:2-3 employs both Rom (9:22-24, 11:33) and 1 Cor (2:1, 6-7). It is remarkable that sometimes Rom is clearly the primary model for the text, e.g. when describing reconciliation through the death of Christ in Col 1:21-22, 2:12-13, but sometimes it is 1 Cor, e.g. when Christ is presented as the mystery of God in Col 1:25-28, 2:2-3. So it cannot be said that either is the prototype for the Christology of Col: both are equally important. It is not possible to know whether the Christology in Col is intentionally modelled on Rom and 1 Cor. The great numbers of agreements may be only due to the fact that 1 Cor and Rom are long letters, containing much material for use.

Table Rom B

Rom	Col
1:20 τὰ γὰρ **ἀόρατα** αὐτοῦ ἀπὸ **κτίσεως** κόσμου ...	1:15 ὅς ἐστιν εἰκὼν τοῦ θεοῦ τοῦ ἀοράτου, πρωτότοκος πάσης **κτίσεως**, ὅτι ἐν αὐτῷ ἐκτίσθη τὰ πάντα ἐν τοῖς οὐρανοῖς καὶ ἐπὶ τῆς γῆς, τὰ ὁρατὰ καὶ **τὰ ἀόρατα** ...
2:9-11 θλῖψις ... ἐπὶ πᾶσαν ψυχὴν ἀνθρώπου τοῦ κατεργαζομένου τὸ κακόν, ... οὐ γάρ **ἐστιν προσωπολημψία** παρὰ τῷ θεῷ.	3:23-25 ... ἐκ ψυχῆς ἐργάζεσθε ... οὐκ **ἔστιν προσωπολημψία**.
4:24-25 ... τοῖς πιστεύουσιν ἐπὶ τὸν ἐγείραντα Ἰησοῦν τὸν κύριον ἡμῶν **ἐκ νεκρῶν**, ὃς παρεδόθη διὰ **τὰ παραπτώματα** ἡμῶν ...	2:12-13 ... ἐν ᾧ καὶ συνηγέρθητε διὰ τῆς πίστεως τῆς ἐνεργείας τοῦ θεοῦ τοῦ ἐγείραντος αὐτὸν **ἐκ νεκρῶν**· καὶ ὑμᾶς νεκροὺς ὄντας [ἐν] τοῖς παραπτώμασιν ... χαρισάμενος ἡμῖν πάντα **τὰ παραπτώματα**.
5:10-11 εἰ γὰρ ἐχθροὶ ὄντες κατηλλάγημεν τῷ θεῷ **διὰ τοῦ θανάτου** τοῦ υἱοῦ αὐτοῦ· ... Ἰησοῦ Χριστοῦ δι᾽ οὗ νῦν τὴν καταλλαγὴν ἐλάβομεν.	1:21-22 Καὶ ὑμᾶς ποτε ὄντας ἀπηλλοτριωμένους καὶ ἐχθροὺς τῇ διανοίᾳ ἐν τοῖς ἔργοις τοῖς πονηροῖς, νυνὶ δὲ ἀποκατήλλαξεν ἐν τῷ σώματι τῆς σαρκὸς αὐτοῦ **διὰ τοῦ θανάτου** ...
6:4 συνετάφημεν οὖν **αὐτῷ** διὰ τοῦ βαπτίσματος εἰς τὸν θάνατον, ἵνα ὥσπερ ἠγέρθη Χριστὸς **ἐκ νεκρῶν** ...	2:12 συνταφέντες **αὐτῷ** ἐν τῷ βαπτισμῷ, ἐν ᾧ καὶ συνηγέρθητε διὰ τῆς πίστεως τῆς ἐνεργείας τοῦ θεοῦ τοῦ ἐγείραντος αὐτὸν **ἐκ νεκρῶν**·
6:6 ... ὁ παλαιὸς ἡμῶν ἄνθρωπος συνεσταυρώθη ...	3:9 ... ἀπεκδυσάμενοι τὸν παλαιὸν ἄνθρωπον ...
6:8 εἰ δὲ ἀπεθάνομεν **σὺν Χριστῷ**, πιστεύομεν ὅτι καὶ συζήσομεν αὐτῷ	2:20 **Εἰ** ἀπεθάνετε **σὺν Χριστῷ** ἀπὸ τῶν στοιχείων τοῦ κόσμου, τί ὡς ζῶντες ἐν κόσμῳ δογματίζεσθε;
6:11 ... **καὶ** ὑμεῖς λογίζεσθε ἑαυτοὺς [εἶναι] **νεκροὺς** μὲν τῇ ἁμαρτίᾳ ζῶντας δὲ τῷ θεῷ ...	2:13 **καὶ** ὑμᾶς **νεκροὺς** ὄντας [ἐν] τοῖς παραπτώμασιν καὶ τῇ ἀκροβυστίᾳ τῆς σαρκὸς ὑμῶν, συνεζωοποίησεν ὑμᾶς σὺν αὐτῷ

8:11 ... τὸ πνεῦμα **τοῦ ἐγείραντος** τὸν Ἰησοῦν **ἐκ νεκρῶν** ... ζῳοποιήσει ...	2:12-13 ... **τοῦ ἐγείραντος** αὐτὸν **ἐκ νεκρῶν**˙ ... συνεζωοποίησεν
8:29 ... τῆς εἰκόνος **τοῦ** υἱοῦ αὐτοῦ, εἰς τὸ εἶναι αὐτὸν πρωτότοκον ἐν πολλοῖς ἀδελφοῖς˙	1:15 ὅς ἐστιν εἰκὼν **τοῦ** θεοῦ τοῦ ἀοράτου, πρωτότοκος πάσης κτίσεως,
8:32-33 ... πῶς οὐχὶ καὶ **σὺν αὐτῷ** τὰ **πάντα ἡμῖν** χαρίσεται; τίς ἐγκαλέσει κατὰ ἐκλεκτῶν **θεοῦ**;	2:13 ... συνεζωοποίησεν ὑμᾶς **σὺν αὐτῷ**, χαρισάμενος **ἡμῖν πάντα** τὰ παραπτώματα.
	3:12-13 Ἐνδύσασθε οὖν, ὡς ἐκλεκτοὶ τοῦ **θεοῦ** ... καθὼς καὶ ὁ κύριος ἐχαρίσατο ὑμῖν
8:34 ... **Χριστὸς** ... ὃς καί **ἐστιν ἐν δεξιᾷ τοῦ θεοῦ**	3:1 ... ὁ **Χριστός ἐστιν ἐν δεξιᾷ τοῦ θεοῦ** καθήμενος˙
9:22-24 εἰ δὲ θέλων **ὁ θεὸς** ... ἵνα γνωρίσῃ τὸν πλοῦτον **τῆς δόξης** αὐτοῦ ... καὶ ἐξ ἐθνῶν	1:27 οἷς ἠθέλησεν **ὁ θεὸς** γνωρίσαι τί τὸ πλοῦτος **τῆς δόξης** τοῦ μυστηρίου τούτου ἐν τοῖς ἔθνεσιν,
11:33 Ὦ βάθος πλούτου καὶ **σοφίας καὶ γνώσεως θεοῦ**˙	2:2-3 ... πλοῦτος τῆς πληροφορίας τῆς συνέσεως, εἰς ἐπίγνωσιν τοῦ μυστηρίου τοῦ **θεοῦ**, Χριστοῦ, ἐν ᾧ εἰσιν πάντες οἱ θησαυροὶ τῆς **σοφίας καὶ γνώσεως** ἀπόκρυφοι.
11:36 ὅτι ἐξ αὐτοῦ καὶ **δι᾿ αὐτοῦ καὶ εἰς αὐτὸν τὰ πάντα**˙	1:16 ... **τὰ πάντα δι᾿ αὐτοῦ καὶ εἰς αὐτὸν** ἔκτισται˙
13:12b-14 ἀποθώμεθα **οὖν** τὰ ἔργα τοῦ σκότους ... ὡς ἐν ἡμέρᾳ εὐσχημόνως περιπατήσωμεν, μὴ κώμοις καὶ μέθαις, ... ἀλλὰ ἐνδύσασθε τὸν κύριον Ἰησοῦν Χριστὸν καὶ τῆς σαρκὸς πρόνοιαν μὴ ποιεῖσθε εἰς ἐπιθυμίας.	3:5-10 Νεκρώσατε **οὖν** τὰ μέλη τὰ ἐπὶ τῆς γῆς, ... ἐπιθυμίαν ... ἐν οἷς καὶ ὑμεῖς περιεπατήσατέ ποτε ... νυνὶ δὲ ἀπόθεσθε ... καὶ ἐνδυσάμενοι τὸν νέον ...
14:17 οὐ γάρ ἐστιν ἡ βασιλεία τοῦ θεοῦ βρῶσις **καὶ** πόσις ...	2:16 Μὴ οὖν τις ὑμᾶς κρινέτο ἐν βρώσει **καὶ** ἐν πόσει ...

Table Rom C

Col	Rom
1:15-16 ὅς ἐστιν εἰκὼν **τοῦ** θεοῦ τοῦ ἀοράτου, πρωτότοκος πάσης **κτίσεως**, ὅτι ἐν αὐτῷ ἐκτίσθη τὰ πάντα ἐν τοῖς οὐρανοῖς καὶ ἐπὶ τῆς γῆς, τὰ ὁρατὰ καὶ **τὰ ἀόρατα**, εἴτε θρόνοι εἴτε κυριότητες εἴτε ἀρχαὶ εἴτε ἐξουσίαι· **τὰ πάντα δι᾽ αὐτοῦ καὶ εἰς αὐτὸν** ἔκτισται·	**8:29** ... τῆς εἰκόνος **τοῦ** υἱοῦ αὐτοῦ, εἰς τὸ εἶναι αὐτὸν πρωτότοκον ἐν πολλοῖς ἀδελφοῖς· **1:20 τὰ** γὰρ **ἀόρατα** αὐτοῦ ἀπὸ **κτίσεως** κόσμου ... **11:36** ὅτι ἐξ αὐτοῦ καὶ **δι᾽ αὐτοῦ καὶ εἰς αὐτὸν τὰ πάντα**.
1:21-22 Καὶ ὑμᾶς ποτε ὄντας ἀπηλλοτριωμένους καὶ ἐχθροὺς τῇ διανοίᾳ ἐν τοῖς ἔργοις τοῖς πονηροῖς, νυνὶ δὲ ἀποκατήλλαξεν ἐν τῷ σώματι τῆς σαρκὸς αὐτοῦ **διὰ τοῦ θανάτου** ...	**5:10-11** εἰ γὰρ ἐχθροὶ ὄντες κατηλλάγημεν τῷ θεῷ **διὰ τοῦ θανάτου** τοῦ υἱοῦ αὐτοῦ· ... Ἰησοῦ Χριστοῦ δι᾽ οὗ νῦν τὴν καταλλαγὴν ἐλάβομεν.
1:27 οἷς ἠθέλησεν **ὁ θεὸς** γνωρίσαι τί τὸ πλοῦτος **τῆς δόξης** τοῦ μυστηρίου τούτου ἐν τοῖς ἔθνεσιν	**9:22-24** εἰ δὲ θέλων **ὁ θεὸς** ... ἵνα γνωρίσῃ τὸν πλοῦτον **τῆς δόξης** αὐτοῦ ... καὶ ἐξ ἐθνῶν
2:2-3 ... πλοῦτος τῆς πληροφορίας τῆς συνέσεως, εἰς ἐπίγνωσιν τοῦ μυστηρίου τοῦ **θεοῦ**, Χριστοῦ, ἐν ᾧ εἰσιν πάντες οἱ θησαυροὶ τῆς **σοφίας καὶ γνώσεως** ἀπόκρυφοι.	**11:33** Ὦ βάθος πλούτου καὶ **σοφίας καὶ γνώσεως θεοῦ**·
2:12-13 συνταφέντες **αὐτῷ** ἐν τῷ βαπτισμῷ, ἐν ᾧ **καὶ** συνηγέρθητε **διὰ** τῆς πίστεως τῆς ἐνεργείας τοῦ **θεοῦ τοῦ ἐγείραντος** αὐτὸν **ἐκ νεκρῶν**· **καὶ** ὑμᾶς **νεκροὺς** ὄντας [ἐν] τοῖς παραπτώμασιν καὶ τῇ ἀκροβυστίᾳ τῆς σαρκὸς ὑμῶν, συνεζωοποίησεν ὑμᾶς **σὺν αὐτῷ**, χαρισάμενος **ἡμῖν πάντα τὰ παραπτώματα**.	**6:4** συνετάφημεν οὖν **αὐτῷ** διὰ τοῦ βαπτίσματος εἰς τὸν θάνατον, ἵνα ὥσπερ ἠγέρθη Χριστὸς **ἐκ νεκρῶν** ... **4:24-25** ... τοῖς πιστεύουσιν ἐπὶ τὸν ἐγείραντα Ἰησοῦν τὸν κύριον ἡμῶν **ἐκ νεκρῶν**, ὃς παρεδόθη διὰ **τὰ παραπτώματα** ἡμῶν ... **8:11** ... τὸ πνεῦμα **τοῦ ἐγείραντος** τὸν Ἰησοῦν **ἐκ νεκρῶν** ... ζωοποιήσει ... **6:11** ... **καὶ** ὑμεῖς λογίζεσθε ἑαυτοὺς [εἶναι] **νεκροὺς** μὲν τῇ ἁμαρτίᾳ ζῶντας δὲ τῷ θεῷ **8:32** ... **σὺν αὐτῷ** τὰ **πάντα ἡμῖν** χαρίσεται;

2:16 Μὴ οὖν τις ὑμᾶς κρινέτο ἐν βρώσει **καὶ** ἐν πόσει ...	**14:17** οὐ γάρ ἐστιν ἡ βασιλεία τοῦ θεοῦ βρῶσις **καὶ** πόσις ...
2:20 **Εἰ** ἀπεθάνετε **σὺν Χριστῷ** ἀπὸ τῶν στοιχείων τοῦ κόσμου, τί ὡς ζῶντες ἐν κόσμῳ δογματίζεσθε;	**6:8 εἰ** δὲ ἀπεθάνομεν **σὺν Χριστῷ**, πιστεύομεν ὅτι καὶ συζήσομεν αὐτῷ
3:1 ... ὁ Χριστός **ἐστιν ἐν δεξιᾷ τοῦ θεοῦ** καθήμενος·	**8:34** ... **Χριστός** ... ὅς καί **ἐστιν ἐν δεξιᾷ τοῦ θεοῦ**
3:5-10 Νεκρώσατε **οὖν** τὰ μέλη τὰ ἐπὶ τῆς γῆς, ... ἐπιθυμίαν ... ἐν οἷς καὶ ὑμεῖς περιεπατήσατέ ποτε ... νυνὶ δὲ ἀπόθεσθε ... καὶ ἐνδυσάμενοι τὸν νέον ...	**13:12b-14** ἀποθώμεθα **οὖν** τὰ ἔργα τοῦ σκότους ... ὡς ἐν ἡμέρᾳ εὐσχημόνως περιπατήσωμεν, μὴ κώμοις καὶ μέθαις, ... ἀλλὰ ἐνδύσασθε τὸν κύριον Ἰησοῦν Χριστὸν καὶ τῆς σαρκὸς πρόνοιαν μὴ ποιεῖσθε εἰς ἐπιθυμίας.
3:9 ... ἀπεκδυσάμενοι τὸν παλαιὸν ἄνθρωπον ...	**6:6** ... ὁ παλαιὸς ἡμῶν ἄνθρωπος συνεσταυρώθη
3:12-13 ... ὡς ἐκλεκτοὶ τοῦ **θεοῦ** ... κύριος ἐχαρίσατο ὑμῖν	**8:32-33** ... τὰ πάντα ἡμῖν χαρίσεται; τίς ἐγκαλέσει κατὰ ἐκλεκτῶν **θεοῦ**;
3:23-25 ... ἐκ ψυχῆς ἐργάζεσθε ... οὐκ **ἔστιν προσωπολημψία**.	**2:9-11** θλῖψις ... ἐπὶ πᾶσαν ψυχὴν ἀνθρώπου τοῦ κατεργαζομένου τὸ κακόν, ... οὐ γάρ **ἐστιν προσωπολημψία** παρὰ τῷ θεῷ.

In spite of the strong evidence for literary dependence between Col and Rom, five resemblances indicating a probable dependence, it has to be noted that texts typical of a letter do not occur among the resemblances: the beginning and conclusion are missing as well as parts where persons are introduced. Instead, the texts deal with teaching, most of all Christology. The finding is compatible with the assumption that, above all, Rom was read aloud and studied again and again among congregations (see p. 23). A/Col might have routinely heard some parts of Rom read aloud and therefore these verses are so familiar to A/Col that he recalls them very well. It cannot be concluded that A/Col was unacquainted with other parts of the letter. It is possible that he had read the whole text of Rom but used only some parts of it.

9.5. 1. Thessalonians

The resemblances between 1 Thess and Col are illustrated in two tables (1 Thess A and 1 Thess B, p. 347). Since Col follows 1 Thess in order, it is not necessary to present the texts in the two tables: in Table 1 Thess B, the agreements can be seen both from the standpoint of 1 Thess and from that of Col.

Table 1 Thess A

1 Thess	Col	1 Thess	Col
1: **2-3**	1:3-5a	4: 1	1:10
6	1:11b	1	2:6-7
10	3:6	3, 5	3:5
2: **12-13**	1:9-10	**12**	4:5
4	3:22-23	5: 25	4:3
9	4:18	27	4:16

Col and 1 Thess have two agreements indicating a probable literary dependence and three resemblances pointing to a possible one. Apart from 1 Thess 1:2-3, which is part of the thanksgiving in the beginning of the letter, all the texts utilized from 1 Thess are exhortations. It was noted that Philem 4-5 is the primary model for the thanksgiving in Col 1:3-8, not 1 Thess 1:2-3. However, the use of the triad faith–love–hope, and in that order, suggests A/Col's acquaintance with 1 Thess 1:2-3 (see pp. 63-64). It is remarkable that 1 Thess is the only letter Col follows in order. When A/Col's method of using the texts is examined more closely, it can be seen that an imitation of 1 Thess usually starts a new passage. The thanksgiving begins in Col 1:3, the intercession in Col 1:9, the warning about the persons who are trying to lead the community astray in Col 2:6, and the catalog of vices in Col 3:5. The only exception is Col 4:5 which occurs in the middle of the exhortations.

Twice, the contexts of the agreements have the same theme. While in 1 Thess 2:12, it is stated that God "calls you into his own kingdom and glory", the kingdom of the Son is described in Col 1:12-14. So it seems that when A/Col in Col 1:9-10 imitates the exhortation from 1 Thess 2:12-13, he also gets the theme for the following passage. In addition, while the exhortation to "behave properly toward outsiders" is followed by the section which discusses problems associated with the parousia in 1 Thess 4:12, in Col 4:5 the counsel to act "wisely toward outsiders" continues with the advice to "making the most of the time". The exact meaning of the words is unclear (see pp. 195-196) but, in any case, the problems concerning the time are referred to in Col 4:5 just as they are in the passage beginning in 1 Thess 4:13. It seems thus that when A/Col imitates the exhortation to behave properly toward outsiders from 1 Thess he also picks up the theme which follows the admonition.

Table 1 Thess B

1 Thess	Col
1:2-3 **Εὐχαριστοῦμεν τῷ θεῷ πάντοτε περὶ** πάντων **ὑμῶν** μνείαν ποιούμενοι ἐπὶ τῶν προσευχῶν ἡμῶν, ἀδιαλείπτως μνημονεύοντες ὑμῶν τοῦ ἔρ-γου τῆς πίστεως καὶ τοῦ κόπου τῆς ἀγάπης καὶ τῆς ὑπομονῆς τῆς ἐλπίδος **τοῦ κυρίου ἡμῶν Ἰησοῦ Χριστοῦ** ἔμπροσθεν τοῦ θεοῦ καὶ πατρὸς ἡμῶν	1:3-5a **Εὐχαριστοῦμεν τῷ θεῷ** πατρὶ **τοῦ κυρίου ἡμῶν Ἰησοῦ Χριστοῦ πάντοτε περὶ ὑμῶν** προσευχόμενοι, ἀκούσαντες τὴν πίστιν ὑμῶν ἐν Χριστῷ Ἰησοῦ καὶ τὴν ἀγάπην ... διὰ τὴν ἐλπίδα ...
2:12-13 ... εἰς τὸ περιπατεῖν ὑμᾶς **ἀξίως** τοῦ θεοῦ ... Καὶ **διὰ τοῦτο καὶ ἡμεῖς** εὐχαριστοῦμεν τῷ θεῷ ...	1:9-10 **Διὰ τοῦτο καὶ ἡμεῖς**, ... περιπατῆσαι **ἀξίως τοῦ** κυρίου εἰς πᾶσαν ἀρεσκείαν,
4:1 ... παρακαλοῦμεν ἐν κυρίῳ Ἰησοῦ, ἵνα καθὼς **παρελάβετε** παρ᾽ ἡμῶν τὸ πῶς δεῖ ὑμᾶς περιπατεῖν καὶ ἀρέσκειν θεῷ, καθὼς καὶ **περιπατεῖτε**, ἵνα περισσεύητε μᾶλλον.	2:6-7 Ὡς οὖν **παρελάβετε** τὸν Χριστὸν Ἰησοῦν τὸν κύριον, ἐν αὐτῷ **περιπατεῖτε**, ἐρριζω-μένοι καὶ ἐποικοδομούμενοι ἐν αὐτῷ καὶ βεβαιούμενοι τῇ πίστει καθὼς ἐδιδάχθητε, περισσεύοντες ἐν εὐχαριστίᾳ.
4:3, 5 ... ἀπὸ τῆς πορνείας ... μὴ ἐν πάθει ἐπιθυμίας ...	3:5 ... πορνείαν ἀκαθαρσίαν πάθος ἐπιθυμίαν κακήν ...
4:12 ἵνα περιπατῆτε εὐσχημόνως **πρὸς τοὺς ἔξω** ...	4:5 Ἐν σοφίᾳ περιπατεῖτε **πρὸς τοὺς ἔξω** ...

The agreements between Col and 1 Thess suggest that 1 Thess was available to A/Col during the writing of Col. Often, when a new parenetical section begins, he imitates Paul's style from 1 Thess. It is surprising that he does not otherwise show any interest in imitating 1 Thess. He may, however, intentionally ignore the teachings of 1 Thess because, for example, problems associated with parousia, which are central in 1 Thess, are no longer relevant for him. The way in which Rom 6:4 is used in Col 2:12-13 shows that his eschatology is different (see pp. 136-137).

9.6. Philippians

Table Phil A

Phil		Col
1:	1	1:2
	1	4:12
	4	1:11b
	5	1:5b-6
	7	4:18
	12	4:7-8
	13, 14, 17	4:18
	21	3:4
	30	2:1
2:	**1-3**	3:12-13
	13	1:29
	30	1:24
3:	**2-3**	2:11
	14	2:18
	14, **19, 21**	3:1-4
	21	1:29
4:	**7**	3:15
	13	1:29
	18	3:20

Between Col and Phil there are two agreements indicating a probable literary dependence and four pointing to a possible one, which occur here and there in Phil (see Table Phil A). From the standpoint of Col, the situation is quite similar: only two of the agreements are located in the catalog of virtues (Col 3:12-13 // Phil 2:1-3, Col 3:15 // Phil 4:7) (see Table Phil C). The number of agreements is not great but compared to the length of Phil, it is more remarkable than those in Rom and 1 Cor (see pp. 222-223).

Table Phil B

Phil	Col
1:12 Γινώσκειν δὲ ὑμᾶς βούλομαι, ἀδελφοί, ὅτι **τὰ κατ' ἐμέ** ...	4:7-8 **Τὰ κατ' ἐμὲ** πάντα γνωρίσει ὑμῖν Τύχικος ὁ ἀγαπητὸς ἀδελφός ... ἵνα γνῶτε τὰ περὶ ἡμῶν ...
2:1-3 ... εἴ τις σπλάγχνα καὶ οἰκτιρμοί, ... τῇ ταπεινοφροσύνῃ ἀλλήλους ἡγούμανοι ὑπερέχοντας ἑαυτῶν	3:12-13 ... σπλάγχνα οἰκτιρμοῦ χρηστότητα ταπεινοφροσύνην πραΰτητα μακροθυμίαν, ἀνεχόμενοι ἀλλήλων ...
2:30 ὅτι διὰ τὸ ἔργον **Χριστοῦ** μέχρι θανάτου ἤγγισεν ... ἵνα ἀναπληρώσῃ τὸ **ὑμῶν** ὑστέρημα τῆς πρός με λειτουργίας.	1:24 ... ἐν τοῖς παθήμασιν ὑπὲρ **ὑμῶν** καὶ ἀνταναπληρῶ τὰ ὑστερήματα τῶν θλίψεων τοῦ **Χριστοῦ** ...
3:2-3 Βλέπετε τοὺς κύνας, ... ἡμεῖς γάρ ἐσμεν ἡ **περιτομή**, οἱ πνεύματι θεοῦ λατρεύοντες καὶ καυχώμενοι **ἐν** Χριστῷ 'Ιησοῦ καὶ οὐκ ἐν σαρκὶ πεποιθότες	2:8, 11 **Βλέπετε** μή τις ὑμᾶς ἔσται ὁ συλαγωγῶν ... 'Εν ᾧ καὶ περιετμήθητε **περιτομῇ** ἀχειροποιήτῳ ἐν τῇ ἀπεκδύσει τοῦ σώματος τῆς σαρκός, **ἐν** τῇ **περιτομῇ** τοῦ Χριστοῦ
3:14, 19-21 ... τὸ βραβεῖον τῆς **ἄνω** κλήσεως ... οἱ **τὰ** ἐπίγεια φρονοῦντες. ... 'Ιησοῦν Χριστόν, ὃς μετασχηματίσει τὸ σῶμα τῆς ταπεινώσεως ἡμῶν σύμμορφον τῷ σώματι τῆς δόξης αὐτοῦ ...	3:1-4 ... τὰ **ἄνω** ζητεῖτε, ... τὰ **ἄνω** φρονεῖτε, μὴ **τὰ** ἐπὶ τῆς γῆς. ... ὅταν ὁ Χριστὸς φανερωθῇ, ... τότε καὶ ὑμεῖς σὺν αὐτῷ φανερωθήσεσθε ἐν δόξῃ.
4:7 καὶ ἡ εἰρήνη τοῦ θεοῦ ... φρουρήσει τὰς καρδίας **ὑμῶν** ...	3:15 **καὶ ἡ εἰρήνη τοῦ** Χριστοῦ βραβευέτω ἐν ταῖς καρδίαις **ὑμῶν**

On two occasions when Paul's situation is described in Col, Phil is used as a model. The description of the sufferings of Paul in Col 1:24 resembles Phil 2:30, which tells how Epaphroditus came close to death for the work of Christ. In addition, both Col 4:7-8 and Phil 1:12 use the same unusual expression τὰ κατ' ἐμέ when referring to the news about Paul. These resemblances, which belong to the frames of the letters, indicate that A/Col was familiar with Phil. However, the resemblances are so few that Phil cannot be a primary model for Col in the same way as Philem, as Kiley contends (see pp. 20). Rather it seems that when A/Col composed his text, every now and then the formulations from Phil came to his mind. Sometimes, especially when the description of the sufferings of Paul in Col 1:24 were modelled on those of Epaphroditus in Phil 2:30, the imitation may have

Table Phil C

Col	Phil
1:24 ... ἐν τοῖς παθήμασιν ὑπὲρ **ὑμῶν** καὶ ἀνταναπληρῶ τὰ ὑστερήματα τῶν θλίψεων τοῦ **Χριστοῦ** ...	**2:30** ὅτι διὰ τὸ ἔργον **Χριστοῦ** μέχρι θανάτου ἤγγισεν ... ἵνα ἀναπληρώσῃ τὸ **ὑμῶν** ὑστέρημα τῆς πρός με λειτουργίας.
2:8, 11 **Βλέπετε** μή τις ὑμᾶς ἔσται ὁ συλαγωγῶν ... Ἐν ᾧ καὶ περιετμήθητε **περιτομῇ** ἀχειροποιήτῳ ἐν τῇ ἀπεκδύσει τοῦ σώματος τῆς σαρκός, **ἐν** τῇ **περιτομή** τοῦ Χριστοῦ	**3:2-3 Βλέπετε** τοὺς κύνας, ... ἡμεῖς γάρ ἐσμεν ἡ **περιτομή**, οἱ πνεύματι θεοῦ λατρεύοντες καὶ καυχώμενοι **ἐν** Χριστῷ Ἰησοῦ καὶ οὐκ ἐν σαρκὶ πεποιθότες
3:1-4 ... τὰ **ἄνω** ζητεῖτε, ... τὰ **ἄνω** φρονεῖτε, μὴ **τὰ** ἐπὶ τῆς γῆς. ... ὅταν ὁ Χριστὸς φανερωθῇ, ... τότε καὶ ὑμεῖς σὺν αὐτῷ φανερωθήσεσθε ἐν δόξῃ.	**3:14, 19-21** ... τὸ βραβεῖον τῆς **ἄνω** κλήσεως ... οἱ **τὰ** ἐπίγεια φρονοῦντες. ... Ἰησοῦν Χριστόν, ὃς μετασχηματίσει τὸ σῶμα τῆς ταπεινώσεως ἡμῶν σύμμορφον τῷ σώματι τῆς δόξης αὐτοῦ ...
3:12-13 ... σπλάγχνα οἰκτιρμοῦ χρηστότητα ταπεινοφροσύνην πραΰτητα μακροθυμίαν, ἀνεχόμενοι ἀλλήλων ...	**2:1-3** ... εἴ τις σπλάγχνα καὶ οἰκτιρμοί, ... τῇ ταπεινοφροσύνῃ ἀλλήλους ἡγούμανοι ὑπερέχοντας ἑαυτῶν
3:15 **καὶ ἡ εἰρήνη τοῦ** Χριστοῦ βραβευέτω ἐν ταῖς καρδίαις **ὑμῶν**	**4:7 καὶ ἡ εἰρήνη τοῦ** θεοῦ ... φρουρήσει τὰς καρδίας **ὑμῶν** ...
4:7-8 **Τὰ κατ᾽ ἐμὲ** πάντα γνωρίσει ὑμῖν Τύχικος ὁ ἀγαπητὸς ἀδελφός ... ἵνα γνῶτε τὰ περὶ ἡμῶν ...	**1:12** Γινώσκειν δὲ ὑμᾶς βούλομαι, ἀδελφοί, ὅτι **τὰ κατ᾽ ἐμέ** ...

been due to intentional recalling of this text from Phil but it is equally possible that it happened unintentionally when A/Col mimicked Pauline style.

9.7. 2. Corinthians

The following table illustrates the resemblances between 2 Cor and Col.

Table 2 Cor A

2 Cor		Col	2 Cor		Col
1:	1-3	1:1-3	6:	7	1:5b
	5	1:24		**14-15, 18**	1:12-13
				17	2:21
2:	9	3:20			
	12	4:3	7:	9	1:24
	14	2:15		15	4:10
3:	6	1:12-13	9:	8	1:10
4:	**4**	1:15	11:	2	1:22
	15	2:7		9	1:6
				23	1:7
5:	**1-3**	2:11			
	10-11	3:22-25	13:	5	1:27
	18	1:20			

The resemblances between Col and 2 Cor are not clustered in any particular part of Col but appear all over the text (see the Appendix). From the standpoint of 2 Cor, the situation is different. The agreements meeting the criteria for a possible or a probable literary dependence are clearly centered in the first half of the letter. Since most scholars now agree that 2 Cor is a composite of parts of at least two originally independent letters,[962] it is reasonable to think that only some parts of the letter are familiar to A/Col.[963]

---

[962] For the question of literary composition of 2 Cor, see Furnish 1984, 30 ss.; L. Aejmelaeus 1987b, 1-108; 2000, 19-26; Betz 1992, 1148-1149.

[963] This assumption is problematic in that there are no manuscripts including only parts of 2 Cor. There is thus no proof that parts of 2 Cor were circulating among congregations independently. Nevertheless, it is possible that some copies of only parts were disseminated.

Table 2 Cor B

2 Cor	Col
1:1-3 Παῦλος ἀπόστολος Χριστοῦ Ἰησοῦ διὰ θελήματος θεοῦ καὶ Τιμόθεος ὁ ἀδελφὸς τῇ ἐκκλησίᾳ τοῦ θεοῦ τῇ οὔσῃ ἐν Κορίνθῳ σὺν **τοῖς ἁγίοις** ... **χάρις ὑμῖν καὶ εἰρήνη ἀπὸ θεοῦ πατρὸς ἡμῶν** καὶ κυρίου Ἰησοῦ Χριστοῦ. Εὐλογητὸς ὁ θεὸς καὶ πατὴρ **τοῦ κυρίου ἡμῶν Ἰησοῦ Χριστοῦ**	1:1-3 **Παῦλος ἀπόστολος Χριστοῦ Ἰησοῦ διὰ θελήματος θεοῦ καὶ Τιμόθεος ὁ ἀδελφὸς τοῖς** ἐν Κολοσσαῖς **ἁγίοις** καὶ πιστοῖς ἀδελφοῖς ἐν Χριστῷ, **χάρις ὑμῖν καὶ εἰρήνη ἀπὸ θεοῦ πατρὸς ἡμῶν**. Εὐχαριστοῦμεν τῷ θεῷ πατρὶ **τοῦ κυρίου ἡμῶν Ἰησοῦ Χριστοῦ** ...
2:12 ... εἰς τὸ εὐαγγέλιον **τοῦ Χριστοῦ** καὶ θύρας μοι ἀνεῳγμένης ἐν κυρίῳ	4:3 ... ἵνα ὁ θεὸς ἀνοίξῃ ἡμῖν θύραν τοῦ λόγου λαλῆσαι τὸ μυστήριον **τοῦ Χριστοῦ**
4:4 ... **ὅς ἐστιν εἰκὼν** τοῦ θεοῦ.	1:15 **ὅς ἐστιν εἰκὼν τοῦ θεοῦ** ...
5:1-3 ... οἰκίαν ἀχειροποίητον αἰώνιον ἐν τοῖς οὐρανοῖς. ... καὶ ἐκδυσάμενοι ...	2:11 ... περιτομῇ ἀχειροποιήτῳ ἐν τῇ ἀπεκδύσει τοῦ σώματος τῆς σαρκός, ἐν τῇ περιτομῇ τοῦ Χριστοῦ
5:10-11 ... ἵνα κομίσηται ἕκαστος τὰ διὰ τοῦ σώματος πρὸς ἃ ἔπραξεν ... **Εἰδότες** οὖν τὸν φόβον τοῦ κυρίου ...	3:22-25 ... ἀλλ᾽ ἐν ἁπλότητι καρδίας φοβούμενοι τὸν κύριον. ... **εἰδότες** ὅτι ἀπὸ κυρίου ... ὁ γὰρ ἀδικῶν κομίσεται ὃ ἠδίκησεν
6:14-15,18 ... ἢ τίς κοινωνία **φωτὶ** πρὸς σκότος; τίς δὲ συμφώνησις Χριστοῦ πρὸς Βελιάρ, ἢ τίς μερὶς πιστῷ μετὰ ἀπίστου; ... καὶ ἔσομαι ὑμῖν εἰς πατέρα καὶ ὑμεῖς ἔσεσθέ μοι εἰς υἱοὺς καὶ θυγατέρας	1:12-13 εὐχαριστοῦντες τῷ πατρὶ τῷ ἱκανώσαντι ὑμᾶς εἰς τὴν μερίδα τοῦ κλήρου τῶν ἁγίων ἐν τῷ **φωτί**· ὃς ἐρρύσατο ἡμᾶς ἐκ τῆς ἐξουσίας τοῦ σκότους καὶ μετέστησεν εἰς τὴν βασιλείαν τοῦ υἱοῦ ...
11:23 διάκονοι **Χριστοῦ** εἰσιν;	1:7 ... ὅς ἐστιν πιστὸς ὑπὲρ ὑμῶν διάκονος τοῦ **Χριστοῦ**

Table 2 Cor C

Col	2 Cor
1:1-3 **Παῦλος ἀπόστολος Χριστοῦ ᾿Ιησοῦ διὰ θελήματος θεοῦ καὶ Τιμόθεος ὁ ἀδελφὸς τοῖς** ἐν Κολοσσαῖς **ἁγίοις** καὶ πιστοῖς ἀδελφοῖς ἐν Χριστῷ, **χάρις ὑμῖν καὶ εἰρήνη ἀπὸ θεοῦ πατρὸς ἡμῶν**. Εὐχαριστοῦμεν τῷ θεῷ πατρὶ **τοῦ κυρίου ἡμῶν ᾿Ιησοῦ Χριστοῦ** ...	1:1-3 **Παῦλος ἀπόστολος Χριστοῦ ᾿Ιησοῦ διὰ θελήματος θεοῦ καὶ Τιμόθεος ὁ ἀδελφὸς** τῇ ἐκκλησίᾳ τοῦ θεοῦ τῇ οὔσῃ ἐν Κορίνθῳ σὺν **τοῖς ἁγίοις** ... **χάρις ὑμῖν καὶ εἰρήνη ἀπὸ θεοῦ πατρὸς ἡμῶν** καὶ κυρίου ᾿Ιησοῦ Χριστοῦ. Εὐλογητὸς ὁ θεὸς καὶ πατὴρ **τοῦ κυρίου ἡμῶν ᾿Ιησοῦ Χριστοῦ**
1:7 ... ὅς ἐστιν πιστὸς ὑπὲρ ὑμῶν διάκονος τοῦ **Χριστοῦ**	**11:23** διάκονοι **Χριστοῦ** εἰσιν;
1:12-13 εὐχαριστοῦντες τῷ πατρὶ τῷ ἱκανώσαντι ὑμᾶς εἰς τὴν μερίδα τοῦ κλήρου τῶν ἁγίων ἐν τῷ **φωτί**· ὃς ἐρρύσατο ἡμᾶς ἐκ τῆς ἐξουσίας τοῦ σκότους καὶ μετέστησεν εἰς τὴν βασιλείαν τοῦ υἱοῦ ...	**6:14-15,18** ... ἢ τίς κοινωνία **φωτὶ** πρὸς σκότος; τίς δὲ συμφώνησις Χριστοῦ πρὸς Βελιάρ, ἢ τίς μερὶς πιστῷ μετὰ ἀπίστου; ... καὶ ἔσομαι ὑμῖν εἰς πατέρα καὶ ὑμεῖς ἔσεσθέ μοι εἰς υἱοὺς καὶ θυγατέρας
1:15 **ὅς ἐστιν εἰκὼν τοῦ θεοῦ** ...	**4:4** ... **ὅς ἐστιν εἰκὼν τοῦ θεοῦ**.
2:11 ... περιτομῇ ἀχειροποιήτῳ ἐν τῇ ἀπεκδύσει τοῦ σώματος τῆς σαρκός, ἐν τῇ περιτομῇ τοῦ Χριστοῦ	**5:1-3** ... οἰκίαν ἀχειροποίητον αἰώνιον ἐν τοῖς οὐρανοῖς. ... καὶ ἐκδυσάμενοι ...
3:22-25 ... ἀλλ᾽ ἐν ἁπλότητι καρδίας φοβούμενοι τὸν κύριον. ... **εἰδότες** ὅτι ἀπὸ κυρίου ... ὁ γὰρ ἀδικῶν κομίσεται ὃ ἠδίκησεν	**5:10-11** ... ἵνα κομίσηται ἕκαστος τὰ διὰ τοῦ σώματος πρὸς ἃ ἔπραξεν ... **Εἰδότες** οὖν τὸν φόβον τοῦ κυρίου ...
4:3 ... ἵνα ὁ θεὸς ἀνοίξῃ ἡμῖν θύραν τοῦ λόγου λαλῆσαι τὸ μυστήριον **τοῦ Χριστοῦ**	**2:12** ... εἰς τὸ εὐαγγέλιον **τοῦ Χριστοῦ** καὶ θύρας μοι ἀνεῳγμένης ἐν κυρίῳ

The two-letter hypothesis, which takes 2 Cor as consisting of parts from two originally separate letters 2 Cor 1-9 and 2 Cor 10-13, was first proposed by Semler in 1776 and still today generally accepted. Since there is only one verbal agreement meeting the criteria for a possible literary dependence between Col and 2 Cor 10-13, the evidence for A/Col's acquaintance with this part of the letter is small. In addition, the verbal agreement between Col 1:7 and 2 Cor 11:23, the use of three words in common, Χριστός, διάκονος, εἰμι, which are very normal in ECL, is one of the weakest of the agreements, classified as just meeting the criteria for a possible literary dependence (see p. 72). Thus, there is not much evidence that A/Col was familiar with 2 Cor 10-13.[964]

Some theories have been suggested which regard 2 Cor 8 and 9 (which include an exhortation on the collection of alms) as an independent letter or two separate epistles. Since no resemblances between Col and 2 Cor 8 have been found and the one between Col 1:10 and 2 Cor 9:8 is only the use of a standard Christian expression (see pp. 74-75), there is no evidence that A/Col was acquainted with 2 Cor 8 or 9.

Accordingly, the verbal agreements reveal A/Col's acquaintance with 2 Cor 1-7 only. The passage 2 Cor 6:14-7:1 has been noted to be a later interpolation (see p. 82-83). The significance of the one verbal agreement meeting the criteria for a possible literary dependence between Col and 2 Cor 6:14-7:1 is problematic to estimate. However, the agreement between 2 Cor 6:14-15, 18 and Col 1:11b-13 cannot be neglected. Though the occurrence of one resemblance is not much in numbers, it is remarkable compared to the length of the text, which includes only six verses. Since we do not know when the interpolation was connected to the text, it is possible that A/Col knew it as part of 2 Cor 1-7, but it is also possible that he knew 2 Cor 6:14-7:1 as an independent fragment.

2 Cor 1-7, excluding 2 Cor 6:14-7:1, includes two agreements with Col indicating a probable literary dependence and three possible ones. The fact that A/Col so many times reveals familiarity with the first part of 2 Cor makes it unlikely that he modifies 1 Cor 1:1-3 in Col 1:1-3. It is more probable that Col 1:1-3 is modelled on 2 Cor 1:1-3, which is its closest parallel (see pp. 62-63). It is surprising that the introduction of Col follows 2 Cor instead that of 1 Cor, which is otherwise often the model for the frame of Col. The reason may be that, like Philem, which is the primary model for Col, 2 Cor also mentions Timothy as a co-sender of the letter. Besides the resemblance between the introductions of Col and 2 Cor, the agreement between Col 4:3 and 2 Cor 2:12, the use of the same image of an open door to proclaim the good news of Christ also, belongs to the frames of the letters. This indicates that A/Col had not only heard some teachings read aloud but had read the letter.

The other texts utilized from 2 Cor deal with Christ. Col 1:15 takes verbatim the formulation ὅς ἐστιν εἰκὼν τοῦ θεοῦ from 2 Cor 4:4, which refers to Christ. Col 3:22-25 mentions the fear of the Lord denoting Christ and describes the judgment according to deeds like 2 Cor 5:10-11. In 2 Cor 5:1-3 the expressions "not made with hands" and "to be unclothed" are used in an eschatological context but A/Col changes the connection and uses the terms to describe the circumcision of Christ in Col 2:11.

---

[964] It is noteworthy that none of the parallels Mitton presents between Eph and 2 Cor 10-13 is remarkable either (see Mitton 1951, 284, 290, 292, 294, 296, 298, 300, 308, 310) which indicates that A/Eph was not acquainted with 2 Cor 10-13.

The tables in chap. 8 gave a wrong impression about the relationship between Col and 2 Cor. The frequency of the occurrences of verbal agreements was low because the numbers of the resemblances were compared to all of 2 Cor while they are clustered in 2 Cor 1-7 only. Though 2 Cor is not a primary model for Col, A/Col still clearly shows acquaintance with 2 Cor 1-7 and every now and then imitates Pauline style from it. Thus, he utilizes it in a similar manner as he does Phil.

9.8. The Septuagint

The following table illustrates all the verbal agreements between Col and the LXX. Though only one of them meets the criteria for a possible literary dependence (Col 2:2-3 // Prov 2:2-6) and none the criteria for a probable one, the resemblances indicate A/Col's acquaintance with several texts from the LXX.

Col	
1:9, 28 **ἐν πάσῃ σοφίᾳ**	Dan 1:4,17 **ἐν πάσῃ σοφίᾳ**
1:11 ἐν πάσῃ δυνάμει δυναμούμενοι κατὰ τὸ κράτος **τῆς δόξης αὐτοῦ** εἰς πᾶσαν ὑπομονὴν καὶ μακροθυμίαν.	1 Kings 26:25 (cf. 1 Macc 5:40) ... καὶ ποιῶν ποιήσεις καὶ δυνάμενος δυνήσει.
1:12-13 εὐχαριστοῦντες τῷ πατρὶ τῷ ἱκανώσαντι ὑμᾶς εἰς τὴν μερίδα τοῦ κλήρου τῶν ἁγίων ἐν τῷ φωτί· ... μετέστησεν εἰς τὴν βασιλείαν τοῦ υἱοῦ τῆς ἀγάπης αὐτοῦ	Isa 2:10, 19, 21 ἀπὸ **τῆς δόξης** τῆς ἰσχύος **αὐτοῦ** Wis 5:5 ... ἐν υἱοῖς θεοῦ καὶ ἐν ἁγίοις ὁ κλῆρος αὐτοῦ ἐστιν;
1:16-18 ὅτι ἐν αὐτῷ ἐκτίσθη τὰ πάντα ἐν τοῖς οὐρανοῖς καὶ ἐπὶ τῆς γῆς ... τὰ πάντα δι᾽ αὐτοῦ καὶ εἰς αὐτὸν ἔκτισται· καὶ αὐτός ἐστιν **πρὸ πάντων** ... ὅς ἐστιν ἀρχή	Prov 8:22-27 κύριος ἔκτισέν με ἀρχὴν ... πρὸ τοῦ τὴν γῆν ποιῆσαι ... **πρὸ** δὲ **πάντων** βουνῶν γεννᾷ με. ... ἡνίκα ἡτοίμαζεν τὸν οὐρανόν
1:19 ὅτι **ἐν αὐτῷ εὐδόκησεν** πᾶν τὸ πλήρωμα κατοικῆσαι	Ps 67:17 LXX ... ὃ **εὐδόκησεν** ὁ θεὸς κατοικεῖν **ἐν αὐτῷ**;
1:21 Καὶ ὑμᾶς ποτε ὄντας ἀπηλλοτριωμένους καὶ ἐχθροὺς τῇ διανοίᾳ **ἐν τοῖς** ἔργοις τοῖς πονηροῖς	Ezek 14:4-5 ... ἐγὼ κύριος ἀποκριθήσομαι αὐτῷ ἐν οἷς ἐνέχεται ἡ διάνοια αὐτοῦ, ... κατὰ τὰς καρδίας αὐτῶν τὰς ἀπηλλοτριωμένας ἀπ᾽ ἐμοῦ **ἐν τοῖς** ἐνθυμήμασιν αὐτῶν.

1:22 ἀποκατήλλαξεν **ἐν** τῷ **σώματι** τῆς **σαρκὸς αὐτοῦ** ...	Sir 23:17 ἄνθρωπος πόρνος **ἐν σώματι σαρκὸς αὐτοῦ**
2:2-3 ἵνα παρακληθῶσιν αἱ καρδίαι αὐτῶν συμβιβασθέντες ἐν ἀγάπῃ καὶ **εἰς** πᾶν πλοῦτος τῆς πληροφορίας τῆς συνέσεως, εἰς **ἐπίγνωσιν** τοῦ μυστηρίου τοῦ **Θεοῦ**, Χριστοῦ, ἐν ᾧ εἰσιν πάντες οἱ θησαυροὶ τῆς **σοφίας** καὶ γνώσεως ἀπόκρυφοι.	**Prov 2:2-6** ... παραβαλεῖς καρδίαν σου εἰς σύνεσιν, ... καὶ ὡς θησαυροὺς ἐξερευνήσῃς αὐτήν, τότε συνήσεις φόβον κυρίου καὶ **ἐπίγνωσιν θεοῦ** εὑρήσεις. ὅτι κύριος δίδωσιν σοφίαν, καὶ ἀπὸ προσώπου αὐτοῦ γνῶσις καὶ σύνεσις· Sir 1:25 Ἐν θησαυροῖς **σοφίας** παραβολαὶ ἐπιστήμης
2:4 ... ἵνα **μηδεὶς** ὑμᾶς παραλογίζηται ...	Bel 7 ... **μηδείς** σε παραλογιζέσθω·
2:7 ἐρριζωμένοι καὶ ἐποικοδομούμενοι ἐν αὐτῷ ...	Pss Sol 14:4, cf. Sir 24:12 ἡ φυτεία αὐτῶν ἐρριζωμένη εἰς τὸν αἰῶνα
2:16 ... **ἐν** μέρει ἑορτῆς ἢ νεομηνίας ἢ σαββάτων·	Ezek 45:17 ... **ἐν** ταῖς ἑορταῖς καὶ ἐν ταῖς νουμηνίαις καὶ ἐν τοῖς σαββάτοις
2:23 ... οὐκ ἐν τιμῇ τινι πρὸς **πλησμονὴν** τῆς σαρκός.	Hos 13:6 ... καὶ ἐνεπλήσθησαν εἰς **πλησμονήν**, καὶ ὑψώθησαν αἱ καρδίαι αὐτῶν·
3:10 ... **κατ' εἰκόνα** τοῦ κτίσαντος **αὐτόν**	Gen 1:27 ... **κατ' εἰκόνα** θεοῦ ἐποίησεν **αὐτόν**
3:19 Οἱ ἄνδρες, ἀγαπᾶτε τὰς γυναῖκας καὶ μὴ πικραίνεσθε πρὸς αὐτας	Eccl 9:9 ἰδὲ ζωὴν μετὰ γυναικός, ἧς ἠγάπησας
3:22 ... μὴ ἐν ὀφθαλμοδουλίᾳ ὡς ἀνθρωπάρεσκοι, ἀλλ' **ἐν ἁπλότητι καρδίας** φοβούμενοι τὸν κύριον.	Pss Sol 4:7, cf. Ps 52:6 ἀνακαλύψαι ὁ θεὸς τὰ ἔργα ἀνθρώπων ἀνθρωπαρέσκων Wis 1:1 ... περὶ τοῦ κυρίου ... **ἐν ἁπλότητι καρδίας** ζητήσατε αὐτόν.
3:23 ... ἐκ **ψυχῆς** ἐργάζεσθε ὡς τῷ κυρίῳ ...	Deut 6:5 καὶ ἀγαπήσεις κύριον τὸν θεόν σου ... ἐξ ὅλης τῆς **ψυχῆς** σου ...
4:5: ... τὸν **καιρὸν** ἐξαγοραζόμενοι.	Dan 2:8 ... **καιρὸν** ὑμεῖς ἐξαγοράζετε

Unlike in the genuine Pauline epistles, the OT citations are never accompanied by an introductory formula. A/Col never quotes the texts[965] but uses them like he does the letters of Paul, borrowing phrases and terms from them. As in Col, the introductory formula is usually missing in Eph also: it occurs only once, in Eph 4:8. Still, A/Eph's exegetical technique of citing the Scriptures resembles more that of Paul than that of A/Col.[966] Though Col lacks clear quotations from the LXX, it cannot be doubted, however, that Col utilizes the texts. Some of the resemblances, e.g. that between Col 3:10 and Gen 1:27, have been called allusions.[967]

9.9. Mark

Col has many more verbal agreements with Mk than with the other Gospels. These appear randomly in Col (see the Appendix). In the following table, the agreements are enumerated from the standpoint of Mk (Table Mk A).[968]

Table Mk A

Mk		Col	Mk		Col
1:	11, 15	1:13	9:	50/Lk 14:34	4:6
4:	**8**	1:6	11:	24	1:9
	4:11	4:3-5			
	20/Mt 13:23/ Lk 8:15	1:5b-6	12:	30/ Deut 6:5	3:23
7:	7	2:22	13:	5/ Mt 24:4	2:8
	4	2:12			
	8	2:8	14:	38/ Mt 36:41	4:2

There appear parallels to Col every now and then in Mk. Some of the texts have synoptic parallels, which could be prototypes of Col, as well as the text of Mk (Mk 4:20, 9:50, 13:5, 14:38, Mk 12:30 cites verbatim Deut 6:5). Sometimes the text of Mk is the closest parallel to Col, which indicates a connection between Col and Mk. Since there is only one resemblance which meets the criteria for literary

965 Lincoln 1982, 48, contends correctly that in Col "no OT citations are used". Cf. Furnish 1992a, 1090: "It is striking, however, that no scriptural texts are quoted or discussed, and that even allusions to Scripture are infrequent."

966 See Lincoln 1982.

967 So Lindemann 1983, 86-87, when stating that in Col all references to the OT are lacking. Cf. Nielsen 1985, 118-119. In contrast Wilson 1997, 127, states that in Col 2:22, A/Col alludes to Isa 29:13, as well as to Ps 110:1 in Col 3:1.

968 The agreement between Mk 16:15 and Col 1:23 is not presented here since Mk 16:15 belongs to the longer ending of Mk which was connected to the Gospel later and thus is unlikely to be familiar to A/Col (see pp. 102-103).

dependence (Col 1:6 // Mk 4:8), the number of agreements is very small compared to those between Col and the authentic Pauline letters. The resemblances are still noteworthy because no other writing outside the Pauline letters has nearly as many verbal agreements with Col as Mk. It has to be noted, however, that the agreements between Mk 1:11,15 and Col 1:13, as well as that between Mk 11:24 and Col 1:9, are, though notable, only independent echoes of Mk which cannot be used as proof for literary dependence. In two cases, agreements are especially remarkable. The following takes a closer look at the relationship between Mk 4 and Col 1 and that between Mk 7 and Col 2, which both have several agreements.

Table Mk B

Mk 4:8	Col 1:5b-6, 10
καὶ ἄλλα ἔπεσεν εἰς τὴν γῆν τὴν καλὴν καὶ ἐδίδου καρπὸν ἀναβαίνοντα **καὶ** αὐξανόμενα καὶ ἔφερεν ἓν τριάκοντα καὶ ἓν ἑξήκοντα καὶ ἓν ἑκατόν.	5b ἣν προηκούσατε ἐν τῷ λόγῳ τῆς ἀληθείας τοῦ εὐαγγελίου 6 τοῦ παρόντος εἰς ὑμᾶς, καθὼς καὶ ἐν παντὶ τῷ κόσμῳ εστὶν καρποφορούμενον καὶ αὐξανόμενον καθὼς καὶ ἐν ὑμῖν, ἀφ' ἧς ἡμέρας ἠκούσατε καὶ ἐπέγνωτε τὴν χάριν τοῦ θεοῦ ἐν ἀληθείᾳ· ... 10 περιπατῆσαι ἀξίως τοῦ κυρίου εἰς πᾶσαν ἀρεσκείαν, ἐν παντὶ ἔργῳ ἀγαθῷ καρποφοροῦντες **καὶ** αὐξανόμενοι τῇ ἐπιγνώσει τοῦ θεοῦ
Mk 4:11	Col 4:3-5
... ὑμῖν **τὸ μυστήριον** δέδοται ... τοῖς ἔξω ἐν παραβολαῖς τὰ πάντα γίνεται.	... ἵνα ὁ θεὸς ἀνοίξῃ ἡμῖν θύραν τοῦ λόγου λαλῆσαι **τὸ μυστήριον** τοῦ Χριστοῦ, δι' ὃ καὶ δέδεμαι, 4 ἵνα φανερώσω αὐτὸ ὡς δεῖ με λαλῆσαι. 5 Ἐν σοφίᾳ περιπατεῖτε πρὸς τοὺς ἔξω ...
Mk 4:20, cf. Mt 13:23, Lk 8:15	
καὶ ἐκεῖνοί εἰσιν οἱ ἐπὶ τὴν γῆν τὴν καλὴν σπαρέντες, οἵτινες ἀκούουσιν τὸν λόγον καὶ παραδέχονται **καὶ** καρποφοροῦσιν ἓν τριάκοντα καὶ ἓν ἑξήκοντα καὶ ἓν ἑκατόν.	

Col 1:5b-6 seems to conflate the parable of the sower (Mk 4:8) and its interpretation (Mk 4:20). The relationship between the texts resembles those found between the undisputed Pauline letters and Col. Similarly, e.g. in Col 3:11 two texts which resemble each other (Gal 3:27-28, 6:15) are conflated from Gal. Since the habit of repeating the words imitated is also characteristic of A/Col, the occurrence of the verbs καρποφορέω and αὐξάνω together again in Col 1:10 also points to

literary dependence. Thus, the agreements between Col 1:5b-6 and Mk 4:8, 20 were noted as indicating that A/Col knew at least the second pre-Markan stage, the parable of the sower and its interpretation together. However, the alternative that he knew Mk or part of Mk was noted to be more probable because the unnatural order of bearing fruit and growing occurs only in Mk and might be Markan redaction (see pp. 69-70).

Col 4:3-5 and Mk 4:11 similarly connect the idea of a dichotomy between insiders and outsiders to the proclamation of the mystery. It was concluded as possible that the resemblance is the result of the use of the same early Christian tradition but the alternative, that Col 4:5 echoes Mk 4:11, was also examined (see p. 195). The fact that A/Col reveals a possible acquaintance both with Mk 4:8 and 11, which belong to the same context, makes it likely that the parable of the sower and its interpretation in Mk 4:1-20 were familiar to A/Col.

Table Mk C

Col	Mk
2:8 Βλέπετε μή τις ὑμᾶς ἔσται ὁ συλαγωγῶν διὰ τῆς φιλοσοφίας καὶ κενῆς ἀπάτης κατὰ **τὴν παράδοσιν τῶν ἀνθρώπων**, κατὰ τὰ στοιχεῖα τοῦ κόσμου καὶ οὐ κατὰ Χριστόν·	7:7 μάτην δὲ σέβονταί με διδάσκοντες **διδασκαλίας ἐντάλματα ἀνθρώπων**. 7:8 ἀφέντες τὴν ἐντολὴν τοῦ θεοῦ κρατεῖτε **τὴν παράδοσιν τῶν ἀνθρώπων.**
2:21 μὴ ἅψῃ μηδὲ γεύσῃ μηδὲ θίγῃς, 2:22 ἅ ἐστιν πάντα εἰς φθορὰν τῇ ἀποχρήσει, κατὰ τὰ **ἐντάλματα** καὶ **διδασκαλίας** τῶν **ἀνθρώπων**	7:18 ... πᾶν τὸ ἔξωθεν εἰσπορευόμενον εἰς τὸν ἄνθρωπον οὐ δύναται αὐτὸν κοινῶσαι 7:19 ὅτι οὐκ εἰσπορεύεται αὐτοῦ εἰς τὴν καρδίαν ἀλλ᾽ εἰς τὴν κοιλίαν, καὶ εἰς τὸν ἀφεδρῶνα ἐκπορεύεται

The verbal agreements between Col 2 and Mk 7 occur in Col in 2:8-23 which includes the warning about the persons who are trying to lead people astray. Mk 7 discusses the controversy over the clean and the unclean which starts with a conversation about eating with defiled hands. The verbal agreement between Col 2 and Mk 7 is not very obvious: none of the resemblances meets the criteria for literary dependence. Nevertheless, the use of the same unusual term "human tradition", παράδοσις τῶν ἀνθρώπων, which occurs only in Col 2:8 and Mk 7:8 in ECL and never in the LXX, points to a connection between the texts. Though minor, the other resemblances clustered in these passages support the dependence. Though Col 2:22a and Mk 7:18-19 do not agree verbally, it is remarkable that they so similarly refer to "things that perish with use", a phrase which also does not have a parallel in the synoptic Gospels (see pp. 151-152).

The resemblances appear in Mk in several stages of the text. While Mk 7:7 is a quotation from Isa 29:13, Mk 7:8 is Markan redaction (see p. 129). Instead, Mk

7:18b-19 probably belongs to the second pre-Markan stage since it seems to be an exposition of the saying in Mk 7:15 which originates with the church (see p. 152). This suggests that, in case there is a connection between Mk and Col, Mk cannot depend on Col but vice versa. Furthermore, it has to be noted that as a quotation from Isa 29:13, Mk 7:8 cannot depend on Col.

The dependence of Col upon Mk 7 would help to interpret the unclear prohibitions in Col 2:21. It is possible that when A/Col writes the prohibitions "Do not handle, Do not taste, Do not touch" he already has in mind the conversation about eating with defiled hands to which he more clearly refers in v. 22. A/Col utilizes the story concerning the controversy over the clean and unclean in Mk 7:1-23, since he has similar problems in mind as the author of Mk. Thus, the prohibitions in Col 2:21, which have no objects, use the command not to touch or eat food with unclean hands as an example of the legalistic commands which are according to human tradition and therefore will perish. Though not strong, there is some evidence that A/Col was familiar with the story concerning the controversy over the clean and unclean in Mk 7:1-23. Accordingly, A/Col reveals acquaintance with two stories in Mk. The evidence is not as clear as in the case of the Pauline letters. However, it may at least partly be due to the fact that, as a writer of a pseudo-Pauline letter, A/Col does not have as strong a reason to imitate Mk as he does the Pauline letters.

10. The Formation and Purpose of Colossians

I have concluded that A/Col was familiar with all the undisputed epistles of Paul (Rom, 1 Cor, 2 Cor, Gal, Phil, 1 Thess, Philem). He also shows knowledge of the LXX by using phrases from it, although he does not explicitly quote the texts. Though the evidence is not as strong as in the case of the Pauline letters, A/Col reveals acquaintance with two stories in Mk: the parable of the sower together with its interpretation in Mk 4 and the controversy over the clean and unclean in Mk 7:1-23. Some of Paul's letters have been more central in the formation of Col than the others. The primary model for the frame of Col is Philem: both the beginning and the conclusion of the letter are partly modelled on Philem and most of the names mentioned in Col seems to be picked up from it. In addition, Paul is described as being in prison in both letters. The frame of Philem is used in order to link the pseudo-Pauline letter to the apostle's life: the author seeks to give the impression that Paul wrote Col about the same time as Philem. The agreement between Philem 23-24 and Col 4:10-14 especially suggests that A/Col had Philem in front of him when writing: all five persons mentioned in Philem 23-24 also occur in Col 4:10-14 and the same epithets, although for different persons, are used.

Since Philem is a letter to a private person, its introductory greeting is not suitable for Col, which is formed to look like a letter addressed to a congregation. Therefore, the greeting of 2 Cor is utilized, which like Philem, mentions Timothy as a co-sender of the letter. Otherwise, the frame of Col is modelled a great deal on 1 Cor. It is not likely, however, that A/Col had either 2 Cor or 1 Cor in front of him when writing but rather he seems to recall them from memory. The exhortations in Col are often modelled on 1 Thess. Col follows 1 Thess in order and an imitation from 1 Thess usually starts a new passage. Sometimes the theme following the exhortation is also similar in Col and 1 Thess. The phenomenon suggests that 1 Thess was available to A/Col during the writing of Col and often when a new parenetical section begins, he imitates Paul's style from 1 Thess.

Gal seems to be intentionally used as the prototype for the warnings against the dangers (Col 2:6-23) and exhortations to believers (Col 3:1-4:1) because the opponents in Gal resemble those confronted in Col. The detail that the agreements indicating literary dependence between Col and Gal are clustered in Col 2:8-3:24 indicates that A/Col had read Gal through before composing this part of his letter, or otherwise was quite familiar with the text. Another explanation for exact imitation may be due to the fact A/Col does not often follow the argumentation of Paul but only picks up the conclusions (see Gal 3:27-28, 6:15). A/Col was unlikely to have had Gal in front of him when writing because he did not follow it in order and also conflated two texts from it (Gal 3:27-28, 6:15). It seems possible that Gal 3:28 has inspired A/Col to form the rules for the household in Col 3:18-4:1. The connection between Col and Gal might also explain the origin of the unique words "erasing the record which stood against us with its legal demands" in Col 2:14. A/Col may have had in mind the description of the law which does not nullify the promise in Gal 3.

When A/Col describes Christ, the texts are usually modelled on 1 Cor or Rom, and sometimes texts from them are conflated. It cannot be said, however, that one is more the prototype for the Christology in Col than the other: sometimes 1 Cor is the primary model, sometimes it is Rom. Both are thus equally important. A/Col seems to be especially impressed with the description of the mystery once hidden but now revealed in 1 Cor 2:1, 6-7 which he employs three times. A/Col reveals himself as well acquainted with 1 Cor and Rom. However, he does not employ at all the frame of Rom or other parts typical of a letter but only texts dealing with theology. This suggests that A/Col might have frequently heard some parts of Rom read aloud, which is compatible with the assumption that Rom, more than any other letter, was read aloud and studied again and again among congregations. Just because A/Col does not utilize certain parts of Rom does not necessarily mean that he was unfamiliar with them.

Both when composing the frame of the letter and when describing Christ, A/Col occasionally seems to imitate Phil and 2 Cor 1-7 (he does not reveal acquaintance with other parts of 2 Cor). Neither Phil nor 2 Cor 1-7 has been a primary model for Col but rather it seems that the texts are familiar to A/Col and when he is writing, the formulations from them come to his mind. It is possible that he sometimes intentionally recalls some texts but normally he may unintentionally follow the Pauline style from these letters without having any specific text in mind.

Though only one of the verbal agreements between Col and the LXX meets the criteria for a possible literary dependence (Col 2:2-3 // Prov 2:2-6) and none the criteria for a probable one, the resemblances indicate A/Col's acquaintance with several texts from the LXX. The OT citations are never accompanied by an introductory formula, unlike in the genuine Pauline epistles, A/Col never clearly quotes the texts but uses them as he uses the letters of Paul, taking phrases and terms from them.

These conclusions fit well together with Schenke's theory about the formation of the Pauline corpus (see p. 23-24). The verbal agreements between Col and other Pauline letters indicate A/Col's acquaintance with 1-2 Cor, Gal, Phil, 1 Thess, and Rom which Schenke views as contained in the first collection. Since Schenke assumes that the corpus did not contain 1 Cor and 2 Cor in the form we know them now but instead a letter to the Corinthians which included 1 Cor and parts from 2 Cor, it is an interesting detail that, on the grounds of the verbal agreements found in this study, A/Col's acquaintance with the whole of 2 Cor is unlikely. In addition, Schenke contends that after the first collection, Col was formed first using the frame of Philem and then Eph was modelled on Col, upon which Eph also has a literary dependence. This assumption is also compatible with my results but I would add that, besides Philem, A/Col shows acquaintance with the first collection of Paul's letters, upon which Col has a literary dependence.

The formation of Col resembles Goodspeed's and his followers' theory about the making of Eph (see pp. 22-23). A/Col seems to have a special attachment to Philem but he also reveals acquaintance with Rom, 1-2 Cor, Gal, Phil, and 1 Thess, as Mitton concluded concerning Eph. Thus A/Col was the first one who familiarized himself with all the genuine letters, not A/Eph. He also probably was the first pseudepigrapher imitating the authentic Pauline letters and was then followed by A/Eph.

The results in chap. 9 shows that Col is not a combination of Paul's letters which utilizes all of them equally. They may suggest that A/Col is better acquainted with some letters than others but we do not know the reason for the phenomenon. It is possible that there was not yet a collection of letters available but single epistles were circulating among congregations. It might also be that the letters were collected together but A/Col was more familiar with some of them than others. However, the alternative, that A/Col had familiarized himself with all the letters but chose only some of them as models for Col, cannot be neglected either. Since Col has at least two agreements indicating literary dependence with all the indisputable Pauline letters although only some of them are used as prototypes for Col, I regard the latter interpretation as the most probable one.

Since Col and Eph seem to be formed similarly and Eph depends on Col, it is very likely that they were written at the same place. Eph is generally taken as being written at Ephesus (see pp. 22-24) which makes it likely that that was the place where Col was also formed. Ephesus is usually regarded as the center of the Pauline school tradition (see p. 15) which increases the likelihood of this suggestion. Though Colossae is probably a pseudo-addressee, Col is directed to Christians in Asia Minor. Since it is ordered to exchange the letters with the community in Laodicea in Col 4:16 and also the neighboring city of Hierapolis is mentioned in Col 4:13, it is probable that Col is aimed at several — or even all congregations — in Asia Minor.

Though A/Col utilizes all the genuine Pauline letters, he does not seem to have the intention of making a summary of Paul's teachings but rather A/Col seems to have his own actual situation in mind. The purpose of Col is to warn the recipients of the letter to take heed against persons who are trying to lead them astray and to preserve the faith in Christ in the form they received it (cf. Col 2:5-7). As is usual at the time, the disciple of Paul writes in the name of his teacher and imitates Paul's own letters. After Paul's death, he reformulates Paul's teaching for a new generation. A/Col seems also to have the notion that Paul's interpretation of Christ is authoritative. Thus, like A/Eph, A/Col also seems to regard Paul's letters as the authoritative tradition (see pp. 45).

The main identifying marks of the persons opposed are "angelic worship" and visions which are both typical of the apocalyptic strands of Christianity among which Rev was written. This charismatic Christianity appeared in Asia Minor as did the Christianity A/Col represents. When condemning those tolerating the eating of meat sacrificed to idols, Rev takes a position which is consistent with the Apostolic Decree (Acts 15:29). In contrast, the prohibitions in Col 2:16, 21 clearly oppose all such regulations concerning food. Therefore, Col seems to represent the debate between two different types of early Christianity: Paul's heritage of

Christian liberty and an apocalyptic visionary group that observed stricter regulations. A/Col defends Paul's heritage against those who demand that Christians observe Jewish habits concerning abstinence from food and drink as well as the observance of holy days. The high Christology of Col, in Christ "the whole fullness of deity dwells bodily" (2:9), may thus oppose the theocentric character of the strands of Christianity among which Rev was written.

The result of this study, demonstrating that A/Col is acquainted with all the indisputable Pauline letters, does not alone help much in defining the date of Col because there is a wide range of opinions about the question of when the epistles were collected together. The way in which the author, on the one hand, imitates the letters but, on the other hand, utilizes their phraseology in new contexts and represents Christology and eschatology differently from Paul indicates, however, that some time has passed since Paul's death. In addition, the use of the term "human tradition" instead of the expression "the traditions of my ancestors" (Col 2:8) may suggest that A/Col is a representative of the second Christian generation and does not have a Pharisaic background (see p. 231). Since Col is earlier than Eph, which is generally dated near the end of the first century,[969] the date of Col cannot be long after the death of Paul. Thus, Col was probably composed in the 80s of the first century.

Since Col is pseudonymous, nothing can be said about the identity of the author with any certainty. His name may appear among the persons mentioned in the letter. It is most likely to be one of those which are not picked up from Philem: Tychicus, Jesus Justus, or Nympha.[970] In Col 4:15 greetings are given to Nympha and the church in her house. Since Nympha is a name of a woman (see p. 205 n. 934), A/Col may thus be female. In my opinion, nothing in the letter suggests that A/Col is a woman but nothing self-evidently indicates that A/Col was a man either. In Col 4:11, Jesus Justus is defined as one of "those of the circumcision", Jewish Christians, among Paul's co-workers. Although it has been noted that A/Col was unlikely to have a Pharisaic background like Paul, it is possible that this Jewish Christian man was A/Col. However, it is remarkable that Jesus Justus as well as Nympha are passed over with a bare mention only while Tychicus is a more central person in Col. He is described as a beloved brother, a faithful minister and a fellow servant in the Lord who will report all the news about Paul and encourage the hearts of the Colossians (Col 4:7-8). Tychicus is thus defined as a messenger of Paul. Therefore, in my opinion it is most likely that Tychicus was the person who

---

[969] See Lohse 1972, 60; Furnish 1992b, 541. Lincoln 1990, lxxiii, prefers a little earlier date, between 80 and 90.

[970] Kiley 1986, 95-97, also regards it as possible that the name of the author could be one of those which do not occur in the co-worker lists in Philem/Phil which he takes as prototypes for Col. In his view, the most probable alternative is Epaphras, who is described in Col 4:12 "as one who has endured much trouble on the community's behalf". Since Epaphras is the first person mentioned in the co-worker list in Philem (23), I would take the position given to him in Col as fictive rather than actual (see p. 205).

composed Col, a message from Paul, which was intended to encourage Paul's followers after his death. It was noted that A/Col does not want to say anything personal about Tychicus in Col 4:7 but defines him with the epithets he usually gives to a respected Christian (see pp. 200). The reason for this could be that the writer does not want to reveal himself. Though we can only make educated guesses about the identity of A/Col, it is clear that he was a defender of Paul's heritage, who wrote Col in order to protect Christian liberty against a group of early Christians who observed holy days and stricter regulations concerning food and drink. He was acquainted with all the genuine Pauline letters and modelled Col on them.

Abbreviations

AASF	Annales Academiae Scientiarum Fennicae
AASF Diss	Annales Academiae Scientiarum Fennicae. Dissertationes Humanorum Litterarum
AB	Anchor Bible
ABD	Anchor Bible Dictionary
A/Col	Author of Colossians
A/Eph	Author of Ephesians
ANRW	Aufstieg und Niedergang der römischen Welt
ATANT	Abhandlungen zur Theologie des Alten und Neuen Testaments
BHT	Beiträge zur historischen Theologie
BN	Biblische Notizen
BNTC	Black's New Testament Commentaries
BSac	Bibliotheca Sacra
ConBNT	Coniectanea Biblica, New Testament Series
CTJ	Calvin Theological Journal
ECL	Early Christian literature
EKKNT	Evangelisch-Katholischer Kommentar zum Neuen Testament
EvQ	Evangelical Quarterly
EvT	Evangelische Theologie
FRLANT	Forschungen zur Religion und Literatur des Alten und Neuen Testaments
HNT	Handbuch zum Neuen Testament
HTKNT	Herders theologischer Kommentar zum Neuen Testament
HTR	Harvard Theological Review
ICC	International Critical Commentary
IDBSup	Supplementary volume to the Interpreter's Dictionary of the Bible
JBL	Journal of Biblical Literature
JSNT	Journal for the Study of the New Testament
JSNTSup	Journal for the Study of the New Testament, Supplement Series.
KEK	Meyers Kritisch-exegetischer Kommentar über das Neue Testament
LCL	Loeb Classical Library
NCB	New Century Bible Commentary
NICNT	The New International Commentary on the New Testament
NovT	Novum Testamentum
NovTSup	Novum Testamentum, Supplements
NTD	Das Neue Testament Deutsch
NTS	New Testament Studies
SBLDS	Society of Biblical Literature Dissertation Series
SBLMS	Society of Biblical Literature Monograph Series
SBM	Stuttgarter biblische Monographien

SC	Sources Chrétiennes.
SUNT	Studien zur Umwelt des Neuen Testaments
SUTS	Suomalainen Uuden testamentin selitys
TDNT	Theological Dictionary of the New Testament
THKNT	Theologischer Handkommentar zum Neuen Testament
TLG	Thesaurus linguae graecae
TLZ	Theologische Literaturzeitung
VC	Vigiliae Christianae
WBC	Word Biblical Commentary
WMANT	Wissenschaftliche Monographien zum Alten und Neuen Testament
WTJ	Westminster Theological Journal
WUNT	Wissenschaftliche Untersuchungen zum Neuen Testament
ZBK	Zürcher Bibelkommentare
ZNW	Zeitschrift für die neutestamentliche Wissenschaft
ZTK	Zeitschrift für Theologie und Kirche
ZWT	Zeitschrift für wissenschaftliche Theologie

Bibliography

1. Texts

The Apostolic Fathers with an English Translation by Kirsopp Lake. Vol I-II. LCL. London – Cambridge, Massachusetts: Harvard University Press 1912-13.

Aristeas to Philocrates. (Letter of Aristeas.) Ed. and Transl. by Moses Hadas. Repr. New York: KTAV Publishing House 1973.

Aristotle, De Mundo. ed. W.L. Lorimer. Aristoteles latinus 11,1-2. Paris: Desclée 1965.

Aristotle, The Nicomachean Ethics. With an English Translation by H. Rackham. LCL. Repr. London – Cambridge, Massachusetts: Harvard University Press 1962.

Aristotle, Parts of Animals. With an English Translation by A. L. Peck. LCL. Revised and Repr. London – Cambridge, Massachusetts: Harvard University Press 1968.

Aristotle, Politics. With an English Translation by H. Rackham. LCL. Repr. London – Cambridge, Massachusetts: Harvard University Press 1977.

Clément D'Alexandrie, Le Pédagogue. Livre III. Traduction de C. Mondésert et C. Matray. Notes de H.-I. Marrou. SC 158. Paris: Les éditions du Cerf 1970.

Epictetus, The Discourses as Reported by Arrian, the Manual, and Fragments with an English Translation by W.A. Oldfather. Vol II. LCL. Repr. London – Cambridge, Massachusetts: Harvard University Press 1959.

Epictetus, Dissertationes ab Arriani Digestae. Recensuit Henricus Schenkl (1916). Bibliotheca scriptorum Graecorum et Romanorum Teubneriana. Nachdr. Stuttgart: B.G. Teubner Verlagsgesellschaft 1965.

Funk, Franciscus Xaverius & Diekamp, Franciscus, Patres Apostolici. Vol II. Textum recensuit adnotationibus criticis exegeticis historicis illustravit versionem latinam prolegomena indices addidit Franciscus Xaverius Funk. Editionem III valde auctam et emendatam paravit Franciscus Diekamp. Tubingae: Libraria Henrici Laupp 1913.

Historia Alexandri Magni (Pseudo-Callisthenes) Vol I. Recensio Vetusta. Edidit Guilelmus Kroll. Berlin: Weidmannsche Buchhandlung 1926.

The Holy Bible containing the Old and New Testaments with the Apocryphal / Deuterocanonical Books. New Revised Standard Version. New York: Oxford University Press 1989.

Iustini Martyris, Apologiae pro christianis. Ed. Miroslav Marcovich. Patristische Texte und Studien Bd. 38. Berlin: De Gruyter 1994.

Josephus with an English Translation by Ralph Marcus, H. St. J. Thackeray, Allen Wikgren. Vol I-IX. LCL. London – New York – Cambridge, Massachusetts: Harvard University Press 1926-1965.

Lucian with an English Translation by A.M. Harmon. Vol IV. LCL. Repr. London – Cambridge, Massachusetts: Harvard University Press 1961.

Novum Testamentum Graece post Eberhard Nestle et Erwin Nestle. Ed. Barbara et Kurt Aland, Johannes Karavidopoulos, Carlo M. Martini, Bruce M. Metzger. 27. revidierte Aufl. Stuttgart: Deutsche Bibelgesellschaft 1993.

Origène, Contre Celse. Tome I-V. Introduction, texte critique, traduction et notes by Marcel Borrett. SC 132, 136, 147, 150, 227. Paris: Les editions du Cerf 1967-76.

Philo with an English Translation by F. H. Colson and G. H. Whitaker. Vol I-IX. LCL. London – Cambridge, Massachusetts: Harvard University Press 1929-1941.

Plato, The Republic. With an English Translation by Paul Shorey. Vol I. Books I-V. LCL. Repr. London – Cambridge, Massachusetts: Harvard University Press 1963.

Plato, The Statesman – Philebus. With an English Translation by Harold N. Fowler. LCL. Repr. London - Cambridge, Massachusetts: Harvard University Press 1962.

Plato, Theaetetus. With an English Translation by Harold North Fowler. LCL. Repr. London – Cambridge, Massachusetts: Harvard University Press 1961.

Plutarch's Moralia in Fifteen Volumes. LCL. London – Cambridge, Massachusetts: Harvard University Press.
Vol II 86B-171F. With an English Translation by Frank Cole Babbit. Repr 1962.
Vol VI 439A-523B. With an English Translation by W.C. Helmbold. Repr 1962.

Vol IX 697C-771E. With an English Translation by Edwin L. Minar, Jr., F.H. Sandbach, and W.C. Helmbold. Repr 1961.

Pseudo-Phocylide, Sentences. Texte établi, traduit et commenté par Pascale Derron. Collection des Universités de France. Paris: Les Belles lettres 1986.

Septuaginta. Id est Vetus Testamentum graece iuxta LXX interpretes edidit Alfred Rahlfs. Volumen I-II. Stuttgart: Deutsche Bibelgesellschaft 1971.

Sibyllinische Weissagungen. Urtext und Übersetzung. Ed. A. Kurfess. Berlin: Heimeran 1951.

Testamentum Iobi. Ed. S.P. Brock. Pseudepigrapha Veteris Testamenti Graece Vol II. Leiden: E. J. Brill 1967.

2. Reference Works

Bachmann, H. & Slaby, W. A., Concordance to the Novum Testamentum Graece of Nestle - Aland, 26th edition, and to the Greek New Testament, 3rd edition. Third Edition. Berlin: de Gruyter 1987.

Bauer, Walter, Griechisch-Deutsches Wörterbuch zu den Schriften des Neuen Testaments und der frühchristlichen Literatur. 6. neu bearbeitete Aufl. Berlin: de Gruyter 1988.

Francis, Fred O. & Sampley, J. Paul, Pauline Parallels. Philadelphia, Pensyl: Fortress Press and Missoula, Mont: Scholars Press 1975.

Hatch, Edwin & Redpath, Henry A., A Concordance to the Septuagint and the Other Greek Versions of the Old Testament (Including the Apocryphal Books). I-II, Supplement. Oxford: Clarendon Press 1897-1906.

Liddell, H. G. & Scott, R., Greek-English Lexicon. A new edition by H. S. Jones with the assistance of Roderick McKenzie. Oxford: Clarendon Press 1953.

Morgenthaler, Robert, Statistik des neutestamentlichen Wortschatzes. 3., um ein Beiheft erweiterte Auflage. Zürich: Gotthelf-Verlag 1982.

Reuter, Rainer, Synopse zu den Briefen des Neuen Testaments. Synopsis of the New Testament Letters. Teil I: Kolosser-, Epheser-, II. Thessalonicherbrief. Vol. I: Colossians, Ephesians, II. Thessalonians. Arbeiten zur Religion und Geschichte des Urchristentums; Bd.5. Frankfurt am Main: Peter Lang 1997.

Strack, H. L. & Billerbeck, P., Kommentar zum Neuen Testament aus Talmud und Midrasch III. München: Beck 1926.

Thesaurus linguae graecae (TLG). Pilot CD Rom#C (CDRM 027300). University of California Irvine 1987.

3. General

Achtemeier, Paul J.
1992 Mark, Gospel of. ABD 4, 541-557.
Aejmelaeus, Anneli
1992 Paavalin perintö 1. Pietarin kirjeessä. In: Aimo annos eksegetiikkaa: piispa Aimo T. Nikolaisen juhlakirja. Toim. Lars Aejmelaeus. Helsinki: Kirjapaja, 205-219.
Aejmelaeus, Lars
1985 Wachen vor dem Ende. Die traditionsgeschichtlichen Wurzeln von 1. Thess 5:1-11 und Luk 21:34-36. Schriften der Finnischen Exegetischen Gesellschaft 44. Helsinki.
1987a Die Rezeption der Paulusbriefe in der Miletrede (Apg 20:18-35). AASF B 232. Helsinki.
1987b Streit und Versöhnung. Das Problem der Zusammensetzung des 2. Korintherbriefes. Schriften der Finnischen Exegetischen Gesellschaft 46. Helsinki.
2000 Schwachheit als Waffe. Die Argumentation des Paulus im Tränenbrief (2. Kor. 10-13). Schriften der Finnischen Exegetischen Gesellschaft 78. Helsinki: The Finnish Exegetical Society. Göttingen: Vandenhoeck & Ruprecht.
Amelungk, Arnold
1899 Untersuchung über Pseudo-Ignatius. ZWT 42, 508-580.
Argall, Randal A.
1987 The Source of a Religious Error in Colossae. CTJ 22, 6-20.
Arnold, Clinton E.
1988 Review of Mark Kiley: Colossians as Pseudepigraphy. EvQ 60, 69-71.
1995 Colossian Syncretism. The Interface Between Christianity and Folk Belief at Colossae. WUNT 2. Reihe 77. Tübingen: J.C.B. Mohr.
Attridge, Harold W.
1989 The Epistle to the Hebrews. Hermeneia. Philadelphia, PA: Fortress Press.
Balch, David L.
1981 Let Wives Be Submissive: The Domestic Code in 1 Peter. SBLMS 26. Atlanta, GA: Scholars Press.
Balz, Horst R.
1969 Anonymität und Pseudepigraphie im Urchristentum. Überlegungen zum literarischen und theologischen Problem der urchristlichen und gemeinantiken Pseudepigraphie. ZTK 66, 403-436.
Bammel, Ernst
1961 Versuch zu Kol 1:15-20. ZNW 52, 88-95.

Barclay, John M. G.
1997 Colossians and Philemon. New Testament Guides. Sheffield: Sheffield Academic Press.
Barnett, Paul
1997 The Second Epistle to the Corinthians. NICNT. Grand Rapids, MI: Eerdmans.
Bauckham, Richard
1983 Jude, 2 Peter. WBC 50. Waco, TX: Word Books.
1988 Pseudo-Apostolic Letters. JBL 107, 469-494.
1992 Jude, Epistle of. ABD 3, 1098-1103.
Baugh, Steven M.
1985 The Poetic Form of Col 1:15-20. WTJ 47, 227-244.

Baum, Armin Daniel
2001 Pseudepigraphie und literarische Fälschung im frühen Christentum. Mit ausgewählten Quellentexten samt deutscher Übersetzung. WUNT 2. Reihe 138. Tübingen: Mohr Siebeck.
Behm, J.
1973 νῆστις, νηστεύω, νηστεία. TDNT 4, 924-935.
Berger, Kl.
1984 Hellenistische Gattungen im Neuen Testament. ANRW II 25.2., 1031-1432.
Best, E.
1997 Who Used Whom? The Relationship of Ephesians and Colossians. NTS 43, 72-96.
Betz, Hans Dieter
1973 2 Cor 6:14-7:1: An Anti-Pauline Fragment? JBL 92, 88-108.
1992 Corinthians, Second Epistle to the. ABD 1, 1148-1154.
1995 Paul's "Second Presence" in Colossians. In: Texts and Contexts. Biblical Texts in Their Textual and Situational Contexts. Essays in Honor of Lars Hartman. Ed. Tord Fornberg and David Hellholm. Oslo – Copenhagen – Stockholm – Boston: Scandinavian University Press, 507-518.
Bigg, Charles
1987 A Critical and Exegetical Commentary on the Epistles of St. Peter and St. Jude. ICC. Repr. Edinburgh: T & T Clark.
Borrett, Marcel
1967 Origène, Contre Celse. Tome I. Introduction, texte critique, traduction et notes. SC 132. Paris: Les éditions du Cerf.
Brown, Milton Perry
1963 The Authentic Writings of Ignatius. A study of linguistic criteria. Durham, NC: Duke University Press.
Brown, Raymond E.
1958 The Semitic Background of the New Testament μυστήριον I. Biblica 39, 426-448.
1959 The Semitic Background of the New Testament μυστήριον II. Biblica 40, 70-87.
Brox, Norbert
1973 Zum Problemstand in der Erforschung der altchristlichen Pseudepigraphie. Kairos 15, 10-23.
1975 Falsche Verfasserangaben. Zur Erklärung der frühchristlichen Pseudepigraphie. Stuttgarter Bibelstudien 79. Stuttgart: Katholisches Bibelwerk.
1976 Pseudo-Paulus und Pseudo-Ignatius; einige Topoi altchristlicher Pseudepigraphie. VC 30, 181-188.
Bruce, F. F.
1988 The Epistles to the Colossians, to Philemon, and to the Ephesians. NICNT. Repr. Grand Rapids, MI: Eerdmans.
1990 The Epistle to the Hebrews. NICNT. Rev. edition. Grand Rapids, MI: Eerdmans.
Büchsel, Friedrich
1974 ἀποκαταλλάσσω. TDNT 1, 258-259.
Bujard, Walter
1973 Stilanalytische Untersuchungen zum Kolosserbrief als Beitrag zur Methodik von Sprachvergleichen. SUNT 11. Göttingen: Vandenhoeck & Ruprecht.
Bultmann, Rudolf
1958 Die Geschichte der synoptischen Tradition. FRLANT 29. 4. Aufl. Göttingen: Vandenhoeck & Ruprecht.
1973a ζάω, ζωή, ζῶον, ζωογονέω, ζωοποιέω, αναζάω. TDNT 2, 832-875.

1973b νεκρός, νεκρόω, νέκρωσις. TDNT 4, 892-895.
Burger, Christoph
1975 Schöpfung und Versöhnung. Studien zum liturgischen Gut im Kolosser- und Epheserbrief. WMANT 46. Neukirchen – Vluyn: Neukirchener Verlag
Caird, G. B.
1966 The Revelation of St. John the Divine. BNTC. London: A & C Black.
1976 Paul's Letters from Prison. NCB. London: Oxford University Press.
Campenhausen, Hans Freiherr von
1968 Die Entstehung der christlichen Bibel. BHT 39. Tübingen: J. C .B. Mohr.
Cannon, G. E.
1981 The Use of Traditional Materials in Colossians: Their Significance for the Problems of Authenticity and Purpose. Diss. (Fuller Theological Seminary) Pasadena, Calif.
Collins, Adela Yarbro
1986 Vilification and Self-Definition in the Book of Revelation. HTR 79, 308-320.
1992 Revelation, Book of. ABD 5, 694-708.
Conzelmann, Hans
1966 Paulus und die Weisheit. NTS 12, 231-244.
1975 1 Corinthians. A Commentary on the First Epistle to the Corinthians. Transl. by James W. Leitch. Hermeneia. Philadelphia, PA: Fortress Press.
1987 Acts of the Apostles. A Commentary on the Acts of the Apostles. Transl. by J. Limburg, A.T. Kraabel, and D. H. Juel. Hermeneia. Philadelphia, PA: Fortress Press.
1990 Der Brief an die Kolosser. In: Die Briefe an die Galater, Epheser, Philipper, Kolosser, Thessalonicher und Philemon. Übersetzt und erklärt von Jürgen Becker, Hans Conzelmann, Gerhard Friedrich. NTD 8. Göttingen: Vandenhoeck & Ruprecht, 176-202.
Cope, Lamar
1985 On Rethinking the Philemon-Colossians Connection. Biblical Research 30, 45-50.
Coutts, J.
1958 The Relationship of Ephesians and Colossians. NTS 4, 201-207.
Crouch, James E.
1972 The Origin and Intention of the Colossian Haustafel. FRLANT 109. Göttingen: Vandenhoeck & Ruprecht.
Dahl, N. A.
1963 Der Epheserbrief und der verlorene, erste Brief des Paulus an die Korinther. In: Abraham unser Vater. Juden und Christen im Gespräch über die Bibel. Hrsg. von Otto Betz, Martin Hengel, and Peter Schmidt. Leiden: E. J. Brill, 63-77.
Deichgräber, Reinhard
1967 Gotteshymnus und Christushymnus in der frühen Christenheit. Untersuchungen zur Form, Sprache und Stil der frühchristlichen Hymnen. SUNT 5. Göttingen: Vandenhoeck & Ruprecht.
Delling, Gerhard
1971 στοιχεῖον. TDNT 7, 670-687.
1973 πλήρωμα. TDNT 6, 298-305.
DeMaris, Richard E.
1994 The Colossian Controversy. Wisdom in Dispute at Colossae. JSNTSup 96. Sheffield: JSOT Press.

Dibelius, Martin
1953 An die Kolosser, Epheser, an Philemon. HNT 12. 3. Aufl. Tübingen: J. C. B. Mohr.
1956 Die Isisweihe bei Apuleius und verwandte Initiationsriten. In: Dibelius: Botschaft und Geschichte Bd. 2. Tübingen, 30-79.
Donaldson, T. L.
1983 Parallels: Use, Misuse and Limitations. EvQ 55, 193-210.
Donelson, Lewis R.
1997 Review of J.D.G. Dunn: The Epistles to the Colossians and to Philemon. A Commentary on the Greek Text. The New International Greek Testament Commentary. Grand Rapids, MI: Eerdmans 1996. JBL 116, 759-760.
Drake, Alfred Edwin
1995 The Riddle of Colossians. Quaerendo Invenietis. NTS 41, 123-144.
Dunderberg, Ismo
1994 Johannes und die Synoptiker. Studien zu Joh 1-9. AASF Diss. 69. Helsinki.
Dunn, James D. G.
1977 Unity and Diversity in the New Testament. An Inquiry into the Character of Earliest Christianity. London: SCM Press.
1993 The Epistle to the Galatians. BNTC. Peabody, MA: Hendrickson.
1995 The Colossian Philosophy: A Confident Jewish Apologia. Biblica 76, 153-181.
1996 The Epistles to the Colossians and to Philemon. A Commentary on the Greek Text. The New International Greek Testament Commentary. Grand Rapids, MI: Eerdmans.
Edelstein, Ludwig
1966 Plato's Seventh Letter. Philosophia Antiqua Vol XIV. Leiden: E. J. Brill .
Enslin, M. S.
1938 "Luke" and Paul. Journal of the American Oriental Society 58, 81-91.
1970 Once again, Luke and Paul. ZNW 61, 253-271.
Fitzer, Gottfried
1971 σύνδεσμος. TDNT 7, 856-859.
Foerster, Werner
1973 εἰρηνοποιέω, εἰρηνοποίος. TDNT 2, 419-420.
Ford, J. Massyngberde
1975 Revelation. Introduction, Translation and Commentary. AB 38. Garden City, NY: Doubleday.
Fornberg, Tord
1977 An Early Church in a Pluralistic Society. A Study of 2 Peter. ConBNT 9. Lund: LiberLäromedel/ Gleerup.
Fung, Ronald Y. K.
1988 The Epistle to the Galatians. NICNT. Grand Rapids, MI: Eerdmans.
Furnish, Victor Paul
1984 II Corinthians. AB 32a. Garden City, NY: Doubleday.
1992a Colossians, Epistle to the. ABD 1, 1089-1095.
1992b Ephesians, Epistle to the. ABD 2, 536-542.
Gabathuler, Hans Jakob
1965 Jesus Christus: Haupt der Kirche – Haupt der Welt. Der Christushymnus Colosser 1, 15-20 in der theologischen Forschung der letzten 130 Jahre. ATANT 45. Zürich: Zwingli Verlag.

Gamble, Harry
1975 The Redaction of the Pauline Letters and the Formation of the Pauline Corpus. JBL 94, 403-418.
1992 Canon, New Testament. ABD 1, 852-861.
Gibbs, John G.
1971 Creation and Redemption. A Study in Pauline Theology. JSNTSup 26. Leiden: E. J. Brill .
Gnilka, Joachim
1971 Der Epheserbrief. HTKNT X/2. Freiburg: Herder.
1978 Das Evangelium nach Markus 1. Teilband. EKKNT II/1. Zürich: Benziger.
1979 Das Evangelium nach Markus 2. Teilband. EKKNT II/2. Zürich: Benziger.
1980 Der Kolosserbrief. HTKNT X/1. Freiburg: Herder.
1982 Der Philemonbrief. HTKNT X/4. Freiburg: Herder.
Goodspeed, Edgar J.
1951 Ephesians and the First Edition of Paul. JBL 70, 285-291.
1974 The Formation of the New Testament. Repr. Chicago: The University of Chicago Press.
Goulder, Michael
1994 A Tale of Two Missions. London: SCM Press.
1995 Colossians and Barbelo. NTS 41, 601-619.
Grundmann, Walter
1974 Der Brief des Judas und der zweiten Brief des Petrus. 4. Print. THKNT XV. Berlin: Evangelische Verlagsanstalt.
1977 Das Evangelium nach Markus. THKNT II. 7. neu bearbeitete Aufl. Berlin: Evangelische Verlagsanstalt.
Gulley, Norman
1971 The Authenticity of the Platonic Epistles. In: Pseudepigrapha I. Ed. Kurt von Fritz. Entretiens sur l'antiquité classique 18. Geneve: Vandceuvres, 103-143.
Guthrie, Donald
1990 New Testament Introduction. Fourth, rev ed. Leicester: Apollos.
Gyllenberg, Rafael
1969 Uuden testamentin johdanto-oppi. Toinen korjattu ja lisätty painos. Helsinki: Otava.
1971 Hebrealaiskirje. SUTS 10. 2. korj. p. Helsinki: Kirjapaja.
Haapa, Esko
1978 Kirkolliset kirjeet. Paavalin kirjeet kolossalaisille, efesolaisille, Timoteukselle ja Tiitukselle. SUTS 9. Helsinki: Kirjapaja.
Harnack, Adolf von
1926 Die Briefsammlung des Apostels Paulus und die anderen vorkonstantinischen christlichen Briefsammlungen. Leipzig: J. C. Hinrichs'sche Buchhandlung.
Hartman, Lars
1985 Kolosserbrevet. Kommentar till Nya testamentet 12. Uppsala: EFS-förlaget.
1986 On Reading Others' Letters. HTR 79, 137-146.
1987 Code and Context: A Few Reflections on the Parenesis of Col 3:6-4:1. In: Tradition and Interpretation in the New Testament: Essays in Honor of E. Earle Ellis for His 60th Birthday. Ed. G. F. Hawthorne and O. Betz. Grand Rapids, MI: Eerdmans, 237-47.
1995 Humble and Confident. On the So-Called Philosophers in Colossians. Studia Theologica 49, 25-39.

1997 Text-Centered New Testament Studies: text-theoretical essays on early Jewish and early Christian literature. Ed. by David Hellholm. WUNT 102. Tübingen: J. C. B. Mohr.

Hays, Richard B.

1989 Echoes of Scripture in the Letters of Paul. New Haven: CT Yale Press.

Hendriksen, William

1971 A Commentary on Colossians & Philemon. London: The Banner of Truth Trust.

Hooker, Morna D.

1973 Were There False Teachers in Colossae? In: Christ and Spirit in the New Testament: in honour of Charles Francis Digby Moule. Ed. by B. Lindars and S. S. Smalley. Cambridge: Cambridge University Press, 315-331.

House, H. Wayne

1992 Heresies in the Colossian Church. Doctrinal Issues in Colossians, Part 1. BSac 149, 45-59.

Hübner, Hans

1997 An Philemon, An die Kolosser, An die Epheser. HNT 12. Tübingen: J. C. B. Mohr.

Jeremias, Joachim

1985 The Parables of Jesus. Revised edition, seventh impr. London: SCM Press.

Johnson, Sherman E.

1960 A Commentary on the Gospel According to St. Mark. BNTC. London: A & C Black.

Joly, Robert

1979 Le Dossier d'Ignace d'Antioche. Université Libre de Bruxelles. Faculté de Philosophie et Lettres LXIX. Brussels: Editions de l'Université de Bruxelles.

Karlsson, Gustav

1956 Formelhaftes in Paulusbriefen? Eranos 54, 138-141.

Käsemann, Ernst

1960 Exegetische Versuche und Besinnung I. Göttingen: Vandenhoeck & Ruprecht.

1965 Essays on New Testament Themes. Transl. by W.J. Montaque. Studies in Biblical Theology 41. 2. impr. London: SCM Press.

Kehl, Nikolaus

1967 Der Christushymnus im Kolosserbrief. Eine motivgeschichtliche Untersuchung zu Kol 1:12-20. SBM 1. Stuttgart: Verlag Katholisches Bibelverk.

Kelhoffer, James A.

2000 Miracle and Mission. The Authentication of Missionaries and Their Message in the Longer Ending of Mark. WUNT 2. Reihe 112. Tübingen: Mohr Siebeck.

Kelly, J. N. D.

1969 A Commentary on the Epistles of Peter and of Jude. BNTC. London: A & C Black.

Kiley, Mark

1986 Colossians as Pseudepigraphy. The Biblical Seminar. Sheffield: JSOT Press.

Klauck, Hans-Josef

1986 2. Korintherbrief. Die Neue Echter Bibel. Kommentar zum Neuen Testament mit der Einheitsübersetzung 8. Würzburg: Echter.

Kleinknecht, H.

1974 θειότης. TDNT 3, 123.

Knox, John

1942 Marcion and the New Testament. An Essay in the Early History of the Canon. Chicago, IL: The University of Chicago Press.

Koskenniemi, Heikki
1956 Studien zur Idee und Phraseologie des griechischen Briefes bis 400 n. Chr. AASF B 102, 2. Helsinki.
Köster, Helmut
1971 σπλάγχνον κτλ. TDNT 7, 548-559.
Kümmel, W. G.
1987 Introduction to the New Testament. Translated by Howard Kee. Revised edition. Sixth impr. London: SCM Press.
Lane, William L.
1991 Hebrews 1-8. WBC 47A. Dallas, TX: Word Books.
Lang, Friedrich
1986 Die Briefe an die Korinther. NTD 7. 16. Aufl. Göttingen: Vandenhoeck & Ruprecht.
Leisegang, H.
1950 Platon 1) Der Philosoph. In: Paulys Realencyclopädie der classischen Altertumswissenschaft. Vierzigster Halbbabd. Stuttgart: Alfred Druckenmüller Verlag, 2342-2537.
Leppä, Heikki
2002 Luke's Critical Use of Galatians. Diss. Helsinki.
Lincoln, Andrew T.
1982 The Use of the OT in Ephesians. JSNT 14, 16-57.
1990 Ephesians. WBC 42. Dallas, TX: Word Books.
1993 The Theology of Ephesians. In: The Theology of the Later Pauline Letters. New Testament Theology. General ed. James D. G. Dunn. Cambridge: Cambridge University Press, 73-172.
1997 The Function of the Household Code in Colossians. A paper presented at the Annual Meeting of the Society of Biblical Literature in San Francisco November 22, 1997.
Lindemann, Andreas
1975 Die Aufhebung der Zeit. Geschichtsverständnis und Eschatologie im Epheserbrief. SUNT 12. Gütersloh: Mohn.
1979 Paulus im ältesten Christentum. Das Bild des Apostels und die Rezeption der paulinischen Theologie in der frühchristlichen Literatur bis Marcion. BHT 58. Tübingen: J. C. B. Mohr.
1983 Der Kolosserbrief. ZBK 10. Zürich: Theologische Verlag.
1985 Der Epheserbrief. ZBK 8. Zürich: Theologische Verlag.
1999 Paulus, Apostel und Lehrer der Kirche: Studien zu Paulus und zum frühen Paulusverständnis. Tübingen: Mohr Siebeck.
Lohmeyer, Ernst
1954 Die Briefe an die Philipper, an die Kolosser und an Philemon. KEK 9. 10th ed. Göttingen: Vandenhoeck & Ruprecht.
Lohse, Eduard
1965 Christusherrschaft und Kirche im Kolosserbrief. NTS 11, 203-16.
1969 Pauline Theology in the Letter to the Colossians. NTS 15, 211-220.
1970 Die Mitarbeiter des Apostels Paulus im Kolosserbrief. In: Verborum Veritas. Festschrift für Gustav Stählin zum 70. Geburtstag. Hrsg. von Otto Böcher und Klaus Haacker. Wuppertal: Theologischer Verlag Rolf Brockhaus.

1971 Colossians and Philemon. A Commentary on the Epistles to the Colossians and to Philemon. Transl. by William R. Poehlmann and Robert J. Karris. Hermeneia. Philadelphia, PA: Fortress Press.
1972 Die Entstehung des Neuen Testaments. Theologische Wissenschaft. Sammelwerk für Studium und Beruf. Band 4. Stuttgart: Kohlhammer.
1973 προσωπολημψία, προσωπολήμτης, προσωπολημτέω, ἀπροσωπολήμτως. TDNT 6, 779-780.
1974 χείρ, χειραγωγέω, χειραγωγός, χειρόγραφον, χειροποίητος, ἀχειροποίητος, χειροτονέω. TDNT 9, 424-437.

Longenecker, Richard N.
1990 Galatians. WBC 41. Dallas, TX: Word Books.

Ludwig, Helga
1974 Der Verfasser des Kolosserbriefes. Ein Schüler des Paulus. Diss. (Georg-August-Universität in Göttingen).

Lührmann, Dieter
1965 Das Offenbarungsverständnis bei Paulus und in paulinischen Gemeinden. WMANT 16. Neukirchen – Vluyn: Neukirchener Verlag.
1978 Der Brief an die Galater. ZBK 7. Zürich: Theologischer Verlag.
1980 Neutestamentliche Haustafeln und antike Ökonomie. NTS 26, 83-97.

Luz, Ulrich
1998 Der Brief an die Kolosser. In: Die Briefe an die Galater, Epheser und Kolosser. Übersetzt und erklärt von Jürgen Becker und Ulrich Luz. NTD 8/1. Göttingen: Vandenhoeck & Ruprecht, 181-244.

Maclean, Jennifer Kay Berenson
1995 Ephesians and the Problem of Colossians: Interpretation of Texts and Traditions in Eph 1,1-2,10. Diss. (Harvard Divinity School, Cambridge 1995). UMI Dissertation Services Ann Arbor Michigan 1999.

Mann, C. S.
1986 Mark: a New Translation with Introduction and Commentary. AB 27. Garden City, NY: Doubleday.

Martin, Ralph P.
1981 Colossians and Philemon. NCB.Grand Rapids, MI: Eerdmans.
1986 2 Corinthians. WBC 40. Waco, TX: Word Books.

Martin, Troy W.
1996a By Philosophy and Empty Deceit. Colossians as Response to a Cynic Critique. JSNTSup 118. Sheffield: Sheffield Academic Press.
1996b Pagan and Judeo-Christian Time-keeping Schemes in Gal 4.10 and Col 2.16. NTS 42, 105-119.

Marxsen, Willi
1963 Einleitung in das Neue Testament. Eine Einführung in ihre Probleme. Gütersloh: Mohn.

Mayerhoff, Ernst Theodor
1838 Der Brief an die Kolosser, mit vornemlicher Berücksichtigung der drei Pastoralbriefe kritisch geprüft. Berlin.

Merkel, Helmut
1987 Der Epheserbrief in der neueren exegetischen Diskussion. ANRW II. 25.4., 3156-3246.

Metzger, Bruce M.
1972 Literary Forgeries and Canonical Pseudepigrapha. JBL 91, 3-14.

Michel, Otto
1971 Σκύθης. TDNT 7, 447-450.
Mitton, C. Leslie
1951 The Epistle to the Ephesians. Its Authorship, Origin and Purpose. Oxford: Clarendon Press.
1955 The Formation of the Pauline Corpus of Letters. London: The Epworth Press.
1983 Ephesians. NCB. Repr. Grand Rapids, MI: Eerdmans.
Montefiore, Hugh
1964 A Commentary on the Epistle to the Hebrews. BNTC. London: A & C Black.
Morton, A. Q. & McLeman, James
1966 Paul, the Man and the Myth. A Study in the Authorship of Greek Prose. London: Hodder & Stoughton.
Moule, C. F. D.
1958 The Epistles of Paul the Apostle to the Colossians and to Philemon. Cambridge Greek Testament Commentaries. Cambridge: Cambridge University Press.
Mowry, Lucetta
1944 The Early Circulation of Paul's Letters. JBL 63, 73-86.
Mullins, Terence Y.
1964 Disclosure. A Literary Form in the New Testament. NovT 7, 44-50.
1984 The Thanksgivings of Philemon and Colossians. NTS 30, 288-293.
Murphy-O'Connor, Jerome
1995 Tradition and Redaction in Col 1:15-20. Revue Biblique 102, 231-241.
Müller, Peter
1988 Anfänge der Paulusschule. Dargestellt am zweiten Thessalonicherbrief und am Kolosserbrief. ATANT 74. Zürich: Theologische Verlag.
Neumann, Kenneth J.
1990 The Authenticity of the Pauline Epistles in the Light of Stylostatistical Analysis. SBLDS 120. Atlanta, GA: Scholars Press.
Nielsen, Charles M.
1985 The Status of Paul and His Letters in Colossians. Perspectives in Religious Studies 12, 103-122.
Nikolainen, Aimo T.
1987 Paavalin kirkolliset kirjeet. Varhaiskristillinen kirkko järjestäytyy. Avaa Uusi testamenttisi 9. Helsinki: Kirjapaja.
O'Brien, Peter Thomas
1977 Introductory Thanksgivings in the Letters of Paul. NovTSup 49. Leiden: E. J. Brill .
1982 Colossians, Philemon. WBC 44. Waco, TX: Word Books.
Oepke, Albrecht
1974 βάπτω, βαπτίζω, βαπτισμός, βάπτισμα, βαπτιστής. TDNT 1, 529-546.
Ollrog, Wolf-Henning
1979 Paulus und seine Mitarbeiter. Untersuchungen zu Theorie und Praxis der paulinischen Mission. WMANT 50. Neukirchen – Vluyn: Neukirchener Verlag.
O'Neill, J. C.
1979 The Source of Christology in Colossians. NTS 26, 87-100.
Pelletier, André
1962 Flavius Josèphe: Adapteur de la Lettre d'Aristée. Études et commentaires 45. Paris: Cerf.
Pesch, Rudolf
1977 Das Markusevangelium. 2. Teil. HTKNT II/2. Freiburg: Herder.

1986 Die Apostelgeschichte. 1. Teilband. EKKNT V/1. Zürich: Benziger.

1989 Das Markusevangelium. 1. Teil. HTKNT II/1. Fünfte Aufl. Freiburg: Herder.

Pfammatter, Josef

1987 Epheserbrief, Kolosserbrief. Die Neue Echter Bibel: Kommentar zum Neuen Testament mit der Einheitsübersetzung Bd. 10 u. 12. Würzburg: Echter.

Pöhlmann, Wolfgang

1973 Die hymnischen All-Prädikationen in Kol 1:15-20. ZNW 64, 53-74.

Pokorný, Petr

1987 Der Brief des Paulus an die Kolosser. THKNT X/1. Berlin: Evangelische Verlagsanstalt.

Preisker, Herbert

1973 ἐμβατεύω. TDNT 2, 535-536.

Räisänen, Heikki

1990 The 'Messianic Secret' in Mark. Translated by Christopher Tuckett. Edinburgh: T & T Clark.

1995 The Nicolaitans: Apoc. 2; Acta 6. ANRW II 26.2., 1602-1644.

Reicke, Bo

1964 The Epistles of James, Peter, and Jude. Introduction, Translation, and Notes. AB 37. Garden City, NY: Doubleday.

Rengstorf, Karl Heinrich

1953 Die neutestamentlichen Mahnungen an die Frau, sich dem Manne unterzuordnen. In: Verbum Dei manet in Aeternum. Eine Festschrift für Prof. D. Otto Schmitz zu seinem siebzigsten Geburtstag am 16. Juni 1953. Witten: Luther-Verlag, 131-145.

Reuter, Rainer

1999 Oral Tradition or Literary Dependence? Some Notes on Luke and First Clement. A paper presented at the International Meeting of the Society of Biblical Literature in Helsinki/Lahti July 20, 1999.

Richards, E. Randolph

1998 The Codex and the Early Collection of Paul's Letters. Bulletin for Biblical Research 8, 151-166.

Rius-Camps, J

1980 The Four Authentic Letters of Ignatius, the Martyr. Orientalia Christiana Analecta 213. Rome: Pontificium Institutum Orientalium Studiorum.

Robinson, J.

1957 A Formal Analysis of Col 1:15-20. JBL 76, 270-287.

Roloff, Jürgen

1984 Die Offenbarung des Johannes. ZBK 18. Zürich: Theologische Verlag.

Roon, A. van

1974 The Authenticity of Ephesians. NovTSup 39. Leiden: E. J. Brill .

Rowland, C.

1987 Christian Origins. An Account of the Setting and Character of the Most Important Messianic Sect of Judaism. 2. impr. London: SPCK.

Royalty, Robert M., Jr.

1997 Dwelling on Visions: On the Nature of the so-called 'Colossians Heresy'. A paper presented at the Annual Meeting of the Society of Biblical Literature in San Francisco November 22, 1997.

Salo, Kalervo

1991 Luke's Treatment of the Law. A Redaction-Critical Investigation. AASF Diss. 57.

Sanders, E. P.
1966 Literary Dependence in Colossians. JBL 85, 28-45.
Sanders, Jack T.
1962 The Transition from Opening Epistolary Thanksgiving to Body in the Letters of the Pauline Corpus. JBL 81, 348-362.
Sandmel, Samuel
1962 Parallelomania. JBL 81, 1-13.
Sappington, Thomas J.
1991 Revelation and Redemption at Colossae. JSNTSup 53. Sheffield: JSOT Press.
Schelkle, Karl Hermann
1964 Die Petrusbriefe Der Judasbrief. HTKNT XIII/2. Freiburg: Herder.
Schenk, Wolfgang
1983 Christus, das Geheimnis der Welt, als dogmatisches und ethisches Grundprinzip der Kolosserbriefes. EvT 43, 139-155.
1987a Der Kolosserbrief in der neueren Forschung (1945-1985). ANRW II 25.4., 3327-3365.
1987b Der Brief des Paulus an Philemon in der neueren Forschung (1945-1987). ANRW II 25.4., 3439-3495.
Schenke, Hans-Martin
1975 Das Weiterwirken des Paulus und die Pflege seines Erbes durch die Paulus-Schule. NTS 21, 505-518.
Schenke, Hans-Martin & Fischer, Karl Martin
1978 Einleitung in die Schriften des Neuen Testaments Vol 1. Die Briefe des Paulus und Schriften des Paulinismus. Gütersloh: Mohn.
Schille, G.
1957 Der Autor des Epheserbriefes. TLZ 82, 325-334.
Schlier, Heinrich
1973 δειγματίζω. TDNT 2, 31-32
1974a ἀνήκει. TDNT 1, 360.
1974b καθήκω. TDNT 3, 437-440.
Schmidt, K. L.
1974 θρησκεία, θρῆσκος, ἐθελοθρησκεία. TDNT 3, 155-159.
Schmithals, Walter
1965 Paulus und Gnostiker: Untersuchungen zu den kleinen Paulusbriefen. Theologische Forschung 35. Hamburg-Bergstedt: Evangelische Verlag.
Schnabel, Eckhard J.
1985 Law and Wisdom from Ben Sira to Paul. A Tradition Historical Enquiry into the Relation of Law, Wisdom, and Ethics. WUNT 2. Reihe 16. Tübingen: J. C. B. Mohr.
Schnackenburg, Rudolf
1982 Der Brief an die Epheser. EKKNT X. Zürich: Benziger.
Schneider, Gerhard
1982 Die Apostelgeschichte. II Teil. HTKNT V/2. Freiburg: Herder.
Schoedel, William R.
1980 Are the Letters of Ignatius of Antioch authentic? A review of R. Weijenborg: Les Lettres d'Ignace d'Antioche (Leiden: E. J. Brill 1969); J. Rius-Camps: The Four Authentic Letters of Ignatius, the Martyr. (Orientalia Christiana Analecta 213. Rome: Pontificium Institutum Orientalium Studiorum 1980), R. Joly: Le Dossier d'Ignace d'Antioche (Université Libre de Bruxelles. Faculté de Philosophie et

Lettres LXIX. Brussels: Editions de l'Université de Bruxelles 1979). Religious Studies Review 6/3, 196-201.
1985 Ignatius of Antioch. A Commentary on the Letters of Ignatius of Antioch. Hermeneia. Philadelphia, PA: Fortress Press.
1992 Ignatius, Epistles of. ABD 3, 383-387.

Schrenk, Gottlob
1973 δίκη, δίκαιος et al. TDNT 2, 178-225.

Schroeder, David
1976 Lists, Ethical. IDBSup, 546-547.

Schweizer, Eduard
1971 The Good News According to Mark. Translated by Donald H. Madvig. London: SPCK.
1982 The Letter to the Colossians. A Commentary transl. by Andrew Chester. London: SPCK.
1988 Slaves of the Elements and Worshipers of Angels: Gal 4:3, 9 and Col 2:8, 18, 20. JBL 107, 455-468.

Shutt, R. James H.
1992 Aristeas, Letter of. ABD 1, 380-382.

Sollamo, Raija
1979 Renderings of Hebrew Semiprepositions in the Septuagint. AASF Diss. 19. Helsinki.
1983 Semitic Interference in Words Meaning "Before" in the New Testament. In: Glaube und Gerechtigkeit. In Memoriam Rafael Gyllenberg (18.6.1893 - 29.7.1982). Hrsgg. Von Jarmo Kiilunen, Vilho Riekkinen und Heikki Räisänen. Schriften der Finnischen Exegetischen Gesellschaft 38. Helsinki, 181-200.

Speyer, Wolfgang
1971 Die literarische Fälschung im heidnischen und christlichen Altertum. Ein Versuch ihrer Deutung. München: Beck.

Stählin, Gustav
1974 ἴσος, ἰσότης, ἰσότιμος. TDNT 3, 343-355.

Standhartinger, Angela
1999 Studien zur Entstehungsgeschichte und Intention des Kolosserbriefes. NovTSup 94. Leiden: E. J. Brill .
2000 The Origin and Intention of the Household Code in the Letter to the Colossians. JSNT 79, 117-130.

Stauffer, E.
1974 βραβεύω, βραβεῖον. TDNT 1, 637-639.

Stuckenbruck, Loren T.
1995 Angel Veneration and Christology. A Study in Early Judaism and the Christology of the Apocalypse of John. WUNT 2. Reihe 70. Tübingen: J. C. B. Mohr.

Sumney, Jerry
1993 Those Who "Pass Judgment": The Identity of the Opponents in Colossians. Biblica 74, 366-388.

Thiering, Barbara
1967 The Acts of the Apostles as Early Christian Art. In: Essays in Honour of G. W. Thatcher 1863-1950. Ed. by E. C. B. MacLaurin. Sydney: Sydney University Press, 139-189.

Thornton, T. C. G.
1989 Jewish New Moon Festivals, Galatians 4:3-11 and Colossians 2:16. The Journal of Theological Studies 40, 97-100.
Trobisch, David
1989 Die Entstehung der Paulusbriefsammlung. Studien zu den Anfängen christlicher Publizistik. Novum testamentum et orbis antiquus 10. Göttingen: Vandenhoeck & Ruprecht.
VanKooten, George
1995 The Literary Phenomenon of 'Conflation' in the Reworking of Paul's Letter to the Colossians by the Author of the Letter to the Ephesians. Including a new Synopsis of the Greek Text of both Letters. Unpublished thesis for the Degree of Master of Arts, University of Durham, England.
Verhoef, Eduard
2001 Pseudepigraphy and Canon. BN 106, 90-98.
Vielhauer, Philipp
1975 Geschichte der urchristlichen Literatur. Einleitung in das Neue Testament, die Apokryphen und die Apostolischen Väter. Berlin: de Gruyter.
Vögtle, Anton
1994 Der Judasbrief / Der 2. Petrusbrief. EKKNT XXII. Düsseldorf: Benziger.
Walker, William O.
1985 Acts and the Pauline Corpus Reconsidered. JSNT 24, 3-23.
Watson, Duane Frederick
1988 Invention, Arrangement, and Style: Rhetorical Criticism of Jude and 2 Peter. SBLDS 104. Atlanta, GA: Scholars Press.
1992 Nicolaitans. ABD 4, 1106-1107.
Wedderburn, A. J. M.
1987 Baptism and Resurrection. Studies in Pauline Theology against Its Graeco-Roman Background. WUNT 44. Tübingen: J. C. B. Mohr.
1993 The Theology of Colossians. In: The Theology of the Later Pauline Letters. New Testament Theology. General ed. James D. G. Dunn. Cambridge: Cambridge University Press, 1-71.
Weidinger, Karl
1928 Die Haustafeln. Ein Stück urchristlicher Paränese. Leipzig.
Weijenborg, Reinoud
1969 Les Lettres d'Ignace d'Antioche. Leiden: E. J. Brill .
Wikenhauser, Alfred & Schmid, Josef
1973 Einleitung in das Neue Testament. 6. Aufl. Freiburg: Herder.
Winter, Sara C.
1987 Paul's Letter to Philemon. NTS 33, 1-15.
Wilckens, Ulrich
1971 σοφία κτλ. TDNT 7, 465-528.
1978 Der Brief an die Römer. Teilband 1. EKKNT VI/1. Zürich: Benziger.
Wilson, Walter T.
1997 The Hope of Glory. Education and Exhortation in the Epistle to the Colossians. NovTSup 88. Leiden: E. J. Brill .
Wright, N.T.
1990 Poetry and Theology in Col 1:15-20. NTS 36, 444-468.
Yates, Roy
1991 Colossians 2.15: Christ Triumphant. NTS 37, 573-591.

Appendix: Parallels to Colossians

Col	Rom	1Cor	2Cor	Gal	Phil	Philem	1Thess
1:1-2		**1:1-3**	**1:1-2**		1:1		
1:3-5a			**1:3**			**4-5**	**1:2-3**
1:5b-6	1:13 1:8		6:7 11:9	2:5,14 4:18,20	1:5		
1:7-8		**4:17**,21	**11:23**			**23**	
1:9-11a	15:14 2:7	**12:8**	9:8				**2:12-13** 4:1
1:11b-14			**6:14-15,** 18 3:6		1:4		1:6
1:15-20	**1:20** **8:29** **11:36**	**8:5-6** 15:24 **11:3** 15:20 **12:27-28** 1:17 10:16	**4:4** 5:18				
1:21-23	**5:10-11** 11:22-23	**15:58**	11:2				
1:24	7:18	7:28	7:9 1:5	4:14	**2:30**		

Gospels	LXX	Others	Col	Col
				1:1-2
				1:3-5a
Mk 4:20/ Mt 13:23/ Lk 8:15 Mt 26:13 **Mk 4:8**				1:5b-6
				1:7-8
Mk 11:24	Dan 1:4,17 1 Kings 26:25/ 1 Macc 5:40 Isa 2:10,19,21		1:3-6	1:9-11a
Mk 1:11,15	Wis 5:5	<u>**Acts 26:18**</u>	1:3	1:11b-14
	Prov 8:22-27 Ps 67:17		1:16	1:15-20
Mk 16:15	Ezek 14:4-5 Sir 23:17			1:21-23
			1:18	1:24

Appendix: Parallels to Colossians

Col	Rom	1Cor	2Cor	Gal	Phil	Philem	1Thess
1:25-28	**9:22-24**	**3:10**		4:19			
	8:10	**4:1**	13:5				
	5:2	**2:6-7**					
		2:1					
1:29-2:1		4:12			2:13		
		9:25			3:21		
					4:13		
	8:9 etc	**11:3**		1:22	1:30		
2:2-3	**11:33**	**2:1**					
2:4-5		**5:3**		3:17 etc			
		14:40					
2:6-7		1:5-6	4:15				**4:1**
		3:9-10	9:12				
2:8-11	15:14	15:24		**4:3-4**			
		8:9	**5:1-3**	5:15	**3:2-3**		
2:12-15	**6:4**		2:14	**1:1**			
	4:24-25						
	8:11						
	6:11						
	8:32						
2:16-23	**14:**3,5,	9:24	6:17	4:9-10	3:14		
	17	5:2					
	6:8	2:1					

Gospels	LXX	Others	Col	Col
			1:23b 1:9 1:22	1:25-28
				1:29-2:1
	Prov 2:2-6 Sir 1:25	2 Thess 2:17	1:27	2:2-3
	Bel 7		1:3-4	2:4-5
	PsSal 14:4 Sir 24:12			2:6-7
Mk 13:5 /Mt 24:4 Mk 7:8			1:16-19 1:22	2:8-11
		Heb 6:1-2	1:21 2:10-11	2:12-15
Mk 7:7	Ezek 45:17 Hos 2:13 Hos 13:6	Heb 10:1 Philo: Conf 190 Lucian: Anach 24	1:10,18,22 2:8	2:16-23

Appendix: Parallels to Colossians

Col	Rom	1Cor	2Cor	Gal	Phil	Philem	1Thess
3:1-4	**8:34**				**3:**14,**19-21** 1:21		
3:5-11	**13:12b-14** 6:13 1:18 **6:6** 1:14	**5:11** **15:28**		**5:19-20** **6:15** **3:27-28**			**4:3,5** 1:10
3:12-15	**8:32-33** 15:7	12:13		**5:22-23**	**2:1-3** **4:7**		
3:16-17	8:11 15:18	14:26 10:31 6:11					
3:18-4:1	12:1-2 14:18 6:16 16:18 **2:9-11**	**14:34-35** 8:5-6	2:9 **5:10-11**	**1:10**	4:18	8 **16**	2:4
4:2-6	12:12		**2:12**				5:25 **4:12**
4:7-9					**1:12**	**10-12**	
4:10-14	10:2 1:1		7:15	2:12-13	1:1	**23-24**	
4:15-18		**16:21-23**			1:7, 13, 14, 17	**2** 10, 13	5:27 2:9

Gospels	LXX	Others	Col	Col
Lk 22:69			2:20,12	3:1-4
	Gen 1:27		3:2 1:21-22 2:2,11	3:5-11
			2:18	3:12-15
			1:25,28,12 1:3,16,3:15	3:16-17
Mk 12:30	Eccl 9:9 PssSol 4:7 Ps 52:6 Wis 1:1 Deut 6:5	Philo: Spec Leg IV Heb 11:8	3:17	3:18-4:1
Mk 14:38 /Mt 26:41 Mk 4:11 Mk 9:50 /Lk 14:34	Dan 2:8		1:25-28	4:2-6
			1:7,2:2	4:7-9
			1:7,9 1:28-29	4:10-14
			1:25	4:15-18

Abstract

This study takes as its starting point the pseudonymity of Colossians (Col): I assume the letter was written by a disciple of Paul, who wrote in Paul's name, after the death of the Apostle. The purpose of this study is to show how the deutero-Pauline author formed the text of Col and why he composed it. I argue that the writer of Col knew and used all the undisputed Pauline letters (Rom, 1 Cor, 2 Cor, Gal, Phil, 1 Thess, Philem). The primary model for the frame of Col is Philem but all other epistles are also utilized. For example, the warnings against those who are trying to lead people astray (Col 2:16-23) are modelled on Gal. In addition, the author of Col reveals acquaintance with the LXX and Mk. In order to find the texts the writer imitates, the whole text of Col is compared with its closest parallels from the authentic Pauline letters. I assume that only verbal and verbatim agreements show possible literary dependence, similar thoughts do not. Thus, only passages which use similar words are placed in parallel.

Colossae is probably a pseudo-addressee. The letter seems to be aimed at a larger circle of readers in Asia Minor rather than to Colossae, which probably was destroyed by an earthquake in A.D. 60-61. The purpose of Col is to warn the recipients of the letter to take heed against persons who are trying to lead them astray and to preserve their faith in Christ (cf. Col 2:5-7). The main identifying marks of the opponents are "angelic worship" and visions. In addition, they demand that Christians observe Jewish habits concerning abstinence from food and drink as well as the observance of holy days. All these characteristics are typical of the apocalyptic strands of Christianity among which the Book of Revelation was written. This charismatic Christianity appeared in Asia Minor as did the Christianity the author of Col represents. Therefore, Col seems to represent the debate between two different types of early Christianity: Paul's heritage of Christian liberty and an apocalyptic visionary group that observed stricter regulations.